INTRODUCTORY RUSSIAN GRAMMAR

JOHN WILEY & SONS, New York ● London ● Syndey ● Toronto

Galina Stilman
Leon Stilman
William E. Harkins
Columbia University

Second Edition

Introductory **Russian Grammar**

Preface

This Russian text attempts to combine the advantages of the traditional grammatical approach to the study of a foreign language with certain features of the modern conversational, inductive method. Basic to this combined approach is the use of a great number and variety of pattern sentences: short, typical Russian sentences which can be used in different ways to provide concentrated and appropriate material for language analysis, reading, and drill. In addition to pattern sentences, all units have been provided with dialogues or readings, often with both. Dialogues may be assigned for presentation in class by two or more students; they may be memorized or not as the teacher prefers. A great variety of drill materials has also been supplied, to the extent that no separate workbook or reader is believed necessary. Thus the book can be used as a first-year textbook which is complete in itself.

The book has been divided into twenty-seven units. Each unit is intended to correspond roughly to one week of a first-year language course on the college level, so that it is possible to finish the book in two semesters of college study, allowing time for review and examination.

Each unit is divided into sections containing grammar, dialogues and readings, summary exercises, and vocabulary. The main or grammar section of each unit is in turn divided into topical sub-units, each of which is provided with its own pattern sentences and drills, which may be used in class, assigned as homework, or both.

It is obvious that the actual use of the book depends very much on the teacher's preferences and the method of instruction employed. Teachers who prefer a more inductive approach may stress memorization and reproduction in class of much of the pattern sentence and dialogue material, while those who follow a more grammatical approach may prefer to use these sections only for illustration and analysis. The number and types of drills and exercises covered in class or assigned as homework will also depend on the preference of the teacher and the method followed, as well as on the amount of class time available.

Where class time is relatively restricted, as in the case of a course meeting only three hours a week, the grammatical approach is recommended over the direct method, with its great demands on time. Narrative readings may be either totally omitted or assigned as homework; checking that the student has read them and understands them may be made through the use of brief quizzes in class. The same procedure may be followed with dialogues. Naturally, this is not ideal, and the teacher may prefer to consider the possibility of completing the book in a longer period of three or four terms. Four terms are definitely recommended for covering the book in high school, and full exploitation of the materials both during class and as homework, followed by frequent class quizzes and reviews, should supply more than enough material to fill the class time.

One important feature of the book is the slow, careful, and systematic presentation of the verbal aspects. By breaking aspect formation into several morphological patterns, we have, we believe, greatly simplified the presentation of one of the most difficult subjects in the teaching of Russian.

Another important advantage is the systematic presentation of phonetics and alphabet as part of the lessons themselves, rather than as a separate section, cut off from grammar and vocabulary. Thus the student learns new letters and sounds as he learns the language itself, not as abstract, unrelated material.

A systematic presentation of the script, proceeding from familiar to unfamiliar letters, has been placed between Units 3 and 4, at the conclusion of the presentation of the printed alphabet and phonetics; ample exercises have been provided.

We believe that the learning of the pronunciation of Russian is significantly aided by the use of a phonetic transcription, which is employed as an auxiliary side by side with the orthographic presentation. Phonetic transcription is especially useful as a reminder to the student of certain phonetic features of the language not represented by its spelling, that is, the reduction of certain vowels by *akanie* and *ikanie*, unvoicing, and so forth. It has simplified the presentation of such morphological patterns as the conjugation of verbs. In devising a system of phonetic transcription we have consciously tried to keep the use of unfamiliar symbols to a minimum.

The treatment of stress on monosyllabic words requires some comment. We were dissatisfied with the general practice of not indicating stress on monosyllables, since in certain contexts many of them are stressed. Furthermore, there is an intermediate stage in which the vowel of a monosyllabic word is not stressed, but still does not undergo reduction by *akanie* or *ikanie*, e.g., the pronouns он and я in certain contexts. Two signs would have been required to indicate these several degrees of reduction. Rather than introduce a system so complicated, we have preferred to follow the practice of indicating as stressed (´) all monosyllabic words which do not undergo vowel reduction.

The vocabulary used is entirely contemporary, and in the choice of words an effort has been made to take into account indications of word-frequency count. Vocabulary reviews have been incorporated. The total vocabulary employed includes approximately 1300 words. A few story-telling words that are obvious cognates of English are not listed in vocabularies.

Although very extensive changes were made for the second edition of this work, we deliberately decided not to change the fundamental approach on which the original edition was based and which met with such gratifying success. In our revision we attempted to treat matters in larger and more related units, and to this end a number of topics were moved: these include the declension of Feminine II nouns, the locative of personal pronouns, the superlative, the declension of family names ending in -ин and -ов, the adverb, age, the verbal prefixes по- and про-, nouns and adjectives of nationality, and so on. A few topics neglected in the first edition were added: these include the verb уме́ть, the prefixes с- and раз-, negative pronouns and adverbs of the type не́чего, не́куда. Grammar topics which have been thoroughly revised in presentation include the reflexive possessive свой, the genitive plural of nouns, the imperative, verbs in -ся, нра́виться and люби́ть, verbs of sitting, standing, and lying, and indirect questions. New phonetics drawings, based on those given in Avenesov and Sidorov, *Russkij jazyk*, Moscow, 1936, and in H. Koneczna and W. Zawadowski, *Obrazy rentgenograficzne glosek rosijskich*, Warsaw, 1956, are also included.

In addition to these changes, the pattern sentences and readings have been systematically revised and much new material has been included. Drills have been tested carefully for suitability of method and many have been changed; in particular, there are fewer drills of the translation type, as opposed to substitution, fill-in, and question-and-answer types. A number of oral drills have been added. Although we did not wish to interfere with the autonomy of the individual classroom instructor, we have tried to make the instructions for drills and exercises more precise.

The new text also places more emphasis on Russian culture and geography.

We acknowledge with sincere gratitude our debt to the many friends and colleagues who have provided helpful advice and criticism. In particular we must thank Professor Francis J. Whitfield, Professor Edward J. Brown, Dr. Allen R. Taylor, and Professor Robert Simmons. The number of valuable suggestions we received in preparing the second edition is almost innumerable, and we are most grateful for them.

In the first edition the co-authors acknowledged the great role played by Professor Leon Stilman as a "virtual third author" of the book. In view of the part he has taken in the preparation of the revised edition, it was decided that his name should now appear on the title page as co-author.

GALINA STILMAN
LEON STILMAN
WILLIAM E. HARKINS

Suggestions for the Use of This Book

The combination of grammar explanation, pattern sentences, drills, readings, and questions provided in each unit of this book constitutes an integrated whole. Though the amount of time and emphasis devoted to each of these sections may vary, no one of these parts should be sacrificed for another.

1. Every grammar explanation given in class should be followed at once with drills supplied after each grammar topic. This will provide an active check and help the instructor and the student to ascertain if the explanation has been correctly understood or if additional explanation is required. It will also give the student the satisfaction of being able to apply at once and use in practice the knowledge he has freshly acquired.

This functional method will help in the quicker assimilation of the newly presented topic and will make theory more concrete and purposeful.

2. Students should carefully study at home pattern sentences and readings and familiarize themselves with the Russian idioms, speech patterns, and sentence structures embodied in them. They should be prepared to translate quickly and idiomatically from either language into the other. They should be ready to answer in class orally or in writing the questions supplied at the end of each reading. The stories may also be used at the instructor's discretion for reading practice or drill in translation, but they are primarily intended for conversational practice. This can be done first through questions and answers, then, gradually, the students must be able to retell the stories in Russian in their own words. This method will help students to master idioms, vocabulary, and sentence patterns in a more effective and natural, as well as more gratifying way.

3. The transliterated passages provided should be used to remind the student of the principles of Russian phonetics and help him further in mastering pronunciation, which should at no time be neglected.

4. Dialogues may be read or acted out by two or more students.

Contents

Unit 12   175

Unit 13   197

Unit 14   210

Unit 15   222

Unit 16   233

Unit 17   251

INTRODUCTORY RUSSIAN GRAMMAR

Phonetics: General character of Russian vowels • Accentuation •
The vowel sounds [a], [o], and [u] • The consonant sound [m] •
The consonant sounds [p], [k], and [t] • The consonant sounds [d], [n],
and [l] • Pronunciation of consecutive vowels • Other consonant
sounds • Unstressed a and o

Unit 1

Phonetics

Introductory. In this and the following units the sounds of the Russian language are presented together with the Russian alphabet as it is used to render these sounds. Russian spelling is far less arbitrary than English, but it is still not a strictly phonetic system. One symbol may have more than one sound value and, conversely, the same sound may be rendered by more than one symbol. This is one of the reasons why it is helpful to use a transcription in which symbols are assigned constant values. Such a transcription is used in this textbook; the value of each symbol will be defined, and transcriptions, whether of separate sounds or of complete words, will always appear in square brackets. The student must remember, for example, that [a] will always be used for the sound ah, never for *a* as in *at* or in *ate*.

There are not many sounds that are exactly alike in English and Russian. In this presentation, Russian sounds are described in terms of their similarities (and dissimilarities) in relation to their closest English equivalents and also in terms of their articulation (position of the tongue, the lips, etc.). With the help of these indications one should be able to approximate correct pronunciation. But it is only through hearing and imitating native speakers that one can advance beyond this "approximate correctness."

1. General character of Russian vowels

Russian, unlike English, does not have long and short vowels. Most so-called "long" vowels in English are actually diphthongs which combine two sounds; one changing, or "gliding off," into the other (as the vowel sounds in *go out, late hour, poor sight*, etc.). Russian vowels do not have this quality; generally they are not diphthongs, but monophthongs, like Spanish or Italian vowels. Graphically, most English long vowels could be compared to curves, Russian vowels to straight lines.

2. Accentuation

Like English, Russian has a strong stress. Only one syllable in a word, however, is accented; secondary accents, such as are often heard in English (e.g., in láboratòry or sécretàry) must be avoided.[1] In normal connected speech unstressed vowels are somewhat less distinct and only slightly shorter than stressed ones. Some vowels actually change their value when unaccented. The values given below are those of the *stressed* variant; the unaccented values will be given later.

The stress in Russian falls, in different words, on different syllables, first, last, or any other. Russian texts do not normally use accent marks; in this text, the stress will always be indicated by an accent over the stress vowel, e.g., á—"stressed **a**."

3. The vowel sounds [a], [o], and [u]

A, a—[a]

The Russian letter **a** in stressed syllables stands for the sound heard in *father*, *palm*. In transcriptions [a] will always be used to denote this sound value.

O, o—[o]

A rather close approximation of Russian **o** (stressed) is the vowel sound in words like *war*, *warm*, and *ward*, pronounced with the initial *w* barely audible. Russian **o** [o] is a back vowel produced with the back portion of the tongue raised toward the soft palate. The lips for this sound protrude somewhat and are rounded (see Illustration 1).

У, y—[u]

This is close to the vowel sound in *woo* or *ooze*. The Russian sound, however, has a deeper, darker quality than the English; this is due to an articulation farther back in the mouth and to more lip rounding. Russian **y** [u] is a back vowel, like [o], but it is produced with the back of the tongue raised more and brought closer to the soft palate than for [o] (see Illustration 2).

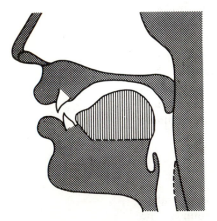

ILLUSTRATION 1. The Vowel [o]

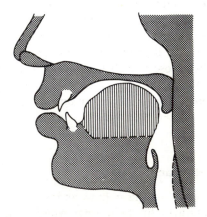

ILLUSTRATION 2. The Vowel [u]

---

[1] A few compound words may have a secondary accent under special conditions; they are an exception.

4. The consonant sound [m]

$$\text{M, м—[m]}$$

Like m in *moon* or *swim*.

5. The consonant sounds [p], [k], and [t]

$$\text{П, п—[p]} \quad\quad \text{К, к—[k]} \quad\quad \text{Т, т—[t]}$$

The Russian sounds [p], [k], and [t] are close to the corresponding English sounds, but not identical with them; the differences are the following:

The sounds [p], [k], and [t] (as in *pool, cool, tool*) are produced by momentarily blocking the passage of the breath, then "exploding" the closure. For [p] this closure is formed by the lips; for [k] by the back portion of the tongue pressed against the roof of the mouth; and for [t] by the tip of the tongue in the front of the mouth. This mechanism is essentially the same in both languages. In Russian, however, the closure is formed with less tension, and the pressure of the breath, as it "explodes" the closure, is weaker. The result, acoustically, in English, is that aspiration (a short breathing sound) usually accompanies the sounds [p], [k], and [t], especially before stressed vowels. In Russian this aspiration is absent.

For English [t] the tip of the tongue touches the teeth-ridge, just above the inner surface of the upper teeth and gums. For Russian [t] the tip of the tongue contacts the inner surface of the upper teeth themselves. The slight difference in the position of the tongue makes for a perceptibly different quality of the sound (see the illustrations below).

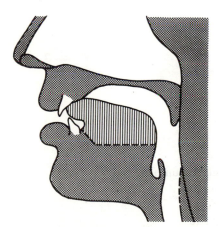 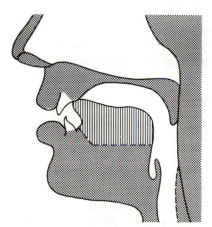

ILLUSTRATION 3. The Russian [t]　　　ILLUSTRATION 4. The English [t]

Read the following words, being careful, for [p], [k], and [t], to avoid aspiration, and for [t], to touch the teeth with the tip of the tongue, making the contact lower than in the English articulation. These examples, and all those in the sections on phonetics in the first three units, are intended as illustrations of sound patterns and need not be memorized.

тут	here	том	tome	пакт	pact
тот	that	там	there	пот	sweat
так	so	ком	lump	па́па	papa
мак	poppy	кум	godfather	пу́ма	puma
как	how	кто	who	ма́ма	mama
кот	tomcat	такт	tact	мука́	flour

6. The consonant sounds [d], [n], and [l]

Д, д—[d]   Н, н—[n]   Л, л—[l]

As for [t], the tip of the tongue must touch the upper teeth, lower than in the English articulation, for [d], [n], and [l]. Russian [l] in the words listed below, whatever its position in the word, is close to English final *l* as in *bill*.

дом	house	но́та	note	ла́мпа	lamp
да	yes	пол	floor	пла́та	pay
Дон	Don River	па́лка	stick	плато́к	kerchief
ду́ма	thought	он	he	тала́нт	talent
да́ма	lady	по́лка	shelf	кла́пан	valve
Ада́м	Adam	ла́па	paw	тума́н	mist
но	but	план	plan	купо́н	coupon
		ку́кла	doll		

7. Pronunciation of consecutive vowels

Two consecutive vowels do not merge into a one-syllable diphthong in Russian, but are pronounced separately, as in:

    кло́ун, clown, pronounced [kló-un], two syllables.
    пау́к, spider, pronounced [pa-úk], two syllables.
    нау́ка, science, pronounced [na-ú-ka], three syllables.

8. Other consonant sounds

С, с—[s]

Like *s* in *so*, but *not s* in *is*.

сок	juice	стол	table	стака́н	glass (tumbler)
сон	dream	стул	chair	со́да	soda
нос	nose	сукно́	cloth	пост	post
слон	elephant	кусо́к	piece	па́ста	paste

З, з—[z]

Like *z* in *zone* or *s* in *rose*.

зал	hall	до́за	dose	мазу́т	heavy oil
замо́к	lock	зонт	umbrella	зано́за	splinter
зо́на	zone	азо́т	nitrogen	каза́к	Cossack
по́за	pose	му́за	Muse	заку́ска	hors-d'oeuvre

В, в —[v]

Like *v* in *velvet*.

вал	wave, billow	ванна	bath	слава	glory
вол	ox	вакса	shoe polish	ваза	vase
волк	wolf	воск	wax	звук	sound
ствол	trunk (of tree)	лава	lava	давно	long ago

Ф, ф—[f]

Like *f* in *fact* or *fun*.

факт	fact	флот	fleet	флакон	bottle
фаза	phase	фут	foot (measure)	кофта	woman's blouse
фат	dandy	фунт	pound	тафта	taffeta
фон	background	фокус	focus	муфта	muff

Г, г—[g]

Like *g* in *get* or *good*, never like *g* in *ginger*.

гага	eider	глаза	eyes	Волга	Volga
агат	agate	глагол	verb	вагон	railroad car
фуга	fugue	глава	chapter	лгун	liar
фагот	bassoon	галка	jackdaw	сага	saga

Б, б—[b]

Like *b* in *boat* or *bath*.

бал	ball (party)	губа	lip	булка	white bread
балкон	balcony	бумага	paper	забота	worry
база	base	буква	letter (of the alphabet)	забава	fun
каблук	heel	табак	tobacco	азбука	alphabet

Р, р—[r]

Russian [r] is "trilled"; it is produced with the tip of the tongue vibrating against the teeth-ridge (usually the contact is lateral, slightly to the right or the left of the median line of the tongue and the teeth-ridge). It is close to the Scottish trilled *r*.

проза	prose	рука	hand	спорт	sport
фраза	phrase	роза	rose	форт	fort
март	March	пар	steam	арфа	harp
рот	mouth	порт	port	марка	stamp

Х, х—[x]

This sound, which has no equivalent in English, will be transcribed as [x] (it must be remembered that [x] in transcription does *not* stand for *ks* or *gz*, the sound value of

English *x*, as in *ax* or *exact*). The Russian sound [x] is close to Castilian Spanish *j* (in *Juan, jota*), German *ch* (in *Bach* or *doch*), or Scottish *ch* (*loch*). This sound is produced by the breath escaping through a narrow passage between the back of the tongue and the back of the mouth (the soft palate); a complete closure at the same point produces [k]. Russian [x] is not a harsh, scraping sound; to avoid harshness, one must be careful not to make too close a contact between the tongue and the soft palate.

мох	moss	зáпах	odor	хор	chorus
мýха	fly	слух	hearing	хвост	tail
Бах	Bach	холм	hill	храп	snoring
дух	spirit	хáта	hut	Пáсха	Easter

9. Unstressed a and o

The sound [o] occurs in Russian only in stressed syllables. Spelling requires **o** in some words and **a** in others in unstressed syllables, but phonetically the two are indistinguishable. However, the sound value of both symbols in an unstressed syllable does vary, depending on the position of this syllable in relation to the syllable under stress.

In the pretonic syllable (the syllable immediately preceding the one on which the stress falls) both **a** and **o** have the value [a] (somewhat less distinct than the stronger articulated stressed [á]):

талáнт [talánt]	talent	карáт [karát]	carat
топóр [tapór]	ax	горá [gará]	mountain
барáн [barán]	ram	доскá [daská]	board
мотóр [matór]	motor	Москвá [maskvá]	Moscow

Both **a** and **o** unstressed are also pronounced [a] in initial position, whether pretonic or not:

аромáт [aramát]	aroma	ананáс [ananás]	pineapple
облакá [ablaká]	clouds	остротá [astratá]	sharpness

In all other positions (i.e., neither in pretonic syllables nor in initial position) both **a** and **o** unstressed have the indistinct, neutral quality of the initial vowel sound in the English words *along* or *upon*, or of the final vowel in *sofa* or *polka*; this sound is called *schwa* in phonetics and is transcribed [ə]:

молокó [məlakó]	milk	óколо [ókələ]	about
головá [gəlavá]	head	кóлокол [kóləkəl]	bell
таракáн [tərakán]	cockroach	кóмната [kómnətə]	room
потолóк [pətalók]	ceiling	пáтока [pátəkə]	molasses

The following table summarizes the sound value of **a** and **o** in relation to stress (pronunciation in initial position is not included):

	PRETONIC SYLLABLE		STRESSED SYLLABLE		
Spelling:	a o	a o	a o	a o	a o
Value:	[ə]	[a]	[á] [ó]	[ə]	[ə]
молокó, milk	м о [m ə]	л о l a	к ó k ó]		
барабáн, drum	б а [b ə]	р а r a	б á н b á n]		
контóра, office		к о н [k a n	т ó t ó	р а r ə]	
палáтка, tent		п а [p a	л á т l á t	к а k ə]	
бáрхатка, velvet ribbon			б á р [b á r	х а т x ə t	к а k ə]
кóлокол, bell			к ó [k ó	л о l ə	к о л k ə l]

PRONUNCIATION DRILL

онá [aná]	she	осá [asá]	wasp
потóм [patóm]	afterwards	окнó [aknó]	window
контóра [kantórə]	office	дóктор [dóktər]	doctor
докторá [dəktará]	doctors	óблако [óbləkə]	cloud
облакá [ablaká]	clouds	панорáма [pənarámə]	panorama
протокóл [prətakól]	protocol	астронóм [astranóm]	astronomer
онó	it	óрган	organ
парадóкс	paradox	остáток	remnant
городóк	small town	мастодóнт	mastodon
водоворóт	whirlpool	полторá	one and a half
кóротко	short	островá	islands
простотá	simplicity	óкна	windows

Phonetics: The sound [j] and the letters й, я, е, ё, and ю • Palatalization of consonants: The soft sign ь and the letters я, е, ё, and ю after
consonants • The vowels и and ы • The letter э • Unstressed е
and я • Open and close variants of [e] • Palatalization before soft
consonants • Grammar: Absence of articles • Absence of link
verbs in present tense • The indefinite demonstrative это • The
word вот • Questions • "Yes" and "No" answers

Unit 2

Phonetics

1. The sound [j] and the letters й, я, е, ё, and ю

The symbol [j] will be used hereafter to transcribe the initial sound heard in *yellow*
or *yonder*, or the final sound in *say* or *boy*. In Russian, the sound [j], when it occurs
after a vowel (in final position or before a consonant), is denoted by the letter **й**
(called "short i"):

май [máj]	May	Толстóй [talstój]	Tolstoy
Дунáй [dunáj]	Danube	гáйка [gájkə]	nut
трамвáй [tramvái]	streetcar	тайгá [tajgá]	taiga
портнóй [partnój]	tailor	пострóйка [pastrójkə]	building

The sound [j] before a vowel is represented by one of the following letters which
stand for the syllable "[j] plus vowel":

Я, я stands for [ja], as *ya* in *yard:*

яхта [jáxtə]	yacht	яблоко [jábləkə]	apple
Ялта [jáltə]	Yalta	маяк [maják]	lighthouse

Е, е stands for [je], as *ye* in *yes:*

Éва [jévə]	Eve
óн éхал [ón jéxəl]	he was riding
óн уéхал [ón ujéxəl]	he rode away, he left
я поéду [já pajédu]	I shall go

Ё, ё stands for [jo], as *yo* in *yore:*

ёлка [jólkə]	Christmas tree	óн поёт [ón pajót]	he sings
заём [zajóm]	loan	óн даёт [ón dajót]	he gives

Note: **ё** occurs only in *stressed* syllables; the accent ['] over **ё** is therefore omitted.

Ю, ю stands for [ju], as *yu* in *Yukon:*

юмор [júmər]	humor	я пою [já pajú]	I sing
каюта [kajútə]	cabin	я даю [já dajú]	I give

2. Palatalization of consonants

Most Russian consonantal sounds occur in two different variants, the "hard" (non-palatalized) and the "soft" (palatalized). The "hard" pronunciation only was described in the preceding unit. Palatalized ("soft") pronunciation will hereafter be indicated in transcriptions by the sign [ˌ] under the letter: [t̞] = palatalized [t], [l̞] = palatalized [l], etc.

Palatalized and non-palatalized consonants are opposed in Russian as different sounds, and the "hardness" or "softness" of one consonant may be the only feature distinguishing two words: e.g., [brat] means *brother*; [brat̞]—*to take*; [úgəl] means *corner*; [úgəl̞]—*coal*.

English does not oppose hard and soft consonants as different sounds. More or less distinct palatalization, however, is occasionally heard in English. Thus, the initial [k] sound in *cool* is close to Russian non-palatalized [k]; in *keel*, on the other hand, it is closer to the Russian palatalized variant, [k̞]. Repeating several times *keel-cool*, one will observe that the initial consonant in *keel* is pronounced with the tongue moved forward and upward, its front close to the hard palate; in *cool*, on the other hand, the tongue is drawn back, leaving a space between its surface and the hard palate. This space works as a resonator; when it is narrowed, the sound produced has a higher pitch.

To "palatalize" a consonant means to pronounce it with the tongue brought close to the hard palate with the acoustic effect of higher pitch.

The position of the tongue for palatalized consonants may be described as that of the English "long *e*" vowel. As a first exercise, make an *ee* . . . sound as in the English word *fee*, and, trying not to change the position of your tongue, pronounce different consonants: *ee . . . tee, ee . . . lee, ee . . . nee*, etc. (see the illustrations below).

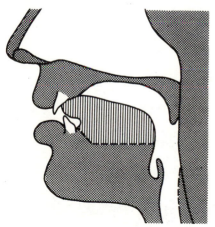

ILLUSTRATION 5.   The Russian [t]

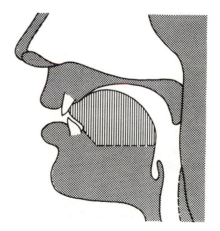

ILLUSTRATION 6.   The Russian [t̞] (palatalized)

Spelling with palatalized consonants. Russian spelling has two ways of indicating palatalization:

(1) When a palatalized consonant is in final position in a word, or is followed by a hard consonant, the special letter ь (the "soft sign") is written after the consonant.

Soft consonant in final position:

брать [bráţ]	to take	(compare hard: брат [brát]	brother)
у́голь [úgəļ]	coal	(compare hard: у́гол [úgəl]	corner)

Soft consonant followed by a hard consonant:

то́лько [tóļkə]	only	(compare hard: то́лком [tólkəm]	sensibly)
го́рько [góŗkə]	bitter	(compare hard: го́рка [górkə]	hill)

(2) When a palatalized consonant is followed by a vowel sound, then the letter representing the vowel also serves to indicate that the consonant is palatalized. The letters used for this double purpose are **я**, **е**, **ё**, and **ю** (and another letter which will be added later in this lesson).

We have seen that initially and after vowels the four letters above mean "j plus vowel." After consonants, however, the same letters mean "palatalized consonant plus vowel." In other words, the sound [a] is written **а** after a hard consonant, but **я** after a palatalized consonant; [o] after a hard consonant is written **о**, after a soft consonant **ё**, etc.[1]

To summarize the meaning of the letters **я**, **е**, **ё**, **ю**:

Initially or after a vowel:	*After a consonant, e.g. л:*
я = [ja]	**ля** = [ļa] (я ля́гу [já ļágu] I shall lie down)
е = [je]	**ле** = [ļe] (лес [ļés] forest)
ё = [jo]	**лё** = [ļó] (лён [ļón] flax)
ю = [ju]	**лю** = [ļu] (люк [ļúk] hatchway)

PRONUNCIATION DRILL

Compare the words in the left column with those in the right.

[l] — [ļ]

класс [klás]	class	кля́сть [kļáşţ]	to curse
покло́н [paklón]	bow	клён [kļón]	maple
лук [lúk]	onion	люк [ļúk]	hatchway
мол [mól]	jetty	моль [móļ]	moth
то́лком [tólkəm]	sensibly	то́лько [tóļkə]	only

[n] — [ņ]

о́н зна́л [ón znál]	he knew	о́н сня́л [ón sņál]	he removed
нос [nós]	nose	нёс [ņós]	carried
ва́нна[2] [vánnə]	bathtub	Ва́ня [váņə]	Johnny

---

[1] Before a **е** in some words of foreign origin, however, there is no palatalization, e.g., те́ннис [téņņis].

[2] Double consonants will be indicated by a double letter in phonetic transcription. They are, however, pronounced as a single long consonant.

внук [vnúk]	grandson	нюх [ņúx]	flair
трон [trón]	throne	тронь [tróņ]	touch!

[d]—[ḑ]

да́та [dátə]	date	дя́дя [ḑáḑə]	uncle
дом [dóm]	house	дёрн [ḑórn]	turf
ду́ма [dúmə]	thought	дю́на [ḑúnə]	dune

[t]—[ţ]

так [ták]	so, thus	пустя́к [puşţák]	trifle
ток [tók]	current	тёк [ţók]	flowed
стук [stúk]	knock	тюк [ţúk]	bundle
тут [tút]	here	ртуть [rtúţ]	mercury

[r]—[ŗ]

ра́да [rádə]	glad	ря́дом [ŗádəm]	beside
ро́за [rózə]	rose	грёза [gŗózə]	daydream
крут [krút]	steep	крюк [kŗúk]	hook
това́р [tavár]	merchandise	слова́рь [slaváŗ]	dictionary

[z]—[ẓ]

зал [zál]	hall	взял [vẓál]	took
взор [vzór]	glance	озёра [aẓórə]	lakes

[s]—[ş]

оса́да [asádə]	siege	я ся́ду [já şádu]	I shall sit down
суда́ [sudá]	vessels	сюда́ [şudá]	here
нос [nós]	nose	ось [óş]	axis, axle
трус [trús]	coward	Русь [rúş]	(Old) Russia

[v]—[ɣ]

вал [vál]	wave	вял [ɣál]	withered
вол [vól]	ox	вёл [ɣól]	led

[m]—[m̧]

ма́сса[2] [mássə]	mass	мя́со [m̧ásə]	meat
мол [mól]	jetty	мёл [m̧ól]	swept

[p]—[p̧]

спал [spál]	he slept	спят [sp̧át]	they sleep
порт [pórt]	port	Пётр [p̧ótr]	Peter
око́п [akóp]	trench	копь [kóp̧]	mine

3. The vowels и and ы

И, и—[i]

The letter **и** ([i] in transcription) stands for the vowel sound in *eve*, *eat*, and *see*. Consonants before **и** are always palatalized.[3] Unlike **я**, **е**, **ё**, and **ю**, however, **и** in initial position or after vowels is not usually preceded by [j]:

и́скра [ískrə]	spark	Ива́н [iván]	Ivan
или [iļi]	or	Ита́лия [itáļijə]	Italy
иска́ть [iskáṭ]	to look for	и́стина [íṣṭinə]	truth
сто́ит [stóit]	costs	хозя́ин [xaẓáin]	host, landlord
лимо́н [ļimón]	lemon	ли́ния [ļíṇijə]	line
рис [ŗís]	rice	диск [dísk]	disk
фи́зика [fíẓikə]	physics	хи́мия [xíṃijə]	chemistry
кино́ [ķinó]	movies	кри́тик [kŗíṭik]	critic
си́льно [ṣíļnə]	strongly		

Ы, ы—[ɨ]

A sound related to [i], but not identical with it, occurs after non-palatalized consonants (never initially or after vowels). The symbol for this sound is **ы**; it will be transliterated [ɨ]. English has no exact equivalent for [ɨ]; as an approximation only, it may be said that [ɨ] is rather close to the English vowel sound in *mill* or *sit*, while the vowel sound in *meal* or *seat* is close to [i]. In English, however, the two sounds differ not only in quality, but also in length, the vowel in *seat* or *meal* being longer, in *sit* or *mill* shorter. In Russian there is no difference in length between **и** [i] and **ы** [ɨ] but only a difference in the quality of the sound. Moreover, Russian **ы** [ɨ] is pronounced with the tongue a little farther back than the sound in *sit* or *mill* but not quite as far back as for the [u] sound in *woo* or *ooze* (see the illustrations below).

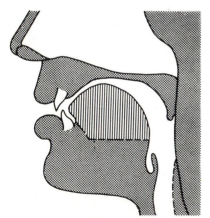

ILLUSTRATION 7. The Vowel [i]

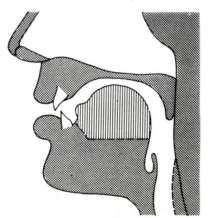

ILLUSTRATION 8. The Vowel [ɨ]

---

[3] Three consonantal sounds that are an exception will be given later.

PRONUNCIATION DRILL

Pronounce the English word, then the Russian word, drawing the tongue a little farther back.

Be careful, in pronouncing the Russian dentals, to place the tip of your tongue against the inner surface of the upper teeth, not the teeth-ridge above the gums as in English (see pages 3 and 4).

English	*Russian*	*English translation*
dim	дым [dɨm]	smoke
till	тыл [tɨl]	rear
click	клык [klɨk]	tusk
nil	ныл [nɨl]	moaned

Compare the words in the left column with those in the right.

стиль [şţíl]	style	остыл [astɨ́l]	grew cold
судить [suḍiţ]	to judge	суды́ [sudɨ́]	courts
ми́ли [ṃíļi]	miles	мы́ли [mɨ́ļi]	(they) washed
си́то [şítə]	sieve	сы́ты [sɨ́ti]	sated
висо́к [ɣisók]	temple (of head)	высо́ко [vɨsókə]	high
кри́зис [kŗíẓis]	crisis	кры́са [krɨ́sə]	rat
Рим [ŗím]	Rome	Крым [krɨ́m]	Crimea
бить [ḅíţ]	to beat	быть [bɨ́ţ]	to be
усни́ [uşņí]	fall asleep (imperative)	сны [snɨ́]	dreams

4. The letter э

Э, э—[e]

One more letter must be added to the vowels given above: the one resembling a reversed **e**, written **э**. This letter forms a pair with the letter **e**; as we know, **e** represents [je] in initial position or after a vowel; after a consonant it recalls that this consonant is palatalized, e.g., **те** [ţe]. The letter **э**, written initially or after a vowel, stands for the sound [e] without a [j]:

ел [jél]	ate	эль [éļ]	name of the letter л
я поеду [já pajédu]	I shall go	поэт [paét]	poet

The letter **э** thus belongs to the series **a**, **o**, **y**, and **ы**. "Reversed e" is not written after consonants (except for a few transliterations of foreign names), however, so that there are no hard counterparts for syllables like **те** [ţe], **де** [ḍe], **ле** [ļe], except in a few non-Russian words spelled with *e*.

The letter **э** is written initially; it occurs, however, only in the different forms of the Russian demonstrative, such as э́тот (*this*), э́ти (*these*), *etc.* and in a number of words of non-Russian origin, e.g.:

э́пос [épəs]	epos	э́хо [éxə]	echo
э́тика [éţikə]	ethics	Э́мма [émmə]	Emma
э́ра [érə]	era	Э́тна [étnə]	Mount Etna

5. Unstressed е and я

In unstressed syllables (with the exception of certain grammatical endings), е and я are pronounced close to [i], and will be transcribed as [i]:

тепéрь [ţipéŗ]	now	телефóн [ţiļifón]	telephone
тянýть [ţinúţ]	to pull	прямóй [pŗimój]	straight

The [j] is preserved if unstressed е or я are initial or follow vowels:

едá [jidá]	food	мы́ знáем [mí znájim]	we know
язы́к [jizík]	language	пóяс [pójis]	belt

Depending on the position in the word and on the tempo of delivery, the sound of unstressed я and е may be further weakened, becoming [ə].

6. Open and close variants of [e]

The sound [e] (е or э stressed) varies somewhat depending on the sound that follows it: [e] is *open* if followed by a non-palatalized consonant (also in final position); *close* if followed by a palatalized consonant. The range of [e] sounds may be said to occupy a place between [a] and [i], with open [e] being nearer to [a] and close [e] nearer to [i]. Open [e] resembles the *e* of English *met*; close [e] the *a* of English *mate*, but without the "y" element of the long English "a" sound.

Close [e] will be transcribed [ę].

Compare words in the left column with those in the right:

[e]		[ę]	
вес [ɣés]	weight	весь [ɣéş]	the whole
плен [pḷén]	captivity	лень [ļéņ]	laziness
э́то [étə]	this	э́ти [éţi]	these
те [ţé]	those	тень [ţéņ]	shadow
где [gḍé]	where	день [ḍéņ]	day

Other vowels too have a somewhat higher quality, due to a narrower articulation, before palatalized consonants, and especially between two palatalized sounds; compare:

[a] in лопáта [lapátə]	spade,	and in пять [pá̧ţ]	five
[o] in тот [tót]	that,	and in тётя [ţó̧ţə]	aunt
[u] in Тýла [túlə]	Tula (town),	and in тюль [ţú̧ļ]	tulle

7. Palatalization before soft consonants

In certain combinations, consonants are palatalized when followed by other palatalized consonants, e.g.:

гость [góşţ]	guest	[ş] before [ţ]	
здесь [ẓḍéş]	here	[ẓ] before [ḍ]	
зóнтик [zóņţik]	umbrella	[ņ] before [ţ]	
индю́к [iņḍúk]	turkey cock	[ņ] before [ḍ]	

The consonant [l] is pronounced hard before palatalized consonants. All consonants remain hard before [g], [k], [x], and [ŗ].

Grammar

1. Absence of articles

Russian has no articles, definite or indefinite, such as *the* and *a* in English.

2. Absence of link verbs in present tense

A sentence present in meaning is formed in Russian without a link verb (*am*, *is*, *are* serve as link verbs in English). Words other than verbs may be used as predicates, e.g., adverbs:

Óн **тýт**.	He is here.
Газéта **тáм**.	The newspaper is there.

or nouns:

Ивáн **дóктор**.	Ivan is a doctor.
Лóндон **пóрт**.	London is a port.
Вóлга **рекá**.	The Volga is a river.

3. The indefinite demonstrative э́то

The word **э́то** introduces something whose name or definition is supplied by the sentence:

Э́то университéт.	*This* (or *that*) *is* a university.
Э́то профéссор Брáун.	*This* (or *that*) *is* Professor Brown.
Э́то Вóлга.	*This* (or *that*) *is* the Volga.
Э́то Óльга и Нúна.	*It's* Olga and Nina.
Э́то профéссор и студéнт.	*It's* a professor and a student.

4. The word вот

The word **вот** points out something or someone present or coming into sight, usually with a gesture in the direction of this object or person:

Вóт перó.	Here's a pen.
Вóт Ивáн!	Here's Ivan! (Here comes Ivan!)
Вóт газéта.	There's the newspaper.

The different uses of **тýт**, **э́то**, and **вот** may be illustrated as follows:

Газéта **тýт**.	The newspaper *is here*.
Дóктор Брáун **тýт**.	Doctor Brown *is here*.

The above are statements about *location* in which **тýт** may mean *here* in this house, apartment, or room, though not necessarily in sight.

Э́то газе́та.	*This is* a newspaper.
Э́то до́ктор Бра́ун.	*This is* Doctor Brown.

These sentences with **э́то** identify an object or a person present, the assumption being that the listener does not know what the object or who the person is.

Во́т газе́та.	*Here's* the (or a) newspaper.
Во́т до́ктор Бра́ун!	*Here's* Doctor Brown!

The first sentence may be uttered while *pointing at* the paper (the listener was looking for it), or *handing* it to the listener. The second sentence may signal the arrival of Doctor Brown, a person known to the listener.

The word **вот** is *never* used in interrogative or negative sentences; its function is limited to asserting the presence of a person or object.

5. Questions

The word order in an interrogative sentence is usually the same as in a declarative sentence, e.g.:

Э́то университе́т?	Is this a university?
Э́то профе́ссор Бра́ун?	Is this Professor Brown?
Во́лга река́?	Is the Volga a river?
Ива́н до́ктор?	Is Ivan a doctor?

In a question the key word is marked by a rising intonation, especially on its stressed syllable.[4] Often, but not always, the last word in a short "yes-or-no" question is the key word; e.g., in **Э́то до́м?**, **до́м** is the key, and suffers the rise.

О́н **ту́т?**	Is he here? (not there)
Газе́та **та́м?**	Is the newspaper over there? (not here)

Questions formed with question words (e.g., **где?**) have *rising* intonation on the question word, *falling* intonation at the end:

Гдé кни́га?	Where is the book?
Кто́ э́то?	Who is that?
—**Кто́** Ива́н? —О́н студе́нт.	—Who is Ivan? —He's a student.

6. "Yes" and "No" answers

Yes in Russian is **да**. In a "yes" answer, the question, or the key word alone, is often repeated after the introductory **да**:

Question	*"Yes" answer*
О́н ту́т?	Да́, о́н ту́т. (or: Да́, ту́т.)
Is he here?	

---

[4] Declarative sentences in Russian have a pronounced falling intonation at the end of the sentence, more so than in English.

Газе́та та́м?	Да́, газе́та та́м. (or: Да́, та́м.)
Is the newspaper there?	
Бра́ун профе́ссор?	Да́, о́н профе́ссор. (or: Да́, профе́ссор.)
Is Brown a professor?	

No in Russian is **нет**; like **да** it is an independent word-phrase. The negative particle, English *not*, is **не**; it is pronounced jointly with the word negated:

не ту́т [ṇitút]	not here
не студе́нт [ṇistuḍént]	not a student
не до́ма [ṇidómə]	not at home
не та́м [ṇitám]	not there

Question	*"No" answer*
Бра́ун профе́ссор?	Не́т, он не профе́ссор.
Is Brown a professor?	
Э́то музе́й?	Не́т, э́то не музе́й.
Is this the museum?	
Библиоте́ка ту́т?	Не́т, библиоте́ка не ту́т. Ту́т музе́й.
Is the library here?	

PATTERN SENTENCES

Read the first nine pairs of sentences until you are thoroughly familiarized with them. Next read the Russian sentences aloud two times. Then cover them and translate back from their English counterparts. Finally, cover the English and translate from the Russian. Do the same with the second group of paired sentences.

1. Э́то кла́сс.
2. Во́т студе́нт; во́т студе́нтка.
3. Во́т сто́л; во́т сту́л; та́м окно́.

4. Э́то стена́; э́то доска́.
5. Во́т кни́га, перо́ и бума́га.
6. —Э́то окно́? —Не́т, э́то не окно́! Э́то доска́. Окно́ та́м.
7. —Э́то потоло́к? —Не́т, э́то не потоло́к! Э́то по́л.
8. —Э́то доска́ или по́лка? —Э́то доска́.

9. —Э́то сту́л или сто́л? —Э́то сту́л. Во́т сто́л.

10. —Э́то ла́мпа? —Не́т, э́то не ла́мпа! Э́то кни́га.
11. Я́ тепе́рь ту́т.
12. —Где́ тепе́рь Ива́н? —О́н до́ма.
13. —Где́ тепе́рь О́льга? —Она́ ту́т. Во́т она́!

1. This is a classroom.
2. Here is a student; here is a co-ed.
3. Here is a table; here is a chair; (over) there is a window.
4. This is a wall; this is a blackboard.
5. Here are a book, a pen, and (some) paper.
6. —Is this a window? —No, it's not a window! It's a blackboard. The window is (over) there.
7. —Is this the ceiling? —No, it's not the ceiling. It's the floor.
8. —Is this a blackboard or a shelf? —It's a blackboard.
9. —Is this a chair or a table? —It's a chair. There is a table!
10. —Is this a lamp? —No, it's not a lamp! It's a book.
11. I am here now.
12. —Where is Ivan now? —He's at home.
13. —Where is Olga now? —She's here. Here she is!

14. —Где теперь Ни́на и А́нна? —Они́ ту́т. Во́т они́!

15. —Во́т до́м. Э́то университе́т? —Да́, э́то университе́т.

16. —Где библиоте́ка? —Библиоте́ка та́м.

17. —Бори́с, вы́ профе́ссор? —Не́т, я́ не профе́ссор. Я́ студе́нт.

18. —Я́ студе́нт? —Не́т, вы́ профе́ссор.

14. —Where are Nina and Anna now? —They are here. Here they are!

15. —Here is a building. Is this the university? —Yes, this is the university.

16. —Where is the library? —The library is (over) there.

17. —Boris, are you a professor? —No, I am not a professor. I'm a student.

18. —Am I a student? —No, you're a professor.

DRILLS

A. *Answer the following questions in Russian, but not just by* **да** *or* **нет**.

1. Где́ Ива́н? О́н до́ма?
2. Где́ тепе́рь Ни́на?
3. Где́ доска́?
4. Э́то окно́ и́ли стена́?
5. Библиоте́ка ту́т?
6. Э́то сту́л и́ли сто́л?
7. Вы́ профе́ссор?
8. Ту́т университе́т и́ли музе́й?
9. Я́ студе́нт?
10. Где́ А́нна и О́льга?
11. Э́то кни́га и́ли газе́та?
12. Э́то музе́й и́ли университе́т?
13. Вы́ тепе́рь до́ма?
14. Я́ до́ктор?
15. Ту́т библиоте́ка?
16. А́нна студе́нт и́ли студе́нтка?

B. *Translate into Russian.*

1. The museum is here.
   The museum is not here.
   This is not the museum.
   The museum's (over) there.
2. This is a newspaper.
   Here's the newspaper.
   The newspaper is here.
3. Anna is not here; she is at home.
   This is not Anna; this is Olga.
   Here are Anna and Olga.
4. Here is the lamp.
   The lamp is here.
   This is not a lamp; this is a window.

Phonetics: The letters ж, ш, ц, ч, and щ • Consonant-vowel
incompatibilities • Palatalization of г, к, and х • Spelling Rules
1–4 • Voiced and voiceless consonants • The separative signs •
The Russian script • The Russian alphabet

Unit **3**

Phonetics

1. The letters ж and ш

Ж, ж —[ž]   Ш, ш —[š]

The letter **ж** (transcribed ž) stands for a sound close to that of *s* in *pleasure* or *z* in *azure*; the letter **ш** (transcribed š) for a sound close to *sh* in *ship*.

The Russian sounds [ž] and [š] are "harder" (that is, they have a lower pitch) than the corresponding English sounds. English [ž] (*s* in *pleasure*) and [š] (*sh* in *ship*) are articulated with the tongue brought close to the frontal part of the roof of the mouth (the hard palate), in a position much like the one for Russian palatalization. The tip of the tongue is on the level of the teeth-ridge. For the Russian articulation the tongue is drawn farther back and its tip (slightly curved upward) is just above the teeth-ridge (see the illustration below).

The sounds denoted in Russian by the letters **ж** (*s* in *pleasure*, but harder) and **ш** (*sh* in *ship*, but harder) are peculiar in that they are never palatalized. The two sounds

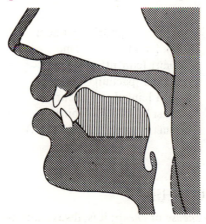

ILLUSTRATION 9.   The Consonants [š], [ž]

are hard even when followed by a "soft sign" (ь). This "soft sign" is purely orthographic and does not affect pronunciation.

The spelling of vowel sounds after ж [ž] and ш [š] is governed by tradition, and does not always reflect the phonetic reality.

Vowel sounds after ж [ž] and ш [š] are written and pronounced as follows. [a] is written **a**: жар [žár] fever; шар [šár] ball, sphere. [o] is written **o** in some words (but only in stressed syllables), **ё** in others, with no difference in pronunciation: прыжóк [prižók] jump; жёлтый [žóltij] yellow; шóпот [šópət] whisper; шёлк [šólk] silk. [u] is written **y**: жук [žúk] beetle; шум [šúm] noise. [e] is written **e**, but without palatalization of the consonant: жест [žést] gesture; шест [šést] pole, staff. Unstressed **e**, normally pronounced [i], sounds like [ɨ] after ж and ш: желéзо [žiḷézə] iron; шестóй [šɨstój] sixth. The letter **ы** is never written after ж and ш, but **и** is pronounced [ɨ] without palatalization: óн жил [ón žɨl] he lived; óн шил [ón šɨl] he sewed.

PRONUNCIATION DRILL

пожáр [pažár]	fire	шáпка [šápkə]	cap
oбжóра [abžórə]	glutton	мешóк [m̦išók]	bag
абажýр [abažúr]	lampshade	шýтка [šútkə]	joke
жир [žír]	fat	широтá [širatá]	breadth
жесть [žéṣṭ]	tin plate	шесть [šéṣṭ]	six
женá [žɨná]	wife	решетó [r̦išitó]	sieve
жёны [žóni]	wives	решётка [r̦išótkə]	lattice

2. The letter ц

Ц, ц—[c]

The letter **ц** (transcribed [c]) stands for the sound *ts* as in *its* or *tz* in *Switzerland*. Like ж [ž] and ш [š], ц [c] is always hard. Both the vowels **и** and **ы** are written after ц (**и** in words of foreign origin, **ы** in native words and in grammatical endings); both **и** and **ы** after ц sound like [ɨ]. Unstressed **e** also has the [ɨ] sound:

PRONUNCIATION DRILL

цирк [círk]	circus	цилúндр [cɨḷíndr]	cylinder
цúник [cíṇik]	cynic	цинк [cínk]	zinc
цензýра [cɨnzúrə]	censorship	цемéнт [cim̦ént]	cement
ценá [cɨná]	price	поцелýй [pacɨlúj]	kiss
цыплёнок [cɨpḷónək]	chick	цынгá [cɨngá]	scurvy
птúца [pṭícə]	bird	птúцы [pṭíci]	birds
конéц [kaṇéc]	end	концы́ [kancí]	ends (pl.)

3. The letters ч and щ

Ч, ч—[č]   Щ, щ—[šč]

The letter **ч** [č] represents the sound of *ch* in *cheese* or *cheap*; it is always soft and is quite close to the English sound.

The letter **щ** stands for a combination of a soft [š] and a soft [č], as in *Danish cheese* pronounced as one word: "*Danishcheese.*" The [č] element tends to be rather weak, and in pronunciation which is perfectly correct and prevalent in the Moscow area, the [č] in **щ** is replaced by a second soft [š], the letter **щ** sounding like *Danish sheep* pronounced as one word: "*Danishsheep.*"

Both [č] and [šč] ([šš]) are always palatalized. Just as **ж** and **ш** remain hard even when followed by a soft sign, so **ч** and **щ** are soft whether followed or not by a soft sign in final position; this soft sign is purely orthographic:

ночь [nóč]	night	врач [vráč]	physician
вещь [véšč]	thing	товáрищ [tavári̦šč]	comrade

The spelling of vowels after **ч** [č] and **щ** [šč] is also rather arbitrary. Vowels after **ч** [č] and **щ** [šč] are written and pronounced as follows:

[a] is written **а** (never **я**!):

час [čás]	hour	пощáда [paščádə]	mercy

[o] is written **ё** and in some words **о**:

чёрный [čórnij]	black	щётка [ščótkə]	brush
крючóк [kr̦učók]	hook	борщóк [bar̦ščók]	a soup

[u] is written **у** (never **ю**!):

чýдо [čúdə]	miracle	щýка [ščúkə]	pike (fish)
я хочý [já xačú]	I want	я тащý [já taščú]	I drag

[e] is written **е**:

честь [čéṣț]	honor	щель [ščél̦]	crack

[i] is written **и**:

читáть [čitáț]	to read	щи [ščí]	cabbage soup
чи́стый [čístij]	clean	щипцы́ [ščipcí]	pliers

[i] is also the sound of unstressed **а** and **е**:

часы́ [čisí]	hours, clock	щади́ть [ščid̦íț]	to show mercy, spare
чемодáн [čimadán]	suitcase	щекá [ščiká]	cheek
чернúла [čir̦n̦ílə]	ink	щенóк [ščinók]	puppy

4. Consonant-vowel incompatibilities

With the three sounds that are always hard: **ж** [ž], **ш** [š], and **ц** [c], and the two that are always soft: **ч** [č] and **щ** [šč], Russian spelling does not make a consistent use of the devices normally showing palatalization. Thus the soft sign is written in certain words after **ж**, **ш**, **ч**, and **щ** in final position, though **ж** and **ш** remain hard despite the soft sign, and **ч** and **щ** are soft even when no soft sign is written after them.

It has been seen also that not all vowel letters are written after the three "always hard" consonants, **ж**, **ш**, and **ц**, and the two "always soft" ones, **ч** and **щ**, nor are those that are written used consistently in terms of palatalization. The combinations of the five consonants with different vowels are given below; **т** [t] has been added as an example of any consonant with a normal range of hard-soft oppositions.

	WITH [a]		WITH [ó][1]		WITH [u]		WITH [i]/[i]		WITH [é]	
	hard	*soft*	*hard*	*soft*	*hard*	*soft*	*hard*	*soft*	*hard*	*soft*
т [t]	та [ta]	тя [ṭa]	тó [tó]	тё [ṭó]	ту [tu]	тю [ṭu]	ты [ti]	ти [ṭi]		те [ṭé]
ж [ž]:	жа [ža]		жó жё [žó]			жу [žu]		жи [ži]		же [žé]	
ш [š]:	ша [ša]		шó шё [šó]			шу [šu]		ши [ši]		ше [šé]	
ц [c]:	ца [ca]		цó [có]			цу [cu]		цы ци [ci]		це [cé]	
ч [ç]:		ча [ça]		чё чó [çó]			чу [çu]		чи [çi]		че [çé]
щ [šç]:		ща [šça]		щё щó [ščó]			щу[šču]		щи [šči]		ще [ščé]

5. Palatalization of г, к, and x

Another group of consonants, known as velars, г [g], к [k], and x [x], can be both palatalized and non-palatalized. They are palatalized, however, only before the vowel sounds [e] and [i], indeed they are *always* palatalized before these vowels. In other words, non-palatalized [g], [k], [x] *never* occur before [i]. Hence the velars г [g], к [k], and x [x] do not appear in the hard-soft oppositions possible with most consonants:

before [a]:	га [ga],	ка [ka],	ха [xa]—hard only
before [o]:	го [go],	ко [ko],	хо [xo]—hard only
before [u]:	гу [gu],	ку [ku],	ху [xu]—hard only
before [i/i]:	ги [gi],	ки [ḳi],	хи [x̦i] —*soft* only
before [e]:	ге [ge],	ке [ḳe],	хе [x̦e] —*soft* only
final:	г[2]	к [k],	x [x] —hard only

Summary of consonant-vowel incompatibilities. Some of the incompatibilities between consonants and vowels mentioned above are phonetic, e.g., the sound [i] is never heard after the sound [ç], nor is the letter ы written after the letter ч. The sound [i], however, is heard after [ž], but a rule of spelling, which is arbitrary, requires it to be written и. The following is a summary of rules for consonant-vowel incompatibilities considered from the viewpoint of *spelling*.

6. Spelling Rules 1–4

SPELLING RULE 1:		Write o	only if stressed after	ж	ш	ц	ч	щ	(Otherwise write e.)	
SPELLING RULE 2:	Never write ы	after		ж	ш		ч	щ	г к х	
SPELLING RULE 3:	Never write я, ю	after		ж	ш	ц	ч	щ	г к х	
SPELLING RULE 4:	Never write ё	after				ц			г к[3] х	

[1] It will be recalled that the vowel sound [o] occurs only under stress. Unstressed, the letter o sounds like a ([a] or [ə]—see page 6).

[2] The pronunciation of г in final position is treated in Section 7 below.

[3] The syllable кё [ḳó] occurs in one verb, ткёт (*weaves*), and in the noun маркёр (billiard marker).

7. Voiced and voiceless consonants

The sound we call "voice" is produced by the breath when, as it passes through the larynx, it makes the vocal cords vibrate. All vowel sounds are "voiced." Some consonants, too, such as [z], [v], [d], [g], are voiced, as if, when articulating them, we were also uttering an indefinite vowel sound. Other consonants (like [s], [f], [t], [k]) are "voiceless"; they are produced with the breath alone, with no vibration of the vocal cords. The difference becomes clear if one compares two consonants articulated in exactly the same manner except that one is voiced and the other voiceless, e.g., *zzz. . .* (voiced) and *sss. . .* (voiceless).

Most Russian consonants fall into pairs in which two sounds (like [z] and [s]) are identical in articulation and differ only in the voice being present in one and absent in the other:

Voiced:	б [b]	в [v]	д [d]	з [z]	ж [ž]	г [g]	—	—	—
Voiceless:	п [p]	ф [f]	т [t]	с [s]	ш [š]	к [k][4]	ц [c][5]	ч [č][5]	щ [ščč][5]

Voiced consonants (both hard and soft) become "unvoiced" when (1) in final position and (2) before voiceless consonants; thus, occasionally they sound like their voiceless counterparts: [b] like [p], [v] like [f], etc.

(1) Unvoicing in final position:

[b] > [p]:	зуб [zúp]	tooth	дробь [dróp]	fraction
[v] > [f]:	ров [róf]	ditch	кровь [króf̧]	blood
[d] > [t]:	сад [sát]	garden	сядь [s̨át̨]	sit down (imperative)
[z] > [s]:	туз [tús]	ace	мазь [más̨]	ointment
[ž] > [š]:	нож [nóš]	knife	рожь [róš]	rye
[g] > [k]:	снег [s̨n̨ék]	snow	луг [lúk]	meadow

(2) Unvoicing before voiceless consonants:

[bk] > [pk]:	скóбка [skópkə]	bracket
[vč] > [fč]:	вчерá [fčirá]	yesterday
[gk] > [xk]:	легкó [l̨ixkó]	easy
[dp] > [tp]:	пóдпись [pótp̨iş]	signature
[žk] > [šk]:	лóжка [lóškə]	spoon
[zk] > [sk]:	ýзко [úskə]	narrow
[bs] > [ps]:	обсудúть [apsud̨ít̨]	to discuss
[vt] > [ft]:	автомобúль [aftəmab̨íl̨]	automobile
[gt] > [kt]:	ля́гте [l̨ákt̨i]	lie down (imperative)
[dk] > [tk]:	лóдка [lótkə]	boat
[žk] > [šk]:	крýжка [krúškə]	mug
[zk] > [sk]:	блúзко [bl̨ískə]	near

On the other hand, voiceless consonants are voiced before **б** [b], **д** [d], **з** [z], **ж** [ž], and **г** [g], i.e., before all voiced consonants except **в** [v]:

---

[4] But **г** is pronounced as [x] before [k], e.g., лёгкий [lóx̨ķij] *easy*; мя́гкий [m̨áx̨ķij] *soft*; also in **Бог** [bóx] *God*.

[5] These have voiced equivalents, but their spellings require two letters: дз [dz], дж [dž], and жж [žž].

[sb] > [zb]:	сбор [zbór]	collection, gathering
[td] > [dd]:	отдéл [aḍḍél]	division, department
[tz] > [dz]:	óтзвук [ódzvuk]	echo
[kž] > [gž]:	тáкже [tágžə]	equally
[sg] > [zg]:	сгибáть [zgibáṭ]	to bend

8. The separative signs

In certain Russian words the sound [j] is heard between a consonant and a vowel, e.g., [şiṃjá], *family*, or [staṭjá], *article*; a sound close to [ṭja] is heard in rapid speech in an English phrase such as " we*t* *y*ard."

In spelling the combination of sounds "consonant + [j] + vowel" is rendered by writing a soft sign **ь** (or a special separative sign **ъ**—see next paragraph) after the consonant, followed by the letter **я** for [ja], **е** for [je], **ё** for [jo], or **ю** for [ju]. The sign *separates* the consonant from the vowel, in order that the latter preserve its initial [j]. Compare:

хотя [xaṭá]	although	—no [j];	but	статья [staṭjá]	article	—[j] before [a]
Пётр [pótr]	Peter	—no [j];	but	пьёт [pjót]	drinks	—[j] before [o]
ключ [kḷúč̣]	key	—no [j];	but	я лью [já ḷjú]	I pour	—[j] before [u]

In a number of words another sign, the "hard" separative sign **ъ**, is used. The consonants **б**, **т**, **д** are *not* palatalized before **ъ**; other consonants usually are.

объявлéние [abjivḷéṇijə]	advertisement
отъéзд [atjést]	departure
подъéхать [padjéxəṭ]	to drive up
съесть [şjéṣṭ]	to eat up
съезд [şjést]	congress
въéхать [vjéxəṭ]	to drive in
объя́тие [abjáṭijə]	embrace

PRONUNCIATION DRILL

Read across.

счáстье [şč̣áṣṭjə]	luck, happiness		чáсти [č̣áṣṭi]	parts
пья́ница [pjáṇicə]	drunkard		пя́тница [páṭṇicə]	Friday
Татья́на [taṭjánə]	Tatiana		тя́нет [ṭáṇit]	pulls
съёмка [şjómkə]	filming		сёмга [şómgə]	smoked salmon
шитьё [šiṭjó]	sewing		тёмный [ṭómnij]	dark
плáтье [pláṭjə]	dress		Кáтя [káṭə]	Katia
съесть [şjéṣṭ]	to eat up		сесть [şéṣṭ]	to sit down
судья́ [suḍjá]	judge		идя́ [iḍá]	walking

PATTERN SENTENCES

Study these sentences carefully until you are prepared to translate from Russian to English and back. Then read the Russian sentences aloud several times for fluency.

1. —Что́ э́то? —Э́то голова́.
2. —Что́ э́то? —Э́то лицо́.
3. —Что́ э́то? —Э́то гла́з.

1. —What is this? —It's a head.
2. —What is this? —It's a face.
3. —What is this? —It's an eye.

4. —Где нóс? —Вóт нóс.

4. —Where is the nose? —Here's the nose.

5. —Это тóже нóс? —Нéт, это не нóс; это рóт.

5. —Is this a nose, too? —No, this is not a nose; it's a mouth.

6. —«Прáвда» газéта или журнáл? —«Прáвда» газéта.

6. —Is *Pravda* a newspaper or a magazine? —*Pravda* is a newspaper.

7. —Чтó это? Это карандáш? —Дá, это карандáш.

7. —What's this? Is it a pencil? —Yes, it's a pencil.

8. —Это тóже карандáш? —Нéт, это не карандáш! Это перó.

8. —Is this a pencil too? —No, it's not a pencil! It's a pen.

9. —Ктó Жýков? —Жýков генерáл.

9. —Who is Zhukov? —Zhukov is a general.

10. —Ктó Брáун? Óн студéнт? —Нéт, óн ужé дóктор.

10. —Who is Brown? Is he a student? —No, he is a doctor already.

11. —Мы́ сейчáс⁶ дóма? —Нéт, мы́ сейчáс тýт.

11. —Are we at home now? —No, we are here now.

12. —Где сейчáс Áнна и Ни́на? Они́ тýт? —Нéт, они́ ужé дóма.

12. —Where are Anna and Nina now? Are they here? —No, they're already at home.

Conversation

Учи́тель и клáсс

Учи́тель. —Дóбрый дéнь! Кáк вы́ поживáете?

—Good day! How are you?

Клáсс. —Óчень хорошó, спаси́бо. Вы́ кáк?

—Very well, thank you. How are you?

У. —Спаси́бо, тóже хорошó. Джóн, покажи́те, где пóл и потолóк.

—I'm well too, thank you. John, show where the floor and the ceiling are.

Джон. —Вóт пóл, вóт потолóк.

—There is the floor, there is the ceiling.

У. —Прáвильно. Тепéрь вы́, Мэ́ри, покажи́те, где доскá.

—Correct (right). Now you, Mary, show (us) where the blackboard is.

Мэ́ри. —Вóт доскá.

—There is the blackboard.

У. —Нéт, это не доскá; это стенá!

—No, that isn't the blackboard; that's the wall!

М. —Áх, дá! Это стенá. Доскá тáм.

—Oh yes! That's the wall. The blackboard is (over) there.

У. —Прáвильно. Повтори́те, пожáлуйста.⁷

—Correct (right). Please repeat.

М. —Это стенá. Доскá тáм.

—That is the wall. The blackboard is (over) there.

У. —Тóм, чтó это?

—Tom, what is that?

Том. —Это лицó.

—That is a face.

У. —А чтó это?

—And what is that?

Т. —Это глáз.

—That's an eye.

У. —Хорошó. Это тóже глáз?

—All right. Is this an eye too?

Т. —Нéт, это не глáз; это рóт.

—No, that's not an eye; that's a mouth.

У. —Покажи́те, где головá и где рукá.

—Show (me) where the head is and where the hand is.

Т. —Вóт головá; вóт рукá.

—Here is the head; here is the hand.

---

⁶ **Сейчáс** and **тепéрь** are nearly synonymous, but **сейчáс** is more common in the sense of *right now, this moment*. **Тепéрь** means *now* in the broader sense of *at present, nowadays, in our times*.

⁷ **Пожáлуйста** (*please*), pronounce [pažálustə].

РОССЍЯ

0   375

Масштаб

Ледовйтый океáн

НОРВЕГИЯ

ШВЕЦИЯ

ФИНЛЯНДИЯ

У Р А Л

С И Б И Р ь

Ленингрáд

Невá

Бáлтийское мóре

•Свердлóвск

Вóлга

•Москвá

ПÓЛЬША

Р   О   С   С   Й   Я

ЧЕХОСЛОВАКИЯ

ВÉНГРИЯ

Днепр

•Кíев

Дон

УКРАЙНА

Хáрьков

•Волгогрáд

РУМЫ́НИЯ

Одéсса

КРЫМ

БОЛГÁРИЯ

Ялта

ГРÉЦИЯ

чёрное мóре

Сóчи

Эльбрýс

К А В К А З

Каспíйское мóре

Бакý•

ТУ́РЦИЯ

ИРÁН

У. —Хорошо́. О́льга, тепе́рь чита́йте, пожа́луйста.

—Fine. Olga, read now, please.

О́льга. —«Во́т ка́рта. Э́то Сове́тский Сою́з. Во́т го́род. Э́то Москва́.»

—"Here is a map. This is the Soviet Union. Here is a city. It is Moscow."

У. —Повтори́те.

—Repeat.

О. —«Во́т ка́рта. Э́то Сове́тский Сою́з. Во́т го́род. Э́то Москва́.»

—"Here is a map. This is the Soviet Union. Here is a city. It is Moscow."

У. —Хорошо́. Тепе́рь пиши́те: «Во́т Ленингра́д, Ки́ев, и Ха́рьков. Во́т река́. Э́то Во́лга. Во́т Сиби́рь и во́т Кавка́з.» Очень хорошо́. Э́то всё; уже́ звоно́к. До свида́ния.

—Fine. Now write: "Here are Leningrad, Kiev, and Kharkov. Here is a river. It's the Volga. Here is Siberia and here is the Caucasus." Very good. That's all; there's the bell already. Good-bye.

DRILLS

A. *Translate into English.*

1. —Ка́к вы пожива́ете? —О́чень хорошо́, спаси́бо.
2. Во́т ка́рта. Во́т го́род Москва́.
3. —Где́ Ки́ев? —Ки́ев та́м. —Пра́вильно.
4. Во́т Сиби́рь, и ту́т река́ Ле́на.
5. Во́т Енисе́й; э́то то́же река́.
6. Чита́йте, пожа́луйста: «Во́т ка́рта. Э́то Сове́тский Сою́з.»
7. —Покажи́те, где́ Во́лга. —Во́т Во́лга. —Пра́вильно.
8. —Где́ Кавка́з? —Во́т Кавка́з. —О́чень хорошо́! Спаси́бо.
9. Уже́ звоно́к. До свида́ния!

B. *Translate into Russian.*

1. —Is Olga at home already? —Yes, she is at home. 2. —Is the pencil also here? —Yes, the pencil is also here. 3. That is the teacher. 4. —Here is the book. —Thank you. 5. —How are you? —Thank you, not very well. 6. The window is (over) there. 7. —Where is the paper? —Here it is. 8. —Is this the floor or the ceiling? —It's the floor. 9. —Who are you? —I'm a student. 10. —What is this? —It's a pen. —Correct. 11. —Good day! How are you? —Fine, thank you! 12. —Where is the wall and where is the window? —The window and the wall are there. 13. —What is that? Is it the bell? —Yes, it's the bell. 14. That's all. Good-bye!

The Russian Script

The letters а, о, е, и, у

А, а   _А а_   И, и   _И и_

О, о   _О о_   У, у   _У у_

Е, е   _Е е_

The letters с, р, в, х

C, c *C c*   В, в *B b*

Р, р *P p*   X, х *X x*

Copy the following words:

Рис, Rice   *Рис*

Ухá, Fish soup   *Уха*

Хéрес, Sherry (Jerez)   *Херес*

Вéра, Éва и Варвáра.   Vera, Eva, and Barbara.

Вера, Ева и Варвара.

В Сахáре сýхо.   In the Sahara it is dry.

В Сахаре сухо

The letters д, п, т

Д, д *D g* or *д*

Note that capital **Д** is written like the English script capital *D*, while the small letter is written like English script small *g* (first variant); the second variant is close to the English *d*.

П, п *П п*

Note that small Russian **п** is written like English *n* in script.

Т, т *T m*

Note that small Russian **т** is written like English *m*.
Copy the following words:

Давйд, David   *Давид*

Пётр, Peter   *Пётр*

Óпера, Opera   *Опера*

Спорт, Sport   *Спорт*

Теа́тр, Theater *Театр*

Write in Russian script:

Ве́ра и Пётр в теа́тре.
Vera and Peter are at the theater.

Варва́ра сестра́ Дави́да.
Barbara is David's sister.

«Аи́да» о́пера Ве́рди.
Aida is an opera by Verdi.

Ту́т в теа́тре поёт хо́р.
Here in the theater a chorus is singing.

The letters к, н, ш

К, к *К к* (not *k*)

Н, н *Н н*

One should be careful not to write small **н** like English *n*, which is the small Russian **п**; the capital letter is like English capital *H*.

Ш, ш *Ш ш*

Note that this letter is written like English *u* with a third vertical stroke.
Copy the following words:

Ко́рсика, Corsica *Корсика*

Кра́ков, Cracow *Краков*

Ни́на, Nina *Нина*

А́нна, Anna *Анна*

Нанки́н, Nanking *Нанкин*

Шах, the Shah *Шах*

Ша́шки, Checkers *Шашки*

Write in Russian script:

О́н шве́д.	He is a Swede.
Она́ хорошо́ поёт.	She sings well.
Нанки́н в Кита́е.	Nanking is in China.
Шу́ра сестра́ Константи́на.	Shura is Konstantin's sister.

The letters г, з, б

Г, г   *Г г*

The capital is like English *T*.

З, з   *З з*   Б, б   *Б б*

Begin the small letter like an o, then continue upward and to the right: *о б*

Copy the following words:

Григóрий, Gregory   *Григорий*

(Note the sign of brevity on the final **и**.)

Бог, God   *Бог*

Зáгреб, Zagreb   *Загреб*

Занзибáр, Zanzibar   *Занзибар*

Write the following words in Russian script:

Рóза и хризантéма.	A rose and a chrysanthemum.
Ивáн Грóзный.	Ivan the Terrible.
Гóрод Бостóн.	The city of Boston.
Йх ребёнок хорошó хóдит.	Their child can walk well.
Егó сестрý зовýт Зúной.	His sister is called Zina.

The letters л, м, я

Л, л   *Л л*

М, м   *М м*

Я, я   *Я я*

Note that small **л**, **м**, and **я** begin with a little hook above the lower line, at about one third of the height of the letters: *л м я*

The letter **я** continues with a loop to the left, then with a vertical stroke:

я я я

Copy the following words, being careful to retain the initial hooks, here indicated by small arrows:

Ли́ма, Lima   *Лима*

Мари́я, Maria   *Мария*

Япо́ния, Japan   *Япония*

Ита́лия, Italy   *Италия*

Write out the following:

Ленингра́д, Ло́ндон, Москва́, Я́лта, Я́ва, Мила́н, Влади́мир Маяко́вский, Ле́в Толсто́й, Я́сная Поля́на, Илиа́да Гоме́ра.

The letters ц and щ

Ц, ц   *Ц ц*   Щ, щ   *Щ щ*

Note that these two letters are written respectively like **и** and **ш**, but with a small loop at the bottom of the last vertical stroke; this loop is much shorter than the "long" letters, such as **р** or **у**:

Цирк, Circus   *цирк*   Щу́ка, Pike   *щука*

Copy the following words:

Цита́та из Цицеро́на.   A quotation from Cicero.

Цитата из Цицерона

Ще́бет пти́ц.   The twitter of birds.

Щебет птиц

Цена́ щётки.   The price of the brush.

Цена щётки

Write out the following words and phrases:

Це́лый ме́сяц.   Цена́ веще́й.
A whole month.   The price of things.

Щека́ ещё распу́хла.
The cheek is still swollen.

Л. В. Ще́рба специали́ст по ру́сской грамма́тике.
L. V. Shcherba is a specialist in Russian grammar.

The letter ч

Ч, ч   *Ч ч*

Copy the following words:

Антóн Пáвлович Чéхов.   Anton Pavlovich Chekhov.

Антон Павлович Чехов

Чёрная шля́па.   A black hat.   *Чёрная шляпа*

Óн врáч.   He is a physician.   *Он врач.*

Write out the following words and phrases:

Си́ние черни́ла.
Blue ink.

Óн говори́т по-чéшски.
He speaks Czech.

Прáга столи́ца Чехословáкии.
Prague is the capital of Czechoslovakia.

Я́йца кýрицу не ýчат.
Eggs don't teach the hen (i.e., elders know better).

The letter ж

Ж, ж   *Ж ж*

The tracing of capital **Ж** can be presented in several stages, as follows:

Ж Ж Ж Ж Ж
1   2   3   4   5

The small letter is ordinarily written like the capital, but smaller in size.
Copy the following words or phrases:

Жóрж живёт в Пари́же.   George lives in Paris.

Жорж живёт в Париже.

Жёлтая кóжа.   Yellow leather.

Жёлтая кожа

Положи́ ножи́ и лóжки на стóл.
Put the knives and the spoons on the table.

Положи ножи и ложки на стол.

Write out the following words:

Её му́ж живёт в Жене́ве.
Her husband is living in Geneva.

Журна́л «Сове́тская же́нщина».
The magazine *Soviet Woman.*

Сего́дня ужа́сно жа́рко.
It's terribly hot today.

The letter ф

Ф, ф

The tracing of capital Ф may be presented in several stages, as follows:

The small letter is, approximately, a *c* combined with an English *p*:

Copy the following words:

Фотогра́фия, Photograph

Фарфо́р, Porcelain

Филосо́фия, Philosophy

Write out the following words:

Фло́т, Fleet   Симфо́ния, Symphony   Фи́зика, Physics
Фами́лия, Family name

The letter э

Э, э

Copy the words below:

Эконо́мика, Economics

Эпо́ха, Epoch

Э́хо, Echo   *Эхо*

Этногра́фия, Ethnography   *Этнография*

Электри́ческая эне́ргия, Electrical energy
Электрическая энергия

Поэ́зия, Poetry   *Поэзия*

Аэропо́рт, Airport   *Аэропорт*

Write out the following words:

Óн поэ́т.   He is a poet.
Óн экономи́ст.   He is an economist.
Э́то э́хо.   That is an echo.
Энциклопе́дия.   Encyclopedia.

The letter ю

Ю, ю   *Ю ю*

This letter may be described as a vertical stroke attached to an o.

Copy the words below:

Ю́рий юри́ст.   Yuri (George) is a lawyer.
Юрий юрист.

Óн лю́бит юриспруде́нцию.   He loves jurisprudence.
Он любит юриспруденцию.

Я́ люблю́ ю́жную приро́ду.   I love southern nature.
Я люблю южную природу.

Они приезжа́ют сюда́ ка́ждую зи́му.　They come here every winter.

Они приезжают сюда каждую зиму

Write out the following words:

Юката́н, Yucatan　　Каю́та, Cabin　　　Рю́мка, Wineglass
Юг, South　　　　　Индю́к, Turkey cock

The letters ь, ы, ъ

These three letters are never written initially and are never capitalized.

ь *ь*　ы *ы*　ъ *ъ*

Note that the small loop, the common feature of the three letters above, comes up to only half the height of the letter:

ь ы ъ

The letter **ы** is a **ь** with another vertical stroke; the **ъ** is like a **ч** with the little loop of the **ь**.

Copy the words below:

Мы́ бы́ли до́ма весь де́нь.　We were at home all day.

Мы были дома весь день.

Кто́ съе́л всё конфе́ты?　Who ate all the candies?

Кто съел все конфеты?

Я́ пью́ то́лько во́ду.　I drink only water.

Я пью только воду.

То́лько ию́ль бы́л о́чень жа́ркий.　Only July was very hot.

Только июль был очень жаркий.

Write out the words below:

Ско́лько сто́ит тако́е объявле́ние?
How much does such an advertisement cost?

Э́тот ковёр о́чень пы́льный.
This rug is very dusty.

То́лько вы́ по́няли его́ объясне́ния.
You alone understood his explanations.

The Russian Alphabet

Printed Letters		Script		Phonetic Transcription	Name of Letter in Phonetic Transcription[8]
А	а	*A*	*a*	a	a
Б	б	*B*	*б*	b	be
В	в	*B*	*в*	v	ve
Г	г	*Г*	*г*	g	ge
Д	д	*Д*	*д*	d	de
Е	е	*E*	*е*	e, je	je
Ё	ё	*Ё*	*ё*	o, jo	jo
Ж	ж	*Ж*	*ж*	ž	že
З	з	*Э*	*з*	z	ze
И	и	*И*	*и*	i	i
Й	й	*Й*	*й*	j	í krátkəjə
К	к	*К*	*к*	k	ka
Л	л	*Л*	*л*	l	el̦
М	м	*М*	*м*	m	em

[8] Contrary to usual Russian phonetic practice, the names of the consonant letters are pronounced hard before the sound [e].

Н н	$\mathscr{H}$ $\mathscr{n}$	n	en
О о	$\mathscr{O}$ o	o	o
П п	$\mathscr{P}$ n	p	pe
Р р	$\mathscr{P}$ p	r	er
С с	$\mathscr{C}$ c	s	es
Т т	$\mathscr{T}$ m	t	te
У у	$\mathscr{U}$ y	u	u
Ф ф	φ φ	f	ef
Х х	$\mathscr{X}$ x	x	xa
Ц ц	$\mathscr{U}$ $\mathscr{y}$	c	ce
Ч ч	$\mathscr{C}$ $\mathscr{r}$	č	če
Ш ш	$\mathscr{U}$ $\mathscr{u}$	š	ša
Щ щ	$\mathscr{U}$ $\mathscr{y}$	šč	šča
ъ[9]	$\mathscr{v}$	—	tv̇órdij znák (hard sign)
ы[9]	$\mathscr{u}$	i̇	i̇
ь[9]	$\mathscr{b}$	[10]	m̦áxkij znák (soft sign)
Э э	$\mathscr{Э}$ $\mathscr{э}$	e	e
Ю ю	$\mathscr{Ю}$ $\mathscr{ю}$	u, ju	ju
Я я	$\mathscr{Я}$ $\mathscr{я}$	a, ja	ja

The student is reminded that the pronunciation of certain of the vowels changes when unstressed. The values given in the table above are for stressed vowels only.

---

[9] Capital forms are not given for these letters since they never begin words.
[10] This sign is subscribed beneath consonants, and indicates their palatalization, e.g., день [d̦ép̦] *day*.

Vocabulary

This is a checklist of words to be learned from the first three lessons.

библиоте́ка library
бума́га paper
вот here is (are), there is (are) (*pointing*)
вы you
газе́та newspaper
где where
глаз eye
голова́ head
да yes
до́ктор doctor
дом house
до́ма at home
доска́ blackboard
журна́л magazine
и and
и́ли or
каранда́ш pencil
класс class, classroom
кни́га book
кто who
ла́мпа lamp
лицо́ face
музе́й museum
мы we
не not
нет no

нос nose
окно́ window
он he
она́ she
они́ they
перо́ pen; feather
пол floor
по́лка shelf, bookshelf
потоло́к ceiling
профе́ссор professor
рот mouth
сейча́с now, right now, this moment
стена́ wall
стол table
студе́нт (male) student
студе́нтка (female) student, co-ed
стул chair
там there
тепе́рь now, at present, at this time
то́же also, too
тут here
университе́т university
что what
э́то this (is), that (is), it (is)
я I

DRILL

Write out the above vocabulary pronouncing each word aloud several times as you do so.

Gender in Russian (introductory) • Personal pronoun, third person
singular • Gender endings of nouns • Hard and soft stem endings •
Personal pronouns • Possessive pronoun-adjectives • Demonstrative pronoun-adjectives • Conjunctions и and а • Conversation

Unit 4

Grammar

1. Gender in Russian (introductory)

Russian has three grammatical genders: masculine, feminine, and neuter. Generally, the gender of a Russian noun depends on its form and has no relation to meaning. This is obviously so with names of inanimate objects, or with abstract nouns, some of which are masculine, others feminine, and still others neuter:

Both **стол** (*table*) and **ум** (*mind*) are masculine.
Both **ко́мната** (*room*) and **нау́ка** (*science*) are feminine.
Both **окно́** (*window*) and **иску́сство** (*art*) are neuter.

In the case of names of male and female beings, the meaning is for the most part reflected in the form: most nouns denoting male and female beings have endings indicative of the corresponding grammatical gender.

2. Personal pronoun, third person singular

The gender of a noun determines the form of the third person pronoun (English *he*, *she*, *it*) that may be used to replace it. The three gender forms of the pronoun in singular are:

for masculine nouns: ОН [ón]
for neuter nouns: ОНО́ [anó]
for feminine nouns: ОНА́ [aná]

The pronouns **он** and **она́** replace not only nouns denoting male and female beings (like *he* and *she* in English), e.g.,

—Где́ до́ктор? —**Он** ту́т.
—Where is the doctor? —*He* is here.

—Где́ сестра́? —**Она́** та́м.
—Where is Sister? —*She* is there.

but also inanimate nouns of the masculine or feminine gender:

—Где университет? —**Он** там.
—Where is the university? —It is there.

—Где книга? —**Она** тут.
—Where is the book? —It is here.

3. Gender endings of nouns

The pattern of the third person pronouns, masculine **он**, neuter **оно́**, feminine **она́**, is followed by very many nouns:

nouns ending in a consonant (like the pronoun **он**) are masculine:
дом   house;

nouns ending in the vowel **-o** (like the pronoun **оно́**) are neuter:
окно́   window;

nouns ending in the vowel **-a** (like the pronoun **она́**) are feminine:
ко́мната   room.

DRILL

Form questions and answers on the pattern of —Где кни́га? —**Она́ та́м,** *substituting for* кни́га *the nouns given below and using the proper form of the personal pronoun* (**он, оно́, она́**) *in the answer.*

каранда́ш	pencil	стул	chair	ма́сло	butter
письмо́	letter	Ива́н	Ivan	река́	river
таре́лка	plate	сестра́	sister	О́льга	Olga
вино́	wine	окно́	window	молоко́	milk
хлеб	bread	телефо́н	telephone	по́лка	shelf
шко́ла	school	кни́га	book	журна́л	magazine

ORAL DRILL

Replace the blank with **он, оно́,** *or* **она́** *as required.*

1. —Это Ива́н? —Да́, это . . . . .
2. —Музе́й здесь? —Не́т, ... там.
3. —Ни́на до́ма? —Да́, ... до́ма.
4. —Где ла́мпа? —Во́т . . . . .
5. —О́льга студе́нтка? —Да́, ... студе́нтка.
6. —Где перо́? —Во́т . . . . .
7. —Бори́с студе́нт? —Не́т, ... профе́ссор.
8. —Где газе́та? —. . . . тут.
9. —Где журна́л? —Во́т . . . . .
10. —Это учи́тель? —Да́, это . . . . .

4. Gender endings continued: The stem and the suffix; hard and soft endings

The three gender forms of the third person pronoun, **он, оно́,** and **она́**, all have the element **он**; it is also present in the plural for all genders, **они́** *they.* The element **он** stands alone in the masculine singular but adds different endings in the other forms. Thus, if the ending **-o** means neuter, the ending **-a** feminine, and **-и** plural, then the absence of any addition to the stem means masculine. A form with no additions to the stem is said to have a *zero ending* when it belongs to a series of related forms which take different endings:

	Masc.	он	suffix *zero*
Sing.	*Neut.*	онó	suffix **-o**
	Fem.	онá	suffix **-a**
Pl. all genders		они́	suffix **-и**

Orthographically, like **он**, the majority of masculine nouns have stems with zero suffixes, while the majority of neuter and feminine nouns have the suffixes **-o** and **-a** respectively.

The vowel suffixes in neuter and feminine nouns are stressed in some words and unstressed in others. Since both **o** and **a** unstressed are [ə], the suffixes, described *phonetically*, for neuter are [ó] or [ə]; for feminine [á] or [ə]:

Neut.	окнó [akn.ó]	window,	but	крéсло [kŗésl.ə]	armchair
Fem.	стенá [ş̣tin.á]	wall,	but	шкóла [škól.ə]	school

Stems of all nouns end in *consonantal sounds*. In the examples given up to now these final stem consonants are *hard*:

телефóн [ţiḷifón.]	stem ending [n] + suffix zero
письмó [piş̣m.ó]	stem ending [m] + suffix [ó]
шкóла [škól.ə]	stem ending [l] + suffix [ə]

Other nouns have *soft* stem endings: palatalized consonants, or the sound [j]. *In terms of sound* rather than spelling, nouns with soft stem endings have the same gender suffixes as nouns of the hard type: masculine zero, neuter [ó] or [ə], feminine [á] or [ə]:

Masc.	учи́тель [učíţiḷ.]	teacher	stem ending [ḷ] + suffix zero
	словáрь [slaváŗ.]	dictionary	stem ending [ŗ] + suffix zero
	музéй [muẓéj.]	museum	stem ending [j] + suffix zero
Neut.	бельё [ḅiḷj.ó]	underwear	stem ending [j] + suffix [ó]
	пóле [pól.ə]	field	stem ending [ḷ] + suffix [ə]
	здáние [zdáņij.ə]	building	stem ending [j] + suffix [ə]
Fem.	земля́ [ẓimḷ.á]	earth	stem ending [ḷ] + suffix [á]
	статья́ [staţj.á]	article	stem ending [j] + suffix [á]
	ку́хня [kúxņ.ə]	kitchen	stem ending [ņ] + suffix [ə]
	идéя [iḍéj.ə]	idea	stem ending [j] + suffix [ə]

One group of nouns of the feminine gender does not conform to the general pattern described above. Nouns of this type, which will be referred to as "Fem. II," end in soft consonants (or in [ž] and [š], which cannot be palatalized). They are written with a soft sign at the end, for example,

соль salt	дверь door	ночь night	мышь mouse

The following sums up the endings of nouns of the three genders:

Masculine: Zero Ending

Spelling: Hard: **any consonant**	*Soft:* **-ь** or **-й**
стол [stól.] table брат [brát.] brother	словáрь [slavár̦.] dictionary учи́тель [učíțil̦.] teacher чай [čáj.] tea музéй [muẓéj.] museum

Neuter: [o] or, if unstressed, [ə]

Spelling: Hard: **-o**	*Soft stressed:* **-ё (-ьё)**
окнó [akn.ó] window крéсло [kr̦ésl.ə] armchair	бельё [b̦il̦j.ó] underwear
	Soft unstressed: **-e**
	пóле [pól̦.ə] field мóре [mór̦.ə] sea здáние [zdán̦ij.ə] building

Fem. I: [a] or, if unstressed, [ə]

Spelling: Hard: **-a**	*Soft:* **-я**
сестрá [șistr.á] sister кóмната [kómnət.ə] room	земля́ [ẓiml̦.á] earth кýхня [kúxn̦.ə] kitchen идéя [id̦éj.ə] idea

Fem. II: Zero Ending; the stem ends in a soft consonant

	Spelling: Soft: **-ь**[1]
	дверь [d̦v̦ér̦] door соль [sól̦.] salt ночь [nóč.] night Сиби́рь [ṣib̦ír̦] Siberia

[1] Fem. II nouns cannot generally be distinguished from masculine nouns ending in a soft consonant, so the gender of nouns of these two types must be memorized. It should be noted, however, that *all* nouns ending in **-жь, -шь, -чь,** and **-щь** are Fem. II; the consonants **ж** and **ш** are, of course, always hard, while **ч** and **щ** are always soft, so that the **-ь** here serves solely as an indication of gender. Nouns ending in **-ж, -ш, -ч,** and **-щ,** *without* a soft sign, are always masculine, e.g., врач *physician,* товáрищ *comrade.*

5. Personal pronouns

Following is a table of Russian personal pronouns:

		Singular		Plural	
1st Pers.		я	I	мы	we
2nd Pers.		ты	you (thou)	вы	you
3rd Pers.	Masc.	он	he, it		
	Neut.	оно́	it (see Sec. 2)	они́	they
	Fem.	она́	she, it		

Like French, German, and other languages (but unlike English), Russian has preserved the second person singular pronoun. This pronoun, **ты**, is used in familiar address between close friends, members of a family, very young people, between and in addressing children, etc. Otherwise the pronoun **вы** is used. **Вы**, the second person plural, serves both for one person in formal address, and also as the actual plural when more than one person is addressed.

Unlike *I* in English, the Russian first person pronoun **я** is not capitalized unless it is at the beginning of a sentence.

PATTERN SENTENCES

1. —Э́то **ты́**, Ива́н? —Да́, э́то **я́**.
2. —**Вы́** профе́ссор Па́влов? —Да́, **я́** Па́влов.
3. **Я́** до́ма и Ива́н то́же. **Мы́** до́ма.
4. **Я́** ту́т и **ты́** ту́т. **Мы́** ту́т.
5. **Ты́** ту́т и О́льга ту́т. **Вы́** ту́т.

6. **О́н** до́ма и **она́** до́ма. **Они́** до́ма.

1. —Is that you, Ivan? —Yes, it's I.
2. —Are you Professor Pavlov? —Yes, I am Pavlov.
3. I'm at home and Ivan is too. We are at home.
4. I'm here and you're here. We are here.
5. You are here and Olga is here. You (both) are here.
6. He's at home and she's at home. They are at home.

ORAL DRILL

Supply the necessary pronouns.

Model: Я́ и Ни́на до́ма. **Мы́** до́ма.
1. Ты́ ту́т и Бори́с ту́т. . . . . ту́т.
2. —Бра́ун и Па́влов та́м? —Да́, ... та́м.
3. —Кто́ вы́? —. . . . учи́тель.

4. —Э́то ты́, О́льга? —Да́, э́то . . . . .
5. —Где́ сейча́с Ни́на и А́нна? —. . . . до́ма.
6. —О́льга ту́т? —Да́, ... ту́т.
7. —Где́ ты́, Бори́с? —. . . . до́ма.

6. Possessive pronoun-adjectives

The Russian possessive pronoun-adjectives agree in gender with the noun denoting the object owned. The distinction between *my* and *mine*, *your* and *yours*, etc. is not made in Russian, and the forms listed below correspond in use to both English forms.

	with *masc.*:	**мо́й** до́м
My and *mine*	with *neut.*:	**моё** письмо́
	with *fem.*:	**моя́** ко́мната

Your and *yours*	with *masc.:*	**твóй** дóм
(correspond to	with *neut.:*	**твоё** письмó
informal **ты**)	with *fem.:*	**твоя́** кóмната
Our and *ours*	with *masc.:*	**нáш** дóм
	with *neut.:*	**нáше** письмó
	with *fem.:*	**нáша** кóмната
Your and *yours*	with *masc.:*	**вáш** дóм
(correspond to pl.	with *neut.:*	**вáше** письмó
or formal **вы**)	with *fem.:*	**вáша** кóмната

These pronoun-adjectives answer questions with *Whose*? The interrogative *whose* also has three gender forms; questions of the type " *Whose . . .* is this?" are usually formed with the word **это** unstressed following **чей**, **чьё**, or **чья́**, e.g.,

	with *masc.:*	**Чéй** это дóм?	Whose house + is *this*?
Whose	with *neut.:*	**Чьё** это письмó?	Whose letter + is *this*?
	with *fem.:*	**Чья́** это кóмната?	Whose room + is *this*?

One will note that the gender forms of the possessive pronoun follow the general pattern described above. In masculine, the different forms are stems with a zero ending. To these stems, neuter adds [ó] and feminine [á] (or, if unstressed, [ə] for both). In the stems [mój] and [tvój] the usual phonetic change [ó] to [a] takes place when the stress shifts to the ending (see page 6):

Masculine: zero		*Neuter:* [ó—ə]		*Feminine:* [á—ə]	
мой	[mój.]	моё	[maj.ó]	моя	[maj.á]
твой	[tvój.]	твоё	[tvaj.ó]	твоя	[tvaj.á]
наш	[náš.]	нáше	[náš.ə]	нáша	[náš.ə]
ваш	[váš.]	вáше	[váš.ə]	вáша	[váš.ə]

The stem of the interrogative has an [é] in the masculine which does not appear in the other forms:

чей	[čéj.]	чьё	[čj.ó]	чья	[čj.á]

PATTERN SENTENCES

Study these sentences carefully until you are prepared to translate from Russian to English and back. Then read the Russian sentences aloud several times for fluency.

1. —**Чéй** это карандáш? —Это **мóй** карандáш.
2. —**Чьё** это перó? —Онó **моё**.
3. —**Чья́** это кóмната? —Это **моя́** кóмната.
4. —**Чéй** это стýл? —Это **вáш** стýл.
5. —Гдé **твóй** дóм? —Óн тáм.
6. —Гдé **нáше** письмó? —Вóт онó.
7. —Ктó это? —Это **моя́** дóчь.
8. —**Чья́** это пóлка? **Вáша**? —Нéт, не **моя́**.

9. —Это **твóй** журнáл? —Дá, **мóй**.
10. —**Чьё** это письмó? — **Нáше.**

1. —Whose pencil is this? —It's my pencil.
2. —Whose pen is this? —It's mine.
3. —Whose room is this? —It's my room.
4. —Whose chair is this? —It's your chair.
5. —Where is your house? —It's over there.
6. —Where is our letter? —Here it is.
7. —Who is that? —That's my daughter.
8. —Whose shelf is this? Yours? —No, (it is) not mine.
9. —Is this your magazine? —Yes, (it is) mine.
10. —Whose letter is this? —Ours.

DRILL

Fill in the blanks under (A) with the proper form of the interrogative **чей** *and those under (B) with the proper Russian form of the possessive pronoun given in English.*

Model: ——**Чéй** это стóл? —**Мóй.**

(A)	(B)		(A)	(B)	
1. .... это кнѝга?	.... ⎫		7. .... это перó?	.... ⎫	
2. .... это дóм?	.... ⎬ (Mine)		8. .... это карандáш?	.... ⎬ (Ours)	
3. .... это окнó?	.... ⎭		9. .... это пóлка?	.... ⎭	
4. .... это журнáл?	.... ⎫		10. .... это окнó?	.... ⎫	
5. .... это газéта?	.... ⎬ (Yours, *sing.*)		11. .... это стýл?	.... ⎬ (Yours, *pl.*)	
6. .... это письмó?	.... ⎭		12. .... это граммáтика?	.... ⎭	

7. Demonstrative pronoun-adjectives

Like English, Russian has two kinds of demonstratives: one used in pointing out objects or persons that are near to the speaker (English *this*); the other, those that are more remote (*that*). In Russian each of the two kinds of demonstratives has three gender forms:

	This (*near*)		*That* (*remote*)	
Masc.	э́тот [étət] дóм	this house	тóт [tót] дóм	that house
Neut.	э́то [étə] окнó	this window	тó [tó] окнó	that window
Fem.	э́та [étə] кóмната	this room	тá [tá] кóмната	that room

The idea "that" in English usage tends to be the more general one, used when nearness or remoteness is not specified or contrasted; in Russian, on the other hand, "this" forms, **э́тот, э́то, э́та,** are more general. The forms **тот, то, та** are used mainly when nearness and remoteness are contrasted, e.g., **Э́та** кóмната моя́, а **тá** (кóмната may be omitted) вáша, *This* room is mine, and *that* one is yours.

The use of the neuter form **э́то** as an indefinite pronoun has been discussed in Unit 2 (page 15). It has been seen that a complete sentence can be formed with the word **э́то** (without gender agreement) and a noun.

> Э́то стóл.   This is a table.
> Э́то кнѝга.   This is a book.

Such sentences can be further elaborated, as with modifiers:

> **Э́то мóй** стол.   This is my table.
> **Э́то моя́** кнѝга.   This is my book.

Such sentences state, about something which is pointed out (**э́то**) that *it* is a table, a book, etc. On the other hand, in **э́тот стóл** or **э́та кнѝга,** a particular table, or book, is pointed out by the demonstrative, but no statement is made about it. The word groups **э́тот сто́л** or **э́та кни́га** are therefore not sentences. To form a sentence a statement must be made, e.g., that the table or the book *is mine*:

Э́тот сто́л мо́й.   This table is mine.
Э́та кни́га моя́.   This book is mine.

Note.   With neuter nouns, the form **э́то** is ambiguous—**э́то** перо́ may mean both *This is a pen* and *This pen*:

Что́ э́то? Э́то перо́.
What is this? *This is a pen.*

Э́то перо́ не моё. То́ перо́ моё.
This pen is not mine. That pen is mine.

PATTERN SENTENCES

Study these sentences carefully until you are prepared to translate from Russian to English and back. Then read the Russian sentences aloud several times for fluency.

1. **Э́тот** студе́нт мо́й сы́н.
2. **Э́та** студе́нтка моя́ до́чь.
3. —**Э́тот** журна́л ва́ш? —Не́т, о́н ва́ш.
4. —**Э́то** перо́ моё. —Не́т, оно́ моё.
5. —Кто́ **э́та** же́нщина? —**Э́то** моя́ ма́ть.
6. **Э́то** газе́та «Пра́вда».
7. —**Э́та** газе́та ва́ша? —Не́т, она́ ва́ша. **Та́** моя́.

8. **Э́тот** сту́л не ва́ш. **То́т** ва́ш.
9. —**Э́то** перо́ моё? —Не́т, **э́то** моё. **То́** ва́ше.

1. This student is my son.
2. This student is my daughter.
3. —Is this magazine yours? —No, it's yours.
4. —This pen is mine. —No, it's mine.
5. —Who is that woman? —It's my mother.
6. This is the newspaper *Pravda*.
7. —Is this newspaper yours? —No, it's yours. That one is mine.
8. This chair isn't yours. That one is yours.
9. —Is this pen mine? —No, this one is mine. That one is yours.

DRILL

Fill in the blanks, using the proper form of the words in boldface in the model sentences.

Model: **Э́тот** до́м **мо́й**. *This* house is *mine.*

1. .... письмо́ .....
2. .... кни́га .....
3. .... сту́л .....
4. .... перо́ .....
5. .... ла́мпа .....
6. .... кре́сло .....
7. .... ку́хня .....
8. .... ко́мната .....

Model: **Э́то** журна́л. **Э́тот** журна́л **ва́ш**. This is a magazine. This magazine is yours.

1. .... кни́га.   .... кни́га .....
2. .... перо́.   .... перо́ .....
3. .... ко́мната.   .... ко́мната .....
4. .... письмо́.   .... письмо́ .....
5. .... сто́л.   .... сто́л .....
6. .... газе́та.   .... газе́та .....

Table of Gender Endings:

Nouns, Third Person Pronouns, Possessive and Demonstrative Pronoun-Adjectives

	Masculine: zero		*Neuter*: [ó]—[ə]		*Feminine*: [á]—[ə]	
Nouns	стол	[stól.]	окнó	[akn.ó]	стенá	[ṣṭin.á]
	учи́тель	[učíṭiḷ.]	бельё	[ḅiḷj.ó]	земля́	[ẓiṃḷ.á]
	музéй	[muẓéj.]	крéсло	[kṛésl.ə]	шко́ла	[škól.ə]
			здáние	[zdáṇij.ə]	идéя	[iḍéj.ə]
3rd Pers. Pron.	он	[ón]	онó	[an.ó]	онá	[an.á]
Poss.	мой, твой	[mój.], [tvój.]	моё, твоё	[maj.ó], [tvaj.ó]	моя́	[maj.á]
	наш, ваш	[náš.], [váš.]	нáше, вáше	[náš.ə], [váš.ə]	твоя́	[tvaj.á]
					нáша	[náš.ə]
					вáша	[váš.ə]
Dem.	э́тот, тот	[ét.ət], [tót]	э́то, то	[ét.ə], [t.ó]	э́та, та	[ét.ə], [t.á]

8. Conjunctions и and а

The conjunction **и** connects several members of a sentence to which the statement made is equally applicable:

Ива́н и Óльга до́ма.   Ivan and Olga are at home.

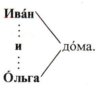   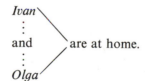

(They are both in the same place. Note that **и** here may be translated as *and* meaning *also*.)

Another conjunction, the separative conjunction **а** (always with a comma before it), is used in Russian when two different statements are made about two members of a sentence:

Ива́н ту́т, а Óльга до́ма.   Ivan is here, and (but) Olga is at home.

Ива́н——ту́т,   *Ivan*——is *here*,

    а   and (but)

Óльга——до́ма.   *Olga*——is *at home*.

(Ivan and Olga are in different places.)

The separative **a** must be used in Russian with statements that are merely different, even when, as in the example above, they are not felt to be conflicting or contrasted; its use is *not optional* as is the use of *but* in English in this example.

The conjunction **a** is also used in sentences of the type "*This is not A, but B*" (or "*This is B, and not A*"):

Она́ не ту́т, а до́ма. (*or:* Она́ до́ма, а не ту́т.)
She is not here, but at home. (*or:* She is at home, and not here.)

Óн не студе́нт, а журнали́ст. (*or:* Óн журнали́ст, а не студе́нт.)
He is not a student, but a journalist. (*or:* He is a journalist, and not a student.)

Questions are often introduced by **a** when inquiring about someone (or something) not yet mentioned, e.g.,

Ива́н ту́т. А где́ Óльга?
Ivan is here. And (but) where is Olga?

И . . . и means *both . . . and:*

Óн и профе́ссор и до́ктор.
He is both a professor and a doctor.

PATTERN SENTENCES

Study these sentences carefully until you are prepared to translate from Russian to English and back. Then read the Russian sentences aloud several times for fluency.

1. Óльга студе́нтка, **и** Ли́дия то́же студе́нтка.
2. Бори́с учи́тель, **а** Вади́м студе́нт.
3. Я́ студе́нт, **и** о́н студе́нт.
4. Я́ учи́тель, **а** о́н студе́нт.
5. Я́ не учи́тель, **а** студе́нт.
6. Я́ студе́нт, **а** не учи́тель.
7. —Я́ учи́тель. **А** кто́ вы́? —Я́ студе́нт.

8. —Мы́ ту́т. **А** где́ они́? —Они́ до́ма.

9. Андре́й Ко́лосов **и** журнали́ст **и** до́ктор.

10. Э́тот до́м на́ш, **а** то́т ва́ш.
11. —Здра́вствуйте!² Прости́те, вы́ до́ктор Бра́ун? —Не́т, я́ не Бра́ун, **а** Сми́т.
12. —**А** ка́к ва́ша фами́лия? —Смирно́в. Я́ то́же до́ктор, ка́к вы́.

1. Olga is a student, and Lydia is a student too.
2. Boris is a teacher, and Vadim is a student.
3. I am a student, and he is a student.
4. I am a teacher, and he is a student.
5. I am not a teacher, but a student.
6. I am a student, and not a teacher.
7. —I am a teacher. And who are you? —I'm a student.
8. —We are here. And where are they? —They are at home.
9. Andrey Kolosov is both a journalist and a doctor.
10. This house is ours, and that one is yours.
11. —Hello! Excuse me, are you Dr. Brown? —No, I am not Brown, but Smith.
12. —And what is your (last) name? —Smirnov. I am a doctor too, like you.

DRILL

A. *Insert* и *and* а *in the blanks as required.*

1. Она́ не секрета́рша, ... учи́тельница.
2. Сестра́ . . . . бра́т до́ма.
3. Ива́н не до́ктор, ... журнали́ст.

1. She is not a secretary, but a teacher.
2. The sister and the brother are at home.
3. Ivan is not a doctor, but a journalist.

---

² The first **в** of **здра́вствуйте!** is not pronounced: [zdrástvujţi].

4. Óльга .... Ивáн брáт .... сестрá.
5. Я́ учи́тель, ... онá секретáрша.
6. Óн .... журнали́ст .... профéссор.
7. Вы́ тýт дóма, ... я́ тýт тóлько гóсть.
8. Áнна .... учи́тельница .... студéнтка.
9. Сы́н .... дóчь тýт, ... отéц .... мáть дóма.
10. Вáш отéц дóктор, ... нáш тóже.
11. Э́то письмó моё, ... тó твоё.
12. Э́та газéта моя́, ... тá вáша.
13. Э́тот журнáл мóй, ... тóт вáш.
14. Э́то пóле нáше, ... тó тóже нáше.
15. Э́то пóле нáше, ... тó нéт.³
16. —Вáш сы́н учи́тель как вы́?
    —Нéт, óн не учи́тель, ... дóктор.

4. Olga and Ivan are brother and sister.
5. I am a teacher, and she is a secretary.
6. He is both a journalist and a professor.
7. You are at home here, and I'm only a guest here.
8. Anna is both a teacher and a student.
9. The son and daughter are here, and the father and mother are at home.
10. Your father is a doctor, and ours is too.
11. This letter is mine, and that one is yours.
12. This newspaper is mine, and that one is yours.
13. This magazine is mine, and that one is yours.
14. This field is ours, and that one is also ours.
15. This field is ours, and that one is not.
16. —Is your son a teacher like yourself?
    —No, he is not a teacher, but a doctor.

B. *Transpose the following sentences according to the model.*

Model: Я́ не дóктор, а профéссор.
          Я́ профéссор, а не дóктор.

1. Я́ не профéссор, а студéнт.
2. Они́ не тýт, а дóма.

3. Бори́с не журнали́ст, а учи́тель.
4. Óльга не учи́тельница, а секретáрша.

Conversation

Read aloud and memorize.

Пáвлов. —Прости́те, кáк вáша фами́лия?
Орлóв. —Моя́ фами́лия Орлóв. А кáк вáша?
П. —Я́ Пáвлов.
О. —Óчень прия́тно. Вы́ профéссор Пáвлов?
П. —Дá. Вы́ тóже профéссор?
О. —Нéт, я́ не профéссор, а журнали́ст. А э́то моя́ дóчь Сóня. Онá тóже журнали́стка, как я́. А э́то моя́ дóчь Ли́дия. Онá учи́тельница. А э́то моя́ женá. Ни́на, э́то профéссор Пáвлов.
Ни́на. —Здрáвствуйте. Óчень прия́тно.
П. —Óчень прия́тно. А вы́ тóже журнали́стка, как вáш мýж?
Н. —Нéт, я́ не журнали́стка, и я́ не учи́тельница. Я́ тóлько женá и мáть.
П. —Э́то óчень хорошó!
Н. —Почемý э́то так хорошó?
П. —Потомý что хорошó, когдá жéнщина дóма.

---

³ The Russian word **не** may not end a sentence; **нет** is used in this position.

Answer the following questions.

1. Кто́ Па́влов?   2. Орло́в то́же профе́ссор, как Па́влов?   3. Кто́ Со́ня? Она́ учи́тельница?   4. Кто́ Ни́на? Она́ то́же журнали́стка, как до́чь и как му́ж? 5. Почему́ э́то хорошо́, что она́ не журнали́стка и не учи́тельница?   6. А кто́ вы́? 7. Ва́ша ма́ть то́же то́лько жена́ и ма́ть?

DRILL

Review translation.

1. —Hello. How are you?   2. —Very well, thank you. And how are you? 3. —Also well, thank you.   4. This is our house; here is the kitchen, and here is my room.   5. —Whose dictionary is this? —It's my dictionary.   6. —And whose letter is this? Is it yours? —It's not mine, but yours.   7. This newspaper is yours, and that one is also yours.   8. —Why are you here? —Because this is my house. 9. This magazine is yours, and that (one) is also yours.   10. This is my room, and that (one) is yours.   11. —Pardon me, what is your (last) name? —My name is Orlov. And what is yours? —Brown. —Glad to know you.   12. Our daughter is both a journalist and a teacher.   13. It's good when a mother is at home.   14. This is your dictionary; and where is mine?

Vocabulary

а and; but
брат brother
газе́та newspaper
гость (*masc.*) guest
до́ктор doctor
дочь (*fem.*) daughter
жена́ wife
же́нщина woman
журнали́ст journalist
журнали́стка woman journalist
здесь here
как how; like, as
когда́ when
ко́мната room
ку́хня kitchen
мать (*fem.*) mother

муж [múš] husband
оте́ц father
письмо́ letter
по́ле field
почему́ why
потому́ что because
секрета́рша secretary
сестра́ sister
слова́рь (*masc.*) dictionary, vocabulary
сын son
так so, thus
то́лько only
хорошо́ well, good
учи́тель (*masc.*) teacher
учи́тельница woman teacher

EXPRESSIONS

Здра́вствуйте! Hello! (How are you?)
Ка́к ва́ша фами́лия? What is your (last) name?
О́чень прия́тно Glad to know you (*lit.*: very pleasant)
Прости́те Excuse me
Э́то хорошо́ That's fine (good)

не ... а not ... but
и ... и both ... and

Unit 5

Grammar

1. Declension (introductory)

In English the relations between words in a sentence are expressed mostly by word order ("John saw Peter," "Peter saw John") or by prepositions ("a letter sent *to* Peter," "a letter sent *by* John"). With nouns, one type of relation may be expressed by using a special form of the world itself: in "John's room" the form "John's" indicates that the relation of "John" to "room" is that of possessor to object possessed. Personal pronouns in English have a wide range of forms denoting different types of relations: he, his, him; they, their, them, etc.

Russian, unlike English, has an extensive system of inflection; that is, nouns, adjectives, and other classes of words take different endings depending on their function in the sentence. These functions, or types of relations, are grouped into cases, and each case has its own endings. To *decline* a noun (or another declinable word) is to combine its stem with the endings of the different cases. Some types of relations are expressed in Russian by a case form (for example, a noun plus a suffix) alone, while others require both a case form and a preposition.

There are in all six cases in Russian, including the nominative. The nominative may be regarded as the basic form; it is in this form that nouns and other words appear when they are isolated from a context, as in dictionaries or vocabularies. The most important function of the nominative in a sentence is that of being the subject.

The other five cases are traditionally listed after the nominative in the following order: genitive, dative, accusative, instrumental, and locative.

Paradigms (sets of case forms) are given below of two masculine and two feminine nouns representing the hard and soft stem ending types of these genders. Both feminines are of class I; the declension of Feminine II will be given later. A neuter noun has not been included since the neuter declension is like the masculine.

It is not necessary to memorize the declensions at this point.

Masculine

	Ending	*Hard:* стол table		*Soft:* слова́рь dictionary	
Nom.	[zero]	стол	[stól.]	слова́рь	[slavár̦.]
Gen.	[a]	стола́	[stal.á]	словаря́	[sləvar̦.á]
Dat.	[u]	столу́	[stal.ú]	словарю́	[sləvar̦.ú]
Acc.	[zero]	стол	[stól.]	слова́рь	[slavár̦.]
Instr.	[om]	столо́м	[stal.óm]	словарём	[sləvar̦.óm]
Loc.	[e]	столе́	[staḷ.é]	словаре́	[sləvar̦.é]

Feminine

		Hard: сестра́ sister		*Soft:* земля́ earth	
Nom.	[a]	сестра́	[şistr.á]	земля́	[żiml̦.á]
Gen.	[i/ɨ]	сестры́	[şistr.ɨ]	земли́	[żiml̦.í]
Dat.	[e]	сестре́	[şistr̦.é]	земле́	[żiml̦.é]
Acc.	[u]	сестру́	[şistr.ú]	зе́млю	[żéml̦.u]
Instr.	[oj]	сестро́й	[şistr.ój]	землёй	[żiml̦.ój]
Loc.	[e]	сестре́	[şistr̦.é]	земле́	[żiml̦.é]

It will be observed that:

(1) In most case forms the hardness or softness of the stem ending is preserved and is shown by spelling. Thus, in the masculine declension, the genitive ending [-a] is spelled **-a** in the hard variant, **-я** in the soft; similarly, dative [-u] is spelled **-y** and **-ю**; instrumental [-om], **-ом** and **-ём**. In the feminine declension we find **-ы**, **-у**, **-ой** in the hard variant, corresponding to **-и**, **-ю**, **-ёй** in the soft. (Unstressed endings, which are slightly different, are not considered here.)

(2) An exception to the above is the suffix **-e**, as in masculine locative and feminine dative and locative. Before the vowel **e** all consonants are palatalized,[1] and the usual hard-soft opposition is lacking in those cases which have **-e** as their ending; thus, the locative case forms **столе́** [staḷ.é] and **сестре́** [şistr̦.é] have soft stem endings even though both nouns are of the hard variant.

(3) Certain changes may occur in the pronunciation of the stem of a noun as it is declined. Thus, in the declension of **стол** [stól], there is a change [ó > a] in the vowel of the stem when the stress shifts to the ending; also, the hard stem ending [l] becomes soft [ḷ] in the locative. These and similar changes, however, are secondary; they are side effects of shifts of stress, of the addition of certain case endings in declension, etc. Except for certain automatic phonetic changes, the stem remains fixed.

2. The locative (prepositional) case of nouns

A. Forms of the locative. Most of the three genders take the ending **-e** in the locative (prepositional) case. A different ending, **-и**, is used by Feminine II nouns and a few others.

---

[1] Except, of course, those consonants which are always hard: **ж, ш,** and **ц.**

			Nominative		Locative
Masc.	hard stem end.		стол	[stól.]	столе́	[staḷ.é]²
	„		стул	[stúl.]	сту́ле	[stúḷ.i]
	soft stem end.		словарь	[slaváṛ.]	словаре́	[sləvaṛ.é]²
	„		гость	[góṣṭ.]	го́сте	[góṣṭ.i]
	„	[j]	музе́й	[muẓéj.]	музе́е	[muẓéj.i]
Neut.	hard stem end.		окно́	[akn.ó]	окне́	[akṇé]
	„		о́зеро	[óẓir.ə]	о́зере	[óẓiṛ.i]
	soft stem end.	[j]	бельё	[ḅiḷj.ó]	белье́	[ḅiḷj.é]
	„		по́ле	[póḷ.ə]	по́ле	[póḷ.i]
Fem. I	hard stem end.		сестра́	[ṣistr.á]	сестре́	[ṣistṛ.é]
	„		ко́мната	[kómnət.ə]	ко́мнате	[kómnət.i]
	soft stem end.		земля́	[ẓimḷ.á]	земле́	[ẓimḷ.é]
	„		ку́хня	[kúxṇ.ə]	ку́хне	[kúxṇ.i]
	„	[j]	иде́я	[iḍéj.ə]	иде́е	[iḍéj.i]
Fem. II			дверь	[d̦ýéṛ.]	две́ри	[d̦ýéṛ.i]
			соль	[sóḷ.]	со́ли	[sóḷ.i]
			ночь	[nóč̦.]	но́чи	[nóč̦.i]
			Сиби́рь	[ṣiḅíṛ.]	Сиби́ри	[ṣiḅíṛ.i]

Note: The word **по́ле** and other words of this type are spelled alike in the nominative and locative; the final unstressed **-e**, however, tends to be pronounced as a neutral sound [ə] in the nominative but with an [i] quality in the locative.

B. Uses of the locative.   As stated earlier, different cases are used with prepositions in some instances and without prepositions in others. The locative case is never used alone, but only with certain prepositions; hence it is often called the "prepositional." There are five prepositions in all that require the use of (or "govern") this case; two of these, **в** and **на**, will be introduced now (a third will be added later in this lesson):

> The basic meaning of **в** is *in*:   in the house—в до́ме
> The basic meaning of **на** is *on*:   on the table—на столе́

Like the adverbs **тут, там, до́ма**, etc., phrases with **в** or **на** and a noun in the locative answer the question **где**? *where? at what place?*

Где?
- в теа́тре [fṭiátṛi]   in (at) the theater
- в шко́ле [fškóḷi]   in (at) the school
- в воде́ [vvaḍé]   (pronounce with a single long [v]) in the water
- на стене́ [nəṣṭiṇé]   on the wall
- на столе́ [nəstaḷé]   on the table

---

² A number of masculine nouns which have the stress on the stem in the nominative shift the stress to the ending in other cases.

Observe in the examples above that a prepositional phrase (a preposition plus a noun in the proper case form) is pronounced as a single word.

The preposition **на**, in addition to its primary meaning, is also used with nouns denoting activities or events one attends rather than actual places (in this use **на** often corresponds to English *at*):

на концéрте	at a concert
на урóке	at a lesson
на рабóте	at work, at one's place of work
на óпере	at an opera
на футбóле	at a football game

But **в**, *at* or *in* a building, an enclosed place:

в теáтре	at (in) the theater
в шкóле	at (in the) school
в библиотéке	at (in) the library
в музéе	at (in) the museum

PATTERN SENTENCES

Study these sentences carefully until you are prepared to translate from Russian to English and back. Then read the Russian sentences aloud several times for fluency.

1. Вóт гóрод. **В гóроде** ýлица.
2. **На ýлице** дóм.
3. **В дóме**[3] квартúра. **В квартúре** кóмната.
4. Эта кóмната—мóй кабинéт.[4] **Я в кабинéте.**
5. Это мóй стóл; **на столé** мóй словáрь.
6. Отéц **на рабóте**, а мáть **в теáтре**.
7. —Гдé мóй карандáш? —Óн **на столé**.
8. —Гдé письмó? —Онó тáм **на стýле**.
9. —Твоя́ сестрá дóма? —Нéт, моя́ сестрá **на концéрте**.
10. —Гдé вáш брáт? —Мóй брáт **в библиотéке** или **в музéе**.
11. Ивáн **на футбóле**, а Óльга **в шкóле на экзáмене**.
12. —«Картúна»—это picture? —Дá, вóт мóй словáрь, а вóт **в словарé** слóво «картúна».
13. Картúна тáм **на стенé**—кóпия; оригинáл **в Москвé, в музéе**.

1. Here is a city. In the city is a street.
2. On the street there is a house.
3. In the house there's an apartment. In the apartment there's a room.
4. This room is my study. I am in the study.
5. This is my table (desk); on the table is my dictionary.
6. Father is at work, and Mother is at (has gone to) the theater.
7. —Where is my pencil? —It's on the table.
8. —Where is the letter? —It's there, on the chair.
9. —Is your sister at home? —No, my sister is at (has gone to) a concert.
10. —Where is your brother? —My brother is at the library or at the museum.
11. Ivan is at a football game, and Olga is at school at an exam.
12. —Is "картúна" *picture*? Yes, here's my dictionary, and here in the dictionary is the word "картúна."
13. The picture there on the wall is a copy; the original is in Moscow, in a museum.

---

[3] Contrast **в дóме** (*in the house*) and **дóма** (*at home*).
[4] In sentences of this type, in which one noun is the subject and a second noun the predicate, a dash is sometimes written to separate the two nouns.

| 14. | Моя́ сестра́ тепе́рь **в Нью-Йо́рке**. | 14. | My sister is in New York now. |

14. Моя́ сестра́ тепе́рь **в Нью-Йо́рке**.
15. —Пётр тепе́рь **в Евро́пе?** —Да́, он **в Пари́же.**
16. Э́то на́ша две́рь, и во́т но́мер **на две́ри**.

17. Во́т крова́ть; **в крова́ти** Ива́н.

14. My sister is in New York now.
15. —Is Peter in Europe now? —Yes, he is in Paris.
16. This is our door, and here is the number on the door.

17. Here is the bed; Ivan is in the bed.

DRILLS

A. *Fill in the blanks in each of the numbered sentences below, using the locative case form of the noun that occurs in the preceding sentence in the nominative.*

Model:

a. Во́т го́род.
   В го́роде у́лица.

b. Во́т шко́ла.

c. Во́т стена́.

1. На . . . . до́м.
2. В . . . . кварти́ра.
3. В . . . . ко́мната.
4. В . . . . сто́л.
5. На . . . . бума́га.
6. На . . . . перо́.

1. В . . . . кла́сс.
2. В . . . . экза́мен.
3. На . . . . моя́ сестра́.

1. На . . . . ка́рта.
2. На . . . . Евро́па.
3. В . . . . Пари́ж.
4. В . . . . мо́й бра́т.

B. *Translate the answers to the following questions into Russian; in the answer use the Russian noun in the nominative case given in parentheses after the English phrase. (Be careful to use proper forms in translating the word* it.)*

1. Где́ ва́ш каранда́ш? It is on the table. (сто́л)
2. Где́ музе́й? It is in the city. (го́род)
3. Где́ ка́рта? It is on the wall. (стена́)
4. Где́ на́ша учи́тельница? She is at school. (шко́ла)
5. Где́ ма́ма? She is in the kitchen. (ку́хня)
6. Где́ ва́ша до́чь? She is at work. (рабо́та)
7. Где́ тво́й бра́т? He is in Europe. (Евро́па)
8. Где́ мо́й слова́рь? It is over there, on the armchair. (кре́сло)
9. Где́ бума́га? It is on the chair. (сту́л)
10. Где́ моё перо́? It is in the study. (кабине́т)
11. Где́ Бори́с? He is in bed. (крова́ть)
12. Где́ му́ха? It's on the door. (две́рь)

C. *Supply the proper preposition (**в** or **на**) for each question and answer it, using a suitable word from the vocabulary you have learned; follow this model.*

Model: —Кто́ **в** кабине́те? —**В кабине́те мо́й оте́ц.**

1. —Кто́ . . . . у́лице? —. . . . .
2. —Кто́ . . . . теа́тре? —. . . . .
3. —Кто́ . . . . экза́мене? —. . . . .
4. —Что́ . . . . ко́мнате? —. . . . .
5. —Кто́ . . . . библиоте́ке? —. . . . .

6. —Кто́ . . . . конце́рте? —. . . . .
7. —Кто́ . . . . кла́ссе? —. . . . .
8. —Кто́ . . . . футбо́ле? —. . . . .
9. —Что́ . . . . ка́рте? —. . . . .
10. —Что́ . . . . музе́е? —. . . . .

3. Locative of third person pronouns

		Nominative	Locative
Sing.	Masc.	он	(в, на) нём [n̦óm]
	Neut.	онó	
	Fem.	онá	(в, на) ней [n̦éj]
Pl. all genders		онú	(в, на) них [n̦íx]

Вóт стóл. **На нём** телефóн.	Here is a table. On it is the telephone.
	(*Or:* There is a telephone on it.)
Вóт окнó. **На нём** мýха.	Here is a window. On it is a fly.
Вóт кнúга. **В ней** кáрта.	Here is a book. There is a map in it.
Вóт чáшка и стакáн. **В них** кóфе.	Here are a cup and a glass. There is coffee in them.

4. Locative of possessive and demonstrative pronoun-adjectives

The locative and other case forms of the possessive and demonstrative pronouns (pronouns used adjectivally and thus referred to as *pronoun-adjectives*) are closely related to those of the third personal pronouns. The possessives and demonstratives take the following endings in the locative:

Masc.⎫
Neut.⎭ **-ом, -ём, -ем**   phonetically [óm]; if unstressed [əm]

Fem. **-ей, -ой**   phonetically [éj] or [ój]; if unstressed [əj]

The locative forms of the different pronouns are given below together with the corresponding nominative forms:

PRONOUNS IN THE LOCATIVE SINGULAR

	Nominative		Locative
	Masculine	Neuter	Masculine and Neuter
3rd Pers. Pron.	он [ón.]	онó [an.ó]	**нём** [n̦.óm]
Possessives	мой [mój.]	моё [maj.ó]	**моём** [maj.óm]
	твой [tvój.]	твоё [tvaj.ó]	**твоём** [tvaj.óm]
	наш [náš.]	нáше [náš.ə]	**нáшем** [náš.əm]
	ваш [váš.]	вáше [váš.ə]	**вáшем** [váš.əm]
Demonstratives	э́тот [ét.ət]	э́то [ét.ə]	**э́том** [ét.əm]
	тот [t.ót]	то [t.ó]	**том** [t.óm]

	Nominative Feminine	Locative
3rd Pers. Pron.	она́ [an.á]	ней [n̡.éj]
Possessives	моя́ [maj.á] твоя́ [tvaj.á] на́ша [náš.ə] ва́ша [váš.ə]	мое́й [maj.éj] твое́й [tvaj.éj] на́шей [náš.əj] ва́шей [váš.əj]
Demonstratives	э́та [ét.ə] та [t.á]	э́той [ét.əj] той [t.ój]

PATTERN SENTENCES

Study these sentences carefully until you are prepared to translate from Russian to English and back. Then read the Russian sentences aloud several times for fluency.

1. Во́т на́ш до́м; **в нём** на́ша кварти́ра.
2. **В э́той** кварти́ре моя́ ко́мната и мо́й кабине́т.
3. **В моём** кабине́те по́лка, кре́сло, и сто́л.
4. —Что́ **на ва́шем** столе́? —**На нём** ла́мпа, телефо́н, бума́га, и каранда́ш.
5. —Кто́ сейча́с **в ва́шей** кварти́ре? —**В не́й** то́лько мо́й оте́ц и моя́ ма́ть.
6. Во́т газе́та «Пра́вда»; **в не́й** моя́ статья́.
7. —Что́ **в э́той** статье́? —**В не́й** моя́ биогра́фия.
8. —Э́то твоё письмо́? —Да́, моё. —Что́ **в твоём** письме́? —Э́то секре́т.

1. Here is our house; in it is our apartment.
2. In this apartment are my room and my study.
3. In my study there are a bookshelf, an armchair, and a desk.
4. —What's on your desk? —On it there are a lamp, a telephone, paper, and a pencil.
5. —Who is in your apartment now? —In it there are only my father and my mother.
6. Here is the newspaper *Pravda*; in it is my article.
7. —What's in that article? —In it is my biography.
8. —Is this your letter? —Yes, mine. —What's in your letter? —That's a secret.

DRILLS

A. *Read aloud, placing the words in parentheses in the locative case. Then write out the phrases.*

в (мо́й до́м) на (э́то окно́) в (моя́ ко́мната)
в (мо́й кабине́т) в (э́то письмо́) в (моя́ статья́)
на (тво́й сто́л) в (то́ письмо́) в (твоя́ ку́хня)
в (на́ш гара́ж) в (моё письмо́) в (на́ша ку́хня)
в (на́ш го́род) на (твоё кре́сло) в (ва́ша статья́)
в (на́ш кла́сс) на (ва́ше кре́сло) на (ва́ша у́лица)
на (э́тот экза́мен) на (на́ше окно́) на (э́та ка́рта)
в (то́т теа́тр) на (то́ окно́) в (та́ газе́та)

B. *Substitute the proper pronoun for the noun used, according to the model.*

Model: Во́т сто́л; на **нём** ла́мпа.

1. Во́т на́ш до́м; в .... мо́й кабине́т.
2. Во́т кни́га; в .... ка́рта.
3. Во́т кре́сло; на .... газе́та.
4. Во́т сту́л; на .... мо́й слова́рь.

5. Вот наш класс; в .... доска.
6. Вот кухня; в .... стол.
7. Вот окно; на .... муха.
8. Вот карта; на .... Москва.

C. *Complete the sentences below by putting the words in parentheses into the locative case.*

1. Словарь на (мой стол).
2. Газета в (твой кабинет).
3. Наша квартира в (этот дом).
4. Школа на (эта улица).
5. Пётр сейчас в (наша школа).
6. Твоя книга на (моё кресло).
7. Почему книга на (это кресло)?
8. Кто сейчас в (ваша комната)?
9. Муха на (моё окно).
10. Доктор сейчас в (та квартира).

5. Past tense of verbs

The Russian verb has only one past tense. In the past tense the verb is not conjugated (does not change according to person—first, second, or third), but agrees in gender and number with its subject; it has three gender forms in the singular and one form for all genders in the plural.

The past tense is formed with a stem which is the same as that of the infinitive. With very few exceptions the infinitive ending of Russian verbs is **-ть** [-ţ]:

работать	to work	stem: работа-
читать	to read	stem: чита-
говорить	to speak	stem: говори-
стоять	to stand	stem: стоя-

Instead of the infinitive ending **-ть** [-ţ], the past tense in all its forms adds to the stem the element **-л** [-l]. No further suffix is added for the masculine; for the neuter **-о** is added after л; for the feminine, **-а**; and for all genders of the plural, **-и** (compare the third person pronoun он, оно, она, они).

Masculine	*Neuter*	*Feminine*	*Plural, All Genders*
работал	работало	работала	работали
читал	читало	читала	читали
говорил	говорило	говорила	говорили
стоял	стояло	стояла	стояли

The following table illustrates the use of the different past forms according to the gender and number of the subject:

Masc. Sing.	Иван стол я (man speaking) ты (to a man) он	стоял [stajá.l.]
Neut. Sing.	кресло оно	стояло [stajá.l.ə]

Fem. Sing.	А́нна ла́мпа я́ (woman speaking) ты́ (to a woman) она́	стоя́ла [stajá.l.ə]
Pl., All Genders	Ива́н и А́нна кре́сло и ла́мпа мы́ вы́ они́	стоя́ли [stajá.ḷ.i]

The Russian forms **стоя́л** or **рабо́тал** may be translated, according to context, as *stood, was standing, did stand, has* (or *had*) *stood*; or *worked, was working, has* (or *had*) *worked*.

Note that the plural forms **стоя́ли** and **рабо́тали** are always used with **вы**, whether it is the actual plural or the "formal."

The verb быть to *be*: past tense.

Infinitive:		**быть**:	To be
Past tense:			
Sing.	*Masc.*	**бы́л**:	Зде́сь **бы́л** сто́л. There was a table here.
	Neut.	**бы́ло**:	Кре́сло **бы́ло** в кабине́те. The armchair was in the study.
	Fem.	**была́**:	Кни́га **была́** на столе́. The book was on the table.
Pl., all genders		**бы́ли**:	Ива́н и О́льга **бы́ли** до́ма. Ivan and Olga were at home.

Sometimes when **бы́л, была́/бы́ли** (literally, *was/were*) are used in conjunction with **в** and **на** they correspond to the English *went to* or *attended*, as in:

Мы́ **бы́ли в** теа́тре. We *went to* (*attended*) the theater.
Я́ вчера́ **бы́л на** конце́рте. I *went to* a concert yesterday.

The negatives *was not, were not* are formed with the **не** particle which is pronounced jointly with the verb. Observe the accentuation (the stress shifting to **не**) in the masculine and neuter singular and in the plural:

не́ был   [ṇébil]
не́ было   [ṇébilə]
не была́   [ṇibilá]
не́ были   [ṇébiḷi]

Note: the negative particle **не** affects the word which immediately follows it.

Positive statement:

Я́ бы́л в теа́тре вчера́.
I went to (was at) the theater yesterday.

Different elements negated:

Я не́ был в теа́тре вчера́.
I *did not go* to the theater yesterday.
   (*lit.*, I was not at the theater yesterday.)

Не я был в теа́тре вчера́, а мо́й бра́т.
It wasn't I who went to the theater yesterday, but my brother.

Я был **не в теа́тре** вчера́, а на конце́рте.
It was *not to the theater* that I went yesterday, but to a concert.
   (*lit.*, I went not to the theater, but to a concert.)

Я был в теа́тре **не вчера́**, а сего́дня.
It was *not yesterday* that I went to the theater, but today.
   (*lit.*, I went to the theater not yesterday, but today.)

The form **бы́ло**, neuter singular, is used when **что?** *what*?, an inanimate interrogative, is the subject, e.g.: **Что́ бы́ло на столе́**? **Всё** meaning *everything* also takes the neuter singular in the past tense: **Всё бы́ло на столе́**. With **кто?**, an animate interrogative, the verb is masculine singular in the past: **Кто́ вчера́ бы́л в теа́тре?**

VERB LIST

быть	to be	говори́ть	to say, tell; speak, talk
стоя́ть	to stand	чита́ть	to read
жить[5]	to live	писа́ть	to write
знать	to know	переводи́ть	to translate
ду́мать	to think	слу́шать	to listen (to)
де́лать	to make, do	рабо́тать	to work

PATTERN SENTENCES

1. Ту́т **стоя́ла** ла́мпа.[6] Где́ она́?

2. Ту́т **стоя́л** сту́л. Где́ о́н?
3. Ту́т **стоя́ло** кре́сло. Где́ оно́?
4. —**Что́ бы́ло** в ко́мнате? —В ко́мнате **бы́л** сто́л.
5. —**Что́ бы́ло** на столе́? —На столе́ **была́** бума́га, а на бума́ге **была́** му́ха!
6. —**Кто́ бы́л** в библиоте́ке? —В библиоте́ке **бы́ли** О́льга и Вади́м. Они́ **рабо́тали** вме́сте.
7. —**Что́ они́ де́лали?** —О́н **чита́л**, а она́ **переводи́ла**.

1. A lamp stood here. (*lit.*, Here stood a lamp.) Where is it?
2. A chair stood here. Where is it?
3. An armchair stood here. Where is it?
4. —What was in the room? —A table was in the room.
5. —What was on the table? —On the table (there) was a paper, and on the paper (there) was a fly!
6. —Who was at the library? —Olga and Vadim were at the library. They were working together.
7. —What were they doing? —He was reading, and she was translating.

---

[5] The verb **жить**, like the verb **быть**, has a shifting stress in the past tense: **жил, жи́ло, жила́, жи́ли**.

[6] Note that in this and the following sentences the inverted order of the Russian sentence corresponds to English sentences in which the subject is used with an *indefinite* article (*a* or *an*). A comparable Russian sentence having the same word order as the usual English sentence would require *the* in translation: Ла́мпа была́ на столе́. *The* lamp was on the table.

8. —А что́ ты́ де́лал? —Я́ писа́л письмо́, и коне́чно слу́шал, что́ они́ говори́ли.

9. —Ка́к они́ говори́ли: по-англи́йски или по-ру́сски? —По-ру́сски, коне́чно!

10. Я́ жи́л в Ло́ндоне, когда́ ва́ш бра́т то́же та́м жи́л.

11. Мы́ не зна́ли, что[7] вы́ вчера́ бы́ли в теа́тре.

12. Вчера́ бы́л конце́рт. Ю́рий бы́л на конце́рте, а Ни́на была́ в теа́тре.

13. —Где́ Анна? —Она́ была́ на уро́ке, а сейча́с она́ в библиоте́ке.

14. —Я́ не́ был в библиоте́ке. Это далеко́ или бли́зко? —О́чень бли́зко.

15. —Вы́ бы́ли в Евро́пе? —Да́, мы́ та́м бы́ли. —Где́ вы́ та́м жи́ли? —Мы́ жи́ли в Ло́ндоне и в[8] Пари́же.

16. —Что́ вы́ та́м де́лали? —Мы́ рабо́тали. Я́ писа́тель, и жена́ моя́ писа́тельница. Мы́ вме́сте писа́ли рома́н. —Как интере́сно!

8. —And what were you doing? —I was writing a letter, and of course I was listening (to) what they were saying.

9. —What (*lit.*, how) were they speaking: (in) English or Russian? —(In) Russian, of course!

10. I was living in London when your brother was living there too.

11. We didn't know that[7] you had been to the theater yesterday.

12. Yesterday there was a concert. Yuri was at the concert, and Nina was at the theater.

13. —Where is Anna? —She was at class, and now she is at the library.

14. —I haven't been to the library. Is it far or near? —Very near.

15. —Have you been to Europe? —Yes, we've been there. —Where did you live there? —We lived in London and (in) Paris.

16. —What were you doing there? —We were working. I am a writer, and my wife is a writer (too). We were writing a novel together. —How interesting!

DRILLS

A. *Supply the correct past tense form of the verb indicated for each of the following three groups.*

(1) быть

   a. Ива́н вчера́ .... на конце́рте.
   b. Ни́на вчера́ .... на конце́рте.
   c. Мы́ вчера́ .... на конце́рте.
   d. В ку́хне .... сто́л.
   e. На столе́ .... кни́га.
   f. На кни́ге .... письмо́.
   g. О́льга сего́дня .... на уро́ке.

(2) жить

   a. —Вы́ .... в Пари́же? —Да́, я́ та́м .....
   b. —Кто́ .... в Ло́ндоне? —Бори́с .... та́м .

---

[7] The word **что** is used as an interrogative pronoun and as a relative pronoun. In both cases it is translated as *what* and is stressed (see Sentence 8). **Что** is also used as a conjunction (see Sentence 11), introducing a clause after *to know, say, think*, etc., and corresponding to *that*. As a conjunction it is unstressed. Note that colloquial English frequently omits the conjunction *that*; in Russian, however, it must not be omitted. Moreover, in Russian there must always be a comma before the **что** introducing a clause.

   Interrog.:   **Что́** о́н чита́л?   *What* was he reading?
   Relative: Я́ не зна́л, **что́** о́н чита́л.   I did not know *what* he was reading.
   Conjunct.:   Я́ зна́л, **что** о́н чита́л по-ру́сски.   I knew (*that*) he was reading in Russian.

[8] Unlike English, Russian usually repeats a preposition before a second object.

   c. —Они́ .... в Нью-Йо́рке? —Не́т, они́ та́м не .....
   d. —Ни́на .... в Москве́? —Да́, она́ та́м .....
   e. —Ты́ .... в Ленингра́де? —Не́т, я́ .... в Москве́.

(3) **стоя́ть**

a. На столе́ .... ла́мпа.	d. На по́лке .... слова́рь.
b. На столе́ .... телефо́н.	e. В ко́мнате .... кре́сло.
c. На по́лке .... кни́га.	f. В ку́хне .... ма́ма.

B. *Supply the correct past tense form of* **де́лать** *in the questions and translate the answers into Russian.*

1. Что́ О́льга вчера́ ....?	She read.
2. Что́ Ива́н вчера́ ....?	He wrote.
3. Что́ э́та студе́нтка вчера́ ....?	She worked.
4. Что́ ты́ вчера́ ....?	I translated.[9]
5. Что́ ты́ и твой бра́т вчера́ ....?	We talked.

6. The preposition о, об, обо *about*

Another preposition which, like **в** and **на**, governs the locative case (though it does not show location) is the preposition **о**. It is written **об** before words beginning with a vowel sound other than initial [j], or, in other words, except **я, е, ё,** or **ю** (sounds [ja], [je], [jo], and [ju]). A prepositional phrase with **о** denotes content or topic:

Я́ ду́мал **о** Бори́се.	I thought about Boris.
О́н писа́л **о** спо́рте.	He wrote about sport.
Мы́ говори́ли **об** А́нне.	We talked about Anna.
Я́ чита́л **об** э́том.	I read about that.
Она́ писа́ла **о ва́с.**	She wrote about you.

The questions *about what?* or *about whom?* are formed in Russian with the preposition **о** plus the locative case of **что** (*what*) or **кто** (*who*):

о чём? about what?   о ко́м? about whom?

Like all prepositions, **о** is pronounced together with the word it governs:

о чём	[ačóm]	о ко́м	[akóm]
о спо́рте	[aspórţi]	об э́том	[abétəm]

The form **обо** is used in the phrases **обо мне́** (*about me*) and **обо всём** (*about everything*), while **об** is used in **об э́том** (*about that*).

The prepositional forms of the personal pronouns used with **о/об/обо** are shown in the box below.

LOCATIVE OF PERSONAL PRONOUNS

Nom.	я	ты	он оно́	она́	мы	вы	они́
Loc.	**обо мне́**	**о тебе́**	**о нём**	**о ней**	**о на́с**	**о ва́с**	**о ни́х**

[9] In this and later drills with the word *I*, always use the gender appropriate to yourself.

PATTERN SENTENCES

1. —**О ко́м** они́ говори́ли? —Они́ говори́ли **о** писа́теле Шо́лохове.[10] Они́ мно́го **о нём** говори́ли.
2. —**О чём**[11] вы́ ду́мали? —Я́ ду́мал **об э́той** пробле́ме. Я́ мно́го **о ней** ду́мал.
3. —**О ко́м**[11] вы́ говори́ли? —Мы́ говори́ли **об** О́льге и **о** Ни́не.
4. —Что́ вы́ **о ни́х** говори́ли? —Э́то секре́т!
5. —**О чём** э́та статья́? —**О** бале́те в Аме́рике.
6. Я́ не зна́л **об э́той** статье́.
7. —Мы́ вчера́ говори́ли **о ва́с**, Ива́н Ива́нович. —Что́ вы́ **обо мне́** говори́ли? —Э́то секре́т!
8. —О́льга Ива́новна! Я́ так мно́го слы́шал **о ва́с** и **о ва́шем** му́же! —**О на́с**?! Э́то интере́сно!

1. —About whom did they talk? —They talked about the writer Sholokhov.[10] They talked a great deal about him.
2. —About what did you think? —I thought about that problem. I thought a great deal about it.
3. —About whom did you speak? —We spoke about Olga and Nina.
4. —What did you say about them? —That's a secret!
5. —What is that article about? —About ballet in America.
6. I didn't know about that article.
7. —We were talking about you yesterday, Ivan Ivanovich. —What did you say about me? —That's a secret!
8. —Olga Ivanovna! I've heard so many things about you and about your husband. —About us?! That's interesting!

DRILLS

A. *Complete the answers below using the correct form of both the preposition* **o** *and the locative of each noun and pronoun listed.*

1. —О чём она́ говори́ла? —Она́ говори́ла **о/об/обо**: мы, вы, я, ты, он, она́, оно́, Ле́нин, Москва́, на́ша рабо́та, э́тот уро́к, твоё письмо́, э́та газе́та.
2. —О ко́м вы́ ду́мали? —Я́ ду́мал **о/об**: вы, Бори́с, О́льга, мо́й учи́тель, моя́ жена́, твоя́ учи́тельница, до́ктор Ива́нов, профе́ссор Ро́бинсон.
3. —О чём ва́ша статья́? —Моя́ статья́ **о/об**: спорт, о́пера, на́ш го́род, э́та пробле́ма, ва́ш профе́ссор, на́ша шко́ла.

B. *Supply the correct form of the third person pronoun.*

1. —Вы́ писа́ли о Че́хове?[12] —Да́, я́ о . . . . писа́л(а).
2. —Вы́ писа́ли об э́той о́пере? —Не́т, я́ о . . . . не писа́л(а).
3. —Вы́ говори́ли о Бори́се и об О́льге? —Да́, мы́ о . . . . говори́ли.
4. —Вы́ говори́ли об э́том письме́? —Не́т, мы́ о . . . . не говори́ли.
5. —Вы́ слы́шали (heard) об э́той кни́ге? —Да́, я́ о . . . . слы́шал(а).
6. —Ты́ слы́шал(а) о на́шем экза́мене? —Да́, я́ о . . . . слы́шал(а).

---

[10] Two words in apposition in Russian (as **писа́тель** and **Шо́лохов** here) are both declined; both take the locative ending in the example above. Михаи́л Алекса́ндрович Шо́лохов (b. 1905) was a leading Soviet novelist who grew up among the Cossacks of the Don. His novel «Ти́хий До́н» (*The Quiet Don*) brought him great popularity both in the Soviet Union and abroad. He won the Nobel Prize for Literature in 1965.

[11] Observe that prepositions and their objects may not be separated in Russian; a Russian sentence may not end with a preposition.

[12] Че́хов, Анто́н Па́влович (1860–1904), a famous Russian writer. Chekhov wrote short stories and plays. The latter include «Ча́йка» *The Sea Gull*, «Дя́дя Ва́ня» *Uncle Vanya*, «Три́ сестры́» *The Three Sisters*, and «Вишнёвый са́д» *The Cherry Orchard*.

Conversation

Read the two conversations aloud several times. Memorize the first conversation.

1. В классе

Андрей. —Борис, ты сегодня был **в** школе?
Борис. —Конечно был![13]

А. —Что вы́ де́лали **на** уро́ке?
Б. —Мы́ как всегда́ чита́ли, писа́ли **на** доске́, переводи́ли, и, коне́чно, говори́ли.
А. —Ка́к сего́дня чита́ла Со́ня?
Б. —Она́ чита́ла ма́ло, но хорошо́, и хорошо́ переводи́ла.
А. —А ка́к говори́ла Ни́на?
Б. —Я́ не слу́шал, но вероя́тно она́, как всегда́, говори́ла мно́го и пло́хо.
А. —А ка́к переводи́л Бо́б?
Б. —О́чень хорошо́. О́н о́чень хорошо́ зна́л уро́к.
А. —Это стра́нно, потому́ что вчера́ о́н о́чень пло́хо чита́л, пло́хо писа́л на доске́, и да́же не слу́шал, о чём говори́л учи́тель.
Б. —Это коне́чно пло́хо, но э́то быва́ет.

2. В библиоте́ке

О́льга сего́дня мно́го рабо́тала и до́ма (at home) и в шко́ле: она́ чита́ла, переводи́ла, слу́шала, что́ говори́л учи́тель, и писа́ла сочине́ние. Сейча́с она́ в библиоте́ке. А Вади́м не́ был в шко́ле, но сейча́с он то́же в библиоте́ке.

Вади́м. —Здра́вствуй, О́льга.
О́льга. —Здра́вствуй, Вади́м. Ка́к ты́ поживае́шь?
В. —Спаси́бо, о́чень хорошо́. А ты́ ка́к?
О. —Пло́хо. Рабо́та, рабо́та, и то́лько рабо́та! Ско́ро экза́мен и я́ тепе́рь всегда́ или в кла́ссе, или в библиоте́ке. А что́ ты́ де́лал? Почему́ ты́ не́ был в шко́ле?
В. —Я́ бы́л на футбо́ле. Бы́ло о́чень интере́сно.
О. —Ско́ро экза́мен, а ты́ бы́л на футбо́ле?!
В. —Ну́, так что́? Почему́ не́т? А сейча́с я́ здесь в библиоте́ке то́лько потому́ что я́ зна́л, что ты́ зде́сь.
О. —Вади́м!
В. —Что́ «Вади́м»? Это пра́вда. Я́ так ра́д, что мы́ зде́сь вме́сте!
О. —Ты́ ра́д, а я́ не ра́да. Когда́ Ни́на Ла́пина была́ здесь, она́ была́ твоя́ герои́ня. А тепе́рь, когда́ Ни́на в Ленингра́де, герои́ня я́! Это то́лько потому́, что она́ далеко́, а я́ бли́зко.
В. —О́льга, э́то непра́вда! Это не та́к!
О. —Коне́чно э́то та́к! Не́т, Вади́м. Ты́ не мо́й геро́й. До свида́ния!

---

[13] Pronoun subjects are sometimes omitted when they are obvious. Their omission is especially frequent in replies to questions in which the verb used in the question is repeated in the reply.

Answer the following questions.

1. Почему́ О́льга тепе́рь всегда́ и́ли в кла́ссе, и́ли в библиоте́ке?   2. Почему́ Вади́м вчера́ не́ был в кла́ссе?   3. Почему́ о́н сейча́с в библиоте́ке?   4. Ка́к бы́ло на футбо́ле?   5. Почему́ Вади́м ра́д?   6. Почему́, когда́ Ни́на была́ в Москве́, она́ была́ геро́йня, а тепе́рь геро́йня О́льга?

DRILL

Review Translation.

1. —Hello, Olga! Where is Mama? —She is now in the kitchen.   2. Nina was there too. They were there together.   3. We stood on the street, and, as usual, talked about our work.   4. In Boston they probably lived in your apartment.   5. —Is the museum far away? —No, it's very close.   6. My brother lived in Moscow, and my sister lived in Leningrad.   7. —Nina is very glad that you are here, and Ivan is not glad. —That's not true! That is not so.   8. —Vadim was at the football (game) today! —Well, what of it? Why not?   9. —What were you speaking about? —About our exam, of course!   10. —About whom was she talking? —About Chekhov, as usual.   11. —Did she speak Russian? —Yes, but she spoke badly.   12. Nina spoke Russian, and Vadim spoke English.

Vocabulary

библиоте́ка library
бли́зко [bļískə] near, close
вероя́тно probably
вме́сте together
всегда́ always
вчера́ [fčirá] yesterday
геро́й hero
геро́йня heroine
го́род city, town
да́же even
далеко́ far (away)
дверь (*fem. II*) door
интере́сно interesting
кабине́т study
карти́на picture
кварти́ра apartment
коне́чно (*pronounce* [kaņéšnə]) of course, certainly
конце́рт concert
крова́ть (*fem. II*) bed
ма́ло little, few
ма́ма mama

мно́го much, many
но but (however)
писа́тель (*masc.*) writer
писа́тельница woman writer
пло́хо bad, badly; poorly
пра́вда truth, true, right
рабо́та work
рад (*masc.*) ра́да (*fem.*) glad
сего́дня (*pronounce* [şivódņə]) today
сейча́с now[14]
ско́ро soon
сочине́ние composition
статья́ [staţjá] article
стра́нно strange
теа́тр theater
у́лица street
уро́к lesson
футбо́л football (soccer)
что [što] (*conj.*) that; (*rel. pron.*) what
шко́ла school
экза́мен [egzáɱin] examination

---

[14] See note on p. 25.

EXPRESSIONS

или . . . или either . . . or
по-англи́йски (in) English
по-ру́сски (in) Russian
говори́ть, чита́ть, писа́ть по-ру́сски to speak, read, write (in) Russian
как всегда́ as always; as usual
Э́то пра́вда. That's right; that's true.
Э́то непра́вда. That's not so; it's not true.
Э́то быва́ет. That happens; that can happen.
Э́то не та́к. That's not so; that's wrong.
Здра́вствуй! Hello! (*familiar*)
Ка́к ты́ пожива́ешь? How are you? (*familiar*)
Ну́, так что́? Well, what of it?

VOCABULARY REVIEW

Places

Аме́рика	Евро́па	Сове́тский Сою́з
Босто́н	Ло́ндон	Москва́
Нью-Йо́рк[15]	Пари́ж	Ленингра́д
Чика́го		Ки́ев
		Сиби́рь (*fem. II*)

The Family

муж	сын
жена́	дочь
оте́ц	брат
мать	сестра́

Professions

студе́нт, -ка
учи́тель, -ница
писа́тель, -ница
журнали́ст, -ка
секрета́рь, секрета́рша
профе́ссор[16]
до́ктор[16]

Buildings

дом
шко́ла
музе́й
теа́тр
библиоте́ка

School

шко́ла
класс
уро́к
доска́
ка́рта

At Home

дом
кварти́ра
ко́мната
кабине́т
ку́хня
стол
стена́
пол
потоло́к
окно́
карти́на
ла́мпа
по́лка

Activities[17]

уро́к
рабо́та
конце́рт

Parts of the Body

голова́
лицо́
рот
нос
глаз
рука́

Adverbs of Place

где?
тут, здесь
там
до́ма
бли́зко
далеко́

Reading Matter

кни́га
журна́л
газе́та
статья́
письмо́
слова́рь (*masc.*)
грамма́тика

Adverbs of Time

когда́?
всегда́
вчера́
сего́дня
ско́ро

---

[15] Only the last part of a hyphenated word is declined: **в** Нью-Йо́рке *in New York*.
[16] These two words are used in the masculine form for feminine members of the profession as well.
[17] These take **на** with the locative: e.g., **на** уро́ке *at the lesson*.

Adjectives, nominative case • List of some commonly used adjectives •
The interrogative adjective какóй • Adjectives and nouns of nationality
• Locative of adjectives • The relative котóрый *who*, *which*,
that • Reading: И тáк всегдá!

Unit **6**

Grammar

1. Adjectives, nominative case

Like the possessives and the demonstratives studied in the preceding unit, Russian adjectives agree in gender, number, and case with the noun they modify. In the examples below, adjectives in boldface are given in the three gender forms of the nominative singular.

Masc.	вáш **нóвый** дóм	your *new* house
Neut.	тó **нóвое** крéсло	that *new* armchair
Fem.	нáша **нóвая** квартúра	our *new* apartment

The form illustrated above by **нóвый** *new* is the most common, though not the only one. Adjectives of this type are stressed on the stem (in this case [nóv.]), and their final stem consonants are *hard*:

		Ending
Masc.	нóв.ый	-ЫЙ
Neut.	нóв.ое	-ОЕ
Fem.	нóв.ая	-АЯ

A variant of the hard group has the stress falling on the ending; its masculine ending is **-óй**, as in молодóй *young*:

		Ending
Masc.	молод.óй	-ÓЙ
Neut.	молод.óе	-ÓЕ
Fem.	молод.áя	-ÁЯ

67

Note: Only the masculine nominative singular is *spelled* differently; all other forms of the **-ой** group are spelled identically with their **-ый** group counterparts.

In a relatively small group of adjectives the stem ends in a *soft* consonant: e.g., **синий** *blue* (stem [şíņ.]); in writing, the softness of the stem ending is shown by the first vowel of the ending:

Ending

Masc.	син.ий	**-ИЙ**
Neut.	син.ее	**-ЕЕ**
Fem.	син.яя	**-ЯЯ**

SUMMARY

		Masculine		*Neuter*		*Feminine*	
Stress on stem:	{ hard	но́вый	-ЫЙ	но́вое	-ОЕ	но́вая	-АЯ
	{ soft	си́ний	-ИЙ	си́нее	-ЕЕ	си́няя	-ЯЯ
Stress on ending: *hard only*		молодо́й	-ОЙ	молодо́е	-ОЕ	молода́я	-А́Я

DRILL

Supply the proper endings of the adjectives in the phrases below.

но́вый new	**большо́й** big	**после́дний** last
нов.... ко́мната	больш.... го́род	послед.... письмо́
нов.... студе́нт	больш.... по́ле	послед.... статья́
нов.... кре́сло	больш.... кварти́ра	послед.... до́ллар
нов.... ку́хня	больш.... кла́сс	послед.... сло́во (word)

си́ний blue	**молодо́й** young	**пе́рвый** first
син.... пла́тье (dress)	молод.... до́ктор	перв.... сло́во
син.... костю́м (suit)	молод.... секрета́рша	перв.... уро́к
син.... шля́па (hat)	молод.... лицо́	перв.... статья́
син.... кре́сло	молод.... студе́нтка	перв.... кни́га

Spelling for Adjectival endings after г, к, х, ж, ш, ч, and щ. The rules given in Unit 3, page 21, on consonant-vowel incompatibilities have several applications to the spelling of adjective endings. These are formulated as Spelling Rules 1 and 2.

The student will recall that certain consonant-vowel incompatibilities underlie certain rules of spelling for combinations of consonant plus vowel (see page 22). In particular, Spelling Rules 1 and 2 apply to the spelling of adjective endings:

Spelling Rule 1: Write **о** *only if stressed* after ж, ш, ц, ч, щ; otherwise write **е**.

Spelling Rule 2: Write **и**, *never* **ы**, after ж, ш, ч, щ, г, к, and х.

Application of spelling rules. (1) If an adjective has a *stressed stem* ending in **ж, ш, ч, щ, г, к,** or **х**, replace the **ы** of the masculine ending **-ый** with an **и** (*Spelling Rule 2*):

	Masculine			Neuter	Feminine
Г	стро́гий	strict		стро́гое	стро́гая
К	ру́сский	Russian	*but no change in*	ру́сское	ру́сская
Х	ти́хий	quiet		ти́хое	ти́хая

(2) In addition to the substitution of **и** for **ы** in the masculine, the substitution of **е** for unstressed **о** in the neuter is required after **ж, ш, ч,** and **щ** (*Spelling Rule 1*):

	Masculine		Neuter	Feminine
Ж	све́жий	fresh	све́жее	све́жая
Ш	хоро́ший	good, nice	хоро́шее	хоро́шая
Ч	горя́чий	hot	горя́чее	горя́чая
Щ	бу́дущий	future	бу́дущее	бу́дущая

(3) Adjectives with stems ending in the seven consonants listed above, but with the stress on the *ending* have normal endings of the stressed type, e.g., дорого́й, дорого́е, дорога́я; плохо́й, плохо́е, плоха́я; большо́й, большо́е, больша́я; чужо́й, чужо́е, чужа́я.

Summary

STEMS ENDING IN Г, К, Х

Masc.	ру́сский	⟵	-ИЙ (not -ЫЙ!)
Neut.	ру́сское		
Fem.	ру́сская		

STEMS ENDING IN Ж, Ш, Ч, Щ[1]

Masc.	хоро́ший	⟵	-ИЙ (not -ЫЙ!)
Neut.	хоро́шее	⟵	-ЕЕ (not -ОЕ!)
Fem.	хоро́шая.		

DRILL

Fill in the correct endings of the following adjectives.

ру́сский Russian	**хоро́ший** good	**большо́й** big
ру́сск.... сло́во	хоро́ш.... автомоби́ль	больш.... до́м
ру́сск.... слова́рь	хоро́ш.... письмо́	больш.... го́род

---

[1] *Note on pronunciation.* The vowel **ы** [i] in unstressed masculine endings is pronounced [ə]: [nóvəj] [trúdnəj], etc.; the **и** required by spelling after **ж** and **ш** does *not* produce palatalization, and also sounds like [ə]: хоро́ший [xaróšəj], све́жий [s̮véžəj].

ру́сск.... студе́нтка	хоро́ш.... журнали́стка	больш.... ко́мната
ру́сск.... грамма́тика	хоро́ш.... до́м	больш.... кре́сло
ру́сск.... го́род	хоро́ш.... кре́сло	больш.... по́ле

лёгкий easy, light	**свéжий** fresh	**ма́ленький** small
лёгк.... пла́тье	свéж.... дéнь	ма́леньк.... дере́вня
лёгк.... уро́к	свéж.... мя́со (meat)	ма́леньк.... кварти́ра
лёгк.... кни́га	свéж.... лицо́	ма́леньк.... сто́л
лёгк.... сло́во	свéж.... ма́сло (butter)	ма́леньк.... по́ле
	свéж.... ро́за (rose)	

Note: A number of soft adjectives ending in **-ний, -нее, -няя** are derived from adverbs of place or from words denoting a certain time, e.g.:

зима́	зи́мний	winter (*adj.*)	зи́мний дéнь a winter day
лéто	лéтний	summer (*adj.*)	лéтняя пого́да summer weather
сего́дня	сего́дняшний	today's	сего́дняшний уро́к today's lesson
вчера́	вчера́шний	yesterday's	вчера́шняя газéта yesterday's newspaper
здéсь	здéшний	of this place, local	здéшняя шко́ла the local school
тепéрь	тепéрешний	present, of this time	тепéрешняя мо́да the present fashion

Observe that, in contrast to English, Russian does not use nouns adjectivally, such as in "a *winter* day." Instead in such cases adjectives are derived from nouns by the addition of one of several suffixes, e.g., **зи́мний** дéнь.

2. List of some commonly used adjectives

америка́нский	American (*adj.*)	после́дний	last
англи́йский	English (*adj.*)	прия́тный	pleasant
бéлый	white	ру́сский	Russian (*adj.*)
большо́й	big, large	свéжий	fresh
вчера́шний	yesterday's (*adj.*)	сего́дняшний	today's (*adj.*)
здéшний	local, of this place	[ṣivódṇišṇij]	
зи́мний	winter (*adj.*)	серьёзный	serious
интерéсный	interesting	[ṣiṛjóznəj]	
краси́вый	beautiful, hand- some, pretty	си́ний	blue
		ску́чный	dull, boring
лёгкий	light; easy	ста́рый	old
[ļóxķij]		стра́нный	strange
лéтний	summer (*adj.*)	тёплый	warm
ма́ленький	little, small	тру́дный	difficult, hard
молодо́й	young	холо́дный	cold
но́вый	new	хоро́ший	good, fine
пéрвый	first	цéлый	whole (*adj.*), entire
плохо́й	bad, poor	чёрный	black

DRILLS

A. *Give the antonyms of the following adjectives. Choose from the list above.*

но́вый	молодо́й	ма́ленький
пе́рвый	тру́дный	холо́дный
плохо́й	интере́сный	зи́мний
бе́лый		сего́дняшний

B. *Supply three suitable adjectives for each of the nouns below and put them in the proper gender form.*

1. . . . .
    . . . . уро́к
    . . . .

2. . . . .
    . . . . газе́та
    . . . .

3. . . . .
    . . . . де́нь
    . . . .

4. . . . .
    . . . . студе́нтка
    . . . .

5. . . . .
    . . . . кварти́ра
    . . . .

6. . . . .
    . . . . сло́во
    . . . .

3. The interrogative adjective како́й

The interrogative adjective meaning *what kind/sort of?*, *what?*, *which?* is in the nominative as follows and is declined like adjectives ending in **-о́й** after **к**.

Masc.	**како́й**
Neut.	**како́е**
Fem.	**кака́я**

—**Како́й** о́н студе́нт? —О́н хоро́ший студе́нт.
—What sort of a student is he? —He is a good student.
—**Кака́я** она́ студе́нтка? —Она́ хоро́шая студе́нтка.
—What sort of a student is she? —She is a good student.

Како́й with another adjective is used in exclamations:

Како́й большо́й го́род!
What a big city!
Како́е большо́е по́ле!
What a big field!

Questions with **како́й** are often formed with **это** (unstressed) and agree in gender and number with the noun. (Compare the following questions with those using **чей** on p. 44.)

—**Како́й** это го́род? —Ленингра́д.
—What city is this? —Leningrad.
—**Кака́я** это река́? —Во́лга.
—What river is this? —The Volga.

Similarly, **тако́й** is used with another adjective to mean *so . . ., such a . . .*:

Э́та кни́га **така́я** интере́сная!
This book is so interesting!
О́н **тако́й** хоро́ший студе́нт!
He is such a good student!

PATTERN SENTENCES

1. —**Кака́я** А́нна до́чь? —Она́ хоро́шая до́чь.

2. —**Како́й** го́род Ки́ев? —Ки́ев краси́вый, ста́рый го́род.

3. —**Кака́я** ко́мната ва́ша, э́та ма́ленькая или та́ больша́я? —Ма́ленькая.

4. —Э́то вчера́шняя газе́та, а где́ сего́дняшняя? —Та́м на столе́.

5. Сего́дня прия́тный ле́тний де́нь. Пра́вда?

6. —**Кака́я** газе́та на столе́, «Пра́вда» или «Та́ймз»? —«Пра́вда».

7. —**Како́й** э́то рома́н? —Э́то «Война́ и ми́р».

8. То́т уро́к бы́л тру́дный, а э́тот лёгкий. Пра́вда?

9. **Како́й** стра́нный вопро́с!

10. **Како́е** хоро́шее, большо́е кре́сло!

11. Во́т све́жее ма́сло и све́жий бе́лый хле́б.

12. Э́та америка́нская журнали́стка **така́я** краси́вая!

---

1. —What kind of daughter is Anna? —She is a good daughter.

2. —What kind of city is Kiev? —Kiev is a beautiful, old city.

3. —Which room is yours, this little one or that big one? —The little one.

4. —This is yesterday's paper, but where is today's? —There on the table.

5. Today is a pleasant summer day. Right?

6. —Which newspaper is on the table, *Pravda* (*Truth*) or the *Times*? —*Pravda*.

7. —What novel is this? —It's *War and Peace*.

8. That lesson was hard, and this one is easy. Right?

9. What a strange question!

10. What a fine, large armchair!

11. Here is fresh butter and fresh white bread.

12. This American newspaperwoman is so beautiful!

DRILL

Fill in the blanks with the suitable form of the word above in the same column.

A. *Model:* —Како́й костю́м ва́ш, э́тот или то́т? —Э́тот мо́й.

1. —. . . . до́м . . . ., ... или . . . .? —. . . . .
2. —. . . . слова́рь . . . ., . . . или . . . .? —. . . . .
3. —. . . . ко́мната . . . ., ... или . . . .? —. . . . .
4. —. . . . газе́та . . . ., ... или . . . .? —. . . . .
5. —. . . . кни́га . . . ., ... или . . . .? —. . . . .
6. —. . . окно́ . . . ., ... или . . . .? —. . . . .
7. —. . . . кре́сло . . . ., ... или . . . .? —. . . . .

B. *Model:* —Кака́я она́ студе́нтка? —Она́ хоро́шая студе́нтка.

1. —. . . . она́ ма́ть? —Она́ . . . . ма́ть.
2. —. . . . о́н учи́тель? —О́н . . . . учи́тель.
3. —. . . . о́н писа́тель? —О́н . . . писа́тель.
4. —. . . . о́н сы́н? —О́н . . . сы́н.
5. —. . . . она́ учи́тельница? —Она́ . . . . учи́тельница.

C. *Model:* Какóй плохóй хлéб!

.... ромáн (novel)!

.... погóда!

.... зимá!

.... лéто!

4. Adjectives and nouns of nationality

Russian has adjectives of nationality, such as **америкáнский** and **англи́йский**. These adjectives, however, are used only as modifiers, as in **америкáнский гóрод**, **англи́йская газéта**. When referring to persons of a given nationality, *nouns* of nationality *must* be used, e.g.:

He is an American. *Or:* He is American.	} Óн америкáнец.
She is an American. *Or:* She is American.	} Онá америкáнка.
He is an Englishman. *Or:* He is English.	} Óн англичáнин.
She is an Englishwoman. *Or:* She is English.	} Онá англичáнка.

The only exception to the above is the Russian nationality; the forms **ру́сск.ий**, **-ая** are used both as modifiers and as nouns denoting Russian nationals, e.g.:

ру́сский журнáл, **ру́сская** кни́га

as well as:

He is Russian. Óн **ру́сский**.

She is Russian. Онá **ру́сская**.

Note that nouns or adjectives of nationality are *not capitalized in Russian*.

PATTERN SENTENCES

1. Джóн Брáун **америкáнец**. Óн **америкáнский** журнали́ст.
2. Нéлли Брáун **америкáнка**. Онá **америкáнская** актри́са.
3. Мóй отéц бы́л **англичáнин**, а моя́ мáть былá **ру́сская**.
4. Отéц говори́л **по-ру́сски**, как **ру́сский**.
5. Моя́ женá **англичáнка**. Мы́ жи́ли в Ливерпýле. Э́то **англи́йский** гóрод.
6. Когдá мы́ тáм жи́ли, я́ говори́л **по-англи́йски**, как **англичáнин**.
7. Сергéй Прокóфьев бы́л **ру́сский**. Óн **ру́сский** компози́тор. А Аарóн Кóпланд **америкáнец**; óн **америкáнский** компози́тор.

1. John Brown is American. He is an American journalist.
2. Nelly Brown is American. She is an American actress.
3. My father was English, and my mother was Russian.
4. Father spoke Russian like a Russian.
5. My wife is English. We lived in Liverpool. That is an English city.
6. When we lived there, I spoke English like an Englishman.
7. Sergei Prokofiev was Russian. He was a Russian composer. And Aaron Copland is American; he is an American composer.

DRILL

Translate the words in parentheses into Russian.

1. —Бóб, вы́ (Russian)? —Нéт, я (American).
2. Бостóн (is an American) гóрод.
3. Мóй отéц (is Russian), а моя́ мáть (is English).
4. Э́тот молодóй (Englishman) мóй студéнт.
5. О́ксфорд (is an English) университéт.
6. Ивáн Петрóв (is Russian). Зóя Петрóва (is Russian).
7. Фóлкнер (is American). Óн óчень интерéсный (American) писáтель.
8. Вóлга (is a Russian) рекá.
9. Мéри (is American). Онá (American) журналúстка.
10. «Нью-Йóрк Тáймз» (is an American) газéта, а «Прáвда» (is a Russian) газéта.
11. Э́та молодáя (American) нáша студéнтка.

5. Locative of adjectives

Adjectives take the following endings in the locative case in the singular:

Masculine *Neuter*	-ом, -ем
Feminine	-ой, -ей

The spelling is generally **-ом** for masculine and neuter and **-ой** for feminine; however, **e** replaces **o** (that is, **-ем** and **-ей** replace **-ом** and **-ой**) in an adjective (1) if its stem ends in a soft consonant (e.g., сúнем, сúней) or in ж, ш, ч, щ and (2) if the stress is on the stem:

хорóшем, хорóшей, *but* большóм, большóй

Compare the adjectival endings with those of the third person singular personal pronoun and the possessive pronouns.

ADJECTIVES AND PRONOUNS IN THE LOCATIVE SINGULAR

	NOMINATIVE		LOCATIVE (with prepositions в, на, о)
	Masculine	*Neuter*	*Masculine and Neuter*
3rd pers. sing.	он	онó	нём [ņ.óm]
Possessives	мой	моё	моём [maj.óm]
Adjectives	нóвый большóй сúний хорóший	нóвое большóе сúнее хорóшее	нóвом [nóv.əm] большóм [baļš.óm] сúнем [şíņ.əm] ⎫ хорóшем [xaróš.əm]⎭ with **e**

	Feminine		
3rd pers. sing.	она́	ней [n.éj]	
Possessives	моя́	мо**е́й** [maj.éj]	} with **e**
Adjectives	но́вая	но́в**ой** [nóv.əj]	
	больша́я	больш**о́й** [baʎš.ój]	
	си́няя	си́**ней** [şíṇ.əj]	
	хоро́шая	хоро́ш**ей** [xaróš.əj]	} with **e**

PATTERN SENTENCES

1. —В како́м до́ме жи́л тво́й дру́г? —О́н жи́л в э́том ма́леньком до́ме.
2. —В како́м го́роде рабо́тал тво́й сы́н? —В Ки́еве.
3. —В како́й газе́те ты́ об э́том чита́ла, в ру́сской или америка́нской? —В зде́шней ру́сской газе́те.
4. Моя́ сестра́ жила́ в э́той ма́ленькой англи́йской дере́вне.
5. —О чём они́ говори́ли? —О но́вом америка́нском фи́льме.
6. —О ко́м вы́ писа́ли в ва́шем после́днем письме́? —О моём ру́сском дру́ге. —О како́м ру́сском дру́ге? —Об Ива́не Петро́ве.
7. —О ко́м вы́ говори́ли? —О молодо́й англи́йской писа́тельнице.
8. —В како́й газе́те была́ э́та статья́, в сего́дняшней или вчера́шней? —В сего́дняшней.
9. —В чём вчера́ была́ О́льга? —Она́ была́ в краси́вом си́нем пла́тье и в си́ней шля́пе.
10. Ста́рая англича́нка жила́ одна́ в большо́й кварти́ре.

1. —In which house did your friend live? —He lived in this small house.
2. —In which city did your son work? —In Kiev.
3. —In which newspaper did you read about this, in a Russian or an American one? —In the local Russian paper.
4. My sister lived in this small English village.
5. —What did they talk about? —About a new American film.
6. —About whom did you write in your last letter? —About my Russian friend. —About which Russian friend? —About Ivan Petrov.
7. —Whom did you talk about? —About a young English woman writer.
8. —In which newspaper was that (this) article, in today's or yesterday's? —In today's.
9. —What was Olga wearing yesterday? —She was wearing a pretty blue dress and a blue hat.
10. The old Englishwoman lived alone in a large apartment.

DRILLS

A. *Fill in the blanks with the proper endings.*

1. Мы́ бы́ли в э́т.... ру́сск.... го́роде.
2. Мы́ бы́ли в э́т.... ру́сск.... теа́тре.
3. Мы́ бы́ли на э́т.... ру́сск.... конце́рте.
4. Мы́ бы́ли в э́т.... ру́сск.... дере́вне.
5. Мы́ говори́ли об э́т.... ру́сск.... же́нщине.
6. Мы́ говори́ли об э́т.... ру́сск.... журнали́стке.
7. Мы́ говори́ли об э́т.... ру́сск.... сло́ве.

B. *Translate the words in parentheses, using the proper endings.*

1. Я́ ду́мал о (your last) рома́не.
2. Я́ ду́мал о (your last) сло́ве.
3. Я́ ду́мал о (your last) кни́ге.
4. Я́ ду́мал о (your last) статье́.

5. Я ду́мал о (our last) письме́.

7. Я ду́мал о (our last) кварти́ре.

6. Я ду́мал о (our last) уро́ке.

C. *Fill in the blanks with the proper forms of* **како́й** *and translate the words in parentheses, using the proper endings.*

1. —О . . . . го́роде вы́ говори́ли? —(About our big city.)
2. —О . . . . уро́ке вы́ говори́ли? —(About our new lesson.)
3. —О . . . . словаре́ вы́ говори́ли? —(About your good dictionary.)
4. —О . . . . кни́ге вы́ говори́ли? —(About your new book.)
5. —О . . . . кварти́ре она́ говори́ла? —(About this small apartment.)
6. —О . . . . кре́сле она́ говори́ла? —(About this one.)[2]
7. —О . . . . статье́ она́ говори́ла? —(About this one.)[2]

6. The relative кото́рый *who, which, that*

Russian uses the relative **кото́рый** to mean *who, which,* or *that.* **Кото́рый** is declined as an adjective. It agrees in gender and number with the noun it replaces. But its *case* depends on its use in its own clause. Note that clauses with **кото́рый** are always set off by commas.

Где́ кни́га, **кото́рая** была́ ту́т на столе́?
Where is the book that was here on the table?

Во́т мо́й бра́т, **кото́рый** жи́л в Нью-Йо́рке.
Here is my brother who lived in New York.

Перо́, **кото́рое** бы́ло на столе́, не моё.
The pen that was on the table is not mine.

До́м, **в кото́ром** о́н жи́л в Ло́ндоне, бы́л о́чень ста́рый.
The house in which he lived in London was very old.

Кварти́ра, **в кото́рой** мы́ жи́ли, была́ о́чень больша́я.
The apartment we lived in[3] was very large.

Это **та́** краси́вая молода́я студе́нтка, **о кото́рой** говори́л ста́рый профе́ссор.
This is that pretty young student the old professor was talking about (about whom the old professor was talking).

Кото́рый *as Interrogative*

Кото́рый also means *which, which one.* It is used to point out or select from a limited number of alternatives, e.g., **Кото́рый** ва́ш сы́н? Which one is your son? Otherwise **како́й** is used, e.g., В **како́м** го́роде вы́ жи́ли? In which town did you live? В **како́й** кни́ге вы́ э́то ви́дели? In which book did you see that?

---

[2] The English word *one* (*big one, new one,* etc.) in these sentences has no correspondent in Russian and must not be translated.

[3] In such sentences as this and the following one, the relative must not be omitted in Russian, although it frequently is omitted in colloquial English.

DRILLS

A. *Transform the two sentences into one by using relative clauses with* **кото́рый**, *according to the models.*

A. *Model:* Где́ мо́й сто́л? О́н стоя́л ту́т.
   Где́ мо́й сто́л, кото́рый стоя́л ту́т?

1. Где́ ва́ша ла́мпа? Она́ стоя́ла ту́т.
2. Где́ ва́ш телефо́н? О́н стоя́л ту́т.
3. Где́ твоё кре́сло? Оно́ стоя́ло ту́т.
4. Где́ э́тот писа́тель? О́н жи́л в на́шем го́роде.

5. Где́ э́та журнали́стка? Она́ жила́ в э́той кварти́ре.
6. Где́ ва́ш бра́т? О́н жи́л в на́шем до́ме.

B. *Model:* Во́т до́м. Мы́ в нём жи́ли.
   Во́т до́м, в кото́ром мы́ жи́ли.

1. Во́т го́род. Мы́ в нём жи́ли.
2. Во́т у́лица. Мы́ на не́й жи́ли.
3. Во́т кварти́ра. Мы́ о не́й говори́ли.
4. Во́т автомоби́ль. Мы́ о нём говори́ли.

5. Во́т студе́нт. Мы́ о нём говори́ли.
6. Во́т студе́нтка. Мы́ о не́й говори́ли.
7. Во́т дере́вня. Мы́ в не́й жи́ли.
8. Во́т музе́й. Мы́ в нём не́ были.

B. *Fill in the blanks with the correct form of* **кото́рый** *and put the words in parentheses into the correct case.*

1. Письмо́, ... бы́ло на (мой) столе́, сейча́с на (ваш).
2. Кни́га, ... была́ в (твоя́) ко́мнате, сейча́с в (твой) кабине́те.
3. Автомоби́ль, ... бы́л в (ваш) гараже́, сейча́с на (на́ша) у́лице.
4. Сту́л, ... бы́л в (наш) ко́мнате, сейча́с на (ва́ша) вера́нде.
5. Сто́л, ... стоя́л в (твой) кабине́те, сейча́с в (моя́) ко́мнате.
6. Кре́сло, ... стоя́ло в (э́тот) кабине́те, сейча́с в (тот).
7. Ла́мпа, ... стоя́ла на (э́та) по́лке, сейча́с на (та).

Conversation

О́н и компози́тор и пиани́ст

Семёнов. —Что́ вы́ вчера́ де́лали, Андре́й?

Ма́слов. —Я́ бы́л вчера́ на о́чень интере́сном конце́рте.

С. —Где́ бы́л э́тот конце́рт?

М. —О́чень бли́зко; в но́вой шко́ле на на́шей у́лице.

С. —А я́ да́же не зна́л, что та́м вчера́ бы́л конце́рт. А кто́ игра́л вчера́?

М. —Во́льский,[4] молодо́й и о́чень тала́нтливый (talented) музыка́нт (musician).

С. —На чём о́н игра́л?

М. —На роя́ле.

С. —Э́то то́т пиани́ст, о кото́ром говори́ла ва́ша жена́, когда́ мы́ бы́ли в Большо́м теа́тре?

---

[4] Some Russian last names have the form of adjectives and are declined as such, e.g., Чайко́вский, Достое́вский: о Чайко́вском, о Достое́вском.

М. —Я не слу́шал, о ко́м и о чём говори́ла О́льга.

С. —А я слу́шал. Пра́вда—я не му́ж.

М. —Да́, коне́чно. Вероя́тно она́ говори́ла о Во́льском. О́н о́чень интере́сный музыка́нт: о́н как Рахма́нинов,[5] и компози́тор (composer) и пиани́ст.

С. —Как жа́ль, что я не зна́л об э́том конце́рте!

М. —Да́, о́чень жа́ль. Э́то бы́л после́дний конце́рт в э́том сезо́не (season).

PRONUNCIATION DRILL

—štó vɨ fčirá ḍéləḷi, andṛéj?

—já bɨl fčirá naóčin iṇṭiṛésnəm kancérṭi.

—gḍé bɨl étət kancért?

—óčiṇ bḷískə; vnóvəj škóḷi, katórəjə nanášij úḷici.

—a ja dáži ṇiznál, štə tám fčirá bɨl kancért.

Answer the following questions in Russian.

1. Како́й бы́л конце́рт, на кото́ром бы́л Ма́слов? 2. Где́ бы́л э́тот конце́рт? 3. Почему́ Семёнов та́м не́ был? 4. Где́ О́льга говори́ла об э́том тала́нтливом музыка́нте? 5. Почему́ Ма́слов не зна́л, о ко́м и о чём говори́ла жена́? 6. А почему́ Семёнов слу́шал, о чём она́ говори́ла? 7. Почему́ жа́ль, что Семёнов не́ был на э́том конце́рте?

Reading

Read through until you are familiar with the story and can answer all the questions. Then read aloud for fluency.

И та́к всегда́!

Как жа́ль, что сего́дня така́я плоха́я и холо́дная пого́да! Э́то, коне́чно, норма́льно: тепе́рь зима́. Но́ вчера́ бы́л тако́й хоро́ший, тёплый де́нь! Я ду́мал, что уже́ ле́то.

Вчера́, вероя́тно, бы́ло о́чень хорошо́ в дере́вне, а я це́лый де́нь бы́л до́ма и рабо́тал! Я переводи́л но́вый америка́нский рома́н. Рома́н э́тот о́чень интере́сный. Э́то рома́н о молодо́й краси́вой же́нщине, кото́рая жила́ одна́ (alone) в большо́м до́ме. Э́тот до́м стоя́л в большо́м краси́вом па́рке. Бы́ло ле́то. Пого́да была́ хоро́шая и тёплая.

Недалеко́, в ма́леньком бе́лом до́ме, жи́л молодо́й тала́нтливый музыка́нт. О́н игра́л на гита́ре, а же́нщина в большо́м до́ме слу́шала, когда́ о́н игра́л. Музыка́нт жи́л оди́н (alone).

---

[5] Рахма́нинов, Серге́й Васи́льевич (1873–1943), Russian pianist and composer.

Э́то то́лько нача́ло (beginning). Рома́н о́чень интере́сный. Но́ как жа́ль, что вчера́, когда́ пого́да была́ хоро́шая, я це́лый де́нь бы́л до́ма и рабо́тал, а сего́дня пого́да така́я плоха́я! И та́к всегда́!

Answer the following questions in Russian.

1. Кака́я сего́дня пого́да? 2. Почему́ э́то норма́льно, что сего́дня хо́лодно?
3. Почему́ я́ ду́мал вчера́, что уже́ ле́то? 4. Где́, вероя́тно, бы́ло хорошо́ вчера́?
5. Что́ я́ вчера́ де́лал? 6. О ко́м э́тот рома́н? 7. В како́м до́ме жила́ герои́ня?
8. Где́ стоя́л э́тот до́м? 9. В како́м до́ме жи́л молодо́й музыка́нт? 10. Что́ де́лал музыка́нт? 11. Како́й это рома́н? 12. Кака́я пого́да была́ вчера́, и кака́я пого́да сего́дня?

DRILLS

A. *Translate into English.*

1. —Како́й автомоби́ль ва́ш, чёрный или бе́лый? —Чёрный. 2. —Чьё си́нее пла́тье та́м на сту́ле? —Моё. 3. —О како́м музыка́нте о́н писа́л в ва́шем журна́ле? —О Проко́фьеве. 4. —На чём она́ игра́ла, на роя́ле, на гита́ре или на балала́йке (balalaika)? —На роя́ле. 5. Во́т то́т но́вый америка́нский рома́н, о кото́ром я́ чита́л в «Пра́вде»,[6] когда́ я́ бы́л в Москве́. 6. Ру́сская писа́тельница, кото́рая жила́ ту́т, тепе́рь в Ленингра́де. 7. —О ко́м вы́ говори́ли? —Мы́ говори́ли о профе́ссоре Семёнове, кото́рый жи́л в Ло́ндоне, когда́ мы́ то́же та́м жи́ли. 8. —О чём э́та кни́га? —О молодо́м до́кторе, кото́рый жи́л и рабо́тал в А́фрике. 9. Студе́нтка, кото́рая говори́ла вчера́ о Че́хове, америка́нка. Она́ говори́ла по-ру́сски. 10. Америка́нец, кото́рый писа́л в на́шем ру́сском журна́ле, писа́л по-ру́сски! Все́ ду́мали, что о́н ру́сский. 11. —Кто́ э́та краси́вая молода́я же́нщина? —Э́то англи́йская журнали́стка.

B. *Translate into Russian.*

1. Ann is an American. She is such a serious student! 2. When she lived in this small apartment, she worked day and night! 3. What a strange woman she is!
4. This new lesson is very easy. 5. My sister, about whom we were speaking, lived in Leningrad. 6. I read that Russian novel about which you were speaking; it is very difficult. 7. The house in which that American lived in Moscow was large and pleasant. 8. My mother was English. When she was young, she spoke Russian, and she played the piano. 9. —Where is the big armchair that stood in this room? —It is on the porch. 10. This butter is still good and fresh, and the bread is also fresh.
11. Yesterday was a warm, pleasant summer day. 12. —Have you thought about that difficult question? —Not yet. 13. My sister was thinking about a new black hat.
14. My mother was (dressed) in a blue summer dress. 15. What a strange word! It's very difficult. 16. About which novel were you speaking? About my first novel or my last (one)? 17. Yesterday was a cold winter day, but we went to (were in) the country.

---

[6] Note that without the qualifying noun *newspaper*, the title is declined.

Vocabulary

(See also the list of some commonly used adjectives on page 70.)

автомоби́ль [aftəmaƀíl] (*masc.*) automobile, car
вера́нда porch
война́ war
вопро́с question
гара́ж [garáš] garage
день (*masc.*) day
дере́вня village; country
друг friend
зима́ winter
костю́м suit
кре́сло armchair
ле́то summer
ма́сло butter; oil
мир peace; world

му́зыка music
мя́со meat
недалеко́ not far (away)
норма́льно normal(ly)
ночь (*fem. II*) night
парк park
перо́ pen, nib; feather
пла́тье [plátjə] dress
пого́да weather
рома́н novel
роя́ль (*masc.*) piano
сло́во word
шля́па hat

EXPRESSIONS

Жа́ль, что . . . It's too bad that . . .
Как жа́ль! What a pity!
игра́ть на (+ *loc.*) to play (an instrument)
быть в (+ *loc.*) to be dressed in
И та́к всегда́! And so it goes! It's always that way!

Genitive case of nouns • Genitive with adverbs of quantity •
Third person pronouns in the genitive • Genitive case of
modifiers • Есть and нет • Nouns with fleeting
o or e • Conversation: На вéчере прéссы

Unit 7

Grammar

1. Genitive case of nouns

The main function of the genitive case in Russian corresponds to that of the English prepositional phrases with *of*, such as *a glass of milk*, *the color of the car*, etc.

начáло **урóка** (*nom.* урóк)	the beginning of the lesson
килогрáмм **мя́са** (*nom.* мя́со)	a kilogram of meat
стакáн **воды́** (*nom.* водá)	a glass of water

The Russian genitive also corresponds to the English possessive form with *'s*: *teacher's*, *Mary's*. (Note, however, the difference in word order between the Russian and the English phrases below.)

áдрес **дóктора** (*nom.* дóктор)	the doctor's address
кóмната **сестры́** (*nom.* сестрá)	the sister's room
фамúлия **гóстя** (*nom.* гость)	the guest's last name

Forms of nouns in the genitive. Nouns take the following endings in the genitive case:

	Spelling	
	Hard	Soft
Masc. and Neut.	**-a**	**-я**
Fem.	**-ы**	**-и**

81

		Nominative	Genitive
Masc.	Hard	стол [stól.] брат [brát.]	стола́ [stal.á] бра́та [brát.ə]
	Soft	слова́рь [slaváṛ.] гость [góṣṭ.] музе́й [muẓéj.]	словаря́ [sləvaṛ.á] го́стя [góṣṭ.ə] музе́я [muẓéj.ə]
Neut.	Hard	окно́ [akn.ó] кре́сло [kṛésl.ə]	о́кна́ [akn.á] кре́сла [kṛésl.ə]
	Soft	бельё [ḅiḷj.ó] по́ле [pól.ə]	белья́ [ḅiḷj.á] поля́ [pól.ə]
Fem. I	Hard	сестра́ [ṣistr.á] ко́мната [kómnət.ə]	сестры́ [ṣistr.ɨ] ко́мнаты [kómnət.ɨ]
	Soft	земля́ [ẓimḷ.á] (earth) ку́хня [kúxṇ.ə] иде́я [iḍéj.ə]	земли́ [ẓimḷ.í] ку́хни [kúxṇ.i] иде́и [iḍéj.i]
Fem. II		дверь [ḍvéṛ.]	две́ри [ḍvéṛ.i]

Spelling Rule 2 applies to the endings of the genitive case of hard feminine nouns (see p. 21); in accordance with this rule we write **-и** not **-ы** after the consonants **г, к, х, ж, ш, ч,** and **щ**:

Nominative		Genitive
кни́га	кни́ги	[kṇíg.i]
студе́нтка	студе́нтки	[stuḍéntḳ.i]
Ма́ша[1]	Ма́ши	[máš.ɨ]
ко́жа (skin, leather)	ко́жи	[kóž.ɨ]

PATTERN SENTENCES

1. Э́то то́лько нача́ло уро́ка.
2. В ку́хне килогра́мм ры́бы.
3. На столе́ кусо́к хле́ба и стака́н воды́.
4. В холоди́льнике была́ то́лько одна́ буты́лка молока́!
5. Во́т дверь ку́хни.
6. Како́й стра́нный цве́т кре́сла!

1. This is only the beginning of the lesson.
2. In the kitchen there is a kilogram of fish.
3. On the table are a piece of bread and a glass of water.
4. In the refrigerator there was only one bottle of milk!
5. Here is the door of the kitchen.
6. How strange the armchair's color is!

---

[1] Nickname of **Мари́я** Mary.

7. —Где со́ль? —Во́т це́лый килогра́мм со́ли!	7. —Where is the salt? —Here's a whole kilo of salt!
8. —**Че́й** это кабине́т? —Профе́ссора Па́влова.	8. —Whose study is this? —Professor Pavlov's.
9. —**Чья́** это ко́мната? —Жены́ Па́влова.	9. —Whose room is this? —Pavlov's wife's.
10. —**Чьё** это письмо́? —Ни́ны.	10. —Whose letter is this? —Nina's.
11. Нача́ло письма́ Ни́ны о́чень интере́сное.	11. The beginning of Nina's letter is very interesting.
12. На моём столе́ пье́са Турге́нева[2] «Ме́сяц в дере́вне».	12. On my table is Turgenev's play *A Month in the Country*.
13. В нача́ле ле́та мы́ бы́ли в Ленингра́де, а в нача́ле зимы́—в Москве́.	13. At the beginning of summer we were in Leningrad, and at the beginning of winter, in Moscow.
14. Э́то ещё не коне́ц войны́.	14. This is not yet the end of the war.
15. О́льга не зна́ла, что е́сть ещё це́лая буты́лка вина́!	15. Olga didn't know that there was still a whole bottle of wine!

DRILLS

A. *Translate the phrases into Russian, working from left to right.*

the doctor's wife	the wife's doctor
the brother's friend	the friend's brother
the sister's teacher	the teacher's sister
the son's professor	the professor's son

B. *Translate the following into Russian.*

1. —Whose apartment is this? —This is Anna's apartment.
2. —Whose dictionary is this? —This is Ivan's dictionary.
3. This is only the beginning of the novel.
4. This is the end of winter.
5. There was a glass of water on the table.
6. —Whose address is this? —This is Professor Pavlov's address.
7. Anna is Dr. Smirnov's wife.
8. Dr. Smirnov is Anna's husband.

2. Genitive with adverbs of quantity

The genitive is used with adverbs of quantity, such as **мно́го** *much, many, a lot;* **ма́ло** *little, few;* **немно́го а** *little;* **ско́лько?** *how much? how many?*:

Ско́лько мя́са в холоди́льнике?
How much meat is in the refrigerator?

На столе́ ма́ло хле́ба.
There is little bread on the table.

---

[2] Турге́нев, Ива́н Серге́евич (1818–1883), a leading Russian novelist and writer of stories and plays. Among his many works, the novel «Отцы́ и де́ти» *Fathers and Sons*, the play «Ме́сяц в дере́вне» *A Month in the Country*, and the story «Пе́рвая любо́вь» "First Love" are outstanding.

В су́пе **ма́ло со́ли**.
There is (too) little salt in the soup.

В буты́лке **немно́го вина́**.
There is a little wine in the bottle.

—**Ско́лько** молока́ пи́л Бо́б? —О́н пи́л **мно́го** молока́ и **ма́ло** воды́.
—How much milk did Bob drink? —He drank a lot of milk and little water.

With adverbs of quantity the verb in the past tense is *neuter singular*:

На столе́ **бы́ло ма́ло** хле́ба.
В стака́не **бы́ло** немно́го воды́.
Ско́лько молока́ **бы́ло** в холоди́льнике?

But with nouns denoting quantities the verb agrees in gender and number with the noun subject:

Та́м **была́** то́лько одна́ **буты́лка**.
В холоди́льнике **бы́л килогра́мм** мя́са.

DRILL

Translate the following sentences into Russian.

1. —How much wine did they drink? —They drank very little wine, but a lot of water.
2. —How much bread was there on the table? —There was only a small piece there.
3. There is still a whole bottle of milk in the kitchen.
4. In the refrigerator there was a big piece of fish.
5. Did you drink milk? There is still a little milk in this glass.
6. Today Nina ate only soup and a little bread, and drank only milk.

3. Third person pronouns in the genitive

The forms of the third person singular pronouns in the genitive are as follows:

	Nominative	Genitive
Masc.	он [ón.]	**его́** [j.ivó]
Neut.	оно́ [an.ó]	
Fem.	она́ [an.á]	**её** [j.ijó]
Pl.	они́ [aṇ.í]	**их** [íx]

Note the pronunciation of **г** as [v] in **его́**.

As has been seen earlier (Unit 4, page 43), possession is expressed by possessive pronoun-adjectives for the first and second persons in the singular and plural. The genitive case, on the other hand, is used when the possessor is referred to by a third person pronoun (*he, she, it, they*) or a noun.

POSSESSION EXPRESSED BY POSSESSIVE PRONOUNS

POSSESSOR: *1st and 2nd Person Pronouns*

Personal prons.		Я	ТЫ	МЫ	ВЫ	
Poss. pron.	M.	мо́й,	тво́й,	на́ш,	ва́ш	сто́л
	N.	моё,	твоё,	на́ше,	ва́ше	кре́сло
	F.	моя́,	твоя́,	на́ша,	ва́ша	кни́га

The possessive pronouns *agree* in gender, number, and case with the object possessed, e.g.,

моя́ кни́**га**
в мо**е́й** кни́**ге**
ва́ш бра́т
о ва́шем му́же

POSSESSION EXPRESSED BY GENITIVE CASE

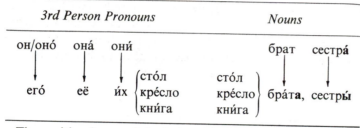

The genitive forms of the 3rd person pronouns as well as of nouns are used *regardless* of gender, number or case; in other words, there is no agreement of that which is possessed, e.g.,

его́ кре́сло   **её** бра́т
на его́ кре́сле   ко́мната **её бра́та**

и́х до́м
в и́х до́ме

Observe that nouns in the genitive case normally *follow* the noun to which they refer, e.g., до́м профе́ссор**а** (literally, *house of the professor*), while pronouns *precede* the noun to which they refer, e.g., **его́** до́м (*his house*).

PATTERN SENTENCES

1. Э́то **его́** ко́мната. Во́т **его́** сто́л и **его́** кре́сло.

2. Я́ бы́л **в его́** ко́мнате.

3. Мы́ говори́ли **о его́** кни́ге, и о кни́ге **его́** бра́та.

1. This is his room. Here are his table and his armchair.

2. I was in his room.

3. We spoke about his book and about his brother's book.

4. Это **её** ко́мната. Во́т **её** сто́л и **её** кре́сло. А во́т сто́л **её** сестры́.

5. Мы́ бы́ли **в её** ко́мнате.

6. Бори́с ду́мал **о её** му́же.

7. Ива́н **её** бра́т; Ни́на **её** сестра́.

8. Во́т Ива́н и Ни́на. Во́т **и́х** шко́ла.

9. Мы́ бы́ли **в и́х** шко́ле.

10. Я́ писа́л **об и́х** шко́ле.

11. Мы́ говори́ли **о её** бра́те и о не́й.

12. Мы́ говори́ли **о его́** сестре́ и о не́м.

13. Мы́ говори́ли **об и́х** шко́ле и о ни́х.

14. Мы́ говори́ли **о его́** жене́, и о сестре́ **его́** жены́.

15. Я́ ду́мал о не́м и **о его́** жене́.

4. This is her room. Here are her table and her armchair. And here is her sister's table.

5. We were in her room.

6. Boris thought about her husband.

7. Ivan is her brother; Nina is her sister.

8. Here are Ivan and Nina. Here is their school.

9. We were in their school.

10. I wrote about their school.

11. We spoke about her brother and about her.

12. We spoke about his sister and about him.

13. We spoke about their school and about them.

14. We spoke about his wife and about his wife's sister.

15. I thought about him and about his wife.

DRILL

Replace the English words in parentheses with the corresponding Russian.

1. Мы́ говори́ли о (his) бра́те и о (his) сестре́.

2. Мы́ говори́ли о (her) бра́те и о (her) сестре́.

3. Мы́ бы́ли в ко́мнате (of his) сестры́.

4. Мы́ бы́ли в ко́мнате (of his) бра́та.

5. Мы́ бы́ли в (their) кварти́ре и говори́ли о (them).

6. Я́ ду́мал о (her and about her) му́же.

7. Я́ ду́мал о (him and about his) жене́.

8. Мы́ говори́ли о (them and about their) сы́не.

9. Мы́ жи́ли в до́ме (of her) бра́та.

10. Я́ чита́л рома́н (of his) сестры́.

4. Genitive case of modifiers

It has been pointed out earlier (Unit 5, page 56) that the case endings of possessives and demonstratives, adjectives, and certain other classes of words are closely related to the corresponding case forms of the third person pronouns. Thus, in the prepositional case, masculine and neuter: нём—моём, э́том, си́нем, большо́м.

The declensional pattern followed by most declinable words other than nouns is called the pronominal declension.

Modifiers (possessives, demonstratives, and adjectives) take the following endings in the genitive case:

Masc. *Neut.*	**-ого, -его**	The consonant **г** is pronounced [v], as in the genitive of the third person pronoun **его́** [jivó].
Fem.	**-ой, -ей**	

The genitive forms of different classes of modifiers are given below together with the nominative forms.

	NOMINATIVE Masculine	Neuter	GENITIVE Masculine and Neuter
3rd Pers. Pron.	он	онó	егó [j.ivó]
Adjectives	нóвый	нóвое	нóвого [nóv.əvə]
	молодóй	молодóе	молодóго [məlad.óvə]
	сѝний	сѝнее	сѝнего [şíṇ.əvə]
	большóй	большóе	большóго [baḷš.óvə]
	рýсский	рýсское	рýсского [rúsk.əvə]
	хорóший	хорóшее	хорóшего [xaróš.əvə]
Possessives	мой	моё	моегó [məj.ivó]
	твой	твоё	твоегó [tvəj.ivó]
	наш	нáше	нáшего [náš.əvə]
	ваш	вáше	вáшего [váš.əvə]
Demonstratives	ѐтот	ѐто	ѐтого [ét.əvə]
	тот	то	тогó [t.avó]
Interrogatives	кто		когó [k.avó]
		что	чегó [č̦.ivó]

Feminine

	оná	еë [j.ijó]
3rd Pers. Pron.	oná	еë [j.ijó]
Adjectives	нóвая	нóвой [nóv.əj]
	молодáя	молодóй [məlad.ój]
	сѝняя	сѝней [şíṇ.əj]
	большáя	большóй [baḷš.ój]
	рýсская	рýсской [rúsk.əj]
	хорóшая	хорóшей [xaróš.əj]
Possessives	моя́	моéй [maj.éj]
	твоя́	твоéй [tvaj.éj]
	нáша	нáшей [náš.əj]
	вáша	вáшей [váš.əj]
Demonstratives	ѐта	ѐтой [ét.əj]
	та	той [t.ój]

Spelling. The endings are spelled **-ого** for masculine and neuter and **-ой** for feminine after hard final stem consonants: ѐтого, ѐтой; нóвого, нóвой; after **ш** and **ж** the endings **-ого, -ой** are written only if the ending is stressed: большóго, большóй.

The endings **-его** for masculine and neuter and **-ей** for feminine are written after soft final stem consonants, e.g., си́**него**, си́**ней**, and also after the sound [j]: мо**его́**, мо**е́й**; тво**его́**, тво**е́й**. In accordance with Spelling Rule 2 (Unit 6, p. 68), **-его**, **-ей** are written also after **ш** and **ж** if the ending is unstressed: на́**шего**, на́**шей**; ва́**шего**, ва́**шей**; хоро́**шего**, хоро́**шей**.

PATTERN SENTENCES

1. —**Чья** авторӳчка на столе́? —Мо**его́** но́в**ого** студе́нт**а**. Э́то **его́** авторӳчка.

2. —**Чей** это а́дрес? —На́**шей** но́в**ой** учи́тельниц**ы**. Э́то **её** а́дрес.

3. На пе́рвом этаже́ кварти́ра на́**шего** хоро́**шего** дрӳг**а** Смирно́в**а** и **его́** жены́. Та́м **их** кварти́ра.

4. Во́т окно́ **его́** больш**о́го** кабине́т**а**, а во́т окно́ **её** больш**о́й** ко́мнат**ы**.

5. Во́т чёрный автомоби́ль **их** го́ст**я**. Кры́ша **его́** чёрн**ого** автомоби́л**я** бе́лая.

6. —Ка́к и́мя[3] тво**его́** ма́леньк**ого** бра́т**а**? —**Его́** и́мя И́горь.

7. —Ка́к а́дрес тво**е́й** рӳсск**ой** учи́тельниц**ы**? —Во́т **её** а́дрес и но́мер телефо́на.

8. —Ка́к назва́ние[3] ва́**шего** после́дн**его** рома́н**а**? —«Коне́ц ми́ра».

9. Мы́ уже́ бы́ли в столи́це Сове́тск**ого** Сою́з**а**, а вы́ ещё не́ были та́м!

10. Я́ давно́ не́ был в столи́це ва́**шей** стран**ы́**.

11. —Кто́ о́н? —О́н реда́ктор газе́ты. —Како́й газе́т**ы**? —Газе́т**ы** «Пра́вда».[4]

12. Нача́ло э́той пье́сы интере́сное.

13. —Ка́к и́мя то́й молодо́й же́нщины? —Како́й же́нщин**ы**? —То́й, о кото́рой мы́ говори́ли вчера́.

14. —Ка́к назва́ние т**ого́** журна́л**а**? —Как**о́го** журна́л**а**? —То**го́**, в кото́ром вы́ ча́сто писа́ли. —Э́то «Но́вый ми́р».

15. Учи́тель, в кварти́ре кото́р**ого** мы́ жи́ли, тепе́рь в Ки́еве.

1. —Whose (fountain) pen is on the table? —My new student's. It's his pen.

2. —Whose address is this? —Our new teacher's. It's her address.

3. On the first floor is the apartment of our good friend Smirnov and his wife. Their apartment is there.

4. Here is the window of his large study, and here is the window of her large room.

5. Here is their guest's black car. The roof of his black car is white.

6. —What is your little brother's name? —His name is Igor.

7. —What is the address of your Russian teacher? —Here is her address and telephone number.

8. —What is the name of your last novel? —*The End of the World.*

9. We have already been to the capital of the Soviet Union, but you still haven't been there!

10. I haven't been to the capital of your country for a long time.

11. —Who is he? —He's the editor of a newspaper. —Which newspaper? —The paper *Pravda.*

12. The beginning of that play is interesting.

13. —What is that young woman's name? —Which woman? —The one we were talking about yesterday.

14. —What is the name of that magazine? —Which magazine? —The one in which you often wrote. —It's *Novy mir.*

15. The teacher in whose apartment we used to live is in Kiev now.

---

[3] **И́мя** means *name*, and is used only of persons. **Назва́ние**, also meaning *name*, is used for inanimates, e.g., objects, places, works of art, abstractions.

[4] The titles of books, organizations, etc., are declined unless they are used with a classifying noun such as рома́н, о́пера, газе́та: —Вы́ бы́ли **на** о́пере «Аи́да»? —Да́, мы́ бы́ли **на** «Аи́де».
Observe also that Russian elliptical (incomplete) sentences continue the grammatical pattern already established. Hence, **како́й** and **газе́ты** are in the genitive case, and are translated *of which newspaper*, even though the word governing the genitive occurs only in a previous sentence.

16. —**Како́го** цве́та ва́ш но́вый костю́м? —Се́-рого.[5]	16. —What's the color of your new suit? (*lit.*, Of what color is your new suit?) —Gray.
17. —Вы́ давно́ здесь? —Не́т, не о́чень, но́ я уже́ ви́дел **мно́го интере́сного**.[6]	17. —Have you been here long? —No, not very, but I've seen many interesting (things) already.
18. Я слы́шал об Ива́не **мно́го хоро́шего**.[6]	18. I've heard much good about Ivan.
19. До свида́ния! **Всего́ хоро́шего!**	19. Good-bye! All the best!
20. Како́й тёплый ве́чер, а у́тро бы́ло тако́е холо́дное!	20. What a warm evening, and the morning was so cold!
21. В нача́ле у́тра не́бо бы́ло се́рое.	21. At the start of the morning the sky was gray.
22. Коне́ц ве́чера—э́то нача́ло но́чи.	22. The end of evening is the beginning of night.

DRILLS

A. *Supply the correct case forms of the words given in parentheses. Then reword the sentences by substituting a pronoun in the genitive, as in the model.*

Model: Че́й это до́м? —Э́то до́м **моего́ бра́та**. Э́то **его́** до́м.

1. —Че́й это автомоби́ль? —Э́то автомоби́ль (мо́й сы́н).
2. —Чьё это пла́тье? —Э́то пла́тье (моя́ жена́).
3. —Чья́ это ко́мната? —Э́то ко́мната (на́ш сы́н).
4. —Че́й это костю́м? —Э́то костю́м (мо́й му́ж).
5. Э́то кварти́ра (ва́ш учи́тель и его́ жена́).
6. Э́то газе́та (до́ктор Петро́в).
7. Э́то кре́сло (тво́й ста́рый го́сть).
8. Э́то кни́га (на́ш хоро́ший учи́тель).
9. Э́то но́вое пла́тье (моя́ ма́ленькая сестра́).
10. Э́то журна́л (на́ша но́вая учи́тельница).
11. Э́то автомоби́ль (на́ш ру́сский го́сть и его́ жена́).

B. *Change the words in the right-hand column to the genitive.*

1. Кака́я цена́ . . .   What is the price of . . .   э́тот си́ний автомоби́ль?
   э́то краси́вое пла́тье?
   э́та ста́рая кни́га?
   э́тот хоро́ший костю́м?

2. Ка́к и́мя . . .   What is the name of . . .   ва́ша ма́ленькая сестра́?
   тво́й ма́ленький бра́т?
   то́т молодо́й писа́тель?

3. Ка́к назва́ние . . .   What is the name of . . .   ва́ш но́вый рома́н?
   э́та ру́сская о́пера?
   её хоро́шая статья́?

---

[5] Some qualities are expressed in the genitive case. **Како́го цве́та . . .?**, literally, *Of what color . . .?* Similarly, **Како́го ро́ста . . .?** is *How tall is . . .?* Костю́м се́рого цве́та=се́рый костю́м *a gray suit*; челове́к высо́кого ро́ста, literally *a person of tall stature, a tall person.*

[6] The neuter singular of adjectives such as хоро́шее, плохо́е, интере́сное, но́вое, ста́рое may be used as *nouns*; when used thus with expressions of quantity the Russian singular may correspond to the plural in English, e.g., **всё хоро́шее** *all the good things*; **мно́го хоро́шего** *much good, many nice things*; **мно́го интере́сного** *much of interest, much that's interesting, many interesting things*; **ма́ло но́вого** *little news, little that is new.* Note questions: **Что́ но́вого?** *What's new?* **Что́ хоро́шего?** *Any good news?*

4. Ка́к а́дрес . . . What is the address of . . . ва́ша молода́я прия́тельница?
наш но́вый учи́тель?
его́ ста́рый до́ктор?
та́ больша́я гости́ница?

5. Есть and нет

(1) **Éсть** (*there is, there are*) is used to express the existence or availability of something or someone:

На на́шей у́лице **есть** гости́ница.
On our street there is a hotel.

—Зде́сь **есть** хоро́шая библиоте́ка? —Да́, **есть**.
—Is there a good library here? —Yes, there is.

—Что́ **есть** в э́том ма́леньком го́роде? —В э́том го́роде **есть** музе́й, **есть** теа́тр, и да́же **есть** стадио́н!
–What is there in this small town? —In this town there is a museum, there is a theater, and there is even a stadium!

Note that Russian declarative sentences of this type usually open with an adverb (e.g., **здесь**) or a prepositional phrase (e.g., **в на́шем го́роде**).

(2) **Есть** is generally used when English employs the *indefinite* article and is generally omitted when English employs the *definite* article:

На э́той у́лице **есть** библиоте́ка.
There is *a* library on this street.

But: Библиоте́ка на э́той у́лице.
The library is on this street.

Note also: —Что́ **есть** на столе́? —На столе́ **есть** перо́.
—What is there on the table? —There is a pen on the table.

—Что́ на столе́? —Перо́ на столе́.
—What is on the table? —The pen is on the table.

(3) In the *past tense*, the verb forms **был, бы́ло, была́, бы́ли** agree with the subject in gender and number.

Что́ **бы́ло** на столе́?
What was (there) on the table?

На столе́ **был** каранда́ш.
There was a pencil on the table.

На столе́ **бы́ло** вино́.
There was wine on the table.

На столе́ **была́** кни́га.
There was a book on the table.

На столе́ **бы́ли** кни́ги (*nom. pl.*).
There were books on the table.

В то́м магази́не **бы́ло** всё.
There was everything in that store.

(4) In a sentence in the *future tense*, **бу́дет** (*third person singular*) and **бу́дут** (*third person plural*) are used. Note that in the future there is agreement in number but not in gender:

На на́шей у́лице **бу́дет** гости́ница.
On our street there will be a hotel.

Зде́сь **бу́дет** хоро́ший музе́й.
There will be a good museum here.

В мое́й ко́мнате **бу́дет** но́вое кре́сло.
There will be a new armchair in my room.

Ско́ро в на́шем го́роде **бу́дут** хоро́шие магази́ны и рестора́ны (*nom. pl.*).
In our city there will soon be good stores and restaurants.

(5) The negative of **есть** is **нет** (*colloq.* **не́ту**), *there is no, there are no*. Nouns, pronouns, and adjectives governed by **нет** take the *genitive case*:

На на́шей у́лице **не́т** гости́ницы.
There is no hotel on our street.

Зде́сь **не́т** библиоте́ки.
There is no library here.

В мое́й ко́мнате **не́т** но́вого кре́сла.
There is no new armchair in my room.

—В холоди́льнике е́сть мя́со? —**Не́т, не́ту** (*colloq.*).
—Is there meat in the refrigerator? —No, there isn't.

—**Чего́ не́т** на столе́? —**Не́т** хле́ба и **не́т** воды́.
—What is not on the table (what is lacking)? —There is no bread or water.

—**Кого́** сейча́с **не́т** до́ма? —**Ни́ны не́т** до́ма.
—Who is not at home now? —Nina is not at home.

(6) To express the negative past *there was no* and *there were no*, the word **нет** is replaced by **не́ было**. The verb is always neuter singular, regardless of the gender and number of the person(s) or thing(s) concerned. Like **нет**, **не́ было** requires the *genitive* case:

—**Чего́ не́ было** в магази́не? —Та́м **не́ было** ры́бы.
—What was (there) not in the store? —There was no fish there.

На столе́ **не́ было** кра́сного вина́.
On the table there was no red wine.

На э́той у́лице **не́ было** шко́лы.
There was no school on this street.

На по́лке **не́ было** кни́г. (кни́г, *gen. pl.*)
On the bookshelf there were no books.

(7) To express the negative future *there will be no*, the word **нет** is replaced by **не бу́дет**. Like **нет**, **не бу́дет** requires the *genitive case*:

> На на́шей у́лице **не бу́дет** гости́ни**цы**.
> There will be no hotel on our street.

> В на́шем го́роде **не бу́дет** музе́**я**.
> There will be no museum in our city.

> В мое́й ко́мнате **не бу́дет** но́в**ого** кре́сла.
> There will be no new armchair in my room.

(8) The negative forms **нет**, **не́ было**, and **не бу́дет** also often serve to denote the absence of *particular* persons or things:

> Ива́**на не́т** до́ма. **Его́ не́т** до́ма.
> Ivan is not at home. He isn't at home.

> Вчера́ Ива́**на не́ было** до́ма. **Его́ не́ было** до́ма.
> Ivan was not at home yesterday. He wasn't at home.

> Моего́ си́него пера́ **не́ было** на столе́. **Его́** та́м **не́ было**.
> My blue pen wasn't on the desk. It wasn't there.

> Кни́ги **не́ было** в мое́й ко́мнате. **Её** та́м **не́ было**.
> The book was not in my room. It wasn't there.

> —**Кого́** сего́дня **не́ было** в шко́ле? —Бори́са **не́ было** в шко́ле.
> —Who wasn't at school today? —Boris wasn't.

Note: In contrast to this use of the genitive, the *nominative* case used with the negative of *to be* often has the sense of *go*, *come*, *visit*, or *attend* in English:

> **Óн** давно́ **не́ был** в Нью-Йо́рке.
> He hasn't been (gone) to New York for a long time (he lives outside it).

But: Тогда́ **его́ не́ было** в Нью-Йо́рке.
> At that time he wasn't (didn't happen to be) in New York (perhaps he lives there).

> Ива́н вчера́ **не́ был** в музе́е.
> Ivan didn't go to the museum yesterday.

But: Ива́**на** вчера́ **не́ было** в музе́е.
> Ivan wasn't at the museum yesterday (I was looking for him there).

DRILLS

A. *Reply to the questions by using the words in the right column; your answers should be complete sentences.*

Model: Что́ бы́ло на столе́? На столе́ бы́л стака́н.

1. Что́ бы́ло в холоди́льнике? мя́со
                               вода́
                               вино́
                               сыр
                               ма́сло

2. Чего́ здесь не́т? ка́рта
                      авто́ру́чка
                      статья́
                      каранда́ш
                      журна́л
                      письмо́

3. Чего́ не́ было на столе́? но́вая ка́рта
                             ру́сская грамма́тика
                             си́няя авто́ру́чка
                             мо́й чёрный каранда́ш
                             ва́ше после́днее письмо́
                             бе́лое вино́
                             его́ статья́

4. Кого́ не́ было в ко́мнате? Ива́н
                              моя́ сестра́
                              на́ш учи́тель
                              его́ това́рищ
                              сове́тский журнали́ст

5. Кого́ за́втра не бу́дет до́ма? Ни́на
                                  Ви́ктор
                                  моя́ жена́
                                  мо́й оте́ц
                                  её сын
                                  она́
                                  они́

B. *Supply the proper form of the words in parentheses.*

1. На твоём столе́ (there is a pencil), а на моём (there is no pencil).
2. Сего́дня, когда́ я была́ в ку́хне, (Olga was not there), но́ ма́ма (was there).
3. Как стра́нно, что вчера́ (Ivan was not at home).
4. На э́той у́лице (there is) францу́зский рестора́н.
5. Э́тот францу́зский рестора́н (is on this street).
6. (Boris was not in Moscow), когда́ я та́м бы́л, но́ о́н ско́ро (will be there).
7. В кабине́те моего́ бра́та (there is) телефо́н, а в моём кабине́те (there is no telephone and there will be no telephone).
8. На его́ столе́ (there is) ла́мпа. На моём столе́ (there was a lamp), но́ тепе́рь на нём (there is no lamp).
9. В на́шем ма́леньком го́роде (there is a doctor), а в ва́шем го́роде (there was no doctor), но́ та́м ско́ро (there will be a doctor).
10. В нача́ле уро́ка (Ivan was not in class).
11. —(Who was not at home), когда́ ты́ та́м бы́л? —(Anna).
12. —(What was missing) на столе́? —(White bread).

C. *Oral Drill. Answer the following questions using the nouns and adjectives that you know.*

1. Чего́ нет в э́том магази́не (store)?
2. Что́ бы́ло в холоди́льнике?
3. Чего́ не́ было в ва́шей кварти́ре?
4. Что́ бу́дет на э́той у́лице?
5. Кого́ вчера́ не́ было в кла́ссе?
6. Кого́ за́втра не бу́дет до́ма?

6. Nouns with fleeting o or e

In declension some masculine nouns drop the vowel **o** or **e** which precedes the final consonant in the nominative:

Nominative		Genitive	Locative
оте́ц	(father)	отца́	об отце́
коне́ц	(end)	конца́	в конце́ (at the end)
потоло́к	(ceiling)	потолка́	на потолке́
кусо́к	(piece)	куска́	в куске́
день	(day)	дня	о дне́

DRILL

Translate the words in parentheses.

1. Ко́мната их го́стя (at the end) коридо́ра.
2. В кабине́те (of Father) большо́й сто́л.
3. В до́ме нет (a piece) хле́ба.
4. (On the ceiling) му́ха.
5. Э́то бы́ло в (end of the day).
6. Мы́ говори́ли (about his father).

Conversation

Read the Russian aloud several times until you are completely familiar with the text. Then answer the questions which follow in Russian.

На ве́чере пре́ссы

Пи́тер Ро́бертс, корреспонде́нт популя́рного америка́нского журна́ла «Тайм» («Вре́мя»), был в Москве́ на ве́чере пре́ссы. На э́том ве́чере говори́ли об Аме́рике и её поли́тике (politics) и о поли́тике Сове́тского Сою́за. На э́том ве́чере был и Ива́н Ива́нович Петро́в, реда́ктор сове́тского журна́ла «Но́вое вре́мя». Петро́в был неда́вно в Аме́рике.

Вот их разгово́р.

Петро́в. —А, Пи́тер! Здра́вствуйте! Како́й прия́тный сюрпри́з: вы́ в Москве́! Э́то здо́рово!

ILLUSTRATION 10. Балéт в Большóм
теáтре в Москвé. (*Tass from Sovfoto.*)

ILLUSTRATION 11. Толстóй в своём
кабинéте. Рисýнок худóжника И. Е.
Рéпина. (*Sovfoto.*)

ILLUSTRATION 12. «В Москвé éсть мнóго
и стáрого и нóвого.» (*Tass from Sovfoto.*)

Ро́бертс. —До́брый ве́чер, Ива́н Ива́нович! Да́, я здесь, в ва́шей столи́це, и о́чень ра́д бы́ть здесь.

П. —Ра́д э́то слы́шать. Вы́ давно́ в Москве́?

Р. —Не́т, не о́чень.

П. —В како́й вы́ гости́нице?

Р. —В Метропо́ле, в це́нтре Москвы́! Метропо́ль хоро́шая ста́рая гости́ница, и рестора́н та́м хоро́ший, и всё бли́зко.

П. —А интере́сный го́род на́ша Москва́, пра́вда?

Р. —Да́, о́чень интере́сный!

П. —Что́ же[7] вы́ ту́т ви́дели? Где́ бы́ли?

Р. —Я́ уже́ мно́го ви́дел, но ещё коне́чно не всё. Я́ бы́л в библиоте́ке Ле́нина.[8] Прекра́сная библиоте́ка! Бы́л коне́чно в Большо́м теа́тре[9] на о́пере «Евге́ний Оне́гин»[10] и на о́пере «Карме́н». «Карме́н» по-ру́сски![11] Э́то бы́ло о́чень интере́сно! И так мно́го интере́сного на Кра́сной пло́щади![12] Кака́я там интере́сная це́рковь![13] Истори́ческий музе́й, и мавзоле́й Ле́нина, где́ Ле́нин как живо́й (as though alive)! И ГУМ[14]—магази́н, о кото́ром я́ уже́ ра́ньше (earlier) мно́го слы́шал.

П. —Вы́ пра́вда уже́ мно́го здесь ви́дели!

Р. —Но́ э́то ещё не всё! Вчера́ я́ бы́л в до́ме Толсто́го, в до́ме а́втора «Войны́ и ми́ра»! Та́м всё та́к, как бы́ло, когда́ Толсто́й та́м жи́л: в его́ кабине́те— его́ библиоте́ка, дива́н, на кото́ром о́н иногда́ спа́л, его́ пи́сьменный сто́л, его́ кре́сло! Ко́мната, в кото́рой писа́л и ду́мал Ле́в Толсто́й!

П. —Да́, в Москве́ е́сть мно́го и ста́рого и но́вого. Но в Вашингто́не, в ва́шей столи́це, то́же е́сть мно́го интере́сного: Библиоте́ка Конгре́сса—прекра́сная библиоте́ка; и кака́я прекра́сная ва́ша Национа́льная галере́я! А в Бе́лом до́ме я́ бы́л в ко́мнате президе́нта Ли́нкольна, и ви́дел та́м крова́ть, на кото́рой Ли́нкольн спа́л! А како́й хоро́ший его́ па́мятник в це́нтре Вашингто́на!

Р. —Ш...Ш...Ш... Я́ не́ был в ко́мнате Ли́нкольна... Пра́вда, я́ в Вашингто́не не тури́ст.

П. —Ш...Ш...Ш... А я́ не́ был в до́ме Толсто́го... Пра́вда, я не тури́ст в Москве́.

---

[7] The unstressed particle **же** has many functions. When used after question words ка́к **же**? что́ **же**? где́ **же**?, it adds a tone of emphasis or interest (sometimes of impatience or perplexity): Что́ **же**? *What then?, Just what?*; Где́ **же**? *So where?*

[8] **Библиоте́ка Ле́нина** or as it is officially called, Госуда́рственная библиоте́ка и́мени Ле́нина (State Library Named for Lenin) is the main library of the Soviet Union and one of the largest in the world.

[9] The Большо́й теа́тр in the center of Moscow is the principal Soviet theater performing opera and ballet.

[10] «Евге́ний Оне́гин», an opera of the well-known novel in verse by Алекса́ндр Серге́евич Пу́шкин, adapted and set to music by the composer Пётр Ильи́ч Чайко́вский and first produced in 1879, has become one of the most popular of Russian operas.

[11] In Russia foreign operas are sung in Russian.

[12] Кра́сная пло́щадь is Red Square. This name appeared as early as 1661 in the notes of a foreign traveller (Meyerberg). Кра́сный, now meaning *red*, in Old Russian meant *beautiful* (now краси́вый).

[13] The church on Red Square is Хра́м Васи́лия Блаже́нного, St. Basil's Cathedral (built from 1555 to 1560).

[14] ГУМ, Госуда́рственный универса́льный магази́н, *State Department Store.* (Госуда́рство *state.*)

PRONUNCIATION DRILL

—á, pítər! zdrástvujṭi! kakój pṛíjátnij ṣurpṛís: vɨ vmaskvé! étə zdórəvə!

—dóbrij véčir, iván ivánič! dá, ja ẓḍéṣ, vvášəj staḷíci, i óčiṇ rát biṭ ẓḍéṣ.

—rát étə slíšəṭ! i vɨ davnó vmaskvé?

—ṇét, ṇióčiṇ.

—fkakój vɨ gaṣṭíṇici?

—vṃitrapóḷi. ṃitrapóḷ stárəjə no udóbnəjə gaṣṭíṇicə, i aná fcéntṛi maskvɨ.

Answer the following questions in Russian.

1. Петро́в уже́ зна́л Ро́бертса? 2. О како́м прия́тном сюрпри́зе говори́л Петро́в? 3. Почему́ Ро́бертс ра́д бы́ть в Москве́? 4. Кака́я гости́ница Метропо́ль, и где́ она́? 5. Что́ Ро́бертс говори́л о Библиоте́ке (и́мени) Ле́нина? 6. Что́ о́н говори́л о Кра́сной пло́щади? 7. Что́ о́н говори́л о до́ме Толсто́го? 8. В како́й галере́е в Вашингто́не бы́л Петро́в? 9. Что́ о́н о не́й говори́л? 10. В како́й ко́мнате о́н бы́л в Бе́лом до́ме? 11. Почему́ Ро́бертс не́ был в ко́мнате Ли́нкольна в Вашингто́не, а Петро́в не́ был в до́ме Толсто́го в Москве́?

DRILLS

A. *Translate into Russian the words in parentheses.*

1. Мы́ жи́ли в гости́нице (in the center of Moscow). 2. Это окно́ (of my father's study), а то́ окно́—окно́ (of our bright kitchen). 3. —Ка́к и́мя (of your girl student)? —(Of which student)? —(The one), кото́рая жила́ (in Olga's apartment). —Её и́мя Ни́на. 4. —Ка́к назва́ние (of that magazine)? —(Of which magazine)? —(The one about which) мы́ сего́дня говори́ли. 5. На столе́ стоя́л стака́н (of water). 6. Где́ коне́ц (of this street)? 7. Ка́к фами́лия (of your good friend)? 8. О́н жи́л в кварти́ре (of our son). 9. Это до́м (of Ivan Ivanovich and his sister). 10. Нача́ло (of her new novel) о́чень интере́сное. 11. —Чья́ кварти́ра на пе́рвом этаже́? —(Our friend Smirnov's). 12. Ка́к и́мя (of that American girl student)? 13. То́т па́мятник стоя́л (in the center of their little town). 14. Я́ бы́л (at my good friend's party). 15. Ка́к назва́ние (of your Soviet book)? 16. Ка́к а́дрес (of your sister Anna)?

B. *Review Translation.*

1. What is his name? 2. What is his brother's name? 3. What is your sister's family name (last name)? 4. What is her father's address? 5. —Good evening! Have you been here long? —All day. 6. It is evening already! 7. It's not yet the end of the world! 8. At the end of summer his son was still in the capital of the Soviet Union. 9. —About whom did you speak? —About your father's doctor. 10. —Is there a restaurant on this street? —No, there is no restaurant here. 11. —What is the color of your new dress? —It's gray. 12. —What is the price of the dress? Is it expensive? —No, it's cheap. 13. —What is the title of his new book about the Soviet Union? —*The New Policy of the Soviet Union.* 14. At the end of the street stood his brother's house. 15. What a strange study! There is no window here! 16. Our son drank much milk but ate little bread. 17. I was recently in the capital of your country, and I saw many interesting things there.

Vocabulary

а́втор [áftər] author
авторучка [aftarúčkə] fountain pen
ве́чер evening; evening party
вино́ wine
вода́ water
вре́мя[15] time
всё (*nom. sing.*) everything, all
гости́ница hotel
давно́ long ago, long since
дешёвый cheap, inexpensive
дорого́й dear, expensive
есть there is, there are
ещё still, yet
и also, too, even
и́мя[15] (first) name
коне́ц (*gen.* конца́) end, finish
кры́ша roof
кусо́к (*gen.* куска́) piece, bit
мавзоле́й mausoleum
молоко́ milk
назва́ние name, title (of objects)
нача́ло beginning, start
не́бо sky, heaven
неда́вно recently, not long ago
но́мер number
па́мятник monument, memorial
пи́сьменный сто́л writing table, desk
поли́тика politics, policy
популя́рный popular

пье́са [pjésə] play, drama
прекра́сный fine, wonderful, excellent
пре́сса press
прия́тель (*fem.* -ница) friend
разгово́р conversation
реда́ктор editor
рестора́н restaurant
ры́ба fish
се́рый gray
ско́лько (+ *gen.*) how much? how many?
сове́тский [saɣécķij] Soviet (*adj.*)
Сове́тский Сою́з [saɣécķij sajús] Soviet Union
соль (*fem. II*) salt
стака́н glass
столи́ца capital
страна́ country, land
суп soup
сыр cheese
тури́ст (*fem.* -ка) tourist
удо́бный convenient, comfortable
уже́ already; yet (in questions)
у́тро morning
францу́зский [francúsķij] French (*adj.*)
хлеб bread
холоди́льник refrigerator
цвет color
цена́ price
центр center

VERBS

ви́деть to see
есть to eat (*past*: ел, е́ло, е́ла, е́ли)
пить to drink (*past*, пил, пи́ло, пила́, пи́ли)
спать to sleep

EXPRESSIONS

До́брый ве́чер! Good evening!
До́брое у́тро! Good morning!
Ка́к ва́ше и́мя? What is your (first) name?
Ка́к назва́ние (+ *gen.*)? What is the name (title) (of) . . . (an object, book, etc.)?
Ка́к а́дрес (+ *gen.*)? What is the address (of) . . .?
Кака́я цена́ (+ *gen.*)? What is the price (of) . . .?
Како́го цве́та (+ *nom.*)? What is the color of . . .? What color is . . .?
в нача́ле (+ *gen.*) at the beginning (of) . . .
в конце́ (+ *gen.*) at the end (of) . . .
весь де́нь all day long
Вы́ давно́ зде́сь? Have you been here long?
Я́ давно́ не́ был . . . I haven't been for a long time . . .
Како́й сюрпри́з! [kakój şurpŗís!] What a surprise! That's wonderful!
Всего́ хоро́шего! Good-bye! (All the best!)

---

[15] A few nouns ending in **-мя** are neuter in gender.

VOCABULARY REVIEW

Found in Buildings

кварти́ра
стена́
пол
потоло́к
кры́ша
дверь (*fem.*)
окно́
ко́мната
ку́хня
кабине́т

Food and Drink

хлеб
молоко́
сыр
мя́со
суп
вода́
вино́
во́дка

Furniture

стол
пи́сьменный сто́л
стул
кре́сло
по́лка
роя́ль (*masc.*)
ла́мпа
холоди́льник

In the City

дом
музе́й
гости́ница
шко́ла
библиоте́ка
университе́т
у́лица
рестора́н
мавзоле́й
магази́н
парк
па́мятник
стадио́н

Clothing

костю́м
пла́тье
шля́па

Colors

бе́лый
чёрный
си́ний
се́рый
кра́сный

Parts of Day

день (*masc.*)
ночь (*fem.*)
у́тро
ве́чер

Reading

кни́га
рома́н
пье́са
газе́та
журна́л
статья́
слова́рь (*masc.*)

Give opposites for the following words.

день
пе́рвый
большо́й
но́вый

ве́чер
тру́дный
молодо́й
зима́

хорошо́
коне́ц
холо́дный
ма́ло
плохо́й

зи́мний
бе́лый
дорого́й
давно́

Accusative singular of nouns and modifiers · Accusative singular of
pronouns · Accusative of time · Present tense of verbs · Negative
expressions · Declension of оди́н *one* · До́лжен *must* · Reading:
Бра́т и сестра́

Unit **8**

Grammar

1. Accusative singular of nouns and modifiers

The accusative case is the case of the direct object. The direct object is the person
or thing which is directly affected by the action of a verb (verbs that take a direct
object are called *transitive*). In the following examples the words in italics are direct
objects: he bought a *book*; we know *John*; she loves her *mother;* he drinks *tea*; we saw
him; they liked *her*.

The direct object in Russian takes the *accusative case.*

A. Masculine. Russian distinguishes between *animate* nouns (persons and
animals) and *inanimate* nouns (things and abstract concepts). *Animate* nouns of
masculine gender have the same forms in the accusative as in the *genitive*. *Inanimate*
masculine nouns have the same forms as in the *nominative:*

	Animate	Inanimate
Nom.	брат	стол ←
Gen.	бра́та ←	стола́
Acc.	бра́та ←	стол ←

The same rule applies to all modifiers of animate masculine nouns (modifiers include
adjectives, possessives, and demonstratives):

	Animate	Inanimate
Nom.	мо́й ма́ленький сы́н	э́тот большо́й сто́л ←
Gen.	моего́ ма́ленького сы́на ←	э́того большо́го стола́
Acc.	моего́ ма́ленького сы́на ←	э́тот большо́й сто́л ←

E.g.:	Во́т ко́мната моего́ ма́ленького сы́на. (*gen.*)
	О́н ви́дел моего́ ма́ленького сы́на. (*acc.*)
But:	О́н ви́дел мо́й большо́й сто́л. (*acc.*)

100

B. Neuter.   All *neuter* nouns and modifiers have in the accusative the same form as in the nominative.

C. Feminine.   *Feminine nouns ending in* **-a** *and* **-я**. This is the only class of nouns having a distinct ending in the accusative singular: this ending is [-u], spelled **-у** after hard consonants (сестра́-сестру́) and **-ю** after soft consonants (ку́хня-ку́хню).[1] *There is no difference between animate and inanimate feminines in the singular.*

Modifiers of feminine nouns.   Hard adjectives end in **-ую**; soft adjectives in **-юю**:

Nom.	но́вая	си́няя
Acc.	но́вую	си́нюю

Feminine demonstratives and possessives in the accusative end in **-у/-ю**:

Nom.	э́та	та	на́ша	ва́ша	моя́	твоя́
Acc.	э́ту	ту	на́шу	ва́шу	мою́	твою́

E.g.:   Она́ зна́ла мою́ молоду́ю секрета́ршу.
Я чита́л э́ту интере́сную кни́гу.
Я ви́дел твою́ си́нюю шля́пу.

Feminine nouns ending in **-ь** (*Fem. II*). These nouns, both animate and inanimate, have the same form in the accusative as in the nominative:

Nom. and *Acc.*   мать   дочь   дверь   ночь, etc.

E.g.:   Я ви́дел ва́шу до́чь.
Я ви́дел Сиби́рь на ка́рте.

To summarize for nouns in the accusative:

Я ви́дел

- бра́та. Masc., anim.: like *gen.*
- сто́л. Masc., inanim.: like *nom.*
- окно́. Neut., (*all*): like *nom.*
- сестру́. / ко́мнату. Fem. I { special *acc.* ending **-у** (or **-ю**, e.g., дере́вню) } same for animate
- ма́ть. / две́рь. Fem. II } like *nom.* and inanimate

2. Accusative singular of pronouns

A. Personal pronouns.   All personal pronouns have an accusative identical in form with the genitive. The forms of the third person pronouns have already been given in Unit 7.

---

[1] Some feminine nouns shift the stress to the first syllable in the accusative: рука́—ру́ку; голова́—го́лову; река́—ре́ку; зима́—зи́му, etc.

GENITIVE AND ACCUSATIVE OF PERSONAL PRONOUNS

Nom.	я	ты	мы	вы	он онó	онá	они́
Gen. and *Acc.*	меня́	тебя́	нас	вас	егó	её	их

E.g.: Óн ви́дел **меня́**. Я́ знáл **её**. Мы́ знáли **их**. Я́ ви́дел **вáс** и **егó**.

B. Interrogative pronouns. **Что?** (*what*) is used in both the nominative and accusative for inanimates,

—**Чтó** вы́ ви́дели? —Нóв**ый** фи́льм.

Когó? (*whom*) is the accusative, as well as the genitive, of **кто?** (*who*),

—**Когó** вы́ ви́дели? —Нóв**ого** дирéктор**а**.

PATTERN SENTENCES

1. Ви́ктор, **чтó** ты́ читáл в библиотéке?
2. Я́ читáл пьéсу Пу́шкина «Бори́с Годунóв».[2]
3. А я́ слы́шал «Бори́с**а** Годунó**ва**» в Большóм теáтре.
4. —**Чтó** вы́ вчерá ви́дели в теáтре? —Мы́ ви́дели нóв**ую** пьéсу Арбáтов**а**.
5. Я́ ужé ви́дел э́ту пьéсу, а Вéра ещё не ви́дела **её**.
6. —**Когó** вы́ ви́дели в теáтре? —Мы́ ви́дели вáш**его** брáт**а** Ивáн**а**, егó жену́, и и́х дóч**ь** Вéру.
7. —Они́ ви́дели **вáс**? —Нéт, мы́ ви́дели **и́х**, нó они́ не ви́дели **нáс**.
8. Отéц Ни́ны знáл Чéхов**а**! Чéхов тогдá жи́л в Я́лте.[3]
9. —**Когó** ещё óн знáл? —Óн знáл Гóрьк**ого**,[4] и óн ви́дел балери́ну Áнну Пáвлову![5] Это всё бы́ло óчень давнó!
10. —Ктó читáл ромáн Толстóго[6] «Войнá и ми́р»? —Мы́ всé читáли «Войну́ и ми́р» и «Áнну Карéнину».

1. Victor, what did you read at the library?
2. I read Pushkin's play *Boris Godunov*.
3. And I heard *Boris Godunov* at the Bolshoy Theater (opera).
4. —What did you see yesterday at the theater? —We saw a new play by (= of) Arbatov.
5. I have already seen that (this) play, but Vera hasn't seen it yet.
6. —Whom did you see at the theater? —We saw your brother Ivan, his wife, and their daughter Vera.
7. —Did they see you? —No, we saw them, but they didn't see us.
8. Nina's father knew Chekhov! Chekhov lived then in Yalta.
9. —Whom else did he know? —He knew Gorky, and he has seen the ballerina Anna Pavlova! That was all very long ago!
10. —Who has read Tolstoy's novel *War and Peace*? —We all have read *War and Peace* and *Anna Karenina*.

---

[2] «Бори́с Годунóв», a verse tragedy by Pushkin about a powerful nobleman who reigned as tsar from 1598 to 1605 during the Time of Troubles. The composer Moussorgsky made the play into an opera.

[3] Я́лта Yalta, a seaport and resort on the Black Sea. The writer Chekhov lived there during the last several years of his life; the Yalta Conference was held there in 1945.

[4] Гóрький, Макси́м, pseudonym of Алексéй Макси́мович Пешкóв (1868–1936), a writer of stories, novels, and plays, known for his series of autobiographical novels.

[5] Пáвлова, Áнна Матвéевна (1882–1931), a famous ballerina, renowned for her classical technique, as displayed in such pieces as "The Dying Swan."

[6] Note that Russian family names ending in **-ий** and **-ой** are declined as adjectives, e.g., Мы́ говори́ли о Толстóм. (Note also the form Гóрького, acc. of Гóрький, in sentence 9 above.) Women members of the same family use the same name, declined as a feminine adjective, e.g., Толстáя.

11. Вчера́ на вечери́нке Ве́ра слу́шала то́лько **меня́**, а не **тебя́** и не Бори́**са**!	11. Yesterday at the party Vera listened only to me, and not to you and to Boris!
12. Э́тот журнали́ст знал президе́нт**а** Тру́ман**а** и его́ жену́ и до́чь.	12. That newspaperman knew President Truman and his wife and daughter.
13. —Кто́ чита́л вече́рнюю газе́ту? Кто́ ви́дел её? —Я́ ви́дел то́лько у́треннюю.	13. —Who has read the evening paper? Who's seen it? —I have seen only the morning paper.
14. Когда́ мы́ бы́ли на бале́те, мы́ ви́дели Ма́ю Плисе́цкую.[7] Ма́я Плисе́цкая о́чень хоро́шая балери́на.	14. When we went to the ballet, we saw Maya Plisetskaya. Maya Plisetskaya is a very fine dancer.
15. А́! Ива́н Ива́нович![8] Ра́д **вас** ви́деть! Я́ так давно́ **вас** не ви́дел!	15. Ah, Ivan Ivanovich! I'm glad to see you! I haven't seen you for so long!

DRILLS

A. *Fill in the form of the direct object of the pronoun which corresponds to the subject of the first sentence.*

Model: Он был в Нью-Йо́рке. Я́ **его́** там ви́дел.

1. Кни́га была́ в кабине́те. Я́ .... та́м ви́дел.
2. Журна́л бы́л на столе́. Я́ .... та́м ви́дел.
3. Они́ бы́ли в Аме́рике. Я́ .... та́м ви́дел.
4. Бори́с бы́л в Москве́. Я́ .... та́м ви́дел.
5. И́х ма́ть была́ на конце́рте. Я́ .... та́м ви́дел.
6. О́льга и Ива́н бы́ли в па́рке. Я́ .... та́м ви́дел.

B. *Fill in the direct object pronouns.*

Model: Почему́, когда́ **она́** говори́ла, ты́ **её** не слу́шал?

1. Почему́, когда́ **мы́** говори́ли, ты́ .... не слу́шал?
2. Почему́, когда́ **я́** говори́л, ты́ .... не слу́шал?
3. Почему́, когда́ **вы́** говори́ли, о́н .... не слу́шал?
4. Почему́, когда́ **ты́** говори́л, о́н .... не слу́шал?
5. Почему́, когда́ **они́** говори́ли, ты́ .... не слу́шал?
6. Почему́, когда́ А́нна говори́ла, ты́ .... не слу́шал?
7. Почему́, когда́ Бори́с говори́л, ты́ .... не слу́шал?

C. *Put the words in parentheses into the correct case form and translate.*

1. Я́ уже́ чита́л (э́та кни́га).
2. Андре́й писа́л (но́вая пье́са).
3. Мы́ вчера́ ви́дели (О́льга Смирно́ва).
4. Я́ ви́дела (она́) на уро́ке.
5. Мы́ не зна́ли (он).
6. Профе́ссор Па́влов зна́л (они́).

---

[7] Плисе́цкая, Ма́я, ballerina in the Bolshoy Theater company. She has danced in the United States several times.

[8] Russian middle names are patronymics, formed from the father's first name with the addition of a masculine or feminine suffix, usually **-ович** for sons and **-овна** for daughters; e.g., Ива́н Ива́**нович** is *Ivan, son of Ivan,* while О́льга Ива́**новна** is *Olga, daughter of Ivan.* See also Unit 11.

7. Они́ зна́ли (профе́ссор Па́влов). Они́ хорошо́ зна́ли (он).
8. Мы́ чита́ли («А́нна Каре́нина»).
9. Моя́ ма́ть зна́ла (э́тот тала́нтливый писа́тель). Она́ ви́дела (он) в Москве́.
10. —Где́ газе́та? —Я́ ви́дел (она́) в кабине́те.
11. —Где́ журна́л? —Я́ не ви́дел (он).
12. —Где́ Андре́й? —Я́ не ви́дел (он).
13. —Где́ ты́ ви́дел (я)? —Я́ ви́дел (ты) на у́лице.
14. Я́ хорошо́ зна́л (ва́ша до́чь О́льга) и (ва́ш ста́рший сы́н Бори́с).
15. Никто́ не зна́л (на́ш но́вый инжене́р).
16. Мы́ вчера́ ви́дели (тво́й ста́рый дру́г).

D. *Translate into Russian.*

1. Did you see the president of our country when he was in your city?
2. No, but I saw him when I was in the capital.
3. Where did Tolstoy write *War and Peace*?
4. He probably wrote that novel in the country.
5. Have you read *Boris Godunov* by (= of) Pushkin?
6. Yes, I have read that play.
7. Where did you see us?
8. I saw you in a store, but you didn't see me.
9. —Whom did you know there? —I knew only their sister.
10. —Did you see our brother? —Yes, I saw him.
11. —Have you seen my book? —Yes, I saw it.

3. Accusative of time

Besides serving as direct object, the accusative case is used to designate:
    a. A period of time in which an action is carried out:

Мы́ рабо́тали та́м **це́лую**[9] **неде́лю**.
We worked there **a** *whole week.*

Сего́дня я́ **весь**[9] **де́нь** чита́л.
Today I read **the** *whole day long.*

    b. Expressions such as *every day*, *every week*, etc.

Ка́ждый ве́чер ма́ма чита́ла вече́рнюю газе́ту.
Every evening Mama read the evening paper.

4. Present tense of verbs

Russian has two conjugations, a first, or **-е-**, conjugation, and a second, or **-и-**, conjugation. The basic endings of the two conjugations in the *present tense* are spelled as follows:

---

[9] In general **це́лый** corresponds to *a whole*; **весь** to *the whole*.

	1st Conjugation	2nd Conjugation
	Singular	*Singular*
1st pers.	-ю	-ю
2nd pers.	-ешь	-ишь
3rd pers.	-ет	-ит
	Plural	*Plural*
1st pers.	-ем	-им
2nd pers.	-ете	-ите
3rd pers.	-ют	-ят

Note that these two sets of endings differ in the vowels (**e** or **и**) in the second and third persons singular and the first and second persons plural; also, the vowel of the third plural ending of the first conjugation (**-ют**) must also be distinguished from that of the second conjugation (**-ят**).

The majority of verbs with infinitives ending in **-ать** or **-ять** belong to the first conjugation. The final **-ть** of the infinitive is dropped, and the present endings of the first conjugation are added:

First Conjugation

чита́.ть *to read*

1st pers.	я чита́ю	мы́ чита́ем
2nd pers.	ты́ чита́ешь	вы́ чита́ете
3rd pers.	о́н (она́, оно́) чита́ет	они́ чита́ют

Russian has only *one* present tense form corresponding to the various forms of the English present: simple, progressive, and emphatic (*I read, am reading, do read*).

Table of First Conjugation Verbs
(conjugated like чита́ть)

Verbs Used in Earlier Lessons		*New Verbs*	
де́лать	to make, do	начина́ть	to begin, start
ду́мать	to think	конча́ть	to end, finish
знать	to know	закрыва́ть	to close, shut
рабо́тать	to work	открыва́ть	to open
слу́шать	to listen (to)	понима́ть	to understand
игра́ть	to play	спра́шивать	to ask, inquire
		отдыха́ть	to rest, relax
		покупа́ть	to buy
		объясня́ть	to explain

Most verbs with infinitives ending in **-ить** belong to the *second* conjugation. The final **-ить** of the infinitive is dropped, and the present endings of the second conjugation are added:

SECOND CONJUGATION

говор.и́ть *to speak, say, talk*

1st pers.	я́ говорю́	мы́ говори́м
2nd pers.	ты́ говори́шь	вы́ говори́те
3rd pers.	о́н (она́, оно́) говори́т	они́ говоря́т

Other second conjugation verbs will be treated in Unit 11.

PATTERN SENTENCES

1. Я́ хорошо́ **зна́ю** э́ту библиоте́ку. Я́ **рабо́таю** та́м ка́ждый ве́чер.

2. Они́ **говоря́т**, что хорошо́ **зна́ют** ва́шу до́чь Ле́ну и ва́шего сы́на Ива́на.

3. —Вы́ **говори́те** по-ру́сски? —Да́, я́ немно́го **говорю́**. А почему́ вы́ **спра́шиваете**?

4. Я́ **спра́шиваю**, потому́ что Ни́на **говори́т**, что вы́ её не о́чень хорошо́ **понима́ете**.

5. —**Зна́ете**, я́ тепе́рь **понима́ю** ка́ждое сло́во, когда́ вы́ не сли́шком бы́стро **говори́те**. —Ка́к я́ ра́д э́то **слы́шать**!

6. —Мы́ тепе́рь **чита́ем** Шекспи́ра. —Каку́ю пье́су вы́ **чита́ете**? —Мы́ **чита́ем** «Га́млета», моноло́г «Бы́ть и́ли не бы́ть». —О́, да́, всё **зна́ют** э́тот моноло́г.

7. Я́ не **понима́ю**, почему́ ты́ **открыва́ешь** окно́, когда́ я́ его́ **закрыва́ю**!

8. Мы́ то́лько **начина́ем** э́тот уро́к, а они́ уже́ **конча́ют** его́!

9. Учи́тель ка́ждую неде́лю **объясня́ет** в кла́ссе но́вый уро́к, а мы́ **слу́шаем**. Когда́ мы́ не **понима́ем**, мы́ **спра́шиваем**.

10. Я́ **понима́ю** почти́ всё, когда́ о́н **говори́т** ме́дленно, но когда́ я́ не **понима́ю**, я́ **спра́шиваю**.

11. —Ни́на, ты́ та́к мно́го **рабо́таешь**! Когда́ ты́ **отдыха́ешь**? —**Зна́ешь**, я́ **отдыха́ю** то́лько когда́ я́ **слу́шаю** му́зыку.

12. —Где́ ты́ **покупа́ешь** газе́ту? —Я́ **покупа́ю** её в кио́ске.

13. Ле́на, ка́к хорошо́ ты́ тепе́рь **игра́ешь на** роя́ле и ка́к хорошо́ ты́ **игра́ешь в** те́ннис! А я́ **игра́ю** то́лько **в** кроке́т![10]

14. Ви́ктор **игра́ет в** футбо́л в на́шей университе́тской кома́нде. В э́той кома́нде всё хорошо́ **игра́ют**.

1. I know that library well. I work there every evening.

2. They say that they know your daughter Lena and your son Ivan well.

3. —Do you speak Russian? —Yes, I speak a little. Why do you ask?

4. I ask because Nina says that you don't understand her very well.

5. —You know, I understand every word now when you don't speak too fast. —How glad I am to hear that!

6. —We are reading Shakespeare now. —Which play are you reading? —We are reading *Hamlet*, the soliloquy "To be or not to be." —Oh, yes, everyone knows that soliloquy.

7. I don't understand why you open the window when I close it!

8. We are just starting this lesson, and they are already finishing it!

9. Every week the teacher explains a new lesson in class, and we listen. When we don't understand, we ask.

10. I understand almost everything when he speaks slowly, but when I don't understand, I ask.

11. —Nina, you work so much! When do you relax? —You know, I relax only when I'm listening to music.

12. —Where do you buy your newspaper? —I buy it at the newsstand.

13. Lena, how well you play the piano now, and how well you play tennis! And I play only croquet!

14. Victor plays soccer on our university team. On that team everybody plays well.

---

[10] The verb **игра́ть** meaning *to play* takes **в** + *accusative* case of *games*, but **на** + *locative* for *musical instruments*, e.g.

	игра́ть **в** те́ннис	to play tennis
But:	игра́ть **на** роя́ле	to play the piano

DRILLS

A. *Fill in the correct endings of the verbs.*

1. Я мно́го рабо́та . . . . .
2. Что́ ты́ спра́шива . . . . ?
3. О чём они́ говор . . . . ?
4. Мы́ ва́с слу́ша . . . . .
5. Они́ отдыха́ . . . . .
6. О́н говор . . . . по-англи́йски.
7. Почему́ ты́ не конча́ . . . . письмо́?
8. Я́ не понима́ . . . . , что́ ты́ говор . . . . .
9. Вы́ хорошо́ объясня́ . . . . грамма́тику.
10. Что́ они́ де́ла . . . . ?
11. Они́ говор . . . . по-ру́сски.
12. Мы́ начина́ . . . . понима́ . . . . .

B. *Change the infinitives in parentheses to the correct forms of the present.*

1. Они́ мно́го (рабо́тать). Я́ то́же мно́го (рабо́тать).
2. Я́ (спра́шивать) его́, где́ о́н (рабо́тать), а о́н (спра́шивать) меня́.
3. —Где́ вы́ (покупа́ть) газе́ту? —Я́ (покупа́ть) её в кио́ске.
4. Они́ (говори́ть) по-ру́сски, а вы́ (говори́ть) по-англи́йски.
5. Я́ (понима́ть) всё, что ты́ (говори́ть), а ты́ меня́ (понима́ть)?
6. Почему́ ты́ не (слу́шать), когда́ я́ (говори́ть)?
7. Я́ всегда́ (слу́шать) ва́с, но́ вы́ не (слу́шать) меня́.
8. Ива́н (закрыва́ть) две́рь, а вы́ (открыва́ть) её!
9. —Что́ вы́ (де́лать)? —Я́ (закрыва́ть) окно́.
10. Мы́ (начина́ть) чита́ть но́вую пье́су.
11. Они́ (конча́ть) писа́ть перево́д.
12. Ты́ (объясня́ть) грамма́тику, но́ я́ не (понима́ть).
13. Они́ (отдыха́ть) в дере́вне, а мы́ (отдыха́ть) в го́роде.
14. Я́ никогда́ не (отдыха́ть); я́ всегда́ (рабо́тать).
15. Вы́ не (рабо́тать), а (говори́ть).
16. —О чём ты́ (ду́мать)? —Я́ не (зна́ть).
17. Вы́ не (слу́шать), когда́ они́ (говори́ть).

C. *Supply the proper forms of the words in parentheses, adding prepositions if appropriate.*

1. О́льга чита́ет (Пу́шкин, Ди́ккенс, Фо́лкнер, Достое́вский, Толсто́й, Маяко́вский).
2. Ива́н игра́ет (гита́ра, роя́ль, балала́йка, футбо́л, баскетбо́л, волейбо́л).
3. Я́ слу́шаю (му́зыка, Ива́н, О́льга, отец, ма́ть, о́пера, учи́тель).

5. Negative expressions

Many negative expressions are formed in Russian by prefixing **ни-** to an interrogative:

Interrogative	*Negative*	*English Translation*
когда́?	никогда́	never, not . . . ever
кто́?	никто́ (*nom.*) никого́ (*gen. and acc.*; *pronounced* [n̦ikavó])	no one, not . . . anyone

что?	ничто́ (*nom.*) ничего́ (*derived from gen. of* что; *pronounced* [n̦ičivó])	nothing, not . . . anything
где?	нигде́	nowhere, not . . . anywhere

When one of the negative expressions formed with **ни-** is used in a sentence, the negative particle **не** must be placed before the verb or other predicate:

> О́н **никогда́ не** рабо́тает.
> He never works.

> Она́ **ничего́ не** зна́ет.
> She knows nothing. (*Or:* She doesn't know anything.)

> **Никто́** об э́том **не** ду́мает.
> No one thinks about that.

Note: When a negative expression is used without a verb, the **не** is, of course, not used:

> —Что́ о́н зна́ет? —**Ничего́!**
> —What does he know? —Nothing!

> —Кого́ о́н зна́ет? —**Никого́.**
> —Whom does he know? —No one.

When the various case forms of **никто́** and **ничто́** are used with prepositions, the **ни-** is written separately and **кто** or **что** takes the case form required by the preposition, which is then placed between the **ни** and the proper case form of **кто** or **что**. For example, with the preposition **о** governing the locative case, **ни о ко́м** means *about no one*, and **ни о чём** *about nothing*.

> —О ко́м вы́ говори́ли? —**Ни о ко́м.**
> —Whom were you speaking about? —(About) No one.

Ни . . . **ни** means *neither . . . nor*:

> Я́ не зна́ю **ни** Петра́ **ни** его́ бра́та.
> I know neither Peter nor his brother. (*Or:* I don't know either Peter or his brother.)

6. Declension of оди́н *one*

Оди́н (*one*) is declined like **э́тот** (pronominal declension); in other words, it agrees in gender and case with the noun it modifies. The **и** of the masculine nominative drops out in other cases:

	Masculine	Neuter	Feminine
Nom. *Gen.*	один одного[11]	одно Same as masc.	одна одной
Acc.	одного[11] *anim.* один *inanim.*	одно	одну
Loc.	в/на/об одном	Same as masc.	в/на/об одной

Один sometimes has the meaning of English *a, a certain*:

> В ва́шем кла́ссе я зна́ю **одну́** о́чень краси́вую де́вушку.
> In your class I know a very pretty girl.

Один also means *alone*.

> Я́ бы́л та́м **оди́н**.   I was there alone.
> Она́ жила́ **одна́**.   She lived alone (by herself).

In this meaning the word may also be used in the plural:

> Они́ жи́ли **одни́**.   They lived alone.

7.   До́лжен *must*

До́лжен agrees in gender and number with the subject and is used with infinitives. Note that the masculine has a fleeting **e** which drops out in the other forms; note also that the stress shifts to the ending in the feminine singular and plural. The past and future tense auxiliaries are unstressed and follow the proper form of **до́лжен**.

> Ива́н **до́лжен** тепе́рь мно́го рабо́тать.
> Ivan must (ought to) work a great deal now.

> Бори́с **до́лжен был** вчера́ рабо́тать.
> Boris had to work yesterday.

> О́н **до́лжен будет** за́втра рабо́тать.
> He will have to work tomorrow.

> А́нна **должна́** тепе́рь мно́го рабо́тать.
> Anna must work a great deal now.

> Она́ не **должна́ была** рабо́тать вчера́.
> She didn't have to work yesterday.

> Она́ не **должна́ будет** так мно́го рабо́тать.
> She won't have to work so much.

> Вы́ не **должны́** так мно́го рабо́тать!
> You mustn't work so much!

---

[11] Pronounced [adnavó].

Они **должны́ бы́ли** вчера́ рабо́тать?
Did they have to work yesterday?

За́втра всё **должны́ бу́дут** рабо́тать.
Tomorrow everyone will have to work.

PATTERN SENTENCES

1. —Я **ничего́ не** понима́ю, когда́ профе́ссор говори́т бы́стро. А ты́? —То́же не́т.

2. —Ни́на и Ле́на, почему́ вы́ **ничего́ не** де́лаете? Вы́ **должны́** рабо́тать как все́.

3. —Где́ ты́ тепе́рь рабо́таешь, А́нна? —Я́ **нигде́ не** рабо́таю. Я́ отдыха́ю.

4. —Не́лли, почему́ ты́ **никогда́ не** говори́шь по-ру́сски? —Я́ ещё так ме́дленно говорю́! —Но тогда́ ты́ **должна́** бо́льше говори́ть.

5. —Ива́н зде́сь **бо́льше не** рабо́тает. Не зна́ю, что́ о́н тепе́рь де́лает.

6. —Ле́на, почти́ ка́ждую неде́лю, покупа́ет но́вую ю́бку, или блу́зку, или но́вое пла́тье! А я́ **никогда́ ничего́ не** покупа́ю!

7. —В дере́вне, где́ мы́ жи́ли, **ничего́ не́** было, и мы́ всё **должны́ бы́ли** покупа́ть в го́роде. Но́ тепе́рь в то́й дере́вне всё е́сть.

8. —Ни́на, ты́ сли́шком мно́го говори́шь. Ты́ **не должна́** так мно́го говори́ть!

9. —**Оди́н** до́ктор говори́т, что всё **должны́** ме́ньше е́сть и бо́льше спа́ть. —А я́ зна́ю **одного́** до́ктора, кото́рый говори́т, что мно́го спа́ть то́же пло́хо!

10. —Я́ зна́ю **одну́** де́вушку, кото́рая ду́мает, что её **никто́ не** понима́ет, и она́ всегда́ одна́!

11. Я́ **бо́льше не** игра́ю ни на роя́ле, ни на балала́йке.

12. Ви́ктор **до́лжен бы́л** игра́ть вчера́ в баскетбо́л, но́ не игра́л.

1. —I don't understand anything when the professor speaks fast. And you? —I don't either.

2. —Nina and Lena, why aren't you doing anything? You must work like everybody else.

3. —Where are you working now, Anna? —I am not working anywhere. I'm taking a rest.

4. —Nellie, why don't you ever speak Russian? —I still speak so slowly! —But then you ought to speak more.

5. —Ivan isn't working here any more. I don't know what he's doing now.

6. —Almost every week Lena buys a new skirt, a blouse, or a new dress. And I never buy anything.

7. —In the village where we lived there was nothing, and we had to buy everything in town. But now there is everything in that village.

8. —Nina, you talk too much. You mustn't talk so much!

9. —A certain doctor says that everyone must eat less and sleep more. —And I know a doctor who says that to sleep a great deal is also bad!

10. —I know a young girl who thinks that no one understands her, and she is always alone!

11. I don't play either the piano or the balalaika any more.

12. Victor was supposed to play basketball yesterday, but he didn't.

DRILLS

A. *Fill in the correct forms of* **оди́н**.

1. А́нна была́ на конце́рте . . . . .
2. Ива́н бы́л до́ма . . . . .
3. Я́ зна́ю . . . . хоро́шего журнали́ста и . . . . хоро́шую журнали́стку.
4. Мы́ говори́ли об . . . . хоро́шем до́кторе.
5. Мы́ жи́ли в . . . . ко́мнате.
6. Они́ жи́ли . . . . .

B. *Translate into English.*

1. Мы́ вчера́ нигде́ не́ были и никого́ не ви́дели. Мы́ весь де́нь бы́ли до́ма одни́.
2. Ни́на ещё никого́ здесь не зна́ет и она́ почти́ всегда́ одна́.
3. Когда́ Ива́н жи́л оди́н, о́н до́лжен был ка́ждое у́тро покупа́ть молоко́, све́жий хле́б, и у́треннюю газе́ту. Тепе́рь всё это покупа́ет его́ жена́.
4. Я́ зна́ю одного́ челове́ка, кото́рый всегда́ рабо́тает, и никогда́ не отдыха́ет! Како́й стра́нный челове́к!
5. Они́ говори́ли об одно́й де́вушке, кото́рую и[12] вы́ хорошо́ зна́ете, но́ о кото́рой я́ да́же никогда́ не слы́шал.
6. Мы́ жи́ли неде́лю в Ленингра́де и почти́ це́лый ме́сяц в Москве́. Мы́ та́м никого́ не зна́ли, и никто́ не зна́л на́с.
7. —Ви́ктор, ты́ до́лжен бо́льше чита́ть и ме́ньше игра́ть в футбо́л. —Я́ не игра́л уже́ це́лую неде́лю! Я́ до́лжен был игра́ть вчера́, но́ не игра́л.
8. Никто́ не понима́ет, почему́ Бори́с ду́мает, что о́н всё зна́ет. Всё зна́ют, что о́н ничего́ не зна́ет.

C. *Translate into Russian.*

1. She sometimes had to live alone.
2. You ought to work more. Why don't you do anything?
3. Why do you never listen when I speak? You must listen to me.
4. She was supposed to speak in class today. She must speak every week.
5. Nowhere did I see her, or (=nor) her sister.
6. Why doesn't he ever play the guitar? I know that he plays volleyball every day.
7. They don't understand anything!
8. —About what are you thinking? —About nothing.
9. —About whom are you thinking —About no one.

Reading

First read the story to yourself and be sure you know the vocabulary. Then read it aloud two times for fluency. Be prepared to answer the questions.

Бра́т и сестра́

Я́ ти́хий, серьёзный челове́к. Я́ ма́ло говорю́, но́ мно́го рабо́таю. Я́ студе́нт и рабо́таю и в университе́те и до́ма. Когда́ я́ не рабо́таю, я́ чита́ю хоро́шую кни́гу или серьёзный журна́л, или слу́шаю класси́ческую му́зыку, как наприме́р Бетхо́вена, Чайко́вского, Шопе́на. Чте́ние и му́зыка—это мо́й о́тдых. Я́ так хорошо́ отдыха́ю, когда́ я́ оди́н!

Но́ моя́ ста́ршая сестра́ Ле́на[13] меня́ не понима́ет. Ле́на хоро́шая де́вушка,

---

[12] И often has the meaning *also, too.*
[13] Ле́на, diminutive of Еле́на.

но она́ ду́мает, что она́ всё зна́ет и всё понима́ет. И она́ ду́мает, что я, её мла́дший брат, до́лжен её слу́шать!

Она́ ча́сто та́к начина́ет разгово́р: «Зна́ешь, Алёша,[14] ты сли́шком мно́го чита́ешь и сли́шком мно́го ду́маешь. Это потому́ что ты́ та́к мно́го быва́ешь[15] оди́н. Никто́ никогда́ тебя́ не ви́дел, ни на вечери́нке ни да́же на футбо́ле! Почему́ ты тако́й стра́нный и ску́чный челове́к! Почему́ ты́ нигде́ не быва́ешь?[15] Почему́ ты́ не как всё?»

Я слу́шаю сестру́, но ничего́ не говорю́. Она́ не должна́ та́к говори́ть. Почему́ я ску́чный? Почему́ я до́лжен бы́ть как все́? И кто́ это «все́»? Почему́ она́ ду́мает, что всё, что де́лают «все́» или то́, что де́лает она́—это хорошо́, а всё, что де́лаю я—это пло́хо! Наприме́р: Ле́на, почти́ ка́ждую неде́лю, покупа́ет но́вую ю́бку или блу́зку, и почти́ ка́ждый ме́сяц, но́вое, иногда́ дорого́е пла́тье—это хорошо́! А когда́ я иногда́ покупа́ю кни́гу, ча́сто дешёвую, или пласти́нку—это пло́хо!

А вы́ зна́ете подру́гу Ле́ны, краси́вую брюне́тку Ни́ну Ла́пину? Вы́ её не зна́ете? Ну́, это ничего́. Вы́ ду́маете, что когда́ Ле́на и Ни́на вме́сте, они́ говоря́т о литерату́ре или о поли́тике? Никогда́! Я иногда́ слу́шаю и́х разгово́р. Вчера́, наприме́р, они́ говори́ли об одно́м молодо́м челове́ке, кото́рого они́ ви́дели на одно́й вечери́нке. Этот па́рень (fellow) о́чень хорошо́ игра́л на гита́ре, и они́ слы́шали, что о́н хорошо́ игра́ет в волейбо́л. Како́й геро́й! И они́ ещё говори́ли об одно́й то́лстой блонди́нке, кото́рую они́ та́м ви́дели. И э́та то́лстая блонди́нка была́ в кра́сном, о́чень у́зком пла́тье! Како́й сканда́л!

Не зна́ю, о ко́м и о чём они́ ещё говори́ли—я не слу́шал.

Не́т, я не понима́ю сестру́, а она́ не понима́ет меня́. Но э́то ничего́: она́ хоро́шая сестра́, то́лько она́ сли́шком мно́го обо мне́ ду́мает.

Answer these questions in Russian.

1. Где́ рабо́тает на́ш геро́й? 2. Что́ де́лает Алёша, когда́ о́н отдыха́ет? 3. Где́ его́ никто́ никогда́ не ви́дел? 4. Ка́к вы́ ду́маете, где́ о́н быва́ет? (Мы́ зна́ем, что о́н серьёзный молодо́й челове́к.) 5. Ка́к ча́сто и что́ покупа́ет Ле́на? 6. Ка́к ча́сто и что́ покупа́ет Алёша? 7. Кто́ Ни́на Ла́пина и кака́я она́ (what is

---

[14] Алёша, diminutive of Алексе́й. Diminutive forms of men's names ending in -a and -я are declined like feminine nouns, e.g., Я зна́ю Алёшу.

[15] The verb быва́ть is an important one with several idiomatic meanings:

(a) *to be, happen, occur* (often, repeatedly, from time to time):

   Ма́ть иногда́ **быва́ла** одна́.   Mother sometimes used to be alone.

(b) *to go, attend, visit* (frequently, from time to time):

   Я́ иногда́ **быва́ю** в Босто́не.   I sometimes go to Boston.

Быва́ть retains the same sense in the negative:

   Ма́ть никогда́ не **быва́ет** одна́.   Mother is never alone.
   Я́ никогда́ не **быва́ю** в Босто́не.   I never go to Boston.

she like)?   8. О чём Ни́на и Ле́на никогда́ не говоря́т?   9. Где́ они́ ви́дели па́рня-геро́я, и что́ они́ о нём говори́ли?   10. Кого́ ещё они́ там ви́дели?   11. Что́ говори́т Алёша в конце́?

PRONUNCIATION DRILL

ja țíxij i șiɍjóznij čilaɣék. ja málə gəvaɍú, no mnógə rabótəju. ja stuḍént i rabótəju i vuņiɣiɍșițéți i dómə. kagdá ja ņirabótəju, ja čitáju xaróšuju kņígu iļi șiɍjóznij žurnál, iļi slúšəju klaşíčiskuju múziku, kak napɍiméɍ ḫetxóɣenə, čijkóvskəvə, šopénə. Čțéņijə i múzikə—étə moj óddix. ja tak xərašó addixáju, kagdá ja aḍín!

DRILLS

A. *Change the words in parentheses to the accusative case, and fill in the blanks with appropriate pronouns.*

1. —Вы́ ви́дели (но́вая гости́ница)?—Да́, я ви́дел . . . . . Во́т . . . . .   2. —Ты́ зна́ешь (мой бра́т)? —Да́, я хорошо́ зна́ю . . . .; . . . . мо́й прия́тель.   3. —Мы́ начина́ем чита́ть (э́та интере́сная кни́га). А они́ конча́ют . . . . . —Чья́ . . . .? —. . . . моя́.   4. —Кто́ всегда́ открыва́ет (э́то окно́)? —Андре́й открыва́ет . . . . . 5. Я́ закрыва́ю (э́та две́рь). Я́ ка́ждый ве́чер закрыва́ю . . . . .   6. Я́ спра́шиваю (ва́ша сестра́ и вы́) о ва́шем бра́те.   7. Бори́с говори́т, что о́н зна́ет (оди́н тала́нтливый инжене́р). Андре́й то́же зна́ет . . . . .   8. Она́ покупа́ет (чёрное пла́тье и кра́сная шля́па).   9. Я́ зна́ю (э́тот рестора́н и ти́хий челове́к), кото́рый та́м рабо́тает.   10. Я́ не понима́ю (ва́ш хоро́ший дру́г). Я́ не понима́ю . . . ., а . . . . не понима́ет . . . . .   11. Вчера́ мы́ ви́дели (на́ш учи́тель и на́ша учи́тельница); мы́ ви́дели . . . . в теа́тре.   12. Мы́ всегда́ покупа́ем (вече́рняя газе́та) в э́том кио́ске.

B. *Review Translation.*

1. When my elder brother is alone at home, he reads the paper.   2. —What paper does he read? —I think that sometimes he reads a Russian paper.   3. You rest too much. That isn't good.   4. She buys meat every day.   5. I know a very pretty brunette, whom I think you also know.   6. He doesn't understand anything, because he never listens.   7. You must not ask Olga what she does.   8. Every morning he opens the store. He opens it very early.   9. I know that young American writer and his pretty wife. I saw them in London at a party.   10. He is very dull and never reads anything.   11. Whom do you know in this town?   12. I know an (= one) old doctor and his eldest son.   13. —Do you know her mother? —No, I never saw her. 14. They are not doing anything; they say that they are resting.   15. Sometimes she asks me, "Whom are you (ты) thinking about? Why don't you ever listen? Why do you close your door?" What a dull conversation!   16. The hat (that) we saw in the store is too expensive.   17. She is buying a cheap hat.   18. Every evening he closes the store late.   19. Olga knows Ivan and Ivan knows Olga.   20. This is very interesting reading; every co-ed should read this book.

Vocabulary

блу́зка [blúskə] blouse
блонди́н (*fem.* -ка) blond(e) (*noun*)
брюне́т (*fem.* -ка) brunette (*noun*)
бо́льше more; бо́льше . . . не no longer, no more
бы́стро fast, quickly
вечери́нка (informal) evening party
вече́рний evening (*adj.*)
все[16] (*pl.*) everyone, all
всё[16] (*neut. sing.*) everything
де́вушка girl
ещё else, in addition
иногда́ sometimes
ка́ждый each, every
кио́ск newsstand
кра́сный red
магази́н store, shop
ме́дленно slowly
ме́ньше less
мла́дший [mlátšij] younger, youngest
му́зыка music
наприме́р for example
неде́ля week

неприя́тный unpleasant
оди́н, одно́, одна́ one, a certain; alone
одни́ (*pl.*) alone
о́тдых [óddix] rest, relaxation
пласти́нка phonograph record
подру́га girl friend
потому́ что because
почти́ almost
ску́чный dull, boring
сли́шком too, excessively
ста́рший elder, eldest; older, oldest
ти́хий quiet, soft (of voice)
тогда́ then, at that time
то́лстый fat, stout, thick
у́зкий [úsķij] narrow
у́тренний morning (*adj.*)
ча́сто often, frequently
челове́к man, person, human being
чте́ние reading
широ́кий wide, broad
эпо́ха epoch, era
ю́бка [júpkə] skirt

VERBS

(For their conjugation see p. 105)

быва́ть (I) to be, happen, occur, go to, frequent (see footnote on p. 112)
говори́ть (II) to speak, talk; tell, say
закрыва́ть (I) to shut, close
конча́ть (I) to finish, end
начина́ть (I) to begin, start
объясня́ть (abjisņáṭ) (I) to explain
отдыха́ть (I) (addixáṭ) to rest, relax
открыва́ть (I) to open
покупа́ть (I) to buy, purchase
понима́ть (I) to understand
спра́шивать (I) to ask, inquire

EXPRESSIONS

ка́к ча́сто? how often?
Ещё бы! I should say so!
Спаси́бо за комплиме́нт! Thanks for the compliment!
почти́ ничего́ hardly anything
почти́ никого́ hardly anyone
Кто ещё! Who else!

---

[16] Все (*everyone*, *all*) is always plural in Russian, e.g., Они́ все бы́ли там. Все зна́ют, что э́то непра́вда. Всё (*everything*) is always neuter singular, e.g., Всё бы́ло на столе́. Всё, что о́н говори́л, бы́ло о́чень интере́сно.

Молодéц! (*expresses praise or approval*) Well done! Good for him (her, you . . .)! (*lit.*, strong *or* fine young fellow)
всё, что everything that
бóльше ничегó nothing else
бóльше никогдá never again

VOCABULARY REVIEW

Adverbs of Time	Adverbs of Place	Adverbs of Quantity
когдá?	где?	скóлько?
никогдá	нигдé	мáло
иногдá	здесь	мнóго
всегдá	тут	немнóго
тогдá	там	бóльше
давнó	дóма	мéньше
недáвно	блúзко	
скóро	далекó	
сейчáс		
тепéрь		

Unit 9

Grammar

1. Dative of nouns

The dative case denotes the recipient or addressee of something that is given, sent, transmitted, or communicated.

A sentence with a *direct object* (the thing given, sent, communicated, etc.) and an *indirect object* (the recipient) may be represented as follows.

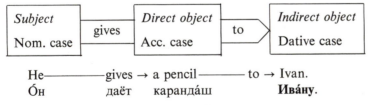

Subject Nom. case	gives	Direct object Acc. case	to	Indirect object Dative case

He————gives → a pencil———— to → Ivan.
Óн   дaёт   карандáш   **Ивáну**.

Or: He gives Ivan a pencil: Óн дaёт **Ивáну** карандáш.

The dative of **кто?** is **комý?**

—**Комý** óн дaёт карандáш? —Ивáну.
—To whom does he give the pencil? —To Ivan.

An indirect object in the dative may also occur in a sentence without a direct object expressed:

Онá писáла Ивáну кáждый дéнь.
She wrote to Ivan every day.

Ending of Nouns in the Dative Case

	Hard	Soft
Masc. ⎱ Neut. ⎰	-у	-ю
Fem. I	-e	-e
Fem. II		-и

	Nominative	Dative
Masc.	стол [stól.] гость [góṣṭ.] музéй [muẓéj.]	столý [stal.ú] гóстю [góṣṭ.u] музéю [muẓéj.u]
Neut.	окнó [akn.ó] пóле [póḷ.ə]	окнý [akn.ú] пóлю [póḷ.u]
Fem. I	женá [žin.á] кýхня [kúxṇ.ə]	женé [žiṇ.é] кýхне [kúxṇ.i]
Fem. II	дверь [ḏvéṛ.]	двéри [ḏvéṛ.i]

Verbs with an Indirect Object in the Dative
(not a complete list)

"Giving"		*"Communicating"*	
давáть (I)	to give (to)	говори́ть (II)	to tell, say (to)
продавáть (I)	to sell (to)	писáть (I)	to write (to)
посылáть (I)	to send (to)	читáть (I)	to read (to)
помогáть (I)	to help (give help to)	объясня́ть (I)	to explain (to)
покупáть (I)	to buy (*for*)	звони́ть (II)	to phone (to)
		покáзывать (I)	to show (to)
		отвечáть (I)	to answer (to)

The verbs посылáть, помогáть, покупáть, объясня́ть, покáзывать, and отвечáть are conjugated in the present like читáть. Говори́ть and звони́ть belong to the second conjugation (see Unit 8). The conjugation of давáть, продавáть, and писáть will be presented later in this unit.

Спрáшивать (*to ask*), unlike отвечáть (*to answer*), takes the *accusative* of the person asked: спрáшивать **когó** but отвечáть **комý**.

PATTERN SENTENCES

1. —**Кому́** вы́ посыла́ете э́ту кни́гу? —Я посы-ла́ю её прия́телю.
2. —**Кому́** он объясня́ет но́вое пра́вило? —Он объясня́ет пра́вило Ви́ктору и Ни́не.
3. Ива́н никогда́ ничего́ не посыла́ет сестре́! Он **никому́** ничего́ не посыла́ет!
4. Они́ посыла́ют приве́т профе́ссору Па́влову и его́ жене́.
5. —**Кому́** ты пока́зываешь на́шу но́вую би-блиоте́ку? —Я пока́зываю её сове́тскому журнали́сту.
6. —**Кому́** ты сейча́с звони́шь? —Я звоню́ до́к-тору Смирно́ву.
7. Жу́ков ча́сто звони́т **по телефо́ну** О́льге. О́льга никогда́ не звони́т инжене́ру Жу́кову.
8. —**Кому́** отвеча́ет студе́нт? —Он отвеча́ет профе́ссору. А профе́ссор отвеча́ет студе́нту.
9. Муж до́лжен помога́ть жене́, а жена́ должна́ помога́ть му́жу.
10. Я помога́ю А́нне де́лать упражне́ние.
11. —**Кому́** ты покупа́ешь пода́рок? —Я поку-па́ю пода́рок бра́ту.

1. —To whom are you sending this book? —I am sending it to a friend.
2. —To whom is he explaining the new rule? —He is explaining the rule to Victor and Nina.
3. Ivan never sends anything to his sister! He sends nothing to anyone!
4. They are sending greetings to Professor Pavlov and his wife.
5. —To whom are you showing our new library? —I am showing it to a Soviet newspaperman.
6. —Whom are you calling now? —I'm calling Dr. Smirnov.
7. Zhukov often telephones Olga. Olga never phones Engineer Zhukov.
8. —Whom is the student answering? —He's answering the professor. And the professor is answering the student.
9. A husband must help his wife, and the wife must help her husband.
10. I'm helping (giving help to) Anna do the exercise.
11. —For whom are you buying a present? —I'm buying a present for my brother.

DRILLS

A. *Translate into English.*

1. Ка́ждое у́тро Ива́н Ива́нович до́лжен объясня́ть секрета́рше, что́ она́ должна́ де́лать весь де́нь. Он объясня́ет, а она́ иногда́ его́ слу́шает, а иногда́ не́т.
2. Ма́ть, ка́ждую неде́лю, покупа́ет пласти́нку и посыла́ет её сы́ну.
3. Ви́ктор, сы́н на́шего до́ктора, кото́рый тепе́рь живёт в Вашингто́не, ча́сто звони́т Ве́ре. Ве́ра почти́ никогда́ не звони́т Ви́ктору.
4. Я пока́зываю прия́телю мою́ статью́, кото́рую он ещё никогда́ не ви́дел, и я всё ему́ объясня́ю.
5. Мы́ посыла́ем телегра́мму Бори́су и Ни́не. Мы́ давно́ их не ви́дели, и ничего́ о ни́х не зна́ем.
6. Он никогда́ не помога́ет отцу́. Пра́вда, он никогда́ никому́ не помога́ет!

B. *Put the words in parentheses into the proper case and translate.*

1. Я помога́ю (бра́т и сестра́).
2. Я слу́шаю (бра́т и сестра́).
3. Он вчера́ ви́дел (профе́ссор Па́влов и его́ жена́).
4. Он помога́ет (профе́ссор Па́влов и его́ жена́).
5. Я спра́шиваю (друг), что́ он де́лает.
6. Я посыла́ю телегра́мму (друг).
7. Почему́ вы́ не звони́те (до́ктор)?

8. Когда́ вы́ ви́дели (до́ктор)?
9. Что́ ты́ объясня́ешь (Ни́на и Бори́с)?
10. Когда́ ты́ ви́дел (Ни́на и Бори́с)?
11. Студе́нт отвеча́ет (профе́ссор), кото́рый спра́шивает (студе́нт).
12. Он спра́шивает (профе́ссор), что́ он до́лжен сейча́с чита́ть.

C. *Translate into Russian.*

1. —Whom are you helping? —I am helping Brother, but he helps no one!
2. —Whom is this student answering? —He is answering the teacher, who is questioning him.
3. —To whom is the teacher explaining the new rule? —To the student (*fem.*), but she doesn't understand anything.
4. —To whom are you showing your new suit? —To Father.
5. —Whom are you calling on the phone? —I am calling (my) secretary.
6. —For whom are you buying this gift? —I'm buying it for a friend.
7. —I don't understand to whom you are telling this. —I'm telling this to Anna.
8. He is showing our apartment to Olga, and to Victor. They have not yet seen our new apartment.
9. I am sending (my) regards to Dr. Semënov and his wife.

2. Dative of pronouns and adjectives

The dative masculine-neuter ending of these forms is spelled **-ому** (hard) or **-ему** (soft). The dative feminine ending is spelled **-ой** (hard) or **-ей** (soft).

ADJECTIVES AND PRONOUNS IN THE DATIVE SINGULAR

	NOMINATIVE		DATIVE
	Masculine	*Neuter*	*Masculine and Neuter*
3rd pers. pron.	он	оно́	ему́ [j.imú]
Adjectives	но́вый си́ний хоро́ший	но́вое си́нее хоро́шее	но́вому [nóv.əmu] си́нему [şíṇ.əmu] хоро́шему [xaróš.əmu]
Possessives	мой твой наш ваш	моё твоё на́ше ва́ше	моему́ [məj.imú] твоему́ [tvəj.imú] на́шему [náš.əmu] ва́шему [váš.əmu]
Demonstratives	э́тот тот	э́то то	э́тому [ét.əmu] тому́ [t.amú]
Interrogatives	кто 	 что	кому́ [k.amú] чему́ [č̦.imú]
	оди́н	одно́	одному́ [adn.amú]

	Feminine	
3rd pers. pron.	она́	ей [j.éj]
Adjectives	но́вая си́няя хоро́шая	но́вой [nóv.əj] си́ней [şíṇ.əj] хоро́шей [xaróš.əj]
Possessives	моя́ твоя́ на́ша ва́ша	мое́й [maj.éj] твое́й [tvaj.éj] на́шей [náš.əj] ва́шей [váš.əj]
Demonstratives	э́та та	э́той [ét.əj] той [t.ój]
	одна́	одно́й [adn.ój]

DATIVE OF PERSONAL PRONOUNS

Nom.	я	ты	он оно́	она́	мы	вы	они́
Dat.	мне	тебе́	ему́	ей	нам	вам	им

PATTERN SENTENCES

1. Дире́ктор пока́зывает го́род но́вому инжене́ру, и всё ему́ объясня́ет.
2. Наш нача́льник пока́зывает конто́ру но́вой секрета́рше, и всё ей объясня́ет.
3. Моя́ ма́ть объясня́ла э́той молодо́й хозя́йке, где она́ обы́чно покупа́ет све́жую ры́бу.
4. Почему́ я до́лжен отвеча́ть э́тому глу́пому челове́ку?
5. Мы должны́ помога́ть на́шему ста́рому отцу́. Он всегда́ помога́л нам.
6. Я иногда́ звоню́ ва́шей мла́дшей сестре́. Я звоню́ ей, но она́ никогда́ не звони́т мне!
7. Вчера́ я звони́л вам, но ва́с не́ было. Я не зна́л, что́ мне де́лать!
8. Ни́на должна́ чита́ть Шекспи́ра, но у неё не́т словаря́. Что́ ей де́лать?
9. Я посыла́ю приве́т вам, ва́шей ми́лой жене́, и ва́шему у́мному ма́ленькому сы́ну.
10. Она́ ча́сто говори́т мне, что её му́ж настоя́щий ге́ний! Я ничего́ ей не отвеча́ю.
11. О́льга обы́чно помога́ет Бори́су и его́ жене́. Почему́ она́ помога́ет им, а не нам?

1. The director is showing the city to the new engineer and is explaining everything to him.
2. Our director is showing the office to the new secretary, and is explaining everything to her.
3. My mother was explaining to this young housewife where she usually buys fresh fish.
4. Why do I have to answer that stupid man?
5. We must help our old father. He has always helped us.
6. I sometimes call up your younger sister. I call her, but she never calls me!
7. Yesterday I phoned you, but you weren't there. I didn't know what to do!
8. Nina must read Shakespeare, but she doesn't have a dictionary. What can she do? (lit., What is there for her to do?)
9. I am sending greetings to you, your dear wife, and your clever little son.
10. She often tells me that her husband is a real genius! I don't answer (anything to) her.
11. Olga usually helps Boris and his wife. Why does she help them, and not us?

DRILLS

A. *Translate into English.*

1. Ка́ждый ве́чер ма́ма чита́ет интере́сную исто́рию мне́ и мое́й ма́ленькой сестре́. Она́ на́м чита́ет, а мы́ её слу́шаем.

2. —Андре́й, кому́ вы́ пока́зывали на́шу но́вую библиоте́ку? —Я пока́зывал её моему́ хоро́шему дру́гу, реда́ктору журна́ла «Но́вый ми́р», тому́, кото́рый пока́зывал на́м Москву́, когда́ мы́ та́м бы́ли.

3. Моя́ ма́ть посыла́ет приве́т то́й ми́лой ти́хой де́вушке, кото́рую она́ ви́дела в ва́шей конто́ре, и, кото́рой она́ помога́ла писа́ть тру́дное письмо́ но́вому нача́льнику.

4. —Како́й подру́ге обы́чно звони́т Ле́на? —Она́ ка́ждый ве́чер звони́т краси́вой брюне́тке Ни́не. И они́ говоря́т, и говоря́т . . . весь ве́чер! О чём—не зна́ю: я́ не слу́шаю.

5. Вы́ не должны́ объясня́ть хоро́шей хозя́йке, где́ и что́ она́ должна́ покупа́ть!

6. Как легко́ и прия́тно объясня́ть грамма́тику у́мному студе́нту, кото́рый слу́шает и всё понима́ет.

7. —Како́му студе́нту вы́ посыла́ете письмо́? —Ива́ну Смирно́ву, на́шему но́вому студе́нту. Я́ посыла́ю тако́е письмо́ ка́ждому но́вому студе́нту.

B. *Put the words in parentheses into the correct case.*

1. Андре́й говори́т (молода́я блонди́нка), что она́ о́чень краси́вая.
2. Профе́ссор объясня́ет (молодо́й музыка́нт), ка́к игра́ть на гита́ре.
3. Вы́ не должны́ говори́ть (настоя́щий писа́тель), ка́к писа́ть рома́н!
4. Ве́ра звони́т (хоро́шая подру́га).
5. Я́ посыла́ю приве́т (твоя́ ми́лая жена́).
6. Мы́ пока́зываем го́род (сове́тская журнали́стка и сове́тский журнали́ст).
7. Мы́ мно́го говори́м о (сове́тская журнали́стка).
8. О́н сли́шком мно́го ду́мает о (краси́вая брюне́тка).
9. Мы́ посыла́ем пода́рок (ты́ и твоя́ ма́ленькая сестра́).

C. *Translate into Russian.*

1. He is sending the magazine to a talented young man.
2. He was telling that to your older brother. I don't know why he was telling that to him.
3. We are showing our school to our new teacher and are explaining everything to him.
4. —Whom is he helping? —He is helping me today.
5. We always help him and his wife, but they never help us.
6. Every day I explain to my husband why we must write to my sister every week. He thinks that that is too often.

3. Adverbs and expressions of state or condition derived from adjectives

Indeclinable forms may be derived from most adjectives by dropping the ending (**-ый, -ой**, etc.), adding **-o** to the stem, and in *some* instances shifting the stress. These forms are used as adverbs and in impersonal expressions of state or condition, e.g.,

(1) Used as an *adverb, modifying a verb*: The form **тихо** (from the adjective **тихий** meaning *quiet* or, when referring to a voice, *low, soft*) may be used thus:

Óн говори́л **тихо**.   He spoke softly.

Here **тихо** modifies the verb **говори́л**.

(2) Used *in an impersonal sentence*:

В до́ме **тихо**.   It is quiet in the house.

In this instance the word **тихо** describes the state or condition of quiet in a certain place. Note that no equivalent of the English *it* is used in the Russian sentence; hence these Russian expressions are truly impersonal.

SOME ADVERBS THAT SHIFT STRESS

Adjective		*Adverb or Impersonal of State or Condition*	
хоро́ший	good	хорошо́	well
плохо́й	bad	пло́хо	badly
весёлый	cheerful, alive	ве́село	cheerfully, lively
лёгкий	easy, light	легко́	lightly, easily
све́тлый	bright, light	светло́	brightly
тёмный	dark	темно́	darkly
у́мный	intelligent	умно́	intelligently
тёплый	warm	тепло́	warmly
холо́дный	cold	хо́лодно	coldly

NOTE: Although the impersonal of state or condition takes the adverbial form in Russian, it is translated by the corresponding adjectival form in English.

A. Adverb

Бори́с о́чень серьёзный студе́нт; о́н всегда́ о́чень **серьёзно** рабо́тает.
Boris is a very serious student; he always works very seriously.

Како́й ску́чный челове́к! Óн так **ску́чно** говори́т!
What a boring person! He speaks so boringly!

(1) The *interrogative* for adverbs and impersonals is **как**:

—**Ка́к** о́н говори́т? —**Бы́стро/тихо/хорошо́.**
—*How* does he speak? —Fast/softly/well.

—**Ка́к** на у́лице? —**Хо́лодно/тепло́/прия́тно.**
—*How* is it outdoors (on the street)? —Cold/warm/pleasant.

(2) **Как** is also used in exclamations:

Как бы́стро о́н говори́т!
How quickly he speaks!

(3) Note the comparable use of **так**:

Óн **так** бы́стро говори́т!
He speaks *so* fast!

B. State or condition

Здéсь **прия́тно**.   It's pleasant here.
На у́лице **хо́лодно**.   It's cold on the street (= outside).
Хорошо́, что вы́ бы́ли тáм. It's good that you were there.

(1) For the past tense, impersonals take a neuter verb (**бы́ло**); for the future, a third person singular verb (**бу́дет**).

Вчерá **бы́ло хо́лодно**.
It was cold yesterday.

Я́ ду́маю, что зáвтра **бу́дет тепло́**.
I think it will be warm tomorrow.

(2) Impersonal expressions may also be used with infinitives:

По-ру́сски **легко́ читáть**, нó **говори́ть тру́дно**.
It's easy to read Russian, but difficult to speak it.

Жи́ть в дерéвне **прия́тно**.
It's pleasant to live in the country.

DRILL

Each of the sentences below should contain, when completed, an adjective and a corresponding adverbial or impersonal form; fill in each blank with the missing adjective, impersonal, or adverb.

1. **У́мный** человéк обы́чно говори́т . . . . .
2. Как . . . . слу́шать **ску́чного** человéка!
3. **Хоро́ший** музыкáнт обы́чно . . . . игрáет.
4. О́льга такáя **бы́страя**! Онá так . . . . всё понимáет!
5. Как **мéдленно** óн всё дéлает! Óн такóй . . . . !
6. Ивáн Ивáнович так **хорошо́** всё объясня́ет! Óн такóй . . . . учи́тель!
7. **Плохо́й** писáтель писáл . . . . .
8. Óн так **хо́лодно** говори́т о стáром отцé. Óн такóй . . . . человéк!
9. По-англи́йски **легко́** говори́ть, потому́ что англи́йский язы́к . . . . .
10. **Весёлый** человéк всё дéлает . . . . .
11. Какóй . . . . вопро́с! Как **глу́по** об э́том спрáшивать!
12. Её мáть óчень **стрáнная**: онá всегдá так . . . . отвечáет по телефо́ну!

PATTERN SENTENCES

Adverbs

1. —Ты́ ду́маешь, что нáш но́вый начáльник **глу́пый**? —Не знáю, нó вчерá óн говори́л óчень **глу́по**!

1. —Do you think that our new superior is stupid? —I don't know, but yesterday he was talking very stupidly!

2. Но́вая секрета́рша **така́я у́мная** и **бы́страя**! Она́ всё де́лает **бы́стро** и **умно́**.
3. —Како́й он музыка́нт? —О́чень **хоро́ший**. —Ка́к он вчера́ игра́л? —О́н о́чень **хорошо́** игра́л Проко́фьева.[1]
4. Андре́й **тако́й холо́дный** челове́к! О́н всегда́ **так хо́лодно** говори́т о сы́не.
5. Ни́на така́я **весёлая**, что она́ да́же рабо́тает **ве́село**.

2. The new secretary is so intelligent and fast! She does everything rapidly and intelligently.
3. —What sort of musician is he? —Very good. —How did he play yesterday? —He played Prokofiev very well.
4. Andrey is such a cold person! He always speaks so coldly about his son.
5. Nina is so cheerful that she even works cheerfully.

Impersonals with infinitives

1. На́ша гости́ница о́чень удо́бная, и **как удо́бно** жи́ть в це́нтре го́рода!
2. Проко́фьев тру́дный компози́тор. Проко́фьева **тру́дно** игра́ть!
3. Англи́йский язы́к не о́чень тру́дный. Говори́ть по-англи́йски **легко́**, но́ писа́ть **тру́дно**.

1. Our hotel is a very convenient one, and how convenient it is to live in the center of town!
2. Prokofiev is a difficult composer. It's hard to play Prokofiev!
3. English isn't very difficult. It's easy to speak English, but hard to write it.

Impersonals of state or condition

1. —Како́й **жа́ркий** де́нь! —Да́, сего́дня о́чень **жа́рко**.
2. Ещё не ве́чер, а в э́той ко́мнате уже́ **темно́**. Э́то така́я **тёмная** ко́мната!
3. Зде́сь **темно́**, потому́ что уже́ **по́здно**.
4. Моя́ ко́мната **све́тлая** и **ую́тная**. В мое́й ко́мнате так **светло́** и **ую́тно**!
5. Зде́сь **светло́**, потому́ что ещё **ра́но**.
6. —Ка́к на у́лице? —**Хо́лодно**! —А в до́ме (=inside) так **тепло́**! Э́то тако́й **тёплый** до́м!
7. —Сего́дня **жа́рко**? —Да́, о́чень.

1. —What a hot day! —Yes, it's very hot today.
2. It's not evening yet, and it's already dark in this room. It's such a dark room!
3. It's dark here because it's late already.
4. My room is bright and cozy. It's so bright and cozy in my room!
5. It's bright here because it's still early.
6. —How is it outside? —It's cold! —But it's so warm inside! This is such a warm house!
7. —Is it hot today? —Yes, very.

DRILL

Replace the English words in parentheses with proper Russian forms.

1. Кли́мат зде́сь (cold). Зде́сь всегда́ (cold).
2. Как (cheerful) в ва́шем до́ме!
3. Э́то о́чень (bright) кварти́ра. В не́й всегда́ (bright).
4. В э́том (boring) го́роде всегда́ (boring).
5. —(Is it cold?) —Не́т, де́нь не (cold).
6. —Бы́ло (interesting) на конце́рте? —Да́, конце́рт бы́л о́чень (interesting).
7. —Вы́ ду́маете, что бу́дет (interesting) в Ме́ксике? —Коне́чно бу́дет (interesting)! Э́то така́я (interesting) страна́!

---

[1] Проко́фьев, Серге́й Серге́евич (1891–1953), distinguished Russian composer. He wrote many symphonies and concertos. His stage works include a ballet for Shakespeare's *Romeo and Juliet* and an opera for Tolstoy's novel «Война́ и ми́р» *War and Peace*.

4. Dative of state or condition

Impersonal sentences of the type **Здесь хо́лодно** (It is cold here) can be made personal by using a noun or pronoun in the *dative case*.

Мне́ хо́лодно.	I feel cold.
Мне́ бы́ло хо́лодно.	I felt cold.
Мне́ бу́дет хо́лодно.	I will feel cold.
Ва́м всегда́ хо́лодно.	You always feel cold.
Здесь ску́чно.	It's boring here.
Мне́ ску́чно.	I'm bored (I feel bored).
А́нне бы́ло ску́чно.	Anna was bored.
Ива́ну бу́дет ску́чно.	Ivan will be bored.
И́м всегда́ ску́чно.	They always feel bored.
Здесь ве́село.	It's cheerful here.
Ни́не ве́село.	Nina feels cheerful.
Ва́м бу́дет ве́село та́м.	You will have a good time there.

Similarly, the dative may be used with infinitives:

Сми́ту тру́дно говори́ть по-ру́сски.
It's hard for Smith to speak Russian (= He has trouble speaking it).

Моему́ бра́ту и **мне́** бы́ло прия́тно э́то слы́шать.
It was pleasant for my brother and me to hear that (= My brother and I were pleased to hear that).

А́нне ничего́ не тру́дно де́лать.
Nothing is hard for Anna to do.

Мне́ бы́ло ску́чно чита́ть э́ту кни́гу.
I was bored reading that book.

PATTERN SENTENCES

1. **Мне́ интере́сно** ва́с **слу́шать**.
2. —**Тебе́ ску́чно?** —Да́, **мне́ ску́чно**. А тебе́? —То́же.
3. Конце́рт бы́л ску́чный, и **на́м** бы́ло **ску́чно**.
4. —**Кому́ хо́лодно?** —Ива́ну.
5. —**Кому́** бы́ло **ве́село** на вечери́нке? —О́льге. **Ей** всегда́ **ве́село**. Она́ весёлая.
6. Ви́ктору **тру́дно говори́ть** по-ру́сски. Ему́ всё **тру́дно**.
7. —Я́ ду́маю, что **ва́м** не о́чень **удо́бно** на э́том сту́ле: о́н тако́й неудо́бный! —**Мне́** о́чень **удо́бно**, пра́вда!
8. Я́ открыва́ю окно́, потому́ что моему́ ма́ленькому сы́ну **жа́рко**.
9. Бори́с тако́й интере́сный. **Мне́** всегда́ **интере́сно** его́ **слу́шать**.

1. It's interesting for me to listen to you.
2. —Are you bored? —Yes, I'm bored. And you? —I am too.
3. The concert was boring, and we were bored.
4. —Who feels cold? —Ivan does.
5. —Who had a good time at the party? —Olga did. She always has a good time. She's a cheerful (lively) person.
6. Victor has trouble speaking Russian. Everything is hard for him.
7. —I think you are not very comfortable on this chair: it is so uncomfortable! —I am very comfortable, really!
8. I'm opening the window because my little son feels hot.
9. Boris is so interesting. I'm always interested listening to him.

5. The adjective ну́жный, ну́жное, ну́жная, ну́жные *necessary*

Э́то **ну́жная** ве́щь.   This is a necessary thing.
Во́т **ну́жные** докуме́нты.   Here are the necessary documents.

6. Ну́жно or на́до (interchangeable)

The words **ну́жно** or **на́до**, followed by an infinitive, both express that *it is necessary* to do something, that something *must/should/has to* be done. **Ну́жно** and **на́до** are used in impersonal constructions. The statement made may be general (*it is necessary . . . , one should . . .* , etc.) or it may refer to a particular person (*it is necessary for someone . . . , someone should . . .* , etc.). In the latter case the noun or pronoun denoting the person is in the *dative*.

To express the past tense **ну́жно/на́до бы́ло** is used; for the future **ну́жно/на́до бу́дет**.

The negatives **не ну́жно** and **не на́до** have a range of meanings varying from *one doesn't have to* to *one musn't, don't!*

The **ну́жно/на́до** construction with the *dative* case is often used in a meaning very close to that of **до́лжен** with the nominative (see Unit 8, p. 109). But in impersonal sentences only **ну́жно** or **на́до** may be used.

Study the examples below carefully.

A. Impersonal statements

Ну́жно всегда́ говори́ть пра́вду.
One must always tell the truth.

Э́то **на́до бы́ло** зна́ть вчера́.
One should have known that yesterday.

Та́м **ну́жно бу́дет** говори́ть по-ру́сски.
It will be necessary to speak Russian there.

Не **ну́жно** сли́шком мно́го е́сть.
People ought not to eat too much.

Не **на́до** та́к говори́ть.
One shouldn't talk that way (= Don't talk like that).

Не **ну́жно** об э́том ду́мать.
One mustn't think about that.

B. Statements with reference to a particular person (+ *dative*)

Ва́м **ну́жно** бо́льше спа́ть.
You should sleep more.

Отцу́ **ну́жно бы́ло** мно́го рабо́тать.
Father had to work a great deal.

Мне́ **на́до бу́дет** бо́льше рабо́тать.
I will have to work more.

—Кому́ э́то **ну́жно** зна́ть? —Мне́ и А́нне.
—Who needs to know that? —Anna and I.

Мне́ э́то не **ну́жно** зна́ть.
I don't need to know that.

Мне́ на́до бу́дет э́то зна́ть за́втра.
I will need to know that (by) tomorrow.

Ви́ктору на́до бо́льше говори́ть по-ру́сски.
Victor needs to speak Russian more.

Ка́ждому челове́ку **на́до** пи́ть, е́сть и спа́ть.
Everyone needs to drink, eat and sleep.

—**На́м ну́жно** бы́ть та́м за́втра? —Не́т, **не ну́жно.**
—Do we have to be there tomorrow? —No, you don't have to.

DRILL

Translate into Russian.

1. I am closing the window because my little sister feels cold.
2. She was alone and she felt bored.
3. You read (*present tense*) too little; you need to read more.
4. I don't need to work now.
5. —Are you cold? —I am a little cold.
6. It was interesting for us to listen to her.
7. It was very interesting for my son to listen to you.
8. Your son is so interesting!
9. She is bored both at home and in class.
10. She is so boring!
11. Why is it necessary for every person to work?
12. One shouldn't think about the war.

7. First conjugation verbs (continued)

First conjugation verbs of the type studied in the preceding unit all have a vowel (**а, я**) before the endings, e.g., чита́ю, чита́ешь; объясня́ю, объясня́ешь, etc.

A large group of verbs have stems which end in a *consonant*. Their endings in the present are spelled somewhat differently from those of the type чита́ть: instead of **-ю** (first singular) and **-ют** (third plural), they take **-у** and **-ут** respectively.

PRESENT TENSE, FIRST CONJUGATION

	писа́ть *to write* (*present stem:* **пиш-**)	жить *to live* (*present stem:* **жив-**)	*Compare* ду́мать *to think* (*present stem:* **дума-**)
		Singular	
1st pers.	я пишу́	живу́	ду́маю
2nd pers.	ты́ пи́шешь	живёшь	ду́маешь
3rd pers.	о́н пи́шет	живёт	ду́мает

Plural

1st pers.	мы́ пи́шем	живём	ду́маем
2nd pers.	вы́ пи́шете	живёте	ду́маете
3rd pers.	они́ пи́шут	живу́т	ду́мают

With this group of "consonant stems," the last consonant of the stem frequently differs from that of the infinitive (infinitive писа́ть: present пишу́), or may disappear entirely in the infinitive, as is the case with the verb жить, conjugated живу́, живёшь, etc.

Every Russian verb follows one of three patterns of stress in the present tense:

(1) *Stress on Stem*	(2) *Stress on Ending* (with **e** > **ё**)	(3) *Shifting Stress:* *Stress on ending in 1st pers. sing.,* *but on stem in all other persons*
ду́мать	жить	писа́ть
(to think)	(to live)	(to write)
ду́маю	живу́	пишу́
ду́маешь	живёшь	пи́шешь
ду́мает	живёт	пи́шет
ду́маем	живём	пи́шем
ду́маете	живёте	пи́шете
ду́мают	живу́т	пи́шут

It is essential, therefore, to memorize three forms of the verb: the *infinitive, first person singular present*, and *second person singular present*. These three forms will be given in the vocabularies for all first conjugation verbs with present stems ending in a consonant, and for all second conjugation verbs with shifting stress.

8. Present tense of дава́ть **to** *give*

The suffix **-ва** disappears in the present tense of the verb. The stress is on the ending, so **e** becomes **ё**:

	Singular	*Plural*
1st pers.	я даю́	мы́ даём
2nd pers.	ты́ даёшь	вы́ даёте
3rd pers.	о́н даёт	они́ даю́т

Продава́ть (*to sell*) is conjugated like **дава́ть**, продаю́, продаёшь, etc.

PATTERN SENTENCES

1. —Кому́ ты́ **пи́шешь**? —Я́ **пишу́** до́ктору Смирно́ву.
2. Андре́й ре́дко **пи́шет** жене́.
3. О́н никому́ не пока́зывает, что́ о́н **пи́шет**.
4. —Како́му бра́ту вы́ **пи́шете**? —Я́ **пишу́** моему́ ста́ршему бра́ту. Я́ **пишу́** ему́ почти́ ка́ждую неде́лю.

1. —To whom are you writing? —I'm writing to Dr. Smirnov.
2. Andrey seldom writes to his wife.
3. He doesn't show anybody what he writes.
4. —To which brother are you writing? —I'm writing to my elder brother. I write him almost every week.

5. —Где вы́ тепе́рь **живёте**? —Я́ **живу́** в Оде́ссе. Это го́род на Чёрном мо́ре.
6. Они́ говоря́т, что **живу́т** в дорого́й гости́нице.
7. —Бори́с никому́ не говори́т, где о́н **живёт**. По-мо́ему э́то о́чень стра́нно. А по-ва́шему? —Не зна́ю; мне́ всё равно́.
8. —Кому́ вы́ **даёте** уро́к му́зыки? —Ка́ждый ве́чер я́ **даю́** уро́к му́зыки Вади́му и О́льге.
9. Они́ **продаю́т** до́м до́ктору Андре́еву.
10. —Что́ **продаю́т** в э́том магази́не? —Говоря́т, что в э́том магази́не е́сть всё.

5. —Where do you live now? —I live in Odessa. That's a city on the Black Sea.
6. They say they live in an expensive hotel.
7. —Boris doesn't tell anyone where he lives. In my opinion (= I think) that's very strange. What do you think? —I don't know; it's all the same to me.
8. —To whom are you giving a music lesson? —Every evening I give a music lesson to Vadim and Olga.
9. They are selling (their) house to Dr. Andreev.
10. —What do they sell in this store? —They say that there is everything in this store.

As can be seen from the last example, the third person plural *without a subject* may be used in the *indefinite* sense of "people," "one," "they," e.g., **Что́ о нём говоря́т?** *What do people say about him?* Sometimes an alternate translation may be passive, as in the sentence above: *What* is sold *in this store?*

DRILLS

A. *Fill in the blanks with the suitable form of the verbs.*

1. Кому́ вы́ пи́ш....?
2. Я́ пиш.... Ива́ну.
3. Они́ ча́сто пи́ш.... отцу́.
4. А́нна и О́льга жив.... в э́том до́ме.
5. Я́ тепе́рь жив.... здесь. Вы́ то́же здесь жив....?
6. Мы́ ка́ждый ме́сяц пи́ш.... на́шему дру́гу Константи́ну Ряби́нину, кото́рый жив.... в Оде́ссе.

B. *Put the words in parentheses into the proper case or tense forms.*

1. Кому́ ты́ (дава́ть) э́тот сове́т (= advice)?
2. Я́ (дава́ть) э́тот сове́т (ты́ и сестра́).
3. —Что́ здесь (продава́ть)? —Всё.
4. Почему́ вы́ (продава́ть) ва́ш автомоби́ль?
5. Мы́ не (продава́ть) его́. Мы́ иногда́ (дава́ть) его́ (Ни́на и её бра́т).
6. Ка́ждое у́тро ма́ть (дава́ть) (сы́н) уро́к му́зыки.

C. *Translate into Russian.*

1. I often lend (= give) my dictionary to Vadim and (to) his wife.
2. I am selling my fountain pen to Boris.
3. Why are you selling your library to Professor Pavlov and not to me?
4. They are writing to Dr. Andreev.
5. To whom are you writing?
6. I am writing to Olga and (to) her sister.
7. He is writing to the young Soviet (woman) writer.
8. He sometimes gives us good advice.

9. In the classroom there was no dictionary.
10. Who is giving Anna the teacher's dictionary?
11. I write to my sister every month. She says that that is not too often.
12. —My friend Andrey is writing a play! —That's terrific!

9. Reflexive possessive свой

Russian has a reflexive possessive, **свой**, which refers back to the subject; **свой** is declined like **мой** or **твой**, and is used as follows:

(1) *With the possessor a noun or third person pronoun in the nominative.* **Свой** must be used, instead of **его́**, **её**, and **их**, when the "possessor" is a noun or a third person pronoun and is at the same time the subject of the clause or sentence, as in the examples below:

Ива́н пи́шет **свое́й** сестре́.
("**его́** сестре́" would mean not his own, but someone else's, sister.)

Ве́ра чита́ла на́м письмо́ **своего́** бра́та.
("**её** бра́та" would mean not her own, but someone else's, brother.)

Они́ говори́ли о **своём** сы́не.
("**их** сы́не" would mean not their own, but someone else's, son.)

In the following examples, arrows indicate the noun denoting the "possessor" to which the possessive refers; these examples show how the use of **свой** helps avoid ambiguity:

Пётр пи́шет Ива́ну и своему́ бра́ту. ("**своему́** бра́ту" here means Peter's brother, since Peter is the subject of the sentence.)

Пётр пи́шет Ива́ну и его́ бра́ту. ("**его́** бра́ту" means Ivan's brother, not Peter's.)

Ве́ра чита́ла мне́ письмо́ О́льги и телегра́мму свое́й сестры́. ("**свое́й** сестры́" means Vera's sister, Vera being the subject.)

Ве́ра чита́ла мне́ письмо́ О́льги и телегра́мму её сестры́. ("**её** сестры́" means Olga's sister, not Vera's.)

(2) *With the possessor in the first or second person in the nominative.* The use of **свой**, which is mandatory when the subject is in the third person, is optional when the subject is in the first or second person:

Я да́л ва́ше письмо́ **своему́** (ог **моему́**) бра́ту.

Ты́ говори́л **своему́** (ог **твоему́**) дру́гу об э́том письме́?

Мы́ говори́ли о письме́ **своего́** (ог **на́шего**) сы́на.

(3) *With the possessor a noun or third person pronoun in the dative*. In constructions with the dative (of the type **ему́ ну́жно**) **свой** must be used when the possessor is denoted by a noun or third person pronoun in the dative:

> **Ему́** ну́жно ча́сто писа́ть **своему́** отцу́.
> It is necessary for *him* to write to *his* father.

> **Ива́ну** бы́ло прия́тно говори́ть о **своём** го́роде.
> It was pleasant for *Ivan* to speak about *his* city.

(4) *In impersonal sentences*. The use of **свой** is mandatory in impersonal constructions involving possession or belonging:

> **Ну́жно зна́ть исто́рию **свое́й** страны́.
> One should know the history of one's country.

Свой should *not* be used when both the possessor and the possessed have the same grammatical function in the sentence, e.g., when both are subjects or both are dative in impersonal constructions.

> О́н и **его́** [*not* **свой**!] бра́т рабо́тают на заво́де.
> He and his brother are working at the factory.

> Вчера́ у на́с был Ива́н и **его́** [*not* **свой**!] дру́г Пётр.
> Yesterday Ivan and his friend Peter were at our house.

> Ива́ну и **его́** [*not* **своему́**!] бра́ту ну́жно бо́льше рабо́тать.
> It is necessary for Ivan and his brother to work more.

Свой may be used only when the possessor and the possessed are in the same clause. For instance, **свой** would be wrong in the two sentences below:

> Ива́н студе́нт, а **его́** [*not* **своему́**!] бра́ту ну́жно рабо́тать на заво́де.
> Ivan is a student, but his brother must work at the factory.

> О́н говори́т, что **его́** [*not* **свое́й**!] сестры́ не́т до́ма.
> He says **that** his sister is not at home.

PATTERN SENTENCES

1. Вади́м ча́сто помога́ет **своему́** отцу́; о́н зна́ет, что **его́** оте́ц о́чень мно́го рабо́тает.

1. Vadim often helps his father; he knows that his father works very hard.

2. О́льга всегда́ ду́мает о **свое́й** сестре́ и о **своём** бра́те.

2. Olga is always thinking about her sister and brother.

3. Ива́н ча́сто даёт А́нне **свой** слова́рь. О́н говори́т, что **его́** слова́рь о́чень хоро́ший.

3. Ivan often lends Anna his dictionary. He says that his dictionary is very good.

4. Они́ ка́ждую неде́лю пи́шут **своему́** сы́ну. Они́ говоря́т, что **и́х** сы́н ре́дко пи́шет **и́м**.

4. Every week they write their son. They say that their son seldom writes to them.

5. Влади́мир ча́сто говори́т о **свое́й** семье́. О́н ду́мает, что **его́** семья́ ско́ро бу́дет зде́сь.

5. Vladimir often talks about his family. He thinks that his family will soon be here.

6. Ири́на даёт **свое́й** сестре́ уро́к францу́зского языка́.

6. Irene is giving her sister a French lesson.

7. Она́ говори́т, что **её** сестра́ уже́ всё понима́ет, когда́ Ири́на ме́дленно говори́т.

7. She says that her sister already understands everything when Irene speaks slowly.

8. Óн всё де́лает **по-сво́ему.**[2] Э́то нехорошо́!

8. He does everything in his own way. That's bad!

DRILL

Replace the English words in parentheses with Russian words.

1. Ива́н даёт (his) слова́рь (to his) учи́телю.
2. Она́ жена́ моего́ бра́та; мо́й бра́т ча́сто покупа́ет пода́рок (for his) жене́.
3. Зи́на жена́ Андре́я; мо́й бра́т покупа́ет пода́рок (for his—Andrew's) жене́.
4. Ве́ра хоро́шая жена́; она́ ча́сто пи́шет (to her) му́жу, и Бори́с то́же ча́сто пи́шет (to her) му́жу.
5. Ви́ктор ча́сто рабо́тает в ко́мнате (of his) сестры́, потому́ что (his) ко́мната тёмная.
6. Ви́ктор ду́мает, что (his) сестра́ о́чень у́мная.
7. Ива́н пи́шет письмо́ (to his) бра́ту. Ива́н зна́ет, что (his) бра́т бу́дет ра́д.
8. Ве́ра в кабине́те (of her) му́жа, и ду́мает о (her) му́же. Она́ ду́мает, что (her) му́ж сли́шком мно́го рабо́тает.
9. Во́т ко́мната му́жа Ве́ры. Почему́ О́льга в ко́мнате (of her) му́жа?
10. Ви́ктор ча́сто даёт А́нне (his) фотоаппара́т.
11. О́н говори́т, что (his) фотоаппара́т о́чень хоро́ший.

Conversation

Кому́ ты́ пи́шешь?

Бра́т. —Кому́ ты́ пи́шешь, Ле́на?

Сестра́. —Я́ пишу́ Ви́ктору.

Б. —Кто́ э́то Ви́ктор?

С. —Э́то оди́н молодо́й челове́к.

Б. —О́чень у́мный отве́т! Я́ понима́ю, что Ви́ктор не де́вушка.

С. —Ты́ пра́вильно э́то понима́ешь.

Б. —А́, я́ зна́ю, кто́ э́то! Э́то то́т па́рень, кото́рого ты́ и Ни́на Ла́пина ви́дели на одно́й вечери́нке, и о́н так хорошо́ игра́ет на гита́ре, и о́н тако́й хоро́ший спортсме́н, и я́ не зна́ю, что́ ещё. Ты́ ему́ пи́шешь?

С. —Ему́.

Б. —Како́й я́ у́мный! А о́н тебе́ пи́шет?

С. —Пи́шет[3]... Иногда́.

---

[2] Note the expression **по-сво́ему** *in one's own way,* e.g.,
Она́ всё де́лает **по-сво́ему.** She does everything her own way. See pattern sentence 7 on page 129.

[3] Pronoun subjects are often omitted in answers to yes-or-no questions, where the same verb is repeated. Here the answer **пи́шет** corresponds to the English *he does,* a shortened form for *he does write.*

—Ты́ бы́л та́м? —Бы́л.　　—Have you been there? —Yes, I have.

Б. —А Ни́не Ла́пиной[4] о́н то́же пи́шет?

С. —Не зна́ю: я́ не спра́шиваю Ви́ктора, кому́ о́н пи́шет, и не спра́шиваю Ни́ну Ла́пину, кто́ ей пи́шет: об э́том беста́ктно (tactless) спра́шивать.

Б. —А ты́ всегда́ такти́чная (tactful)?

С. —А ты́ не зна́л?

Б. —Не́т, не зна́л. Но́, коне́чно, всё, что ты́ де́лаешь, хорошо́! Ну́, а Ни́на пи́шет э́тому Ви́ктору?

С. —Го́споди, Алёша! Я́ же тебе́ говорю́, что я́ никогда́ об э́том не спра́шиваю: э́то и беста́ктно и мне́ всё равно́.

Б. —Гм... Тебе́ э́то всё равно́? А ты́ зна́ешь, что твоя́ Ни́на и тво́й Ви́ктор бы́ли вме́сте в теа́тре Сати́ры, и бы́ли на Центра́льном стадио́не, и в Па́рке культу́ры и о́тдыха,[5] и бы́ли...

С. —Го́споди! Не́т, я́ не зна́ла!

Б. —Ле́ночка![6] Прости́ меня́! Я́ же зна́ю, что тебе́ э́то не всё равно́. Заче́м же я́ всё э́то расска́зываю!

С. —Ничего́, Алёша, пра́вда ничего́. Ты́ зна́ешь, э́тот Ви́ктор неинтере́сный па́рень: о́н не о́чень хорошо́ игра́ет на гита́ре, и о́н не о́чень хоро́ший спортсме́н, и о́н никогда́ ничего́ не чита́ет, ни-че́-го́? О́чень ску́чный па́рень!

PRONUNCIATION DRILL

—kamú ti píšiš, ļénə?

—ja pišú γíktəru.

—γíktər, étə tót məladój čilaγék katórəvə ti i ņínə lápinə ņidávnə γíḑiļi nəadnój γičiŗínķi, i katórij tək xərašó igrál nəgitáŗi? Ti jimú píšiš?

Answer these questions in Russian.

1. Что́ де́лает Ле́на? 2. Кто́ Ви́ктор? 3. Ви́ктор пи́шет Ле́не? 4. О́н Ни́не то́же пи́шет? 5. Почему́ Ле́на не спра́шивает, кто́ кому́ пи́шет? 6. Где́ бы́ли вме́сте Ни́на и Ви́ктор? 7. Почему́ Алёша вдру́г говори́т Ле́не: «Ле́ночка, прости́ меня́?» 8. Ка́к Ле́на объясня́ет Алёше, что «э́то ничего́», что́ о́н ей расска́зывает о Ви́кторе и Ни́не?

Reading

Письмо́ ста́рому дру́гу

Сего́дня пра́здник, и поэ́тому я́ не на слу́жбе. Я́ до́ма, и пишу́ письмо́ своему́ ста́рому дру́гу Константи́ну.

Мне́ нелегко́ писа́ть э́то письмо́: я́ так давно́ не писа́л ему́, что да́же не зна́ю, о чём ему́ писа́ть.

---

[4] Masculine last names ending in **-ов** and **-ин** and their feminine counterparts, **-ова** and **-ина**, have a mixed declension: some cases are declined like nouns, others like adjectives (see Unit 11).

[5] Па́рк культу́ры и о́тдыха *Park of culture and rest.* Such parks usually have a theater, restaurants, tennis courts, volleyball courts, tables for chess players, children's playgrounds; almost all Soviet cities have such a park.

[6] Ле́ночка (from Ле́на) one of the endearing forms of Russian diminutives:

Ни́на—Ни́ночка, Со́ня—Со́нечка, Воло́дя—Воло́дечка, Алёша—Алёшенька.

Но́ во́т моё письмо́:

Дорого́й Ко́стя![7]

Ка́к ты́ пожива́ешь? Я́ ре́дко тебе́ пишу́, но́ ча́сто о тебе́ ду́маю [Э́то не
о́чень оригина́льное нача́ло, но́ ничего́—та́к всё пи́шут]. Но́ ты́ же зна́ешь, как
мно́го я́ рабо́таю. Я́ ве́сь де́нь на слу́жбе. Слу́жба моя́ в це́нтре го́рода, а живу́
я́ далеко́. Ка́тя,[8] моя́ жена́, как ты́ зна́ешь, хоро́шая у́мная же́нщина, но́ плоха́я
хозя́йка, и её здоро́вье то́же не о́чень хоро́шее. Поэ́тому я́ до́лжен помога́ть ей
по (= about) хозя́йству. Мне́ тру́дно рабо́тать и на слу́жбе и до́ма, но́ что́
мне́ де́лать? Помога́ть жене́—коне́чно норма́льно.

На́ша до́чь Ве́ра никогда́ не помога́ет Ка́те по хозя́йству. Она́ почти́ ве́сь
де́нь в шко́ле, а до́ма—телеви́зор, телефо́н, ра́дио (она́ слу́шает то́лько джа́з и
лёгкую му́зыку). Ка́ждый ве́чер она́ звони́т свое́й подру́ге О́льге, или своему́
прия́телю Вади́му, или они́ звоня́т ей, и они́ говоря́т и говоря́т ве́сь ве́чер.
Когда́ я́ говорю́, что по-мо́ему э́то нехорошо́, жена́ отвеча́ет мне́, что всё э́то
норма́льно; что я́ не понима́ю до́чь, что Ве́ра хоро́шая де́вушка, она́ молода́я
и весёлая, а я́—ста́рое поколе́ние и не понима́ю но́вое! Я́ ничего́ не говорю́
Ве́ре, и она́, коне́чно, всё де́лает по-сво́ему.

На́ш сы́н Серёжа[9] бы́л в университе́те, бы́л на слу́жбе, но́ ему́ всё ску́чно!
Тепе́рь о́н пи́шет! О́н ду́мает, что о́н настоя́щий писа́тель! Я́ не зна́ю, ни ка́к
о́н пи́шет, ни о чём—о́н мне́ никогда́ ничего́ не пока́зывает. Ка́те о́н пока́зывает,
и она́ ду́мает, что о́н настоя́щий ге́ний, и до́лжен писа́ть. И я́ ничего́ не говорю́
сы́ну, и сы́н живёт по-сво́ему.

Ну́, тепе́рь ты́ всё зна́ешь обо мне́ и о мое́й семье́ и понима́ешь, почему́ мне́
тру́дно ча́сто тебе́ писа́ть. Но́ почему́ ты́ так ре́дко мне́ пи́шешь? Мне́ так
интере́сно зна́ть, ка́к ты́ живёшь, ка́к твоя́ семья́ и ка́к твоё здоро́вье.

Приве́т тебе́ и твое́й семье́,
Тво́й Воло́дя[10]

Answer the following questions in Russian.

1. Почему́ Влади́мир (а́втор письма́) сего́дня не на слу́жбе?   2. Почему́ о́н
не зна́ет, о чём писа́ть своему́ дру́гу Константи́ну?   3. Почему́ о́н до́лжен
помога́ть жене́?   4. Почему́ и́х до́чь Ве́ра не помога́ет по хозя́йству?   5. Что́
об э́том ду́мает оте́ц?   6. Что́ об э́том ду́мает ма́ть?   7. Почему́ Серёжа не
на слу́жбе и не в университе́те?   8. Почему́ оте́ц не зна́ет, о чём пи́шет сы́н?
9. О чём Влади́мир спра́шивает своего́ дру́га в конце́ письма́?

DRILLS

A.   *Replace the English in parentheses with the Russian interrogative in its proper*
form.

1. (Who) объясня́ет грамма́тику?   2. (Whom) о́н зна́ет?   3. (To whom) они́
даю́т э́тот слова́рь?   4. (What) студе́нтку вы́ ви́дели?   5. (To what) прия́телю
вы́ даёте сове́т?   6. (Who) бы́л та́м?   7. (What) журна́л вы́ чита́ете?   8. (What)

---

[7] Ко́стя, diminutive of Константи́н.
[8] Ка́тя, diminutive of Екатери́на (Catherine).
[9] Серёжа, diminutive of Серге́й.
[10] Воло́дя, diminutive of Влади́мир.

редáктора онá вúдела? 9. (What) журналúстка былá на вечерúнке? 10. (To what) журналúстке вы даёте сегóдня урóк? 11. (To whom) ты продаёшь твоё перó? 12. (To what) студéнту ты объясняешь прáвило? 13. (What) вáше úмя? 14. (What) вы дéлаете? 15. (What) вáша фамúлия?

B. *Review Translation.*

1. I need to work, but there is no work! What am I to do? 2. Every person needs to eat. 3. I was bored at the theater. The play was so boring! 4. Why don't they ever write to their father? He writes to them every week. 5. —What are you giving her? —I am giving her my textbook. 6. —What are you selling to Boris? —I am selling him my old car. 7. It is too hard for him always to speak Russian, and therefore he often speaks English. For Ivan it is easy: he is Russian. 8. —What are people saying about her? —Many good things. 9. —What is sold in this store? —Everything. 10. I think (= in my opinion) it is strange that he doesn't write to his son. He has not written to him in a long time. 11. I write to my son, but not too often. 12. We didn't talk about anything.

Vocabulary

англúйский English (*adj.*)
гéний genius
глýпый stupid, foolish
джаз jazz
дирéктор director
жáркий hot
здорóвье health
инженéр engineer
истóрия history; story
контóра office
мúлый nice, sweet, kind, likable
настоящий real
начáльник chief, superior, boss
нелегкó not easy, hard
нехорошó not good, bad
обычно usually
оригинáльный original
отвéт answer, reply
пáрень (*gen.* пáрня) (*colloq.*) fellow
подáрок (*gen.* подáрка) gift
пóздно [póznə] late; it's late
поколéние generation
поэтому therefore, so

прáвило rule
прáздник [práʐņik] holiday
привéт (+*dat.*) greeting(s), regards
рáдио radio
рáно early; it's early
рéдко [ŗétkə] rarely, seldom
свéтлый (*adv.*, светлó) bright, light
семья family
слýжба work, service, job
совéт advice, counsel; council
талáнтливый talented
телевúзор television set
телегрáмма telegram
телефóн telephone
тёмный (*adv.*, темнó) dark
ýмный (*adv.*, умнó) intelligent, sensible, clever
упражнéние exercise
учéбник textbook
уютный cozy
фотоаппарáт camera
хозяйка housewife; hostess; landlady
хозяйство housekeeping; household economy

VERBS

In the vocabulary below and throughout the book, the verbs are given in the infinitive with a dot separating the stem from the ending; the conjugation type, I or II, is also given. The first and second persons singular are given only when there is shift of stress (see p. 128) or some irregularity in the conjugation.

да.ва́.ть (I: да.ю́,-ёшь) to give
звон.и́ть (II) (+ *dat.*) to ring; call (on the telephone)
объясня́.ть (I) to explain
отвеча́.ть (I) (+ *dat.*) to answer, reply
пока́зыва.ть (I) to show
покупа́.ть (I) to buy
помога́.ть (I) to help
посыла́.ть (I) to send
прода.ва́.ть (I: прода.ю́,-ёшь) to sell

EXPRESSIONS

Что́ мне́ де́лать? What should I do? What am I to do?
Мне́ всё равно́. I don't care. It's all the same to me.
А тебе́ не всё равно́? Isn't it all the same to you? What do you care?
Ка́к ва́ше здоро́вье? How is your health?
помога́ть по хозя́йству to help with the housework (at housekeeping)
посыла́ть приве́т (+ *dat.*) to send greetings (regards)
посыла́ть телегра́мму (+ *dat.*) to send a telegram
звони́ть по телефо́ну (+ *dat.*) to call on the telephone
Я́ так давно́ не писа́л. I haven't written for so long.
Го́споди! Good Lord! Heavens!
по-мо́ему in my opinion (= I think)
по-сво́ему in one's own way

VOCABULARY REVIEW

Adverbs of Manner	Adverbs of Time
как?	когда́?
бы́стро	всегда́
ме́дленно	никогда́
хорошо́	ре́дко
пло́хо	иногда́
нехорошо́	обы́чно
умно́	ча́сто
глу́по	
интере́сно	ра́но
ску́чно	по́здно
ве́село	
стра́нно	давно́
	неда́вно
	ско́ро

Future tense of быть *to be* • Prepositions до, после, без, and кроме •
The preposition у with genitive • У + genitive—*at the house of* •
Possession expressed by у with genitive • Нужен • Numerals 2,
3, 4 • Modal verbs хотеть and мочь • Conversation: Анна
читает Чехова • Reading: Что ему ещё нужно?

Unit **10**

Grammar

1. Future tense of быть *to be*

The complete conjugation of the verb **быть** (*to be*) in the future is:

	Singular	*Plural*
1st pers.	я буду	мы будем
2nd pers.	ты будешь	вы будете
3rd pers.	он будет	они будут

PATTERN SENTENCES

1. —Если завтра **будет** холодно,[1] где вы **будете**?
   —Мы **будем** дома.

2. Завтра в магазине **будет** французский сыр.

3. Завтра **не будет** французского сыра.

4. —Если Вадим и Ольга **будут** в библиотеке завтра, я может быть тоже там **буду**; я ещё не знаю.

5. Мы **будем** очень рады вас видеть.

6. —Экзамен **будет** завтра? —Нет, завтра **не будет** экзамена; экзамен был вчера.

7. Завтра Ивана **не будет** дома; он **будет** весь день в деревне.

8. —Иван завтра **будет** в классе? —Нет, **не будет**.

1. —If it's cold tomorrow,[1] where will you be?
   —We'll be at home.

2. Tomorrow there will be French cheese at the store.

3. Tomorrow there will be no French cheese.

4. —If Vadim and Olga will be at the library tomorrow, perhaps I will be there too; I don't know yet.

5. We will be very glad to see you.

6. —Will the exam be tomorrow? —No, there will be no exam tomorrow; the exam was yesterday.

7. Ivan won't be at home tomorrow; he is going to be in the country all day.

8. —Will Ivan be in class tomorrow? —No, he won't.

---

[1] **Если** always takes the future in Russian if the meaning is future, although the corresponding English is usually present.

DRILLS

A. *Translate into English.*

1. Он ещё не зна́ет, где́ он бу́дет за́втра. Мо́жет быть он бу́дет здесь, а мо́жет быть нет.
2. За́втра на́с весь де́нь не бу́дет до́ма. Мы́ бу́дем в дере́вне.
3. Ива́н вчера́ не́ был в библиоте́ке. Мо́жет быть он бу́дет та́м за́втра.
4. Когда́ я́ бы́л в библиоте́ке, Ива́на та́м не́ было. Стра́нно! Я́ ду́мал, что о́н та́м весь де́нь.
5. Если за́втра бу́дет жа́рко, я́ бу́ду весь де́нь до́ма.
6. —Вы́ ду́маете, что та́м никого́ не бу́дет? —Это тру́дно зна́ть.
7. В кабине́те звони́л телефо́н, но́ та́м никого́ не́ было.
8. Мы́—моя́ жена́ и я́—бу́дем о́чень ра́ды ва́с ви́деть.

B. *Fill in the blanks with proper forms of the future tense of the verb* to be.

1. Где́ вы́ .... за́втра?
2. За́втра я́ .... до́ма.
3. Где́ сего́дня .... Ива́н?
4. О́н .... в библиоте́ке.
5. Мы́ .... в шко́ле. Вы́ то́же та́м ....?
6. Да́, мы́ то́же .... та́м.
7. Кто́ ещё та́м ....?
8. Та́м .... Ива́н и А́нна.
9. —Где́ вы́ .... за́втра? —Я́ ещё не зна́ю, где́ я́ .....
10. —Бори́с, ты́ .... до́ма? —Да́, ...

C. *Translate into Russian. Remember that the word* there *in* there is, there will be, *is an expletive and has no equivalent in Russian* (*see p. 90*).

1. There is a library here.
2. There is no library here.
3. There will be a library here.
4. There will be no library here.
5. We will be at home tomorrow.
6. He will not be at home.
7. —Who will be at the opera tomorrow? —Ivan and Anna will be there.
8. We will be very glad to see them.

2. Prepositions до, по́сле, без, and кро́ме

The following prepositions govern the *genitive* case:

до	before, till, until, up to
по́сле	after
без	without
кро́ме	except, besides

До войны́ они́ жи́ли в Москве́, а **по́сле** войны́ в Оде́ссе.
Before the war they lived in Moscow, and after the war in Odessa.

Петро́в бы́л в Евро́пе **без жены́**.
Petrov was in Europe without his wife.

О́н е́л всё **кро́ме мя́са**.
He ate everything except meat.

The accusative forms of the personal pronouns given in Unit 8 are also the genitives: меня́, тебя́, нас, and вас; без меня́, кро́ме ва́с, etc.

Personal pronouns of the third person (его́, её, их) prefix an н- when they follow a preposition of which they are the object:

без него́	without him
без неё	without her
кро́ме ни́х	besides them

But when его́, её, and и́х are possessives and modify a noun which is governed by a preposition, the prefix н- is *not* added.

Contrast:

без него́	without him,	*but:*	без его́ сы́на	without his son
без неё	without her,	*but:*	без её отца́	without her father
кро́ме ни́х	besides them,	*but:*	кро́ме и́х бра́та	besides their brother

PATTERN SENTENCES

До, по́сле

1. **По́сле** теа́тра о́н бу́дет до́ма.
2. —Гдé вы́ бу́дете **по́сле** уро́ка? —Я бу́ду в рестора́не.
3. **По́сле** рабо́ты я ничего́ не де́лаю; я отдыха́ю.
4. —Гдé вы́ бы́ли **до** обе́да? —Я бы́л в музе́е, а **до** э́того я бы́л до́ма.
5. **До** войны́ они́ жи́ли в Ки́еве.

1. After the theater he will be at home.
2. —Where will you be after class? —I'll be at the restaurant.
3. After work I do nothing; I relax.
4. —Where were you before dinner? —I was at the museum, and before that I was at home.
5. Before the war they lived in Kiev.

Без, кро́ме

1. О́льга была́ в Я́лте **без** Вади́ма.
2. Они́ бы́ли та́м **без него́** и **без его́** бра́та.

3. Вади́м бы́л в теа́тре **без** Ни́ны.
4. О́н бы́л та́м **без неё** и **без её** подру́ги.

5. О́н бы́л на конце́рте **без свое́й** жены́.
6. Всé бу́дут на конце́рте **кро́ме** А́нны.
7. Всé бу́дут та́м **кро́ме неё** и **кро́ме её** подру́ги.

8. На столе́ е́сть всё **кро́ме** хле́ба.
9. О́н сего́дня ничего́ не пи́л **кро́ме** молока́.
10. Зи́на была́ то́лстая, и поэ́тому она́ е́ла хле́б **без** ма́сла, и пила́ ко́фе **без** молока́.

1. Olga was in Yalta without Vadim.
2. They were there without him and without his brother.
3. Vadim was at the theater without Nina.
4. He was there without her and without her friend.
5. He was at the concert without his wife.
6. Everyone will be at the concert except Anna.
7. Everyone will be there except her and her girl friend.
8. On the table there's everything except bread.
9. Today he didn't drink anything except milk.
10. Zina was fat, and so she ate bread with no butter and drank coffee without milk.

DRILLS

A. *Translate into English.*

1. —Кто́ бы́л та́м кро́ме ва́с? —Кро́ме на́с та́м никого́ не́ было.
2. —Что́ вы́ е́ли кро́ме мя́са? —Ничего́. Кро́ме мя́са почти́ ничего́ не́ было.
3. На́м ску́чно жи́ть без неё и без её сестры́, но что́ де́лать?

4. Я сего́дня ничего́ не е́л кро́ме хле́ба и сы́ра.

5. Мы́ бы́ли в рестора́не без А́нны. Та́м бы́ли все́ кро́ме неё.

6. Оте́ц тепе́рь живёт оди́н без Вади́ма и без О́льги. Ему́ ску́чно без ни́х!

B. *Translate the words in parentheses.*

1. —Что́ вы́ де́лали (before the lesson)? —Я́ писа́л перево́д (without a dictionary).

2. Я́ ви́дел Андре́я (before the concert and after the concert).

3. Они́ жи́ли в Аме́рике (before the war), а (after the war) они́ жи́ли в Евро́пе.

4. (After the theater) мы́ бу́дем до́ма.

5. Она́ была́ та́м (without Ivan and without Anna).

6. (After work) я́ бу́ду зде́сь.

7. Мы́ тепе́рь живём (without Olga). На́м ску́чно (without her), а е́й ску́чно (without us).

8. —Кто́ бу́дет до́ма (besides Father and Zina)? —(Except for them) та́м никого́ не бу́дет.

9. И́м тру́дно жи́ть (without him and without her), а ему́ тру́дно (without them).

10. Мы́ бы́ли в Евро́пе (before them).

11. Она́ бу́дет та́м (without her brother).

12. Э́тот журнали́ст ничего́ не ви́дел (besides Moscow and Leningrad).

13. (After dinner) мы́ говори́ли о поли́тике, и (after that) о литерату́ре.

14. Мы́ никогда́ та́м не́ были (before that).

15. На столе́ ничего́ не́ было (except meat), и мы́ должны́ бы́ли е́сть мя́со (without bread).

16. (After dinner) мы́ рабо́тали. А (after work) мы́ отдыха́ли.

3. The preposition у with genitive

Another preposition governing the genitive is у. Its basic meaning is *by, near, at*:

> У о́зера была́ больша́я гости́ница.
> There was a big hotel by the lake.

> Ива́н стоя́л у доски́ и писа́л.
> Ivan stood at the blackboard and wrote.

> У окна́ стоя́ло си́нее кре́сло.
> By the window stood a blue armchair.

> На́ша да́ча стоя́ла у реки́.
> Our summer cottage stood by the river.

> О́н чита́л у окна́.
> He was reading by the window.

4. У + genitive—*at the house of*

Phrases with the preposition у perform another important function: with nouns or pronouns designating persons, these phrases are used to express "visiting—, being with—, seeing someone, being at someone's place or house" (compare French *chez*, German *bei*).

Сего́дня я́ обе́даю у сестры́.
Today I'm having dinner at my sister's.

Кто́ у ва́с вчера́ бы́л?
Who was at your place yesterday?

Кто́ у ва́с за́втра бу́дет?
Who will be at your place tomorrow?

Prepositional phrases with у (у меня́, у отца́, etc.) may be combined with other prepositional phrases to indicate location:

У меня́ в ко́мнате есть дива́н.
There is a sofa in my room.

У на́с в го́роде хоро́шая библиоте́ка.
There's a good library in our town.

Телефо́н у отца́ в кабине́те.
The telephone is in Father's study.

The genitive of кто is кого́ [kavó], therefore у кого́ is *at whose house?*

—У кого́ вы́ бы́ли вчера́? —У моего́ бра́та.
—At whose house were you yesterday? —At my brother's.

PATTERN SENTENCES

1. —У кого́ вы́ живёте? —Я́ живу́ у Бори́са.

2. Мы́ тепе́рь живём у отца́, а Ни́на живёт у А́нны.

3. Твоя́ кни́га у меня́ на столе́.

4. Э́та же́нщина рабо́тает у на́с и у на́шего бра́та.

5. У отца́ в кабине́те большо́й пи́сьменный сто́л.

6. Мы́ вчера́ бы́ли у ва́шего учи́теля.

7. У како́го до́ктора о́н вчера́ бы́л? —О́н бы́л у своего́ ста́рого до́ктора.

8. О́н вчера́ рабо́тал у меня́.

1. —At whose house do you live? —I live at Boris's.

2. We're living at Father's now, and Nina is living at Anna's.

3. Your book is on my desk.

4. That woman works at our place and at our brother's.

5. In Father's study there is a large desk.

6. Yesterday we were at your teacher's.

7. —At which doctor's was he yesterday (which doctor did he go to see yesterday)? —He was at his old doctor's.

8. He worked at my place yesterday.

DRILLS

A. *Translate into English.*

1. —У кого́ живёт его́ ма́ть? —Она́ живёт у свое́й мла́дшей сестры́.

2. —У кого́ рабо́тает ва́ш ста́рший бра́т? —О́н рабо́тает у до́ктора Смирно́ва.

3. Вчера́ все́ бы́ли у на́с.

4. За́втра все́ бу́дут у но́вого учи́теля.

5. У кого́ вы́ ви́дели э́ту кни́гу?

B. *Translate into Russian.*

1. I shall be at your place tomorrow.
2. They lived at our place.

3. He will soon be at the doctor's.
4. She will be at my brother's.

5. At whose house are they living now?
6. She is working at Professor Robinson's.

7. All except the secretary were at his place.
8. We lived at his son's.

5. Possession expressed by у with genitive

The Russian verb **име́ть** (*to have*) is seldom used (its use is discussed in Unit 21). Ordinarily possession is expressed in Russian by the preposition **у** with the *genitive* of the possessor and the object or objects possessed in the *nominative*. Often, the word **есть** is used in this construction:

У до́ктор**а** **есть** телефо́н.
The doctor has a telephone.

У моего́ бра́т**а** **есть** ру́сский слова́рь.
My brother has a Russian dictionary.

A. Use of есть. (1) The word **есть** is generally used in **у** phrases when the name of the object can be preceded by the indefinite article, that is, *a* or *an* (as can be seen above).

These constructions are similar to those with **есть** already discussed in Unit 7, Sec. 5 (p. 90), except that a "**у** + *gen.*" phrase is now used rather than an expression of place or time. Compare the two examples above with:

В то́й ко́мнате **есть** телефо́н.
In that room there is a telephone.

В библиоте́ке **есть** ру́сский слова́рь.
In the library there is a Russian dictionary.

The question *Who has . . .?* is rendered by the prepositional phrase with **у кого́ (есть)?**

У кого́ **есть** слова́рь?   Who has a dictionary?

(2) When the particular object referred to is one that was previously mentioned, and known to be owned by someone, then **есть** is not needed and is generally *omitted*. (In English this definiteness may be expressed by the article *the, my, the doctor's, Ivan's,* etc.)

У кого́ слова́рь?
Who has *the* dictionary? (The one just mentioned or seen. It may be the doctor's or Ivan's.)

У кого́ **есть** слова́рь?
Who has *a* dictionary?

(3) Phrases *with* **есть** usually refer to actual ownership, while those without **есть** may signify mere possession, often temporary:

У меня́ **есть** слова́рь, но́ о́н сейча́с у моего́ бра́та.
I have (own) a dictionary, but it is now at my brother's (in my brother's possession).

(4) The word **есть** is *not* used when the "having" itself is regarded as obvious or is taken for granted, and when the statement concerns itself only with some quality or characteristic.

> У Óльги приятный голос.
> Olga has a pleasant voice.

> У Ивáна длинный нóс.
> Ivan has a long nose.

(5) Having an illness is also expressed without **есть**:

> У моегó брáта аппендицит.
> My brother has appendicitis.

B. Past and future tenses. To use the phrase "**у**+*genitive*" in a sentence in the affirmative past tense, the forms **был, было, была, были** must be included. The verb agrees in gender and number with the thing (or things) possessed:

> У брáта **был** телефóн.   Brother had a telephone.
> У отцá **была** машина.   Father had a car.
> У Нины **было** кресло.   Nina had an armchair.

An affirmative sentence showing future possession is formed with **у**+*gen.*+ **будет/будут**:

> У брáта **будет** телефóн.   Brother will have a telephone.
> У отцá **будет** машина.   Father will have a car.

C. Negative. In the negative, **нет** is used. The thing *not* possessed is in the *genitive*:

> У брáта **есть** телефóн.   Brother has a telephone.
> *But:* У брáта **нет** телефóн**а**.   Brother has no telephone.

> У отцá **есть** машина.   Father has a car.
> *But:* У отцá **нет** машин**ы**.   Father has no car.

The past tense, negative, of the **у** construction employs **не было** and the *genitive*, regardless of the gender and number of the object:

> У брáта **не было** телефóн**а**.   Brother had no telephone.
> У отцá **не было** машин**ы**.   Father had no car.
> У Нины **не было** кресл**а**.   Nina had no armchair.

The future tense, negative, employs **не будет** and the genitive:

> У брáта **не будет** телефóн**а**.   Brother will have no telephone.
> У отцá **не будет** машин**ы**.   Father will have no car.

D. У with third person pronouns. Third person pronouns governed by **у** (and other prepositions) prefix **н-** (see section 1 above):

> У **н**егó есть сын.   He has a son.
> У **н**её есть дóчь.   She has a daughter.
> У **н**их есть дóм.   They have a house.

But when **егó**, **её** and **их** modify a noun in the genitive which itself is governed by **y**, then **н-** is not added:

	У **негó** éсть дóм.	He has a house.
But:	У **егó** брáта éсть дóм.	His brother has a house.
	У **неё** éсть сы́н.	She has a son.
But:	У **её** сестры́ éсть сы́н.	Her sister has a son.
	У **ни́х** éсть маши́на.	They have a car.
But:	У **и́х** дрýга éсть маши́на.	Their friend has a car.

E. The use of свой as own. *Note:* **Свой** is used in sentences of the type **y негó (éсть)** to emphasize possession or ownership:

У ни́х éсть **свóй** дóм.
They have *their own* house.

У Джóна нéт **своéй** маши́ны; э́то маши́на егó отцá.
John does not have a car *of his own*; that is his father's car.

PATTERN SENTENCES

1. У профéссора éсть сы́н.
2. У сестры́ éсть э́та пласти́нка.
3. У Ни́ны éсть брáт, а у Бори́са нéт брáта. У негó никогдá нé было брáта.
4. —У тебя́ éсть сестрá? —Дá, éсть.
5. У А́нны нéт сестры́.
6. У неё никогдá нé было сестры́.
7. Ни́на не сестрá А́нны.
8. —У вáс éсть э́тот учéбник? —У нáс бы́л э́тот учéбник, нó тепéрь у нáс егó нéт.
9. Я́ дýмаю, что у нáс скóро бýдет э́тот учéбник.
10. —У когó éсть словáрь? —Ни у когó нéт словаря́.
11. —У когó мóй словáрь? —Óн у Бори́са. —Бори́с, у тебя́ мóй словáрь? —Дá, óн у меня́.
12. У когó éсть «Вечéрняя Москвá»? —Ни у когó.

1. The professor has a son.
2. Sister has that record.
3. Nina has a brother, but Boris has no brother. He never had a brother.
4. —Do you have a sister? —Yes, I have.
5. Anna has no sister.
6. She never had a sister.
7. Nina is not Anna's sister.
8. —Do you have that textbook? —We had that textbook, but now we don't have it.
9. I think that we will soon have that textbook.
10. —Who has a dictionary? —No one has a dictionary.
11. —Who has my dictionary? —Boris has it. —Boris, do you have my dictionary? —Yes, I have it.
12. —Who has *Evening Moscow*? —No one.

DRILLS

A. *Translate into English.*

1. У Вади́ма и у О́льги ничегó нéт, у ни́х никогдá ничегó нé было, и у ни́х никогдá ничегó не бýдет.
2. Бори́с говори́т, что у негó éсть хорóший францýзский учéбник, нó óн тепéрь у Андрéя.
3. —Андрéй, у тебя́ учéбник Бори́са? —Дá, óн у меня́.

4. Говоря́т, что у ни́х ско́ро всё бу́дет.
5. —О́льга, где́ газе́та? —Она́ сейча́с у меня́.
6. —У кого́ е́сть интере́сная кни́га? —Ни у кого́ не́т интере́сной кни́ги.
7. У ни́х тогда́ был о́чень хоро́ший учи́тель, но никто́ не зна́ет, где́ о́н тепе́рь.
8. —У Ива́на никогда́ не́ было маши́ны? —Не́т,[2] у него́ была́ маши́на, но́ тепе́рь у него́ не́т маши́ны.
9. У Бори́са маши́на его́ отца́.

B. *Answer the following questions in complete sentences.*

1. У ва́с е́сть бра́т?
2. У ва́с е́сть сестра́?
3. У ва́с кварти́ра или то́лько ко́мната?
4. У ва́с больша́я или ма́ленькая ко́мната?
5. Что́ е́сть у ва́с в ко́мнате?
6. У ва́с е́сть авторучка?
7. У ва́с е́сть телефо́н?
8. У ва́с или у ва́шего отца́ е́сть маши́на?
9. У кого́ е́сть ру́сско-англи́йский слова́рь?
10. Мо́й слова́рь у ва́с?
11. У кого́ е́сть сего́дняшняя газе́та?
12. У кого́ е́сть фотоаппара́т?
13. У ва́шей сестры́ е́сть му́ж?
14. У неё хоро́ший му́ж?
15. У ва́шего бра́та е́сть сы́н?
16. У ва́с е́сть каранда́ш и бума́га?
17. Мо́й каранда́ш у ва́с?
18. У ва́с е́сть э́тот уче́бник?
19. У ва́с е́сть ка́рта Сове́тского Сою́за?
20. У кого́ е́сть журна́л «Но́вый ми́р»?

C. *Translate into Russian.*

1. Vadim has a little sister.
2. He had a little sister.
3. They had no little sister.
4. I have no little sister.
5. She had a new apartment.
6. We will soon have a new apartment.
7. Who had a new house?
8. Her friend has a blue car.
9. His doctor has no car.
10. Anna had a good doctor.
11. Do you have a good doctor?
12. Who has a good doctor?
13. I don't have a good doctor.
14. We will have a big summer house.

6. Ну́жен

This word corresponds literally to the English word *necessary*. As we have seen in the preceding unit, the neuter form **ну́жно** is used with infinitives to express necessity or obligation: Мне́ **ну́жно** рабо́тать; Ва́м **ну́жно** э́то зна́ть, etc.

The agreeing forms **ну́жен**, **ну́жно**, **нужна́**, **нужны́** are used to express the idea rendered in English by the verb *need*. **Ну́жен** agrees in gender and number with the object needed, which is in the *nominative* case; the person who needs it is in the *dative*:

Present

О́льге **ну́жен** слова́рь.	Olga needs a dictionary.
Ива́ну **нужна́** маши́на.	Ivan needs a car.
Мне́ **ну́жно** кре́сло.	I need an armchair.
Ему́ **нужна́** рабо́та.	He needs work.
Они́ **на́м** нужны́.	We need them.

---

[2] Russian always uses **нет** to contradict the negative assumption of a negative question; here **нет** may be translated *No, that's not so.*

Observe in the last sentence above that when the object or person needed is designated by a pronoun, that pronoun comes first in the sentence.

Past

О́льге ну́жен **был** слова́рь.	Olga needed a dictionary.
Ива́ну нужна́ была́ маши́на.	Ivan needed a car.
Мне́ ну́жно было кре́сло.	I needed an armchair.
Ему́ нужна́ была́ рабо́та.	He needed work.
Они́ **на́м** бы́ли нужны́.	We needed them.

Future

О́льге ну́жен бу́дет слова́рь.	Olga will need a dictionary.
Ива́ну нужна́ бу́дет маши́на.	Ivan will need a car.
Мне́ ну́жно бу́дет кре́сло.	I will need an armchair.
Ему́ нужна́ бу́дет рабо́та.	He will need work.
Они́ **на́м** бу́дут нужны́.	We will need them.

Negative

О́льге **не** ну́жен слова́рь.	Olga doesn't need a dictionary.
Ива́ну **не** нужна́ была́ маши́на.	Ivan didn't need a car.
Мне́ не ну́жно бу́дет кре́сло.	I won't need an armchair.
Ей не нужна́ бу́дет рабо́та.	She won't need work (a job).
Они́ **на́м** бо́льше **не** нужны́.	We no longer need them.

DRILLS

A. *Translate into English.*

1. Вчера́шняя газе́та никому́ не нужна́; её уже́ все́ чита́ли.
2. Бори́с ну́жен отцу́, а оте́ц ну́жен Бори́су; они́ рабо́тают вме́сте.
3. Где́ Ве́ра и Серёжа? Они́ на́м ско́ро бу́дут нужны́.
4. —Кому́ ну́жен слова́рь? —О́н ну́жен А́нне. Она́ чита́ет Толсто́го, и е́й ещё тру́дно чита́ть без словаря́; она́ не все́ понима́ет.
5. У кого́ газе́та? Она́ нужна́ отцу́; о́н её ещё не чита́л.
6. Ива́н говори́т, что мы́ за́втра бу́дем ему́ нужны́; ему́ бу́дет нужна́ на́ша по́мощь.
7. —Ива́н, вы́ бы́ли на́м о́чень нужны́ вчера́. Где́ вы́ бы́ли? На́м так ну́жен бы́л ва́ш сове́т! —Как жа́ль, что я́ не зна́л, что я́ ва́м та́к бы́л ну́жен!

B. *Form sentences with the words according to the models given.*

Model: У меня́ не́т ко́мнаты. Мне́ нужна́ ко́мната.
Same for: учи́тель, маши́на, телефо́н, кре́сло.

Model: У на́с не́ было молока́. На́м ну́жно было молоко́.
Same for: учи́тельница, телеви́зор, кни́га, шля́па.

Model: У сестры́ та́м не бу́дет рабо́ты. Ей нужна́ бу́дет рабо́та.
Same for: холоди́льник, кварти́ра, прия́тель.

7. Numerals 2, 3, 4

два (*masc. and neut.*)
две (*fem.*) } two
три   three
четы́ре   four

The word *two* has two gender forms: два́ for the masculine and neuter, and две́ for the feminine. (We recall that the numeral оди́н, (*one*) has three gender forms—see p. 109.) Numerals above two have only one gender form.

Nouns with these numerals take the genitive singular.

        два́ до́ма (*masc.*)
        два́ окна́ (*neut.*)
But: две́ ла́мпы (*fem.*)
        три́
        четы́ре } до́ма, окна́, ла́мпы

With numerals and other expressions of quantity the word есть is generally omitted from the "*have*" and "*there are*" constructions:

На столе́ два́ карандаша́.   На столе́ мно́го хле́ба.
У него́ три́ сы́на.   У него́ мно́го хле́ба.

When the past tense of быть (and of some other verbs) *precedes* a numeral plus noun, it most often takes the *neuter singular* form бы́ло, e.g.,

На столе́ **бы́ло** два́ карандаша́.
On the table there were two pencils.

But when it *follows* the numeral plus noun, it takes the *plural* бы́ли, e.g.,

Два́ карандаша́ **бы́ли** на столе́, а оди́н бы́л на сту́ле.
Two pencils were on the table, and one was on the chair.

The future tense follows the same pattern:

В но́вой кварти́ре **бу́дет** четы́ре ко́мнаты.
There will be four rooms in the new apartment.

Четы́ре ко́мнаты **бу́дут** на пе́рвом этаже́.
Four rooms will be on the first floor.

PATTERN SENTENCES

1. В кабине́те **три́** ла́мпы.
2. В мое́й ко́мнате **два́** окна́.
3. На столе́ **две́** ча́шки и **два́** стака́на.
4. У на́шей сосе́дки **два́** сы́на. Оди́н живёт здесь, а друго́й в Оде́ссе.

1. There are three lamps in the study.
2. My room has two windows.
3. On the table are two cups and two glasses.
4. Our neighbor (woman) has two sons. One lives here and the other in Odessa.

5. На по́лке **четы́ре** кни́ги.
6. У меня́ **две́** соба́ки: одна́ бе́лая, а друга́я чёрная.
7. Мы ви́дели пье́су Че́хова «**Три́** сестры́».
8. У ка́ждого челове́ка **две́** ноги́, **две́** руки́, **два́** гла́за, **два́** у́ха, но́ то́лько одна́ голова́.
9. Ни́не нужны́ ещё[3] **два́** кре́сла.
10. В э́том до́ме **четы́ре** этажа́.
11. У на́с в ста́рой кварти́ре **бы́ло две́** ко́мнаты.
12. А в на́шей но́вой кварти́ре **бу́дет четы́ре** ко́мнаты.

5. There are four books on the shelf.
6. I have two dogs: one is white and the other black.
7. We saw Chekhov's play *Three Sisters*.
8. Each person has two feet, two hands, two eyes, two ears, but only one head.
9. Nina needs two more armchairs.
10. This house has four stories.
11. Our old apartment had two rooms.
12. And our new apartment will have four rooms.

DRILLS

A. *Supply the correct form of the numerals and change the nouns in parentheses to the proper case form.*

1. У Ни́ны 2 (сестра́).
2. У меня́ 2 (брат).
3. У дире́ктора 3 (секрета́рша).
4. На пи́сьменном столе́ бы́ло 2 (словарь).
5. У соба́ки 4 (нога́).
6. В и́х кварти́ре 2 (ко́мната).

B. *Translate into Russian.*

1. There are two dictionaries on my desk; one is English and the other is Russian.
2. I need two more lamps.
3. My room has three windows.
4. There are four apartments in this house.
5. He has two sisters; one lives in Leningrad and the other in Moscow.
6. We had two telephones.

8. Modal verbs хоте́ть and мочь

Хоте́ть means *to want, wish, desire*. In the singular it is conjugated as having a first conjugation consonant stem (with the stem **хоч-**) but in the plural as a second conjugation verb (with the stem **хот-**). The past tense is regular хоте́л, о, -а, -и.

Singular (*1st conjugation*)	*Plural* (*2nd conjugation*)
я́ хочу́	мы́ хоти́м
ты́ хо́чешь	вы́ хоти́те
о́н хо́чет	они́ хотя́т

(1) **Хоте́ть** is followed by a noun in the *accusative* case or by an infinitive.

Я́ хочу́ э́ту кни́гу.   I want that book.
Мы́ хоти́м **рабо́тать**.   We want to work.

(2) It is followed, however, by the *genitive* of words expressing abstractions (*fame, happiness*, etc.), and of words denoting divisible matter, in other words, when the word *some* is appropriate.

Вы́ хоти́те хле́ба?   Do you want *some* bread?

---

[3] Note that **ещё** may be translated also as *more, besides, in addition*, but its basic meaning does not change.

Мочь (*to be able, can*) is a first conjugation verb of the type having a consonant stem. The stems of both the first person singular and the third person plural end in **г**; the stems of the other forms of the present tense end in **ж**.

я могу́	мы́ мо́жем
ты́ мо́жешь	вы́ мо́жете
о́н мо́жет	они́ мо́гут

Past tense: **мог, могло́, могла́, могли́.**

Мочь is used with the infinitive to mean *can*:

Вы́ мо́жете бы́ть та́м за́втра?	Can you be there tomorrow?
О́н не мо́г рабо́тать.	He couldn't work.

PATTERN SENTENCES

Хоте́ть

1. —Что́ вы́ тепе́рь **хоти́те** чита́ть? —Мы́ **хоти́м** чита́ть Пу́шкина.
2. О́н ничего́ не **хо́чет** де́лать.
3. —Андре́й, ты́ **хо́чешь** молока́? —Не́т, ничего́ не **хочу́**.
4. Ни́на, **хо́чешь** хле́ба? —Да́, **хочу́**.
5. Вчера́ на конце́рте я́ **хоте́л** спа́ть.
6. —Кто́ **хо́чет** е́сть? Зи́на, ты́ **хо́чешь**? —Не́т, не **хочу́**.
7. Ири́на о́чень[4] **хоте́ла** ва́с ви́деть! Где́ вы́ бы́ли?

1. —What do you want to read now? —We want to read Pushkin.
2. He doesn't want to do anything.
3. —Andrey, do you want some milk? —No, I don't want anything.
4. —Nina, do you want some bread? —Yes, I do.
5. Yesterday at the concert I felt like sleeping (= was sleepy).
6. —Who wants to eat (= who's hungry)? Zina, do you? —No, I don't.
7. Irina wanted to see you very much! Where have you been?

Мочь

1. —Я́ хочу́ писа́ть, но́ не **могу́**. —Ты́ не **мо́жешь** или не хо́чешь? —Я́ не **могу́**, потому́ что у меня́ не́т бума́ги.
2. Вы́ не **мо́жете** чита́ть э́ту кни́гу без словаря́?
3. Вчера́ у Ива́на в ко́мнате игра́ло ра́дио, и мы́ не **могли́** спа́ть. Никто́ не **мо́г** спа́ть.
4. Ни́на вчера́ не **могла́** игра́ть в те́ннис; её раке́тка у О́льги.

1. —I want to write, but can't. —You can't or you won't? —I can't, because I have no paper.
2. Can't you read that book without a dictionary?
3. Yesterday the radio was playing in Ivan's room, and we couldn't sleep. No one could sleep.
4. Yesterday Nina couldn't play tennis; Olga had her racket.

---

[4] **О́чень** (*not* **о́чень мно́го**) is used when intensity and not quantity is involved, as with verbs of wanting, liking, hoping, etc., whereas English uses *very much* in both instances. E.g., О́н **о́чень** хо́чет писа́ть. He *very much* wants to write. *But:* О́н **о́чень мно́го** пи́шет. He writes *very much* (= a great deal).

DRILLS

A. *Fill in the proper forms of the verbs indicated.*

Хоте́ть (*present*)

1. О́н всегда́ . . . . спа́ть.
2. Почему́ вы́ не . . . . отвеча́ть?
3. —Что́ ты́ . . . .? —Я́ . . . . говори́ть.
4. —Кто́ . . . . два́ до́ллара? —Все́ . . . .

5. —Что́ вы́ . . . .? —Я́ ничего́ не . . . . .
6. —Мы́ . . . . зна́ть пра́вду. Вы́ то́же . . . .?
   —Коне́чно! Всё . . . . .

Мочь (*present*)

1. Сего́дня я́ не . . . . чита́ть.
2. Почему́ ты́ не . . . .?
3. Мы́ не . . . . бы́ть до́ма весь де́нь.

4. Всё . . . . э́то де́лать и вы́ то́же . . . . .
5. Ива́н не . . . . бы́ть зде́сь за́втра.

Мочь (*past*)

1. Ива́н не . . . . бы́ть в кла́ссе.
2. А́нна не . . . . бы́ть в кла́ссе.

3. Мы́ не . . . . бы́ть в кла́ссе.
4. Она́ не . . . . бы́ть в кла́ссе.

B. *Translate into Russian.*

1. I cannot eat soup without bread.
2. Vadim wanted to play the piano, but he couldn't; it was too late.
3. Nina wanted to read, but she couldn't; it was already dark.
4. They want to sleep, but they can't! It's so hot!
5. Nobody knows what she wants!
6. —What do you want? —I don't want anything.
7. —We want to play soccer, and you? —I want to also.
8. Why don't they want to do anything?
9. Why can't they work?
10. They couldn't work; it was so cold.
11. Nina couldn't sleep after the concert.
12. How strange! No one could!

Conversation

А́нна чита́ет Че́хова

А́нна. —Бо́б, мо́жет быть ты́ зна́ешь, у кого́ е́сть ру́сско-англи́йский слова́рь? У меня́ не́т, а о́н мне́ о́чень ну́жен. Я́ про́сто не зна́ю, что́ мне́ де́лать!

Бо́б. —Ты́ спра́шивала в университе́тском кни́жном магази́не? Мо́жет быть о́н у ни́х е́сть.

А. —Коне́чно, спра́шивала. Вчера́ у ни́х не́ было словаря́, и они́ не зна́ют, когда́ о́н у ни́х бу́дет!

Б. —А зачём о́н тебе́ та́к ну́жен?

А. —А во́т заче́м: я хочу́ чита́ть Че́хова в оригина́ле. Ру́сского писа́теля на́до чита́ть по-ру́сски. Че́хов в перево́де—не Че́хов. Во́т! Но́ я́ ещё не могу́ чита́ть без словаря́.

Б. —А мо́жет быть ты́ мо́жешь?

А. —Я́ говорю́ тебе́, что не могу́. Мне́ э́то ещё тру́дно. Я хочу́ понима́ть ка́ждое сло́во, кото́рое пи́шет Че́хов. Ка́ждое сло́во, понима́ешь?

Б. —Понима́ю. Зна́ешь что́? Хо́чешь мо́й? Он мне́ сейча́с не ну́жен.

А. —Пра́вда? Е́сли о́н тебе́ сейча́с не ну́жен, о́чень хочу́! Большо́е тебе́ спаси́бо!

Б. —Не́ за что!

PRONUNCIATION DRILL

—bób, móžit biț ti znájiš, ukavó jéşț rúskə-angļísķij slavár̩? uṃiṇá ṇét, a on mṇe óčiṇ núžən. ja próstə ṇiznáju, štó mṇe ḑéləț!

—ti sprášəvələ vuṇiɣirşiţétskəm ķṇížnəm məgaẓíṇi? móžit biț on uṇíx jéşț.

—kaṇéšnə, sprášəvələ. fčirá uṇíx ṇébilə sləvar̩á, i aṇi ṇiznájut, kagdá on uṇíx búḑit.

Answer the following questions in Russian.

1. Чего́ у А́нны не́т? 2. Заче́м А́нне ну́жен ру́сско-англи́йский слова́рь? 3. Где́, ду́мает Бо́б, е́сть тако́й слова́рь? 4. О́н у ни́х е́сть? А е́сли не́т, когда́ о́н у ни́х бу́дет? 5. Когда́ Бо́б слы́шит то́, что А́нне говоря́т в кни́жном магази́не, что́ о́н е́й говори́т?

Reading

Что́ ему́ ещё ну́жно?

В но́вой кварти́ре, в кото́рой тепе́рь живу́т Кали́нины (the Kalinins), четы́ре ко́мнаты: спа́льня, столо́вая,[5] гости́ная,[5] и ко́мната и́х сы́на Ю́рика. В кварти́ре, коне́чно, е́сть ку́хня и ва́нная.[5]

Ю́рик (его́ настоя́щее и́мя Ю́рий) у́мный па́рень, и хоро́ший, приле́жный учени́к. Но́ во́т како́й у него́ хара́ктер: о́н эгои́ст! О́н ре́дко быва́ет дово́лен, и ему́ всегда́ что́-нибудь (something) ну́жно.

В ста́рой кварти́ре, в кото́рой бы́ло то́лько две́ ко́мнаты, у Ю́рика была́ ма́ленькая и тёмная ко́мната, и о́н, коне́чно, хоте́л большу́ю и све́тлую. Тепе́рь у него́ така́я ко́мната, как о́н хоте́л.

Хотя́ инжене́р-эле́ктрик Кали́нин, оте́ц Ю́рика, не о́чень бога́тый челове́к, о́н и его́ жена́ покупа́ют сы́ну то́, что сы́ну ну́жно, и то́, что о́н хо́чет. И́м не всегда́ легко́ э́то де́лать, но́ у ни́х то́лько оди́н сы́н, и они́ ра́ды де́лать то́, что ему́ прия́тно.

У Ю́рика тепе́рь крова́ть, а не ма́ленький у́зкий дива́н, как э́то бы́ло в ста́рой кварти́ре. В его́ ко́мнате тепе́рь е́сть кре́сло, два́ сту́ла, две́ по́лки: одна́ высо́кая,

---

[5] See footnote 7, p. 152.

а друга́я ни́зкая. Ю́рик тепе́рь хо́чет не просто́й сто́л, как у него́ есть, а настоя́-
щий пи́сьменный, и они́ покупа́ют ему́ тако́й сто́л. У него́ да́же е́сть тепе́рь
ковёр, пра́вда ма́ленький, но—ковёр! В ко́мнате е́сть две́ ла́мпы: одна́ на
пи́сьменном столе́, а друга́я у крова́ти (= by the bed). Тепе́рь у него́ есть всё,
что ему́ ну́жно, и в ко́мнате о́чень прия́тно. На ни́зкой по́лке стои́т гло́бус
(globe). На одно́й стене́ ка́рта Сове́тского Сою́за и портре́т Пу́шкина, а на
друго́й, у две́ри, больша́я фотогра́фия: Ю́рик и его́ три́ това́рища игра́ют в
баскетбо́л.

Но́ тепе́рь Ю́рик говори́т, что его́ те́ннисная раке́та сли́шком ста́рая, и что
ему́ нужна́ но́вая! Оте́ц покупа́ет ему́ но́вую раке́тку. А вчера́ Ю́рик бы́л у своего́
това́рища Сергея Моро́зова, и ви́дел у него́ япо́нский фотоаппара́т, и тепе́рь о́н
то́же хо́чет тако́й! Но́ оте́ц Серге́я диплома́т, и ему́ легко́ покупа́ть всё, что сы́н
хо́чет. Гм . . . .[6] говори́т оте́ц Ю́рика. Гм . . . . говори́т ма́ть . . . .

Э́то коне́ц расска́за. Бу́дет у Ю́рика япо́нский фотоаппара́т, и́ли не́т?

Answer these questions in Russian.

1. Кака́я была́ и́х ста́рая кварти́ра? 2. Кака́я профе́ссия у Кали́нина? 3. По-
чему́ говоря́т, что у Ю́рика не о́чень хоро́ший хара́ктер? 4. Почему́ роди́тели
(= parents) покупа́ют сы́ну всё, что о́н хо́чет? 5. На чём спа́л Ю́рик в ста́рой
кварти́ре? 6. На чём о́н тепе́рь спи́т? 7. На како́м столе́ стои́т одна́ ла́мпа?
8. Где́ гло́бус? 9. Где́ фотогра́фия, на кото́рой четы́ре това́рища игра́ют в
баскетбо́л? 10. Почему́ ему́ нужна́ но́вая раке́тка? 11. Че́й сы́н Серге́й
Моро́зов?

Answer from your own experience.

1. У ва́с це́лая кварти́ра и́ли то́лько ко́мната? 2. Что́ есть в ва́шей ко́мнате
(и́ли кварти́ре)? 3. У ва́с есть всё, что ва́м ну́жно? 4. На чём вы́ спи́те?
5. Како́й сто́л в ва́шей ко́мнате? 6. Что́ ва́м ещё ну́жно? 7. Како́й у ва́с
хара́ктер?

Vocabulary

бога́тый rich, wealthy
ва́нная[7] bathroom
высо́кий high, tall
гости́ная[7] living room
дово́лен (*fem.* дово́льна; *pl.* дово́льны) satisfied,
  content, pleased
дово́льно (*adv.*) rather, fairly, enough
друго́й other, another; different
е́сли if

за́втра tomorrow
зачем what for, why
кни́жный магази́н bookstore
ковёр (*gen.* ковра́) rug, carpet
лени́вый lazy
маши́на machine; car
ме́бель (*fem.*; *no plural*) furniture
недово́лен (*like* дово́лен) dissatisfied
ни́зкий [ṇísḳij] low

---

[6] Гм . . . . is pronounced *hmmm . . .*, and expresses doubt or hesitation.
[7] These words are declined as adjectives, though they function as do nouns; the noun ко́мната is
  understood to accompany them:

  Мы́ бы́ли в гости́ной.   We were in the *living room*.

нога́ leg, foot
обе́д dinner
перево́д translation
по́мощь (*fem.*) help, aid
приле́жный diligent, industrious
про́сто simply
расска́з (short) story
роди́тели (*pl.*) parents
ру́сско-англи́йский Russian-English
соба́ка dog
совсе́м quite, entirely

совсе́м не (нет) not at all
сосе́д (*fem.* сосе́дка [saşétkə]) neighbor
спа́льня bedroom
столо́вая[7] dining room
това́рищ (*masc. used for both genders*) comrade, friend
у́хо ear
учени́к (*fem.* учени́ца) pupil[8]
хара́ктер disposition, character
хотя́ although, though
ча́шка cup

VERBS

хоте́ть (*irr.*, see p. 148) to want, wish, desire
мочь (I: могу́, мо́жешь, . . . мо́гут) to be able (can)

EXPRESSIONS

мо́жет быть maybe, perhaps
Не мо́жет бы́ть! It can't be! I can't believe it!
бо́льше не no more, no longer
ещё оди́н (одна́, одно́, *etc.*) one more, another, an additional
большо́е спаси́бо many thanks
Не́ за что! Don't mention it (in reply to thanks)!
Я про́сто не зна́ю. I simply don't know.
Что́ мне́ де́лать? What am I to do?

VOCABULARY REVIEW

Parts of the Body	Clothing	Furnishings	
голова́	пла́тье	ме́бель	ковёр
лицо́	костю́м	стол	карти́на
нос	шля́па	пи́сьменный сто́л	по́лка
глаз	блу́зка	стул	ра́дио
рот	ю́бка	кре́сло	телефо́н
у́хо		крова́ть	телеви́зор
рука́		ла́мпа	холоди́льник
нога́		дива́н	

Rooms	Occupations	Food and Drink	Buildings
гости́ная	учи́тель/-ница	хлеб	дом
столо́вая	профе́ссор	мя́со	шко́ла
ва́нная	студе́нт/-ка	сыр	теа́тр
ку́хня	учени́к/учени́ца	ры́ба	музе́й
спа́льня	до́ктор	молоко́	библиоте́ка
кабине́т	инжене́р	вода́	магази́н
	писа́тель/-ница	вино́	кни́жный магази́н
	журнали́ст/-ка	во́дка	гости́ница
			рестора́н

---

[8] The word студе́нт/-ка refers only to university students; учени́к/учени́ца and шко́льник/шко́льница refer to elementary or secondary students.

In the Classroom	Geography (nouns)	Geography (adjectives)
учи́тель	Росси́я	ру́сский
учи́тельница	Сове́тский Сою́з	сове́тский
учени́к	Сиби́рь (*fem.*)	англи́йский
учени́ца	Аме́рика	европе́йский
доска́	Евро́па	францу́зский
учéбник	Кита́й	америка́нский
слова́рь		
уро́к	**Russian Cities**	**For Reading**
	Ленингра́д	чте́ние
профе́ссор	Москва́	кни́га
студе́нт/-ка	Ки́ев	рома́н
	Одéсса	пье́са
		расска́з
	Adverbs of Time	статья́
	когда́	газе́та
	всегда́	журна́л
	ча́сто	
	иногда́	
	ре́дко	
	никогда́	

Give opposites of the following:

све́тлый	блонди́н/-ка	молодо́й	продава́ть
ни́зкий	ме́ньше	ску́чный	рабо́тать
лени́вый	бы́стро	хоро́ший	но́вый
прия́тный	бе́лый	лёгкий	ма́ленький
у́мный	мла́дший	ночь	у́тро
пло́хо	о́тдых	после́дний	ле́то
нача́ло	ле́тний	конча́ть	мно́го
жа́ркий	дешёвый	закрыва́ть	широ́кий
ра́но	неда́вно	отвеча́ть	

Second conjugation verbs (continued) • Instrumental case of nouns •
Instrumental of pronouns and adjectives • The preposition с with the
instrumental • Predicate instrumental • Instrumental of time •
Russian names • Давно́ and до́лго • Conversation 1: Я звони́л
вам у́тром, днём и ве́чером • Conversation 2: В рестора́не
«Во́лга» • Reading: Всё э́то бы́ло давно́

Unit 11

Grammar

1. Second conjugation verbs (continued)

A. Stress patterns of the second conjugation. Like verbs of the first conjugation, second conjugation verbs have three possible stress patterns for the present
tense: (1) stress on the stem throughout; (2) stress on the ending throughout; and (3)
a shifting stress—on the ending in the infinitive and first person singular and on the
last syllable of the stem in all other forms of the present.

	(1) *Stress on Stem*	(2) *Stress on Ending*	(3) *Shifting Stress*
	по́мнить	**стоя́ть**	**кури́ть**
	(to remember)	(to stand)	(to smoke)
1st sing.	я по́мню	я стою́	я курю́
2nd sing.	ты по́мнишь	ты стои́шь	ты ку́ришь (←stress shifts)
3rd sing.	он по́мнит	он стои́т	он ку́рит
1st pl.	мы по́мним	мы стои́м	мы ку́рим
2nd pl.	вы по́мните	вы стои́те	вы ку́рите
3rd pl.	они́ по́мнят	они́ стоя́т	они́ ку́рят

B. Л after labial consonants. Second conjugation verbs with stems ending in
the labial consonants **б, в, м, п,** and **ф** have an **л** inserted after the labial consonant
in the first person singular, e.g., in **спать** *to sleep,* and **люби́ть** *to love*:

спать *to sleep*	**люби́ть** *to love, like*
я сплю́	я люблю́
ты спи́шь	ты лю́бишь (← stress shifts)
он спи́т	он лю́бит
мы спи́м	мы лю́бим
вы спи́те	вы лю́бите
они́ спя́т	они́ лю́бят

155

C. Since the vowel letters **я** and **ю** may not be written after the consonants **ж, ц, ч, ш,** and **щ** (see Spelling Rule 3 on p. 22), verbs with stems ending in these consonants have in the first person singular the ending **-у** (not **-ю**) and in the third person plural **-ат** (not **-ят**).

<table>
<tr><td></td><td>Compare</td></tr>
<tr><td>держа́ть to hold, keep</td><td>говори́ть to speak, talk</td></tr>
<tr><td>я́ держу́</td><td>я́ говорю́</td></tr>
<tr><td>ты́ де́ржишь (← stress)</td><td>ты́ говори́шь</td></tr>
<tr><td>о́н де́ржит</td><td>о́н говори́т</td></tr>
<tr><td>мы́ де́ржим</td><td>мы́ говори́м</td></tr>
<tr><td>вы́ де́ржите</td><td>вы́ говори́те</td></tr>
<tr><td>они́ де́ржат</td><td>они́ говоря́т</td></tr>
</table>

Similarly:

> лежа́ть *to lie* (*recline*), *be lying*: я́ лежу́, ты́ лежи́шь, . . . они́ лежа́т
>
> слы́шать *to hear*: я́ слы́шу, ты́ слы́шишь, . . . они́ слы́шат

Remember that лежа́ть, слы́шать, держа́ть (like many verbs ending in **-жать** or **-шать**) are *second conjugation*, not first

> *But:* слу́шать, **I**: слу́шаю, слу́шаешь *to listen*

D. Consonant changes. In the second conjugation, *mutations* of the final consonant of the stem affect *the first person only*. For example, final **д** of the stem becomes **ж** in the first person singular.

<table>
<tr><td>сиде́ть to be sitting</td><td>ви́деть to see</td></tr>
<tr><td>я́ сижу́</td><td>я́ ви́жу</td></tr>
<tr><td>ты́ сиди́шь</td><td>ты́ ви́дишь</td></tr>
<tr><td>о́н сиди́т</td><td>о́н ви́дит</td></tr>
<tr><td>мы́ сиди́м</td><td>мы́ ви́дим</td></tr>
<tr><td>вы́ сиди́те</td><td>вы́ ви́дите</td></tr>
<tr><td>они́ сидя́т</td><td>они́ ви́дят</td></tr>
</table>

PATTERN SENTENCES

1. —Я́ не **ви́жу**, где́ они́ **стоя́т**, а вы́ **ви́дите**? —Да́, я́ **ви́жу**.

1. —I don't see where they are standing. Do you see? —Yes, I do.

2. —Вы́ **ви́дите**, где́ **лежи́т** мо́й слова́рь? —Не́т, не **ви́жу**. —О́н **лежи́т** на сту́ле.

2. —Can you see where my dictionary is lying? —No, I can't. —It's lying on the chair.

3. Две́ газе́ты и два́ журна́ла **лежа́т** на дива́не.

3. Two newspapers and two magazines are lying on the sofa.

4. Когда́ я́ слу́шаю ра́дио, я́ всегда́ **сижу́** на э́том дива́не.

4. When I listen to the radio, I always sit on this couch.

5. Почему́ они́ **сидя́т** так далеко́?

5. Why do they sit so far away?

6. —Что́ вы́ **де́ржите** в руке́? —Я́ **держу́** два́ до́ллара.

6. —What are you holding in your hand? —I am holding two dollars.

7. —Вы́ ку́рите? —Да́, я́ курю́, но́ ма́ло. До́ктор говори́т, что я́ совсе́м не до́лжен кури́ть, но́ э́то тру́дно, когда́ всё ку́рят.

7. —Do you smoke? —Yes, I smoke, but (only a) little. The doctor says that I shouldn't smoke at all, but that's hard (to do) when everyone smokes.

8. —Вы́ хорошо́ спи́те? —Не́т, я́ пло́хо сплю́. Когда́ жа́рко, почти́ всё пло́хо спя́т.

8. —Do you sleep well? —No, I sleep badly. When it's hot almost everyone sleeps badly.

9. —Алло́! Алло́! Я́ ва́с не слы́шу. А вы́ меня́ слы́шите? —Да́, я́ ва́с хорошо́ слы́шу.

9. —Hello, hello! I don't hear you. Do you hear me? —Yes, I hear you (very) well.

10. —Вы́ лю́бите Толсто́го? — Да́, о́чень люблю́. По-мо́ему, всё его́ лю́бят.

10. —Do you like Tolstoy? —Yes, very much. I think everybody likes him.

11. Мы́ о́чень лю́бим сиде́ть до́ма.

11. We like to stay at home very much.

12. У А́нны Ива́новны о́чень плоха́я па́мять. Она́ сего́дня не по́мнит, что бы́ло вчера́!

12. Anna Ivanovna has a very bad memory. She doesn't remember today what happened yesterday!

DRILLS

A. *Supply the correct forms of the verb in parentheses in the present tense for questions and answers.*

1. —Кого́ вы́ (ви́деть)? —Мы́ . . . . и́х.
2. —Кого́ Ива́н . . . .? —О́н . . . . своего́ прия́теля.
3. —Кого́ я́ . . . .? —Вы́ . . . . учи́теля.
4. —Кого́ они́ . . . .? —Они́ . . . . Ива́на.
5. —Кого́ мы́ . . . .? —Вы́ . . . . О́льгу.
6. —На чём вы́ (сиде́ть)? —Мы́ . . . . на дива́не.
7. —На чём о́н . . . .? —О́н . . . . на кре́сле.
8. —На чём ты́ . . . .? —Я́ . . . . на сту́ле.
9. —На чём она́ . . . .? —Она́ . . . . на кре́сле.
10. —На чём они́ . . . .? —Они́ . . . . на дива́не.
11. —На чём я́ . . . .? —Ты́ . . . . на крова́ти.
12. —Почему́ ты́ не (спа́ть)? —Потому́ что я́ не (хоте́ть).
13. —Почему́ Ива́н не . . . .? —Потому́ что о́н не . . . . .
14. —Почему́ вы́ не . . . .? —Потому́ что я́ не . . . . .
15. —Почему́ О́льга не . . . .? —Потому́ что она́ не . . . . .
16. —Почему́ они́ не . . . .? —Потому́ что они́ не . . . . .
17. —Почему́ мы́ не . . . .? —Потому́ что вы́ не . . . . .
18. —Почему́ я́ не . . . .? —Потому́ что ты́ не . . . . .

B. *Supply the correct present tense form of* **люби́ть** *and translate the infinitives in parentheses.*

1. —Что́ о́н (люби́ть)? —О́н . . . . (to smoke).
2. —Что́ я́ . . . .? —Вы́ . . . . (to sleep).
3. —Что́ они́ . . . .? —Они́ . . . . (to listen).
4. —Что́ она́ . . . .? —Она́ . . . . (to play).
5. —Что́ Ива́н . . . .? —О́н . . . . (to eat).
6. —Что́ вы́ . . . .? —Я́ . . . . (to rest).

C. *Supply the correct present tense form of the verbs in parentheses.*

1. Я́ ничего́ не (по́мнить).
2. Они́ ничего́ не . . . . .
3. Ты́ ничего́ не . . . . .
4. Мы́ ничего́ не . . . . .
5. Она́ ничего́ не . . . . .
6. Вы́ ничего́ не . . . . .

7. Чтó онѝ (держáть)?
8. Чтó ты́ ....?
9. Чтó вы́ ....?

10. Чтó я́ ....?
11. Чтó Óльга ....?
12. Чтó мы́ ....?

D. *Translate into English.*

1. Мóй отéц всегдá дéржит э́тот докумéнт в своём пи́сьменном столé.
2. Дóктор держáл Сергéя двé недéли дóма в кровáти.
3. —Вы́ пóмните истóрию, котóрую Вади́м расскáзывал на послéдней вечери́нке? —Нéт, не пóмню. Я́ егó не слу́шал.
4. Я́ не понимáю, о чём вы́ говори́те.
5. Как стрáнно, что онѝ нáс ещё пóмнят! Онѝ так давнó нáс не ви́дели!
6. —Почему́ ты́ так мнóго ку́ришь? —Я́ не могу́ не кури́ть.
7. Я́ не понимáю, почему́ мы́ вáс тепéрь так рéдко ви́дим.
8. —Ты́ ви́дишь, что тáм на пóлке стоя́т двé кни́ги, а учéбник лежи́т на столé. —Дá, ви́жу.
9. Пóсле обéда отéц лю́бит лежáть на дивáне, котóрый стои́т в моéй кóмнате.
10. —Чтó вáм пи́шет Ивáн? —Óн нáм совсéм не пи́шет.

E. *Replace the infinitives in parentheses with the proper form of the present tense and translate.*

1. Я́ не (пóмнить), гдé онѝ (жить), а онѝ не (пóмнить), гдé я́ (жить)!
2. Я́ не (понимáть), что вы́ (говори́ть), а вы́ не (понимáть), что я́ (говори́ть).
3. Я́ не (хотéть) слы́шать, что онѝ (говори́ть), а онѝ не (хотéть) слы́шать, что я́ (говори́ть).
4. —Ты́ (слы́шать), что я́ (говори́ть)? —Дá, я́ (слы́шать), что ты́ (говори́ть).
5. Онѝ не (понимáть), почему́ мы́ и́х не (слы́шать), а мы́ не (понимáть), почему́ онѝ нáс не (слы́шать).
6. —Ктó (спать) в э́той кóмнате? —Здéсь я́ (спать), а онѝ (спать) в кабинéте.
7. —Почему́ ты́ (стоя́ть)? —Потому́ что вы́ (стоя́ть) и всé (стоя́ть).
8. —Я́ не (люби́ть) стоя́ть. —А чтó вы́ (люби́ть)? —Я́ (люби́ть) лежáть.
9. Мы́ не (ви́деть), что óн (держáть) в рукé.
10. Я́ (ви́деть), что онѝ (держáть) прогрáмму.
11. —Я́ не (пóмнить), вáш брáт (кури́ть) или нéт? —В моéй семьé всé (кури́ть). Как стрáнно, что вы́ не (пóмнить)!
12. —Чтó ты́ (дéлать)? —Я́ (сидéть) и (писáть) письмó сестрé.
13. Онѝ почти́ всегдá (сидéть) дóма. Онѝ (писáть), (кури́ть), или (спать).
14. —Я́ не (пóмнить), гдé вы́ (жить). —Я́ (жить) в тóм высóком дóме.

F. *Translate into Russian.*

1. —What are you writing? —I am writing a translation.
2. —Do you see him often? —We don't see him at all.
3. I don't remember where she lives. Perhaps you remember?
4. She lives at Anna's, and I live there too. We live in a large apartment.
5. I see Boris almost every day, and I am always glad to see him.
6. We never see Nina. Only Lena sees her.
7. I hear very well what you are saying. Do you hear me?
8. They say that they remember us well. But I don't remember them.
9. They have a good memory. That's (вот) why they remember everything.
10. I don't understand why you smoke! You shouldn't smoke!

11. Everybody smokes; that's (вот) why I smoke too.
12. —Why am I sitting while you are standing? —Everybody is sitting except me.
13. —What is he holding? —He is holding two dictionaries.
14. I have a good memory; I remember well the monument you are talking about.
15. I often write to my family.
16. His father and mother live far (away) and see their son rather seldom.

2. Instrumental case of nouns

The instrumental case is used to express the means, instrument, manner, or agent by which an action is performed.

Я пишу́ **перо́м**.
I write *with* (by means of) a pen (*instrument*).

Я посыла́ю письмо́ **по́чтой**.
I am sending the letter *by* mail (*means*).

О́н говори́т **гро́мким го́лосом**.
He speaks in a loud voice (*manner*).

ENDINGS OF NOUNS IN THE INSTRUMENTAL SINGULAR

	Hard	Soft
Masc. \ Neut. ∫	**-ом**	**-ём** (unstr. **-ем**)
Fem. I	**-ой**	**-ёй** (unstr. **-ей**)[1]
Fem. II		**-ью**

NOUNS IN THE INSTRUMENTAL SINGULAR

	NOMINATIVE	INSTRUMENTAL
Masc.	стол [stól.] гость [góşţ.] музе́й [muẓéj.]	столо́м [stal.óm] го́стем [góşţ.əm] музе́ем [muẓéj.əm]
Neut.	окно́ [akn.ó] по́ле [pól̦.ə]	окно́м [akn.óm] по́лем [pól̦.əm]
Fem. I	жена́ [žin.á] ку́хня [kúxṇ.ə]	жено́й [žin.ój] ку́хней [kúxṇ.əj]
Fem. II	ночь [nóč̦.]	но́чью [nóč̦.ju]

[1] The feminine instrumental has the alternate ending **-ою/-ею**, which is used mostly in poetry.

The *unstressed* instrumental endings, masculine and neuter [-əm] and feminine [-əj], are always written -ем and -ей respectively for nouns with stems ending in ж, ш, ц, ч, and щ (according to Spelling Rule 1, unstressed o cannot be written after these letters):

Masc.	му́ж—му́жем ме́сяц—ме́сяцем това́рищ—това́рищем (comrade)	(but: но́ж—ножо́м) (but: оте́ц—отцо́м) (but: бо́рщ—борщо́м) (a soup)
Neut.	со́лнце—со́лнцем (sun)	(but: лицо́—лицо́м)
Fem.	кры́ша—кры́шей (roof) да́ча—да́чей (summer cottage)	(but: душа́—душо́й) (soul) (but: свеча́—свечо́й) (candle)

PATTERN SENTENCES

(Note that the instrumental of что is **чем**, of кто is **кем**.)

1. —**Чём** вы́ пи́шете, перо́м или карандашо́м?
   —Я́ всегда́ пишу́ перо́м.
2. О́н де́лает же́ст руко́й.
3. —**Чём** Ни́на пи́шет на доске́? —Она́ пи́шет ме́лом, как все́.
4. О́н де́ржит шля́пу руко́й, потому́ что ве́тер.
5. Андре́й па́льцем пока́зывает на ка́рте, где́ о́н жи́л.
6. Оте́ц о́чень дово́лен² О́льгой и Ка́тей.
7. Учи́тельница дово́льна Ива́ном и Андре́ем.
8. Профе́ссор недово́лен студе́нтом, а студе́нт недово́лен профе́ссором.
9. Ива́н е́л варе́нье ло́жкой.
10. —**Кём** дово́льна ма́ть? —Ни́ной.

1. —What do you write with, a pen or a pencil?
   —I always write with a pen.
2. He is making a gesture with his hand.
3. —What does Nina write with on the blackboard?
   —She writes with chalk, as everybody does.
4. He is holding his hat with his hand because it's windy.
5. Andrey is pointing out on the map with his finger where he used to live.
6. Father is very pleased with Olga and Katya.
7. The teacher is pleased with Ivan and Andrey.
8. The professor is dissatisfied with the student, and the student is dissatisfied with the professor.
9. Ivan ate the jam with a spoon.
10. —With whom is Mother pleased? —With Nina.

DRILL

Put the words in parentheses into the proper case form and translate.

1. На доске́ все́ пи́шут (мел).
2. Я́ держу́ бума́гу (рука́).
3. Мы́ ду́маем (голова́).
4. Профе́ссор дово́лен (А́нна).
5. Мы́ дово́льны (до́ктор).
6. Студе́нтка недово́льна (профе́ссор).
7. Ма́ть недово́льна (Ива́н).
8. Я́ никогда́ не пишу́ (каранда́ш).

---

² Note that дово́лен and недово́лен require the instrumental without preposition (see section 4 below).

9. Что́ о́н де́лает (нога́)?
10. Мы́ дово́льны (го́сть).
11. Они́ бы́ли о́чень дово́льны (дере́вня).
12. Учи́тель дово́лен (Ка́тя), но́ недово́лен (О́льга).
13. Я́ пока́зываю (па́лец), где́ мо́й до́м.
14. —Че́м о́н е́л су́п? —Коне́чно, (ло́жка).

3. Instrumental of pronouns and adjectives

ENDINGS OF ADJECTIVES IN THE
INSTRUMENTAL CASE

	Hard	*Soft*
Masc. *Neut.*	-ым	-им
Fem.	-ой[3]	-ей[3]

ADJECTIVES AND PRONOUNS IN THE INSTRUMENTAL SINGULAR

	NOMINATIVE *Masculine*	*Neuter*	INSTRUMENTAL *Masculine and Neuter*
3rd pers. pron.	он	оно́	им [ím]
Adjectives	но́вый си́ний хоро́ший ру́сский	но́вое си́нее хоро́шее ру́сское	но́вым [nóv.im] си́ним [sí.ṇim] хоро́шим [xaróš.im] ру́сским [rúṣķ.im][4]
Possessives	мой наш	моё на́ше	мои́м [maj.ím] на́шим [náš.im]
Demonstratives	э́тот тот	э́то то	э́тим [éṭ.im] тем [ṭ.ém]
Interrogatives	кто	что	кем [ķ.ém] чем [č̦.ém]
Numeral 1	оди́н	одно́	одни́м [adṇ.ím]

[3] The feminine forms have the alternate endings -ою (hard) and -ею (soft) throughout this declension, but these forms are largely poetic.
[4] Adjectives with stems ending in г, к, х have the ending -им in the masculine-neuter instrumental (Spelling Rule 2).

	Feminine	
3rd pers. pron.	она́	ей [j.éj] or éю [j.éju]
Adjectives	но́вая си́няя хоро́шая	но́вой [nóv.əj] си́ней [şíṇ.əj] хоро́шей [xaróš.əj]
Possessives	моя́ на́ша	мое́й [maj.éj] на́шей [náš.əj]
Demonstratives	э́та та	э́той [ét.əj] той [t.ój]
Numeral 1	одна́	одно́й [adn.ój]

INSTRUMENTAL OF PERSONAL PRONOUNS

Nom.	я	ты	он оно́	она́	мы	вы	они́
Instr.	мной	тобо́й	им	ей	на́ми	ва́ми	и́ми

PATTERN SENTENCES

1. —Каки́м карандашо́м ты́ пи́шешь, кра́сным или чёрным? —Чёрным.
2. —Каки́м ме́лом вы́ лю́бите писа́ть? —Коне́чно, бе́лым! —А я́ люблю́ писа́ть жёлтым.
3. —Како́й руко́й пи́шет Бори́с? —Óн пи́шет ле́вой.
4. Óн ещё не уме́ет писа́ть перо́м.
5. Ле́на о́чень дово́льна свое́й но́вой си́ней шля́пой.
6. Мы́ о́чень дово́льны на́шим но́вым профе́ссором, и о́н дово́лен на́ми.
7. Они́ недово́льны свои́м ста́ршим сы́ном.
8. Профе́ссор о́чень дово́лен мно́й, и я́ дово́льна и́м.
9. Почему́ вы́ говори́те таки́м ти́хим го́лосом?
10. Изда́тель дово́лен её после́дним рома́ном.

1. What sort of pencil do you write with, a red or a black one? —With a black one.
2. —What kind of chalk do you like to write with? —With white chalk, of course! —But I like to write with yellow chalk.
3. —Which hand does Boris write with? —He writes with his left hand.
4. He still doesn't know how to write with a pen.
5. Lena is very pleased with her new blue hat.
6. We are very pleased with our new professor, and he is pleased with us.
7. They are displeased with their eldest son.
8. The professor is very pleased with me, and I am pleased with him.
9. Why do you speak in such a low voice?
10. The publisher is pleased with her last novel.

DRILLS

A. *Put the words in parentheses into the correct case and translate.*

1. Я́ пишу́ (жёлтый ме́л).
2. Ни́на пи́шет (чёрный каранда́ш).
3. Я́ не люблю́ писа́ть (но́вое перо́).
4. Бори́с пока́зывает (то́лстый па́лец) на ка́рте, где́ о́н жи́л.
5. Ка́к ты́ мо́жешь писа́ть (ле́вая рука́)?
6. Я́ не могу́ рабо́тать (одна́ рука́).
7. Мы́ дово́льны (но́вый слова́рь).
8. Áнна дово́льна (си́нее пла́тье).

B. *Substitute according to the model.*

Model: Áнна довóльна порфéссором.
Профéссор довóлен Áнной.

1. **Нóвый учи́тель** довóлен Бори́сом.
2. **Мы́** довóльны на́шим дóктором.
3. **Óн** довóлен ва́ми.

4. **Нóвый дирéктор** довóлен нóвой секрета́ршей.
5. **Твóй профéссор** довóлен тобóй?
6. **Они́** довóльны на́ми.

4. The preposition с with the instrumental

(1) With the instrumental case, the preposition **с** means *with*, *along with*, *together with*:

Студéнт говори́т **с профéссором**.
The student is talking *with* the professor.

Я́ пью́ ча́й **с лимóном**.
I drink tea *with* lemon.

Вчера́ я рабóтал **с бра́том** [zbrátəm].
I worked *with* my brother yesterday.

(2) When *with* cannot be replaced by *along with* or *together with* in an English sentence, the instrumental is used *without a preposition*:

Я́ пишу́ **карандашóм**.
I write with a pencil (*by means of a pencil*).

Óн довóлен **свои́м дóктором**.
He is pleased with his doctor.

But: Óн рабóтает **с дóктором** [zdóktərəm].
He works with the doctor (*together with the doctor*).

(3) With a double object **с** (like other Russian prepositions) is usually repeated:

Я́ бы́л та́м **с** бра́том и **с** егó прия́телем.
I was there with my brother and (with) his friend.

(4) The form **со** is used before certain words beginning with a consonant cluster, e.g.,

со мнóй (*with me*)
со всéй семьёй (*with the whole family*).

(5) The preposition **с** is used with the instrumental of abstract nouns to form phrases of the type:

с удовóльствием	with pleasure
с аппети́том	with an appetite
с трудóм	with difficulty

But: Óн говори́т грóмким гóлосом (without **с**).
He speaks in a loud voice.

(6) The following idiomatic expressions are very typical in Russian and are used frequently:

Мы́ с . . . . (+ instr.) (someone) and I
Вы́ с . . . . (+ instr.) (someone) and you

Сего́дня **мы́ с бра́том** [zbrátəm] бы́ли в музе́е.
Today my brother and I went to the museum.

Вы́ с жено́й [žžinój] давно́ в Аме́рике?
Have you and your wife been in America long?

(7) After the preposition **с** (as after other prepositions), the declined forms of the third person pronouns have a prefixed **н-**.

с ним	with him, it
с ней	with her, it
с ни́ми	with them

	Я́ ча́сто говори́л **с ни́ми**.	I often spoke with them.
But:	**Я́** говори́л **с и́х** сы́ном.	I spoke with their son.

PATTERN SENTENCES

1. —**С ке́м** ты́ была́ в теа́тре? —Я́ была́ с одни́м дру́гом. Мы́ сиде́ли **ря́дом с а́втором** пье́сы!

2. Вади́м живёт тепе́рь **с отцо́м**. О́н живёт **с ни́м** уже́ два́ ме́сяца.[5]

3. О́льга была́ **с А́нной** в рестора́не, а пото́м она́ была́ **с ней** у до́ктора.

4. Мы́ хоти́м игра́ть в волейбо́л **с ва́ми**. Вы́ хоти́те игра́ть **с на́ми**?

5. Вади́м не хо́чет рабо́тать **со мно́й**, и я́ не хочу́ рабо́тать ни **с ни́м**, ни **с** его́ глу́пым дру́гом.

6. —**С ке́м** бы́л Бори́с вчера́ на вечери́нке? —О́н бы́л **со мно́й** и **с** мое́й мла́дшей сестро́й Ве́рочкой.

7. —**С че́м** Ива́н Ива́нович обы́чно пьёт ча́й, **с лимо́ном** или **с молоко́м**? —О́н пьёт ча́й то́лько **с са́харом**.

8. О́льга Ива́новна, как и я́, лю́бит пи́ть ча́й без са́хара, но́ **с варе́ньем**.

9. В францу́зском рестора́не мы́ снача́ла е́ли заку́ску, а пото́м о́чень вку́сное мя́со **с карто́фелем** и **с сала́том**.

1. —With whom were you at the theater? —With a friend. We sat beside the author of the play!

2. Vadim now lives with his father. He has been living with him for two months now.[5]

3. Olga was at the restaurant with Anna, and then went with her to the doctor's.

4. We want to play volleyball with you. Do you want to play with us?

5. Vadim doesn't want to work with me, and I don't want to work either with him or with his stupid friend.

6. —With whom was Boris at the party yesterday? —He was with me and my younger sister Verochka.

7. —With what does Ivan Ivanovich usually take his tea, with lemon or milk? —He drinks tea only with sugar.

8. Olga Ivanovna, like me, likes to drink tea without sugar, but with jam.

9. At the French restaurant we first ate hors-d'œuvres, and then very delicious meat with potatoes and salad.

---

[5] When a period of time is given, Russian verbs in the present tense correspond to the English verbs in the *present perfect* tense, e.g.,

Мы́ ту́т **живём** две́ неде́ли.	We *have been living* here for two weeks.
Мы́ ту́т давно́ **живём**.	We *have been living* here for a long time.

10. Но́вый инжене́р говори́т по-англи́йски пра́-
вильно, но **с ру́сским** акце́нт**ом**, и я́ с трудо́м
его́ понима́ю.

11. Смирно́в, как всегда́, е́л **с больши́м** удово́ль-
стви**ем** и **с** аппети́т**ом**.

12. —**С че́м** вы́ пьёте ко́фе? —Я́, как и вы́, пью́
ко́фе **с** молоко́**м** и **с** са́хар**ом**.

10. The new engineer speaks English correctly, but
with a Russian accent, and I have difficulty
understanding him (understand him with
difficulty).

11. Smirnov, as always, ate with great enjoyment
and appetite.

12. —With what do you drink coffee? —I, like
you, drink coffee with milk and sugar.

DRILLS

A. *Translate into English.*

Хотя́ А́нна живёт тепе́рь в до́ме ря́дом с на́шим, она́ о́чень ре́дко у на́с
быва́ет. На́м с жено́й жа́ль, что мы́ так ре́дко её ви́дим, и так ре́дко с не́й раз-
гова́риваем. Она́ така́я ми́лая и у́мная де́вушка!

Га́ля, сестра́ мое́й жены́, живёт в одно́й кварти́ре с А́нной и рабо́тает вме́сте
с не́й в Истори́ческом музе́е. Га́ля говори́т, что дире́ктор музе́я о́чень дово́лен
рабо́той А́нны.

У А́нны мно́го рабо́ты: она́ весь де́нь на слу́жбе, а ве́чером (in the evening) она́
ча́сто помога́ет по хозя́йству одно́й ста́рой же́нщине, у кото́рой плохо́е здоро́вье,
и кото́рая совсе́м одна́. Хорошо́, что э́та же́нщина живёт в кварти́ре ря́дом с
кварти́рой, где живёт А́нна.

А́нна, коне́чно, устаёт (gets tired), но Га́ля говори́т, что она́ дово́льна свое́й
жи́знью, дово́льна свое́й интере́сной рабо́той в музе́е, и ра́да, что мо́жет помо-
га́ть челове́ку, кото́рому так нужна́ её по́мощь.

Жа́ль, что мы́ давно́ не ви́дели э́ту ми́лую де́вушку.

B. *Give answers to the questions asked, supplying the correct case form of the words in
the right-hand column.*

Вопро́с		**Отве́т**	
С че́м	вы́ е́ли хле́б? вы́ пи́ли ча́й? вы́ пи́ли ко́фе? вы́ е́ли мя́со?	С	(сы́р) (са́хар) и с (варе́нье) (молоко́) (карто́фель) и с (сала́т).
С ке́м	бы́л Бори́с в Босто́не? была́ А́нна в Москве́? вы́ бы́ли на конце́рте? оте́ц говори́л по́сле обе́да? Ро́берт говори́т по-ру́сски?	О́н бы́л с (сестра́). . . . . с (дру́г). . . . . с (Ве́ра). . . . . с (го́сть). . . . . с (Ива́н).

C. *Put the nouns and pronouns in parentheses into the correct form.*

1. —Ке́м оте́ц недово́лен? —О́н недово́лен (я́ и ты́).
2. О́н хо́чет серьёзно говори́ть с (ты́ и я́).
3. —Ке́м учи́тель дово́лен? —О́н дово́лен (о́н и она́).
4. —С ке́м вы́ хоти́те рабо́тать? —Я́ хочу́ рабо́тать с (о́н) и с (она́).
5. —С ке́м А́нна ви́дела Бори́са? —Она́ ви́дела его́ с (вы).

6. Óн хо́чет говори́ть с (они́) и с (вы).
7. Кто́ хо́чет рабо́тать с (мы)?
8. Почему́ вы́ не разгова́риваете с (она́)?

D. *Translate into Russian.*

1. —What did you eat the bread with? —I ate it with butter and cheese.
2. —With whom did you work? —I worked with her and (with) her silly brother.
3. —What do you write with in class? —I usually write with my old pen.
4. —Why don't you want to speak with me? —I don't want to speak with you because I am displeased with you.
5. I never drink coffee with sugar. I like black coffee.
6. —With whom is he talking on the phone? —He's talking with his young secretary.
7. He is very pleased with this secretary.
8. Anna cannot live with her sister, (and) therefore she lives with Nina's sister. She lives with her sister in a small and cheap apartment.

5. Predicate instrumental

In *John was a student* the words *was a student* form the predicate, and *student* is said to be the *predicate noun*.

(1) Predicate nouns in Russian usually take the instrumental case when the link verb **быть** is in the past or in the future tense:

Её ма́ть была́ актри́**сой**.
Her mother was an actress.

Её му́ж бы́л хоро́**шим** инжене́**ром**.
Her husband was a good engineer.

Она́ бу́дет актри́**сой**.
She will be an actress.

Я́ ду́маю, что о́н бу́дет хоро́**шим** инжене́**ром**.
I think he will be a good engineer.

Я́ тогда́ бы́л ещё студе́нт**ом**.
At that time I was still a student.

Ра́ньше Петербу́рг бы́л столи́**цей**, а тепе́рь столи́ца Москва́.
Saint Petersburg was formerly the capital, but now the capital is Moscow.

Э́та пло́щадь ра́ньше была́ це́нтр**ом** го́рода.
This square used to be the center of the city.

But in the present tense: Её ма́ть актри́**са**. Её му́ж хоро́**ший** инжене́р.

(2) Adjectives in the predicate are also sometimes in the instrumental:

Когда́ Толсто́й бы́л молод**ы́м**, о́н бы́л офице́р**ом**.
When Tolstoy was young, he was an officer.

(3) Nouns and adjectives always take the instrumental case with **быть** in the *infinitive*, as in:

Тру́дно **бы́ть** хоро́шим инжене́р**ом**.

Бра́т мое́й подру́ги хо́чет (or хоте́л) **бы́ть** диплома́т**ом**.

—**Ке́м** хо́чет **бы́ть** А́нна? —А́нна хо́чет **бы́ть** учи́тельниц**ей**. Я́ ду́маю, что она́ бу́дет хоро́ш**ей** учи́тельниц**ей**.

Когда́ мо́й сы́н бы́л ма́леньк**им**, о́н хоте́л **бы́ть** адмира́л**ом** или милиционе́р**ом** (policeman).

6. Instrumental of time

The *instrumental* of the noun serves as an adverb of time in the following phrases:

Nominative		*Instrumental*	
весна́	spring	весно́й	in spring
ле́то	summer	ле́том	in summer
о́сень (*fem.*)	fall, autumn	о́сенью	in fall
зима́	winter	зимо́й	in winter
у́тро	morning	у́тром	in the morning
день (*masc.*)	day, afternoon	днём	in the daytime; in the afternoon
ве́чер	evening	ве́чером	in the evening
ночь (*fem.*)	night	но́чью	at night

Note the expressions:

сего́дня у́тром	this morning
вчера́ ве́чером	last evening
сего́дня ве́чером	tonight (this evening)

Russian is more consistent than English in using ве́чер (ве́чером) for the period between 6:00 and about 12:00 P.M.

Вчера́ ве́чером мы́ бы́ли в теа́тре.
Last night we went to the theater.

But: Я́ пло́хо спа́л **но́чью**.
I slept badly last *night*.

PATTERN SENTENCES

1. **Зимо́й** в Ленингра́де быва́ет о́чень хо́лодно, и зима́ та́м дли́нная.
2. **Ле́том** та́м иногда́ быва́ет жа́рко, но́ ленингра́дское ле́то дово́льно коро́ткое.
3. Я́ люблю́ ру́сскую весну́. **Весно́й** осо́бенно хорошо́ в дере́вне.

1. In winter in Leningrad it's (usually) very cold and the winter there is a long one.
2. In summer there it's sometimes hot, but the Leningrad summer is rather short.
3. I love the Russian spring. In spring it's especially nice in the country.

4. Пу́шкин о́чень люби́л о́сень. О́н всегда́ мно́го писа́л **о́сенью**.

5. У́тро сего́дня бы́ло холо́дное; ра́но **у́тром** бы́л да́же сне́г.

6. Вчера́ **ве́чером** бы́л у меня́ Бори́с, и мы́ с ни́м ве́сь ве́чер говори́ли о ру́сской литерату́ре.

7. Кака́я тёмная но́чь! Я́ люблю́ рабо́тать **но́чью**, когда́ всё спя́т и всё ти́хо.

8. **Но́чью** бы́ло хо́лодно, а **днём** бы́ло тепло́, как ле́том!

9. В газе́те «Вече́рняя Москва́» всегда́ е́сть на после́дней страни́це отде́л спо́рта.

10. В Сове́тском Сою́зе да́же **зимо́й** продаю́т моро́женое на у́лице.

4. Pushkin loved autumn very much. He always wrote a great deal in autumn.

5. This morning was cold; early in the morning it even snowed.

6. Last evening Boris was at my place, and we talked all evening about Russian literature.

7. What a dark night! I like to work at night when everyone's asleep and everything is quiet.

8. At night it was cold, but during the daytime it was warm, like summer!

9. In the newspaper *Evening Moscow* there is always a sports section on the last page.

10. In the Soviet Union they sell ice cream on the street even in wintertime.

DRILL

Translate into English.

1. Вчера́ ве́чером мы́ с Ле́ной обе́дали у Бори́са. Кро́ме на́с та́м никого́ не́ было.

2. Я́ хочу́ ка́ждое у́тро за́втракать с ва́ми. Я́, как и вы́, люблю́ ра́но за́втракать.

3. Ле́том А́нна живёт в дере́вне у своего́ ста́ршего бра́та, а зимо́й она́ живёт в го́роде совсе́м одна́.

4. О́льга лю́бит жи́ть в дере́вне зимо́й, осо́бенно когда́ быва́ет мно́го сне́га.

5. Вчера́ у́тром Андре́я не́ было в кла́ссе. Э́то быва́ет о́чень ре́дко.

6. Весно́й мы́ бу́дем в Москве́. Я́ люблю́ ру́сскую весну́. Тако́й весны́ нигде́ не́т!

7. Вчера́ ве́чером мы́ с бра́том обе́дали в италья́нском рестора́не. Мы́ с ни́м дово́льно ча́сто та́м обе́даем.

8. У́тром Андре́й рабо́тает в библиоте́ке, а днём—до́ма.

9. В «Вече́рней Москве́» мо́й бра́т чита́ет то́лько после́днюю страни́цу.

7. Russian names

«А́нна Ива́новна Ива́нова»
«Ива́н Ива́нович Ива́нов»

In addition to the *first name* (**и́мя**) and the *family name* (**фами́лия**), Russians also use the *patronymic* (**о́тчество**), a form derived from the father's first name by adding the suffix **-ович** (or **-евич** or **-ич**) in the *masculine*, and **-овна** (**-евна**) in the *feminine*, thus:

Ива́н Ива́нович
Ivan, Ivan's son

А́нна Ива́новна
Anna, Ivan's daughter

Бори́с Петро́вич
Boris, Peter's son

Мари́я Петро́вна
Marie, Peter's daughter

Серге́й Андре́евич
Sergey, Andrew's son

Еле́на Андре́евна
Helen, Andrew's daughter

The first name followed by the patronymic is a very commonly used form of address. In rapid speech, the patronymic suffix is often slurred or contracted, e.g., Ива́нович is pronounced [ivánič]; Андре́евна is pronounced [andŗévnə].

The first name alone (or, quite frequently, a diminutive, such as Ва́ня for Ива́н, Пе́тя for Пётр, Ко́ля for Никола́й, О́ля for О́льга, Та́ня for Татья́на) is used between friends and relatives, or in addressing young people and children.

Note. Most Russian family names end in **-ов/-ев, -ин,**[6] or **-ский.**[7] The latter, those ending in **-ский,** have the ending **-ская** for females, and are declined like adjectives.

Family names ending in **-ов/-ев** and **-ин** have the endings **-ова/-ева** and **-ина** for the feminine. The declension of these names follows a mixed pattern that uses some nominal and some adjectival endings:

	Masculine		*Feminine*	
Nom.	Петро́в	} like nouns	Петро́ва	like nouns
Gen.	Петро́ва		Петро́вой }	like adjs.
Dat.	Петро́ву		Петро́вой }	
Acc.	Петро́ва		Петро́ву	like nouns
Instr.	Петро́вым	like adjs.	Петро́вой }	like adjs.
Loc.	Петро́ве	like nouns	Петро́вой }	

Family names ending in a consonant (except those ending in **-ов/-ев** and **-ин**) are declined as nouns in the masculine, but they are indeclinable in the feminine:

Я живу́ у Ива́на Ива́новича Бе́рга.

But: Я живу́ у А́нны Ива́новны Бе́рг.

Or: Я зна́ю Ро́берта Бра́уна и Не́лли Бра́ун.

The Russian equivalents of *Mr.* and *Mrs.* are **господи́н** and **госпожа́**; they are not in use in the Soviet Union (except when addressing foreigners). The terms used instead are **това́рищ** (*comrade*) for both sexes, and **граждани́н** for *citizen* and for the female citizen, **гражда́нка** (with the last name).

8. Давно́ and до́лго

(1) *With the past tense,* **давно́** refers to something that occurred long ago, or, when the verb is in the negative, to something which has *not* occurred in a long time:

Всё это бы́ло **давно́**.
All that happened long ago.

Я **давно́** ему́ не писа́л.
I haven't written to him for a long time.

Мы́ **давно́** не́ были в теа́тре.
We haven't been to the theater for a long time.

---

[6] Че́хов, Па́влов, Турге́нев, Соловьёв, Пу́шкин, Ле́нин.
[7] Чайко́вский, Достое́вский.

(2) *With the present tense,* **давно** refers to an action or state initiated in the past but *continuing* in the present:

> Вы́ **давно́** здесь?
> Have you been here long?

> Ива́н **давно́** живёт в Ленингра́де.
> Ivan has been living in Leningrad for a long time.

(3) **До́лго**, meaning *a long time*, refers to the *duration* of an action or condition:

> О́н **до́лго** жи́л в Сове́тском Сою́зе, почти́ всю́ жи́знь.
> He lived in the Soviet Union for a long time, almost all his life.

> Я́ вчера́ **до́лго** говори́л по телефо́ну с Бори́сом.
> Yesterday I talked for a long time on the phone with Boris.

> О́н всегда́ **до́лго** говори́т по телефо́ну.
> He always talks a long time on the phone.

Conversation

1. Я́ звони́л ва́м у́тром, днём и ве́чером

Юрий. —Я́ звони́л ва́м вчера́, Серге́й Петро́вич. Я́ звони́л у́тром, днём, и да́же по́здно ве́чером, но никто́ не отвеча́л.

Серге́й. —Что́ бы́ло вчера́? Ах, да́! У́тром О́льга Андре́евна, моя́ жена́, была́ у свое́й сестры́, а я́ бы́л у своего́ изда́теля.

Ю. —У изда́теля?

С. —Да́. Я́ говори́л с ни́м о мое́й но́вой кни́ге «Эволю́ция социали́зма».

Ю. —«Эволю́ция социали́зма»! Кака́я интере́сная те́ма! О́чень интере́сная! А я́ да́же не зна́л, что у ва́с ско́ро бу́дет но́вая кни́га! О́чень ра́д. И вы́ говори́ли с изда́телем це́лый де́нь? Я́ ва́м звони́л днём—никого́ не́ было.

С. —Не́т, Юрий Бори́сович. Я́ бы́л у изда́теля то́лько у́тром, а днём мы́ с жено́й покупа́ли ме́бель. В на́шей ста́рой кварти́ре бы́ло две́ ко́мнаты, а в но́вой четы́ре. Поэ́тому у на́с ма́ло ме́бели.

Ю. —Но́вая кни́га, но́вая кварти́ра, но́вая ме́бель . . . . Всё но́вое! Это́ же но́вая жи́знь! «Эволю́ция жи́зни»! Здо́рово!

С. —Почему́ же не́т? Это́ всегда́ хорошо́.

Ю. —Ещё бы!

Questions to be answered instantly and quickly.

1. С ке́м говори́л у́тром Серге́й Петро́вич? 2. Кака́я те́ма его́ но́вой кни́ги? 3. Где была́ у́тром его́ жена́? 4. Что́ они́ де́лали днём? 5. Почему́ и́м нужна́ ещё ме́бель?

—ja zvaṇíl vam fčirá, şirgéj pitróɣič. ja zvaṇíl útrəm, dṇóm, i dážə póznə ɣéčirəm, no ṇiktó ṇiatɣičál.

—čtó bílə fčirá? áx, dá! útrəm şɣitlánə andŗéjivnə, majá žɨná, bɨlá usvajéj şistrɨ, a já bil usvajivó izdáţiḷə.

—uizdáţiḷə?

—dá. ja gəvaŗíl şṇím amajéj nóvəj kṇígi "evaḷúcijə səcialízmə."

2. В рестора́не «Во́лга»

Ю. —А где́ же вы́ бы́ли ве́чером?

С. —Ве́чером мы́ у́жинали с господи́ном Джо́нсоном и с госпожо́й Джо́нсон. Ро́берт Джо́нсон то́же исто́рик, как я́. Мо́жет быть вы́ чита́ли его́ кни́гу «Эволю́ция капитали́зма»?

Ю. —Не чита́л, но слы́шал о не́й. Говоря́т, что кни́га интере́сная. Но́ тепе́рь я́ хочу́ слы́шать о вчера́шнем ве́чере. Вы́ у ни́х у́жинали?

С. —Не́т, не у ни́х, а в рестора́не «Во́лга». Зна́ете, рестора́н ря́дом с «Но́вым теа́тром», где́ мы́ с ва́ми у́жинали весно́й. По́мните?

Ю. —Я́ не у́жинал та́м ни весно́й, ни ле́том, ни о́сенью, ни зимо́й. Я́ да́же никогда́ не слы́шал об э́том рестора́не.

С. —Ну что́ вы́ говори́те, Ю́рий Бори́сович! Мы́ с ва́ми е́ли та́м бефстро́ганов (Beef Stroganoff), и пи́ли прекра́сное кры́мское (Crimean) вино́.

Ю. —Не зна́ю, с ке́м вы́ е́ли бефстро́ганов, и с ке́м вы́ пи́ли кры́мское вино́, но э́то бы́ло не со мно́й. Но́ всё равно́. Расскажи́те, что вы́ та́м е́ли, како́е бы́ло меню́. Люблю́ слу́шать, когда́ говоря́т о еде́ (еда́, food, eating)!

С. —С удово́льствием. Снача́ла—заку́ска: осетри́на (sturgeon), сёмга (salmon), и, коне́чно, селёдка (herring). У́жин без селёдки—не у́жин.

Ю. —Пра́вильно! А вы́ ничего́ не пи́ли?

С. —Ну, что́ вы! Джо́нсоны и я́ пи́ли во́дку, а пото́м вино́. О́льга Андре́евна ничего́ не пила́. Она́ совсе́м не пьёт. Я́ пью́, но ма́ло.

Ю. —Ну́, а по́сле заку́ски?

С. —Мы́ всё е́ли настоя́щий украи́нский бо́рщ. А́х, како́й э́то бы́л бо́рщ! Настоя́щая поэ́ма!

Ю. —Люблю́ бо́рщ! А что́ по́сле борща́?

С. —Жена́ е́ла ры́бу с карто́фельным пюре́ (mashed potatoes), а Джо́нсоны и я́— о́чень вку́сное мя́со с жа́реным (fried) карто́фелем и с о́чень вку́сным сала́том.

Ю. —И э́то всё?

С. —Не́т, что́ вы! Пото́м бы́ло сла́дкое.[8] Мы́ с Ро́бертом е́ли на сла́дкое кофе́йное моро́женое; Не́лли, госпожа́ Джо́нсон, е́ла шокола́дное моро́женое, а жена́ е́ла компо́т. Она́ говори́т, что компо́т бы́л немно́жко сли́шком сла́дкий, но вку́сный. По́сле э́того мы́ с жено́й пи́ли ча́й с варе́ньем, а Джо́нсоны—ко́фе.

Ю. —Как я́ ви́жу, «Во́лга» совсе́м не плохо́й рестора́н, и мне́ о́чень жа́ль, что меня́ не́ было с ва́ми.

---

[8] **Сла́дкое** *dessert* (literally *sweet*); here the adjective is used as a noun, and is in the neuter because the neuter noun **блю́до** (*dish*) is understood. **На сла́дкое** *for dessert*.

Answer these questions in Russian.

1. Почему́ Сергея́ Петро́вича и О́льги Андре́евны не́ было до́ма вчера́ ве́чером?
2. Почему́ Серге́й Петро́вич расска́зывает своему́ прия́телю, что они́ всё е́ли в рестора́не?
3. По́сле чего́ они́ е́ли борщ?
4. Они́ всё е́ли мя́со с жа́реным карто́фелем?
5. Они́ всё е́ли моро́женое на сла́дкое (= for dessert)?
6. Како́й был компо́т?
7. С чем они́ пи́ли чай?
8. Како́й рестора́н «Во́лга»?
9. Что Ю́рий Бори́сович говори́т в конце́ разгово́ра?

Reading

Всё э́то бы́ло давно́

Я о́чень люблю́ разгова́ривать с мои́м хоро́шим дру́гом Луне́вым. Он о́чень у́мный челове́к; у него́ была́ интере́сная жизнь, и он так интере́сно уме́ет обо всём расска́зывать.

Анто́н Анто́нович исто́рик, и одно́ вре́мя он был диплома́том. Он был везде́; он мно́го ви́дел и мно́го зна́ет. Он был в А́фрике, в Аме́рике, жил в Аргенти́не; он зна́ет А́зию, и дово́льно до́лго жил в Кита́е.

Зимо́й мы ча́сто сиди́м с ним ве́чером в его́ кабине́те, пьём чай с ро́мом (rum) и́ли с варе́ньем, и́ли туре́цкий (Turkish) ко́фе; ку́рим и разгова́риваем. Я сижу́ ти́хо, мно́го курю́, ма́ло говорю́, пью свой чай, и с больши́м удово́льствием слу́шаю Анто́на Анто́новича.

Он говори́т ти́хим и прия́тным го́лосом, ку́рит туре́цкую тру́бку, и расска́зывает о свое́й жи́зни.

У него́ прекра́сная па́мять. Он хорошо́ по́мнит всё, что ви́дел, с кем и о чём разгова́ривал.

Когда́ он был ещё шко́льником, он ви́дел после́днего ру́сского царя́. Пото́м, когда́ он был уже́ студе́нтом, он ви́дел и слы́шал Ле́нина. Э́то бы́ло тру́дное вре́мя: была́ война́, была́ револю́ция. Но он тогда́ был молоды́м, а молодо́му всё легко́ и интере́сно.

Когда́ он был диплома́том, он быва́л в Ло́ндоне, в Пари́же, в Вашингто́не, в Пеки́не. Он был в Я́лте, когда́ там бы́ли Ру́звельт, Че́рчиль и Ста́лин. Луне́в ча́сто разгова́ривал с президе́нтом Ру́звельтом и иногда́ с Че́рчилем. Э́то бы́ло интере́сное вре́мя. Но всё э́то бы́ло давно́.

Тепе́рь Луне́в живёт в э́том ма́леньком го́роде и пи́шет кни́гу обо всём, что он зна́ет и что он ви́дел. Он живёт здесь со свое́й жено́й Елизаве́той Петро́вной. Елизаве́та Петро́вна помога́ет ему́ писа́ть: они́ мно́го ви́дели вме́сте, и у неё то́же хоро́шая па́мять. Она́ лю́бит рабо́тать с му́жем. Она́ ча́сто сиди́т с на́ми и то́же с интере́сом слу́шает му́жа. Ря́дом с Луне́вым, на жёлтом кре́сле, лежи́т и́ли сиди́т их соба́ка Ма́шка, и с больши́м удово́льствием слу́шает своего́ хозя́ина. Она́ о́чень дово́льна свои́м хозя́ином. Ме́сто на жёлтом кре́сле её, и никто́ кро́ме неё не до́лжен там сиде́ть.

На столе́ стои́т ла́мпа с си́ним абажу́ром (shade), стои́т буты́лка с ро́мом, и лежи́т ка́рта ми́ра. Лунёв па́льцем пока́зывает на́м на ка́рте Кита́й, Аргенти́ну, Аме́рику. Мы́ всё сиди́м ти́хо и слу́шаем его́, иногда́ всю но́чь до утра́.

Answer these questions in Russian.

1. Лунёв всегда́ бы́л диплома́том? 2. Где́ и когда́ они́ обы́чно разгова́ривают? 3. Что́ они́ ещё де́лают когда́ разгова́ривают? 4. Ке́м Лунёв бы́л, когда́ о́н ви́дел царя́, и ке́м бы́л о́н, когда́ о́н ви́дел Ле́нина? 5. Кого́ о́н ещё ви́дел и зна́л? 6. О́н всю́ жи́знь жи́л в Кита́е? 7. О чём Лунёв пи́шет кни́гу, и с ке́м о́н её пи́шет? 8. Почему́ его́ жена́ мо́жет ему́ помога́ть? 9. Ка́к всё его́ слу́шают? 10. Кто́ Ма́шка, и где́ её ме́сто? 11. Чём Лунёв пока́зывает на́м на ка́рте, где́ о́н бы́л?

DRILL

Review Translation.

1. —With whom were you there last evening? —With her and with her sister. 2. I am very pleased with her. 3. —Did you speak with him this morning? —Yes, and I am very pleased with him. 4. I want to work with you. Do you want to work with me? 5. In the spring we always live at Olga's. 6. Spring in Europe is usually nice. 7. I don't know where he was in the summer, but I do know that the summer was very hot. 8. —Where will you be in the fall? —If the fall is (= will be) nice, we will be in the country. 9. Tonight the Russian historian will be at the theater with his pretty wife. She is American. 10. She works with Anna in the morning, but in the afternoon she works alone. 11. When I work late in the evening, I don't sleep at night. 12. Her son wants to be a writer, and her daughter wants to be a teacher. 13. That good student always listens to the professor with great interest. 14. When he was young, he lived at one time with his family in China. 15. —Who was he? —He was an engineer. 16. My father was a teacher, and I want to be a teacher. 17. —Why do you smoke? —I can't help smoking. 18. We have been living in America three months.

Vocabulary

А́зия Asia
алло́! hello! (on the telephone)
аппети́т appetite
А́фрика Africa
борщ borsch (a kind of soup)
буты́лка bottle
варе́нье [vaɾéɲjə] jam, preserves
везде́ everywhere
весна́ spring
ве́тер (*gen.* ве́тра) wind; it's windy
вку́сный delicious, tasty (вкус, taste)
во́дка [vótkə] vodka
го́лос voice

господи́н Mr.
госпожа́ Mrs.
дива́н sofa, couch
дли́нный long
до́лго long, for a long time
жёлтый [žóltij] yellow
жизнь (*fem.*) life
жест gesture
за́втрак breakfast
заку́ска appetizer, hors-d'œuvres
изда́тель (*masc.*) publisher
интере́с interest
исто́рик historian

картóфель (*masc., no pl.*) potato(es)
корóткий (*adv.* кóротко) short, brief
кóфе (*masc., indeclinable*) coffee
лéвый left
лимóн lemon
лóжка [lóškə] spoon
мел chalk
мéсто place
морóженое (*adj. used as noun*) ice cream
неплóхо not bad(ly)
óсень (*fem.*) autumn, fall
пáлец (*gen.* пáльца) finger, toe
пáмять (*fem.*) memory
потóм[9] then, next; later, afterwards
прáвый right
президéнт president
Россúя Russia
рядом nearby, next door

рядом с (+ *instr.*) beside, next to, alongside
салáт salad
сáхар sugar
слáдкое (*adj. used as a noun*) dessert
сначáла at first, first
снег snow
совсéм [safşém] quite, entirely
совсéм не (нéт) not at all
странúца page
товáрищ (*masc., used for both sexes*) comrade
трýбка [trúpkə] pipe
труд labor
удовóльствие pleasure
ýжин supper
хозяин master; host; landlord
царь (*masc.*) tsar
чай tea
шкóльник (*fem.* шкóльница) schoolboy, -girl

VERBS

(See also Section 1)
зáвтракать (I)[10] to have breakfast (lunch)
обéдать (I)[10] to have dinner
пить (I: пью, пьёшь) to drink
разговáривать (I)[10] to converse, have a conversation, talk
расскáзывать (I)[10] to narrate, tell (a story); р. о (+ *loc.*) tell about (someone or something)
ýжинать (I) to have supper
умéть (I: умéю, умéешь) to know how to (+ *inf.*)

EXPRESSIONS

сидéть дóма to stay at home
расскажúте tell (*imperative*)
однó врéмя at one time
всю нóчь all night
тáк что so that
всё ещё still
Ну чтó вы говорúте! (Чтó вы!) expresses disagreement or surprise
не могý не (+ *inf.*) I can't help (doing something)
с трудóм with difficulty
с удовóльствием with pleasure
с интерéсом with interest
как и я like me
на слáдкое for dessert

---

[9] Потóм (*then*) is used for the next of a series of actions or events, whereas тогдá (*then*) means *at that time*, e.g., Это бы́ло до войны́; я тогдá бы́л ещё совсéм молоды́м. That was before the war; *then* I was still quite young. *But:* Я сначáла бы́л в шкóле, а потóм в университéте. First I was in school, and *then* at the university.

[10] First conjugation verbs conjugated like читáть are designated by the symbol (I) without forms of the present tense. First conjugation verbs with consonant stems (like писáть) are designated by the same symbol plus the first and second persons singular, e.g., писáть (I: пишý, пúшешь).

Declension of nouns in singular (review) • Genitive masculine in
-у/-ю • Locative masculine in -ý/-ю́ • Dative and locative ending
-ии • Declension of Fem. II nouns in singular (review) • Declension
of neuter nouns in -мя, singular • Indeclinable nouns • The
preposition на and the locative (supplement) • Declension of personal
pronouns (review table) • Adjective and pronoun-adjective declensions
in the singular (review) • Superlative of adjectives with са́мый •
Reading: В Сове́тском Сою́зе

Unit 12

Grammar

1. Declension of nouns in singular (review)

In Unit 5, page 51, a preliminary survey was given of the three classes of Russian noun declensions. All the regular case forms in the singular of the first two classes of nouns have been presented, and will be reviewed and supplemented in this unit. Feminine nouns ending in **-ь** (Fem. II) will be reviewed in Section 5 below.

MASCULINE, NEUTER, AND FEM. I NOUNS

	Masculine		*Neuter*		*Fem. I*	
	Hard	Soft	Hard	Soft	Hard	Soft
Nom.	дом	роя́ль	окно́	по́ле	ко́мната	ку́хня
Gen.	до́ма	роя́ля	окна́	по́ля	ко́мнаты[3]	ку́хни
Dat.	до́му	роя́лю	окну́	по́лю	ко́мнате	ку́хне
Acc.	дом[1]	роя́ль[1]	окно́	по́ле	ко́мнату	ку́хню
Instr.	до́мом[2]	роя́лем	окно́м	по́лем	ко́мнатой[4] (-ою)	ку́хней (-ею)
Loc.	до́ме	роя́ле	окне́	по́ле	ко́мнате	ку́хне

2. Genitive masculine in -у/-ю

Some masculine nouns denoting divisible matter (like foodstuffs, tobacco) take an alternate genitive ending **-у/-ю**, rather than the usual **-а/-я**, when the genitive is used for a *partitive* sense, i.e., when we speak of large or small quantities of some item, or a particular amount of it. Among the most commonly used of these nouns are:

[1] Masculine animate nouns have the accusative like the genitive: сы́на, го́стя, etc.
[2] Spelling Rule 1 applies: това́рищем.
[3] Spelling Rule 2 applies: кни́ги, да́чи, etc.
[4] Spelling Rule 1 applies: у́лицей, да́чей, etc.

175

Nominative	Genitive	Partitive genitive
са́хар	са́хара	са́хару
рис	ри́са	ри́су (rice)
таба́к	табака́	табаку́ (tobacco)
сыр	сы́ра	сы́ру
чай	ча́я	ча́ю
шокола́д	шокола́да	шокола́ду (chocolate)
суп	су́па	су́пу
But: хлеб	хле́ба	хле́ба

Partitive genitive forms are used with adverbs such as **ско́лько, мно́го, немно́го, ма́ло**, with expressions of measurable quantities (**кило́** *kilogram*; **ча́шка** *cup*, **таре́лка** *plate*, **кусо́к** *piece*), and also when an unspecified amount of something is called for, such as when we employ *some* or *any* in English.

DRILL

Supply the proper case endings of the words in parentheses.

1. В ку́хне мно́го (хлеб) и кило́ (са́хар).
2. В холоди́льнике éсть немно́го (сыр).
3. На столé ча́шка (чай) и кусо́к (хлеб).
4. —Хо́чешь (су́п)? —Да́, я хочу́ таре́лку (су́п), немно́го (мя́со), и стака́н (молоко́).

3. Locative masculine in -у́/-ю́

Some hard masculine nouns (mostly of one syllable) end in **-у́** in the locative singular after the preposition **в** and **на**. This ending is *always* stressed:

пол	на полу́	on the floor
сад	в саду́	in the garden
лес	в лесу́	in the woods
у́гол	в углу́	in the corner
бе́рег	на берегу́	on the shore, bank
мост	на мосту́	on the bridge
порт	в порту́	in (the) port
ряд	в пе́рвом ряду́	in the first row
Крым	в Крыму́	in the Crimea
Дон	на Дону́	on the Don, in the Don region
год	в про́шлом году́	(in the) last year
	в э́том году́	(in) this year
	в бу́дущем году́	(in) next year

Similarly, a few soft masculine nouns of one syllable ending in **-й** have a locative singular in **-ю́** with **в** and **на**:

рай	в раю́	in paradise
край	на краю́	on the edge

With the preposition **о**, these nouns end in **-е** (usually unstressed): о са́де, etc.

PATTERN SENTENCES

1. Вот у́гол мое́й у́лицы. Я живу́ в до́ме на пра́вом углу́, а на ле́вом углу́ апте́ка.

2. У нас есть ма́ленькая да́ча на берегу́ реки́.

3. У нас там большо́й сад. Я люблю́ рабо́тать в на́шем саду́.

4. Вот на́ша да́ча. Там по́ле и недалеко́ лес.

5. Как прохла́дно ле́том в лесу́!

6. Вот река́ и мост. Чья маши́на стои́т на мосту́? Где милиционе́р? Маши́на не должна́ стоя́ть на мосту́!

7. В про́шлом году́, ле́том, А́нна была́ в Крыму́. Она́ расска́зывает о Кры́ме мно́го интере́сного.

8. Ива́н рабо́тает в э́том году́ в ленингра́дском порту́. Он ещё не зна́ет, где он бу́дет рабо́тать в бу́дущем году́.

9. —В како́м ряду́ вы сиде́ли вчера́ на конце́рте? —В пе́рвом ряду́.

10. Они́ лю́бят говори́ть о своём са́де. Я ещё не́ был в их саду́.

1. Here is the corner of my street. I live in the house on the right corner, and on the left corner is a drugstore.

2. We have a small summer cottage on the bank of a river.

3. We have a large garden there. I like to work in our garden.

4. Here is our summer cottage. There is a field over there, and not far off, a wood.

5. How cool it is in the summer in the woods!

6. Here is the river and the bridge. Whose car is parked on the bridge? Where is a policeman? A car should not be parked on a bridge!

7. Last year, in summer, Anna was in the Crimea. She tells many interesting things about the Crimea.

8. Ivan is working this year at the Leningrad port. He doesn't know yet where he will work next year.

9. —In which row did you sit yesterday at the concert? —In the first row.

10. They like to talk about their garden. I haven't been in their garden yet.

DRILL

Answer in complete sentences, using the word given in the right-hand column in your answer.

Вопро́с	Отве́т
Model: Где прия́тно бы́ть, когда́ жа́рко?	(лес)—Прия́тно бы́ть в лесу́.
1. Где Шо́лохов писа́л «Ти́хий До́н»?	(Дон)
2. Где вы лю́бите рабо́тать ле́том?	(сад)
3. На чём лежи́т ковёр?	(пол)
4. На чём стои́т ла́мпа?	(стол)
5. Где стои́т на́ша да́ча?	(бе́рег)
6. Где стои́т милиционе́р?	(у́гол)
7. Где я ви́жу челове́ка?	(мост)
8. Где вы ви́дели А́нну?	(шко́ла)
9. Где Я́лта?	(Крым)
10. Где вы бы́ли вчера́ днём?	(го́род)
11. Где вы рабо́тали сего́дня у́тром?	(библиоте́ка)
12. Когда́ вы бы́ли в Крыму́?	(про́шлый го́д)
13. Где рабо́тает Андре́й?	(порт)
14. Когда́ они́ бу́дут здесь?	(бу́дущий го́д)

4. Dative and locative ending -ии

Nouns of all three genders with the following nominative endings:

Masc. **-ий** [-ij]
Neut. **-ие** [-ijə]
Fem. **-ия** [-ijə]

have in the locative case the ending **-ии** [-ii].

Thus:

Nominative	Locative
ге́ний	ге́нии (о ге́нии)
зда́ние	зда́нии (о зда́нии)
Росси́я	Росси́и (в Росси́и)

The ending **-ии** is pronounced as two distinct **и**'s [-ii], without slurring but without a break.

Likewise, *feminine* nouns ending in the nominative in **-ия** take the ending **-ии** in three cases, the genitive and the dative as well as the locative, e.g., (*nom.*) **Росси́я**, (*gen., dat., loc.*) **Росси́и**.

For complete paradigms of these nouns see Appendix A, p. 472.

PATTERN SENTENCES

1. Росси́я огро́мная страна́.
2. В Росси́и была́ револю́ция.
3. Он был в Росси́и по́сле револю́ции.
4. Ра́ньше Смирно́в жил во Фра́нции.[5] Он говори́т, что Фра́нция замеча́тельная страна́.
5. Я бо́льше люблю́ Ита́лию. Мы ра́ньше жи́ли в Ита́лии.
6. Ле́том А́нна была́ с бра́том в А́нглии. Они́ о́чень лю́бят А́нглию.
7. За́втра бу́дет интере́сная ле́кция о ру́сской исто́рии. Я бу́ду на э́той ле́кции.
8. Вчера́ ве́чером на собра́нии я ви́дел Лунёва.
9. Я никогда́ не́ был во Флори́де, но я был в Калифо́рнии в про́шлом году́. По-мо́ему, Калифо́рния о́чень краси́вая.

1. Russia is an immense country.
2. There was a revolution in Russia.
3. He was in Russia after the revolution.
4. Formerly, Smirnov lived in France. He says that France is a wonderful country.
5. I like Italy more. We used to live in Italy.
6. In the summer Anna was in England with her brother. They like England very much.
7. Tomorrow there will be an interesting lecture on Russian history. I will be at that lecture.
8. Last night I saw Lunyov at the meeting.
9. I have never been in Florida, but last year I was in California. I think California is very beautiful.

DRILL

Translate into Russian.

1. My father loves Russia.
2. He lived in Russia for a whole year. He was in Siberia, in the Crimea, and in the Don (region).

---

[5] The form **во** is used in place of **в** before certain words beginning with a consonant cluster especially when the first consonant is **в** or **ф**.

3. I wrote Maria about our work at the university.
4. We spoke a great deal about Russian history and about the Russian Revolution.
5. Yesterday there was a lecture about England. I was at that lecture.
6. I have never been in Italy, but I have heard many good things about Italy.
7. The concert was in this tall building.
8. In the morning I was at a meeting.
9. —Where were you last year? —In France.

5. Declension of Fem. II nouns in singular (review)

These nouns, which end in a soft consonant, are declined as follows:

	жизнь *life*	дверь *door*	часть *part*
Nom.	жизнь	дверь	часть
Gen.	жи́зни	две́ри	ча́сти
Dat.	жи́зни	две́ри	ча́сти
Acc.	жизнь	дверь	часть
Instr.	жи́знью	две́рью	ча́стью
Loc.	жи́зни	две́ри	ча́сти

Two nouns **мать** (*mother*) and **дочь** (*daughter*), insert **-ер-** before the ending in all cases other than the nominative and accusative singular:

Nom.	мать	дочь
Gen.	ма́тери	до́чери
Dat.	ма́тери	до́чери
Acc.	мать	дочь
Instr.	ма́терью	до́черью
Loc.	ма́тери	до́чери

Note that all Fem. II nouns have an accusative like their nominative.

6. Declension of neuter nouns in -мя, singular

Ten neuter nouns end in **-мя** in the nominative singular (they must not be confused with feminines!). The most used are **и́мя** *first name*, **вре́мя** *time*, **пла́мя** *flame*, **зна́мя** *banner*, and **пле́мя** *tribe*. These nouns insert the syllable **-ен-** between the stem and the ending of all case forms except the nominative and accusative singular.

	и́мя *first name*	вре́мя *time*
Nom.	и́мя	вре́мя
Gen.	и́мени	вре́мени
Dat.	и́мени	вре́мени
Acc.	и́мя	вре́мя
Instr.	и́менем	вре́менем
Loc.	и́мени	вре́мени

PATTERN SENTENCES

1. Ле́том ма́ть живёт у свое́й до́чери в А́нглии.

2. Она́ лю́бит жи́ть со свое́й до́черью.

3. Когда́ они́ не вме́сте, ма́ть почти́ ка́ждый де́нь пи́шет до́чери, а до́чь пи́шет ма́тери.

4. Во́т на ка́рте Сиби́рь. В э́той ча́сти Сиби́ри зима́ о́чень дли́нная и холо́дная, а ле́то совсе́м коро́ткае.

5. —Ско́лько вре́мени живёт ва́ш прия́тель То́мсон в Ита́лии? —Почти́ всю́ жи́знь. О́н о́чень дово́лен свое́й жи́знью та́м.

6. О́н лю́бит расска́зывать о свое́й жи́зни, хотя́, по-мо́ему, его́ жи́знь не осо́бенно интере́сная.

7. Те́ма пье́сы, кото́рую я́ вчера́ ве́чером ви́дела, любо́вь и сме́рть.

8. Э́то не о́чень оригина́льная те́ма; все́ пи́шут о любви́ и сме́рти.

9. —У ва́с сего́дня днём бу́дет вре́мя со мно́й рабо́тать? —Днём у меня́ не бу́дет вре́мени, но ве́чером бу́дет.

10. —Вы́ ви́дите ту́ зелёную две́рь? —Да́, ви́жу. —Како́й но́мер на две́ри? —Та́м не́т но́мера.

11. В про́шлом году́ они́ жи́ли в ста́рой ча́сти го́рода, а в э́том году́ они́ живу́т в но́вой ча́сти.

1. In summer the mother lives with her daughter (= at her daughter's house) in England.

2. She likes to live with her daughter.

3. When they aren't together, the mother writes to the daughter almost every day, and the daughter writes to the mother.

4. Here on the map is Siberia. In this part of Siberia winter is very long and cold, and summer is quite short.

5. —How long (= how much time) has your friend Thomson lived in Italy? —Almost all his life. He is very content with his life there.

6. He likes to talk about his life, although, in my opinion, his life isn't particularly interesting.

7. The subject of the play which I saw yesterday evening is love and death.

8. That's not a very original subject; everybody's writing about love and death.

9. —Will you have time to work with me this afternoon? —This afternoon I won't have time, but this evening I will.

10. —Do you see that green door? —Yes, I do. —What is the number on the door? —There's no number there.

11. Last year they lived in the old part of the city, and this year they are living in the new part.

DRILL

Put the nouns in parentheses into the proper case.

1. Андре́й лю́бит лежа́ть в (крова́ть).
2. Ма́ть дово́льна но́вой (крова́ть).
3. У него́ не́т (мать).
4. О́н бы́л та́м без (мать) и без (сестра́).
5. Она́ живёт с (мать) и с (сестра́).
6. Я́ люблю́ её (дочь).
7. Я́ люблю́ говори́ть с её (дочь).
8. Я́ ча́сто говорю́ о её (дочь).
9. У кого́ е́сть (вре́мя)?
10. У меня́ не́т (вре́мя).
11. Что́ вы́ де́лаете с ва́шим (вре́мя)?
12. У э́той соба́ки не́т (и́мя).
13. Я́ дово́льна мои́м (и́мя).
14. Она́ всегда́ ду́мает о (смерть).
15. Ма́ть ча́сто расска́зывает о свое́й (жизнь).
16. Она́ говори́т, что она́ дово́льна свое́й (жизнь).
17. Я́ посыла́ю пода́рок мое́й (ма́ть и до́чь).

7. Indeclinable nouns

Nouns of non-Russian origin are declined in Russian only if they end in a consonant (like телефо́н or автомоби́ль) or in -а/-я (like дра́ма or револю́ция). Nouns ending in the vowels -е, -и, -о, and -у are *not* declined; most of them are of neuter gender (all listed below except two):

желе́	jelly	метро́	subway
кафе́	café	пальто́	topcoat, overcoat
ко́фе (*masc.*)	coffee	ра́дио	radio
ви́ски	whisky	фо́то	photo
такси́	taxi	кенгуру́ (*masc.*)	kangaroo
кино́	movie house	рагу́	ragout, stew

Also indeclinable are foreign geographical or personal names ending in the vowels listed above, e.g., Миссу́ри, Ве́рди, Чика́го, Пикассо́, Ке́ннеди. Similarly, place names in the Soviet Union but of non-Russian origin, like Баку́[6] (Baku) or Со́чи[7] (Sochi), are indeclinable.

PATTERN SENTENCES

1. Во́т стои́т **такси́**. Я́ никого́ не ви́жу в **такси́**.
2. Мы́ ви́дели профе́ссора Па́влова на ста́нции **метро́**.
3. Моско́вское **метро́** о́чень удо́бное и дово́льно бы́строе.
4. Про́шлым ле́том мы́ жи́ли в Я́лте, а Кали́нины жи́ли в **Со́чи**. Мы́ почему́-то не о́чень лю́бим **Со́чи**.
5. Мы́ вчера́ бы́ли в **кино́** и ви́дели замеча́тельный францу́зский фи́льм.
6. Сего́дня прохла́дно; почему́ ты́ без шля́пы и без **пальто́**? Где́ твоё **пальто́**?
7. Мо́й сы́н живёт в Ха́рькове, а до́чь в **Баку́**. (**Баку́** на берегу́ Каспи́йского мо́ря.)
8. Я́ бы́л в **Чика́го**, но́ не́ был в **Бу́ффало**.

---

1. There is a taxi standing. I don't see anyone in it.
2. We saw Professor Pavlov at the subway station.
3. The Moscow subway is very convenient and rather fast.
4. Last summer we lived in Yalta, and the Kalinins lived in Sochi. For some reason we don't like Sochi very much.
5. Yesterday we went to the movies and saw a wonderful French film.
6. Today it's cool; why are you without a hat and coat? Where is your coat?
7. My son is living in Kharkov, and my daughter in Baku. (Baku is on the shore of the Caspian Sea.)
8. I have been in Chicago, but I haven't been in Buffalo.

DRILL

Answer in complete sentences, using the nouns in the right-hand column.

	Вопро́с	**Отве́т**
1.	Где́ ты́ бы́л, Ива́н?	(теа́тр)
2.	Где́ А́нна?	(кино́)
3.	Где́ вы́ бы́ли вчера́?	(конце́рт)
4.	Где́ вы́ ви́дели Андре́я?	(такси́)
5.	Чего́ у ва́с не́т?	(костю́м)
6.	Чего́ не́т у Алёши?	(пальто́)

---

[6] An important center of oil industry on the Caspian Sea.
[7] A resort city on the Black Sea.

7. Чего́ нет у Ни́ны? (шля́па)
8. Где́ вы́ бы́ли весно́й? (Чика́го)
9. Где́ слу́жит (= work) ва́ш бра́т? (Вашингто́н)
10. Чего́ нет у сестры́? (ра́дио)
11. О чём вы́ говори́те? (Я́лта и Со́чи)
12. Где́ река́ Ле́на? (Сиби́рь)
13. Где́ вы́ живёте? (Баку́)
14. Где́ вы́ ви́дели А́нну? (метро́)

8. The preposition на and the locative (supplement)

The preposition на and not в (with the locative case) is used to express location with some nouns, including certain geographical names:

по́чта	на по́чте	at the post office
заво́д	на заво́де	at the plant
фа́брика	на фа́брике	at the factory
вокза́л	на вокза́ле	at the terminal
ста́нция	на ста́нции	at the station
Кавка́з	на Кавка́зе	in the Caucasus
Дон	на Дону́	in the Don region
Ура́л	на Ура́ле	in the Urals
Украи́на	на Украи́не	in the Ukraine

(See Unit 5, page 54, for the use of на with nouns denoting activities or events, and section 3, this unit, for -у in the locative after в and на.)

PATTERN SENTENCES

1. Ни́на слу́жит **на** по́чте, а Ива́н слу́жит в ба́нке.
1. Nina works at the post office, and Ivan works at the bank.

2. Сы́н А́нны Ива́новны рабо́тает **на** большо́м заво́де, а до́чь слу́жит в апте́ке.
2. Anna Ivanovna's son works at the big plant, and the daughter works in a drugstore.

3. Когда́ мы́ бы́ли в Сове́тском Сою́зе, мы́ бы́ли в Крыму́, но́ не́ были **на** Кавка́зе. У на́с бы́ло ма́ло вре́мени.
3. When we were in the Soviet Union, we visited the Crimea, but weren't in the Caucasus. We had little time.

4. И́х до́чь живёт **на** Украи́не.
4. Their daughter lives in the Ukraine.

5. Она́ хорошо́ зна́ет Украи́ну: она́ жила́ **на** Украи́не це́лый го́д.
5. She knows the Ukraine well: she lived in the Ukraine a whole year.

6. Джо́нсон бы́л везде́: он бы́л в Сиби́ри, **на** Ура́ле, и **на** Кавка́зе, но́ он почему́-то не́ был в Крыму́.
6. Johnson has been everywhere: he has been in Siberia, in the Urals, and in the Caucasus, but for some reason he hasn't been in the Crimea.

7. Писа́тель Шо́лохов жи́л **на** Дону́, и та́м о́н писа́л сво́й рома́н «Ти́хий До́н».
7. The writer Sholokhov lived on the Don and there he wrote his novel *The Silent Don*.

8. Я́ всегда́ покупа́ю газе́ту в кио́ске **на** ста́нции.
8. I always buy my newspaper at the newsstand at the station.

DRILL

Answer in complete sentences, using the word given in the right-hand column in your answer.

Вопро́с	Отве́т
Model: Где́ вы́ живёте?	(Босто́н)—Я́ живу́ в Босто́не.

1. Где́ рабо́тает Ива́н? — (заво́д)
2. Где́ вы́ слу́жите? — (по́чта)
3. Где́ живёт Ива́н Петро́вич? — (Москва́)
4. Где́ вы́ покупа́ете пла́тье? — (магази́н)
5. Где́ вы́ обыкнове́нно ви́дите А́нну? — (ста́нция)
6. Где́ Ки́ев? — (Украи́на)
7. Где́ ча́сто жи́л Че́хов? — (Я́лта)
8. Где́ ты́ живёшь ле́том? — (Кавка́з)
9. Где́ Зи́мний дворе́ц (Winter Palace)? — (Ленингра́д)
10. Где́ ты́ бу́дешь сего́дня ве́чером? — (теа́тр)
11. Где́ Бори́с? — (конце́рт)
12. Где́ ты́ обыкнове́нно рабо́таешь днём? — (библиоте́ка)
13. Где́ зима́ дли́нная? — (Сиби́рь)
14. Где́ ва́жный металлурги́ческий це́нтр? — (Ура́л)

9. Declension of personal pronouns (review table)

SINGULAR	*1st person*	*2nd person*	*3rd person*	
Nom.	я	ты	он оно́	она́
Gen.	меня́	тебя́	его́	её
Dat.	мне	тебе́	ему́	ей
Acc.	меня́	тебя́	его́	её
Instr.	мной, мно́ю[8]	тобо́й, тобо́ю[8]	им	ей, е́ю[8]
Loc.	обо мне́	о тебе́	о нём	о не́й

PLURAL			
Nom.	мы	вы	они́
Gen.	нас	вас	их
Dat.	нам	вам	им
Acc.	нас	вас	их
Instr.	на́ми	ва́ми	и́ми
Loc.	о на́с	о ва́с	о ни́х

[8] The forms ending in **-ю** are alternate forms which occur mostly in the literary and poetic language.

10. Adjective and pronoun-adjective declensions in the singular (review)

Most adjectives are of the hard type and have the stress on the stem; some, however, have the accent on the ending, which, for masculine nominative, is **-о́й** instead of **-ый** of the unstressed variant. A relatively small group of adjectives follows the soft pattern.

Hard means that the final consonant of the stem is hard, and *soft* means that this consonant is soft (it is most often a soft **н** [ņ]). The vowels appearing after the final consonant in the different case and gender forms follow the usual pattern (*the soft endings are never accented*):

Hard: -а- -о- -у- -ы-
Soft: -я- -е- -ю- -и-

The endings of masculine and neuter adjectives in cases other than the nominative closely resemble the corresponding case forms of **он** and **оно́** (in the feminine, the similarity with the declension of **она́** is not consistent).

	Masculine—Neuter			Feminine		
		Hard	Soft		Hard	Soft
Nom.	[он/оно́]	но́вый/но́вое	си́ний/си́нее	[она́]	но́вая	си́няя
Gen.	его́	но́вого	си́него	её	но́вой	си́ней
Dat.	ему́	но́вому	си́нему	ей	но́вой	си́ней
Acc.	его́	[Like Nom. or Gen.]		её	но́вую	си́нюю
Instr.	им	но́вым	си́ним	ей	но́вой	си́ней
Loc.	нём	но́вом	си́нем	ней	но́вой	си́ней

Hard type with stress on the ending:

	Nom.	*Gen.*	*Dat.*	*Acc.*	*Instr.*	*Loc.*
Masc. *Neut.*	молодо́й молодо́е	молодо́го	молодо́му	—	молоды́м	молодо́м
Fem.	молода́я	молодо́й	молодо́й	молоду́ю	молодо́й	молодо́й

The spelling of the endings differs from the patterns given above in adjectives with stems ending in **г, к,** and **х** and in **ж, ч, ш,** and **щ**. In terms of spelling, the first group may be regarded as basically hard and the second (if the stress is *not* on the ending) as basically soft. In both groups there are a few deviations from the regular patterns in accordance with the spelling rules (see Unit 3, p. 22).

Stems in г, к, and х, basically *hard* pattern. The masculine declension presents two deviations:

	Normal hard *masc. endings*	*Stems in* г, к, х, *e.g.,* **ру́сский**
Nom.	**-ый**	ру́сский (no **ы** after г, к, х!)
Gen.	-ого	normal
Dat.	-ому	normal
Acc.	[Like Nom. or Gen.]	
Instr.	**-ым**	ру́сским (no **ы** after г, к, х!)
Loc.	-ом	normal

Neuter has the normal hard ending **-ое** in the nominative and accusative, and is like masculine in the other cases. Feminine follows the normal pattern.

Stem in ж, ч, ш, and щ (stress on the stem), basically *soft* pattern. Masculine and neuter, e.g., хоро́ший, хоро́шее, follow the normal soft pattern (see above). Feminine presents two deviations:

	Normal soft *fem. endings*	*Stems in* ж, ч, ш, щ, *e.g.,* **хоро́шая**
Nom.	**-яя**	хоро́шая (no я after ж, ч, ш, щ!)
Gen.	-ей	normal
Dat.	-ей	normal
Acc.	**-юю**	хоро́шую (no ю after ж, ч, ш, щ!)
Instr.	-ей	normal
Loc.	-ей	normal

Some adjectives with stems in г, к, х and ж, ч, ш, щ have stressed endings, e.g., плохо́й, плохо́е, плоха́я; большо́й, большо́е, больша́я. They follow the regular hard pattern with only one exception: the instrumental ending in masculine and neuter is **-им**, not **-ым**.

It must be understood that the rules given above concern spelling, not pronunciation. Thus, the sounds [š] and [ž] remain hard even when the vowels **и** and **e** are written after them; and the sounds [č] and [ṣ̌č] remain soft even when followed by **a** or **y**.

Pronoun-adjective declension. Pronoun-adjectives have a declension which is similar to, but not entirely identical with, the adjective declension. The forms of the nominative and some forms of the accusative are distinct.

(1) *Declension of demonstratives.*

э́тот *this* (singular)

	Masculine	*Neuter*	*Feminine*
Nom.	э́тот	э́то	э́та
Gen.	э́того	like masc.	э́той
Dat.	э́тому	like masc.	э́той
Acc.	like Nom. or Gen.	э́то	э́ту
Instr.	э́тим [9]	like masc.	э́той
Loc.	э́том	like masc.	э́той

---

[9] This stem becomes soft in the instrumental [éṭ.].

Одни́ (*one*) is declined like э́тот, but has final stress (одного́, одному́, etc.). The vowel **и** drops out in all cases other than the masculine singular nominative.

тот *that* (singular)

	Masculine	Neuter	Feminine
Nom.	тот	то	та
Gen.	того́	like masc.	той
Dat.	тому́	like masc.	той
Acc.	like Nom. or Gen.	то	ту
Instr.	тем [10]	like masc.	той
Loc.	том	like masc.	той

(2) *Declension of possessives.*

мой *my*, *mine* (singular)

	Masculine	Neuter	Feminine
Nom.	мой	моё	моя́
Gen.	моего́	like masc.	мое́й
Dat.	моему́	like masc.	мое́й
Acc.	like Nom. or Gen.	моё	мою́
Instr.	мойм	like masc.	мое́й
Loc.	моём	like masc.	мое́й

Твой (*your*, *yours*) and **свой** (*one's own*) are declined like **мой**.

наш *our*, *ours* (singular)

	Masculine	Neuter	Feminine
Nom.	наш	на́ше	на́ша
Gen.	на́шего	like masc.	на́шей
Dat.	на́шему	like masc.	на́шей
Acc.	like Nom. or Gen.	на́ше	на́шу
Instr.	на́шим	like masc.	на́шей
Loc.	на́шем	like masc.	на́шей

Ваш (*your*, *yours*) is declined like **наш**.

(3) *Declension of definites.*

весь *all* (singular)

	Masculine	Neuter	Feminine
Nom.	весь	всё	вся
Gen.	всего́	like masc.	всей
Dat.	всему́	like masc.	всей
Acc.	like Nom. or Gen.	всё	всю
Instr.	всем	like masc.	всей
Loc.	всём	like masc.	всей

---

[10] This stem becomes soft in the instrumental [ṭ.].

(4) *Declension of interrogative pronouns.*

	кто *who*	**что** *what*
Nom.	кто	что
Gen.	кого	чего
Dat.	кому	чему
Acc.	кого	что
Instr.	кем	чем
Loc.	ком	чём

PATTERN SENTENCES

1. **Вся** на́ша семья́ живёт тепе́рь вме́сте.
2. Ма́ть должна́ ду́мать **обо всей** семье́.
3. Хоро́шая хозя́йка должна́ **всё** по́мнить и должна́ **обо всём** ду́мать.
4. Учи́тель недово́лен **всем** кла́ссом. О́н ка́ждый де́нь говори́т э́то **всему́** кла́ссу.
5. Ива́н Ива́нович люби́мый учи́тель **всего́** кла́сса.

1. All our family is living together now.
2. The mother has to think about the whole family.
3. A good housewife must remember everything and must think about everything.
4. The teacher is dissatisfied with the whole class. Every day he tells the whole class that.
5. Ivan Ivanovich is the favorite teacher of the whole class.

DRILL

Put the words in parentheses in the correct case and translate.

1. У меня́ не́т (ве́сь те́кст).
2. У меня́ не́т (ве́сь перево́д).
3. Я до́лжен ду́мать обо (всё).
4. Я ви́дел (вся семья́).
5. Я ви́дел (вся пье́са).
6. Я дово́лен (вся семья́).
7. Я до́лжен ду́мать обо (вся семья́).

11. Superlative of adjectives with са́мый

One type of superlative is formed by using the adjective **са́мый** with the basic adjective. Both **са́мый** and the basic adjective are declined:

Э́то **са́мая дорога́я** гости́ница в го́роде.
This is the most expensive hotel in town.

Они́ живу́т в **са́мой дорого́й** гости́нице.
They live in a most expensive hotel.

Во́т **са́мый интере́сный** рома́н э́того писа́теля.
Here is the most interesting novel of this writer.

Э́то рома́н об одно́м **са́мом обыкнове́нном** челове́ке.
This is a novel about a most ordinary person.

—С ке́м вы́ говори́ли? —С мои́м **са́мым у́мным** ученико́м.
—With whom were you speaking? —With my brightest pupil.

DRILL

Combine each of the incomplete sentences under A with the first, and then with the second phrase under B using the proper case forms.

A.

Я говори́л о . . . .
Я говори́л с . . . .
Я ви́дел . . . .
Я дово́лен . . . .
Я объясня́ю пра́вило . . . .

B.

1. моя́ са́мая у́мная студе́нтка
2. мо́й са́мый у́мный студе́нт

Reading

В Сове́тском Сою́зе

This reading is in three parts. Study the first part carefully; read it over several times, familiarizing yourself with the vocabulary and the content, and then answer the questions, first in writing and then aloud. Do the same with the second and third parts.

Пе́рвая ча́сть (First Part)

Вы́ вероя́тно ви́дели высо́кое зда́ние ря́дом с университе́том на углу́ э́той у́лицы. В э́том зда́нии на пе́рвом этаже́ на́ш студе́нческий клу́б.

Вчера́ у на́с та́м бы́ло собра́ние. На э́том собра́нии Бо́б Кла́рк, студе́нт, кото́рый изуча́ет ру́сский язы́к и литерату́ру, чита́л докла́д о Сове́тском Сою́зе, где́ он бы́л в э́том году́ о́сенью. О́н бы́л та́м два́ ме́сяца.

Мне́ бы́ло о́чень интере́сно слу́шать Бо́ба, та́к как я о́чень ма́ло зна́ю об э́той стране́. Во́т всё, что я зна́ю: в Росси́и была́ револю́ция. До револю́ции та́м бы́л ца́рь, а по́сле револю́ции у ни́х бы́л во́ждь Ле́нин. По́сле Ле́нина вождём бы́л Ста́лин, и во вре́мя Ста́лина бы́л «ку́льт ли́чности» (cult of personality). По́сле Ста́лина бы́л Хрущёв. По́сле него́—два́ вождя́ вме́сте. Пото́м . . . не зна́ю. Я зна́ю, что во вре́мя Второ́й мирово́й войны́ (the Second World War) Сове́тский Сою́з бы́л на́шим сою́зником (ally). Я зна́ю, что э́то тепе́рь респу́блика, что э́то огро́мная страна́, са́мая больша́я в ми́ре. Та́м коммуни́зм и та́м о́чень хо́лодно.

Это почти́ всё, что я зна́ю, и я слу́шал докла́д с больши́м интере́сом.

Ленингра́д

Снача́ла Кла́рк бы́л в Ленингра́де, бы́вшей (former) столи́це Росси́и. До царя́ Петра́ Пе́рвого (или Вели́кого)[11] столи́цей была́ Москва́, как тепе́рь. Но́ Росси́и ну́жен бы́л по́рт, и в де́льте (delta) реки́ Невы́, у Фи́нского зали́ва,[12] Пётр

---

[11] **Пётр Пе́рвый (Вели́кий)** *Peter I (the Great),* 1672–1725. Peter I was a great reformer who introduced many European customs into Russian life.

[12] **Фи́нский зали́в.** The Gulf of Finland is the gulf of the Baltic Sea into which the Neva empties.

ILLUSTRATION 13.   Зи́мний дворе́ц (Эрмита́ж). (*Tass from Sovfoto.*)

ILLUSTRATION 14.   Ку́хня в голла́ндском сти́ле в Ле́тнем дворце́ Петра́ Вели́кого (нача́ла 18-го ве́ка). (*Sovfoto.*)

Вели́кий основа́л (founded) но́вый го́род: Петербу́рг[13] (тепе́решний Ленингра́д).

Кла́рк говори́т, что Ленингра́д, мо́жет быть, са́мый краси́вый го́род в Евро́пе. Он расска́зывал об одно́м осо́бенно краси́вом зда́нии—э́то Зи́мний дворе́ц (the Winter Palace), где до револю́ции жи́л ца́рь. В Зи́мнем дворце́ знамени́тый музе́й Эрмита́ж.[14] Гла́вная у́лица Ленингра́да—широ́кий и дли́нный Не́вский проспе́кт. В одно́м конце́ Не́вского—Адмиралте́йство (the Admiralty), и ря́дом с ни́м больша́я пло́щадь, где стои́т знамени́тый па́мятник[15] Петру́ Вели́кому: Пётр на ло́шади (on a horse) на скале́ (rock), и на э́той скале́, у ноги́ ло́шади, огро́мная змея́ (snake)! В дово́льно центра́льной ча́сти го́рода—Ле́тний са́д. В Ле́тнем саду́ стои́т краси́вый и просто́й Ле́тний дворе́ц Петра́. Пётр люби́л просту́ю жи́знь, и ча́сто жи́л в э́том дворце́.

Во́т где ещё бы́л Кла́рк, и что о́н ещё ви́дел в э́том замеча́тельном го́роде: о́н бы́л в кварти́ре-музе́е Пу́шкина. В э́той кварти́ре жи́л, и по́сле дуэ́ли у́мер (died) вели́кий поэ́т. Кла́рк бы́л в кварти́ре, в кото́рой одно́ вре́мя, до револю́ции, жи́л Влади́мир Ильи́ч Ле́нин. О́н бы́л в кварти́ре-музе́е знамени́того физио́лога Ива́на Петро́вича Па́влова[16] и в Институ́те эксперимента́льной медици́ны, в кото́ром Па́влов рабо́тал. О́н ви́дел до́м, кото́рый Достое́вский опи́сывает (describes) в своём рома́не «Преступле́ние и Наказа́ние» (*Crime and Punishment*). Э́то до́м, в кото́ром Раско́льников, геро́й рома́на, убива́ет (kills) стару́ху (old woman). Э́то мо́й люби́мый рома́н, и я хорошо́ по́мню описа́ние до́ма и описа́ние стару́хи и преступле́ния.

Я о́чень хочу́ ви́деть э́тот го́род и всё то, о чём расска́зывал Кла́рк!

Answer these questions in Russian.

1. Где зда́ние, в кото́ром студе́нческий клу́б? 2. На како́м этаже́ клу́б? 3. Где вчера́ бы́ло собра́ние? 4. Что́ бы́ло вчера́ на собра́нии? 5. Кто́ Бо́б Кла́рк? 6. Когда́ и ско́лько вре́мени бы́л Кла́рк в Сове́тском Сою́зе? 7. Почему́ мне́ бы́ло интере́сно его́ слу́шать? 8. Почему́ Пётр Вели́кий основа́л Петербу́рг, и где о́н его́ основа́л? 9. Где музе́й Эрмита́ж? 10. Что́ на большо́й пло́щади ря́дом с Адмиралте́йством? 11. Где Ле́тний дворе́ц, како́й о́н, и почему́ Пётр люби́л та́м жи́ть? 12. Когда́ жи́л Ле́нин в кварти́ре, о кото́рой расска́зывал Бо́б? 13. Кто́ бы́л Ива́н Петро́вич Па́влов? 14. В како́м рома́не Достое́вский опи́сывает до́м, о кото́ром говори́л Бо́б, и кто́ Раско́льников?

Втора́я ча́сть (*Second Part*)

Москва́

Москва́ столи́ца Сове́тского Сою́за, полити́ческий и культу́рный це́нтр

---

[13] **Петербу́рг** (in former parlance, Са́нкт-Петербу́рг) was founded by Peter the Great in 1703. It was renamed Петрогра́д during World War I in order to avoid the Germanic **-бу́рг**, of which the Slavic **-гра́д** (*city*) is the equivalent. After Lenin's death in 1924 the city was renamed once again, and became Ленингра́д. Six years earlier, in 1918, Moscow once again became the capital.

[14] *The Hermitage* is one of the most famous art museums in the world.

[15] Monuments to persons are referred to with the name of the person memorialized in the dative case: па́мятник Ли́нкольну, Пу́шкину, Достое́вскому. The word **па́мятник** is derived from **па́мять** (*memory*).

[16] *Pavlov, Ivan Petrovich* (1849–1936), world-famous physiologist, especially noted for his theory of conditioned reflex.

ILLUSTRATION 15.   Моско́вский Кре́мль и Москва́-река́. (*Tass from Sovfoto.*)

страны́. В Москве́, в са́мом большо́м го́роде Сою́за, мно́го интере́сного, и ста́рого и но́вого.

Гости́ница «Росси́я», где у Кла́рка была́ хоро́шая ко́мната с ва́нной, са́мая но́вая и са́мая больша́я гости́ница столи́цы. «Росси́я» стои́т в о́чень интере́сной ча́сти го́рода: она́ стои́т у Москвы́-реки́, ря́дом с Кра́сной пло́щадью и Кремлём.

Кремль,[17] э́та истори́ческая часть го́рода, люби́мое ме́сто Кла́рка в Москве́. Э́то ме́сто бы́ло нача́лом Москвы́. В Кремле́ всё интере́сно. Ка́ждая це́рковь, ка́ждое зда́ние—па́мятник ру́сской исто́рии. Тепе́рь там, в большо́м Кремлёвском дворце́ (palace) Верхо́вный Сове́т (Supreme Soviet), ва́жный о́рган сове́тского прави́тельства.

Боб ви́дел всё то́, о чём говори́л на ве́чере пре́ссы Пи́тер Ро́бертс, но так как он жи́л в Москве́ три неде́ли, а Ро́бертс то́лько две́, Боб ви́дел бо́льше, чем (than) Ро́бертс.

Кла́рк бы́л в Моско́вском Худо́жественном Теа́тре[18] на пье́се Че́хова «Три́ сестры́». Так как он уже́ ра́ньше чита́л э́ту пье́су, он понима́л всё без большо́го труда́. Все́ игра́ли (acted) о́чень хорошо́, но осо́бенно хорошо́ игра́ла о́чень молода́я актри́са, кото́рая игра́ла ро́ль Ири́ны, мла́дшей сестры́.

В Большо́м теа́тре, на бале́те «Лебеди́ное о́зеро»[19] (Swan Lake) Чайко́вского, танцева́ла знамени́тая балери́на Ма́йя Плисе́цкая. Как замеча́тельно она́ танцева́ла!

В Третьяко́вской галере́е,[20] где, мо́жет быть, са́мая больша́я колле́кция ру́сского иску́сства (art), Кла́рк ви́дел знамени́тую ико́ну (icon) худо́жника (artist, painter) Андре́я Рублёва, на кото́рой три́ а́нгела. Э́та ико́на «Тро́ица» (The Trinity) са́мая краси́вая ико́на во всей галере́е. В кни́ге «Ру́сское иску́сство» Боб ви́дел ра́ньше репроду́кцию карти́ны худо́жника Левита́на «Золота́я о́сень» (Golden Autumn). А тепе́рь он ви́дел оригина́л э́той карти́ны на стене́ галере́и!

Кла́рк, коне́чно, ви́дел и «но́вую Москву́». Он бы́л в огро́мном Центра́льном стадио́не, бы́л в бы́стром и удо́бном моско́вском метро́, где, как говори́л его́ гид-перево́дчик, «во́здух всегда́ све́жий, как в дере́вне».

В огро́мном но́вом Моско́вском университе́те весёлый и у́мный студе́нт-матема́тик Андре́й Во́лков всё ему́ пока́зывал и объясня́л. Андре́й хорошо́ зна́ет англи́йский язы́к, кото́рый он изуча́ет уже́ четы́ре го́да. И, хотя́ он матема́тик, он дово́льно хорошо́ зна́ет америка́нскую и англи́йскую литерату́ру. Его́ люби́мый писа́тель Хе́мингуэй, но Бе́рнарда Шо́у (Shaw) и Ма́рка Тве́на (Twain) он то́же зна́ет и лю́бит. Боб и Андре́й говори́ли о литерату́ре, о но́вой матема́тике. Андре́й расска́зывал о своём университе́те, а Боб о своём, и они́ бы́ли о́чень дово́льны свои́м разгово́ром.

---

[17] **Кремль** (*masc.*). The Kremlin is the walled historical part of Moscow located in the center of the city. On one side the wall separates the Kremlin from Red Square, on the other side from the embankment of the Moscow River. Inside the Kremlin there are many famous old churches and historical buildings. Several buildings date from the fifteenth century. Some of the old and new buildings are now used by the Soviet government.

[18] **Моско́вский Худо́жественный Теа́тр.** The celebrated Moscow Art Theater was founded by Stanislavsky and Nemirovich-Danchenko in 1898. This theater produced all Chekhov's plays, and is closely connected with his name. The white *sea gull* (**ча́йка**) in honor of Chekhov's play of the same name still decorates the theater curtain and has become the emblem of the Art Theater.

[19] **Лебеди́ное о́зеро**, *Swan Lake*, a famous ballet by Tchaikovsky on a fairy-tale subject. **Ле́бедь** *swan*.

[20] **Третьяко́вская галере́я.** The Tretiakov Gallery contains a very large collection of Russian art, from early icons to the works of contemporary artists. Among the icons are several by the famous Russian master Andrei Rublev (1360–1430).

Answer these questions in Russian.

1. Что́ вы́ зна́ете о гости́нице «Росси́я»? 2. Что́ вы́ мо́жете рассказа́ть о Кремле́? 3. В како́м зда́нии Кремля́ Верхо́вный Сове́т? 4. В како́м моско́вском теа́тре мо́жно (one can) ви́деть пье́су Че́хова, и в како́м теа́тре мо́жно ви́деть бале́т и́ли слы́шать о́перу? 5. Чью́ ро́ль игра́ла в пье́се «Три́ сестры́» молода́я актри́са? 6. Кто́ Ма́йя Плисе́цкая, и в како́м бале́те её ви́дел Бо́б? 7. Ка́к назва́ние знамени́той ико́ны, и почему́ у э́той ико́ны тако́е назва́ние? Кто́ худо́жник? 8. Что́ Бо́б ви́дел в кни́ге «Ру́сское иску́сство»? 9. Что́ о́н говори́т о моско́вском метро́? 10. Что́ о́н расска́зывал об Андре́е Во́лкове? Како́й о́н, что́ о́н изуча́ет, и что́ о́н лю́бит?

Тре́тья ча́сть (*Third Part*)

Украи́на

По́сле Москвы́ Бо́б бы́л почти́ неде́лю в Ки́еве,[21] в столи́це Украи́нской респу́блики.

Ки́ев о́чень краси́вый го́род на высо́ком берегу́ Днепра́. Ки́ев и Дне́пр игра́ли ва́жную ро́ль в исто́рии Росси́и. В Ки́еве, в Днепре́, Кня́зь (prince) Влади́мир крести́л[22] сво́й наро́д (people, nation), кото́рый до э́того бы́л язы́ческим (pagan).

В Ки́еве говоря́т по-украи́нски и по-ру́сски (украи́нский то́же славя́нский [Slavic] язы́к, как ру́сский).

Перево́дчик и ги́д Кла́рка, Ива́н Руде́нко, студе́нт Ки́евского университе́та, не о́чень хорошо́ говори́л по-англи́йски, и поэ́тому они́ говори́ли по-ру́сски: америка́нец с америка́нским акце́нтом, а украи́нец—с украи́нским! Но́ Бо́б хорошо́ понима́л Ива́на, а Ива́н Бо́ба. Кла́рк ви́дел с Ива́ном мно́го интере́сного. Они́ бы́ли на украи́нской о́пере, где́ Ива́н до́лжен был всё переводи́ть. Они́ бы́ли на конце́рте украи́нской му́зыки, где́ пе́л замеча́тельный хо́р. Они́ почти́ це́лый де́нь бы́ли в Софи́йском собо́ре,[23] и Руде́нко, кото́рый лю́бит архитекту́ру и иску́сство (art), интере́сно расска́зывал Бо́бу исто́рию э́той замеча́тельной це́ркви. Бо́б бу́дет до́лго по́мнить э́ту неде́лю в Ки́еве.

Кро́ме Ки́ева, Бо́б ви́дел на Украи́не то́лько ещё оди́н го́род: Ха́рьков. Ха́рьков тепе́рь ва́жный индустриа́льный це́нтр. Бо́б бы́л та́м на большо́м тра́кторном заво́де, на автомоби́льном заво́де, и на большо́м хими́ческом. Хотя́ о́н не инжене́р и не хи́мик, ему́ бы́ло интере́сно ви́деть сове́тскую инду́стрию, а не то́лько чита́ть о не́й.

Кли́мат

О кли́мате Сове́тского Сою́за Кла́рк говори́т, что, когда́ о́н бы́л в Ленингра́де, та́м бы́ло уже́ дово́льно хо́лодно: в Москве́ бы́ло прохла́дно, на Ура́ле о́н да́же ви́дел сне́г (snow), а на берегу́ Чёрного мо́ря—наприме́р в Я́лте, в Крыму́, и в Со́чи, на Кавка́зе—бы́ло ещё тепло́ как ле́том. Коне́чно, на Эльбру́се, на са́мой высо́кой горе́ (mountain) Кавка́за, бы́л сне́г (snow) как всегда́.

---

[21] Ки́ев бы́л пе́рвой столи́цей Руси́. (Ру́сь ста́рое назва́ние Росси́и.)

[22] **Крести́л**, *baptized, christianized.* The christianizing of the Russian people occurred in 988 A.D.

[23] Софи́йский Собо́р, the St. Sophia Cathedral, begun in 1037, has been remodelled over the centuries, most recently in 1690. The cathedral possesses magnificent frescoes and mosaics, some from the eleventh century.

ILLUSTRATION 16. Мозáика в Софи́йском Собóре в Ки́еве. (*Tass from Sovfoto*.)

ILLUSTRATION 18. Трáкторный завóд в Хáрькове. (*Novosti from Sovfoto*.)

ILLUSTRATION 17. Метрó в Ки́еве. (*Sovfoto*.)

Ни в Сибири, ни в средней (Central) Азии, Кларк не был, так как у него было слишком мало времени.

По-моему, все были довольны этим докладом, и я теперь ещё больше хочу знать русский язык.

Answer these questions in Russian.

1. Столицей чего был Киев раньше? 2. Какой князь крестил свой народ в Днепре? 3. Кто Руденко? 4. Почему Руденко мог так интересно рассказывать о Софийском соборе? 5. Почему Боб был на автомобильном заводе в Харькове? 6. Было везде ещё тепло как летом? 7. Где кроме Урала он видел снег?

DRILL

Review Translation.

1. About me and about you (*sing.*). 2. About you (*pl.*) and about us. 3. About her and about her mother and her daughter. 4. About everything. 5. With me and with him. 6. With his mother and with his sister. 7. With the whole family. 8. —How long did he live in the Ukraine? —A year in Kiev, where he worked in a drugstore, and a year in Kharkov, where he worked in a post office. 9. Yalta is on the shore of the Black Sea. 10. They don't know Siberia at all; they have never been in Siberia. 11. The Soviet Union is the biggest country in the world. 12. The main street is to the left, and Red Square to the right. 13. I seldom write to my mother, because I have no time, but I always think about her. 14. —Do you know his mother? —No, for some reason I know only his sister. 15. He wants to be an historian. 16. When Tolstoy was young, he lived in the Caucasus. He was an officer then. 17. She says that the Russian language, which she is studying this year, is the most beautiful language that she knows! 18. My old dog always lies on the floor next to the chair on which I am sitting; that is his favorite place. 19. They are writing a book with me. 20. Today is a fine spring day. 21. I am very pleased with my life. 22. It is interesting for him to work in this plant; it is the largest plant in this city. 23. He is not a famous historian, but he knows very much about Russian history and especially about the Russian Revolution.

Vocabulary

аптека drugstore
банк bank
берег shore, coast, bank (of a river)
важный important
великий great
вождь (*masc.*) leader
воздух air
гид guide
главный main, chief
год year
гражданин (*fem.* гражданка) citizen
дача summer cottage

доклад report, talk, speech
завод plant, factory
замечательный remarkable, wonderful
здание building
зелёный green
знаменитый famous, celebrated
кино (*neut. indecl.*) movies, movie theater
климат climate
клуб club
лекция lecture
лес woods, forest
любимый favorite, beloved

любо́вь (*fem. II*) (*loc.* любви́; *instr.* любо́вью) love

метро́ (*neut. indecl.*) subway

мо́ре sea

мост bridge

нале́во on (to) the left

напра́во on (to) the right

но́мер number; hotel room

обыкнове́нный usual, ordinary

огро́мный huge, enormous, immense

осо́бенно especially

пальто́ (*neut. indecl.*) coat, overcoat

перево́дчи.к (*fem.* -ца) interpreter, translator

пло́щадь (*fem. II*) square

по́чта post office; mail

просто́й simple, plain

прохла́дно cool

про́шлый past, last

ра́ньше earlier, formerly, before (*adv.*)

револю́ция revolution

рис rice

роль (*fem. II*) role, part

сад garden; orchard

са́мый the most

смерть (*fem. II*) death

собра́ние meeting; collection

ста́нция station

такси́ (*neut. indecl.*) taxi

таре́лка plate

те́ма theme, subject

у́гол (*gen.* угла́) corner; angle

университе́т university

фильм film

часть (*fem. II*) part

VERBS

изуча́ть (I) to learn, study (*trans.*)

служи́ть (II: служу́, слу́жишь) to serve, work, be employed

EXPRESSIONS

ско́лько вре́мени? how long?

во вре́мя (+ *gen.*) during

та́к как since, as, because

почему́-то for some reason

чита́ть докла́д to give a talk

игра́ть ро́ль to play a part

ещё бо́льше even more

в про́шлом году́ last year

в э́том году́ this year

в бу́дущем году́ next year

GEOGRAPHICAL TERMS

А́нглия England

англи́йский English (*adj.*)

Дон Don (river)

Ита́лия Italy

Кавка́з Caucasus (mountains)

моско́вский of Moscow (*adj.*)

Сиби́рь (*fem.*) Siberia

Украи́на Ukraine

Ура́л Urals (mountains)

Фра́нция France

Nominative plural of nouns • Nominative plural of pronoun-
adjectives • Nominative plural of adjectives • Masculine nouns
with nominative plurals in -á/-я • Nominative plurals in -ья •
Miscellaneous categories of nominative plurals • Reciprocal pronoun
друг друга • Conversation: Бе́дная продавщи́ца! • Reading for
plurals

Unit 13

Grammar

1. Nominative plural endings of most nouns

Nominative Plural	Hard	Soft
Most *masc.*, all *fem.*	**-ы**	**-и**
Some *masc.*, all *neut.*	**-а**	**-я**

		Singular	Plural
Type 1: -ы or -и	*Masc.*	студе́нт [stuḍént.] гость [góşţ.] музе́й [muẓéj.] оте́ц (aţéc)	студе́нты [stuḍént.i] го́сти [góşţ.i] музе́и [muẓéj.i] отцы́ (atcí)
	Fem. I	стена́ [şţin.á] кни́га [kṇíg.ə] ку́хня [kúxṇ.ə] ле́кция [ḷekcij.ə]	сте́ны [şţén.ɨ] кни́ги[1] [kṇíg.i] ку́хни [kúxṇ.i] ле́кции [ḷékcɨj.i]
	Fem. II	дверь [ḍvéṛ.]	две́ри [ḍvéṛ.i]
Type 2: -а or -я	*Masc.*	hard: дом [dóm] soft: учи́тель [učíţiḷ.]	дома́ [dam.á] учителя́ [učiţiḷ.á]
	Neut.	hard: кре́сло [kṛésl.ə] soft: { по́ле [póḷ.ə] { зда́ние [zdáṇij.ə]	кре́сла [kṛésl.ə] поля́ [paḷ.á] зда́ния [zdáṇij.ə]

[1] Spelling Rule 1 (page 68) applies.

DRILL

Put the following nouns in the nominative plural.

ко́мната	телефо́н	учи́тельница
студе́нт	музе́й	кварти́ра
исто́рик	кре́сло	геро́й
инжене́р	пло́щадь	ку́хня
студе́нтка	гость	собра́ние

Shifting stress in plural nouns.

Nouns frequently undergo a shift of stress in the plural; in the feminine and neuter this helps to distinguish the nominative plural from the genitive singular, e.g.,

Nom. Sing.	*Gen. Sing.*	*Nom. Pl.*
стена́	стены́	сте́ны
страна́	страны́	стра́ны
рука́	руки́	ру́ки
нога́	ноги́	но́ги
голова́	головы́	го́ловы
река́	реки́	ре́ки
окно́	окна́	о́кна
ме́сто	ме́ста	места́ [ṃistá]
сло́во	сло́ва	слова́ [slavá]
по́ле	по́ля	поля́ [paḷá]
мо́ре	мо́ря	моря́ [maṛá]

In some words the vowel **e** of the stem becomes **ё** under stress:

жена́	жены́	жёны
сестра́	сестры́	сёстры
звезда́	звезды́	звёзды
о́зеро	о́зера	озёра

Note the plurals of words with fleeting **o** or **e**:

коне́ц	конца́	концы́
оте́ц	отца́	отцы́
кусо́к	куска́	куски́
ковёр	covpа́	ковры́
день	дня	дни

DRILL

Write the following nouns in the nominative plural with the proper stresses. Then read each noun aloud first in the singular and then in the plural.

стол (stress shifts)	страна́	голова́
сад (stress shifts)	рука́	мо́ре
окно́	нога́	жена́

по́ле	сестра́	письмо́
река́	ме́сто	сло́во
стена́	каранда́ш	о́зеро (lake)

2. Nominative plural of pronoun-adjectives

It has been seen that the third person pronoun **они́** is used for *all three genders* in the plural. The same is true of the plural of pronouns and adjectives; none of these have distinct gender forms in the plural.

Like **они́**, the possessives, the demonstrative **э́тот**, and the numeral **оди́н** take the ending **-и** in the plural:

Singular	*Plural*
мой [mój.]	**мои́** [maj.í]
твой [tvój.]	**твои́** [tvaj.í]
свой [svój.]	**свои́** [svaj.í]
наш [náš.]	**на́ши** [náš.i]
ваш [váš.]	**ва́ши** [váš.i]
чей, чья, чьё [stem čj.]	**чьи** [čj.í]
э́тот [ét.ət]	**э́ти** [éṭ.i][2]
оди́н [aḍín]	**одни́** [aḍṇí][2]

The demonstrative **тот** has the plural **те**.[2] **Весь** (all) has the plural **все**, all genders. The following sentences illustrate these pronouns in the singular and the plural:

Во́т ва́ш студе́нт.	Во́т ва́ши студе́нты.
Э́то моя́ шля́па.	Э́то мои́ шля́пы.
Э́тот слова́рь на́ш.	Э́ти словари́ на́ши.
Чья́ кни́га на столе́?	Чьи́ кни́ги на столе́?

3. Nominative plural of adjectives

In the nominative plural, hard adjectives take the ending **-ые** (но́вые). Soft adjectives take the ending **-ие** (си́ние). With adjectives with stems ending in the consonants **г, к, х, ж, ш,** and **щ** the ending is spelled **-ие** (ру́сские, хоро́шие):

Masculine Singular	*Plural All Genders*
но́вый [nóv.əj]	но́вые [nóv.iji]
молодо́й [məlad.ój]	молоды́е [məlad.íji]
како́й [kak.ój]	каки́е [kaḳ.íji]
ру́сский [rúsḳ.ij]	ру́сские [rúsḳ.iji]
хоро́ший [xaróš.ɨj]	хоро́шие [xaróš.ɨji]
си́ний [ṣíṇ.ij]	си́ние [ṣíṇ.iji]

[2] Note that the final stem consonants of these words soften in the plural. For the use of **оди́н**, see p. 108.

E.g.: Во́т на́ши но́вые студе́нты.
Э́то хоро́шие молоды́е инжене́ры.
Все́ э́ти ру́сские писа́тели интере́сные.
Каки́е краси́вые си́ние кре́сла!

DRILLS

A. *Supply the proper endings of the plural and translate.*

1. В э́том го́роде е́сть дли́нн... у́лиц....
2. Э́тот писа́тель пи́шет ску́чн... рома́н....[3]
3. Э́то на́ш... но́в... студе́нт....
4. —Кто́ э́т... молод... тури́ст...? —Они́ ру́сск....
5. —Чь'... э́т... ма́леньк... ма́льчик...? Они́ ва́ш...? —Да́, мо'....
6. В э́той шко́ле хоро́ш... учени́к.'...
7. Я́ чита́ю рома́н «Дн'... и но́ч...».
8. На́м нужны́ удо́бн... кре́сл....
9. Мо'... сёстр... пи́шут мне́ коро́тк... пи́сьм....
10. В э́той ко́мнате бо́льш'... о́кн....
11. Как'... огро́мн... пол'...!
12. В на́шей кварти́ре бо́льш'... све́тл... ко́мнат....
13. У неё краси́в... ру́к....
14. У него́ хоро́ш... секрета́рш....
15. —Де́вочк...! Чь'... э́т... но́в... кни́г...? —На́ш....
16. Я́ люблю́ ни́зк... крова́т....

B. *Form plurals of the following.*

э́тот у́мный студе́нт
то́ высо́кое зда́ние
твоя́ приле́жная учени́ца
мо́й у́зкий боти́нок
на́ш глу́пый ма́льчик

э́тот сове́тский писа́тель
ва́ш но́вый уче́бник
твоё дли́нное пальто́
на́ш си́ний автомоби́ль
э́та удо́бная крова́ть

э́то тру́дное пра́вило
ру́сский ца́рь
чьё окно́?
э́та америка́нская семья́
вся́ кни́га

C. *Translate into Russian.*

1. What long novels!
2. Everyone likes comfortable apartments.
3. In Italy we saw old narrow streets.
4. These little boys are my pupils.
5. Who are these little girls? They are my sister's pupils.
6. I love green fields.
7. Whose are these blue notebooks?
8. Where do you buy your armchairs?
9. These words were his last.
10. My students are very good. They are intelligent and diligent.
11. The United States of America is a huge country.

4. Masculine nouns with nominative plurals in -á/-я́

Following are some of the more important nouns taking **-á/-я́** in the masculine nominative plural. This ending is stressed throughout the plural in the masculine (in contrast to the genitive singular of these words, which has stress on the stem):

Nominative Singular	Nominative Plural	
до́м	дома́	houses
по́езд	поезда́	trains
го́род	города́	cities

---

[3] The accusative plural of *inanimate* nouns, all genders, is the same as the nominative plural.

лес	леса́	forests
ве́чер	вечера́	evenings
бе́рег	берега́	shores
го́лос	голоса́	voices
цвет	цвета́	colors
но́мер	номера́	numbers
а́дрес	адреса́	addresses
глаз	глаза́	eyes
до́ктор	доктора́	doctors
профе́ссор	профессора́	professors
дире́ктор	директора́	directors
учи́тель	учителя́	teachers

DRILLS

A. *Change the words in parentheses to plural and translate.*

1. На э́той у́лице то́лько (ни́зкий до́м).
2. В э́том го́роде (дли́нная у́лица).
3. В Сиби́ри (огро́мный лес).
4. Я люблю́ (ста́рый истори́ческий го́род).
5. В на́шей кварти́ре (больша́я ко́мната).
6. (Э́тот по́езд тако́й ме́дленный.)
7. (Бе́рег) Во́лги о́чень (краси́вый).
8. У на́с вчера́ бы́ли (францу́зский профе́ссор).
9. У меня́ есть (хоро́ший студе́нт).
10. В э́той шко́ле (серьёзный учи́тель).
11. В э́том го́роде есть (хоро́ший до́ктор).
12. (Чья́ э́та ру́сская газе́та?)
13. (Како́й дли́нный ве́чер!)
14. На полу́ лежа́т (ста́рый журна́л).

B. *Translate into Russian.*

1. Where are those old forests?
2. These good students are mine.
3. I love big cities.
4. Whose are these new cars?
5. The trains here are very fast.
6. Do you have good teachers?
7. Do you see those red walls?
8. The shores of the Black Sea are very beautiful.
9. These doctors are very expensive.
10. Who are these professors?
11. We need new tables.
12. Whose teachers are they?
13. What nice homes!
14. They buy expensive lamps.
15. Our professors are very serious.
16. She has blue eyes.

5. Nominative plurals in -ья

A few masculine and neuter nouns form nominative plurals in **-ья**. Some of these undergo change of stem or shift of stress:

Nominative Singular	Nominative Plural	
брат	бра́тья [brát jə]	brothers
стул	сту́лья [stúḷ jə]	chairs
лист	ли́стья [ḷíṣṭ jə]	leaves[4]

_____

[4] But **листы́** *sheets* (*of paper*).

With shift of stress:

муж	мужья́ [mužjá]	husbands
перо́	пе́рья [péɽjə]	pens, feathers
де́рево	дере́вья [d̦iɽéɣjə]	trees

With change of stem:

| друг | друзья́ [druz̦já] | friends |
| сын | сынонвья́ [sɨnaɣjá] | sons |

DRILLS

A. *Translate the words in parentheses.*

1. Бори́с (friend) Вади́ма. Бори́с и Вади́м (are friends).
2. Мои́ (sons) живу́т в А́нглии: оди́н (son) живёт в Ло́ндоне, а два́ (sons) в Ливерпу́ле.
3. Мои́ (brothers) мно́го рабо́тают: два́ (brothers) слу́жат в ба́нке, а оди́н в апте́ке.
4. Все́ э́ти (chairs) о́чень дороги́е.
5. В на́шем саду́ ста́рые и то́лстые (trees).
6. Все́ (leaves) на э́том де́реве уже́ жёлтые.

B. *Translate into Russian.*

1. They say that they are our friends.
2. Whose brothers are they?
3. In what store do (they) sell cheap chairs?
4. My sons seldom write to me.
5. In our forest there are thick, tall trees.
6. These chairs are not comfortable.
7. Does she have friends?
8. Their sons work in this factory.
9. Nina's brothers live in Italy.
10. The leaves on this old tree are red.
11. Our friends were then in Europe.
12. Here are our husbands.

6. Miscellaneous categories of nominative plurals

The following words are not irregular in the nominative plural but require special attention:

Nominative Singular		Nominative Plural	
мать		ма́тери	mothers
дочь		до́чери	daughters
вре́мя		времена́	times
и́мя		имена́	names
челове́к	person	лю́ди	people
ребёнок	child[5]	де́ти	children

Сосе́д (*neighbor*) has the irregular nominative plural сосе́ди (soft throughout the plural).

DRILLS

A. *Read and translate.*

1. Все́ ма́тери ду́мают, что и́х де́ти замеча́тельные.
2. Мо́й му́ж всегда́ говори́т, что на́ш ребёнок глу́пый, а все́ други́е де́ти у́мные.
3. Андре́й и И́горь друзья́ мое́й до́чери. Э́то краси́вые имена́, пра́вда?

---

[5] There is a word дитя́ (neuter singular) for *child*, but it is now archaic and poetic.

4. Ма́ма говори́т, что Ива́н Петро́вич о́чень ми́лый **челове́к**. Пра́вда, ма́ма ду́мает, что все́ **лю́ди** ми́лые.
5. —Во́т сосе́ди мое́й ста́ршей до́**чери**. —Ка́к и́х **имена́**? —Не зна́ю, но́ зна́ю, что они́ америка́нцы.
6. Ма́ленький Ко́ля зна́ет все́ **времена́** го́да! Он зна́ет, что е́сть четы́ре вре́мени го́да: о́сень, зима́, весна́, и ле́то.
7. —Вы́ бу́дете за́втра на конце́рте? —Не́т, у меня́ не́т ни биле́та ни вре́**мени**.
8. —У ни́х е́сть **де́ти**? —Да́, е́сть. У ни́х оди́н **ребёнок**.
9. Э́ти **де́ти** ещё не уме́ют писа́ть.

B. *Put in the plural.*

1. Во́т её до́чь и её сы́н.
2. Он мо́й дру́г.
3. Э́тот ребёнок на́ш.
4. На́ша ма́ть о́чень хоро́шая.
5. Како́й у́мный челове́к!
6. Како́е краси́вое и́мя!
7. Во́т на́ш ти́хий сосе́д.
8. Мо́й бра́т хоро́ший му́ж.
9. Како́е тру́дное вре́мя!
10. Э́то де́рево о́чень ста́рое.

C. *Give the singular of the word in parentheses and then put the sentence in the plural.*

1. —Кто́ э́тот (American)? —Он учи́тель.
2. —Кто́ э́та (American)? —Она́ тури́стка.
3. Э́тот (American) го́род о́чень краси́вый.
4. Э́то (American) о́зеро о́чень большо́е.
5. Э́тот (American) на́ш дру́г.
6. Во́т на́ша студе́нтка; она́ (American).

D. *Translate into Russian.*

1. This is my mother's room.
2. Here are our mothers.
3. Her daughters are very beautiful.
4. This is our daughter's friend.
5. We have friends in Moscow.
6. They never have time!
7. —How long did your neighbors live in Europe? —A whole year.
8. —Where are your sons? —They are at my mother's.
9. We have good neighbors.
10. I like Russian names.

E. *Translate the words in parentheses and mark the stress. Remember that the numerals 2, 3, and 4 take the genitive singular.*

Вопро́с	Отве́т
1. У ва́с е́сть сёстры?	Да́, у меня́ (two sisters).
2. В коридо́ре е́сть о́кна?	Да́, та́м (three windows).
3. В ва́шей ко́мнате е́сть кре́сла?	Да́, в мое́й ко́мнате (four armchairs).
4. У неё е́сть до́чери?	Да́, у неё (two daughters).
5. Зде́сь е́сть озёра?	Да́, зде́сь (two lakes).
6. Все́ ва́ши бра́тья студе́нты?	Не́т, то́лько (two brothers).
7. Все́ э́ти поля́ ва́ши?	Не́т, то́лько (three fields).
8. Все́ э́ти дома́ но́вые?	Не́т, то́лько (four houses).

7. The reciprocal pronoun друг дру́га

The reciprocal pronoun **дру́г дру́га** corresponds to the English *one another, each other*. The first word never changes; the second is declined:

Gen. дру́г дру́га
Dat. дру́г дру́гу

Acc.	дру́г дру́га
Instr.	дру́г дру́гом
Loc.	дру́г о дру́ге

E.g.: Они́ лю́бят **дру́г дру́га**. They like each other.

Мы́ помога́ем **дру́г дру́гу**. We help one another.

Prepositions are inserted between the two words:

Мы́ мно́го разгова́риваем **дру́г с дру́гом**.

Вади́м и О́льга ча́сто ду́мают **дру́г о дру́ге**.

DRILL

Translate into Russian.

1. We love each other.
2. Boris and Anna often talk with one another.
3. Do they send each other letters?

4. They do not like one another.
5. We do not understand one another.
6. They seldom talk about one another.

Conversation

Бе́дная продавщи́ца!

В магази́не. **Покупа́тельница.** (Же́нщина с неприя́тным лицо́м и неприя́тным го́лосом.) **Продавщи́ца.** (О́чень молода́я де́вушка с прия́тным лицо́м и прия́тным го́лосом.)

Покуп. —Де́вушка,[6] у ва́с е́сть ле́тние костю́мы и пла́тья?

Прод. —Коне́чно, е́сть. У на́с о́чень большо́й вы́бор. Како́го цве́та вы́ хоти́те костю́м и како́го цве́та пла́тье?

Покуп. —Я́ ещё не зна́ю. Покажи́те мне́, что́ у ва́с е́сть.

Прод. —Како́й ва́ш разме́р? Во́т, пожа́луйста. Зде́сь костю́мы, а зде́сь блу́зки и пла́тья. Ви́дите: ю́бки тепе́рь у́зкие, а жаке́ты коро́ткие и широ́кие. Это са́мая после́дняя мо́да! О́чень краси́во.

Покуп. —Да́, ви́жу. Ужа́сная мо́да! И каки́е высо́кие це́ны! Это сли́шком до́рого! У ва́с е́сть други́е костю́мы?

Прод. —У на́с е́сть и дешёвые. Во́т э́ти костю́мы у на́с то́лько два́ дня́. Чёрные, наприме́р, о́чень краси́вые. Ви́дите: ю́бки широ́кие, а жаке́ты у́зкие. После́дняя мо́да!

Покуп. —Это то́же после́дняя мо́да? По-мо́ему, я́ ви́дела э́ти костю́мы в про́шлом году́. А ско́лько вре́мени вы́ зде́сь слу́жите?

Прод. —Кто́, я́?

Покуп. —Да́, вы́.

Прод. —Я́? . . . два́ дня́.

---

[6] **Де́вушка** is the usual form of address for younger saleswomen, women office workers, post office clerks, etc., in the Soviet Union.

ILLUSTRATION 19.   Магази́н да́мского пла́тья в Москве́. (*Tass from Sovfoto.*)

Answer the following questions in Russian.

1. Что́ ну́жно покупа́тельнице? 2. Кака́я после́дняя мо́да? 3. Почему́ да́ма не покупа́ет пе́рвый костю́м, кото́рый ей пока́зывает продавщи́ца? 4. Како́й вопро́с да́ма задаёт продавщи́це? 5. Почему́ она́ его́ задаёт?

Reading

Го́род

Что́ есть в ка́ждом большо́м го́роде?

В ка́ждом большо́м го́роде есть больши́е и ма́ленькие дома́ и зда́ния; есть дли́нные и коро́ткие у́лицы. Есть у́лицы широ́кие и у́зкие. В ка́ждом го́роде есть гла́вная у́лица: в Москве́, наприме́р, э́то у́лица Го́рького (Gorky Street), в Ленингра́де знамени́тый Не́вский проспе́кт (Nevsky Prospect).

В ка́ждом большо́м го́роде есть теа́тры, музе́и, па́рки, пло́щади, па́мятники; есть дешёвые и дороги́е рестора́ны и гости́ницы; есть шко́лы, институ́ты, библиоте́ки, и университе́т; есть обыкнове́нные магази́ны и есть универма́ги.

В ка́ждом го́роде—большо́м или ма́леньком—есть лю́ди бога́тые и есть бе́дные, есть лю́ди счастли́вые и есть несча́стные.

Answer the following questions in Russian.

1. Каки́е больши́е города́ вы зна́ете? 2. В большо́м го́роде всё дома́ больши́е? 3. Все́ рестора́ны в э́том го́роде дешёвые? 4. Кака́я гла́вная у́лица э́того го́рода? 5. В э́том го́роде все́ лю́ди бога́тые? 6. Что́ вы зна́ете о Не́вском проспе́кте?

Шко́ла

В ка́ждой шко́ле есть кла́ссные ко́мнаты, есть ученики́ и учени́цы, есть учителя́ и учи́тельницы. Учителя́ объясня́ют уро́ки в кла́ссе. Они́ объясня́ют пра́вила, и задаю́т уро́ки (зада́ния)—кото́рые ученики́ должны́ гото́вить до́ма—и даю́т отме́тки.

Приле́жные, у́мные ученики́ слу́шают то́, что говори́т учи́тель, хорошо́ де́лают зада́ния, и обыкнове́нно получа́ют хоро́шие отме́тки.

Лени́вые ученики́ ничего́ не де́лают. Таки́е ученики́ получа́ют плохи́е отме́тки, но э́то им всё равно́.

Answer the following questions in Russian.

1. Что́ де́лают учителя́ в кла́ссе? 2. Каки́е ученики́ слу́шают учи́теля? 3. Что́ ученики́ должны́ де́лать до́ма? 4. Что́ получа́ют лени́вые ученики́?

Университе́т

В ка́ждом университе́те есть аудито́рии и библиоте́ки, есть студе́нты, студе́нтки, и профессора́.

Профессора́ чита́ют ле́кции. Студе́нты запи́сывают то́, что ва́жно и пото́м, до́ма, чита́ют свои́ запи́ски. Иногда́ по́сле ле́кции они́ задаю́т вопро́сы профе́ссору.

В конце́ го́да все́ студе́нты должны́ сдава́ть экза́мены. Хоро́шие студе́нты выде́рживают экза́мены, а плохи́е не́т.

Answer the following questions in Russian.

1. Что́ де́лают профессора́? 2. Что́ запи́сывают студе́нты во вре́мя ле́кции? 3. Что́ они́ иногда́ де́лают по́сле ле́кции? 4 Что́ все́ студе́нты де́лают в конце́ го́да?

Универма́г

В универма́ге продавцы́ и продавщи́цы продаю́т ра́зные ве́щи, как наприме́р: пла́тья, ю́бки и блу́зки, гото́вые костю́мы, пиджаки́, брю́ки, руба́шки, шля́пы, боти́нки. Покупа́тели покупа́ют э́ти ве́щи. Вы́бор в магази́не большо́й.

Во́т э́тому высо́кому господи́ну нужны́ руба́шки. Продавщи́ца спра́шивает, како́й его́ разме́р и пока́зывает ему́ руба́шки, но высо́кий господи́н говори́т, что э́ти руба́шки сли́шком дороги́е. Тогда́ она́ пока́зывает ему́ други́е, дешёвые, и о́н и́х покупа́ет.

Нале́во—отде́л ме́бели. Та́м продаю́т столы́, сту́лья, буфе́ты, ра́зные кре́сла, крова́ти, кни́жные по́лки, и ковры́. Во́т молода́я па́ра покупа́ет ме́бель. Она́ хо́чет э́ти сту́лья, а му́ж хо́чет те́. Жена́ хо́чет си́ние кре́сла, а о́н хо́чет зелёные. Они́ спо́рят. Продавщи́ца ду́мает: мо́жет быть э́то и́х пе́рвый спо́р, но, коне́чно, не после́дний.

Напра́во отде́л посу́ды. Та́м продаю́т стака́ны, ча́шки, таре́лки, ва́зы. Во́т э́той то́лстой же́нщине в жёлтом пла́тье нужны́ бе́лые ча́шки. Продавщи́ца говори́т е́й, что сего́дня в магази́не е́сть то́лько си́ние и зелёные, но за́втра бу́дут и бе́лые и кра́сные. Но же́нщина в жёлтом пла́тье о́чень недово́льна: е́й нужны́ ча́шки сего́дня, а не за́втра!

Answer the following questions in Russian.

1. Кто́ продаёт в универма́ге? 2. Кто́ покупа́ет та́м ра́зные ве́щи? 3. Каки́е, наприме́р, ве́щи покупа́ют в магази́не? 4. Что́ ну́жно высо́кому господи́ну? 5. Како́й вопро́с задаёт ему́ продавщи́ца? 6. Почему́ о́н не покупа́ет те́ руба́шки, кото́рые она́ ему́ снача́ла пока́зывает? 7. Каки́е о́н покупа́ет? 8. Како́й вы́бор в э́том отде́ле? 9. Что́ мы́ ви́дим в отде́ле ме́бели? 10. Что́ покупа́ет молода́я па́ра и о чём они́ спо́рят? 11. Что́ ду́мает продавщи́ца, когда́ слы́шит э́тот спо́р? 12. Что́ мы́ ви́дим в отде́ле посу́ды? 13. Что́ ну́жно то́лстой же́нщине в жёлтом пла́тье? 14. Что́ е́й говори́т продавщи́ца? 15. Почему́ покупа́тельница так недово́льна?

DRILL

Review Translation.

1. We need good doctors. 2. In summer the trees are green, but in fall their leaves are yellow or red. 3. These students write down all that their professors say. 4. I think that that is unnecessary. They must write down only what (= that which) is

important. 5. Boris needs new suits. He says that all his expensive suits are already old. 6. The saleswomen in this department store are very good. 7. The old cities that we saw in Italy were very interesting. 8. Her sons write letters to me every week. Sometimes I answer, and sometimes I don't (answer). But they don't care. 9. Sergey has friends who live in our house. 10. In our capital there are beautiful parks, monuments, museums, long streets, and comfortable and expensive hotels. 11. She has beautiful eyes. 12. —Do you have any sons? —Yes, I have two sons: one is an engineer and the other is a writer. 13. My brothers and their wives live in the center of Boston. 14. He likes to buy shirts, suits, and overcoats. 15. All schoolboys and schoolgirls must prepare their lessons every day. That is very important. 16. These are very difficult rules. 17. Some students get good grades, and other students get poor grades. 18. They like one another very much and often talk with one another on the phone. 19. We need white plates and blue cups. 20. We always buy furniture and china in this department store.

Vocabulary

аудито́рия auditorium, lecture room
бе́дный poor
боти́н.ок (*gen.* -ка) shoe
брю́ки (*pl. only*) trousers
буфе́т buffet; cupboard; lunchstand
вдруг suddenly
вещь (*fem. II*) thing
внима́ние attention
вы́бор choice, selection
глубо́кий deep
гора́ mountain
гото́вый ready
де́вочка (little) girl
де́рево tree
де́ти (*pl. only*) children
зада́ние task, assignment
запи́ска note
знамени́тый famous, celebrated
лист leaf (*pl.* ли́стья); sheet (*pl.* листы́)
лю́ди (*pl. only*) people
ма́льчик boy
мо́да fashion, style
несча́стный [niščásnɨj] unhappy, unfortunate
объясне́ние [abjasņéņijə] explanation
о́зеро lake

отде́л [aḍḍél] department
отме́тка grade, mark
па́ра couple, pair
пе́сня song
пиджа́к jacket, coat
по́езд train
покупа́тель (*fem.* -ница) customer
посу́да (*coll.*) dishes, china
продав.е́ц (*gen.* -ца́) salesman
продавщи́ца saleswoman
разме́р size, measure
ра́зный (*mostly pl.*) various, different[7]
ребён.ок (*sing. only*) (*gen.* -ка) child
руба́шка shirt
Соединённые Шта́ты Аме́рики United States of America (*abbrev.* США, U.S.A.)
спор argument
студе́нческий student (*adj.*)
счастли́вый [ščislívɨj] happy, fortunate
тетра́дь (*fem. II*) copybook, school notebook
то́нкий thin, fine
ужа́сный terrible, horrible
универма́г (универса́льный магази́н) department store

---

[7] Observe that ра́зные means *different* in the sense of *various*, while други́е means *different* in the sense of *other*.

VERBS

гото́вить (II: гото́влю, гото́вишь) to prepare, to cook
задава́ть (I: задаю́, задаёшь) to assign; задава́ть вопро́с to ask a question
запи́сывать (I) to note down
получа́ть (I) to receive, get
спо́рить (II: спо́рю, спо́ришь) to argue

EXPRESSIONS

одни́ . . . други́е some . . . others
то́, что what; that which
Что́ де́лать? What can one do? What is to be done?
чита́ть ле́кцию to give a lecture, to lecture
сдава́ть (I: сдаю́, сдаёшь) экза́мен to take an exam
выде́рживать экза́мены to pass exams[8]
вре́мя го́да season
гото́вый костю́м ready-made suit
са́мый после́дний very latest

---

[8] But: Он вы́держал экза́мены. He passed the exams.

Unit 14

Grammar

1. The category of aspect in the Russian verb

The Russian verb system distinguishes only three tenses: a present, a past, and a future. There is in addition to tense, however, another category in the Russian verb system, that of *aspect*.

Nearly all Russian verbs are of either the *imperfective* or the *perfective* aspect. All verbs given until now have been *imperfective*.

Imperfective verbs are used to describe:

(1) actions in progress over a period of time without any reference to completion or termination (*He was*, or *is, writing letters*); (2) actions performed repeatedly (*He writes*, or *wrote, home every week—often*); and (3) actions spoken of in general terms, without reference to an actual performance at any particular time (*My father spoke five languages; she buys her hats in Paris*).

Perfective verbs are used to describe actions that have been or will be brought to completion or termination (*She bought a hat; I will write you tomorrow*).

In very general terms, then, an imperfective verb says that an action is (was or will be) in progress (continuously or as a series of repeated acts). A perfective verb says that an action has been or will be performed, something has been or will be done.

In most cases imperfective and perfective verbs fall into pairs in which the two verbs are identical (or very close) in meaning but different in aspect. One such pair is **писа́ть** and **написа́ть**; both verbs mean *to write*, the first being *imperfective* and the second *perfective*.

The English and the Russian verb systems are based on different kinds of distinctions and no precise equivalence between the two sets of forms can be established; the correlations, however, are as follows (considering the past tense only):

Yesterday he *was writing* all day.
Вчера́ о́н **писа́л** весь де́нь. (*imperf.*)

He *wrote* (*used to write*) every day.
О́н **писа́л** ка́ждый де́нь. (*imperf.*)

He *wrote* (*used to write*) Russian and English very well.
Óн óчень хорошó **писáл** по-рýсски и по-англи́йски. (*imperf.*)

He *wrote* (*has written*) this letter this morning.
Óн **написáл** э́то письмó сегóдня у́тром. (*perf.*)

He *wrote* to Olga yesterday.
Óн вчерá **написáл** Óльге. (*perf.*)

2. Aspect and tense

Perfective verbs speak of actions that have reached (or will reach) a terminal point, not of actions as processes unfolding in time; they have, therefore, no present tense, since "present" means that an action is currently in progress, or that a state or condition is present "now," at the time when the statement is made.

Perfective verbs have only two tenses: a past (meaning that something has been done) and a future (meaning that something will be done).
Imperfective verbs have all three tenses: present, past, and future.

Formation of tenses.   Perfective verbs do not have any special endings different from those of imperfective verbs.
(1) *The past tense* forms are similar for both aspects; thus:

> *Imperfective:*   писáл, писáло, писáла, писáли.
> *Perfective:*   написáл, написáло, написáла, написáли.

(2) *In the future tense perfective verbs* are conjugated with the same types of endings as imperfective verbs in the present: thus написáть is conjugated exactly like писáть, but it has a *future* meaning:

> **Я напишу́,** etc.
> I *shall* write, *shall* have written, etc.

(3) *The future of imperfective verbs* is formed with the future of the auxiliary verb **быть** and the infinitive:

> **Я бу́ду писáть, ты́ бу́дешь писáть,** etc.
> I shall write, shall be writing; you will write.

The difference in meaning between the two aspect forms in the future parallels the difference between them in the past tense:

Imperfective Future

Зáвтра я бу́ду **писáть** весь дéнь. ⎫
I'll write (be writing) all day tomorrow. ⎬ (action in progress)

Óн бу́дет нáм чáсто **писáть**. ⎫
   (or: кáждую недéлю, etc.) ⎬ (repeated action)
He will write to us often (every week, etc.). ⎭

Я бу́ду ва́м **писа́ть** то́лько по-ру́сски. ⎱ (action in general, not one
I will write to you only in Russian. ⎰ specific performance)

Perfective Future

Я́ ему́ **напишу́** за́втра. ⎱ (future completed action)
I will write to him tomorrow. ⎰

The same distinction applies to the use of the *infinitive*:

В кла́ссе мы́ должны́ **писа́ть** по-ру́сски. ⎱ (*imperf.*)
In class we must write in Russian. ⎰ (action in general)

Я́ до́лжен за́втра ему́ **написа́ть**. ⎱ (*perf.*)
I must write to him tomorrow. ⎰ (action to be completed)

To sum up the aspect and tense system:

IMPERFECTIVE ASPECT		
Past	*Present*	*Future*
an action *was* in progress: óн писа́л	an action *is* in progress: óн пи́шет	an action *will be* in progress: óн бу́дет писа́ть

PERFECTIVE ASPECT	
Past	*Future*
an action *has been* completed: óн написа́л	an action *will be* completed: óн напи́шет

3. Forms of the aspects

Perfective verbs differ from corresponding imperfective verbs in several ways; there is no one definite pattern in this type of correlation.

(1) In the case of the verbs **писа́ть—написа́ть**, the difference between the two aspect forms is that the perfective has a *prefix*, **на-**, while the imperfective has none. Many other verbs have non-prefixed imperfectives with perfectives formed by adding one of several prefixes e.g.:

Imperfective	*Perfective*
чита́ть (чита́ю—pres.)	**про**чита́ть (прочита́ю—future)
де́лать (де́лаю—pres.)	**с**де́лать [zdélət] (сде́лаю—future)
игра́ть (игра́ю—pres.)	**сы**гра́ть[1] (сыгра́ю—future)
звони́ть (звоню́—pres.)	**по**звони́ть (позвоню́—future)
гото́вить (гото́влю—pres.)	**при**гото́вить (пригото́влю—future)

---

[1] When a prefix consisting of a consonant like **с-** (or ending in a consonant like **под-** or **от-**) is combined with a verb beginning with **и** not only is the consonant not softened, the **и** instead becomes **ы**: **с** + игра́ть = сыгра́ть. The same is true *phonetically* when **с, от,** or **под** as prepositions precede a noun beginning in **и-**, e.g., с Ива́ном [sivánəm].

In these examples the prefixes change only the aspect of the verbs; their meaning remains unchanged. (In other combinations, prefixes may affect not only the aspect of a verb, but its meaning as well.)

(2) A small number of pairs consist of two verbs derived from different roots; two such pairs are given below:

Imperfective: **брать**   *Perfective:* **взять** (*to take*)

Present	Past	Future	Past
беру́	брал	возьму́	взял
берёшь	бра́ло	возьмёшь	взя́ло
берёт	брала́	возьмёт	взяла́
берём	бра́ли	возьмём	взя́ли
берёте		возьмёте	
беру́т		возьму́т	

The other pair, **говори́ть/сказа́ть**, has two aspectual forms that differ somewhat in meaning. The imperfective **говори́ть** means *to speak*, *talk*, and also *to say*, *tell*. The perfective **сказа́ть** has only the latter meaning: *to say*, *tell*.

Imperfective: **говори́ть**   *Perfective:* **сказа́ть**

Present	Past	Future	Past
говорю́	говори́л	скажу́	сказа́л
говори́шь	говори́ло	ска́жешь	сказа́ло
говори́т	говори́ла	ска́жет	сказа́ла
говори́м	говори́ли	ска́жем	сказа́ли
говори́те		ска́жете	
говоря́т		ска́жут	

PATTERN SENTENCES

Чита́ть (*imperfective*), **прочита́ть** (*perfective*).

1. Алёша **чита́л** вчера́ весь де́нь, и **прочита́л** ве́сь э́тот дли́нный рома́н.
2. Ле́на **прочита́ла** то́лько полови́ну э́того рома́на.
3. За́втра, е́сли у неё бу́дет вре́мя, она́ **прочита́ет** ещё две́ главы́.
4. Мы́ **бу́дем** ка́ждый де́нь **чита́ть** ру́сскую газе́ту; на́м нужна́ пра́ктика.
5. А́нна то́лько что **прочита́ла** ва́шу интере́сную статью́.
6. Ле́том я́ **чита́л** Достое́вского. Я́ **прочита́л** рома́ны «Идио́т» и «Бра́тья Карама́зовы».

1. Alyosha was reading all day yesterday, and read that whole long novel.
2. Lena has read only half of that novel.
3. If she has time tomorrow, she will read two more chapters.
4. We shall read a Russian newspaper every day; we need practice.
5. Anna has just read your interesting article.
6. In the summer I was reading Dostoyevsky. I read the novels *The Idiot* and *The Brothers Karamazov*.

DRILLS

A. *Choose the correct form of the verb and translate.*

1. Я́ (бу́ду чита́ть/прочита́ю) ва́м своё письмо́.
2. Тепе́рь вы́ должны́ (чита́ть/прочита́ть) то́лько по-ру́сски.
3. Ле́на (чита́ла/прочита́ла) вчера́ пе́рвую главу́, и тепе́рь бу́дет чита́ть втору́ю.

4. Снача́ла я́ (бу́ду чита́ть/прочита́ю) письмо́, а пото́м мы́ бу́дем разгова́ривать.

5. Я́ до́лжен (чита́ть/прочита́ть) его́ письмо́, тогда́ я́ бу́ду зна́ть, о чём (о́н пи́шет/напи́шет).

6. Когда́ я́ бу́ду во Фра́нции, я́ (бу́ду чита́ть/прочита́ю) то́лько францу́зские газе́ты.

B. *Translate into Russian.*

1. I have read only half of his letter.
2. We shall read a lot in the summer.
3. He will read us her letter.
4. I shall read you what Father writes.
5. I've read only two words, but I already know what he wants.
6. I shall read less in the winter.

PATTERN SENTENCES

Писа́ть (*imperfective*), написа́ть (*perfective*).

1. О́н уже́ два́ го́да **пи́шет** кни́гу, но́ пока́ о́н **написа́л** то́лько пе́рвую главу́.

2. О́н вероя́тно **бу́дет писа́ть** её ещё го́д или два́.

3. —Вы́ зна́ете, что́ Ко́ля **написа́л** свое́й сестре́? —Зна́ю. О́н са́м **прочита́л** мне́ своё письмо́.

4. Вы́ зна́ете, что э́та молода́я писа́тельница **написа́ла** уже́ два́ рома́на?

5. Когда́ я́ наконе́ц **напишу́** мою́ статью́, я́ сама́ ва́м её **прочита́ю**.

6. —Мы́ за́втра обо всём **напи́шем** отцу́. —Вы́ ка́ждый де́нь говори́те, что **напи́шете** ему́ за́втра.

7. Я́ **писа́л** четы́ре часа́, и **написа́л** то́лько э́то письмо́! Де́ло в то́м, что я́ о́чень ме́дленно **пишу́**.

8. Я́ **прочита́л** его́ статью́. По-мо́ему о́н совсе́м не уме́ет **писа́ть**!

1. He has been writing a book now (in progress) for two years, but so far he has written (finished writing) only the first chapter.

2. He will probably be writing it for another year or two.

3. —Do you know what Kolya wrote to his sister? —I know. He read me his letter himself.

4. Do you know that this young writer has written two novels already?

5. When I finally get my article written, I shall read it to you myself.

6. —Tomorrow we will write to Father about everything. —Every day you say that you'll write to him tomorrow.

7. I've been writing for four hours, and I've written only this letter. The thing is that I write very slowly.

8. I have read his article. In my opinion, he doesn't know how to write at all!

DRILLS

A. *Choose the correct form of the verb and translate.*

1. Вчера́ Ве́ра (писа́ла/написа́ла) два́ часа́.
2. О́н говори́т, что (о́н напи́шет/бу́дет писа́ть) на́м ка́ждый де́нь.
3. Я́ должна́ за́втра (писа́ть/написа́ть) Бори́су.
4. Когда́ вы́ (бу́дете писа́ть/напи́шете) Ни́не о её до́чери?
5. Я́ вчера́ (написа́л/писа́л) весь де́нь.
6. Я́ е́й ско́ро (бу́ду писа́ть/напишу́).

B. *Translate into Russian.*

1. He wrote Father a long letter.
2. The children say that they will write to us often.
3. I wrote to Nina yesterday, and will write her again tomorrow.
4. Lena wrote for three hours, and wrote only two letters.
5. I will write an article about that. I know how to write!

PATTERN SENTENCES

Де́лать (*imperfective*), сде́лать (*perfective*).

1. —Что́ вы́ де́лали вчера́? —Я ничего́ не де́лал. Я отдыха́л.
2. Мы́ са́ми ещё не зна́ем, что мы́ **бу́дем де́лать** ле́том.
3. Мо́й му́ж всё лю́бит **де́лать** са́м. О́н, наприме́р, са́м **сде́лал** э́ти по́лки.
4. —Почему́ ты́ ещё не **сде́лал** э́то упражне́ние? —У меня́ не́ было вре́мени. Я́ **сде́лаю** его́ ве́чером.
5. Я́ не зна́ю, что́ мне́ **де́лать** с Ко́лей. О́н тако́й эго́ист!
6. Где́ моё перо́? Что́ ты́ с ни́м **сде́лал**?
7. Мэ́ри хорошо́ говори́т по-францу́зски, но́ она́ ещё **де́лает** оши́бки.
8. Вчера́ в кла́ссе она́ **сде́лала** две́ оши́бки.
9. Как хорошо́ уме́ть всё **де́лать**!

1. —What did you do yesterday? —I didn't do anything. I relaxed.
2. We ourselves don't know yet what we shall be doing in the summer.
3. My husband likes to make everything himself. For instance, he made these shelves himself.
4. —Why haven't you done that exercise yet? —I had no time. I'll do it this evening.
5. I don't know what to do with Kolya. He is so selfish!
6. Where is my pen? What have you done with it?
7. Mary speaks French well, but she still makes mistakes.
8. In class yesterday she made two mistakes.
9. How fine it is to know how to do everything!

DRILLS

A. *Choose the correct form of the verb and translate.*

1. Я́ ещё не зна́ю, что́ я (бу́ду де́лать/сде́лаю) за́втра.
2. Что́ ты́ (де́лал/сде́лал)!
3. О́н обы́чно хорошо́ перево́дит, но́ э́тот перево́д о́н (де́лал/сде́лал) пло́хо.

4. Я́ должна́ (де́лать/сде́лать) э́то упражне́ние! Сего́дня у меня́ не́т вре́мени, но́ за́втра я́ его́ (сде́лаю/бу́ду де́лать).

B. *Translate into Russian.*

1. —Anna, why did you make this mistake again? —For some reason I always make this mistake.
2. He doesn't know yet what he will do in the winter.
3. We did that every day in class.
4. Yesterday we did all that we had to do.
5. What did you do with the letter?
6. —What did you do yesterday? —We read.

PATTERN SENTENCES

Игра́ть (*imperfective*), сыгра́ть (*perfective*).

1. Молодо́й пиани́ст вчера́ прекра́сно **игра́л**. О́н осо́бенно хорошо́ **сыгра́л** ва́льс Шопе́на.
2. Мы́ вчера́ **игра́ли** в те́ннис с Ива́ном. Мы́ **сыгра́ли** четы́ре па́ртии.
3. Я́ **сыгра́ю** ва́м мело́дию, кото́рую я́ то́лько что слы́шал.
4. По́сле конца́ семе́стра я́ **бу́ду** ка́ждый де́нь **игра́ть** в те́ннис.

1. The young pianist played (was playing) marvelously yesterday. He played a waltz by Chopin especially well.
2. I played tennis yesterday with Ivan. We played four games.
3. I shall play you a tune that I have just heard.
4. After the end of the semester, I shall play tennis every day.

5. Óн наконéц **сыгрáл** сонáту, котóрую я тáк люблю!

5. He finally played the sonata I like so much!

6. Ивáн óчень хорошó **игрáет** в шáхматы. Я **сыгрáл** с ни́м вчерá двé пáртии.

6. Ivan plays chess very well. I played two games with him yesterday.

DRILLS

A. *Choose the correct form of the verb and translate.*

1. Вчерá мóй мýж (игрáл/сыгрáл) вéсь вéчер в кáрты.

2. А я (игрáла/сыгрáла) тóлько двé пáртии, и бóльше я не хотéла (игрáть/сыгрáть).

3. Éсли хоти́те, я пóсле обéда (бýду игрáть/сыгрáю) нóвое тангó.

4. Éсли хоти́те, я чáсто (бýду игрáть/сыгрáю) вáм.

B. *Translate into Russian.*

1. They never play cards.
2. My son played tennis with Anna in summer.
3. Yesterday they played three games, and she didn't want to play any more.

4. I shall play only one game and then I shall work.
5. He will play with us in winter.
6. We often played cards in winter.

PATTERN SENTENCES

Брáть (*imperfective*), **взять** (*perfective*).

1. Лéна всегдá **берёт** всё мои́ вéщи!
2. Зимóй онá чáсто **бралá** мои́ кни́ги!
3. Вчерá онá **взялá** мóй учéбник.
4. Éсли онá зáвтра опя́ть егó **возьмёт**, я скажý мáме.
5. Óсенью Алёша **бýдет брáть** урóки англи́йского языкá.
6. Покá óн **взя́л** тóлько четы́ре урóка.

7. Я **взя́л** э́ту пласти́нку у Ни́ны.[2] Я чáсто **берý** у неё[2] пласти́нки.

1. Lena always takes all my things!
2. In the winter she often took my books!
3. Yesterday she took my school book.
4. If she takes it again tomorrow, I'll tell Mama.
5. In the fall Alyosha will take English lessons.
6. So far he has taken (finished taking) only four lessons.
7. I took (borrowed) that record from Nina. I often borrow records from her.

DRILLS

A. *Choose the correct form of the verb and translate.*

1. В прóшлом годý я кáждый дéнь (брáл/взя́л) кни́ги в библиотéке.
2. Гдé мóй словáрь? Ктó (брáл/взя́л) егó?
3. Лéтом я (возьмý/бýду брáть) урóки тéнниса.
4. Они́ зáвтра (возьмýт/бýдут брáть) нáш автомоби́ль.

5. Мы́ иногдá (брáли/взя́ли) и́х автомоби́ль.
6. Вчерá Ивáн (брáл/взя́л) у меня́ послéдний дóллар.
7. Какýю шля́пу вы́ (бýдете брáть/возьмёте) у мáтери, бéлую или чёрную?

---

[2] **Брáть/взять** (*to take from*) takes у + genitive.

B. *Translate into Russian.*

1. Zoya took my hat; I will take yours.
2. Who took the letter that was lying on my desk?
3. He always used to take my textbooks.
4. I know that you have no dictionary, but you can always take mine.
5. They will take your records tomorrow night.
6. Will you take meat or fish?
7. I am going to take French lessons in the spring.

PATTERN SENTENCES

Говори́ть (*imperfective*), **сказа́ть** (*perfective*).

1. Андре́й то́лько что **сказа́л** О́льге, что о́н её лю́бит.
2. На́ш нача́льник лю́бит **говори́ть**. Вчера́ на собра́нии о́н мно́го **говори́л** и, как обы́чно, не **сказа́л** ничего́ ва́жного.[3]
3. Оте́ц то́лько что мне́ **сказа́л**, что учи́тель **говори́л** с ни́м обо мне́.
4. Я́ **скажу́** е́й, что она́ не должна́ та́к **говори́ть** с ма́терью.
5. На́ш ма́ленький Ко́ля ещё не **говори́т**. О́н мо́жет то́лько **сказа́ть** «па́па» и «ма́ма».
6. Когда́ жена́ мне́ **ска́жет**,[4] что́ она́ хо́чет де́лать за́втра, я́ ва́м сейча́с же позвоню́.
7. Е́сли вы́ ему́ э́то **ска́жете**,[4] вы́ бу́дете непра́вы. Э́то бу́дет большо́й оши́бкой.
8. Я́ ему́ **сказа́л**, что о́н о́чень хорошо́ **говори́т** по-ру́сски.

1. Andrey has just told (said to) Olga that he loves her.
2. Our boss likes to talk (speak). Yesterday at the meeting he spoke a great deal, and, as usual, said nothing important.
3. Father has just told me that the teacher spoke with him about me.
4. I will tell her that she should not talk to (speak that way with) her mother.
5. Our little Kolya doesn't speak yet. He can say only "papa" and "mama."
6. When my wife tells me what she wants to do tomorrow, I will call you up right away.
7. If you tell him that, you will be wrong. It will be a great mistake.
8. I told him that he speaks Russian very well.

DRILLS

A. *Choose the correct form of the verb and translate.*

1. Кто́ вчера́ (говори́л/сказа́л) на собра́нии?
2. Кто́ за́втра (бу́дет говори́ть/ска́жет) на собра́нии?
3. Когда́ вы́ (бу́дете говори́ть/ска́жете) Серге́ю, что экза́мен бу́дет за́втра?
4. За́втра профе́ссор (бу́дет говори́ть/ска́жет) о сме́рти Пу́шкина весь ча́с.
5. Ива́н на́м за́втра (бу́дет говори́ть/ска́жет), где́ о́н живёт.

B. *Translate into Russian.*

1. Does her little daughter talk already?
2. Who said that the concert was dull?
3. I shall tell him that his article is very good.
4. She always talks a great deal.
5. They will not tell him what the professor said of him.
6. Zoya told me that she speaks English well.

---

[3] **Ничего́** (*nothing*) takes the genitive case of adjectives.
[4] Observe again that Russian uses the future (usually perfective) with **когда́, е́сли, ка́к то́лько** to refer to a future action, though English generally employs the present.

Conversation

Серёжа написа́л рома́н!

Бори́с. —Вади́м, ты́ зна́ешь Серёжу Козло́ва?

Вади́м. —Я́ его́ ма́ло зна́ю, но́ я́ мно́го о нём слы́шал.

Б. —Что́ ты́ о нём слы́шал?

В. —Ра́зные ве́щи.

Б. —Как наприме́р?

В. —Наприме́р, говоря́т, что о́н большо́й эгои́ст.

Б. —Почему́ о́н эгои́ст?

В. —Говоря́т, что оте́ц Серёжи совсе́м не бога́тый челове́к, а Серёжа, кро́ме писа́ния, ничего́ не хо́чет де́лать и не хо́чет помога́ть отцу́. О́н почему́-то ду́мает, что бу́дет знамени́тым писа́телем. Но́ я́ слы́шал, что пока́ о́н ничего́ хоро́шего не написа́л и, вероя́тно, ничего́ хоро́шего не напи́шет. Оте́ц, коне́чно, недово́лен сы́ном, но́ ма́ть (как все́ ма́тери) ду́мает, что её сы́н ге́ний. Во́т что о нём говоря́т.

Б. —А что́ ты́ о нём ду́маешь? Мне́ говори́ли, что ты́ его́ не лю́бишь. Э́то пра́вда?

В. —Не́т, э́то не совсе́м та́к, но, сказа́ть пра́вду, о́н меня́ про́сто ма́ло интересу́ет (interests). Как я́ тебе́ уже́ сказа́л ра́ньше, я́ его́ ма́ло зна́ю. Я́ ду́маю, что о́н про́сто лени́вый па́рень.

Б. —А я́ до́лжен тебе́ сказа́ть, Вади́м, что ты́ непра́в, и лю́ди, кото́рые ду́мают как ты́, то́же непра́вы, а права́ его́ ма́ть.

В. —Ты́ хо́чешь сказа́ть, что о́н ге́ний? Я́ зна́ю, Бори́с, что ты́ его́ почему́-то лю́бишь.

Б. —Де́ло совсе́м не в э́том, а де́ло в то́м, что о́н настоя́щий писа́тель.

В. —Э́то но́вость! Но́ почему́ ты́ э́то говори́шь?

Б. —Слу́шай (listen). Вчера́ ве́чером я́ бы́л в на́шем студе́нческом клу́бе. Бы́ло ещё дово́льно ра́но, и кро́ме меня́ и Серёжи та́м никого́ не́ было. Серёжа сиде́л в углу́ и ду́мал.

В. —Вероя́тно у него́ в голове́ бы́л пла́н бу́дущего рома́на.

Б. —Не́т, не пла́н в голове́, а рома́н на бума́ге.

В. —Я́ не ве́рю.

Б. —Я́ зна́ю, что ты́ ске́птик. Ты́ мо́жешь мне́ не ве́рить, но э́то фа́кт. Серёжа уже́ написа́л четы́ре главы́! Две́ о́н мне́ вчера́ прочита́л. По-мо́ему, о́н пи́шет замеча́тельную ве́щь.[5]

В. —Э́то действи́тельно но́вость. О чём же э́тот рома́н?

Б. —Э́то рома́н о молодо́м тала́нтливом хи́мике, кото́рый слу́жит на заво́де на Ура́ле. Васю́шкин (э́то фами́лия хи́мика) сде́лал одно́ о́чень ва́жное откры́тие. Э́то откры́тие не́которое вре́мя должно́ бы́ть секре́том. Э́то о́чень ва́жно. Но де́ло в то́м, что об э́том секре́те, кро́ме Васю́шкина, зна́ет то́лько машини́стка Ната́ша. Она́ рабо́тает в заводско́й конто́ре. Васю́шкин и Ната́ша лю́бят дру́г дру́га.

---

[5] **Вещь** is used to refer to a work of literature, music, art.

В. —Ну́, коне́чно! Как оригина́льно! Что́ да́льше?

Б. —Слу́шай. В лаборато́рии, кро́ме Васю́шкина, е́сть ещё друго́й хи́мик, Кири́ллов. Кири́ллов не тако́й тала́нтливый, как Васю́шкин, и о́н э́то зна́ет. О́н большо́й интрига́н (intriguer). О́н ненави́дит Васю́шкина. Кири́ллов зна́ет, что Васю́шкин всю́ зи́му по́здно ве́чером рабо́тал оди́н в лаборато́рии. Кири́ллову о́чень ва́жно узна́ть (to find out, perf.), каки́е откры́тия сде́лал Васю́шкин.

В. —Ну́, что́ да́льше?

Б. —Не зна́ю. Я́ тебе́ сказа́л, что Серёжа прочита́л мне́ вчера́ то́лько две́ главы́. Но́ о́н сказа́л мне́, что е́сли геро́и его́ рома́на на́с интересу́ют (interest), о́н прочита́ет на́м ещё две́ главы́ сего́дня ве́чером. О́н сде́лает э́то с удово́льствием. Или, е́сли хо́чешь, я́ возьму́ у него́ э́ти гла́вы, и ты́ са́м и́х прочита́ешь.

В. —Где́ о́н бу́дет чита́ть?

Б. —В клу́бе.

В. —Я́ бу́ду та́м. Я́ хочу́ слы́шать, ка́к о́н чита́ет, и меня́ интересу́ет, что́ бу́дет с Васю́шкиным и с его́ откры́тием.

Чита́йте э́ти вопро́сы и отвеча́йте на ни́х (read these questions and answer them).

1. Ке́м Серёжа хо́чет бы́ть? 2. Почему́ говоря́т, что о́н эгои́ст? 3. Почему́ Бори́с ду́мает, что Вади́м не лю́бит Серёжу? 4. Вади́м действи́тельно его́ не лю́бит? 5. Что́ бы́ло вчера́ ве́чером? 6. Кто́ Васю́шкин? 7. Где́ о́н рабо́тает? 8. Что́ о́н сде́лал? 9. Кто́ Ната́ша, и где́ она́ рабо́тает? 10. О чём она́ зна́ет? 11. Расскажи́те, что́ вы́ зна́ете о Кири́ллове. 12. Почему́ Бори́с не зна́ет, что́ бу́дет да́льше? 13. Что́ Серёжа сде́лает с удово́льствием? 14. Почему́ Вади́м бу́дет ве́чером в клу́бе?

DRILLS

A. *Read the following sentences and be ready to explain the use of the aspects.*

1. Она́ сказа́ла, что бу́дет ча́сто на́м писа́ть. Но́ она́ написа́ла на́м то́лько одно́ коро́ткое письмо́. 2. До войны́, когда́ Серге́й жи́л с ма́терью в Крыму́, о́н иногда́ писа́л Зи́не. 3. По́сле войны́ о́н написа́л ей то́лько два́ письма́. 4. —Что́ тебе́ пи́шет Та́ня? —Когда́ я́ прочита́ю её письмо́, я́ тебе́ скажу́. 5. Я́ не зна́ю, что́ де́лать: я́ сего́дня должна́ прочита́ть э́ту кни́гу, но у меня́ так ма́ло вре́мени! 6. Все́ э́ти дни́ Андре́й ничего́ не де́лал, но вчера́ о́н наконе́ц сде́лал все́ упражне́ния и да́же сде́лал дли́нный и тру́дный перево́д. 7. —В и́х кварти́ре никогда́ не звони́л телефо́н; но вчера́, когда́ я́ бы́л у ни́х, телефо́н вдру́г позвони́л. —Кто́ э́то бы́л? —Э́то была́ оши́бка! 8. Я́ позвоню́ О́льге по́сле уро́ка. 9. Я́ бу́ду ча́сто ей звони́ть: она́ така́я ми́лая де́вушка! 10. —Кто́ взя́л мо́й уче́бник? —Я́ взя́л его́: о́н мне́ бы́л о́чень ну́жен. —А у тебя́ не́т уче́бника? —Коне́чно е́сть, но Зо́я всегда́ его́ берёт.

B. *Choose the correct form of the two forms given in parentheses.*

1. О чём профе́ссор вчера́ (говори́л/сказа́л)? 2. Когда́ вы́ (бу́дете говори́ть/ска́жете) на́м, когда́ бу́дет экза́мен? 3. Что́ она́ (бу́дет де́лать/сде́лает) всё ле́то? 4. Мы́ (бу́дем писа́ть/напи́шем) ва́м ча́сто. 5. Когда́ вы́ (бу́дете бра́ть/возьмёте) ва́шу ла́мпу? 6. О́н уже́ (де́лал/сде́лал) всё, что бы́ло ну́жно. 7. Я́ (бу́ду

звони́ть/позвоню́) ва́м за́втра у́тром. 8. Сего́дня ве́чером она́ (бу́дет бра́ть/ возьмёт) моё чёрное пла́тье. 9. Ле́том я (бу́ду бра́ть/возьму́) кни́ги в библиоте́ке ка́ждую неде́лю. 10. Я (бу́ду чита́ть/прочита́ю) тебе́ мою́ статью́, как то́лько я её (бу́ду писа́ть/напишу́). 11. Он бы́стро (гото́вил/пригото́вил) уро́к и написа́л письмо́. 12. Когда́ я (бу́ду гото́вить/пригото́влю) уро́к, я ва́м (бу́ду звони́ть/ позвоню́).

C. *Translate into Russian.*

1. —When did you write this letter? —I wrote it last night. 2. I'll tell you what I think about it when I read (shall have read) it. 3. —What are you going to (will) do tomorrow? —I will work. 4. He will take my car tonight. 5. I am going to tell him that in the spring I shall often take his car. 6. Who is going to speak about Shakespeare at the meeting? 7. She talked a great deal, but didn't say with whom she had been at the movies. 8. I did everything yesterday, and today I will rest. 9. He read three articles before dinner. 10. I will be at home after class and will read Chekhov all evening. 11. —Whose dictionary did you take? —I always take Boris's dictionary. 12. —When and where did he write this wonderful novel? —He wrote it in Italy before the war. He was working on it (= was writing it) for four years. 13. I must write at once to my mother! 14. He made three mistakes in his translation.

Vocabulary

бу́дущий future, next
выраже́ние expression
глава́ chapter; head, chief
глаго́л verb
действи́тельно indeed, in fact, really, actually
де́ло matter, affair, business
заводско́й factory (*adj.*)
машини́ст (*fem.* -ка) machinist; typist
наконе́ц finally, at last
непра́в, неправа́, непра́вы wrong (*as predicate adjective only*)
но́вость (*fem.*) (piece of) news
но́вости (*pl.*) news
опя́ть again
откры́тие discovery
оши́бка mistake
па́ртия game; (political) party

писа́ние writing
план plan
пока́ so far, to now; as long as; for the time being
полови́на (+ *gen.*) half
прав, права́, пра́вы right (*as predicate adjective only*)
пра́ктика practice
сам, само́, сама́, са́ми oneself: myself, yourself, himself, themselves, etc.
сейча́с же at once, immediately
секре́т secret
хи́мик chemist
час hour
ша́хматы (*fem. pl.*) chess
эгои́ст (*fem.* -ка) selfish person, egoist

VERBS

(For new perfectives see pp. 212–213.)
брать (imperf., I: бер.у́, -ёшь), взять (perf., I: возьм.у́, -ёшь) б./в. у (+ *gen.*) to take from someone
ве́рить (imperf., II: ве́р.ю, -ишь), пове́рить (perf., II) to believe (+ *dat.*)
ненави́деть (imperf. only, II: ненави́.жу, -дишь) to hate

EXPRESSIONS

то́лько что (+ *past*) (have) just
как то́лько as soon as
игра́ть в ка́рты to play cards
хоте́ть сказа́ть to mean, mean to say
Де́ло в то́м, что . . . The thing is that . . .
Не в э́том де́ло. That's beside the point, that's not the point.
не́которое вре́мя for some time
Что́ да́льше? What next?
Что́ бу́дет с . . . (+ *instr.*)? What will happen to . . .? What will become of . . .?

Unit **15**

Grammar

1. Aspects (continued)

In the preceding lesson we have seen that perfective verbs can be formed from imperfectives through the addition of one of a number of prefixes, e.g., imperfective **писа́ть**, perfective **написа́ть**. We have also seen that in exceptional cases a pair of verbs with different roots can be related, e.g., imperfective **говори́ть**, perfective **сказа́ть**; or imperfective **брать**, perfective **взять**.

(1) In other cases, the two verbs have identical stems, but differ in the elements that follow the stem (suffixes) both in the infinitive and the personal forms of the conjugation, thus:

Imperf.	конча́ть (I: конча́.ю, -ешь)
Perf.	ко́нчить (II: ко́нч.у, -ишь)
Imperf.	объясня́ть (I: объясня́.ю, -ешь)
Perf.	объясни́ть (II: объясн.ю́, -и́шь)

(2) Sometimes there are also differences in the stem vowel (often **a** alternates with **o**), or differences in the final stem consonant:

Imperf.	спра́шивать (I: спра́шива.ю, -ешь)
Perf.	спроси́ть (II: спрошу́, спро́сишь)
Imperf.	отвеча́ть (I: отвеча́.ю, -ешь)
Perf.	отве́тить (II: отве́чу, отве́тишь)

(3) In the preceding lesson it has been indicated that a prefix added to a verb changes its aspect, e.g., imperfective писа́ть, perfective написа́ть. The same verb писа́ть, however, may take other prefixes as well, e.g., за-, пере-, под-; the resulting verbs, записа́ть, переписа́ть, подписа́ть, are perfective; but besides changing the aspect

to perfective, these prefixes, unlike **на-**, also add new meanings to **писа́ть**: thus **записа́ть** means *to note down*; **переписа́ть** means *to rewrite, transcribe*; **подписа́ть** means *to underwrite, subscribe, sign*.

Obviously, such perfective verbs as записа́ть, переписа́ть, подписа́ть, formed with "meaningful" prefixes, must have corresponding imperfectives that would mean not simply *to write*, but *to note down*, *to rewrite*, or *to sign*. Perfective verbs thus formed with "meaningful" prefixes are "de-perfectivized" by the insertion of a suffix; in the case of the prefixed forms of писа́ть (and of many other verbs), the suffix **-ыва-** (or **-ива-**) is used. Thus are formed the imperfective verbs запи́сывать, перепи́сывать, подпи́сывать.

To sum up:

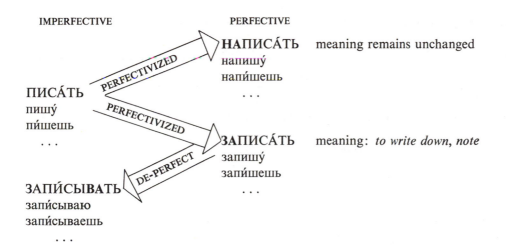

IMPERFECTIVE   PERFECTIVE

НАПИСА́ТЬ   meaning remains unchanged
напишу́
напи́шешь
. . .

ПИСА́ТЬ
пишу́
пи́шешь
. . .

ЗАПИСА́ТЬ   meaning: *to write down, note*
запишу́
запи́шешь
. . .

ЗАПИ́СЫВАТЬ
запи́сываю
запи́сываешь
. . .

The procedure described above is used to form imperfective-perfective pairs of prefixed verbs identical in meaning, and differentiated as to aspect by their suffixes.

All imperfective prefixed verbs with an inserted **-ыва-** or **-ива-** are conjugated like **чита́ть,** regardless of the original perfective form. Thus:

запи́сываю
запи́сываешь, etc.

Learn the verbs in the table below and their conjugation. Most of these verbs have already been presented in their imperfective aspect forms.

IMPERFECTIVE (*Infinitive and Present Tense*)	PERFECTIVE (*Infinitive and Future Tense*)
конча́ть (I: конча́.ю, -ешь) to end, finish	ко́нчить (II: ко́нч.у, -ишь)
получа́ть (I: получа́.ю, -ешь) to receive, obtain, get	получи́ть (II: получу́, полу́чишь)

IMPERFECTIVE	PERFECTIVE
(*Infinitive and Present Tense*)	(*Infinitive and Future Tense*)
объясня́ть (I: объясня́.ю, -ешь) to explain	объясни́ть (II: объясн.ю́, -и́шь)
отвеча́ть (I: отвеча́.ю, -ешь) to answer, reply	отве́тить (II: отве́чу, отве́тишь)
запи́сывать (I: запи́сыва.ю, -ешь) to note down	записа́ть (I: запишу́, запи́шешь)
перепи́сывать (I: перепи́сыва.ю, -ешь) to copy, rewrite	переписа́ть (I: перепишу́, перепи́шешь)
пока́зывать (I: пока́зыва.ю, -ешь) to show	показа́ть (I: покажу́, пока́жешь)
расска́зывать (I: расска́зыва.ю, -ешь) to narrate, tell	рассказа́ть (I: расскажу́, расска́жешь)
спра́шивать (I: спра́шива.ю, -ешь) to ask, inquire	спроси́ть (II: спрошу́, спро́сишь)
начина́ть (I: начина́.ю, -ешь) to begin, start	нача́ть (I: начн.у́, -ёшь)

(4) The imperfective verb **дава́ть** (*pres.:* **даю́, даёшь**), meaning *to give*, has an irregular perfective, **дать**, which is conjugated as follows:

Perfective Future	*Perfective Past*
дам	дал
дашь	да́ло
даст	дала́
дади́м	да́ли
дади́те	
даду́т	

The imperfective prefixed verb **продава́ть** (*to sell*) is conjugated like **дава́ть**, and its perfective **прода́ть** is conjugated like **дать** for the perfective future. The stress in the past tense falls on the prefix for all except the feminine: про́дал, про́дало, продала́, про́дали.

(5) The verb **нача́ть** inserts an **н** throughout the future tense: начну́, начнёшь, etc. (This **н** is also found in all forms of the imperfective начина́ть.) Its past tense is на́чал, на́чало, начала́, на́чали.

(6) The perfective verbs **показа́ть** and **рассказа́ть** are conjugated in the future exactly like сказа́ть: покажу́, пока́жешь; расскажу́, расска́жешь, etc.

There is a tendency for the stress to shift to the ending of the past tense in the feminine: была́, жила́, дала́, продала́, начала́, брала́, взяла́, etc.

PATTERN SENTENCES

Объясня́ть (*imperfective*), **объясни́ть** (*perfective*).

1. Их ста́рый учи́тель всегда́ хорошо́ **объясня́л** им пра́вила грамма́тики.
2. Па́вел **объясни́л** мне́, почему́ ему́ бы́ло так ску́чно на ле́кции.
3. Мне́ бы́ло тру́дно **объясни́ть** учи́телю, почему́ я сде́лал э́ту глу́пую оши́бку.
4. Я́ **объясню́** Ни́не, ка́к сде́лать э́тот перево́д.
5. Её роди́тели **объясня́т** ей, что́ она́ должна́ бу́дет де́лать в дере́вне.
6. На ка́ждом уро́ке я́ **бу́ду объясня́ть** ва́м грамма́тику.
7. О́н не уме́ет **объясня́ть** тру́дные пра́вила.

1. Their old teacher always explained rules of grammar to them well.
2. Paul explained to me why he was so bored at the lecture.
3. I had trouble explaining to the teacher why I made that stupid mistake.
4. I shall explain to Nina how to do that translation.
5. Her parents will explain to her what she will have to do in the country.
6. At every class session I shall explain the grammar to you.
7. He doesn't know how to explain difficult rules.

DRILLS

A. *Choose the correct form of the verb and translate.*

1. Я́ (бу́ду объясня́ть/объясню́) ва́м, где́ я́ покупа́ю ры́бу.
2. Я́ тепе́рь зна́ю э́то пра́вило; учи́тель хорошо́ (объясня́л/обясни́л) мне́ его́.
3. Как ску́чно ка́ждый де́нь (объясня́ть/объясни́ть) секрета́рше, что́ она́ должна́ де́лать!
4. О́н наконе́ц (объясня́л/объясни́л) на́м сво́й но́вый пла́н.
5. Мо́й нача́льник (бу́дет объясня́ть/объясни́т), что́ я́ до́лжен сде́лать с э́тим докуме́нтом.

B. *Translate into Russian.*

1. Who will explain this rule to you?
2. She explained to me why she doesn't want to work here.
3. When the teacher was explaining grammar, I didn't listen.
4. If you want, I'll explain my plan to you.
5. Every day he will explain a new rule to us.

PATTERN SENTENCES

Отвеча́ть (*imperfective*), **отве́тить** (*perfective*). These verbs take the *dative* of persons, but **на** + *accusative* for questions, letters, etc.

1. Мне́ бы́ло легко́ **отве́тить** учи́телю; его́ вопро́с был о́чень лёгкий, и я́ бы́стро и пра́вильно отве́тил **на** его́ вопро́с.
2. Я́ **отве́чу** Ива́ну, когда́ у меня́ бу́дет[1] вре́мя.
3. Когда́ же они́ наконе́ц **отве́тят на** все́ э́ти вопро́сы?
4. Е́сли о́н бу́дет задава́ть[1] мне́ глу́пые вопро́сы, я́ не **бу́ду** ему́ **отвеча́ть**.

1. I had no trouble answering (it was easy for me to answer) the teacher; his question was very easy and I answered his question quickly and correctly.
2. I shall answer Ivan when I have time.
3. When will they finally answer all these questions?
4. If he is going to ask me silly questions, I am not going to answer him.

---

[1] Remember that the *future* tense must be used in Russian subordinate clauses beginning with **е́сли** and **когда́**, although the present tense is used in English with future meaning, e.g.: Когда́ я́ получу́ отве́т, я́ ва́м позвоню́. When I *get* the answer, I will call you up.

5. Я неда́вно написа́л А́нне, и она́ сейча́с же мне́ **отве́тила**.

5. Recently I wrote to Anna and she at once answered me.

6. Лунёв ре́дко **отвеча́л** своему́ бра́ту **на** его́ пи́сьма, но вчера́ о́н вдру́г **отве́тил** ему́ дли́нным письмо́м.

6. Lunyov rarely answered his brother's letters, but yesterday he suddenly answered him with a long letter.

DRILLS

A. *Choose the correct form of the verb and translate.*

1. Почему́ вы́ не (отвеча́ли/отве́тили) на его́ письмо́?
2. Я́ (бу́ду отвеча́ть/отве́чу) сего́дня ве́чером.
3. Когда́ вы́ (отвеча́ли/отве́тили) на э́то письмо́?
4. Я́ (отвеча́л/отве́тил) вчера́ у́тром.
5. Е́сли ты́ бу́дешь писа́ть мне́, я́ коне́чно (бу́ду отвеча́ть/отве́чу) тебе́.

B. *Translate into Russian.*

1. He never answers my letters.
2. He usually answered the teacher quickly and well.
3. He didn't answer your question.
4. —Have you answered him? —Not yet. I'll answer soon.
5. They will answer the letter tomorrow.
6. Why don't you answer Anna's letters?
7. I couldn't answer that question.

PATTERN SENTENCES

Спра́шивать (*imperfective*), спроси́ть (*perfective*).

1. Что́ ты́ **отве́тишь** учи́телю, е́сли о́н тебя́ **спро́сит**, почему́ тебя́ вчера́ не́ было в кла́ссе?

1. What will you answer the teacher if he asks you why you weren't in class yesterday?

2. О́н никогда́ об э́том не **спра́шивает**.

2. He never asks about that.

3. Вчера́ Ка́тя **спроси́ла** меня́ о ва́с.

3. Yesterday Katya asked me about you.

4. —Е́сли они́ тебя́ **спро́сят**, что́ ты́ де́лал всё ле́то, что́ ты́ им **отве́тишь**? —Я́ **отве́чу** пра́вду.

4. —If they ask you what you were doing all summer, what will you answer them? —I shall answer the truth.

5. Я́ **спрошу́** отца́, с ке́м о́н хо́чет сего́дня рабо́тать в саду́.

5. I shall ask Father with whom he wants to work today in the garden.

DRILLS

A. *Choose the correct form of the verb and translate.*

1. Ты́ (спра́шивал/спроси́л) Бори́са, где́ о́н бы́л вчера́?
2. Не́т ещё, но́ я́ (бу́ду спра́шивать/спрошу́) его́.
3. Ле́на (спра́шивала/спроси́ла) меня́, почему́ я́ не была́ на вечери́нке.
4. Я́ ещё не (спра́шивала/спроси́ла) Ле́ну, где́ она́ была́ вчера́.
5. Вы́ (бу́дете спра́шивать/спро́сите) Ле́ну, где́ она́ покупа́ет пласти́нки?

B. *Translate into Russian.*

1. I asked Nina who was at her party.
2. I shall ask my sister what she is going to do tomorrow.
3. I never ask to whom she writes, and she never tells me about it.

4. We often asked Boris about you.
5. Why didn't you ask Ivan Ivanovich where he had been last night?
6. Perhaps they will ask us what we think of them.
7. If they ask, what will you tell them?

PATTERN SENTENCES

Начина́ть (*imperfective*), нача́ть (*perfective*).
Конча́ть (*imperfective*), ко́нчить (*perfective*).

These verbs are followed by the *accusative* case, or, if by a verb, the *imperfective infinitive.*

1. Зо́я неда́вно **начала́** рабо́тать на по́чте. На заво́де она́ **начина́ла** рабо́тать о́чень ра́но, а тепе́рь она́ **начина́ет** по́зже.
2. Андре́й вдру́г **на́чал** писа́ть ле́вой руко́й, и Ка́тя вдру́г **начала́** кури́ть!
3. Вы́ должны́ **нача́ть** говори́ть по-ру́сски!
4. Я́ **ко́нчил** чита́ть пе́рвую главу́.
5. Зимо́й я́ **конча́л** рабо́тать дово́льно по́здно.
6. Когда́ ты́ **ко́нчишь** э́ту ску́чную рабо́ту?
7. Я́ ещё не зна́ю, когда́ я́ её **ко́нчу**; я́ то́лько неда́вно её **на́чал**.
8. Мы́ ско́ро **начнём** но́вую жи́знь!

1. Recently Zoya began to work at the post office. At the plant she used to start work very early, but now she starts later.
2. Andrey has suddenly begun to write with his left hand, and Katya has suddenly begun to smoke!
3. You must start speaking Russian!
4. I have finished reading the first chapter.
5. In the winter I used to finish working rather late.
6. When will you finish that boring work?
7. I don't know yet when I'll finish it; I only began it recently.
8. We shall soon begin a new life!

DRILLS

A. *Choose the correct form of the verb and translate.*

1. За́втра я́ (бу́ду начина́ть/начну́) чита́ть но́вую главу́.
2. Тепе́рь Ива́н ка́ждое у́тро (бу́дет начина́ть/начнёт) рабо́тать ра́ньше.
3. Ле́том я́ о́чень ра́но (начина́ла/начала́) сво́й де́нь.
4. Когда́ вы́ (бу́дете начина́ть/начнёте) писа́ть статью́?
5. Я́ давно́ (конча́л/ко́нчил) её.
6. Ка́к то́лько я́ (бу́ду конча́ть/ко́нчу) писа́ть э́то письмо́, я́ сейча́с же (бу́ду начина́ть/начну́) друго́е.
7. Ни́на то́лько что (конча́ла/ко́нчила) гото́вить уро́ки.

B. *Translate into Russian.*

1. We must begin a new life!
2. I will start reading the second chapter at once.
3. My brothers finished their work.
4. In the fall they used to finish working quite late.
5. First I will finish writing the letter, and then I will read it to you.
6. —When will you finish reading this play? —I haven't started it yet.
7. —Have you finished reading that novel? —Not yet.
8. I started writing a letter to my mother, but I haven't finished it yet.
9. I always begin working early and finish late.

PATTERN SENTENCES

Дава́ть (*imperfective*), дать (*perfective*).

1. —Кто́ **да́ст** мне́ папиро́су? —Я́ **да́м** тебе́, е́сли у меня́ е́сть.	1. —Who will give me a cigarette? —I will give you one if I have any.
2. —Ты́ мне́ **да́шь** ру́бль и́ли два́? —Я́ могу́ **да́ть** тебе́ да́же четы́ре рубля́.	2. —Will you give me a ruble or two? —I can even give you four rubles.
3. А́нна лю́бит **дава́ть** сове́ты.	3. Anna likes to give advice.
4. —Оля,² что́ ты́ сде́лала с мое́й газе́той? —Я́ её прочита́ла и **дала́** ма́ме, а ма́ма, когда́ прочита́ет, **да́ст** её тебе́.	4. —Olya, what did you do with my paper? —I read it and gave it to Mama, and Mama, when she finishes, will give it to you.
5. Эта ми́лая да́ма **дава́ла** А́нне уро́ки му́зыки два́ го́да.	5. That nice lady gave Anna music lessons for two years.
6. Вчера́ она́ **дала́** ей после́дний уро́к. Осенью она́ опя́ть **бу́дет дава́ть** ей уро́ки.	6. Yesterday she gave her the last lesson. In the fall she will be giving her lessons again.
7. —Если ва́м нужны́ бу́дут де́ньги, мы́ ва́м **дади́м**. —Большо́е спаси́бо! —Не́ за что.	7. —If you (will) need money, we will give you (some). —Many thanks! —You're welcome.

DRILLS

A. *Choose the correct form of the verb and translate.*

1. Я́ не люблю́ (дава́ть/да́ть) уро́ки.
2. Кто́ (дава́л/да́л) тебе́ уро́ки зимо́й?
3. Зи́на (дава́ла/дала́) мне́ три́ уро́ка те́нниса.
4. Оте́ц (бу́дет дава́ть/да́ст) мне́ де́ньги ка́ждый ме́сяц.
5. Кто́ (дава́л/да́л) тебе́ э́тот до́ллар?
6. Я́ (бу́ду дава́ть/да́м) тебе́ моё пальто́ за́втра ве́чером.
7. Кому́ вы́ (бу́дете дава́ть/дади́те) э́ту кни́гу?

B. *Complete the following sentences, supplying the proper form of* дать.

1. Мне́ нужны́ де́ньги. Вы́ мне́ . . . . ?
2. Мне́ нужны́ де́ньги. Ты́ мне́ . . . . ?
3. Мне́ нужны́ де́ньги. Кто́ мне́ . . . . ?
4. Мне́ нужны́ де́ньги. Оте́ц и ма́ть мне́ . . . . .
5. Вчера́ мне́ нужны́ бы́ли де́ньги. А́нна мне́ . . . . .
6. Вчера́ мне́ нужны́ бы́ли де́ньги. Бори́с мне́ . . . . .
7. Вчера́ мне́ нужны́ бы́ли де́ньги. Они́ мне́ . . . . .

2. Prepositions из and от with the genitive

The prepositions из, meaning *out of, from*, and от, meaning *from, away from*, both take the *genitive* case.

Из is used with most places, while от is used with persons:

—**Отку́да** э́то письмо́? —Письмо́ **из** Москвы́.
—Where is that letter from? —The letter is from Moscow.

---

² Оля is the diminutive of О́льга, *Olga*.

—**От кого́** э́то письмо́? —Письмо́ **от бра́та.**
—Whom is that letter from? —The letter is from Brother.

Я получи́л телегра́мму **от сестры́ из А́нглии.**
I got a telegram from my sister in (from) England.

PATTERN SENTENCES

Получа́ть (*imperfective*), **получи́ть** (*perfective*).

1. Серёжа наконе́ц **получи́л** отве́т **из Москвы́.**
2. Я ду́маю, что они́ за́втра **полу́чат** телегра́мму **из Оде́ссы.**
3. До войны́ он ча́сто **получа́л** пи́сьма **от своего́ дру́га.**
4. —**От кого́** вы **получи́ли** э́тот замеча́тельный пода́рок? —Я **получи́ла** его́ **от** мое́й ста́ршей до́чери.
5. Когда́ я **получу́** отве́т **от дире́ктора**, я вам сейча́с же позвоню́.
6. Я ду́маю, что ты тепе́рь ча́сто **бу́дешь получа́ть** пи́сьма **от Бори́са.**
7. —**Отку́да** э́то письмо́? —Оно́ **из Я́лты.** Я **получи́ла** его́ вчера́.

1. Seryozha finally got an answer from Moscow.
2. I think that tomorrow they will get a telegram from Odessa.
3. Before the war he often got letters from his friend.
4. —From whom did you get that wonderful present? —I got it from my elder daughter.
5. When I get an answer from the director, I'll phone you at once.
6. I think that now you will be getting letters from Boris often.
7. —Where does this letter come from? —It comes from Yalta. I got it yesterday.

DRILLS

A.   *Choose the proper form of* **получа́ть/получи́ть** *and translate.*

1. —Зи́на, от кого́ ты . . . . э́ти де́ньги? —Я . . . . их от отца́. Я ду́маю, что я ско́ро . . . . ещё.
2. Ра́ньше Ива́н ча́сто . . . . пода́рки из Аме́рики.
3. Как то́лько я . . . . письмо́ от Ни́ны, я вам сейча́с же позвоню́. Я всегда́ вам звоню́, когда́ . . . . от неё пи́сьма.
4. Оте́ц не ду́мает, что мы бу́дем ча́сто . . . . пи́сьма от Серёжи. Мо́жет быть мы . . . . одно́ или два́ письма́.

B.   *Translate into Russian.*

1. I often receive letters from my mother.
2. I used to receive a letter from her every week.
3. Yesterday our friend received this letter from Leningrad.
4. Nina thinks that tomorrow she will receive an answer from Moscow.
5. When I get an answer from Boris, I will tell you.
6. —From where is that telegram? —From New York.

3.   Tenses in reported speech

In Russian the tense used in reported discourse (indirect quotation) is the same as that used in the original statement. E.g.:

Original statement in the present tense:
      (Ivan speaking) «Я **пишу́** письмо́ бра́ту.»

Reported by another as an indirect quotation:

Ива́н сказа́л, что о́н **пи́шет** письмо́ бра́ту.

(Contrast English: Ivan said that he *was writing* a letter to his brother.)

Original statement in the past tense:

(Ivan speaking) «Я́ **написа́л** письмо́ бра́ту.»

Reported by another:

Ива́н сказа́л, что о́н **написа́л** письмо́ бра́ту.

(Compare English: He said that he *had written* a letter to his brother.)

Original statement in the future:

(Ivan speaking) «Я́ **напишу́** письмо́ бра́ту.»

Reported by another:

Ива́н сказа́л, что о́н **напи́шет** письмо́ бра́ту.

(Contrast English: He said that he *would write* a letter to his brother.)

In colloquial English the conjunction *that* is often omitted in indirect quotation, e.g., "He said he would answer you soon." In Russian, however, the conjunction **что** must *never* be omitted: О́н сказа́л, **что** о́н ско́ро ва́м отве́тит.

DRILLS

A. *Translate into English.*

1. Я́ спроси́л Ива́на, ско́лько вре́мени о́н живёт в э́том го́роде. О́н отве́тил, что живёт зде́сь три́ го́да.
2. Сего́дня у́тром я́ писа́л письмо́.
3. Бори́с спроси́л меня́, кому́ я́ пишу́.
4. Я́ отве́тил, что пишу́ ма́ме.
5. Вчера́ о́н мне́ сказа́л, что о́н пи́шет но́вый рома́н.
6. Вчера́ о́н мне́ сказа́л, что о́н написа́л но́вый рома́н.
7. Вчера́ о́н мне́ сказа́л, что о́н ско́ро напи́шет но́вый рома́н.
·8. Ма́ть спроси́ла Ива́на в письме́, почему́ о́н так ре́дко пи́шет своему́ бра́ту. О́н отве́тил в письме́, что у него́ не́т вре́мени ему́ писа́ть.
9. О́н рассказа́л на́м, где́ о́н бы́л, и что́ о́н де́лал.
10. О́н сказа́л на́м, что за́втра о́н бу́дет до́ма весь де́нь.
11. Когда́ я́ ви́дел Ве́ру, она́ мне́ сказа́ла, что она́ чита́ет Че́хова и спроси́ла меня́, что́ я́ чита́ю. Я́ отве́тил, что чита́ю Солжени́цына.[3]

B. *Translate into Russian.*

1. He said that he was writing an article about that.
2. They said that they would write to us if they had time.
3. He wrote (to) us that he wanted to see us.

---

[3] Alexander Solzhenitsyn, a contemporary Soviet author, famed in the Western world for his novels *The First Circle, Cancer Ward,* and his role in Soviet literary circles, was awarded the Nobel Prize for Literature in 1970.

4. The director said that I would get a letter about that tomorrow.

5. When I saw her yesterday, she said that she was now working in a factory.

6. He wrote to us in a letter that Leningrad was very beautiful and clean.

C. *Read and translate.*

1. В бу́дущем году́ мы́ **продади́м** на́ш до́м и бу́дем жи́ть у сы́на, кото́рый живёт в дере́вне со[4] свое́й семьёй. 2. —Кому́ ты́ **прода́шь** твои́ францу́зские кни́ги? —Я́ **прода́м** и́х одному́ францу́зскому журнали́сту. 3. О́н **рассказа́л** на́м вчера́ о́чень интере́сную исто́рию, кото́рую я́ **расскажу́** ва́м по́сле уро́ка. 4. Она́ должна́ была́ **переписа́ть** э́тот дли́нный перево́д, потому́ что бума́га, на кото́рой она́ его́ **написа́ла**, была́ гря́зная. Она́ взяла́ чи́стую бума́гу и всё **переписа́ла**. 5. Я́ бы́л вчера́ на́ о́чень интере́сной ле́кции и **записа́л** ка́ждое сло́во, кото́рое я́ слы́шал. 6. Я́ зна́ю одного́ студе́нта, кото́рый никогда́ ничего́ не **запи́сывает**, но кото́рый лю́бит задава́ть вопро́сы. 7. —Вы́ слы́шали но́вость? Смирно́вы **про́дали** сво́й до́м. И́м нужны́ были де́ньги. —Кто́ ва́м э́то **рассказа́л**? —Мы́ **получи́ли** от ни́х коро́ткое письмо́, в кото́ром они́ на́м об э́том **пи́шут**. —Как жа́ль! Э́то бы́л замеча́тельный ста́рый до́м и, как всё говори́ли, настоя́щий истори́ческий па́мятник. 8. Воло́дя показа́л мне́ маши́ну, кото́рую ему́ **про́дал** оди́н его́ дру́г.[5] 9. —Э́тому дру́гу нужны́ были де́ньги. —А я́ ду́мал, что э́то бы́л пода́рок от его́ жены́. 10. Я́ возьму́ чи́стый ли́ст бума́ги и **перепишу́** письмо́, кото́рое я́ **написа́л** дире́ктору. 11. Снача́ла я́ **покажу́** его́ мое́й жене́, а пото́м я́ да́м его́ ва́м. 12. —Что́ вы́ **отве́тите** э́тому глу́пому ма́льчику, е́сли о́н ва́с **спро́сит**, о чём вы́ говори́ли с его́ ма́терью? —Я́ **отве́чу** ему́, что э́то секре́т, и что о́н не до́лжен меня́ об э́том **спра́шивать**, потому́ что я́ всё равно́ ему́ ничего́ не **расскажу́**.

D. *Give the correct Russian verb form of the words in parentheses, and translate the whole sentence into English.*

1. Во́т продавщи́ца, кото́рая (sold) мне́ э́ту кни́жную по́лку. 2. Ни́на (will work) в универса́льном магази́не; она́ (will sell) ме́бель. 3. Я́ (will sell) тебе́ моё вече́рнее пла́тье. 4. Я́ (will tell) Вади́му, что о́н пло́хо (did) э́тот перево́д. 5. Что́ (answered) ма́ма тебе́, когда́ ты́ (asked) её, о чём она́ (talked) со мно́й? 6. Когда́ ты́ (will answer) твоему́ дру́гу? 7. Я́ (will copy) моё упражне́ние. 8. —Вы́ уже́ (answered) ва́шему ученику́, от кото́рого вы́ (received) вчера́ письмо́? —Да́, я́ ему́ (answered) и (wrote) ему́ обо всём. 9. Мы́ (will write down) а́дрес ва́шего до́ктора. 10. Кто́ та́к хорошо́ (explained) ва́м э́то тру́дное пра́вило? 11. Весно́й они́ (will start) рабо́тать о́чень по́здно. 12. Они́ (will finish) сего́дня в три́ часа́. 13. Я́ (shall tell) ва́м интере́сную исто́рию, кото́рую мне́ вчера́ (told) одна́ ми́лая де́вушка. 14. Э́тот молодо́й челове́к о́чень лю́бит (to ask) вопро́сы. 15. —Кто́ (copied) э́то упражне́ние? —Я́ (copied) его́. Я́ всегда́ (copy) то́, что я́ (write). 16. Вы́ ча́сто (will receive) пи́сьма от меня́.

E. *Review Translation.*

1. When did he tell you that, before or after class? 2. When they get my letter, I shall already be in Siberia. 3. —From whom did you get that telegram? —I got it from Anna from London. 4. I will explain this to you; I like explaining. 5. After

---

[4] The preposition с takes the form **со** before **свой** and a few other words beginning in a consonant cluster, e.g., со мно́й, со все́ми.

[5] **Оди́н его́ дру́г** *a friend of his.*

dinner they will explain everything to you.   6. Here is a greeting from the Soviet Union.   7. Where is the answer from Professor Robinson?   8. He wrote me only one letter from Leningrad.   9. He wrote down their address.   10. Last year I started to work in this small school.   11. Tomorrow I shall tell you everything about my life.   12. This year we received two letters from her from Italy, and one from France. 13. We heard that he had received a letter from our old director, and that next year he will work in our factory.   14. They all know that she will live alone, as she lived before the war.   15. They asked the young engineer whose those factories were. 16. Bob always got poor grades, but yesterday he got a good one.   17. If you don't write to her at once, she won't answer you.   18. When I write this article, I'll give it at once to my daughter; she will give it to her husband, and then they will give it to you. 19. As soon as you get it from them, you will give it to Vladimir.   20. —What did you get from them? —From whom? —From Vadim and Nina, of course. —Before I used to get many good things, but now I got a book from her, and nothing from him. 21. —When will you start working in the new office? —I will start next year.   22. Everybody will start working early tomorrow.   23. We got your wonderful present. Many thanks!   24. They told us that the streets of the city were very dirty.   25. They said they would answer us soon.

Vocabulary

второй second (*adj.*)
грязный dirty
дама lady
деньги (*pl.*) money
доллар dollar

откуда? from where?
папироса[6] cigarette
позже later
рубль (*masc.*) ruble
чистый clean, pure

VERBS

(See pp. 223–224.)

---

[6] **Папиросы** have the typical Russian cardboard mouthpiece. The word **сигарета** is used for a cigarette without the built-in mouthpiece.

Genitive plural of nouns • Genitive plurals of adjectives and other
modifiers • Uses of the genitive plural • Numerals, 5–39
Masculine nouns with a zero ending in the genitive • *Once a week,*
twice a month, etc. • Clock time • Age • Accusative plural
Genitive as direct object of negated verbs • Conversation: В котором
часу́ • Reading: На да́че у Ла́пиных

Unit 16

Grammar

1. Genitive plural of nouns

There are three types of noun endings in the genitive plural; unlike most noun endings encountered so far, their selection is not generally determined by gender.

A. 1st type; bare stem *(zero ending).* The genitive plural form of nearly all hard neuter nouns, and of Fem. I nouns, hard and soft, is the bare stem of these nouns; this stem is obtained by dropping the final vowel sound of the nominative singular:

	Nominative Singular	*Genitive Plural*
Neut., hard	сло́во [slóv.ə]	слов [slóf.]
Fem. I { *hard*	рука́ [rúk.á]	рук [rúk.]
soft { неде́ля [ņiḍéḷ.ə]	неде́ль [ņiḍéḷ.]
фами́лия [faṃíḷij.ə]	фами́лий [faṃíḷij.]

1. Type: **неде́ля—неде́ль**. In spelling, the final **-я** of the nominative singular is a sign both of the final vowel sound ([ə] in this example) and of the softness of the preceding consonant [ḷ]; in the genitive plural, the final vowel sound is dropped, and the softness of the end consonant is then indicated by the sign **-ь** (i.e., [ḷə] is written **ля**; [ḷ] final is written **ль**).

2. Type: **фами́лия—фами́лий**. In spelling, the final **-я** of the nominative singular stands for [jə]. Dropping the final vowel sound to form the genitive plural leaves the sound [j] in final position; it is rendered by the letter **-й** (i.e., [ijə] is written **-ия**; [ij] is written **-ий**).

Similarly: иде́я [iḍéj.ə]   иде́й [iḍéj]

233

Neuter nouns in **-ие** follow the same pattern:

зда́ние [zdáṇij.ə]   зда́ний [zdáṇij.]

Fleeting **o** *and* **e** *inserted in the genitive.*   Those nouns which have *zero* endings in the genitive plural (i.e., hard neuters and Fem. I, hard and soft) often have an inserted vowel **o** or **e** between two consonants in final position. Some of these are:

Nominative Singular	Genitive Plural
окно́ [akn.ó]	о́кон [ókən.]
кре́сло [kṛésl.ə]	кре́сел([kṛéşəl.]
письмо́ [pişm.ó]	пи́сем [píşəm.]
по́лка [pólk.ə]	по́лок [pólək.]
ча́шка [čášk.ə]	ча́шек [čášək.]
де́вушка [ḍévušk.ə]	де́вушек [ḍévušək.]
сестра́ [şistr.á]	сестёр [şişṭór.]

B. 2nd type: hard masculines. The ending **-ов** is added to the stem of hard masculines and pronounced [óf], or if unstressed, [əf].

стол [stól]	столо́в [stal.óf]
студе́нт [stuḍént]	студе́нтов [stuḍéntəf]

A variant of the ending **-ов** is **-ев**; masculine nouns ending in the nominative singular in a vowel plus [j], that is, a vowel plus spelled **-й**, take this ending: [girój]— [girój.əf] геро́й—геро́**ев**.

C. 3rd type: soft masculines and others. The ending **-ей** is added to the stem (pronounced [éj] if stressed; if unstressed, [əj]). This type includes soft masculines ending in **-ь**; masculines ending in **-ж, -ч, -ш,** and **-щ**; Fem II nouns (in **-ь**); and a few soft neuters:

Examples:

учи́тель [učíṭiḷ.]	учителе́**й** [učiṭiḷ.éj]
нож [nóš.]	ноже́**й** [naž.éj]
врач([vráč.]	враче́**й** [vrač.éj]
това́рищ [taváṛişč̣.]	това́рищ**ей** [taváṛişč̣.əj]
мо́ре [móṛ.ə]	мор**е́й** [maṛ.éj]
ночь [nóč̣.]	ноче́**й** [nač̣.éj]

The main classes of nouns may be grouped as follows according to the type of ending they take in the genitive plural (other special cases of genitive plural formation will be given later):

GENITIVE PLURAL OF NOUNS

	Nominative Singular	Type I Bare stem; "zero" ending	Type II -ов/-ев	Type III -ей
Masc.	стол →	столо́в		
	учи́тель			→ учителе́й
	геро́й →		геро́ев	
	нож			→ ноже́й
Neut.	сло́во → слов			
	по́ле →			→ поле́й
	зда́ние → зда́ний			
Fem. I	ко́мната → ко́мнат			
	неде́ля → неде́ль			
	фами́лия → фами́лий			
Fem. II	дверь			→ двере́й

DRILLS

A. *The following are examples of the various types of genitive plurals. Identify the nominative plural of each, and mark its stress.*

Zero Ending	Zero Ending— Fleeting Vowel Inserted	-ов/-ев	-ей
рек	студе́нток	студе́нтов	гостей́
гор	таре́лок	домо́в	писа́телей
мест	де́вочек	расска́зов	дней
карти́н	ло́жек (spoons)	ученико́в	това́рищей
кварти́р	ви́лок (forks)	отцо́в	врачей́
жён	сосе́док	музе́ев	море́й
карт	сестёр	ге́ниев	ночей́
учени́ц	о́кон		
озёр	пи́сем		
назва́ний	кре́сел		
иде́й	по́лок		
имён	ча́шек		
времён	де́нег (money; *pl. only*)		
	ку́хонь		

B. *Place the following nouns in the genitive plural. Mark the stress. You may refer to the lists above if necessary.*

дом	геро́й	мо́ре	же́нщина	музе́й	учени́ца
гость	ле́кция	слова́рь	ви́лка	газе́та	фами́лия
де́вушка	сестра́	лес	оте́ц	ге́ний	ви́лка
шко́ла	кни́га	жена́	писа́тель	таре́лка	назва́ние
кре́сло	ло́жка	собра́ние	писа́тельница	учени́к	врач
и́мя	де́ньги	ку́хня	иде́я	вре́мя	

2. Genitive plurals of adjectives and other modifiers

Adjectives and other modifiers end in **-ых/-их** for all genders (compare the genitive plural form of the third person pronoun **их**).

Nominative Singular Masculine	*Genitive Plural (All Genders)*
но́вый	но́вых
кра́сный	кра́сных
си́ний	си́них
хоро́ший	хоро́ших
ру́сский	ру́сских
како́й	каки́х
тако́й	таки́х
мой	мои́х
наш	на́ших
э́тот (*nom. pl.* э́ти)	э́тих
тот (*nom. pl.* те)	тех
весь (*nom. pl.* все)	всех
оди́н (*nom. pl.* одни́)	одни́х

DRILL

Change the following phrases from nominative plural to genitive plural.

но́вые учителя́	э́ти ученики́	на́ши высо́кие зда́ния
после́дние гла́вы	э́ти широ́кие поля́	э́ти интере́сные ле́кции
хоро́шие учени́цы	все́ но́вые автомоби́ли	те́ широ́кие озёра
англи́йские журна́лы	все́ си́ние ковры́	на́ши краси́вые жёны
мои́ ста́рые роди́тели	хоро́шие иде́и	одни́ на́ши друзья́
ва́ши ножи́		

3. Uses of the genitive plural

Like the genitive singular, the genitive plural is used:

Possessively (belonging or pertaining to):

    ко́мната сестры́—ко́мната сестёр
    цена́ костю́ма—цена́ костю́мов

After certain prepositions:

    без окна́—**без** о́кон
    из ко́мнаты—**из** ко́мнат

от ва́шего до́ктора—**от** ва́ших докторо́в
кро́ме э́того студе́нта—**кро́ме** э́тих студе́нтов
до/по́сле уро́ка—**до/по́сле** уро́ков
для (for) мое́й сестры́—**для** мои́х сестёр
о́коло (near) э́того до́ма—**о́коло** э́тих домо́в
у сестры́—**у** сестёр

With **нет** (**не́ было, не бу́дет**):

У на́с **не́т** э́той кни́ги.—У на́с **не́т** э́тих кни́г.

With expressions of quantity: As has been seen in Unit 7, the genitive is used with indefinite expressions of quantity.

(1) The genitive *singular* is used with nouns denoting divisible matter, that is, substances which cannot be counted, but can be measured:

ско́лько воды́, вина́, хле́ба?
мно́го воды́, вина́, хле́ба
ма́ло воды́, вина́, хле́ба

(2) The genitive *plural* is used with **ско́лько, мно́го, ма́ло, не́сколько** (*several*), and **сто́лько** (*so much, so many*) when the noun denotes something that *can be counted:*

ско́лько стака́нов, ча́шек, ноже́й?
мно́го пи́сем, студе́нтов, ко́мнат
ма́ло кни́г, докторо́в, теа́тров
не́сколько журна́лов, де́вушек, автомоби́лей, имён
сто́лько кни́г, веще́й, студе́нтов

(3) All these expressions of quantity take a neuter singular verb in the past and a singular verb in the future when the verb comes first, e.g.,

На столе́ стоя́ло **не́сколько** стака́нов.

PATTERN SENTENCES

1. У Ива́на бы́ло **мно́го** кни́г.
2. В Голла́ндии не́т го́р.
3. У него́ мно́го де́нег.
4. В на́шем до́ме не́т кварти́р.
5. Ма́ть не спала́ мно́го ноче́й.
6. В э́той ко́мнате не́сколько двере́й.
7. В на́шей ку́хне ма́ло о́стрых ноже́й; у на́с то́лько два́ о́стрых ножа́.
8. В э́том магази́не не́ было кра́сных каранда́ше́й.
9. Зде́сь бы́ло ма́ло хоро́ших враче́й.
10. В СССР[1] мно́го озёр.

1. Ivan had many books.
2. There are no mountains in Holland.
3. He has much money.
4. There are no apartments in our house.
5. Mother didn't sleep for many nights.
6. In this room there are several doors.
7. There are few sharp knives in our kitchen; we have only two sharp knives.
8. In that store there were no red pencils.
9. There were few good physicians here.
10. In the U.S.S.R. there are many lakes.

---

[1] **СССР** (indecl.) is *U.S.S.R.* The full form is Сою́з Сове́тских Социалисти́ческих Респу́блик, Union of Soviet Socialist Republics.

11. Я ча́сто получа́ю пи́сьма **от** мои́х учени́ц и **от** и́х роди́телей.
12. Во́т оте́ц все́х э́тих ма́леньких ма́льчиков.
13. На собра́нии не́ было ни ва́ших, ни мои́х ученико́в.
14. Та́м никого́ не́ было, **кро́ме** на́ших профессоро́в.
15. Ни́на не мо́жет жи́ть **без** свои́х подру́г.
16. —**Для кого́** вы́ купи́ли э́ти блу́зки? —Я́ купи́ла э́ти блу́зки **для** мои́х сестёр.
17. Что́ вы́ бу́дете де́лать **по́сле** экза́менов?
18. О́н зна́ет **сто́лько** анекдо́тов!
19. **О́коло** больши́х гости́ниц ча́сто быва́ет мно́го маши́н.
20. Я́ получи́л письмо́ **от** мои́х роди́телей.
21. У на́с студе́нты **из** ра́зных городо́в.
22. Я́ до́лжен прочита́ть э́ти две́ кни́ги **до** экза́менов.

11. I often get letters from my girl pupils and from their parents.
12. Here is the father of all those little boys.
13. Neither your pupils nor mine were at the meeting.
14. No one was there except our professors.
15. Nina can't live without her girl friends.
16. —For whom did you buy those blouses? —I bought these blouses for my sisters.
17. What will you be doing after the examinations?
18. He knows so many anecdotes!
19. Near large hotels there are often many cars.
20. I got a letter from my parents.
21. We have students from different cities.
22. I must read these two books before the exams.

DRILLS

A. *Place the words in parentheses in the genitive plural.*

1. У на́с вчера́ бы́ло мно́го (интере́сные го́сти).
2. В э́том ме́сяце бы́ло ма́ло (хоро́шие дни́).
3. В Ита́лии мно́го (ста́рые города́).
4. Ле́том Ни́на прочита́ла не́сколько (интере́сные рома́ны).
5. В э́том рома́не не́т (настоя́щие геро́и).
6. У на́с не́т (всё э́ти журна́лы).
7. У на́с мно́го (ненужные ве́щи).
8. В и́х кварти́ре не́сколько (больши́е ко́мнаты).
9. О́коло (э́ти дома́) не́т (хоро́шие магази́ны).

B. *Complete the following questions and answers in the plural, according to the model.*

	Вопро́с	Отве́т
Model:	У ва́с е́сть **кни́ги**?	Не́т, у на́с не́т **кни́г**.

Same for: словари́, тетра́ди, де́ньги, но́вости, сёстры, врачи́, у́мные студе́нты, вече́рние газе́ты, кра́сные кре́сла, о́стрые ножи́, хоро́шие учителя́.

C. *Translate into Russian.*

1. There are several large windows in your living room.
2. How many sisters does he have?
3. —How many pencils do you see on the table? —I see only three pencils.
4. —For whom did you buy these textbooks? —For my students.
5. There were no new letters on my desk.
6. How many blue plates and cups do you have?
7. We have neither blue cups nor plates.
8. There are no big forests near big cities.
9. —How many weeks did you stay (live) in the Crimea? —We stayed there three weeks.
10. New York has (in New York there are) several good libraries.
11. He knows many Russian words, but he speaks slowly.

12. I bought these books for my comrades.
13. Near those new summer cottages there are many woods.
14. Our students have few good textbooks.

4. Numerals 5–39

It has been seen that the numerals *two, three,* and *four* take the genitive *singular* e.g.,

два́/две́, три́, четы́ре до́м**а**, сло́в**а**, кни́г**и**

The numerals 5 and above govern the genitive *plural*, e.g.,

пя́ть (5) дом**о́в**
оди́ннадцать (11) сло́**в**
три́дцать (30) кни́**г**

The numerals from 5 through 10 are as follows:

5	пять	8	во́семь
6	шесть	9	де́вять
7	семь	10	де́сять

The numbers from 11 through 19 are formed with *a basic numeral* + **на** + **дцать** (a contraction of **де́сять** *ten*); the first numeral loses its final **-ь**, if any:

11	оди́ннадцать	15	пятна́дцать
12	двена́дцать	16	шестна́дцать
13	трина́дцать	17	семна́дцать
14	четы́рнадцать	18	восемна́дцать
		19	девятна́дцать

The numbers 20 and 30 are formed with *the basic numeral* + **-дцать**:

20	два́дцать	30	три́дцать

Compound numerals are formed as in English (but without a hyphen):

21 два́дцать оди́н (одно́, одна́)
32 три́дцать два́ (две́)
35 три́дцать пя́ть
36 три́дцать ше́сть
etc.

The *last* digit (i.e., the units digit) of the compound numeral determines the number and case of the noun, e.g.,

(21) два́дцать оди́н до́м
    ,,   одно́ сло́во *nom. sing.*
    ,,   одна́ кни́га

(22) два́дцать **два́** до́ма, сло́ва
    ,,   **две́** кни́ги
(23) два́дцать **три́** до́ма, сло́ва, кни́ги *gen. sing.*
(24) два́дцать **четы́ре** до́ма, сло́ва, кни́ги

(25) два́дцать **пя́ть** домо́в, сло́в, кни́г } gen. pl.
(26) два́дцать **ше́сть** домо́в, сло́в, кни́г } gen. pl.

All numerals except **оди́н** take *adjectives* in the genitive *plural*:

три́ больши́х го́рода
четы́ре но́вых заво́да
пя́ть хоро́ших ученико́в

With 2, 3, and 4 the *nominative plural* of adjectives may be used optionally for *feminines*:

три́ хоро́ших/хоро́шие газе́ты

5. Masculine nouns with a zero ending in the genitive plural

A small number of hard masculine nouns have a *zero* ending in the genitive plural, that is, their genitive plural is identical with the nominative singular. These include the nouns **раз** (*time, occasion*), **солда́т** (*soldier*), **боти́нок** (*shoe*), and **глаз** (*eye*).

	ско́лько **ра́з**?	how many times?
	пя́ть **ра́з**	five times
But:	два́ **ра́за** (*gen. sing.*)	twice

As stated in Unit 13, the nominative plural of **челове́к** (*person*) is **лю́ди** (*people*). The genitive plural is **люде́й**. But with numerals (5 and above), as well as with **ско́лько** and **не́сколько**, the genitive plural form **челове́к**, identical with the nominative singular, is used:

—Ско́лько та́м бы́ло **челове́к**? —Та́м бы́ло се́мь **челове́к**.

But: Та́м бы́ло мно́го **люде́й**.
О́н жи́л у э́тих **люде́й**.

The genitive plural of **ле́то** (*summer*), **лет**, is used with numerals (5 and above) and *all* other expressions of quantity as a suppletive[2] genitive plural of **год** (*year*):

	ско́лько **ле́т**?	how many years?
	мно́го **ле́т**	many years
	во́семь **ле́т**	eight years
But:	два́ **го́да** (*gen. sing.*)	two years

6. Once a week, twice a month, etc.

This is expressed by **в** + the *accusative* of the unit of time:

ра́з **в** неде́лю	once a week
два́ ра́за **в** де́нь	twice a day
де́сять ра́з **в** го́д	ten times a year
ча́с **в** де́нь	an hour a day
три́ часа́ **в** неде́лю	three hours a week

---

[2] Suppletives are words unrelated in form but linked together in one declensional or conjugational pattern, e.g., *be, am, was,* in English.

DRILLS

A. *Read and translate.*

1. На нашей у́лице **се́мь** но́вых домо́в и **не́сколько** ста́рых.
2. В э́том до́ме **семна́дцать** удо́бных кварти́р.
3. У нас **пя́ть** ма́леньких ко́мнат и **две́** больши́х.
4. У отца́ в кабине́те **де́сять** высо́ких и больши́х кни́жных по́лок, а у меня́ в ко́мнате то́лько **две́** ма́леньких по́лки.
5. Я́ куплю́ **пятна́дцать** бе́лых ча́шек и **двена́дцать** таре́лок.
6. У меня́ **два́дцать се́мь** ру́сских кни́г, а у бра́та **три́дцать четы́ре**.
7. —Ско́лько вы́ заплати́ли за э́ту пласти́нку? —Я́ заплати́ла за неё **пя́ть** до́лларов. Я́ ре́дко плачу́ бо́льше за пласти́нки. —Для кого́ вы́ купи́ли её? —Я́ купи́ла её для мои́х дочере́й.
8. —Ско́лько сто́ит ко́мната с ва́нной в ва́шей гости́нице? —Мы́ пла́тим за ко́мнату **три́дцать** до́лларов в неде́лю.
9. —А ско́лько вы́ пла́тите? —Я́ плачу́ ме́ньше: то́лько **два́дцать пя́ть** до́лларов.
10. —Ско́лько сто́ят э́ти боти́нки (shoes)? —Они́ сто́ят **пятна́дцать** до́лларов.
11. В неде́ле **се́мь** дне́й.
12. —Ско́лько дне́й в ме́сяце? —**Три́дцать** или **три́дцать оди́н**, а в феврале́ (February) то́лько **два́дцать во́семь**.
13. —Ско́лько челове́к бы́ло на собра́нии? —Та́м бы́ло **пятна́дцать челове́к**.
14. —Ско́лько ле́т тому́ наза́д вы́ бы́ли в Сове́тском Сою́зе? —Два́ го́да тому́ наза́д.
15. —Ско́лько ра́з вы́ бы́ли в Евро́пе? —Я́ та́м бы́л **пя́ть ра́з**, а моя́ жена́ то́лько **два́ ра́за**.
16. —Ско́лько часо́в в де́нь вы́ рабо́таете? —Обыкнове́нно **во́семь** часо́в, не ме́ньше. —Я́ не зна́л, что вы́ сто́лько рабо́таете.
17. **Ра́з** в неде́лю у меня́ уро́к му́зыки и **три́ ра́за** в неде́лю уро́к ру́сского языка́.

B. *Form questions and answers in the plural, according to the model, using the numerals given in parentheses.*

Вопро́с	Отве́т
Model: —Ско́лько у ва́с ко́мнат?	—У на́с ше́сть ко́мнат.

Same for: (7) кре́сла, (4) кни́жные по́лки, (12) ма́ленькие ло́жки, (6) но́вые ви́лки, (8) си́ние таре́лки, (2) больши́е ковры́, (3) дли́нные столы́, (5) дороги́е ла́мпы, (2) широ́кие о́кна.

C. *Translate into Russian.*

1. I saw several blue cars in the garage.
2. At the meeting yesterday I saw six Soviet reporters.
3. —How many knives do you see? —I see eight knives.
4. I lived in England twenty-eight years, and my brother lived there twenty-one years.
5. I don't know all these people.
6. I saw six people who were playing cards.
7. My neighbor has three large rooms, and we have only two.

8. —How many years have you been working here? —Twenty-two years. —And I have been working here twenty-five years.
9. I have already read that book several times.
10. I've read it three times.
11. There were several soldiers on the train.
12. I have no new shoes.
13. I write to my mother two or three times a week.
14. That newspaperman writes four articles a month.

7. Clock time

Кото́рый ча́с? (*or*: **Ско́лько сейча́с вре́мени?**) *What time is it?*

Ча́с. (*nom. sing.*)	One o'clock.
Два́ часа́. (*gen. sing.*)	Two o'clock.
Три́ часа́.	Three o'clock.
Четы́ре часа́.	Four o'clock.
Пя́ть часо́в. (*gen. pl.*)	Five o'clock.
etc.	etc.
Двена́дцать часо́в.	Twelve o'clock.

Бы́ло is used for the past (except with *one*); **бу́дет** for the future:

Бы́ло два́ часа́.	It was two o'clock.
Бы́ло де́сять часо́в.	It was ten o'clock.
Ско́ро бу́дет де́сять часо́в.	It will soon be ten o'clock.
But: Бы́л ча́с.	It was one o'clock.

В кото́ром часу́? (*or*: **В како́е вре́мя?**) *At what time?*

В ча́с.	At one o'clock.
В два́ часа́.	At two o'clock.
В пя́ть часо́в.	At five o'clock.
Ро́вно в де́сять часо́в.	At ten o'clock sharp.
etc.	etc.

Instead of the English system of using A.M. and P.M., the day is divided into four parts, designated by the genitives **утра́**, **дня́**, **ве́чера**, and **но́чи**:

В ча́с дня́.	At 1:00 P.M.
В ше́сть часо́в ве́чера.	At 6:00 P.M.
В ча́с но́чи/утра́.	At 1:00 A.M.
В ше́сть часо́в утра́.	At 6:00 A.M.
etc.	

PATTERN SENTENCES

1. —**В кото́ром часу́** вы́ встаёте ка́ждый де́нь? —Я́ обы́чно встаю́ **в се́мь часо́в**.

1. —At what time do you get up every day? —I usually get up at seven o'clock.

2. За́втра пра́здник и я́ не зна́ю, **в кото́ром часу́** я́ вста́ну. Я́ не люблю́ ра́но встава́ть.

2. Tomorrow is a holiday and I don't know at what time I will get up. I don't like to get up early.

3. —**В кото́ром часу́** ты́ бу́дешь в рестора́не? —Я́ бу́ду ро́вно **в ча́с**.

3. —At what time will you be at the restaurant? —I'll be there at one o'clock sharp.

4. Зимо́й **в се́мь часо́в утра́** ещё быва́ет темно́.	4. In winter it's still dark at seven o'clock in the morning.
5. Бы́ло **четы́ре часа́**, когда́ я ко́нчил писа́ть письмо́.	5. It was four o'clock when I finished writing the letter.
6. Ско́ро бу́дет **де́вять часо́в**, а ещё светло́!	6. It will soon be nine, and it's still light!
7. Уже́ **оди́ннадцать**, а А́нны ещё не́т до́ма!	7. It's eleven already, and Anna isn't home yet!

DRILL

Translate into Russian.

1. Tomorrow is a holiday and I shall get up at ten.
2. —What time is it? —It is four o'clock.
3. And I thought it (was) already five.
4. —At what time did you have supper after the theater? —We had supper at eleven o'clock.
5. We usually have dinner exactly at seven o'clock.
6. Yesterday at one o'clock I had lunch with Boris and his wife.
7. —At what time did you see her? —At nine o'clock in the morning.
8. At 10 p.m. he was not home yet.
9. It was two o'clock when I saw them.
10. It will soon be eight.

ORAL DRILL

Answer from your own experience.

1. В кото́ром часу́ вы́ обы́чно встаёте?
2. В кото́ром часу́ у ва́с пе́рвый уро́к?
3. В кото́ром часу́ после́дний?
4. Что́ вы́ обы́чно де́лаете в се́мь часо́в утра́?
5. Что́ вы́ обы́чно де́лаете в се́мь часо́в ве́чера?
6. Ско́лько часо́в в де́нь вы́ быва́ете в шко́ле?
7. Ско́лько часо́в вы́ спи́те?
8. Ско́лько кни́г и журна́лов в ме́сяц вы́ покупа́ете?
9. Ско́лько ра́з в неде́лю вы́ быва́ете в библиоте́ке?
10. Ско́лько часо́в в де́нь ва́м ну́жно для ва́ших зада́ний?
11. Вы́ пи́шете мно́го пи́сем в ме́сяц?
12. От кого́ вы́ получа́ете пи́сьма?
13. Ско́лько ра́з в де́нь вы́ быва́ете в рестора́не?
14. Ско́лько экза́менов у ва́с бу́дет в конце́ семе́стра?
15. С ке́м вы́ мо́жете говори́ть по-ру́сски для пра́ктики?
16. Како́й у ва́с са́мый интере́сный предме́т (subject) в шко́ле?

8. Age

The *person* or *object* whose age is given is in the *dative case*.

—Ско́лько **ва́м** ле́т? —**Мне́** девятна́дцать ле́т.
—How old are you? —I am nineteen.

Моему́ бра́ту Ива́ну два́дцать два́ го́да.
Мое́й сестре́ Со́не два́дцать оди́н го́д.

—Ско́лько лет э́тому до́му? —Ему́ три́дцать лет.

—How old is this house? —It is thirty years old.

The past uses the *neuter singular* **бы́ло** (but **был** if the final digit of the numeral is **оди́н**); the future is always **бу́дет**.

> На́шему отцу́ **бы́ло** тогда́ три́дцать пять лет.
> Our father was thirty-five at that time.
>
> Мне́ ско́ро **бу́дет** два́дцать лет.
> I will soon be twenty.
>
> *But:* **Ему́** тогда́ **был** два́дцать оди́н год.
> He was twenty-one years old then.

DRILLS

A. *Express the ages of the following, according to the model.*

Model: На́ша мать (35)—На́шей ма́тери три́дцать пять лет.

Твоя́ подру́га (18)	Э́то де́рево (30)
Твой това́рищ (24)	Э́тот па́мятник (33)
Э́та студе́нтка (21)	Э́та шко́ла (39)
Ваш мла́дший брат (11)	Наш ста́рший сын (4)

B. *Translate into Russian.*

1. She will soon be ten.   2. My little sister will soon be four.   3. He will soon be seventeen.   4. I was fifteen at that time.   5. Ivan was twenty-two at that time.

9. Accusative plural

We have seen (Unit 8, page 100) that in the masculine singular (but not in the other genders) the accusative coincides in form with the nominative for *inanimate* nouns and with the genitive for nouns *animate* in meaning.

In the plural, the animate-inanimate distinction and the rule that the accusative is like the nominative for inanimate nouns, and like the genitive for animates, applies to nouns of all genders.

		ACCUSATIVE SINGULAR		
Masc.	*Inan.:*	Я ви́дел сто́л.	like *Nom. Sing.*	**Animate-Inanimate Distinction**
	Anim.:	Я ви́дел **студе́нта**.	like *Gen. Sing.*	
Neut.	*Inan.:*	Я ви́дел письмо́.	like *Nom. Sing.*	
	Anim.:	Я ви́дел **дитя́**.[3]		
Fem. I	*Inan.:*	Я ви́дел ко́мнату.	[u]-ending	
	Anim.:	Я ви́дел **де́вушку**.		
Fem. II	*Inan.:*	Я ви́дел две́рь.	like *Nom. Sing.*	
	Anim.:	Я ви́дел **дочь**.		

[3] The word **дитя́** (*child*), which may be regarded as the only example of an animate neuter noun, is very rarely used in the singular.

ACCUSATIVE PLURAL

Masc.	*Inan.:*	Я ви́дел столы́.	like *Nom. Pl.*
	Anim.:	Я ви́дел **студе́нтов**.	like *Gen. Pl.*
Neut.	*Inan.:*	Я ви́дел пи́сьма.	like *Nom. Pl.*
	Anim.:	Я ви́дел **дете́й**.	like *Gen. Pl.*
Fem. I	*Inan.:*	Я ви́дел ко́мнаты.	like *Nom. Pl.*
	Anim.:	Я ви́дел **де́вушек**.	like *Gen. Pl.*
Fem. II	*Inan.:*	Я ви́дел две́ри.	like *Nom. Pl.*
	Anim.:	Я ви́дел **дочере́й**.	like *Gen. Pl.*

Animate-Inanimate Distinction

PATTERN SENTENCES

1. Алёша опя́ть купи́л но́вую пласти́нку. Óн лю́бит покупа́ть пласти́нки.
2. Мы́ óчень лю́бим э́ту ми́лую де́вочку.
3. Я люблю́ э́тих ми́лых де́вочек. Э́то до́чери люде́й, кото́рых я зна́ю мно́го ле́т.
4. —Вы́ зна́ете э́тот огро́мный заво́д? —Да́, я хорошо́ зна́ю э́тот заво́д, и я зна́ю его́ дире́ктора.
5. Я зна́ю э́ти хими́ческие заво́ды, и я хорошо́ зна́ю и́х директоро́в.
6. Вчера́ я в пе́рвый ра́з ви́дела её краси́вую сестру́.
7. Я уже́ не́сколько ра́з ви́дел её мла́дших сестёр.
8. —Вы́ зна́ете на́шу но́вую машини́стку? —Я зна́ю все́х ва́ших машини́сток.
9. Я люблю́ ста́рые дере́вья, кото́рые расту́т в э́том саду́. В на́шем саду́ не́сколько таки́х дере́вьев.

1. Alyosha has bought another new record. He likes to buy records.
2. We like that sweet little girl very much.
3. I like those nice girls. They are the daughters of people whom I have known for many years.
4. —Do you know that huge plant? —Yes, I know that plant well and I know its director.
5. I know those chemical plants and I know their directors well.
6. Yesterday I saw her pretty sister for the first time.
7. I've seen her younger sisters several times already.
8. —Do you know our new typist? —I know all your typists.
9. I like the old trees which grow in this garden. In our garden there are several such trees.

DRILL

Put the words in parentheses into the proper form.

Зи́на ви́дела -
- (ва́ша но́вая блу́зка).
- (ва́ши но́вые блу́зки).
- (ва́ша но́вая подру́га).
- (ва́ши но́вые подру́ги).
- (э́тот ма́ленький го́род).
- (э́тот ма́ленький ма́льчик).
- (э́ти ма́ленькие ма́льчики).
- (э́ти ма́ленькие учени́цы).

$$\text{Мы́ зна́ем} \begin{cases} \text{(эти сове́тские журнали́сты).} \\ \text{(эта сове́тская газе́та).} \\ \text{(эта сове́тская журнали́стка).} \\ \text{(эти сове́тские студе́нтки).} \end{cases}$$

10. Genitive as direct object of negated verbs

It will be recalled that the word **нет** governs the *genitive* case (see p. 91), e.g.,
В на́шем го́роде **нет** теа́тра; У меня́ **нет** словаря́.

The direct object of a negated verb is also generally in the *genitive* case, e.g.,

Я́ **не** е́л мя́са.	I ate no meat.
Óн **не** зна́ет ру́сского языка́.	He doesn't know any Russian.
Они́ никогда́ **не** чита́ют газе́т.	They never read any papers.
Я́ **не** по́мню и́х имён.	I don't remember their names.
Я́ **не** бу́ду задава́ть тру́дных вопро́сов.	I won't ask any hard questions.
Я́ **не** зна́ю здесь ни одно́й краси́вой де́вушки.	I don't know a single pretty girl here.
Óн **не** получи́л отве́та.	He got no answer.

However, in referring to a particular, individualized object or person, the accusative *may* be used, especially in colloquial speech.

Óн ещё **не** чита́л мою́ статью́.	He hasn't read my article yet.
Я́ **не** зна́ю его́ жену́.	I don't know his wife.
Я́ **не** куплю́ э́то кре́сло.	I won't buy this armchair.
А́нна **не** лю́бит э́тот цве́т.	Anna doesn't like this color.

DRILL

Translate into Russian, putting the object in the genitive case.

1. I never saw such big stores.
2. He drinks no milk.
3. We have not yet seen his new car.
4. I didn't see any interesting books there.
5. She bought no bread.
6. Sonya doesn't like cheap restaurants.
7. I have not yet read this magazine.
8. She never buys expensive presents.
9. I didn't get that letter.
10. They don't drink French wine.

Conversation

В кото́ром часу́

Андре́й. —Боб, ты́ недоста́точно говори́шь по-ру́сски. Тебе́ нужна́ пра́ктика. Два́ ра́за в неде́лю мы́ для пра́ктики бу́дем разгова́ривать по-ру́сски. Я́ бу́ду твои́м учи́телем и бу́ду задава́ть тебе́ вопро́сы, а ты́ бу́дешь игра́ть ро́ль ученика́. Сего́дня, е́сли хо́чешь, бу́дет на́ш пе́рвый уро́к.

Боб. —Э́то прекра́сная иде́я! Но́ я́ зна́ю, как ма́ло у тебя́ вре́мени!

А. —Ничего́, для э́того у меня́ бу́дет доста́точно вре́мени.

Б. —Но́ зна́ешь, мне́ бу́дет тру́дно отвеча́ть на твои́ вопро́сы: я́ зна́ю сли́шком ма́ло сло́в и де́лаю сли́шком мно́го оши́бок!

А. —Во́т поэ́тому тебе́ нужна́ пра́ктика! Вопро́сы бу́дут просты́е. Слу́шай (listen)! **В кото́ром часу́** ты обыкнове́нно встаёшь?

Б. —Я встаю́ **в се́мь**.

А. —А почему́ тебе́ ну́жно так ра́но встава́ть?

Б. —Потому́ что я́ живу́ дово́льно далеко́ от шко́лы.

А. —Понима́ю. **В кото́ром часу́** у тебя́ пе́рвый уро́к?

Б. —Пе́рвый уро́к **в де́вять часо́в**.

А. —А в како́е вре́мя после́дний?

Б. —Иногда́ **в три́**, а иногда́ **в четы́ре часа́**.

А. —Ты́ ви́дишь, как хорошо́ ты́ отвеча́ешь! Бу́дем продолжа́ть. Ско́лько часо́в в де́нь ты́ в шко́ле?

Б. —Ше́сть или се́мь часо́в в де́нь.

А. —А что́ ты́ обы́чно де́лаешь в **ше́сть часо́в**?

Б. —**В ше́сть часо́в утра́** я́ сплю́, **а в ше́сть часо́в ве́чера** я́ у́жинаю.

А. —Прекра́сно. Сего́дня пра́здник. Ты́ и сего́дня вста́л **в се́мь**?

Б. —Не́т, что́ ты! Я́ вста́л **в двена́дцать**... Не́т, **в ча́с**.

А. —**В ча́с**! Здо́рово! Ско́лько же часо́в ты́ спа́л?

Б. —То́лько де́сять. Э́то не так мно́го. Люблю́ спа́ть!

А. —Кто́ не лю́бит! Ну во́т, ви́дишь, что ты́ мо́жешь отвеча́ть на мои́ вопро́сы. Го́споди! Уже́ **пя́ть часо́в**! Э́то коне́ц уро́ка. Мы́ бу́дем продолжа́ть на́ш разгово́р в друго́й ра́з.

Б. —Большо́е тебе́ спаси́бо за по́мощь!

А. —Не́ за что. До ско́рого.

PRONUNCIATION DRILL

—bób, ti n̦idastátəčnə gəvar̦íš parúski. țib̦é nužná prákțikə. dvá rázə ṵn̦id̦él̦u mi dl̦iprákțiki búd̦im rəzgavár̦ivəț parúski. ja búdu tvajím uč̦íțiĺəm i búdu zədaváț țib̦é vaprósi, a ti búd̦iš igráț ról̦ uč̦in̦iká. šivódn̦ə, jéșl̦i xóč̦iš, búd̦it náš pérvij urók.

—étə pr̦ikrásnəjə id̦éjə! no ja znáju, kak málə uțib̦á vr̦émin̦i!

Answer these questions in Russian.

1. Почему́ Андре́й бу́дет два́ ра́за в неде́лю разгова́ривать с Бо́бом по-ру́сски? 2. Кака́я ро́ль бу́дет у Андре́я, и каку́ю ро́ль бу́дет игра́ть Бо́б? 3. Что́ во вре́мя уро́ка до́лжен бу́дет де́лать Андре́й, и что́ до́лжен бу́дет де́лать Бо́б? 4. Почему́ Бо́б ду́мает, что ему́ э́то бу́дет тру́дно? 5. В кото́ром часу́ Бо́б встаёт? 6. Почему́ о́н до́лжен так ра́но встава́ть? 7. О́н до́лжен всегда́ э́то де́лать? 8. В кото́ром часу́ после́дний уро́к в шко́ле? 9. Ско́лько часо́в в де́нь о́н быва́ет в шко́ле? 10. Что́ о́н де́лает в ше́сть часо́в утра́ и что́ в ше́сть часо́в ве́чера? 11. Когда́ они́ бу́дут продолжа́ть сво́й разгово́р?

Reading

На да́че у Ла́пиных

У меня́ е́сть подру́га, Ни́на Ла́пина. Мы́ зна́ем дру́г дру́га уже́ мно́го ле́т. Мы́ бы́ли с не́й в шко́ле, а тепе́рь мы́ с не́й в университе́те. Мне́ тепе́рь два́дцать ле́т, а Ни́не два́дцать оди́н го́д.

Недалеко́ от Москвы́, среди́ (among) лесо́в и поле́й, е́сть ме́сто Переде́лкино.

В Переделкине, где живёт много известных писателей (там жил знаменитый поэт Борис Пастернак, автор романа «Доктор Живаго»), у родителей Нины есть дача. Это большой деревянный, старый дом. Никто даже не знает, сколько этому дому лет. Вокруг дома сад, в котором растут старые красивые деревья.

В этом большом, но уютном доме много больших и маленьких комнат, много дверей, узких и длинных коридоров, несколько балконов, несколько комнат для гостей. Мебель в доме довольно старомодная и везде много разных нужных и ненужных вещей, много книг и картин.

Для меня всегда настоящий праздник жить у Лапиных, у этих милых, интересных людей. Хозяин дома, Александр Павлович Лапин, писатель. Он написал несколько романов и пьес. Он весёлый и тёплый человек, что[4] довольно необыкновенно для известного писателя. Он любит людей, собак, лошадей, кошек и даже детей! Во дворе его дачи (двор большой) две лошади и четыре собаки. Две кошки и одна собака живут в доме.

Александр Павлович очень любит природу. Летом, когда погода хорошая, он встаёт рано, иногда в шесть часов, иногда даже раньше. Он сидит на веранде, на своём любимом месте, видит розовое небо, видит, как встаёт солнце. Он любит писать рано утром, когда всё тихо кругом, и только птицы поют. Другие жители (inhabitants) дома встают позже, одни в девять, а другие в десять и даже в одиннадцать.

Елена Борисовна Лапина, как и её муж, любит людей, и у них всегда можно (one can) встретить писателей, поэтов, музыкантов, художников (painters), певцов (singers). В доме всегда есть молодёжь: подруги Нины и товарищи Бориса, сына Лапиных. (Борису восемнадцать лет.) Там всегда много шума, смеха, и споров. Гости пьют чай, обедают, ужинают на веранде, рассказывают друг другу разные анекдоты, играют в шахматы, в карты, гуляют в лесу, ловят рыбу.[5] Молодёжь поёт песни, играет в теннис, в крокет, читает друг другу стихи своих любимых поэтов. Вечером все любят сидеть в кабинете Александра Павловича. В этой большой, уютной комнате много хороших и редких книг, много фотографий разных знаменитых людей, есть несколько картин знаменитых художников, среди (among) них картины пейзажиста[6] Левитана.[7] Левитан любимый русский художник Лапина. Там, в этом кабинете, поэты и писатели часто читают свои вещи и критикуют (criticize) друг друга.

Много интересных и талантливых людей встретила я в этом весёлом, шумном доме!

Answer the following questions in Russian.

1. Сколько времени Нина и её подруга знают друг друга?   2. Что вы теперь знаете о Переделкине?   3. Почему видно, что дача Лапиных довольно старая? 4. Почему у Лапиных всегда много молодёжи?   5. Кого можно у них встретить? 6. Что гости делают целый день?   7. Почему можно сказать об Александре

---

[4] **Что** here means *which is*. **Что** (stressed) may be used as a relative pronoun without a definite antecedent.

[5] **Ловить** (II: ловлю, ловишь) *to catch*; **ловить рыбу** *to fish*.

[6] **Пейзаж** *landscape*; **пейзажист** *landscape painter*.

[7] **Левитан, Исаак Ильич**, a late nineteenth-century painter celebrated for his typically Russian landscapes.

Па́вловиче, что о́н тёплый челове́к? 8. Что́ есть в кабине́те Ла́пина? 9. Кто́ Левита́н? 10. Что́ го́сти де́лают в кабине́те?

DRILL

Review Translation.

1. —How much does that shirt cost? —I paid five dollars for it; I never pay more for shirts. 2. I met him several times on a noisy, lively street in Paris. 3. —How old is he? —He is thirty years old, and his wife is twenty-three. 4. —At what time did you meet him? —I met him yesterday at 7:00 P.M., and I shall meet him tomorrow at 10:00 A.M. 5. —How many Russian books do you have? —I have no Russian books. 6. —Are there (any) tall houses on your street? —Yes, on my street there are several tall houses. 7. There were no mountains and no forests where we lived. 8. But there were many lakes, fields, and rivers. 9. —How many legs does a dog have? —A dog has four legs. 10. Near our house there are several good stores. 11. —For whom are you writing down that address? —I am writing it down for my sisters. 12. —For whom did you buy these coats? —I bought them for my secretaries. 13. Chekhov didn't write novels; he wrote (short) stories. 14. Bob has never read those stories. 15. I have never seen Chekhov's plays. 16. My daughters were in the Caucasus eleven months ago. 17. I've told you twenty times not to do that. 18. Near the house (there) grow big trees. One tree is twenty-five years old. 19. Around the house there are many fields and woods. 20. Boris is only seventeen.

Vocabulary

весёлый (*adv.* ве́село) cheerful, merry, lively
ви́лка fork
вокру́г (*adv.* or *prep.* + *gen.*) around, all around
врач physician
двор court, yard
деревя́нный wooden, made of wood
для (+ *gen.*) for, for the sake of
доста́точно sufficient(ly)
за (+ *acc.*) for, in exchange for
иде́я idea
изве́стный well-known
коридо́р hall, corridor
ко́шка cat
ло́шадь (*fem. II*) horse
молодёжь (*fem. II, coll.*) young people
не́бо (*pl.* небеса́) sky, heaven
недоста́точно insufficient(ly)
не́сколько (+ *gen.*) several, some, a few
нож knife
о́коло (+ *gen.*) near, in the vicinity of
о́стрый sharp
певе́ц (*gen.* -ца́; *fem.* -и́ца) singer
поэ́т poet
приро́да nature

пти́ца bird
раз time, occasion
ра́нний (*adj.*) early
ре́дкий rare
ро́вно exactly, precisely
роди́тели (*pl.*) parents
ро́зовый pink, rosy
смех laughter
солда́т soldier
со́лнце [со́нцэ] sun
СССР [эсэсэсе́р] U.S.S.R. (short for Сою́з Сове́тских Социалисти́ческих Респу́блик Union of Soviet Socialist Republics)
старомо́дный old-fashioned
стих (line of) verse
стихи́ verses, poems
сто́лько (+ *gen.*) so much, so many
тому́ наза́д ago
у́жин supper
ую́тный cozy
фотогра́фия photograph
худо́жник painter, artist
шум noise
шу́мный noisy

VERBS

встава́ть (imperf., I: встаю́, -ёшь), встать (perf., I: вста́н.у, -ешь) to get up, stand up, arise

встреча́ть (imperf., I), встре́тить (perf., II: встре́.чу, -тишь) to meet, encounter

гуля́ть (imperf., I), погуля́ть (perf., I) to stroll, take a walk, go for walks

забыва́ть (imperf., I), забы́ть (perf., I: забу́д.у, -ешь) to forget

купи́ть (perf., II: куплю́, ку́пишь) to buy[8]

петь (imperf., I: по.ю́, -ёшь), спеть (perf., I) to sing

продолжа́ть (imperf., I) to continue, go on (+ *inf.*)

плати́ть (imperf., II: плачу́, пла́тишь), заплати́ть (perf., II) to pay (+ *dat. of person*): п. за + *acc.* to pay for

расти́ (imperf., I: расту́, растёшь) (Note the change of stem *a* to *o* in the past: рос, -ло́, -ла́, -ли́) to grow

сто́ить (imperf., II) to cost, to be worth. **Ско́лько сто́ит . . .?** How much does it cost (is it worth)?

у́жинать (imperf., I), поу́жинать (perf., I) to have supper

---

[8] Купи́ть (perf.) is unusual in that it does not retain the prefix по- of the imperfective покупа́ть.

Unit **17**

Grammar

1. Determinate and indeterminate imperfectives

(1) Most Russian verbs have only one form of the imperfective aspect to express two kinds of meaning; this form is used:

(a) For actions in actual progress at some particular time:

> When I saw him, he *was reading*.
> Когда́ я его́ ви́дел, о́н **чита́л**.

> —What *is he doing* now? —He *is reading*.
> —Что́ о́н тепе́рь де́лает? —О́н **чита́ет**.

(b) For actions spoken of without reference to actual performance at any particular time, that is, when the action may be habitual or recurring, or when it may be regarded as a potentiality.

He *reads* a lot.	О́н мно́го **чита́ет**.
He *read* (used to read) a lot.	О́н мно́го **чита́л**.
He *reads* Russian	О́н **чита́ет** по-ру́сски.
(*i.e.*, he *can* read Russian).	
My father *read* Russian.	Мо́й оте́ц **чита́л** по-ру́сски.

(2) Unlike most other Russian verbs, one specific group of verbs has *two* kinds of imperfective forms for these two functions. The verbs of this group are related in meaning: they describe different kinds of *going* and of *carrying*.

(a) One of these imperfective forms (usually called *determinate*) refers to the action of *going* or *carrying* in actual progress at some particular time and in a definite direction.

(b) The other form (usually called *indeterminate*) is used when actual progress or definite direction are not implied. This form denotes actions of *going* or *carrying* that are habitual, recurring, potential, etc.

251

2. Verbs of *going by one's own means*

Russian uses one set of verbs for going (or coming) by one's own means, *without* the help of any conveyance, and another set of verbs for going (or coming) with the help of a conveyance, be it a car, train, bicycle, or horse. Each of these two kinds of going may be referred to as *indeterminate* or *determinate imperfective* verbs, or even as *perfective* verbs (some of which will be given later in this lesson).

For going *by one's own means*, the two imperfective forms are as follows:

	Indeterminate	Determinate
Inf.	ходи́ть (II)	идти́ (I)
Pres.	хожу́	иду́
	хо́дишь	идёшь
	хо́дит	идёт
	хо́дим	идём
	хо́дите	идёте
	хо́дят	иду́т
Past	ходи́л, ходи́ло,	шёл, шло,
	ходи́ла, ходи́ли	шла, шли

The *indeterminate* ходи́ть is used to render *go* (on foot), *walk*, in such sentences as:

He *goes* to the library every day—хо́дит
He *went* (used to go) there every day—ходи́л
He *walks* a lot—хо́дит
Their little boy *walks* (can walk)—хо́дит

The *determinate* идти́ is used to render *am going, was going*, etc. (if the going is on foot), in such sentences as:

I *am going* home—иду́
When I saw him, he *was going* home—шёл

3. Adverbs and prepositional phrases of destination

English *where* is rendered in Russian by где or куда́. *Where* (где) refers only to the place *in which* someone or something is or was, or some action is or was performed. *Where* in the sense of *destination* (place *to which*) is expressed by куда́.

A question with где may be answered by a phrase with в or на and the name of the place *where* in the *locative* case:

—Где́ Ива́н?	—Where is Ivan?
—О́н в саду́.	—He is *in the garden.*
Or: —О́н на концѐрте.	—He is *at a concert.*

A question with куда́ may be answered by a phrase with the same prepositions в or на, but the name of the place (place *to* which someone or something is moving) in the *accusative* case:

—Куда́ идёт Ива́н?	—Where is Ivan going?
—О́н идёт в са́д.	—He is going *to the garden.*
Or: —О́н идёт на концѐрт.	—He is going *to a concert.*

Phrases with **в** or **на** + *locative* express *location*; phrases with **в** or **на** + *accusative* express *direction* or *destination*.

Questions with **где**? and **куда**? may also be answered with adverbs:

Question: **Где?** (location)
where?

Answer: **здесь** or **тут** **там**
here *there*

Question: **Куда?** (destination)
where?

Answer: **сюда** **туда**
here (coming this way) *there* (going that way)

Two commonly used adverbial forms express *home*, one **дома**, as location; the other **домой**, as destination:

Location:

—*Where* is he? —He is *at home*. —**Где** óн? —Óн **дома**.

Destination:

—*Where* are you going? —**Куда** вы идёте?
—I am going *home*. —Я иду **домой**.

Going *along* a street, road, etc. is expressed by **идти** with the preposition **по** + *dative*, e.g., Они шли **по** главной улице, *they walked along the main street*. **По** + *dative* with **ходить** is used to express going without a definite destination:

ходить **по** комнате
to walk up and down a room

ходить **по** городу
to walk about a town

PATTERN SENTENCES

Ходить

1. Их ребёнок ещё не говорит и не **ходит**.
2. Óн óчень скóро начнёт говорить и **ходить**.
3. Я всегда мнóго **хожу**; я люблю **ходить**.
4. Моя жена не любит готóвить, и мы часто **хóдим в** рестора́н.
5. Я люблю **ходить по** главной улице, где мнóго магазинов.
6. Мы раньше **ходили** в театр раз или даже два раза **в** неделю, но теперь мы **хóдим** тóлько **раз в** месяц.
7. Мóй младший сын **хóдит в** эту шкóлу, а старший **хóдит в** университет.
8. Когда óн думает, óн любит **ходить по** кóмнате.

1. Their child doesn't talk yet and it doesn't walk.
2. Very soon it will begin to talk and to walk.
3. I always walk a great deal; I like to walk.
4. My wife doesn't like to cook, and we often go to a restaurant.
5. I like to walk along the main street, where there are many stores.
6. We used to go to the theater once or even twice a week, but now we go only once a month.
7. My younger son goes to (attends) this school, and the elder one goes to the university.
8. When he thinks, he likes to walk up and down the room.

Идти

1. —Зóя, **кудá** ты **идёшь?** —Я́ **идý** в кабинéт. Моя́ кни́га в кабинéте.
2. —**Кудá** вы́ **идёте?** —Мы́ **идём** в тý аптéку. —Я́ тóже **тудá** идý.
3. Порá **идти́** обéдать! Ктó **идёт** со мнóй в ресторáн?
4. —**Кудá идёт** Кóля? —Óн **идёт домóй.** —Гдé егó дóм? —Óколо шкóлы, на углý.
5. —Зачéм кóшка **идёт** в кýхню? —Онá **идёт тудá** пи́ть молокó.
6. —Вы́ ви́дите, ктó **сюдá идёт?** —Дá, ви́жу. Это товáрищ Петрóв.
7. —**Кудá** вы́ **идёте** пóсле урóка? —Я́ **идý** в ресторáн. Я́ всегдá обéдаю в ресторáне.
8. Когдá я́ **шёл** на стáнцию, я́ встрéтил нáшего дирéктора. Óн тóже **шёл тудá.**
9. —Я́ вчерá рабóтал в библиотéке. —Дá, я́ ви́дел вáс, когдá вы́ **тудá шли́.** Ктó с вáми **шёл?** —Со мнóй **шлá** Вéра.
10. —**Кудá** вы́ спеши́те? —Я́ дóлжен бы́ть дóма в пя́ть.
11. Нáм порá **идти́ домóй.**

1. —Zoya, where are you going? —I'm going to the study. My book is in the study.
2. —Where are you going? —We're going to that drugstore. —I'm going there too.
3. It's time to go for dinner! Who's coming (going) with me to the restaurant?
4. —Where is Kolya going? —He's going home. —Where is his home? —Near the school, on the corner.
5. —Why is the cat going to the kitchen? —It's going there to drink milk.
6. —Do you see who's coming here? —Yes, I see. It's Comrade Petrov.
7. —Where are you going after class? —I'm going to a restaurant. I always have dinner at a restaurant.
8. When I was on my way to the station, I met our director. He was going there, too.
9. —I was working at the library yesterday. —Yes, I saw you when you were on your way there. Who was going with you? —Vera was going with me.
10. —Where are you hurrying? —I must be at home at five.
11. It's time for us to go home.

DRILLS

A. *Choose the correct form of the verbs in parentheses, and translate.*

1. С кéм вы́ обыкновéнно (хóдите/идёте) в теáтр?
2. Я́ обыкновéнно (хожý/идý) оди́н.
3. Сегóдня вéчером мы́ (хóдим/идём) в кинó.
4. Кáк вы́ (хóдите/идёте), мéдленно или бы́стро?
5. Я́ всегдá (хожý/идý) бы́стро. Я́ не люблю́ (ходи́ть/идти́) мéдленно.
6. С кéм вы́ (ходи́ли/шли́) вчерá, когдá я́ вáс встрéтил?
7. Я́ (ходи́л/шёл) с отцóм.
8. Я́ вчерá встрéтил Андрéя, когдá óн (ходи́л/шёл) в библиотéку.
9. Веснóй бáбушка кáждый дéнь (ходи́ла/шлá) в пáрк.
10. Мы́ чáсто (хóдим/идём) в кинó.

B. *Form two series of sentences, one with* **Я́ идý** . . . , *the other with* **Я́ бы́л** . . . , *the correct preposition* (**в** *or* **на**), *and each of the nouns below in the proper case form:*

Model: Я́ идý в университéт. Я́ бы́л в университéте.

Same for: кóмната, концéрт, здáние, лéкция, сáд, урóк, пóчта, завóд, собрáние, музéй, пáрк.

C. *Choose the correct word in parentheses, and translate.*

1. Ива́н, (куда́/гдé) ты́ идёшь?
2. Ни́на, (куда́/гдé) ты́ рабо́таешь?
3. Ива́н Ива́нович, (куда́/гдé) вы́ живёте?
4. (Куда́/гдé) вы́ идёте?
5. Мы́ идём (туда́/та́м).
6. Вы́ то́же идёте (туда́/та́м)?
7. Мы́ за́втракали (туда́/та́м).
8. (Куда́/гдé) рабо́тает Ива́н?
9. (Куда́/гдé) о́н идёт?
10. О́н идёт (здéсь/сюда́).
11. О́н живёт (здéсь/сюда́).

D. *Translate the words in parentheses.*

1. —Куда́ (are going) дéти? —Они́ (are going) в шко́лу; они́ (go) в шко́лу ка́ждое у́тро.
2. —Куда́ ты́ (are going)? —Я́ (am going) на рабо́ту; я́ (go) на рабо́ту ка́ждый дéнь.
3. Ко́ля хо́чет (to go) домо́й.
4. —С кéм вчера́ вéчером (was walking) Вéра? —Она́ (was walking) одна́.
5. Мы́ (were going) в кино́ и встрéтили Ива́на.
6. О́н то́же (was going) туда́.
7. —Куда́ вы́ (are going) сего́дня по́сле обéда? —Мы́ (are going) в теа́тр; мы́ (go) в теа́тр ра́з или два́ ра́за в мéсяц.

E. *Translate the words in parentheses.*

1. Ко́ля идёт (home).
2. Мы́ (are going to the drugstore). На́м ну́жно купи́ть аспири́н (at the drugstore).
3. Мы́ (are going to the restaurant). Мы́ обéдаем (at the restaurant).
4. —Я́ (am going to the library). Вы́ то́же (are going there)? —Да́, я́ тепéрь рабо́таю (there).
5. Я́ ви́жу Ива́на; о́н идёт (here).
6. Я́ не зна́л, что о́н живёт (here).
7. Ко́шка всегда́ спи́т (here). Во́т она́ идёт (here).

4. Verbs of *riding*

As we have seen at the beginning of Section 2, Russian distinguishes two kinds of going: going by one's own means or walking, and going or riding in a car, train, on horseback, etc. Like the verb for going by one's own means, the basic verb which denotes riding also has two imperfective forms: *indeterminate* and *determinate*. It also has perfective forms, which will be given later. The two imperfective forms are as follows:

	Indeterminate	*Determinate*
Inf.	**éздить** (II)	**éхать** (I)
Pres.	éзжу [jéžžu]	éду
	éздишь	éдешь
	éздит	éдет
	éздим	éдем
	éздите	éдете
	éздят	éдут

The past tense of both verbs is regular: éздил, etc; éхал, etc.

5. Riding in a vehicle

The vehicle used in travel is expressed by **на** + *locative*:

ездить/ехать на поезде — to go by train

ездить/ехать $\begin{Bmatrix} \text{на автомобиле} \\ \text{на машине} \end{Bmatrix}$ — to go by car

ездить/ехать на автобусе — to go by bus

Мы ехали в Москву на поезде.
We were going by train to Moscow.

Я всегда езжу на работу на машине.
I always go to work by car.

But **в** + *locative* is normally used when it is a question of location, and not of use of a vehicle as a means for travel (compare English *by car* vs. *in a car*):

Мы сидели **в** автомобиле.
We were sitting in a car.

Я встретил моего учителя **в** поезде.
I met my teacher on the train.

PATTERN SENTENCES

Ездить

1. Я **езжу** в Одессу два раза в год. В Одессе живёт мой сын.
2. Мой муж часто **ездит** в Калифорнию. Его родители живут в Калифорнии. Он едет туда **через** неделю.
3. Смирновы каждое лето **ездят** в Крым. Их дочь живёт в Крыму. Они едут туда **через** месяц.
4. Они любят **ездить** по городу в своём новом автомобиле.
5. Я живу далеко и каждый день **езжу** на работу на поезде. Но сегодня я еду на машине.
6. Мы никогда не **ездим** слишком быстро; это опасно!
7. Ольга никогда не **ездит** на метро. Она **ездит** только на такси.
8. Они любят **ездить** и много **ездят**.

1. I go to Odessa twice a year. My son lives in Odessa.
2. My husband often goes to California. His parents live in California. He is going there a week from now.
3. Every summer the Smirnovs go to the Crimea. Their daughter lives in the Crimea. They are going there a month from now.
4. They like to ride around town in their new car.
5. I live far away, and every day I go to work by train. But today I am going by car.
6. We never drive too fast; it's dangerous!
7. Olga never takes the subway. She takes only taxis.
8. They like to travel and they travel a great deal.

Ехать

1. Я вчера **ехал на** поезде из Ленинграда в Москву.
2. В поезде я встретил Миллера. Он тоже **ехал** туда.

1. Yesterday I was going by train from Leningrad to Moscow.
2. On the train I met Miller. He was going there too.

3. Послезáвтра я éду в дерéвню **на** маши́не. Ктó **éдет** со мнóй?

3. Day after tomorrow I am going to the country by car. Who's coming with me?

4. —Как мнóго маши́н! Кудá **éдут** всé э́ти лю́ди? —Они́ **éдут** на футбóл.

4. —How many cars there are! Where are all these people going? —They're going to a soccer game.

5. Они́ **éхали** óчень бы́стро и не ви́дели меня́.

5. They were driving very fast and didn't see me.

6. Из Одéссы мы́ **éдем** в Ки́ев, а из Ки́ева мы́ **éдем** в Москвý на пóезде.

6. From Odessa we are going to Kiev, and from Kiev we are going to Moscow by train.

DRILLS

A. *Choose the correct form of the verb in parentheses, and translate.*

1. Мы́ сегóдня (éздим/éдем) в Бостóн.
2. Мы́ чáсто (éздим/éдем) тудá.
3. Я́ никогдá не (éзжу/éду) во Флори́ду.
4. Э́тот журнали́ст (éздит/éдет) в Берли́н нéсколько рáз в гóд.
5. Здрáвствуйте! Кудá вы́ сейчáс (éздите/éдете)? Я́ сейчáс (éзжу/éду) на вокзáл.
6. Андрéй никогдá не (éздит/éдет) бы́стро.
7. Мы́ лю́бим (éздить/éхать).

B. *Choose the correct form of the verb in parentheses, and translate.*

1. Вади́м (идёт/éдет) в дерéвню.
2. Я́ зáвтра (идý/éду) в Филадéльфию.
3. Я́ (идý/éду) в столóвую.
4. Собáка (идёт/éдет) на верáнду.
5. Мы́ (идём/éдем) в Лóндон.
6. Я́ ви́дел, как Вади́м (шёл/éхал) на автомоби́ле.
7. Когдá вы́ (идёте/éдете) в СССР?
8. Áнна (идёт/éдет) в аптéку.
9. Мáма (идёт/éдет) в кýхню.

C. *Translate into Russian.*

1. We are going to Europe.
2. We are going to the study.
3. Who is going to the country?
4. We are all going there by car.
5. When I saw Olga she was riding very fast.
6. —Where are you going? —I am going to Boston.
7. —Is your wife going there, too? —No, she is going to California.
8. I am going to the living room, and they are going to the kitchen.
9. My grandmother is going to the garden. She likes to be in the garden.
10. The Kalinins are going to Odessa. Their daughter lives in Odessa.
11. We often go to England.
12. We're going there tomorrow.
13. They were driving slowly when I saw them.
14. —Where do you go every summer? —We go to the country.
15. We are going there soon.
16. My husband goes to work by train, and I go by car.
17. Today I, too, am going by train.
18. Do you often go to Kiev?
19. I go there five or six times a year.

6. Adverbs and prepositional phrases of destination (continued)

A. Persons as goal of motion. In Section 3 it has been seen that Russian distinguishes location (в or на + *locative*) from destination (в or на + *accusative*).

If the destination is a person ("going to see someone," "to someone's place"), then it is expressed by the preposition к and the name of the person visited in the *dative*:

Óн идёт к дóктору. {He is going to the doctor.
He is going to the doctor's (house, office, etc.).
He is going to see the doctor.

The usage corresponds to the locational у + *genitive*:

Óн тепéрь у дóктора.   Now he is at the doctor's.

B. Motion from a place. Direction "from a place" is expressed by three prepositions, all governing the *genitive* case. These prepositions correspond in the following way to those used to express motion *to* a place:

	Going to		*Going from*	
Place	в + acc.	в дерéвню	из + gen.	из дерéвни
	на + acc.	на пóчту	с + gen.	с пóчты
Person	к + dat.	к дóктору	от + gen.	от дóктора

К and с have the forms ко and со before certain words beginning with a consonant cluster, e.g., ко мнé (*to me*), ко всéм (*to everyone*). Со is used before a number of words beginning with a consonant cluster, especially when the first consonant is с or з, e.g., со столá, *from the table*.

The different prepositions and case forms expressing *being at, in, going to,* and *going from* present the following regular correspondences:

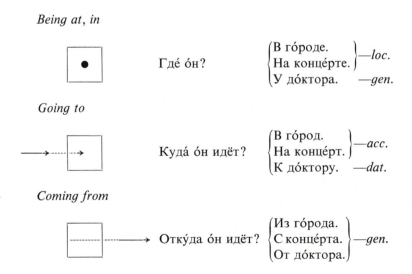

Being at, in

Гдé óн? {В гóроде.
На концéрте.} —*loc.*
У дóктора. —*gen.*

Going to

Кудá óн идёт? {В гóрод.
На концéрт.} —*acc.*
К дóктору. —*dat.*

Coming from

Откýда óн идёт? {Из гóрода.
С концéрта.
От дóктора.} —*gen.*

C. Adverbs of Direction.

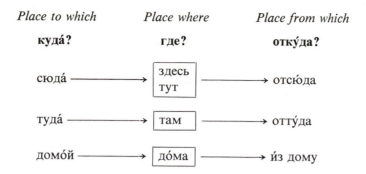

Place to which	Place where	Place from which
куда́?	где?	отку́да?
сюда́ ⟶	здесь тут	⟶ отсю́да
туда́ ⟶	там	⟶ отту́да
домо́й ⟶	до́ма	⟶ и́з дому

D. Getting things or persons. "To go for something or someone," "to go to get something or someone," is expressed by a verb of motion + **за** + *instrumental*:

Я иду́ в библиоте́ку **за кни́гой.**
I'm going to the library *for a book.*

Я иду́ в кабине́т **за карандашо́м.**
I'm going to the study *for a pencil.*

Мы идём **за Ни́ной.**
We are going for (to get) Nina.

PATTERN SENTENCES

1. —**К кому́** вы идёте сего́дня ве́чером? —Мы идём **к Ни́не.**
2. Мы идём **к ней** в се́мь часо́в.
3. —**Отку́да** вы идёте? —Мы идём **от Ни́ны.** Мы **у неё** обе́дали.
4. Мы идём в библиоте́ку **за Бори́сом.**
5. —**Куда́** ты идёшь? —Я иду́ **к до́ктору Смирно́ву.** Я хожу́ **к нему́** ра́з в ме́сяц.
6. Я вчера́ бы́л **у до́ктора Смирно́ва.**
7. Я сейча́с иду́ **от до́ктора Смирно́ва.**
8. —**Отку́да** вы идёте? —Мы идём **из теа́тра.** —Мы то́же идём **отту́да!** Стра́нно, что мы ва́с не ви́дели **в теа́тре.**
9. Мы шли́ **в ба́нк,** а они́ шли́ **из ба́нка.**
10. А́нна была́ **на собра́нии.** Когда́ она́ **шла с собра́ния,** она́ встре́тила Бори́са.
11. Послеза́втра мы все́ идём **на собра́ние.**

1. —To whose place are you going tonight? —We are going to Nina's.
2. We are going to her place at 7:00.
3. Where are you coming from? —We're coming from Nina's. We had dinner at her place.
4. We are going to the library for Boris.
5. —Where are you going? —I'm going to Dr. Smirnov's. I go to see him once a month.
6. Yesterday I was at Dr. Smirnov's (I visited him).
7. Now I am coming from Dr. Smirnov's.
8. —Where are you coming from? —We're coming from the theater. —We're coming from there, too! Strange that we didn't see you in the theater.
9. We were going to the bank, and they were coming from the bank.
10. Anna was at the meeting. When she was coming away from the meeting, she met Boris.
11. Day after tomorrow we're all going to a meeting.

12.	Газéта лежáла **на** столé; я взялá её **со** столá. Словáрь стоя́л **на** пóлке; я взялá егó **с** пóлки.	12.	The newspaper was lying on the table; I took it off the table. The dictionary was standing on the shelf; I took it off the shelf.
13.	—Кудá вы́ идёте? —Я́ иду́ **на** пóчту **за** мáркой. —А я иду́ **с** пóчты. Я́ купи́л мáрки **на** пóчте и сейчáс иду́ **домóй**.	13.	—Where are you going? —I'm going to the post office for a stamp. —And I'm coming from the post office. I bought stamps at the post office, and now I am going home.
14.	—Бори́с, **за чéм** ты́ идёшь в магази́н? —Я́ иду́ **за** крáсным винóм.	14.	—Boris, what are you going to the store for? —I'm going for red wine.
15.	—Кудá ты́ идёшь **отсю́да?** —К Вади́му.	15.	—Where are you going from here? —To Vadim's.

DRILLS

A. *Translate the words in parentheses.*

1. Мы́ идём (to the store for a magazine).
2. Мы́ идём (from the store).
3. Ни́на идёт (to the post office for a stamp).
4. Ни́на идёт (from the post office).
5. Я́ тепéрь служу́ (at the post office).
6. Мáма éдет (to Anna's).
7. Онá бýдет жи́ть (at Anna's).
8. Мáма éдет сюдá (from Anna's).
9. Мы́ идём (to Vadim's).
10. Мы́ бýдем обéдать (at Vadim's).
11. Я́ иду́ (to Ivan's).
12. Я́ люблю́ рабóтать (at Ivan's).
13. Ктó идёт (to Dr. Makarov's)?
14. Я́ бы́л вчерá (at Dr. Makarov's).
15. Зóя идёт (to Lena's for a book).
16. Онá бýдет у́жинать (at Lena's).

B. *Translate into Russian.*

1. —Where are you coming from now? —From home.
2. We were at the drugstore; we are coming from there.
3. I am coming from Dr. Makarov's.
4. They are coming from Anna's.
5. —Where are you going? —We are going to Moscow.
6. We live in Moscow.
7. We are coming from Moscow.
8. Anna is going to Leningrad.
9. She lives in Leningrad.
10. Where is she coming from now?
11. She is coming from Leningrad now.
12. We are going to the concert.
13. We were at the concert.
14. We are now coming from the concert.

7. Perfectives of determinate *going* verbs, with prefix по-

Perfectives of the verbs *to go* (*walk*) and *to ride* are formed with the prefix **по-**:

	To go (*walk*)	*To go* (*ride*)
Inf.	**пойти́**	**поéхать**
Future	пойду́ пойдёшь, etc.	поéду поéдешь, etc.
Past	пошёл, пошлó, etc.	поéхал, etc.

These forms are used as perfectives of the verbs **идти́** and **е́хать**, that is, they are used to denote a single trip. As with other perfectives, the "present" form of their conjugation has future meaning. Observe the difference in the use of these perfectives from that of the determinate imperfective:

Perfective

—Где́ Ива́н? —О́н **пошёл** в шко́лу.
—Where is Ivan? —He's *gone* to school.

Мо́й сы́н **пое́хал** в Ленингра́д.
My son *has gone* to Leningrad.

Determinate Imperfective

О́н **шёл** в шко́лу, когда́ я́ его́ встре́тил.
He *was on his way* to school when I met him.

Когда́ о́н **е́хал** в Ленингра́д, о́н встре́тил в по́езде Андре́я.
When he *was going* to Leningrad, he met Andrey on the train.

The determinate imperfective (**бу́ду идти́**, etc.) is seldom used in the future, though it occurs in certain idioms (see page 263).

The present tense of **идти́** (**е́хать**) *or* the future tense of **пойти́** (**пое́хать**) may often be used interchangeably. This is similar to English:

За́втра я́ **пойду́** в музе́й.
Tomorrow I *shall go* to the museum.

Or:

За́втра я́ **иду́** в музе́й.
Tomorrow *I'm going* to the museum.

Here are several situations where the perfective future *must* be used:

If *going* in the future follows the completion of another action:

Я́ **напишу́** э́то письмо́ и **пойду́** на по́чту.
I shall write this letter and go to the post office.

Мы́ **пое́дем** с ва́ми, но́ ра́ньше мы́ **ко́нчим** на́шу рабо́ту.
We shall go with you, but first we shall finish our job.

With **когда́** or **е́сли** in a clause with future meaning:

Когда́ вы́ **пое́дете** в дере́вню, мы́ **пое́дем** с ва́ми.
When you *go* to the country, we *shall go* with you.

Я́ ещё не зна́ю, **когда́** мы́ **пойдём** к Ве́ре.
I don't know yet when we *are going* to Vera's.

Е́сли за́втра бу́дет хоро́шая пого́да, мы́ **пое́дем** за́ город.
If the weather is good tomorrow, we'll go out of town.

PATTERN SENTENCES

1. —Андрей дома? —Нет, его нет; он **пошёл** к Борису за словарём.
2. Я видел его, когда он **шёл** туда. Он **шёл** по правой стороне улицы.
3. —Где Анна? —Она **пошла** в магазин за молоком. Вы не видели её, когда она туда **шла**?
4. Мы пообедали и **пошли** в театр. Мы **шли** быстро, так как не хотели опоздать.
5. Мы пообедаем и **пойдём** в гости к Анне.
6. —Куда вы **пошли** после театра? —Мы **пошли** прямо домой.
7. —Мы позавтракаем и **пойдём** в музей. Хотите **пойти** с нами? —Спасибо, после завтрака я должен **пойти** к доктору.
8. Иван кончит перевод и **пойдёт** в кино.

9. Я должен завтра **поехать** в деревню к матери. Вы хотите **поехать** со мной?
10. Завтра я не могу. Я **поеду** в деревню послезавтра.
11. —Где Иван Иванович? —Он **поехал** в Киев. —Его жена **поехала** с ним? —Нет, он **поехал** один.
12. Я кончу статью через два дня и **поеду** отдыхать.

1. —Is Andrey at home? —No, he's not; he's gone to Boris's to get a dictionary.
2. I saw him on his way (going) there. He was walking on the right side of the street.
3. —Where's Anna? —She went to the store for milk. Didn't you see her on her way there?
4. We had dinner and went to the theater. We walked fast, since we didn't want to be late.
5. We shall have dinner, and shall go visit Anna.
6. —Where did you go after the theater? —We went straight home.
7. —We shall have lunch and shall go to the museum. Do you want to go with us? —Thanks, after lunch I have to go to the doctor's.
8. Ivan will finish the translation and go to the movies.
9. Tomorrow I must go to the country to Mother's. Do you want to go with me?
10. I can't tomorrow. I shall go to the country the day after tomorrow.
11. —Where's Ivan Ivanovich? —He's gone to Kiev. —Did his wife go with him? —No, he went alone.
12. I will finish the article in two days and go off to have a rest.

DRILL

A. *Choose the correct form of the verb in parentheses and translate.*

1. Мне было скучно и я (шёл/пошёл) к Борису.
2. Я (шёл/пошёл) к нему по этой улице.
3. Мы вчера (шли/пошли) в театр.
4. Когда мы туда (шли/пошли), было холодно.
5. Ольги нет дома. Она (шла/пошла) в аптеку за аспирином.
6. Я встретил её на улице, когда она туда (шла/пошла).
7. Зачем их сын (ехал/поехал) в Лондон?
8. Когда вы (едете/поедете) в Москву, мы (едем/поедем) с вами.
9. Я кончу писать этот роман через месяц и (еду/поеду) на Кавказ.
10. Они купят дом в Крыму и (едут/поедут) туда весной.

B. *Choose the proper form of the verbs* **пойти** *or* **поехать**, *past or future.*

1. —Где Коля? —Он .... к товарищу в Киев.
2. Когда я кончу книгу, я .... в библиотеку, а потом я .... домой.
3. Сначала мы .... в столовую, а потом в кабинет.
4. —Где Зина? —Она .... в деревню.

5. —Кто́ .... с не́й? —Она́ .... одна́. —Тогда́ я то́же туда́ ..... Вы́ .... со мно́й? —Хорошо́, мы́ то́же .....

6. —Куда́ .... ма́ма? —В ку́хню.

8. Idiomatic uses of the verb идти́

This verb is used in the following expressions and many others of a similar nature:

Вре́мя идёт.	Time goes by (passes).
Часы́ иду́т.	The watch (clock) is going.
До́ждь идёт.	It is raining.
Сне́г идёт.	It is snowing.
Фи́льм (карти́на) идёт.	A movie is running.
Пье́са идёт.	A play is running.
По́езд идёт.	The train is going.
But: Автомоби́ль е́дет.	The car is going.

PATTERN SENTENCES

1. Как бы́стро **идёт** вре́мя!
2. Мне́ бы́ло ску́чно, и вре́мя **шло́** ме́дленно.
3. Вчера́ **шёл** до́ждь и сего́дня опя́ть **идёт** до́ждь! За́втра вероя́тно опя́ть бу́дет **идти́** до́ждь! Что́ за кли́мат!
4. Зима́ была́ о́чень холо́дная, и ка́ждый де́нь **шёл** сне́г.
5. Э́ти часы́ не **иду́т**.
6. Мои́ часы́ **иду́т** пра́вильно, а ва́ши часы́ спеша́т.
7. Ка́к **иду́т** дела́?
8. Пи́сьма иногда́ **иду́т** ме́дленно.
9. Э́то письмо́, наприме́р, **шло́** пя́ть дне́й из Филаде́льфии.
11. Э́тот по́езд **идёт** бы́стро.
10. Отсю́да в Пари́ж телегра́мма **идёт** три́ часа́.
12. Фи́льм «До́н Жуа́н» **шёл** в це́нтре го́рода го́д тому́ наза́д. Тепе́рь о́н **бу́дет идти́** в э́том кино́.
13. Не́бо бы́ло си́нее, со́лнце свети́ло, и вдру́г **пошёл** до́ждь!
14. По́езд до́лго стоя́л на ста́нции, и наконе́ц **пошёл**.

1. How rapidly time goes by!
2. I was bored and time passed slowly.
3. Yesterday it was raining, and today it's raining again! Tomorrow it will probably rain again! What a climate!
4. Winter was very cold, and it snowed every day.
5. This watch is not running.
6. My watch is correct, and yours is fast.
7. How are things going?
8. Letters sometimes travel slowly.
9. This letter, for example, took five days coming from Philadelphia.
10. This train is going fast.
11. From here to Paris a telegram takes three hours.
12. The film *Don Juan* was playing downtown a year ago. Now it will be running in this theater.
13. The sky was blue, the sun was shining, and all of a sudden it started to rain!
14. The train stood in the station for a long time, and finally started to go.

DRILL

Translate into Russian.

1. Last year it rained almost every day.
2. My watch isn't running.
3. It snowed early in the morning.
4. Without you time will go slowly.
5. The trains are not running today.
6. It took the telegram five hours to get here.
7. This play was running two years ago.
8. I don't know what is playing in this theater.
9. In summer time goes fast.
10. Where does this train go?

9. The adverb пешко́м

Note. The verbs ходи́ть/идти́ are used to denote going when the means of going is uncertain or irrelevant:

> Мы́ ча́сто хо́дим в теа́тр.
> We often go to the theater (this does not necessarily exclude going in a vehicle).

> Мне́ ну́жно пойти́ к до́ктору.
> I must go to see the doctor (I may conceivably go in a vehicle).

> Я́ люблю́ ходи́ть в го́сти.
> I like to go visiting (how is unimportant).

This usage is impossible, however, if distance precludes:

> Мы́ лю́бим е́здить в Евро́пу.
> We love to go to Europe.

Where there is contrast or emphasis, the adverb пешко́м, meaning *on foot*, is used with ходи́ть/идти́:

> Они́ пое́хали на маши́не, а мы́ пошли́ пешко́м.
> They went by car and we went on foot (= we walked).

> Мо́й сы́н хо́дит в шко́лу.
> My son goes to (attends) school (he may go by bus).

But: Мо́й сы́н хо́дит в шко́лу пешко́м.
> My son *walks* to school (goes to school on foot).

Reading

Пикни́к.

Сего́дня пра́здник, и все́ Кали́нины, то́ есть ма́ть, оте́ц, и сы́н до́ма. Сего́дня отцу́ не ну́жно идти́ на слу́жбу, Ю́рику не ну́жно идти́ в шко́лу, а ма́тери—в магази́н.

Пого́да замеча́тельная: со́лнце све́тит (shines), не́бо си́нее. Но́ в го́роде шу́мно и ду́шно. Что́ Кали́нины бу́дут де́лать ве́сь де́нь?

Анто́н Никола́евич пойдёт у́тром за газе́той и прочита́ет её с нача́ла до конца́. Пото́м о́н бу́дет смотре́ть телеви́зор, пото́м о́н возьмёт журна́л «Огонёк»[1] и пойдёт в сво́й кабине́т, где́ о́н, вероя́тно, бу́дет спа́ть до обе́да на своём зелёном дива́не. Ску́чно!

Ири́на Петро́вна бу́дет до́лго говори́ть по телефо́ну, снача́ла со свое́й ма́терью, пото́м с подру́гой, пото́м она́ пойдёт в ку́хню и начнёт гото́вить обе́д. По́сле обе́да она́ пойдёт к сосе́дке и бу́дет говори́ть с не́й о друго́й сосе́дке. Ску́чно!

Ю́рику, и́х сы́ну, то́же бу́дет о́чень ску́чно: оди́н его́ това́рищ пое́хал в дере́вню

---

[1] A popular Soviet illustrated magazine.

к свое́й ба́бушке; у друго́го това́рища грипп. Ю́рик бу́дет ходи́ть из ко́мнаты в ко́мнату и бу́дет с утра́ до ве́чера задава́ть отцу́ и ма́тери ма́ссу вопро́сов.

Кали́нины мо́гут пойти́ в кино́, кото́рое о́коло и́х до́ма. Но́ та́м идёт ста́рая карти́на, кото́рую они́ уже́ ви́дели, а други́е кино́ сли́шком далеко́ от ни́х. Они́, коне́чно, мо́гут пойти́ в го́сти, но́ и э́то ску́чно.

И во́т что они́ реши́ли сде́лать: они́ пое́дут за́ город! Они́ все́ лю́бят приро́ду, а недалеко́ от Москвы́ е́сть замеча́тельные места́. Они́ пое́дут в Переде́лкино (как мы́ зна́ем, э́то краси́вое ме́сто среди́ поле́й и лесо́в).

До́м, где живу́т Кали́нины, не о́чень далеко́ от вокза́ла, и они́ пошли́ на вокза́л пешко́м. По доро́ге на вокза́л они́ встре́тили Ива́нова, кото́рый шёл со свои́м сы́ном Воло́дей за газе́той. Когда́ Кали́нины рассказа́ли Ива́нову о своём пла́не, Ива́нов вдру́г реши́л, что о́н с Воло́дей то́же пое́дет с ни́ми за́ город. Все́, а осо́бенно ма́льчики, бы́ли о́чень дово́льны.

Тепе́рь и́м ну́жно было спеши́ть, та́к как бы́ло уже́ дово́льно по́здно, и они́ могли́ опозда́ть на по́езд. Они́ пое́хали на вокза́л на авто́бусе.

На вокза́ле они́ купи́ли биле́ты. Кали́нин хоте́л заплати́ть за все́ биле́ты. Но́, по́сле до́лгих спо́ров, Ива́нов заплати́л за сво́й биле́т и за биле́т своего́ сы́на. Пото́м они́ спроси́ли, где́ по́езд, кото́рый идёт в Переде́лкино. И́м сказа́ли но́мер платфо́рмы, и через три́ мину́ты они́ уже́ сиде́ли в удо́бном ваго́не, а через де́сять мину́т уже́ е́хали в Переде́лкино.

Электри́ческий по́езд, на кото́ром они́ е́хали, шёл о́чень бы́стро. Роди́тели сиде́ли и разгова́ривали, а ма́льчики стоя́ли все́ вре́мя у окна́ и смотре́ли на заво́ды, колхо́зы,[2] поля́ и леса́. Они́ с интере́сом смотре́ли на доро́гу, кото́рая шла́ паралле́льно с по́ездом. По э́той доро́ге е́хало мно́го автомоби́лей. Ма́льчики бы́ли о́чень дово́льны, что и́х по́езд идёт так бы́стро, а автомоби́ли е́дут ме́дленно.

Ро́вно через ча́с они́ уже́ бы́ли в Переде́лкине. На вокза́ле они́ купи́ли хле́б, соси́ски, не́сколько бутербро́дов с ма́слом, с ветчино́й и с колбасо́й. Они́ купи́ли та́кже пи́во, вино́, минера́льную во́ду, и фру́кты.

С вокза́ла вся́ компа́ния пошла́ пря́мо в ле́с.

Как чу́дно в дере́вне! Во́здух чи́стый и све́жий. В лесу́ прохла́дно и ти́хо, то́лько пти́цы пою́т. Во́т моното́нный и гру́стный го́лос куку́шки (cuckoo): ку-ку́, ку-ку́. Е́сли вы́ хоти́те зна́ть, ско́лько ле́т вы́ ещё бу́дете жи́ть, вы́ должны́ сосчита́ть ско́лько ра́з куку́шка ска́жет ку-ку́. Но́ заче́м счита́ть?

Они́ до́лго гуля́ли по лесу́, пото́м по по́лю. Бы́ло уже́ два́ часа́, когда́ они́ на́чали е́сть. Бутербро́ды и фру́кты бы́ли о́чень вку́сные, и все́ е́ли с больши́м аппети́том, осо́бенно ма́льчики. Пото́м они́ лежа́ли и отдыха́ли в высо́кой траве́. По́сле о́тдыха они́ пошли́ гуля́ть по бе́регу реки́.

Но́ как бы́стро идёт вре́мя! Уже́ почти́ ве́чер! Пора́ е́хать обра́тно в го́род. Как гру́стно! На́ши друзья́ пошли́ на вокза́л. Они́ бы́ли о́чень дово́льны свои́м днём.

Чита́йте э́ти вопро́сы и отвеча́йте на ни́х по-ру́сски.

1. Кака́я была́ пого́да? 2. Почему́ в го́роде бы́ло не осо́бенно прия́тно? 3. Что́ Кали́нин бу́дет де́лать, е́сли о́н бу́дет весь де́нь до́ма? 4. Что́ бу́дет де́лать его́ жена́? 5. Что́ бу́дет де́лать Ю́рик? 6. Почему́ Кали́нины не пошли́

---

[2] **Колхо́з** *collective farm* (abbreviation from коллекти́вное хозя́йство).

в кино́, а реши́ли пое́хать за́ город?   7. Когда́ они́ встре́тили Ива́нова и Воло́дю?
8. Куда́ шёл Ива́нов?   9. Почему́ внача́ле Кали́нины шли, а не е́хали?   10. По-
чему́ они́ пото́м реши́ли пое́хать на по́езде?   11. Что́ они́ сде́лали на вокза́ле?
12. Что́ де́лали ма́льчики в по́езде? На что́ они́ смотре́ли из окна́?   13. Что́
Кали́нины купи́ли в Переде́лкине?   14. Опиши́те (describe), ка́к бы́ло в дере́вне,
и что́ они́ та́м де́лали?   15. Како́й го́лос у куку́шки?   16. Что́ ну́жно де́лать,
когда́ слы́шишь, как куку́шка куку́ет?   17. Ка́к шло вре́мя в дере́вне?   18. По-
чему́ и́м бы́ло гру́стно, и че́м они́ бы́ли дово́льны?

DRILL

Review Translation.

1. Every spring they go to Odessa.   2. Every day I go to school.   3. He likes to
ride fast.   4. President Truman always walked fast.   5. When I saw her she was
walking with Vadim.   6. I saw him when he was going to the drugstore.   7. We shall
have dinner, and then shall go to the movie, which is nearby.   8. From the movie we
shall go to a restaurant.   9. Are you going home? I shall come with you.   10. —Where
are you going? —I am going to Odessa. —I shall go with you.   11. From Italy we'll
go to the Soviet Union.   12. —Where are you going? —We're going to the store.
13. We go to the store several times a day.   14. —Where is Anna going? —She's
going to the post office.   15. She works at the post office.   16. She is coming from the
post office.   17. —Where are those young men going so fast? —They are going to the
factory.   18. They go there every day.   19. They work at this factory.   20. Now
they are coming from the factory.   21. Day after tomorrow we are going to see
Professor Pavlov and his wife. They live nearby.   22. We shall have dinner at Professor
Pavlov's.   23. We are coming from Professor Pavlov's.   24. Ivan is coming here from
Leningrad.   25. Here is a letter from him.   26. —And where is Olga coming from?
—She's coming from Odessa.   27. Here is a letter from her.   28. She often goes to
Odessa. She goes there several times a year.   29. She was walking along the street
with her husband.   30. They like to drive about town.   31. How late it is! It's time
to go to sleep.

Vocabulary

ба́бушка (*gen. pl.* -ек) grandmother
биле́т ticket
бутербро́д sandwich
ветчина́ [γiččiná] ham
вокза́л [vagzál] terminal, station
гру́стный [grúsnəj] sad, mournful
де́ло matter, business, affair
дела́ (*pl.*) business, affairs
дождь (*masc.*) rain
доро́га road, way, route
ду́шно stuffy

колбаса́ sausage
колхо́з collective farm
куда́? to where?
ма́р.ка (*gen. pl.* -ок) stamp
ма́сло butter, oil
ма́сса mass, great quantity of (*colloq.*)
обра́тно back, in return
опа́сный dangerous
отку́да? from where?
отсю́да from here
отту́да from there

пешко́м on foot
пи́во beer
пора́ (+ *dat.* + *inf.*) it's time to
послеза́втра day after tomorrow
прохла́дно cool
пря́мо straight, directly
соси́с.ка (*gen. pl.* -ок) frankfurter
сторона́ side, direction
сюда́ (to) here

та́кже [tágžə] in addition, as well, likewise
трава́ grass
туда́ (to) there
фрукт fruit
фру́кты fruits, fruit (*coll.*)
час.ы́ [čisí] (*masc. pl.*) (*gen.* -о́в) watch, clock[3]
через (+ *acc.*) from now, after, at the end of, in a (period of time); across
чу́дно marvelous, wonderful

VERBS

опа́здывать (imperf., I), опозда́ть (perf., I) to be late; **опозда́ть на уро́к** to be late for class; **опозда́ть на по́езд** to be late for a train

поза́втракать (perf. of **за́втракать**, I) to have breakfast, lunch

пообе́дать (perf. of **обе́дать**, I) to have dinner

реша́ть (imperf., I), **реши́ть** (perf., II: **реш.у́, -и́шь**) to decide

смотре́ть (imperf., II: **смотрю́, смо́тришь**), посмотре́ть (perf., II) to watch, look; **смотре́ть на** (+ *acc.*) to look at

спеши́ть (imperf., II: **спеш.у́, -и́шь**), поспеши́ть (perf., II) to hurry

счита́ть [ščitáṭ] (imperf., I), **сосчита́ть** [səščitáṭ] (perf., I) to count; consider[4]

EXPRESSIONS

и́з дому from home
за́ город (to go) out of town, to the country
по доро́ге on the way
всё вре́мя all the time
то́ есть that is
с нача́ла до конца́ from beginning to end
с утра́ до ве́чера from morning to evening
идти́/ходи́ть/пойти́ в го́сти to go visiting, visit
Часы́ спеша́т. The watch (clock) is fast.

VOCABULARY NOTE

The English preposition *for* corresponds in Russian to several prepositions governing different cases. Observe the following usage:

(1) For = for the sake of, purpose, goal, beneficiary—**для** + *gen.*

—Для кого́ вы́ э́то купи́ли? —Я́ э́то купи́л для ва́с.
Э́то ко́мната для госте́й.
Э́то но́ж для хле́ба.
О́н э́то сде́лал для своего́ бра́та.

(2) For = in exchange for—**за** + *acc.*

Спаси́бо за ва́шу по́мощь.
Я́ заплати́ла до́ллар за э́ту кни́гу.

---

[3] The plural is used to denote a timepiece.
[4] Imperfective only in the sense of *consider*, when it takes a predicate instrumental, e.g., Я́ счита́ю Бори́са хоро́шим студе́нтом.

(3) For = go for, after, to get—**за** + *instr*.

     Ива́н пошёл **за** газе́той.
     Я́ иду́ в апте́ку **за** аспири́ном.
     Мы́ идём **за** Ива́ном.

VOCABULARY REVIEW

Еда́—Food

заку́ска	карто́фель (*masc.*, *sing. only*)
суп	сала́т
борщ	компо́т
хлеб	фру́кты
ма́сло	моро́женое
мя́со	са́хар
ветчина́	варе́нье
колбаса́	сыр
соси́ски	бутербро́д
ры́ба	сла́дкое

Напи́тки—Drinks

вода́
минера́льная вода́
молоко́
ко́фе (*masc.*, *indecl.*)
чай
ви́ски (*neut.*, *indecl.*)
пи́во
вино́
во́дка

Imperative mood • Ordinal numerals 1 to 20 • Days of the week •
Conversation: «Повторе́ние—ма́ть уче́ния» • Accusative of time with
на and через • *Going* verbs with the prefixes при- and у- • Reading:
Во́т моя́ семья́!

Unit **18**

Grammar

1. The imperative mood

The imperative is the form of the verb used to express commands or requests:
Go! Write! Help me!

The words emphasized in the examples below are imperatives:

Да́й мне́ каранда́ш.	*Give* me a pencil.
Закро́й две́рь.	*Close* the door.
Откро́й окно́.	*Open* the window.
Возьми́ тетра́дь.	*Take* your notebook.
Купи́ хле́ба.	*Buy* (some) bread.
Не забу́дь купи́ть хле́б.	*Don't forget* to buy bread.

The imperatives in the above examples are in the *singular:* they are used when speaking to one person addressed as **ты**.

Plural forms, corresponding to **вы**, both as the polite form and as the actual plural, are obtained by adding **-те** to the singular forms:

Singular, corresponding to **ты**	*Plural,* corresponding to **вы**
дай	да́йте
закро́й	закро́йте
откро́й	откро́йте
возьми́	возьми́те
купи́	купи́те
забу́дь	забу́дьте

A. Formation of the imperative. The imperative of very many verbs is, *in terms of phonetics*, the bare stem of the present (or perfective future) conjugation; other verbs add **-и** [i] to form their imperative. *In terms of spelling*, three types of ending must be distinguished: (1) **-й**, (2) **-ь**, (3) **-и**.

(1) *Imperatives ending in* **й**[j].[1] Verbs with conjugation stems ending in a *vowel* form their imperative by adding the letter -**й** to the stem:

Pres.	чита́.ю	откро́.ю	уме́.ю
	чита́.ешь	откро́.ешь	уме́.ешь
	чита́.ет	откро́.ет	уме́.ет
Imp. sing.	чита́.й!	откро́.й!	уме́.й!

(2) *Imperatives ending in a soft consonant* (*cons.* + **ь**). The imperative of verbs with present conjugation stems ending in a single consonant and with the stress falling on that *stem* is the bare stem with the final consonant softened; the softening is shown in writing by adding a -**ь**:

Pres.	вста́н.у	бу́д.у
	вста́н.ешь	бу́д.ешь
	вста́н.ет	бу́д.ет
Imp. sing.	встань!	будь!

(3) *Imperatives ending in* -**и**[i]. (a) Verbs whose stems end in a consonantal *cluster* and whose stress falls on the stem form their imperative by adding an -**и**[i] to the stem:

Pres.	по́мн.ю
	по́мн.ишь
	по́мнит
Imp. sing.	по́мн.и!

(b) Verbs whose present stem ends in a consonant take a stressed -**и**[í] *if the stress falls on the ending in all personal forms or in the first person singular only:*

	Stress on ending		*Shifting stress*	
Pres.	говор.ю́	возьм.у́	пиш.у́	смотр.ю́
	говор.и́шь	возьм.ёшь	пи́ш.ешь	смо́тр.ишь
	говор.и́т	возьм.ёт	пи́ш.ет	смо́тр.ит
Imp. sing.	говор.и́!	возьм.и́!	пиш.и́!	смотр.и́!

Note: Changes in the final consonant of the stem or a consonant addition in the first person singular, frequent in the second conjugation, do not affect the imperative:

Pres.	куп.лю́	сиж.у́
	ку́п.ишь	сид.и́шь
	ку́п.ит	сид.и́т
Imp. sing.	куп.и́!	сид.и́!

---

[1] The [j] *sound*, represented by the letter **й** in the imperative, really belongs *phonetically* to the stem of the verb. This becomes obvious if we consider the examples given above in phonetic transcription:

	čitáj.u	atkrój.u	uṃéj.u
	čitáj.iš	atkrój.iš	uṃéj.iš
	čitaj.it	atkrój.it	uṃéj.it
Imper.	čitáj.	atkrój.	uṃéj.

The imperative is, consequently, the bare stem considered phonetically, with the final [j] of the stem rendered in spelling by the letter **й**.

With second conjugation verbs the plural imperative is often the same as the second person plural present (or perfective future), e.g.: **вы́ говори́те** *you say*, **говори́те!** *speak!* or *say!* With such verbs the use or omission of the pronoun **вы** and the intonation will indicate which form is being used. With other second conjugation verbs the place of stress distinguishes the imperative: **ку́пите** *you will buy*, but **купи́те!** *buy!*

(4) The following imperative forms require special attention:

Infinitive		*1st Person Sing.*	*Imperative*	
дава́ть	(imperf.)	даю́	дава́й, -те	give!
встава́ть	(imperf.)	встаю́	встава́й, -те	get up!
дать	(perf.)	дам	дай, -те	give!
пить	(imperf.)	пью	пей, -те	drink!
помо́чь	(perf.)	помогу́	помоги́, -те	help!

The verbs **е́хать** and **пое́хать** lack imperatives. The substitute forms **поезжа́й, -те** are used.

To summarize the rules governing the formation of the imperative:

I. If the conjugation stem *ends in a vowel, the letter* **-й** *is added.*

    чита́.ю, чита́.ешь . . . чита́.й (чита́.йте)

(The **й** stands for the sound [j] which is present in the conjugation: [čitáj.u, čitáj.iš . . . čitáj.])

II. If the conjugation stem *ends in a single consonant,* and
(a) *the stress falls on the stem, a soft sign,* **-ь**, *is added.*

    вста́н.у, вста́н.ешь . . . встан.ь (встан.ьте)

Exception: conjugation stems ending in a consonantal cluster add **-и**:

    по́мн.ю, по́мн.ишь . . . по́мн.и (по́мн.ите)

(b) *the stress falls on the ending* throughout the conjugation, or in the first person singular only (shifting stress), a *stressed* **-й** *is added.*

    говор.ю́, говор.и́шь . . . говор.и́ (говор.и́те)
    пиш.у́, пи́ш.ешь . . .   пиш.и́ (пиш.и́те)

The rules for spelling of imperative forms may be presented in tabular form, as follows:

I. *Vowel stem-ending*   add **-й**

(The letter **й** represents the [j] sound present in the stem.)

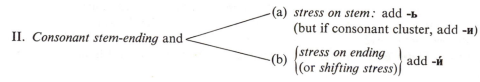

II. *Consonant stem-ending* and
    (a) *stress on stem:* add **-ь**
        (but if consonant cluster, add **-и**)
    (b) { *stress on ending* (or *shifting stress*) } add **-й**

B. Aspect with imperatives. Verbs of both aspects form imperatives. The perfective aspect is generally used for single, definite actions:

Напиши́те свою́ фами́лию!
Write your name!

Скажи́те мне́, куда́ вы́ идёте?
Tell me, where are you going?

Закро́й все́ о́кна!
Close all the windows!

The imperfective imperative is used for *general* rules, commands, or requests:

Пиши́ мне́ ча́сто.
Write me often.

Говори́те всегда́ пра́вду.
Always tell the truth.

Закрыва́йте о́кна, когда́ хо́лодно.
Close the windows when it's cold.

The imperfective imperative is regularly used for *negative* commands:

Не говори́те мне́, что́ я́ до́лжен де́лать!
Don't tell me what I have to do!

Не ду́майте, что о́н ва́м помо́жет.
Don't expect him to help you.

Note: The perfective imperative is used negatively in warnings, in the sense of "be careful not to":

Не потеря́й де́ньги, кото́рые я́ тебе́ да́л.
Don't lose the money I gave you.

Не забу́дь купи́ть ма́сла.
Don't forget to buy butter.

The imperfective imperative is sometimes used to soften commands. This use is particularly common with a few verbs employed in polite suggestions and invitations:

Приходи́те к на́м.   Come to see us.
Сади́тесь.   Sit down.

PATTERN SENTENCES

1. **Пойди́** сюда́.
2. **Повтори́те** э́то сло́во ещё ра́з.
3. **Повторя́йте** за мно́й всё, что я́ говорю́.
4. **Спроси́те** его́, когда́ о́н бу́дет до́ма.
5. **Не спра́шивайте** её о её здоро́вье.
6. —**Сде́лай** сейча́с же всё, что тебе́ ну́жно сде́лать, и **пойди́** спа́ть. —**Помоги́** мне́, тогда́ я́ всё сде́лаю бы́стро.

1. Come here.
2. Repeat this word once more.
3. Repeat after me everything that I say.
4. Ask him when he will be at home.
5. Don't ask her about her health.
6. —Do at once all that you have to do, and go to bed. —Help me, then I'll do everything quickly.

7. **Не де́лай** так мно́го оши́бок!

8. Вади́м, **закро́й** пожа́луйста окно́; на у́лице о́чень шу́мно.

9. Всегда́ **открыва́й** окно́ но́чью, и **спи** с откры́тым окно́м.

10. **Не дава́йте** мне́ сове́тов. Я́ э́того не люблю́.

11. —**Да́й** мне́ сове́т: что́ купи́ть Зи́не? —**Купи́** ей пласти́нку, но́ **не покупа́й** класси́ческой му́зыки.

12. **Не забу́дьте** спроси́ть Зи́ну, ка́к а́дрес Ве́ры.

13. **Не забыва́йте** на́с, и **пиши́те** ча́сто.

14. **Отвеча́й** на вопро́сы ко́ротко и я́сно.

15. **Отве́ть** неме́дленно на э́то письмо́. **Начни́** писа́ть сейча́с же.

16. —**Объясни́те**, пожа́луйста, что́ зна́чит э́то сло́во. —**Посмотри́те** в словаре́.

17. **Не объясня́йте** ребёнку тру́дных веще́й.

18. **Скажи́те** А́нне, что я́ не могу́ бы́ть у неё в четы́ре часа́, но́ **не говори́те** ей почему́.

19. **Бу́дьте** добры́, **переда́йте** мне́ со́ль и пе́рец.

20. —**Расскажи́те** на́м, что́ вы́ ви́дели вчера́ в теа́тре. —Никому́ **не расска́зывайте**, но́ я та́м спа́л!

21. Где́ де́ти? **Посмотри́те**, что́ они́ де́лают.

22. **Не смотри́те** на потоло́к, а **смотри́те** в кни́гу!

23. **Попроси́**[2] Бори́са пойти́ за газе́той.

24. **Спроси́**[3] его́, когда́ о́н пойдёт за газе́той, и **попроси́** его́ купи́ть и хле́ба.

25. Е́сли тебе́ нужны́ де́ньги, **попроси́** у отца́.

26. —**Извини́те**, что я́ не позвони́л ва́м, как обеща́л. —А в чём де́ло? —**Не спра́шивайте!**

27. **Дово́льно игра́ть! Пойди́** рабо́тать!

7. Don't make so many mistakes!

8. Vadim, close the window, please; it's very noisy outdoors (on the street).

9. Always open the window at night, and sleep with an open window.

10. Don't give me advice. I don't like it.

11. —Give me advice: what should (am) I (to) buy Zina? —Buy her a record, but don't buy any classical music.

12. Don't forget to ask Zina what Vera's address is.

13. Don't forget us and write often.

14. Answer the questions briefly and clearly.

15. Answer this letter immediately. Begin to write at once.

16. —Please explain what that word means. —Look in the dictionary.

17. Don't try to explain hard things to a child.

18. Tell Anna that I can't come to see her at four o'clock, but don't tell her why.

19. Be so kind (as to) pass me the salt and pepper.

20. —Tell us what you saw yesterday in the theater. —Don't tell anyone, but I was asleep there!

21. Where are the children? Look (and see) what they're doing.

22. Don't look at the ceiling, but look at your book!

23. Ask Boris to go for the paper.

24. Ask him when he's going for the paper, and ask him to buy bread as well.

25. If you need money, ask Father.

26. —Excuse me for not phoning (that I didn't phone) you as I promised. —What was the matter? —Don't ask!

27. Stop playing! (Enough playing!) Go and work!

DRILLS

A. *Form imperatives, imperfective and perfective, of the following verbs.*

do, read, write, explain, begin, repeat, look, buy, open, shut, say, tell (narrate), show, take, give, be (imperfective only), forget, answer, drink (imperfective only), help.

---

[2] **Проси́ть/попроси́ть** means *to ask* someone (in *accusative*) to do something (*infinitive*) and *to ask for* something (in *accusative*) *from* someone (in **у** + *genitive* form). In other words, it takes the *accusative* of the person asked + the *infinitive* of the favor asked, e.g., Я́ попроси́л А́нну мне́ **помо́чь.** But when an object is requested, it is put in the *accusative* case, while the person from whom it is requested is then expressed by **у** + *genitive*, e.g., Я́ попроси́л у А́нны кни́гу.

[3] Note that **спра́шивать/спроси́ть** means *to ask a question.* It governs the *accusative* of the person asked, or **у** + *genitive*, e.g., Я́ спрошу́ у сы́на, где́ его́ прия́тель живёт.

B. *Say the following sentences aloud, supplying the proper imperatives.*

Model: Попроси́ Бори́са закры́ть окно́.
      —Бори́с, пожа́луйста, **закро́й** окно́.

1. Граждани́н, бу́дьте любе́зны, попроси́те ва́шего сосе́да закры́ть окно́.
   —Пожа́луйста, ... окно́.
2. Зи́на, скажи́ Вади́му, что́ о́н до́лжен прочита́ть.
   —Вади́м, ... после́днюю фра́зу.
3. А́нна, попроси́ Вади́ма объясни́ть тебе́ э́то пра́вило.
   —Вади́м, пожа́луйста, ...
4. Ива́н Ива́нович, попроси́те Алёшу откры́ть кни́гу и нача́ть чита́ть.
   —Алёша, ...
5. Попроси́ твои́х роди́телей писа́ть на́м ча́сто.
   —Пожа́луйста, ...
6. Попроси́те Ро́бертса рассказа́ть ва́м э́ту исто́рию.
   —Господи́н Ро́бертс, пожа́луйста, ...
7. —Я́ хочу́ показа́ть ва́м на́ш но́вый до́м.
   —Да́, пожа́луйста, ...
8. Попроси́ А́нну да́ть тебе́ де́ньги.
   —А́нна, пожа́луйста . . . . .
9. О́ля, е́сли ты́ хо́чешь взя́ть мою́ кни́гу, ... её.
10. Е́сли вы́ хоти́те повтори́ть уро́к, ... его́.
11. Е́сли вы́ хоти́те купи́ть э́то пла́тье, ... его́.
12. Е́сли вы́ хоти́те покупа́ть пла́тья в Пари́же, ... и́х та́м.
13. Е́сли ты́ до́лжен написа́ть реда́ктору, ... ему́.
14. Е́сли ты́ хо́чешь писа́ть расска́зы, ... расска́зы.
15. Е́сли ты́ хо́чешь говори́ть, ... !
16. Е́сли ты́ хо́чешь сказа́ть е́й, что ты́ её лю́бишь, ... е́й!

2. Ordinal numerals 1 to 20

Cardinals	Ordinals	
оди́н	пе́рвый	first
два	второ́й	second
три	тре́тий	third
четы́ре	четвёртый	fourth
пять	пя́тый	fifth
шесть	шесто́й	sixth
семь	седьмо́й	seventh
во́семь	восьмо́й	eighth
де́вять	девя́тый	ninth
де́сять	деся́тый	tenth
оди́ннадцать	оди́ннадцатый	eleventh
двена́дцать	двена́дцатый	twelfth
трина́дцать	трина́дцатый	thirteenth
четы́рнадцать	четы́рнадцатый	fourteenth
пятна́дцать	пятна́дцатый	fifteenth

шестна́дцать	шестна́дцатый	sixteenth
семна́дцать	семна́дцатый	seventeenth
восемна́дцать	восемна́дцатый	eighteenth
девятна́дцать	девятна́дцатый	nineteenth
два́дцать	двадца́тый	twentieth

Ordinals are *adjectives*, and agree in gender, number, and case with the noun to which they refer:

Э́то **деся́тая** глава́.
This is the tenth chapter.

Я́ то́лько что начала́ **деся́тую** главу́.
I have just begun the tenth chapter.

Во́т **седьмо́й** эта́ж.
Here is the seventh floor.

Мы́ живём на **седьмо́м** этаже́.
We live on the seventh floor.

Достое́вский жи́л в **девятна́дцатом** ве́ке.
Dostoevsky lived in the nineteenth century.

The ordinal **тре́тий** (*third*) has a special type of soft declension with stem [tr̯ét̯j-] in all forms except the nominative singular masculine. This declension is the same as that of the pronoun-adjective **чей, чьё, чья** (stem [čj-]):

	SINGULAR			PLURAL
	Masculine	*Neuter*	*Feminine*	*All Genders*
Nom.	тре́тий	тре́тье	тре́тья	тре́тьи
Gen.	тре́тьего	like masc.	тре́тьей	тре́тьих
Dat.	тре́тьему	like masc.	тре́тьей	(тре́тьим)
Acc.	like Nom. or Gen.	тре́тье	тре́тью	like Nom. or Gen.
Instr.	тре́тьим	like masc.	тре́тьей	(тре́тьими)
Loc.	тре́тьем	like masc.	тре́тьей	(тре́тьих)

PATTERN SENTENCES

1. Пётр **Пе́рвый**, и́ли, ка́к его́ называ́ют, Пётр Вели́кий, основа́л го́род Петербу́рг.
2. Ца́рь Никола́й **Второ́й** бы́л после́дним ру́сским царём.
3. Ца́рь Алекса́ндр **Тре́тий** бы́л отцо́м царя́ Никола́я **Второ́го**.
4. Англи́йский коро́ль Гео́рг **Шесто́й** бы́л отцо́м англи́йской короле́вы Елизаве́ты **Второ́й**.

1. Peter I, or, as he is called, Peter the Great, founded the city of St. Petersburg.
2. Tsar Nicholas II was the last Russian tsar.
3. Tsar Alexander III was the father of Tsar Nicholas II.
4. The English king George VI was the father of the English queen Elizabeth II.

5. У Ива́на **Четвёртого**, или Ива́на Гро́зного, как его́ называ́ют, бы́ло семь жён.

6. А у англи́йского короля́ Ге́нриха **Восьмо́го** бы́ло шесть жён.

7. На пра́вой стороне́ у́лицы четы́ре до́ма. Мы́ живём в **четвёртом** до́ме от угла́.

8. Мы́ живём на **седьмо́м** этаже́, а мои́ роди́тели живу́т на **девя́том**.

9. Я́ э́то слы́шу в **пе́рвый** ра́з.

10. Я́ э́то повторя́ю во **второ́й** и в после́дний ра́з!

5. Ivan IV, or Ivan the Terrible (Dread), as he is called, had seven wives.

6. And the English king Henry the Eighth had six wives.

7. On the right side of the street there are four houses. We live in the fourth house from the corner.

8. We live on the seventh floor, and my parents live on the ninth.

9. I am hearing that for the first time.

10. I repeat that for the second and last time!

DRILLS

A. *Answer the following questions in Russian.*

1. Кто́ основа́л Петербу́рг?
2. Что́ вы́ зна́ете о царе́ Никола́е Второ́м?
3. У како́го ру́сского царя́ бы́ло семь жён?
4. На како́м этаже́ вы́ живёте?
5. На како́м этаже́ у на́с тепе́рь уро́к?

B. *Translate the words in parentheses.*

1. Я́ говорю́ о моём (second) сы́не.
2. Я́ пишу́ моему́ (second) сы́ну.
3. Мы́ чита́ем (the second) главу́.
4. О́н бы́л в Я́лте со свое́й (second) жено́й.
5. Я́ повторя́ю э́то в (third) ра́з.
6. Я́ уже́ чита́ю (the third) ру́сскую кни́гу.
7. Мы́ купи́ли маши́ну на́шему (fourth) сы́ну.
8. Я́ ви́дел э́то сло́во на (the fifth) страни́це.
9. Мы́ живём на (the fourteenth) этаже́, а А́нна живёт на (the fifteenth).
10. Мы́ то́лько что ко́нчили (the seventeenth) уро́к в на́шем уче́бнике и начина́ем (the eighteenth).
11. Мы́ живём в (the twentieth) ве́ке.

3. Days of the week

These are nouns, and follow the rules for genders and declension which apply to other nouns. They are not capitalized in Russian:

понеде́льник	Monday	пя́тница	Friday
вто́рник	Tuesday	суббо́та	Saturday
среда́	Wednesday	воскресе́нье	Sunday
четве́рг	Thursday		

Time when with days of the week is expressed by the preposition **в** + *accusative* (**во** with вто́рник):[4]

В пя́тницу я́ бы́л в теа́тре.
Во вто́рник я́ пое́ду в Ленингра́д.

В про́шл**ую** суббо́т**у** его́ не́ было до́ма.
Last Saturday he wasn't at home.

---

[4] Remember, however, that with the preposition **в** the names of months and years are in the *locative* case, e.g., в про́шлом ме́сяце, в бу́дущем году́, в двадца́том ве́ке.

В э́тот понеде́льник я́ бу́ду в Босто́не.
This Monday I will be in Boston.

В бу́дущую сре́ду (note stress) я́ иду́ в теа́тр.
Next Wednesday I am going to the theater.

в э́тот де́нь   on this (that) day
в то́т де́нь   on that day
                        etc.

Conversation

«Повторе́ние—ма́ть уче́ния» (*"Repetition is the mother of learning"*)

А́лан. —У меня́ плоха́я па́мять и мне́ тру́дно запо́мнить назва́ния дней неде́ли. Бу́дьте добры́, помоги́те мне́.

Бори́с. —Э́то о́чень легко́ и про́сто. Е́сли хоти́те, я́ ва́м помогу́.

А. —Э́то бу́дет о́чень любе́зно с ва́шей стороны́. Но́ для э́того ну́жно мно́го вре́мени и терпе́ния.

Б. —Я́ э́то сде́лаю с больши́м удово́льствием. У меня́ е́сть своя́ систе́ма. Слу́шайте и повторя́йте. **Пе́рвый** де́нь неде́ли—э́то **понеде́льник**. **Понеде́льник**—э́то «Monday». «On Monday»—**в понеде́льник**. Повтори́те два́ ра́за:
>   То́м **в понеде́льник** по́здно вста́л,
>   И в шко́лу о́чень опозда́л.

А. (Повторя́ет).

Б. —О́чень хорошо́. Тепе́рь запо́мните, что второ́й де́нь неде́ли—**вто́рник**. Э́то про́сто и логи́чно, пра́вда?

А. —Да́, э́то легко́ запо́мнить: **второ́й** де́нь неде́ли—э́то **вто́рник**.

Б. —«On Tuesday»—**во вто́рник**. Скажи́те два́ ра́за:
>   Мы́ **в понеде́льник** мно́го е́ли,
>   **Во вто́рник** я́ лежа́л в посте́ли.

А. (Повторя́ет).

Б. —По́сле **вто́рника** идёт тре́тий де́нь, **среда́**. Среда́—э́то середи́на (middle) неде́ли. «On Wednesday»—**в сре́ду**. Повтори́те два́ ра́за:
>   Мы́ идём к Бори́су **в сре́ду**,
>   Бу́дем е́сть бифште́кс к обе́ду.

А. (Повторя́ет).

Б. —Отли́чно. Тепе́рь **четвёртый** де́нь—**четве́рг**. Повтори́те три́ ра́за:
>   Мы́ **в четве́рг** в теа́тре бы́ли,
>   А что́ ви́дели—забы́ли.

А. (Повторя́ет).

Б. —Хорошо́. Како́й де́нь идёт по́сле четвёртого? Коне́чно **пя́тый!** Пя́тый де́нь— **пя́тница**. Повтори́те не́сколько ра́з:
>   **В пя́тницу** шёл до́ждь весь де́нь:
>   Мне́ рабо́тать бы́ло ле́нь.

А. (Повторя́ет).

Б. —Шестой день—**суббота**. Слово «суббота» происходит (comes) от слова «Sabbath». Это легко запомнить. Правда?

А. —Да, это не трудно. Я уверен, что я запомню это слово без труда. У вас есть стих для **субботы**?

Б. —Есть:

Мы будем отдыхать **в субботу**,
Забудем школу и работу.

А. —Я повторю это два раза. (Повторяет).

Б. —Отлично. Теперь седьмой и последний день, **воскресенье**.

А. —Это невозможно запомнить!

Б. —Почему «невозможно»? Всё возможно. Я уверен, что вы легко это запомните. Есть такая русская поговорка: «повторение—мать учения». Повторите это слово несколько раз.

А. —Это конечно правильно. А что значит «**воскресенье**»?

Б. —Это значит «resurrection». Теперь повторите:

Воскресенье, воскресенье,
Жду тебя я с нетерпеньем.

А. —Ура! Я всё помню: понедельник, вторник, среда, четверг, пятница, суббота, воскресенье! Ура! Я вас очень благодарю за помощь. Это очень любезно с вашей стороны.

Б. —Не стоит благодарности. Я всегда рад вам помочь. Не забывайте поговорку «повторение—мать учения».

Назовите все дни недели. Начните с понедельника.

4. Accusative of time with на and через

A. На with accusative. The preposition **на** is used with the *accusative* case to specify a period of time subsequent to an action such as going, giving, taking, lending, etc.:

Они **поехали** в Москву **на** неделю.
They went to Moscow *for* a week (to spend a week).

Я **взял** эту книгу **на** два дня.
I took that book *for* two days (to keep it two days).

The corresponding question is **на сколько** + *gen.*:

На сколько времени он поехал в Москву?
For how long has he gone to Moscow?

When the period of time is that of the duration of the action itself, the accusative *without* the preposition is used. In such cases the English preposition *for* may usually be omitted.

—Сколько времени вы читали? —Я читал **три часа**.
—(For) how long did you read? —I read (for) three hours.

B. Через with accusative. The preposition **через**, as has been seen in Unit 17, is used with the accusative in the sense of *in* (but not *within*), *after*, *at the end of*.

Через неде́лю о́н пое́дет во Фра́нцию.
In (after—at the end of) a week he will go to France.
(*or:* A week from now he will go to France.)

DRILLS

A. *Чита́йте э́ти вопро́сы и отвеча́йте на ни́х по-ру́сски.*

1. Како́й де́нь в середи́не неде́ли?
2. В како́й де́нь лю́ди отдыха́ют?
3. Како́й де́нь происхо́дит от сло́ва «Sabbath»?
4. Како́й пя́тый де́нь неде́ли?
5. В кото́ром часу́ у ва́с пе́рвый уро́к во вто́рник?
6. На ско́лько часо́в вы́ хо́дите в шко́лу?
7. В кото́ром часу́ вы́ обыкнове́нно встаёте в понеде́льник?
8. На ско́лько часо́в вы́ хо́дите в библиоте́ку?
9. Ско́лько часо́в в де́нь вы́ рабо́таете?
10. В кото́ром часу́ вы́ обы́чно обе́даете?
11. Воскресе́нье четвёртый де́нь неде́ли?
12. На ско́лько вре́мени вы́ е́дете в Сове́тский Сою́з?
13. На ско́лько дне́й вы́ взя́ли э́ту кни́гу?
14. Вы́ надо́лго е́дете в Аргенти́ну?
15. **Через** ско́лько вре́мени вы́ прие́дете обра́тно?

B. *Переведи́те (translate) с англи́йского на ру́сский.*

1. I will take Anna's car for a few days.
2. I was in London for a few days last year.
3. I am going to Victor's for two hours.
4. I am going to work there for two hours.
5. I will come back after two hours.
6. I am going to Europe in a week.
7. For how long are you going?
8. I am going for a month.
9. How long will you stay (live) at your sister's?
10. I am going to stay at her place for two weeks, not more.
11. We lived in the Ukraine for three years. We are going back there in four months.
12. —For how many months are you going there?
    —For two.

5. *Going* verbs with the prefixes при- and у-

In Unit 15 it was seen that the addition of a prefix to a basic verb may change both the aspect and the meaning of the verb.

The basic verbs of *going* take a variety of prefixes that express different shades of meaning: coming, going away, going out, leaving, arriving, etc. Thus, the prefix **при-** is added to *going* verbs to express the idea of *coming, arriving,* while the prefix **у-** is added to express *leaving, going away.* The distinction between going by one's own means and riding is retained with the compounds of these verbs. However, prefixed or compound, verbs of *going* possess *only one imperfective* form, which serves for both the *determinate* and *indeterminate* functions of the imperfective.

The two imperfective forms of the basic verb when joined to a prefix produce imperfective verbs from indeterminates, and perfectives from determinates:

A. Verbs of *coming, arriving.*

Prefix + *indeterminate* imperfective → *compound imperfective*
при- + ходи́ть   → **приходи́ть**
                       (*det.* and *indet.*)

Prefix + *determinate* imperfective → *compound perfective*
при- + идти́   → **прийти́** (or **придти́**)

} to come, arrive (on foot)

The corresponding compounds for riding are formed with **-езжа́ть** (instead of the indeterminate imperfective е́здить) and **е́хать**:

при- + -езжа́ть → **приезжа́ть** (imperf.)
при- + е́хать → **прие́хать** (perf.)
to come, arrive (not on foot)

The four verbs, all with the general meaning of *coming, arriving*, are conjugated as follows:

	Imperfective (Present)	Perfective (Future)
On foot	**приходи́ть** прихожу́ прихо́дишь прихо́дит прихо́дим прихо́дите прихо́дят	**прийти́** приду́ придёшь придёт придём придёте приду́т
By vehicle	**приезжа́ть** приезжа́ю приезжа́ешь приезжа́ет приезжа́ем приезжа́ете приезжа́ют	**прие́хать** прие́ду прие́дешь прие́дет прие́дем прие́дете прие́дут

Except for **прийти́**, the past tense is regularly formed from the infinitive. The past tense of **прийти́** is like that of **идти́**:

пришёл, пришло́, пришла́, пришли́

The verb **прие́хать** lacks an imperative; the imperfective imperative **приезжа́й, -те** is used in its place.

Observe that the imperfective forms have both *indeterminate* and *determinate* functions:

Indeterm. Function: Óн ча́сто **прихо́дит** к на́м.
He often *comes* to see us.

Compare: Óн ча́сто **хо́дит** в теа́тр.
He often *goes* to the theater.

Determ. Function: Сего́дня óн **прихо́дит** к на́м к обе́ду.
Today he's *coming* to our house for dinner.

Compare: Сего́дня óн **идёт** в теа́тр.
Today he's *going* to the theater.

The "present" tense of the perfective has future meaning:

Perf.: Я ду́маю, что о́н **придёт**.
I think that he *will come*.

Compare: О́н говори́т, что **пойдёт** с на́ми в теа́тр.
He says that he *will go* to the theater with us.

B. Verbs of *going away, leaving*. The prefix **у-** gives a set of verbs with the general meaning of *going away, leaving*.

	Imperfective (Present)	Perfective (Future)
On foot	**уходи́ть** ухожу́ ухо́дишь etc.	**уйти́** уйду́ уйдёшь etc.
By vehicle	**уезжа́ть** уезжа́ю уезжа́ешь etc.	**уе́хать** уе́ду уе́дешь etc.

The past tense of **уйти́** is **ушёл, ушло́, ушла́, ушли́**.

The perfective **уе́хать** lacks an imperative; the imperfective **уезжа́й, -те** is used in its place.

In summary:

		Imperfective	Perfective
Arriving (**при-**)	*on foot*	приходи́ть	прийти́
	by vehicle	приезжа́ть	прие́хать
Leaving (**у-**)	*on foot*	уходи́ть	уйти́
	by vehicle	уезжа́ть	уе́хать

PATTERN SENTENCES

Приходи́ть/прийти́

1. Ка́ждый ра́з, когда́ я **прихожу́** в э́тот рестора́н, я встреча́ю э́того то́лстого господи́на.
2. Иногда́ о́н **прихо́дит** сюда́ со свое́й до́черью.
3. Смирно́вы тепе́рь ре́дко сюда́ **прихо́дят**. Ра́ньше они́ **приходи́ли** дово́льно ча́сто.

1. Every time I come to this restaurant I meet that stout gentleman.
2. He comes here sometimes with his daughter.
3. The Smirnovs now come here infrequently. Formerly they came rather often.

4. Когда́ моя́ до́чь жила́ бли́зко, она́ ча́сто ко мне́ **приходи́ла**.
5. Профе́ссор Па́влов всегда́ **приходи́л** к нам со свое́й жено́й.
6. В сре́ду Зо́я **пришла́** к обе́ду.
7. До́ктор до́лжен был **прийти́** в час, но не **пришёл**.
8. Я́ **приду́** к ва́м в пя́тницу в четы́ре часа́.
9. —Вы́ ду́маете, что Андре́й ско́ро **придёт**? —Через два́дцать мину́т.
10. Они́ сказа́ли, что **приду́т** к нам к обе́ду. **Приходи́те** то́же, е́сли ва́м удо́бно.
11. —В кото́ром часу́ вы́ **прихо́дите** со слу́жбы? —Я́ **прихожу́** домо́й в ше́сть.

4. When my daughter lived near, she often came to (see) me.
5. Professor Pavlov always used to come to (see) us with his wife.
6. On Wednesday Zoya came to dinner.
7. The doctor was supposed to come at one, but didn't come.
8. I shall come to see you on Friday at four o'clock.
9. —Do you think that Andrey will come soon? —In twenty minutes.
10. They said that they would come to our place for dinner. You come too, if it suits you.
11. —At what time do you come from work? —I come home at six.

Уходи́ть/уйти́

1. Я́ обыкнове́нно **ухожу́** и́з дому[5] в се́мь часо́в.
2. Почему́ Смирно́вы уже́ **ухо́дят**? Ещё ра́но.
3. Когда́ А́нна **уходи́ла**, она́ сказа́ла, что ско́ро опя́ть придёт.
4. Она́ то́лько что **ушла́**. Её сы́н **ушёл** с не́й.
5. Я́ **уйду́** через два́ часа́.
6. Все́ ско́ро **уйду́т**, и мы́ бу́дем одни́.
7. Е́сли вы́ бу́дете та́к говори́ть, мы́ **уйдём**.

1. I usually leave home at seven o'clock.
2. Why are the Smirnovs leaving already? It's still early.
3. When Anna was leaving, she said that she would come (back) again.
4. She has just left. Her son has left with her.
5. I shall leave in two hours.
6. Everybody will leave soon and we shall be alone.
7. If you are going to talk that way, we shall leave.

DRILLS

A. *Choose the correct verb and translate.*

Приходи́ть/прийти́

1. Зимо́й я́ (приходи́л/пришёл) домо́й в ше́сть.
2. Тепе́рь я́ всегда́ (прихожу́/приду́) ра́ньше.
3. А́нна вчера́ (приходи́ла/пришла́) к нам в три́ часа́.
4. В кото́ром часу́ Андре́й сего́дня (приходи́л/пришёл) в библиоте́ку?
5. За́втра я́ (бу́ду приходи́ть/приду́) к ва́м ра́но у́тром.
6. Ле́том Ива́н (бу́дет приходи́ть/придёт) к нам ча́сто.

Уходи́ть/уйти́

1. Секрета́рша сего́дня по́здно (уходи́ла/ушла́) из конто́ры.
2. Ра́ньше она́ (уходи́ла/ушла́) в четы́ре часа́.
3. Когда́ я́ рабо́тал на заво́де, я́ (уходи́л/ушёл) и́з дому в пя́ть часо́в утра́.
4. Тепе́рь я́ (ухожу́/уйду́) и́з дому в во́семь.
5. Оте́ц (бу́дет уходи́ть/уйдёт) сего́дня ра́но из конто́ры.
6. Мы́ тепе́рь ка́ждый де́нь (бу́дем уходи́ть/уйдём) ро́вно в де́вять.

---

[5] **Уходи́ть/уйти́ и́з дому** *to leave home.* Note the stress on **и́з** in this idiom. Contrast **из до́ма** *out of the house,* e.g., Они́ вы́шли **из** до́ма. They came out of the house.

B. *Replace the English verb in parentheses with the proper Russian verb form.*

Приходи́ть/прийти́

1. Когда́ Андре́й жи́л бли́зко, о́н ча́сто (came) к Ива́ну. 2. Тепе́рь, когда́ о́н живёт далеко́, о́н ре́дко к нему́ (comes). 3. О́н (came) в суббо́ту и сказа́л, что (would = will come) в четве́рг. 4. Вчера́ Зи́на (came) к А́нне, и они́ вме́сте (came) ко мне́. 5. Они́ сказа́ли, что ско́ро опя́ть (would = will come) ко мне́. 6. Они́ обы́чно (come) в воскресе́нье. 7. Они́ тепе́рь (will come) ка́ждую неде́лю. 8. Мы́ (will come) к ва́м в суббо́ту, и мы́ (will come) ча́сто. 9. Как то́лько вы́ (come = will come) домо́й, позвони́те мне́. 10. Как то́лько я́ (come = will come) домо́й я ва́м позвоню́.

Уходи́ть/уйти́

1. —Почему́ Андре́й уже́ (is leaving)? —Его́ ждёт жена́. О́н до́лжен (to leave). 2. —Кто́ уже́ (left)? —Ни́на (left) и Бори́с (left). 3. Они́ (left) вме́сте. 4. Они́ всегда́ (leave) ра́но. 5. —Вы́ то́же (are leaving)? —Не́т, мы́ (will leave) когда́ всё (will leave). 6. Я́ (will leave) с ва́ми. 7. Де́ти ка́ждый де́нь (leave) и́з дому в во́семь, а я́ (leave) немно́го по́зже.

PATTERN SENTENCES

Приезжа́ть/прие́хать

1. —Я́ **прие́ду** к тебе́ в дере́вню, а ты́ **прие́дешь** ко мне́ в го́род!

2. Ты́ **приезжа́й** ко мне́ в дере́вню ле́том, а я **прие́ду** к тебе́ в го́род зимо́й.

3. Почему́ вы́ бо́льше не **приезжа́ете** к на́м, в Я́лту, как вы́ **приезжа́ли** к на́м ра́ньше?

4. **Приезжа́йте!** Мы́ живём в то́м же до́ме, и у ва́с бу́дет та́ же ко́мната. **Прие́дете?**

5. Я́ обеща́ю ва́м, что мы́ ско́ро **прие́дем**, и что бу́дем тепе́рь ча́сто к ва́м **приезжа́ть**.

6. Ни́на написа́ла на про́шлой неде́ле, что она́ **прие́дет** сюда́ в сре́ду, но не **прие́хала**! Она́ так ча́сто **приезжа́ла** в про́шлом году́!

7. Смирно́вы обеща́ли **прие́хать**, и **прие́хали**! И́х сы́н Серге́й **прие́хал** с ни́ми.

8. Из Ки́ева мы́ е́дем в Оде́ссу по́ездом,[6] а из Оде́ссы в Я́лту парохо́дом.[6] Мы́ **приезжа́ем** туда́ в сре́ду у́тром. Как то́лько **прие́дем**, пошлём тебе́ телегра́мму.

1. —I will come to see you in the country, and you will come to see me in town!

2. You (will) come to see me in the country in summer, and I will come to see you in town in winter.

3. Why don't you come to see us any more in Yalta as you did (come) formerly?

4. Come to see us! We live in the same house, and you will have the same room. Will you come?

5. I promise you that we will come soon and that now we will come to see you often.

6. Nina wrote last week that she would come here on Wednesday, but she didn't come! She came so often last year!

7. The Smirnovs promised to come and they did come! Their son Sergey came with them.

8. From Kiev we're going to Odessa by train, and from Odessa to Yalta by boat. We're arriving there on Wednesday morning. As soon as we arrive we'll send you a telegram.

---

[6] The instrumental case may also be used to express by what means one travels, e.g.: Мы́ е́дем в Вашингто́н по́ездом. We are going to Washington by train.

Уезжа́ть/уе́хать

1. —Ири́на, когда́ ты **уезжа́ешь**? —Я́ **уезжа́ю** через неде́лю. Я́ наве́рно **уе́ду** во вто́рник.

2. —А вы́, Ива́н Ива́нович, не **уезжа́ете**? —Мы́ с жено́й всегда́ **уезжа́ем** на ле́то. Я́ ду́маю, что мы́ **уе́дем** в конце́ ме́сяца.

3. Они́ о́чень хотя́т **уе́хать** из го́рода, и они́ **уе́дут** на два́, три́ ме́сяца.

4. Я́ позвони́ла Ири́не не́сколько дне́й тому́ наза́д, и мне́ сказа́ли, что она́ **уе́хала** из Москвы́ в про́шлый вто́рник. Её бра́т **уе́хал** в то́т же де́нь, но́ не с не́й.

1. —Irina, when are you going away? —I'm going in a week. I will probably leave on Tuesday.

2. —And you, Ivan Ivanovich, aren't you going too? —My wife and I always go away for the summer. I think we're leaving at the end of the month.

3. They very much want to leave the city, and they will leave for two or three months.

4. I called Irina a few days ago and they told me that she had left Moscow last Tuesday. Her brother had left on the same day, but he didn't go with her.

DRILLS

Replace the English verb in parentheses with the proper Russian verb form and translate.

Приезжа́ть/прие́хать

1. Мы́ вчера́ (came) в Нью-Йо́рк. А́нна (came) с на́ми.
2. Э́тот ра́з мо́й оте́ц (didn't come) в го́род.
3. О́н (used to come) сюда́ ра́з в го́д.
4. О́льга всегда́ (came) с ни́м.
5. Они́ иногда́ (came) в Нью-Йо́рк на оди́н де́нь. Я́ не зна́ю, когда́ они́ опя́ть (will come) сюда́.
6. —Когда́ вы́ (will come) к на́м в Кры́м? —Мы́ (will come) ле́том.
7. Мы́ (will come) к ва́м ча́сто.
8. Я́ о́чень хочу́ (to come) к тебе́, и ско́ро (will come).

Уезжа́ть/уе́хать

1. Андре́й (left) из Москвы́. Зи́на (left) с ни́м. Они́ (left) вме́сте.
2. Мы́ ско́ро (are leaving). А когда́ вы́ (are leaving)?
3. Они́ (are leaving) из го́рода через две́ неде́ли. Они́ (are leaving) на три́ неде́ли.
4. Когда́ они́ (will leave) из Босто́на, О́льга бу́дет жи́ть в и́х кварти́ре.
5. Е́сли зде́сь бу́дет жа́рко, мы́ (will leave) отсю́да и вы́ то́же (will leave)!
6. Я́ о́чень хочу́ (to leave)! Я́ ско́ро (will leave).

Reading

Во́т моя́ семья́!

Мо́й му́ж, Серге́й Фёдорович Со́мов. О́н экономи́ст. У него́ хоро́шее положе́ние в экономи́ческом ми́ре, где́ его́ счита́ют отли́чным экспе́ртом. О́н пи́шет статьи́ для журна́ла «Вопро́сы Эконо́мики» и чита́ет ле́кции в Экономи́ческом Институ́те.

Я—Со́фья Миха́йловна Со́мова. Мать, жена́, дома́шняя хозя́йка (housewife), два ра́за в неде́лю рабо́таю в де́тской библиоте́ке. Домрабо́тница[7] прихо́дит к нам три ра́за в неде́лю, на три часа́, а семья́ у меня́ больша́я и рабо́ты мно́го.

Людми́ла, ста́ршая до́чь. Шко́льница, 16 лет.

Кири́лл, ста́рший сын. Шко́льник, 15 лет.

Ири́на, втора́я до́чь. Шко́льница, 12 лет.

Йгорь, мла́дший сын. Шко́льник, 9 лет.

Мой муж уе́хал во вто́рник в Болга́рию (Bulgaria), в Со́фию.[8] Он сейча́с пи́шет статью́ об экономи́ческом положе́нии Болга́рии во вре́мя Вели́кой оте́чественной войны́[9] и о её тепе́решнем положе́нии. Для э́той статьи́ ему́ нужны́ не́которые материа́лы и докуме́нты, кото́рых здесь нет. Он зна́ет не́сколько славя́нских (Slavic) языко́в, осо́бенно хорошо́ болга́рский, и мо́жет без словаря́ чита́ть да́же са́мые тру́дные статьи́ и кни́ги. Он уе́хал на де́сять дней.

Я о́чень хоте́ла пое́хать с ним, но как я могу́?

Answer these questions quickly.

1. Кака́я специа́льность у Со́мова?   2. Почему́ у него́ хоро́шее положе́ние? 3. Кака́я те́ма статьи́, кото́рую он пи́шет?   4. Почему́ он до́лжен был пое́хать в Болга́рию?   5. Ско́лько славя́нских языко́в он зна́ет?   6. Чего́ хоте́ла Со́фья Миха́йловна?   7. Почему́ она́ не могла́ э́того сде́лать?

Мой день

Понеде́льник. У́тро. Я на ку́хне, гото́влю за́втрак. Спешу́. В во́семь часо́в де́ти должны́ уйти́ из до́му. Е́сли уйду́т по́зже, опозда́ют в шко́лу. Вре́мя идёт бы́стро, осо́бенно у́тром. Спешу́.

Го́лос Йгоря из ко́мнаты:

—Ма́ма!

—Что тебе́? (What do you want?)

—Дай мне чи́стую руба́шку.

—Откро́й шкаф и возьми́ сам. Ты же зна́ешь, на како́й по́лке лежа́т в шкафу́ руба́шки. Ири́на, помоги́ ему́!

Го́лос Ири́ны:

—Вот, так всегда́: «Ири́на помоги́, Ири́на сде́лай, Ири́на купи́».

—Хорошо́, Ири́на. Не помога́й, не де́лай, не покупа́й, не на́до!

—Ма́ма, ты же прекра́сно зна́ешь, что я помогу́!

—Спаси́бо, Йрочка.

Го́лос Людми́лы:

—Ма́ма!

—Что тебе́?

—Ты мо́жешь дать мне пять рубле́й? Дай, пожа́луйста.

—Заче́м тебе́?

—Мой класс хо́чет купи́ть пода́рок Зинаи́де Ива́новне. Она́ ухо́дит в конце́ уче́бного го́да.

---

[7] **Домрабо́тница (дома́шняя рабо́тница)** *cleaning woman, servant.*

[8] **Со́фия—столи́ца Болга́рии.**

[9] The Great Fatherland War (World War II), as it is usually called in the Soviet Union.

—Почему́ она́ ухо́дит? Она́ така́я хоро́шая учи́тельница! Я ви́жу, как мно́го ты зна́ешь по исто́рии.[10]

—Но э́то её три́дцать шесто́й год в на́шей шко́ле!

—О́чень жа́ль, что она́ должна́ уйти́. Возьми́ де́ньги в моём столе́.

Го́лос Кири́лла:

—Ма́ма.

—Что́ тебе́?

—Я приду́ из шко́лы с Бори́сом Моро́зовым. Мы придём в шесть к у́жину. Он мо́жет придти́ к у́жину?

—Коне́чно. То́лько приходи́те ра́ньше. Не опа́здывайте. Де́ти! Иди́те за́втракать!

Мы за́втракаем в ку́хне. Я люблю́ на́ши шу́мные весёлые за́втраки, хотя́ ча́сто мо́жно слы́шать мой го́лос: «Не шуми́», «переда́й хлеб И́горю», «закро́й холоди́льник», «возьми́ ещё молока́», «ну, конча́йте», «иди́те». «И́горь, не забу́дь кало́ши», «не опа́здывайте», «Людми́ла, не забу́дь де́ньги», «И́горь, не разгова́ривай во вре́мя уро́ка».

Уф! Ушли́! В ку́хне гря́зная посу́да, везде́ беспоря́док (disorder). Домрабо́тница прихо́дит то́лько три ра́за в неде́лю на три часа́, а семья́ больша́я и рабо́ты мно́го. И её день то́лько за́втра.

Сейча́с я должна́ пойти́ в магази́н. Бу́ду стоя́ть в о́череди (line) за мя́сом, бу́ду стоя́ть в о́череди за молоко́м и ма́слом, пото́м за хле́бом, пото́м...

Звоно́к в дверь. Бо́же мой! Кто э́то? Наве́рное Соро́кин. С ним так тру́дно разгова́ривать! Он ста́рый, пло́хо слы́шит, всё забыва́ет, у него́ совсе́м бо́льше нет па́мяти. Мой муж, когда́ слы́шит его́ го́лос, сейча́с же ухо́дит. А мне его́ жа́ль. Он совсе́м одино́кий и никому́ не ну́жен. Он был дру́гом моего́ отца́, зна́ет меня́ с де́тства (since my childhood) и лю́бит меня́ как дочь.

Открыва́ю дверь. Так и есть! Э́то он!

—Здра́вствуйте, Леони́д Па́влович! Как хорошо́, что вы пришли́! Что́ у вас но́вого?

—Ничего́ у меня́ нет но́вого, Со́нечка.[11] Ста́рость и бо́льше ничего́. А что́ у тебя́ но́вого, мой а́нгел? Я так давно́ тебя́ не ви́дел!

—Ну, как давно́! Сего́дня понеде́льник, а вы бы́ли здесь в суббо́ту.

—Ра́зве я был у тебя́ позавчера́? Не по́мню, Со́нечка. У меня́ тепе́рь совсе́м нет па́мяти; всё забыва́ю. А где́ же наш дорого́й Серге́й Фёдорович?

—Я ведь в пя́тницу вам всё рассказа́ла! Серге́й во вто́рник уе́хал в Болга́рию, в Со́фию.

—Не слы́шу, куда́?

—В Болга́рию, Болга́рию.

—А заче́м он туда́ пое́хал?

—Вы забы́ли? Я ведь вам всё рассказа́ла! Он пи́шет статью́ об экономи́ческом положе́нии Болга́рии и ему́ нужны́ материа́лы, кото́рых здесь нет.

—Не слы́шу. О чём он пи́шет?

—Я расскажу́ вам в друго́й раз. Хоти́те ча́ю?

—Нет, спаси́бо, Со́нечка. Я пойду́. Я приду́ к тебе́ за́втра. Приве́т Серге́ю Фёдоровичу.

---

[10] **По** + *dative* often means *in the field of*. Here: **по исто́рии** *in the field of history*.

[11] **Со́нечка**, an affectionate name for **Со́ня**, which in turn is a diminutive of **Со́фья** *Sophia*.

Слáва Бóгу,[12] ушёл! Бéдный старúк!

Идý в магазúн, в одúн, в другóй. Стою́ в óчереди, в однóй, в другóй. Всё купúла. Пришлá домóй. Гóсподи, скóлько дóма рабóты! Домрабóтница придёт тóлько зáвтра. Ужé пóздно. Я должнá спешúть.

Телефóн.

—Аллó, слýшаю. Ктó говорúт?

—Сóфья Михáйловна, это я, Зóя. Я звоню́ вáм из дéтской библиотéки. Сегóдня ведь мóй дéнь. Я совсéм однá сейчáс, а рабóты óчень мнóго. Óльга придёт мнé помогáть тóлько чéрез чáс. Вы мóжете прийтú на чáс?

—Нó Зóичка, я тóже однá и у меня тóже мнóго рабóты! Зúна, нáша домрабóтница, придёт тóлько зáвтра. В четы́ре придёт из шкóлы Úгорь, и я не люблю́, когдá никогó нéт дóма, когдá он прихóдит. Мóй дéнь в библиотéке тóлько зáвтра.

—Я знáю, дорогáя. Нó пожáлуйста приходúте, пожáлуйста! Я не знáю, чтó мнé дéлать, так мнóго рабóты!

—Хорошó, придý. Нó тóлько на чáс!

—Спасúбо, спасúбо!

Прихожý из библиотéки. В кýхне гря́зная посýда, в квартúре беспоря́док. Úгорь ужé дóма. Óн говорúт, что тóлько что звонúли из шкóлы, что у Ирúны мáленькая температýра и её посылáют домóй и что бýдет лýчше, éсли я пойдý за нéй. Пойдý.

Телефóн! Это из Болгáрии!

—Аллó, это ты́, Серёжа?

—Аллó, Сóнечка, ты́ меня слы́шишь?

—Слы́шу, слы́шу. А ты́ меня?

—Дá, довóльно хорошó. Нý, чтó у вáс? Кáк вы́ всé?

—Всё хорошó, всё нормáльно. Кáк ты́?

—Прекрáсно! Статья́ идёт хорошó. Вúдел мнóго интерéсного. Погóда прекрáсная. А дóма прáвда всё хорошó? Ты́ не слúшком мнóго рабóтаешь?

—Нéт, нéт, чтó ты! Знáешь, Úгорь получúл хорóшую отмéтку по арифмéтике, а Людмúла написáла хорóшее сочинéние на тéму «рóль лúчности в истóрии».

—Молодцы́! Целую́ вáс всéх. Хочý ужé бы́ть дóма!

Идý в шкóлу за Ирúной.

Это бы́л довóльно обыкновéнный дéнь.

Отвéтьте на эти вопрóсы по-рýсски.

1. Чтó дóлжен сдéлать Úгорь, éсли емý нужнá рубáшка? 2. Ктó Ирúна? 3. Почемý онá недовóльна? 4. Зачéм Людмúле нужны́ дéньги? 5. В чьём столé лежáт дéньги? 6. Почемý мáть считáет, что Зинаúда Ивáновна хорóшая учúтельница? 7. Кáк мóжно описáть (describe) зáвтраки в кýхне? 8. Почемý у Сóфьи Михáйловны так мнóго рабóты? 9. Почемý Сóмов ухóдит, как тóлько слы́шит гóлос Сорóкина? 10. Почемý Сóфье Михáйловне егó жáль? 11. Почемý Сорóкин лю́бит Сóфью Михáйловну? 12. Чегó Сорóкин не пóмнил? 13. Чтó Сóфья Михáйловна дéлает пóсле разговóра с Сорóкиным? 14. Ктó, откýда и зачéм позвонúл éй, как тóлько онá пришлá из магазúна? 15. Почемý Сóфья Михáйловна былá недовóльна, что Зóя просúла её прийтú в библиотéку?

---

[12] **Слáва Бóгу** *Thank God* (literally, *Glory to God*).

16. Что Игорь рассказал матери, когда она пришла из магазина? 17. Откуда и от кого был последний телефонный звонок? 18. Что муж рассказал жене, и что жена рассказала мужу?

DRILLS

A. *Give a suitable Russian word or phrase for the English in parentheses, and translate.*

1. Они только что (came to see us). 2. Виктор придёт (to dinner). 3. Мы придём (to see you) завтра утром. 4. После лекции он пришёл (to see me). 5. Он был (at my place) в три часа. Он скоро (left my place). 6. Они будут рады, когда он (will leave them). 7. Когда вы придёте (to see us)? 8. Было поздно, когда Нина (left her). 9. Если ты завтра будешь (at home), я приду (to your place) и буду обедать (at your place). 10. Он вчера в первый раз пришёл (to Vadim's) и (left him) через час. 11. Я был (at Anna's), когда Зина пришла (to her place). 12. Я приду (in two hours). 13. Я буду работать (for two hours). 14. Я уйду (after two hours). 15. Я приду (at two o'clock). 16. Мы уезжаем (in a week). 17. Мы будем жить там (a week). 18. Мы уезжаем (for a week). 19. Она пришла (for an hour). 20. Она сидит у нас уже (for three hours). 21. Ольга пришла к нам (for a book). 22. Он будет здесь (until Tuesday or Wednesday). 23. (After the theater) мы пойдём прямо домой.

B. *Review Translation.*

1. Last month when he arrived from Madrid, he came at once to see us. 2. She just came from the director. 3. From his study she came to my room. 4. They left school early today. 5. From where did he come, from Odessa or from Leningrad? 6. When I came to his room, he wasn't there. 7. Next month he will get (arrive) here from Africa. 8. I am leaving in two days. 9. When they leave Boston next year, who is going to live in their house? 10. She left the concert before the end. 11. She had just left for Moscow for a week. 12. We came here from France. 13. —When did he leave there? —Last Wednesday. 14. Come to see us on Monday. 15. Memorize the names of the days of the week. 16. Be so kind (as to) help me. 17. Excuse me, I have no time. 18. What's new with you? 19. Take this money and give it to your son. 20. Don't give money to your little daughter.

Vocabulary

ангел angel	минута minute
бифштекс beefsteak	мировой world (*adj.*)
Бог[13] [бóх] God	наверно probably, surely
век century	надолго for a long time
возможно possible	невозможно impossible
король (*masc.*) king	нетерпение impatience
королева queen	одинокий lonely
любезный gracious, pleasant, polite	отличный excellent

[13] The word Бог has the vocative (a special form for direct address) Боже! In the Soviet Union, Бог is spelled with lower case б.

о́чередь (*fem. II*) line, queue, turn
парохо́д ship, steamboat
повторе́ние repetition
погово́рка (*gen. pl.* **-ок**) saying, proverb
позавчера́ day before yesterday
положе́ние position, situation
пра́вильный correct
ра́зве? can it be that . . .? (expresses surprise or
    disbelief)

ра́зве . . . не? surely?
середи́на middle
ста́рость (*fem. II*) old age
терпе́ние patience
уве́рен, -а, -ы sure, certain
уче́ние study, studying
це́рк.овь (*fem. II, gen.* **-ви**) church
чита́тель (*fem.* **-ница**) reader
я́сный clear

VERBS

благодари́ть (imperf., II: **благодар.ю́, -и́шь**), поблагодари́ть (perf., II) to thank (+ *acc. of person*
    thanked; **за** + *acc. of object of thanks*)
ждать (imperf., I: **жд.у, -ёшь**), подожда́ть (perf., I) to wait for[14]
закры́ть (perf. of **закрыва́ть**, I: **закро́.ю, -ешь**) to close, shut
запомина́ть (imperf., I), запо́мнить (perf., II: **запо́мн.ю, -ишь**) to memorize, learn (by heart)
извиня́ть (imperf., I), извини́ть (perf., II: **извин.ю́, -и́шь**) to excuse
называ́ть (imperf., I) назва́ть (perf., I: **назов.у́, -ёшь**) to name, call
осно́вывать (imperf., I), основа́ть (perf., I, **осну.ю́, -ёшь**) to found, establish
откры́ть (perf. of **открыва́ть**, I: **откро́.ю, -ешь**) to open
передава́ть (imperf., I: **переда.ю́, -ёшь**), переда́ть (perf., like **дать**) to transfer, pass, hand on,
    transmit, convey
повторя́ть (imperf., I), повтори́ть (perf., II: **повтор.ю́, -и́шь**) to repeat
помо́чь (perf. of **помога́ть**, I: like **мочь**) to help (+ *dat. of person helped*)
послу́шать (perf. of **слу́шать**, I) to listen, obey (+ *acc.*)
предпочита́ть (imperf., I) to prefer
проси́ть (imperf., II: **прошу́, про́сишь**), попроси́ть (perf., II) to ask (for), request, beg (for)

EXPRESSIONS

с ва́шей стороны́ on your part
Бу́дьте добры́ . . .⎫
Бу́дьте любе́зны . . .⎭ Be so good as to (+ *imper. or infin.*)
к обе́ду to dinner, for dinner
Мне́ бы́ло ле́нь (+ *infin.*) I didn't feel like . . .; I felt too lazy to . . .
Что́ зна́чит . . .? What does . . . mean?
Не сто́ит (благода́рности). Don't mention it.
Мне́ его́ (*acc.*) бы́ло жа́ль. I felt sorry for him.
то́т же, то́ же, та́ же, the same[15]
Та́к и е́сть. So it is.
Что́ у ва́с но́вого? What's new with you?
Сла́ва Бо́гу! Thank God!
Бо́же мо́й! My God! My goodness!

---

[14] With the verb **ждать**, masculine and neuter nouns are normally in the genitive. Feminine nouns,
    in particular animates, show a strong tendency to take the accusative rather than the genitive,
    e.g.:
                    Я́ жду́ по́езда.   I'm waiting for a train.
        But: Я́ жду́ жену́.   I'm waiting for my wife.
[15] The first part **тот/то/та** is declined; the particle **же** is invariable, e.g., Они́ обе́дали в **то́м же**
    рестора́не, что мы́. They dined in the same restaurant we did.

Unit 19

Grammar

1. Verbs in -ся

Many Russian verbs add the suffix **-ся** or **-сь** to all their forms. The suffix **-ся** is added to verb forms ending in a consonant, and **-сь** to those ending in a vowel. No verb with the **-ся/-сь** suffix may be used transitively; in other words, it may not take a direct object.

Verbs with the suffix **-ся/-сь** may be divided into several groups according to function.

(1) *Transitive* verbs add **-ся/-сь** when used *intransitively*. One example of such a verb pair is **начина́ть/нача́ть** (*to begin, start*), with **-ся**: начина́ться/нача́ться.

The forms without **-ся** are used only when the action is directed toward an object:

Я́ на́чал э́ту рабо́ту в де́вять часо́в утра́.
I *started* that work at 9:00 A.M.

Учи́тель всегда́ **начина́ет** уро́к во́время.
The teacher always *begins* the lesson on time.

If there is no object, then the forms with **-ся** must be used:

Моя́ рабо́та **начина́ется** в де́вять часо́в.
My work *starts* at 9:00.

Уро́к всегда́ **начина́ется** во́время.
The lesson always *begins* on time.

Note on pronunciation. The combinations **-ться** (in the infinitive) and **-тся** (third person singular and plural) are pronounced [с:ə], i.e., a long **ц** + **ə**.

Similarly with **конча́ться/ко́нчиться, открыва́ться/откры́ться, закрыва́ться/закры́ться**.

Мы́ **конча́ем** рабо́тать в пя́ть часо́в.
We *finish* working at five o'clock.

Наш рабо́чий де́нь **конча́ется** в пя́ть часо́в.
Our working day *finishes* at five o'clock.

Хозя́ин **открыва́ет** магази́н в де́вять часо́в.
The owner *opens* his store at nine o'clock.

Его́ магази́н **открыва́ется** в де́вять.
His store *opens* at 9:00.

О́н **закрыва́ет** магази́н в ше́сть.
He *closes* the store at 6:00.

Магази́н **закрыва́ется** в ше́сть.
The store *closes* at 6:00.

(2) Some verbs acquire a *reflexive* meaning with the **-ся/-сь** suffix; in other words, the action of the verb is directed toward the subject itself:

	Ма́ть **одева́ет** ребёнка.	The mother is dressing the child.
But:	Ма́ть **одева́ется**.	The mother is dressing (herself).
	Я́ **мо́ю** посу́ду.	I am washing the dishes.
But:	Я́ **мо́юсь**.	I am washing (myself).

(3) Sometimes the addition of the **-ся/-сь** suffix gives a *reciprocal* meaning, when several subjects perform a mutual action:

Мы́ о́чень ре́дко **ви́димся**.
We see each other very seldom.

Они́ ча́сто **встреча́лись** зимо́й.
They often met in the winter.

(4) A number of verbs occur *only* with the **-ся/-сь** suffix; many of these describe emotions or behavior expressing emotion:

боя́ться	to fear, be afraid of
наде́яться	to hope
смея́ться	to laugh
улыба́ться	to smile

In English such verbs may sometimes take a direct object, e.g., *to fear*, but not in Russian. **Боя́ться** takes the *genitive* case (compare English *be afraid of*):

Э́тот учени́к **бои́тся** экза́мена.
That student is afraid of the exam.

(5) Another commonly used verb in **-ся** is **каза́ться** (*to seem*):

каза́ться (I: кажу́сь, ка́жешься) to seem

The predicate complement of this verb is in the *instrumental*:

О́н **каза́лся** о́чень молоды́м.
He seemed (looked) very young.

The *dative* case is used for the person to whom something appears:

> Э́ти вопро́сы **мне́ ка́жутся** стра́нными.
> These questions seem strange to me.

More often this verb is used in the third person singular as an impersonal: **ка́жется** (*pres.*), **каза́лось** (*past*):

> Мне́ **ка́жется**, что я́ сде́лал оши́бку.
> I think (it seems to me) that I've made a mistake.

Also parenthetically, between commas:

> Вы́, **ка́жется**, зна́ете мою́ сестру́.
> I believe you know my sister. (*or:* You, it seems, know my sister.)

(6) The verb **занима́ться** (*to study, be engaged in*) takes a predicate complement in the *instrumental*:

> —**Че́м** вы́ **занима́етесь**? —Геогра́фией.
> —What are you studying? —Geography.

(7) Another common verb in **-ся** is **называ́ться** *to be called* (not of persons):

> Ка́к **называ́ется** ва́ш уче́бник?
> What is your textbook called?

> Э́та пти́ца **называ́ется** куку́шкой.
> This bird is called a cuckoo.

Note that the predicate complement here, too, takes the *instrumental*.

(8) In the third person the suffix **-ся** sometimes denotes that an action is *normally* or *correctly* done in a certain way:

> Сло́во «то́лько» **пи́шется** с мя́гким зна́ком.
> The word "tol'ko" is written with a soft sign.

> В сло́ве «по́здно» бу́ква д не **произно́сится**.
> In the word "pozdno" the letter *d* is not pronounced.

Conjugation of verbs in -ся.

мы́ться (I) *to wash* (*oneself*)

мо́юсь	мо́емся
мо́ешься	мо́етесь
мо́ется	мо́ются

Past: мы́лся, мы́лось, мы́лась, мы́лись
Imperative: мо́йся, мо́йтесь

боя́ться (II) *to fear, be afraid of*

бою́сь	бои́мся
бои́шься	бои́тесь
бои́тся	боя́тся

Past: боя́лся, боя́лось, боя́лась, боя́лись
Imperative: бо́йся, бо́йтесь

The verbs **смея́ться** (*to laugh*) and **надея́ться** (*to hope*) drop the vowel **я** in the present tense and all forms derived from the present, such as the imperative.

смея́ться *to laugh*		**надея́ться** *to hope*	
смею́сь	смеёмся	надѐюсь	надѐемся
смеёшься	смеётесь	надѐешься	надѐетесь
смеётся	смею́тся	надѐется	надѐются

Past: смея́лся, смея́лась, etc.   *Past:* надѐялся, надѐялась, etc.
Imperative: смѐйся, смѐйтесь   *Imperative:* надѐйся, надѐйтесь

PATTERN SENTENCES

1. На на́шей у́лице **откры́лся** но́вый рестора́н. Я зна́ю челове́ка, кото́рый его́ откры́л.

2. Э́тот рестора́н **открыва́ется** в по́лдень и **закрыва́ется** в по́лночь.

3. Его́ рабо́чий де́нь **начина́ется** в во́семь утра́ и **конча́ется** в во́семь ве́чера. Он рабо́тает двена́дцать часо́в в де́нь!

4. Я то́чно не зна́ю, ка́к **пи́шутся** и ка́к **произно́сятся** не́которые слова́.

5. Мне́ ка́жется, что я́ **пишу́** и **произношу́** и́х непра́вильно.

6. Ра́ньше о́н **каза́лся** мне́ о́чень счастли́вым челове́ком, а тепе́рь о́н мне́ **ка́жется** несча́стным.

7. На́м с жено́й **каза́лось**, что вы́ недово́льны на́ми.

8. Мы́ случа́йно **встре́тились** с Вади́мом на ле́кции.

9. У́тром ма́ть **мо́ет** и **одева́ет** дете́й, а пото́м сама́ **мо́ется** и **одева́ется**.

10. Ве́чером, по́сле у́жина, ма́ть **раздева́ет** и **мо́ет** дете́й, а пото́м сама́ **раздева́ется** и **мо́ется**.

11. За́втра я́, как обы́чно, вста́ну ра́но, **помо́юсь**, **оде́нусь** и поза́втракаю.

12. Э́ти сёстры **одева́ются** одина́ково.

13. Она́ **бои́тся** всего́ и все́х, а её му́ж ничего́ и никого́ не **бои́тся**.

14. Ива́н **бои́тся провали́ться** на экза́мене, и поэ́тому мно́го **занима́ется**. О́н **надѐется** получи́ть хоро́шие отме́тки.

1. On our street a new restaurant has opened. I know the man who opened it.

2. This restaurant opens at noon and closes at midnight.

3. His working day begins at 8:00 in the morning and ends at 8:00 at night. He works twelve hours a day!

4. I don't know exactly how some words are spelled and how they are pronounced.

5. It seems to me that I spell and pronounce them wrong.

6. He used to seem a very happy person to me, but now he seems unhappy.

7. It seemed to my wife and me that you were displeased with us.

8. We met Vadim by chance at a lecture.

9. In the morning the mother washes and dresses the children, and then washes and dresses herself.

10. In the evening, after supper, the mother undresses and washes the children, and then undresses and washes herself.

11. Tomorrow, as usual, I will get up early, wash, dress, and have breakfast.

12. Those sisters dress alike.

13. She is afraid of everything and everybody, but her husband is not afraid of anything or anyone.

14. Ivan is afraid of failing the exam, so he is studying hard. He is hoping to get good marks.

15. —Ско́лько вре́мени о́н **занима́лся** матема́-тикой? —Я́ то́чно не зна́ю, но́ **ка́жется** о́чень до́лго.

16. Мы́ **наде́ялись**, что о́н придёт, но о́н не пришёл. Что́ на́м тепе́рь де́лать?[1]

17. Все́ лю́бят, когда́ Ни́ночка **смеётся**: у неё тако́й весёлый сме́х и тако́е смешно́е выра-же́ние лица́!

15. —How long did he study mathematics? —I don't know exactly, but it seems a very long time.

16. We hoped that he would come, but he didn't (come). What should we do now?

17. Everyone likes it when Ninochka laughs: she has such a merry laugh and such a funny expression (of the face)!

DRILLS

A. *Supply the proper form of the verb and translate the English words in parentheses.*

Каза́ться (*present tense*)

1. Э́тот челове́к мне́ .... (interesting).
2. Э́та же́нщина мне́ .... (intelligent).
3. Э́тот студе́нт .... (intelligent).
4. Э́тот фи́льм мне́ .... (strange).

Наде́яться (*present tense*)

1. Я́ ...., что вы́ (will come).
2. Мы́ ...., что о́н (will come).
3. Ты́ ...., что все́ (will come).
4. Все́ ...., что ты́ (will come).
5. О́н ...., что я́ (will come).
6. Они́ ...., что никто́ не (will come).

Наде́яться (*past tense*)

1. Ива́н ...., что всё ра́но (would = will leave).
2. Ни́на ...., что её сестра́ ра́но (would leave).
3. Кто́ ...., что ты́ ра́но (would leave)?
4. Они́ ...., что я́ ра́но (would leave).
5. Все́ ...., что мы́ ра́но (would leave).

Боя́ться (*present tense*)

1. Вы́ меня́ ....?
2. Они́ меня́ ....
3. Кто́ меня́ ....?
4. Ты́ меня́ ....?
5. Она́ меня́ ....
6. Все́ меня́ ....
7. Никто́ меня́ не ....
8. Я́ тебя́ ....
9. Я́ никого́ не ....
10. Я́ ничего́ не ....

Боя́ться (*past tense*)

1. Вы́ меня́ ....?
2. Она́ меня́ ....
3. О́н меня́ ....
4. Кто́ меня́ ....?
5. Все́ меня́ ....

B. **Одева́ться** (*present and past tenses*)

1. На́ши де́ти ме́дленно ....
2. Вы́ ме́дленно ....
3. Мы́ ме́дленно ....
4. Ты́ хорошо́ ....
5. Она́ хорошо́ ....
6. Кто́ хорошо́ ....?
7. Зде́сь все́ хорошо́ ....

---

[1] The dative with infinitive connotes various shades of possibility, probability, obligation, etc., e.g., **Что́ мне́ де́лать?** *What can I do? What am I to do? What shall I do?* **Куда́ на́м идти́?** *Where are we to go? Where should we go?* etc.

Одéться (*past tense*)

1. Дéти бы́стро . . . . .
2. Ни́на бы́стро . . . . .

3. Кто́ бы́стро . . . . ?
4. Всé бы́стро . . . . .

Одéться (*future tense*)

1. Я́ бы́стро . . . . .
2. Дéти бы́стро . . . . .
3. Óн бы́стро . . . . .

4. Мы́ бы́стро . . . . .
5. Кто́ бы́стро . . . . ?
6. Вы́ бы́стро . . . . .

B. *Отвéтьте на э́ти вопро́сы по-ру́сски.*

1. Ско́лько врéмени вы́ занима́етесь[2] ру́сским языко́м?
2. С кéм вы́ занима́етесь?
3. Кого́ или чего́ вы́ бои́тесь?
4. Что́ вы́ должны́ дéлать, когда́ вы́ встаёте?
5. Éсли вы́ хоти́те получа́ть хоро́шие отмéтки, что́ вы́ должны́ дéлать?
6. Что́ должна́ дéлать ма́ть у́тром и вéчером, éсли у неё éсть ма́ленький ребёнок?

C. *Change the verbs in parentheses to the correct form of the present, past, or future as appropriate, and translate.*

1. Концéрты ра́ньше (начина́ться) в дéвять.
2. Концéрт (нача́ться) через пя́ть мину́т.
3. Магази́ны тепéрь (закрыва́ться) в шéсть часо́в.
4. Я́ вчера́ (просну́ться) в во́семь часо́в. Я́ бы́стро (помы́ться), (одéться), и пошёл в шко́лу.
5. Тепéрь я́ всегда́ (просыпа́ться) в сéмь часо́в. Я́ бы́стро (встава́ть), (мы́ться), и (одева́ться).
6. Всé уро́ки обыкновéнно (конча́ться) в 4 ч., но́ вчера́ они́ (ко́нчиться) в 3.
7. За́втра уро́ки (ко́нчиться) как всегда́.

D. *Choose one of the following verbs in* **-ся** *and employ it in the proper form:*
боя́ться, закрыва́ться, занима́ться, каза́ться, надéяться, одева́ться, открыва́ться, смея́ться, *or the perfective, if the verb has one.*

1. Пётр ещё не пришёл, но́ я́ . . . . , что о́н придёт.
2. Бори́с о́чень мно́го . . . . ; о́н хотéл получи́ть хоро́шие отмéтки.
3. Его́ отéц ужа́сный человéк, и я́ ра́ньше . . . . его́. Но́ тепéрь я́ его́ бо́льше не . . . . .
4. Ра́ньше мнé . . . . , что Бо́б хоро́ший студéнт, а тепéрь мнé . . . . , что о́н лени́вый.
5. Всé его́ костю́мы о́чень дороги́е; о́н о́чень хорошо́ . . . . .
6. Они́ . . . . , что вы́ ско́ро приéдете к ни́м.
7. О́льга . . . . , что вы́ придёте, но́ вы́ не пришли́.
8. Мы́ бу́дем . . . . всю но́чь: за́втра у на́с экза́мены.
9. —Почему́ вы́ не закры́ли двéрь? —Э́та двéрь не . . . . .

---

[2] **Ско́лько врéмени,** like **давно́,** takes the present tense in Russian when the reference is to a period of time beginning in the past and coming up to the present, e.g., **Ско́лько врéмени** вы́ ужé здéсь **живёте?** *How long have you been living here?*

10. —Почему́ вы́ не открыва́ете э́то окно́? —Потому́ что оно́ не . . . . . —Я́ его́ откро́ю. Во́т ви́дите, оно́ . . . . .

11. Я́ . . . . , что о́н не придёт! О́н мне́ о́чень ну́жен.

12. Бу́дем . . . . , что всё бу́дет хорошо́.

13. Всё . . . . , что ва́м бу́дет ску́чно на э́той ле́кции.

14. Де́ти уже́ вста́ли, но́ они́ ещё не . . . . . Они́ . . . . через де́сять мину́т.

2. Люби́ть and нра́виться, to *like* and to *love*

In addition to the verb **люби́ть**, introduced in earlier lessons, Russian has another verb with the general meaning to *like*, to *love*; this is the verb **нра́виться**.

As we have seen, the verb **люби́ть** is transitive and takes a direct object, e.g., —Я́ люблю́ ма́му. With **нра́виться**, on the other hand, the "person liking something" is denoted by a noun or pronoun in the *dative* case, while the person or object liked is the subject of the sentence in the *nominative* case. (In other words, a construction with **нра́виться** says that something or someone "appeals *to me, to him*," etc., "is pleasing *to me, to him*," etc.)

In general, the use of **люби́ть** corresponds to *love* or *be fond of*, while **нра́виться** corresponds to *like*:

Ива́н лю́бит О́льгу.	Ivan *loves* Olga.
Мы́ лю́бим свою́ страну́.	We *love* our country.
Мне́ нра́вится ва́ша после́дняя статья́.	I *like* your last article.
А́нне нра́вится моё но́вое пла́тье.	Anna *likes* my new dress.
Мне́ не нра́вится э́та карти́на.	I don't *like* that picture.

Under the following conditions, however, **люби́ть** is used where *to like* is normally used in English:

(1) When expressing personal taste, habit, or preference (rather than judgment), particularly where familiar objects or generic categories are concerned, or where famous authors or works are referred to:

Я́ люблю́ сы́р.	I *like* cheese.
А́нна лю́бит жёлтый цве́т.	Anna *likes* the color yellow.
Я́ люблю́ Шекспи́ра.	I *like* Shakespeare.
Мо́й сы́н лю́бит му́зыку.	My son *likes* music.

(2) With infinitives:

О́н лю́бит рабо́тать но́чью.	He *likes* to work at night.

(3) In negative expressions: **не** + **люби́ть** corresponds to *not to like* or *to dislike*.

Я́ не люблю́ сы́ра.	I *don't like* cheese.
О́н не лю́бит рабо́тать но́чью.	He *dislikes* working at night.
Я́ не люблю́ э́того челове́ка.	I *dislike* that person.

In reference to persons, the difference between **люби́ть** and **нра́виться** is generally one of degree, as in English: **люби́ть** corresponding to *to love* or *to be fond of* and **нра́виться** to *to like*.

Aspects and tenses. Both **люби́ть** and **нра́виться** form perfectives with **по-**. With **люби́ть** the perfective has an inchoative meaning: *to begin, get to, come to like* (something or someone).

> Я́ ра́ньше не **люби́л** Ита́лии, а тепе́рь я́ **полюби́л** её.
> Formerly I didn't like Italy, but now I've gotten to like it.

The past tense of the perfective **понра́виться** speaks of a favorable reaction upon first contact (continuing, unless otherwise specified, into the present):

> —Ка́к ва́м **понра́вилась** пе́рвая ле́кция? —Мне́ о́чень **понра́вилась**.
> —How did you like the first lecture? —I liked it very much.

> Ма́тери не **понра́вилось**, ка́к ей отве́тил сы́н.
> The mother didn't like the way her son answered her.

> Мне́ **понра́вилась** и́х до́чь.
> I liked their daughter (she made a good impression on me).

> Тури́стам о́чень **понра́вился** Пари́ж.
> The tourists liked Paris very much.

Perfective future:

> Е́сли Финля́ндия мне́ не **понра́вится**, я́ отту́да уе́ду.
> If I don't like Finland, I shall leave.

The past tense of the imperfective **нра́виться** rather suggests liking in the past, no longer experienced in the present (*I used to like*):

> Мне́ о́чень **нра́вился** э́тот рома́н, когда́ я́ была́ молодо́й.
> I used to like that novel very much when I was young.

> Бори́су тогда́ **нра́вилась** Ни́на.
> Boris liked Nina then.

With both **люби́ть** and **нра́виться** (and some other verbs like **наде́яться**, **хоте́ть**), the word **о́чень** is used for increased intensity (*never* **о́чень мно́го**).

> Я́ **о́чень** люблю́ свою́ ма́ть.
> Студе́нтке **о́чень** нра́вится э́тот молодо́й профе́ссор.
> На́м **о́чень** понра́вился фи́льм, кото́рый мы́ вчера́ ви́дели.

PATTERN SENTENCES

Люби́ть/полюби́ть

1.	На́ш сы́н **лю́бит** матема́тику.	1. Our son likes mathematics
2.	Я́ **люблю́** весну́.	2. I like the spring.
3.	Я́ **люблю́** цветы́.	3. I like flowers.
4.	Они́ не **лю́бят** иностра́нцев.	4. They don't like foreigners.
5.	Я́ не **люблю́** хо́лода.	5. I don't like cold.
6.	**Люблю́** мо́ре!	6. I love the sea!
7.	Она́ не **лю́бит** свою́ слу́жбу.	7. She dislikes her job.
8.	Я́ не **люблю́** писа́ть пи́сьма.	8. I dislike writing letters.

9. Кто́ не лю́бит де́ньги!
10. Она́ никогда́ не люби́ла сы́на.
11. Он жи́л не́сколько ле́т в Сан-Франци́ско и о́чень полюби́л э́тот го́род.

9. Who doesn't like money!
10. She never loved her son.
11. He lived in San Francisco for a few years and took a strong liking to that city.

Нра́виться/понра́виться

1. Мне́ о́чень нра́вится ва́ша но́вая кварти́ра.
2. Мне́ нра́вится, ка́к о́н игра́ет Шопе́на.
3. Мне́ не нра́вится его́ отве́т.
4. Мне́ не нра́вится э́та шля́па; покажи́те мне́ другу́ю.
5. Ка́к ва́м э́то нра́вится!
6. О́н мне́ о́чень нра́вится как учи́тель, но мне́ не понра́вилось его́ объясне́ние э́того пра́вила.
7. —Ка́к е́й понра́вилась жи́знь в дере́вне? —О́чень понра́вилась.
8. —Вы́ ви́дели пье́су «Ви́д с моста́»? —Да́, она́ мне́ не понра́вилась.
9. О́н е́й никогда́ не нра́вился.
10. Ра́ньше мне́ нра́вился э́тот рома́н; тепе́рь не зна́ю.
11. Е́сли Калифо́рния е́й не понра́вится, она́ мо́жет уе́хать.

1. I like your new apartment very much.
2. I like the way he plays Chopin.
3. I don't like his answer.
4. I don't like that hat; show me another one.
5. How do you like that! (Expresses disapproval.)
6. I like him very much as a teacher, but I didn't like his explanation of that rule.
7. —How did she like life in the country? —She liked it very much.
8. —Did you see the play *A View from the Bridge*? —Yes, it didn't appeal to me.
9. She never liked him.
10. Formerly I used to like that novel; now I don't know.
11. If she doesn't like California, she can leave.

Compare лю́бить *and* нра́виться

1. —Ни́на, тебе́ нра́вится э́та кварти́ра? —Нра́вится; я́ люблю́ больши́е кварти́ры.
2. А́нне нра́вится э́то жёлтое пла́тье; она́ о́чень лю́бит жёлтый цве́т.
3. Я́ люблю́ Шостако́вича, но его́ после́дняя симфо́ния мне́ не нра́вится.
4. Я́ о́чень люблю́ Ни́ну, но мне́ не нра́вится, ка́к она́ одева́ется.

1. —Nina, do you like this apartment? —I like it; I like large apartments.
2. Anna likes this yellow dress; she is very fond of yellow (color).
3. I like Shostakovich, but I don't like his last symphony.
4. I am very fond of Nina, but I don't like the way she dresses.

DRILLS

A. *Insert proper forms of* нра́виться/понра́виться *in the blank spaces.*

Present Tense

1. Я́ ва́м ....?
2. Ты́ мне́ ....
3. Она́ тебе́ ....?
4. Они́ мне́ ....
5. Вы́ мне́ ....
6. Никто́ мне́ не ....

Perfective Past

1. Ни́не .... фи́льм.
2. Ива́ну .... пье́са.
3. И́х де́ти тебе́ ....?
4. Кому́ .... расска́з?
5. Каки́е города́ тебе́ ....?
6. Отцу́ .... Москва́.
7. Кто́ тебе́ ....?
8. Что́ тебе́ ....?
9. Никому́ не .... э́тот расска́з.

B. *Give the suitable form of the following verbs, and supply a pronoun whenever needed:* **нра́виться/понра́виться; люби́ть/полюби́ть.**

1. Влади́мир .... занима́ться но́чью.
2. Мы́ .... гуля́ть в лесу́.
3. Мне́ не .... твой но́вый костю́м.
4. Когда́ я́ прие́хал в Ло́ндон в пе́рвый ра́з, он мне́ о́чень не .....
5. Тепе́рь мне́ .... Ло́ндон.
6. На́м ...., ка́к ва́ш бра́т вчера́ сыгра́л ва́льс Чайко́вского.
7. На́ш учи́тель не о́чень .... Чайко́вского.
8. Мо́й бра́т ви́дел вчера́ пье́су Самуэ́ля Бе́кета, и она́ .... не ...., хотя́ о́н .... э́того писа́теля.
9. Вчера́ на вечери́нке О́льга говори́ла то́лько с Бори́сом. Ка́жется, о́н о́чень ....
10. Купи́ пла́тье то́лько, е́сли оно́ ....
11. О́льга .... шокола́д.
12. —Ива́н Ива́нович, ка́к .... вчера́шний конце́рт? —Та́к себе.

C. *Translate into Russian.*

1. I saw her brother for the first time yesterday, and liked him very much.
2. I used to like to travel, but now I no longer like (it).
3. —How do you like this cheese? —So-so; I am not very fond of cheese.
4. If we don't like the high mountains, we shall go to the seashore. My parents like both the mountains and the seashore.
5. I like to study at night; at night it is so quiet!
6. Our teacher is very fond of Turgenev's novel *Fathers and Children*[3] but his students don't like Turgenev.
7. I liked that novel very much when I read it for the first time.
8. Last year we traveled around Europe; I liked France and Italy very much.
9. —How do you like our new teacher? —Not very much. He likes to ask difficult questions.
10. —How do you like the film that you saw last evening? —I didn't like it at all, but my brother liked it.

3. Dative, instrumental, and locative plural of nouns, adjectives, and pronoun-adjectives

Each of these cases uses one plural form for all three genders; the pronouns and adjectives closely resemble the endings of the nouns. The following table presents the endings of these case forms:

	PLURAL				
	Nouns	*3rd Person Pronouns*	*Adjectives*	*Pronoun-Adjectives*	
Dat.	**-ам/-ям**	им	**-ым/-им**	**-им**	**-ем**
Instr.	**-ами/-ями**	и́ми	**-ыми/-ими**	**-ими**	**-еми**
Loc.	**-ах/-ях**	их	**-ых/-их**	**-их**	**-ех**

[3] More commonly known in English as *Fathers and Sons*.

A. Nouns.

	Nominative Singular	Nominative Plural	Dative Plural	Instrumental Plural	Locative Plural
Masc.	студе́нт до́ктор день учи́тель геро́й	студе́нты доктора́ дни учителя́ геро́и	студе́нтам доктора́м дням учителя́м геро́ям	студе́нтами доктора́ми дня́ми учителя́ми геро́ями	студе́нтах доктора́х днях учителя́х геро́ях
Neut.	окно́ по́ле	о́кна поля́	о́кнам поля́м	о́кнами поля́ми	о́кнах поля́х
Fem. I	де́вушка ку́хня	де́вушки ку́хни	де́вушкам ку́хням	де́вушками ку́хнями	де́вушках ку́хнях
Fem. II	крова́ть	крова́ти	крова́тям	крова́тями	крова́тях

The following nouns have dative, instrumental, and locative plural forms which follow the nominative *plural*.

Nominative Singular	Nominative Plural	Dative Plural	Instrumental Plural	Locative Plural
брат	бра́тья	бра́тьям	бра́тьями	бра́тьях
стул	сту́лья	сту́льям	сту́льями	сту́льях
перо́	пе́рья	пе́рьям	пе́рьями	пе́рьях
де́рево	дере́вья	дере́вьям	дере́вьями	дере́вьях
лист	ли́стья	ли́стьям	ли́стьями	ли́стьях
муж	мужья́	мужья́м	мужья́ми	мужья́х
сын	сыновья́	сыновья́м	сыновья́ми	сыновья́х
друг	друзья́	друзья́м	друзья́ми	друзья́х
сосе́д	сосе́ди	сосе́дям	сосе́дями	сосе́дях
вре́мя	времена́	времена́м	времена́ми	времена́х
и́мя	имена́	имена́м	имена́ми	имена́х
мать	ма́тери	матеря́м	матеря́ми	матеря́х
дочь	до́чери	дочеря́м	дочерьми́	дочеря́х
(ребёнок)	де́ти	де́тям	детьми́	де́тях
(челове́к)	лю́ди	лю́дям	людьми́	лю́дях

The distinct instrumental ending **-ьми́** serves for four nouns: дочерьми́, детьми́, людьми́, and лошадьми́.

B. Third Person pronouns, adjectives, and pronoun-adjectives.

Nominative Plural	Dative Plural	Instrumental Plural	Locative Plural
они́	им	и́ми	их
но́вые	но́вым	но́выми	но́вых
си́ние	си́ним	си́ними	си́них
хоро́шие	хоро́шим	хоро́шими	хоро́ших
ру́сские	ру́сским	ру́сскими	ру́сских
мои́	мои́м	мои́ми	мои́х
на́ши	на́шим	на́шими	на́ших
одни́	одни́м	одни́ми	одни́х
э́ти	э́тим	э́тими	э́тих
те	тем	те́ми	тех
все	всем	все́ми	всех

C. Time expressions with по and dative plural.

The preposition **по**+the dative plural of names of days of the week, and the words **у́тро**, **ве́чер**, and **ночь**, imply regular repetition of an action during those periods:

Мы́ всегда́ до́ма **по** вечера́м.
Evenings we're always at home.

По четверга́м я́ хожу́ в кино́.
On Thursdays I go to the movies.

О́н тепе́рь рабо́тает **по** ноча́м.
He works nights now.

PATTERN SENTENCES

Dative Plural

1. Со́ня посла́ла де́ньги свои́м ста́рым роди́телям.
2. О́льга Петро́вна купи́ла пода́рки все́м свои́м де́тям.
3. Учи́тельница объясня́ет пра́вила но́вым ученика́м.
4. Роди́телям ча́сто ка́жется, что и́х де́ти о́чень у́мные.
5. **По** вто́рникам мы́ ча́сто хо́дим к на́шим сосе́дям в го́сти.

1. Sonya sent money to her old parents.
2. Olga Petrovna bought presents for all her children.
3. The teacher explains rules to the new pupils.
4. Parents often think their children are very intelligent.
5. On Tuesdays we often go to visit our neighbors.

ORAL DRILL

Supply correct forms of the dative plural.

1. В э́том кла́ссе у́мные студе́нты и студе́нтки. Кому́ учи́тель объясня́ет пра́вила? . . . . и . . . . .
2. У нас есть но́вые друзья́. Кому́ мы пи́шем? Мы пи́шем . . . .
3. Тут живу́т мои́ дороги́е роди́тели. Я ча́сто хожу́ к . . . .
4. У Ни́ны есть хоро́шие подру́ги. Ни́на покупа́ет пода́рки . . . .
5. Мои́ бра́тья и сёстры живу́т далеко́. Я ча́сто пишу́ . . . . и . . . . .
6. Всё мои́ профессора́ задаю́т мне вопро́сы. Я отвеча́ю . . . .

PATTERN SENTENCES

Instrumental Plural

1. Мы слу́шаем и слы́шим уша́ми.	1. We listen and hear with our ears.
2. Мы ви́дим и смо́трим глаза́ми.	2. We see and look with our eyes.
3. —Чем мы берём ве́щи? —Мы берём их па́льцами.	3. —What do we take things with? —We take take them with our fingers.
4. Ра́ньше лю́ди всё де́лали рука́ми, а тепе́рь всё де́лают маши́нами.	4. Formerly people used to do everything with their hands, but now they do everything with machines.
5. —Каки́ми ножа́ми мясни́к ре́жет мя́со? —Он ре́жет ра́зными ножа́ми—больши́ми и ма́ленькими.	5. —What kind of knives does the butcher cut meat with? —He cuts with different kinds of knives—big and little ones.

Instrumental with the preposition **с**

1. —С кем Серёжа и Алёша бы́ли на вечери́нке? —Они́ бы́ли там **с те́ми** же ми́лыми де́вушк**ами**, **с кото́рыми** они́ бы́ли на ле́кции.	1. —With whom were Seryozha and Alyosha at the party? —They were there with the same nice girls with whom they were at the lecture.
2. Вчера́ мы бы́ли в теа́тре и случа́йно встре́тились **с** на́шими ста́рыми друзья́ми Лунё́выми.	2. Yesterday we went to the theater and by chance met our old friends, the Lunyovs.
3. Я вчера́ обе́дала в рестора́не **со** все́ми мои́ми бра́тьями и сёстрами и **с** их детьми́.	3. Yesterday I had dinner at a restaurant with all my brothers and sisters and their children.

DRILL

Place the words in the right-hand column in the instrumental.

Они́ дово́льны . . . . .
> всё студе́нты
> свои́ но́вые друзья́
> на́ши де́ти
> э́ти кни́ги
> кра́сные кре́сла

Мы рабо́тали там с (со) . . . . .
> молоды́е доктора́
> сове́тские писа́тели
> хоро́шие инжене́ры
> у́мные де́вушки
> всё учителя́
> но́вые друзья́
> ва́ши сыновья́

PATTERN SENTENCES

Locative Plural

1. В э́тих но́вых дома́х живу́т бога́тые лю́ди.
2. Колхо́зники и колхо́зницы живу́т в колхо́зах. Они́ рабо́тают в колхо́зных поля́х, сада́х и леса́х.
3. В бога́тых колхо́зах есть мя́со, ры́ба, моло́чные проду́кты и о́вощи.
4. Расскажи́те на́м о но́вых францу́зских пье́сах и фи́льмах, кото́рые вы́ ви́дели во Фра́нции.
5. Я́ ду́маю, что мы́ говори́м о те́х же лю́дях.
6. Я́ о́чень люблю́ Соединённые Шта́ты. Я́ мно́го ле́т живу́ в Соединённых Шта́тах.

1. Rich people are living in those new houses.
2. Men and women collective farmers live in kolkhozes. They work in the kolkhoz fields, gardens, and woods.
3. In well-to-do kolkhozes they have meat, fish, milk products, and vegetables.
4. Tell us about the new French plays and films which you saw in France.
5. I believe that we're talking about the same people.
6. I am very fond of the United States. For many years I have been living in the United States.

ORAL DRILL

Read the statement and answer the question which follows in terms of the statement.

1. Я́ люблю́ мои́х у́мных, приле́жных студе́нтов. О ко́м я́ ду́маю?
2. Андре́й никогда́ не жи́л в больши́х города́х. В каки́х города́х о́н жи́л?
3. У меня́ есть хоро́шие друзья́. О ко́м я́ ча́сто говорю́?
4. Она́ лю́бит дороги́е, удо́бные гости́ницы. Где́ она́ лю́бит жи́ть?
5. В э́том го́роде огро́мные заво́ды. Где́ рабо́тают э́ти рабо́чие?
6. У А́нны есть свои́ де́ньги. О чём она́ мно́го ду́мает?
7. Моя́ ма́ть лю́бит мои́х дете́й. О ко́м она́ всем расска́зывает?
8. Профе́ссор зна́ет все́ э́ти фа́кты. О чём о́н пи́шет?

4. Prepositions за, перед, над, под, ме́жду with the instrumental[4]

A. За *behind, beyond, on the other side of.*

За на́шим до́мом есть са́д.
Behind our house there is a garden.

За реко́й есть ма́ленькая дере́вня.
There is a small village on the other side of the river.

О́н сиде́л за мно́й.
He sat behind me.

Ива́н шёл за мно́й.
Ivan walked behind me (he followed me).

It will be remembered that за with the instrumental is also used to express "going for," "going to buy," "going to get," etc.:

Ива́н пошёл в магази́н за хле́бом.
Ivan went to the store for bread.

---

[4] Two of these prepositions, за and под, also take the accusative case when they express direction; this will be treated in Unit 24.

Ива́н пришёл **за** мн**ой**.
Ivan came for me (to get me).

Idioms with **за***:*

за́ городом
(be) out of town, in the country

сиде́ть за столо́м
to be at the table

за за́втраком, за обе́дом, за у́жином
at breakfast, at dinner, at supper

за угло́м
(be) around the corner

заграни́цей (adverb formed with за + instr. of **грани́ца** *border*)
(be) abroad

B. Перед *in front of; before (for place and time).*

Place:

Перед до́мом стоя́л автомоби́ль.
In front of the house stood a car.

Time:

Перед уро́ком мы́ кури́ли в коридо́ре.
Before class we smoked in the hall.

Перед is close in its time sense to **до** (+ *genitive*); **до** means *before* (any time before), while **перед** is used mostly for *just before* or *immediately before*.

Я́ мно́го рабо́тал **до** обе́да.
I worked a lot before dinner (all the time before; unspecified).

Я́ вы́мыл ру́ки **перед** обе́дом.
I washed my hands before dinner (when dinner was ready).

C. Над *above, over.*

Над гора́ми ту́чи.
There are clouds above the mountains.

На́ша кварти́ра **над** магази́ном.
Our apartment is over the store.

Idioms with **над***:*

рабо́тать над *to work at.*

О́н на́чал **рабо́тать над** но́вым рома́ном.
He started working on a new novel.

смея́ться над *to laugh at, make fun of.*

На́ш учи́тель никогда́ не **смеётся над** на́шими оши́бками.
Our teacher never makes fun of our mistakes.

D. Под *below, under, underneath.*

Кни́га лежа́ла **под** столо́м.
The book was lying under the table.

With names of towns, **под** means *near*:

У ни́х е́сть да́ча **под** Москво́й.

The forms **передо**, **надо**, and **подо** (instead of **перед**, **над**, and **под**), are required before the pronoun **мной**.

Передо мно́й стена́. Надо мно́й потоло́к. Подо мно́й по́л.

E. Ме́жду *between.*

На́ш университе́т стои́т **ме́жду** реко́й и городски́м па́рком.
Our university stands between the river and the city park.

Э́то **ме́жду на́ми**, коне́чно.
This, of course, is between us.

Ме́жду про́чим.
By the way, incidentally.

PATTERN SENTENCES

1. У ка́ждого челове́ка должна́ бы́ть кры́ша **над** голово́й.
2. В на́шей столо́вой **над** столо́м больша́я старомо́дная ла́мпа.
3. **Над на́ми** се́рые ту́чи, а та́м, **над** зелёными леса́ми и поля́ми, си́нее не́бо.
4. Как прия́тно, когда́ **под** нога́ми мя́гкий ковёр!
5. **Под** э́тими больши́ми дере́вьями да́же в жа́ркий де́нь не жа́рко!
6. Моя́ соба́ка лю́бит спа́ть **под** мои́м дива́ном.
7. **За** на́шим до́мом ма́ленький дво́р, а перед до́мом са́д.
8. Ну́жно мы́ть ру́ки **перед** едо́й.
9. **Перед** дива́ном стои́т сто́лик, а на сто́лике ва́за с кра́сными цвета́ми.
10. Я́ ви́жу велосипе́д **за** де́ревом.
11. И́х дере́вня та́м **за** реко́й.

1. Each man must have a roof over his head.
2. In our dining room there is a large old-fashioned lamp above the table.
3. Above us are gray clouds, and there, over the green woods and fields, is blue sky.
4. How pleasant to have a soft carpet under the feet!
5. Under those big trees it is not hot, even on a hot day!
6. My dog likes to sleep underneath my sofa.
7. Behind our house is a small yard, and in front of the house is a garden.
8. One must wash his hands before eating.
9. In front of the sofa is a little table, and on the table a vase with red flowers.
10. I see a bicycle behind the tree.
11. Their village is over there on the other side of the river.

12. Мы́ шли́ **за ва́ми**.
13. На́ш до́м **ме́жду** шко́лой и ба́нком.
14. **Ме́жду** о́кнами по́лка с ру́сскими кни́гами.

12. We were walking behind you.
13. Our house is between the school and the bank.
14. Between the windows there is a bookshelf with Russian books.

IDIOMATIC USAGES

ме́жду

1. Его́ после́дняя пье́са, по-мо́ему, о́чень ску́чная, но́ э́то, коне́чно, **ме́жду на́ми**.
2. Я́ забы́л ва́м, **ме́жду про́чим**, сказа́ть, что в четы́ре меня́ не бу́дет до́ма.
3. **Ме́жду про́чим**, вы́ отве́тили на его́ письмо́?

1. His last play, in my opinion, is very boring, but that, of course, is between ourselves.
2. I forgot to tell you, by the way, that at four I won't be at home.
3. Incidentally, did you answer his letter?

над

1. —**Над че́м** о́н смеётся? —**На́до мно́й, над те́м**, что я́ сказа́л.
2. —**Над че́м** вы́ тепе́рь рабо́таете? —**Гла́вным о́бразом над** диссерта́цией.

1. —What is he laughing at? —At me, at what I said.
2. —What are you working on now? —For the most part on a dissertation.

за

1. Мы́ сиде́ли **за столо́м** и у́жинали, когда́ Ко́ля пришёл ко мне́ за сигаре́тами.
2. Снача́ла Зо́я пошла́ на по́чту **за ма́рками**, а пото́м в магази́н **за проду́ктами**.
3. Мы́ сейча́с идём **за Бори́сом**, и пото́м придём всё вме́сте к ва́м.

1. We were sitting at the table and having supper when Kolya came to see me to get cigarettes.
2. First Zoya went to the post office for stamps, and then to the grocery store for food.
3. We are on our way to pick up Boris now, and then we'll all come together to your place.

DRILLS

A. *Fill in suitable prepositions.*

1. Моя́ крова́ть стои́т .... окно́м и по́лкой.
2. .... на́шим до́мом стои́т маши́на.
3. .... на́ми кры́ша.
4. О́н рабо́тает .... но́вым рома́ном.
5. О́н говори́л с профе́ссором .... ле́кцией.
6. Смирно́вы живу́т .... угло́м.
7. Зо́я пришла́ .... обе́дом и ушла́ .... обе́да.
8. Ма́ть посла́ла меня́ .... молоко́м.
9. Я́ пришёл к ва́м .... сове́том.
10. Журна́л лежа́л на полу́ .... столо́м.
11. .... дива́ном сто́лик, а .... дива́ном карти́на.
12. Я́ сиде́л .... отцо́м и ма́терью.
13. .... на́ми си́нее не́бо.
14. Почему́ кни́ги лежа́т .... столо́м, а не .... столе́?
15. Ты́ всегда́ смеёшься .... мно́й!
16. Вы́ на́с не ви́дели; мы́ сиде́ли .... ва́ми.

B. *Complete the sentences by putting the words on the right in the proper case.*

Больши́е ту́чи бы́ли над .....

те́ дома́
широ́кое по́ле
моя́ голова́
на́ши го́ловы
высо́кие го́ры

Conversation

Кла́ссная ко́мната, 9 часо́в утра́

Учи́тельница. —Доброе у́тро!

Класс. —Доброе у́тро!

У. —Ну́, ка́к вы́ сего́дня пожива́ете?

К. —Хорошо́, спаси́бо. —Та́к себе. —Не осо́бенно хорошо́. —Ничего́.

У. —Ну́, ра́да э́то слы́шать. Како́й чуде́сный де́нь сего́дня! Почти́ весна́! Пра́вда?

К. —Мм... да́...

У. —Фили́пп, откро́йте кни́гу и начни́те чита́ть.

Фили́пп. —«Бы́ло ра́ннее весе́ннее у́тро. Москва́ ещё спала́.»

У. —Неплохо́. Но произноше́ние ещё не совсе́м пра́вильное: в сло́ве «Москва́» «о́» произно́сится как «а́». Объясни́те мне́, како́е е́сть пра́вило фоне́тики? Вы́ ведь всё зна́ете э́то пра́вило.

К. —Когда́ не́т ударе́ния на «о́», «о́» произно́сится как «а́». Но недоста́точно зна́ть пра́вило, на́м нужна́ пра́ктика.

У. —Коне́чно нужна́! Говори́те дру́г с дру́гом по-ру́сски, ходи́те на ру́сские фи́льмы, расска́зывайте мне́ по-ру́сски всё, что ва́м прихо́дит в го́лову, занима́йтесь бо́льше. А сейча́с, для пра́ктики, повтори́те три́ ра́за «Москва́».

К. —Москва́, Москва́, Москва́.

У. —Дово́льно. Тепе́рь почти́ хорошо́. Не́лли, тепе́рь вы́ чита́йте.

Не́лли. —«На у́лицах и в дома́х бы́ло ещё ти́хо. То́лько в одно́м до́ме, за Москво́й-реко́й...»

У. —Совсе́м не пло́хо, Не́лли. Но мя́гкое «л» (эль) в сло́ве «то́лько» вы́ произно́сите твёрдо как в сло́ве «по́лка». Произнеси́те всё вме́сте не́сколько ра́з «то́лько, ско́лько, то́лько, ско́лько».

К. —То́лько, ско́лько, то́лько, ско́лько, то́лько, ско́лько.

У. —Дово́льно. Тепе́рь почти́ хорошо́. По́мните, что когда́ вы́ пи́шете э́ти слова́—они́ пи́шутся с мя́гким зна́ком по́сле эль. Тепе́рь закро́йте кни́ги и расскажи́те, каки́ми слова́ми начина́ется расска́з, и что́ идёт да́льше. А́нна, начни́те расска́зывать.

А́нна. —Я́ не по́мню все́х сло́в и выраже́ний. Тру́дно всё запо́мнить!

У. —Почему́ тру́дно? Вы́ про́сто недоста́точно занима́етесь. Во́т и всё. Вы́ должны́ бо́льше рабо́тать над зада́ниями, и тогда́ ва́м всё бу́дет легко́, и запомина́ть и расска́зывать, и... получа́ть хоро́шие отме́тки. Но́ вы́ предпочита́ете спра́шивать «что́ зна́чит то́, что́ зна́чит э́то»!

А. —Что́ зна́чит предпочита́ете?

У. —Э́то зна́чит «prefer». Бо́б, расскажи́те вы́ на́м, на како́м заво́де рабо́тал молодо́й инжене́р-меха́ник Андре́й Ко́лосов?

К. —Бо́ба не́т в кла́ссе!

У. —Его́ не́т? Кто́ из ва́с зна́ет, что с ни́м?

Том. —Я́ ви́дел его́ вчера́. Мы́ случа́йно встре́тились в кино́ и, ме́жду про́чим, ви́дели замеча́тельный япо́нский фи́льм. Во́т как фи́льм начина́ется: япо́нский при́нц лю́бит европе́йскую де́вушку, но оте́ц э́того при́нца и ма́ть э́той де́вушки...

У. (Звонóк.) —Кáк, ужé? —Как бы́стро кóнчился урóк! Мы́ кóнчим диктáнт в другóй рáз. На зáвтра прочитáйте ещё двé главы́, переведи́те двáдцать предложéний, и знáйте отвéты на вопрóсы. Занимáйтесь, занимáйтесь, занимáйтесь. До зáвтра!

К. —До зáвтра.

Отвéтьте на вопрóсн по-рýсски.

1. Каки́ми словáми начинáется расскáз, котóрый ученики́ прочитáли на сегóдня? 2. Почемý ученики́ не совсéм прáвильно произнóсят нéкоторые словá? 3. Чтó знáчит «предпочитáть»? 4. Почемý Áнна не мóжет отвéтить учи́тельнице на её вопрóс? 5. Почемý Бóб не мóг отвéтить на вопрóс учи́тельницы? 6. Éсли ученики́ хотя́т дéлать успéхи (progress) и получáть хорóшие отмéтки, чтó они́ должны́ дéлать?

DRILLS

A. *First read each sentence to yourself and make sure you understand it. Then read it aloud in Russian and translate in into idiomatic English.*

1. По вечерáм Ви́ктор лю́бит занимáться в своéй ти́хой кóмнате. 2. —Чéм óн тепéрь занимáется? —Глáвным óбразом математикой и рýсским языкóм. 3. Всё, что вы́ здéсь ви́дите, Ивáн Ивáнович сдéлал свои́ми рукáми. 4. В Соединённых Штáтах, глáвным óбразом в мáленьких городáх, недостáточно врачéй. Это, мéжду прóчим, тáк почти́ во всéх странáх ми́ра. 5. Я́ не пóмню, каки́ми словáми начинáется её письмó, нó я́ пóмню, что начáло письмá показáлось мнé стрáнным. 6. Никомý не нрáвится нáш нóвый начáльник. Всё егó почемý-то боя́тся и надéются, что óн не дóлго бýдет с нáми. 7. —Лéна, я надéюсь, что ты́ приéдешь к нáм в дерéвню в бýдущую суббóту? Приезжáй! —Бою́сь, что не приéду. Я́ рабóтаю над трýдным доклáдом, котóрый я́ должнá прочитáть через недéлю в нáшем клýбе. 8. Мéжду прóчим, вы́ мóжет быть случáйно знáете áдрес Петрóва? Éсли вы́ егó знáете, бýдьте добры́, дáйте мнé егó. 9. Мнé кáжется стрáнным, что óн всéх и всегó бои́тся! Кáжется, никтó ничегó плохóго емý никогдá не сдéлал. 10. Передáйте привéт всéм нáшим друзья́м. 11. Я́ ви́жу, что Óля купи́ла цветы́, но бою́сь, что онá забы́ла купи́ть папирóсы; тогдá я́ должнá бýду пойти́ за папирóсами! 12. Лéна хорошó одевáется. У неё прекрáсный вкýс.

B. *Review Translation.*

1. In front of me is a yellow armchair and behind me is a blue sofa. 2. I am standing behind the yellow armchair and in front of the blue sofa. 3. They live above us. 4. There is a soft, thick rug in my room; the rug is beneath the table and the armchair. 5. At the concert Nina was sitting between Olga and Ivan. 6. Whose children are playing in front of our windows? 7. It seems they are not afraid of us, but we are afraid of them. 8. —Incidentally, who lives in these expensive hotels? —Mostly Americans. 9. I didn't like what he said! 10. Our Aunt Vera always needs money. For some reason she never has any money. Last night she again came to us for money. 11. —How long did she work on her book? —It seems, for a very long time.

12. Those two girls dress alike.   13. —By the way, what do you do evenings? —I often study at my sister's. Sometimes we study together.   14. He thinks about his friends and likes to send presents to all his old friends.   15. I don't like the presents which I received.

Vocabulary

весе́нний spring (*adj.*)
вкус taste
внима́тельный attentive
всё-таки all the same, still, nevertheless
гро́мкий loud
звон.о́к (*gen.* -ка́) bell
знак sign
мя́гкий [ɱа́х̣кij] soft
мясни́к butcher
непра́вильно incorrect(ly), wrong
о́вощи (*masc. pl.*; *gen. pl.* овоще́й) vegetables
одина́ково alike, identically, in the same way
по́лдень (*masc.*) noon
по́лночь (*fem.*) midnight
предложе́ние sentence; proposition, offer
проду́кты (*masc. pl.*) produce, products

произноше́ние pronunciation
рабо́чий work (*adj.*), working; workman (*adj. used as noun*)
случа́йно by chance
смешно́й funny
сто́лик little table
твёрдый hard, firm
то́чно exactly[5]
ту́ча (storm) cloud
ударе́ние accent, stress
уж (уже́) already
у́ши (*nom. pl. of* у́хо) ears
цвет.о́к (*gen.* -ка́; *pl.* цвет.ы́, -о́в, etc.)[6] flower
чуде́сный marvelous, wonderful
япо́нский Japanese (*adj.*)

VERBS

(For other reflexive verbs see Section 1.)

занима́ться (imperf., I) to study, be occupied with (+ *instr.*)
каза́ться (imperf., I: кажу́сь, ка́жешься) to seem, appear (+ *instr.*)
мыть (imperf., I: мо́.ю, -ешь), помы́ть or вы́мыть (perf., I) to wash (*trans.*)
одева́ть (imperf., I), оде́ть (perf., I: оде́н.у, -ешь) to dress (*trans.*)
переводи́ть (imperf., II: перевожу́, перево́дишь), перевести́ (perf., I: перевед.у́, -ёшь; past: перевёл, перевело́, etc.) to translate
поня́ть (perf. of понима́ть, I: пойм.у́, -ёшь; past: по́нял, поняла́, по́няли) to understand, comprehend, grasp
посла́ть (perf. of посыла́ть, I: пошл.ю́, -ёшь) to send
произноси́ть (imperf., II: произн.ошу́, -о́сишь), произнести́ (perf., I: произнес.у́, -ёшь; past: произнёс, произнесло́, etc.) to pronounce
просыпа́ться (imperf., I), просну́ться (perf., I: просн.у́сь, -ёшься) to wake up (*intrans.*)
ре́зать (imperf., I: ре́ж.у, -ешь) to cut, cut up
раздева́ть (imperf., I), разде́ть (perf., I: разде́н.у, -ешь) to undress (*trans.*)
собира́ть (imperf., I), собра́ть (perf., I: собер.у́, -ёшь) to collect, gather (*trans.*)
собира́ться, собра́ться to assemble (*intrans.*), come together, get ready to (+ *infin.*)

---

[5] **Ро́вно** is used with specific measurements in the sense of *exactly*, e.g., **ро́вно** в се́мь часо́в, *but* Я то́чно не зна́ю, *I don't know exactly.*
[6] Note that the word for *color* is **цвет**; *plural* цвет.а́, -о́в, etc.

EXPRESSIONS

та́к себе́ so-so

ме́жду про́чим by the way, incidentally

гла́вным о́бразом chiefly, for the most part

по це́лым дня́м for days on end

провали́ться (perf., II) на экза́мене to fail an exam

вы́держать (perf., II) экза́мен to pass an exam

наде́яться на (+ *acc.*) to rely on

сиде́ть за столо́м to be at the table

опа́здывать/опозда́ть на ча́с to be an hour late

Что́ идёт да́льше? What comes next?

Что́ с ним? What is the matter with him?

кто́ из ва́с? who of you?

До за́втра. Good-bye till tomorrow.

The verbal prefixes по- and про- • Verbs of position: *lying, sitting, standing* • The verb становиться/стать • Masculine nouns in -a and -я • Genitive plural of nouns (supplement) • Nouns and adjectives of nationality • Declension of masculine nouns in -анин/-янин • Review of declension in the plural • Adjectival words expressing quantity • Conversation 1: Познакóмьтесь пожáлуйста • Conversation 2: На приёме у Орлóвых

Unit 20

Grammar

1. The verbal prefixes по- and про-

A. По-.   Many verbs may form a perfective using the prefix **по-**. With some verbs, this prefix, while it changes the aspect, does not affect the meaning of the basic verb; the following are among imperfective-perfective pairs in which the two forms differ in aspect only:

Imperfective	*Perfective*
обéдать	пообéдать
зáвтракать	позáвтракать
совéтовать	посовéтовать
вéрить	повéрить
звонúть	позвонúть
смотрéть	посмотрéть
etc.	

With very many verbs, on the other hand, **по-** produces perfectives meaning *limited duration:* an action has been performed, or a state or condition has lasted "for a while" and then has been terminated, but without any goal, result, or conclusion having been reached.

погуля́ть	to go for a walk, walk for a while
порабóтать	to do some work
поговорúть	to have a talk
поспáть	to take a nap
подýмать	to think a while, give some thought
почитáть	to read for a while
etc.	

311

Perfectives with **по-** are especially frequent with verbs describing actions that do not ordinarily lead to any result or completion; such are verbs of state or condition, in particular, verbs of position (*sitting, lying, standing*):

сиде́ть—посиде́ть	to sit for a while
лежа́ть—полежа́ть	to lie (rest) for a while
стоя́ть—постоя́ть	to stand for a while

B. Про-. Verbs of state or condition (including *sitting, lying, standing*) may also be prefixed with **про-**; forms with **про-** are used when it is felt that the time spent in a state or condition (or position) has been long (sometimes excessively long); these verbs are transitive, and the time spent must always be indicated in the accusative (if not necessarily expressed in units of time):

Он **просиде́л** у на́с весь ве́чер.

Он **пролежа́л** два́ ме́сяца в больни́це.

Он **простоя́л** всю доро́гу.

Он **про́жил** всю жи́знь в Москве́.

Note also:

побы́ть—пробы́ть   to stay, spend some time somewhere

PATTERN SENTENCES

по- (*time limitation*)

1. **Почита́йте** газе́ту; я ско́ро приду́ обра́тно.

2. Я **посижу́** и **покурю́**, а ты́ пока́ оде́нься.

3. Я **полежу́** и мо́жет быть **посплю́**, а пото́м мы́ **поговори́м**.

4. На́шим де́тям бу́дет хорошо́ **пожи́ть** две́ или три́ неде́ли в дере́вне.

5. Мы́ **про́жили** та́м два́дцать ле́т!

1. Read the newspaper for a while; I'll soon come back.

2. I'll sit a while and have a smoke, and meanwhile you get dressed.

3. I'll lie down for a while and maybe I'll sleep a bit, and then we'll have a talk.

4. It will be good for our children to spend two or three weeks in the country.

5. We lived there for twenty years!

по- (*simple perfective*)

6. —**Поду́майте** об э́той пробле́ме и **позвони́те** мне́. —Ла́дно. **Поду́маю** и **позвоню́**.

7. Тру́дно **пове́рить**, что е́й уже́ три́дцать ле́т! Я́ не **пове́рил** е́й, когда́ она́ мне́ э́то сказа́ла.

8. Ко́ля, ка́жется, в саду́. **Посмотри́**, что́ он та́м де́лает.

9. —Мы́ е́дем за́втра в дере́вню? —**Посмо́трим** кака́я бу́дет пого́да.

10. **Послу́шайте**, что́ она́ говори́т!

6. —Think over that problem and call me up. —All right. I'll think it over and call.

7. It's hard to believe that she's thirty already! I didn't believe her when she told me that.

8. Kolya's in the garden, I think. Look and see what he's doing there.

9. —Are we going to the country tomorrow? —We'll see what the weather will be like.

10. Listen to what she's saying!

2. Verbs of position: *lying, sitting, standing*

Three verbs denoting position: **лежа́ть**, **сиде́ть**, and **стоя́ть**, have been given earlier. They form their perfectives by prefixing **по-**, with the meaning of limitation in time: **полежа́ть**, **посиде́ть**, **постоя́ть** *to lie, sit,* and *stand* "*for a while,*" "*for a certain period of time.*" The prefix **про-** also produces perfectives, usually signifying a longer period of time spent lying, sitting, or standing.

The three verbs of position are of the second conjugation.

To lie		To sit		To stand	
Imperf.	*Perf.*	*Imperf.*	*Perf.*	*Imperf.*	*Perf.*
лежа́ть	**полежа́ть**	**сиде́ть**	**посиде́ть**	**стоя́ть**	**постоя́ть**
Present	*Future*	*Present*	*Future*	*Present*	*Future*
лежу́	полежу́	сижу́	посижу́	стою́	постою́
лежи́шь	etc.	сиди́шь	etc.	стои́шь	etc.
лежи́т		сиди́т		стои́т	
лежи́м		сиди́м		стои́м	
лежи́те		сиди́те		стои́те	
лежа́т		сидя́т		стоя́т	

Past

лежа́л	полежа́л	сиде́л	посиде́л	стоя́л	постоя́л
лежа́ло	etc.	сиде́ло	etc.	стоя́ло	etc.
лежа́ла		сиде́ла		стоя́ла	
лежа́ли		сиде́ли		стоя́ли	

Imperative

лежи́	полежи́	сиди́	посиди́	сто́й	посто́й
лежи́те	полежи́те	сиди́те	посиди́те	сто́йте	посто́йте

Another set of three verbs is used to denote *assuming* a lying, sitting, or standing position, i.e., lying down, sitting down, and standing up. The imperfectives of two of these new verbs, **ложи́ться** (*to lie down*) and **сади́ться** (*to sit down*), have the **-ся** element, which although absent in their perfectives, **лечь** and **сесть**, does not alter their basic meanings. These two perfective verbs present certain irregularities in both the present stem and the past tense, as will be seen from the conjugation patterns below:

To lie down		To sit down		To stand up	
Imperf.	*Perf.*	*Imperf.*	*Perf.*	*Imperf.*	*Perf.*
ложи́ться	**лечь**	**сади́ться**	**сесть**	**встава́ть**	**встать**
Present	*Future*	*Present*	*Future*	*Present*	*Future*
ложу́сь	ля́гу	сажу́сь	ся́ду	встаю́	вста́ну
ложи́шься	ля́жешь	сади́шься	ся́дешь	встаёшь	вста́нешь
ложи́тся	ля́жет	сади́тся	ся́дет	встаёт	вста́нет
ложи́мся	ля́жем	сади́мся	ся́дем	встаём	вста́нем
ложи́тесь	ля́жете	сади́тесь	ся́дете	встаёте	вста́нете
ложа́тся	ля́гут	садя́тся	ся́дут	встаю́т	вста́нут

Past

ложи́лся	лёг	сади́лся	сел	встава́л	встал
ложи́лось	легло́	сади́лось	се́ло	встава́ло	вста́ло
ложи́лась	легла́	сади́лась	се́ла	встава́ла	вста́ла
ложи́лись	легли́	сади́лись	се́ли	встава́ли	вста́ли

Imperative

ложи́сь	ляг	сади́сь	сядь	встава́й	встань
ложи́тесь	ля́гте	сади́тесь	ся́дьте	встава́йте	вста́ньте

Idiomatic uses of verbs of position.

(1) As has already been seen, the verbs **стоя́ть** and **лежа́ть** are commonly used to describe the position of certain objects, when in English the link verbs *is* and *are* are more common:

Слова́рь **стои́т** на по́лке.	The dictionary *is* on the shelf.
Стака́ны **стоя́т** на столе́.	The glasses *are* on the table.
Газе́та **лежи́т** на полу́.	The newspaper *is* on the floor.

(2) The imperfective **сиде́ть** and the perfectives **посиде́ть** and **просиде́ть**, often translate, especially in colloquial speech, as *to stay*, or *to spend time*:

Они́ лю́бят **сиде́ть** до́ма.	They like to stay at home.
Посиди́те у нас ещё немно́го!	Stay with us a little longer!
Вчера́ они́ **просиде́ли** у нас весь ве́чер.	Yesterday, they spent the whole evening with us.

(3) The verb **ложи́ться/лечь**, with or without the infinitive **спать**, *to sleep*, often means *to go to bed*:

Мы **ложи́мся** ра́но.	We go to bed early.
Вчера́ мы **легли́** о́чень по́здно.	Yesterday we went to bed very late.
О́н всегда́ **ложи́лся** в де́сять.	He always went to bed at ten.

(4) The verb **сади́ться/сесть** with **на** + *accusative* renders *to get on* or *to take a train, a bus*, etc.:

Мы **ся́дем на** авто́бус на то́м углу́.	We'll get on the bus at that corner.
Где́ вы **се́ли на** по́езд?	Where did you take the train?
Я́ всегда́ е́зжу в Ленингра́д на по́езде, а в Ленингра́де **сажу́сь на** авто́бус.	I always go to Leningrad by train, but in Leningrad I take the bus.

PATTERN SENTENCES

сади́ться/сесть

1. Я́ никогда́ не **сажу́сь** на э́тот сту́л; на нём неудо́бно **сиде́ть**. Я́ **ся́ду** на то́т.
2. На э́то кре́сло никто́ не **сади́тся**. На нём лю́бит **сиде́ть** то́лько на́ша соба́ка.
3. Ни́на **сиде́ла** на дива́не, пото́м **вста́ла** с дива́на и **се́ла** на сту́л.
4. Она́ **посиде́ла** на сту́ле, пото́м **вста́ла** со сту́ла и опя́ть **се́ла** на дива́н.
5. И та́к она́ **сади́лась** и **встава́ла**, **сади́лась** и **встава́ла** не́сколько ра́з!
6. —**Сади́тесь**,[1] пожа́луйста! —Спаси́бо. Я́ хочу́ **се́сть** ря́дом с ва́ми. Хорошо́? —Коне́чно!
7. Я́ **ся́ду** у окна́, а вы́ **ся́дьте** ря́дом. Мы́ поси́ди́м та́м, поговори́м, и пойдём в кабине́т порабо́тать.
8. Приходи́те! Мы́ уже́ **сади́мся** за сто́л.

1. I never sit down on that chair; it's uncomfortable to sit on it. I'll sit down on that one.
2. No one sits on that chair. Only our dog likes to sit on it.
3. Nina was sitting on the couch, then got up from the couch and sat down on a chair.
4. She sat on the chair for a while, then got up from the chair and sat down again on the couch.
5. And so she sat down and got up, sat down and got up several times!
6. —Sit down please! —Thank you. I would like to sit beside you. All right? —Of course!
7. I will sit down at the window, and you sit by me. We will sit there a little, have a talk, and (then) go to the study to work for awhile.
8. Come! We're already sitting down at the table.

ложи́ться/лечь

1. Ири́на лю́бит **ложи́ться** ра́но и **встава́ть** ра́но.
2. Ле́том она́ **ложи́лась** в де́сять и **встава́ла** в ше́сть.
3. Илья́ Ильи́ч **ложи́тся** ра́но, просыпа́ется по́здно, и до́лго **лежи́т** в крова́ти.
4. Вчера́ он **лёг** в де́сять, как всегда́, но́ не мо́г спа́ть, и до́лго **лежа́л** и ду́мал.
5. Вчера́ она́ **легла́** в оди́ннадцать и **вста́ла** в се́мь.

1. Irina likes to go to bed early and get up early.
2. In summer she would go to bed at ten and get up at six.
3. Ilya Ilyich goes to bed early, wakes up late, and (then) lies in bed for a long time.
4. Yesterday he went to bed at ten, as usual, but couldn't sleep and lay (there) and thought for a long time.
5. Yesterday she went to bed at eleven and got up at seven.

---

[1] The imperfective imperative of this verb is preferable as a polite invitation.

6. На́ши де́ти **ложа́тся** в во́семь, и пото́м **лежа́т** и разгова́ривают дру́г с дру́гом!

7. —Когда́ ты́ сего́дня **ля́жешь**? —Я́ ля́гу, как всегда́. —А мы́ **ля́жем** ра́ньше и **вста́нем** ра́ньше. Споко́йной но́чи! Иду́ спа́ть.[2]

8. Де́ти, уже́ по́здно! Пора́ **ложи́ться**! **Ложи́тесь** сейча́с же!

9. —Я́ **полежу́** немно́жко, а ты́ **посиди́** здесь. —Коне́чно, **полежи́**, а я́ **посижу́**.

10. О́н **полежа́л** пя́ть мину́т и опя́ть **вста́л**.

11. В воскресе́нье Ива́н **пролежа́л** ве́сь де́нь в крова́ти.

6. Our children go to bed at eight and then lie (there) and talk to one another!

7. —When will you go to bed today? —I'll go at my usual time. —And we'll go earlier and get up earlier. Good night! I'm going to bed.

8. Children, it's late already! Time to go to bed! Go to bed at once!

9. —I will rest (= lie) awhile, and you sit here a while. —Of course, lie, and I'll sit.

10. He lay for five minutes and (then) got up again.

11. On Sunday Ivan spent the whole day in bed.

DRILL

A. *Translate the English words in parentheses into Russian.*

1. —Ива́н, в кото́ром часу́ ты́ тепе́рь (go to bed)? —Я́ тепе́рь (go to bed at eleven).

2. —Ива́н, когда́ ты́ (did go to bed) вчера́? —Я́ (went to bed at ten).

3. —Ива́н, в кото́ром часу́ ты́ (did go to bed) на про́шлой неде́ле? —Я́ (went to bed at twelve), но́ на бу́дущей неде́ле я́ (will go to bed at ten).

4. —Ива́н, в кото́ром часу́ ты́ (will go to bed) за́втра? —За́втра я́ (will go to bed at ten).

5. —В кото́ром часу́ вы́ тепе́рь (go to bed)? —Мы́ тепе́рь (go to bed at one o'clock).

6. —В кото́ром часу́ вы́ (did go to bed) вчера́? —Мы́ (went to bed at twelve).

7. —В кото́ром часу́ вы́ (did go to bed) на про́шлой неде́ле? —Мы́ (went to bed at eleven).

8. —В кото́ром часу́ вы́ (will go to bed) за́втра? —Мы́ (will go to bed at ten).

9. —О́льга, когда́ ты́ (did go to bed) вчера́? —Я́ (went to bed at ten).

10. —В кото́ром часу́ ты́ обы́чно (did go to bed) на про́шлой неде́ле? —Я́ (went to bed at twelve), но́ на бу́дущей неде́ле я́ (will go to bed at ten).

B. *Translate the English words in parentheses into Russian.*

1. —Здра́вствуйте, Ива́н! (Sit down) на дива́н. —Спаси́бо, я́ (will sit down) на сту́л. Я́ предпочита́ю (to sit) на сту́ле.

2. О́н тепе́рь никогда́ не (sits down) на э́тот дива́н.

3. Ива́н пришёл ко мне́ в кабине́т, (sat down) на кре́сло, кото́рое стои́т в углу́, вста́л с него́, и (sat down) на сту́л о́коло моего́ стола́.

4. Ско́ро пришла́ его́ жена́ и (sat down) на сту́л о́коло его́ сту́ла, и они́ (sat) и разгова́ривали.

5. Пото́м они́ (got up and sat down) на дива́н, и (sat) на дива́не до обе́да.

---

[2] **Идти́/пойти́ спа́ть** is used only for a single time (**ходи́ть спа́ть** is *never* used), e.g., Иди́ спа́ть! or О́н сейча́с идёт спа́ть, Go to bed! or He's going to bed now. **Ле́чь спа́ть** (perfective) is also said of going to bed once, e.g., Я́ хочу́ ле́чь спа́ть, I want to go to bed. **Ложи́ться (спа́ть)** (imperfective) is used in general, e.g., Я́ бу́ду тепе́рь ра́но ложи́ться спа́ть, From now on I'll be going to bed early.

3. The verb станови́ться/стать

This verb has two basic meanings: (1) *to place oneself* (standing) and (2) *to become*. As with ложи́ться/лечь and сади́ться/сесть, the imperfective of this verb has **-ся** while the perfective lacks it.

Imperfective: **станови́ться**		*Perfective:* **стать**	
Present		*Future*	
становлю́сь	стано́вимся	ста́ну	ста́нем
стано́вишься	стано́витесь	ста́нешь	ста́нете
стано́вится	стано́вятся	ста́нет	ста́нут
Past		*Past*	
станови́лся, станови́лось, etc.		стал, -о, -а, -и	
Imperative		*Imperative*	
станови́сь!	станови́тесь!	стань!	ста́ньте!

(1) The verb pair **станови́ться/стать** should be distinguished from **встава́ть/встать**, which means *to stand up, to get up, to arise.*

Óн сиде́л на дива́не, пото́м вста́л с дива́на и ста́л у две́ри.
He was sitting on the sofa, then got up from the sofa and stood (placed himself) by the door.

Снача́ла óн стоя́л ря́дом с отцо́м, а пото́м ста́л у окна́.
At first he was standing near Father, and then he stood (placed himself) by the window.

Перед теа́тром была́ о́чередь. Мы́ ста́ли в о́чередь и простоя́ли в о́череди два́дцать пя́ть мину́т.
In front of the theater there was a line. We got (placed ourselves) into the line and stood in line for twenty-five minutes.

Ста́ньте в о́чередь!
Get into the line!

In all these examples the persons who "placed themselves" near the window or in a line were already in a "standing position."

(2) The verb **станови́ться/стать** is most common in the sense of *to become*. In this use it may take an adverb, or a predicate noun or an adjective in the *instrumental*:

Стано́вится хо́лодно.
It's getting (becoming) cold.

Мне́ ста́ло ску́чно.
I got (became) bored.

Óн ста́л изве́стным исто́риком.
He became a well-known historian.

О́льга ста́ла хоро́шей хозя́йкой.
Olga has become a good housekeeper.

Note: The perfective **стать** is also used with imperfective infinitives and then has the meaning *to start* or *to take to.*

Óн **ста́л** ча́сто опа́здывать.
He has taken to being late often.

Óн **ста́л** хорошо́ говори́ть по-ру́сски.
He has started to speak Russian well.

Я́ не **ста́ну** с ва́ми об э́том спо́рить.
I am not going (starting) to argue with you about that.

DRILL

Переведи́те с англи́йского на ру́сский.

1. It is getting cold.
2. It got cold.
3. Soon it will get cold.
4. If you get cold, I'll shut the window.
5. —It's growing dark. —Yes, it's getting late.
6. My son wants to become a teacher.
7. He became a famous actor.
8. When he becomes a doctor he will live in New York.
9. He thinks that he will soon get rich.
10. My son started getting good grades.

4. Masculine nouns in -a and -я

A number of nouns denoting male persons end in **-a** or **-я** and are declined like feminine nouns with the same endings. Among these nouns are:

мужчи́на   man (a male)
де́душка   grandfather
дя́дя   uncle
па́па   papa

as well as most nicknames of men: Ко́ля (Никола́й), Са́ша (Алекса́ндр), Ва́ся (Васи́лий), Ва́ня (Ива́н), Бо́ря (Бори́с), etc.

Modifiers, verbs in the past tense, and pronouns in connection with these nouns take *masculine* endings:

Мо́й люби́мый **дя́дя** неда́вно прие́хал; **о́н** давно́ у на́с не́ **бы́л**.
На́ш де́душка жи́л в Москве́; **я́ его́** хорошо́ по́мню.

PATTERN SENTENCES

1. **Мо́й** де́душка и де́душка Бори́са живу́т в то́м же го́роде.
2. Я́ ча́сто быва́ю с ма́мой и па́п**ой** у мо**его́** де́душки и у мое́й ба́бушки.
3. Я́ хорошо́ зна́ю де́душку и ба́бушку Ива́на. Я́ люблю́ разгова́ривать с его́ де́душк**ой** и ба́бушкой.
4. В теа́тре идёт пье́са Че́хова «Дя́дя Ваня». Мы́ вчера́ ви́дели «Дя́дю Ва́ню».
5. Я́ ви́жу из окна́ высо́к**ого** мужчи́ну и высо́кую же́нщину.

1. My grandfather and Boris's grandfather live in the same city.
2. My mama and papa and I often visit my grandfather and grandmother.
3. I know Ivan's grandfather and grandmother well. I like to converse with his grandfather and grandmother.
4. At the theater a play by Chekhov called *Uncle Vanya* is playing. Yesterday we saw *Uncle Vanya.*
5. From the window I see a tall man and a tall woman.

6. —Ты́ зна́ешь э́того мужчи́ну и э́ту же́нщину? —Я́ зна́ю **его́**, но́ не зна́ю её.

7. Я́ бы́л на собра́нии с тётей Ве́рой и с дя́дей Ко́лей. Та́м бы́ло мно́го мужчи́н и ма́ло же́нщин.

8. Не все́ мужчи́ны уме́ют гото́вить, но́ я́ зна́ю мужчи́н, кото́рые прекра́сно гото́вят.

6. —Do you know that man and that woman? —I know him, but I don't know her.

7. I was at the meeting with Aunt Vera and Uncle Kolya. There were many men there and few women.

8. Not all men know how to cook, but I know some men who cook very well.

DRILL

Переведи́те с англи́йского на ру́сский.[3]

1. Seventeen men and nine women work in this small plant.
2. Kolya has two uncles and two aunts.
3. Do you like your uncle and your aunt?
4. This is our uncle's house.
5. I remember well our grandfather and our grandmother.
6. Kolya writes often to his grandfather and to his grandmother.
7. —For whom did you buy these candies? —I bought them for Mama and Daddy.
8. She was talking with a small fat man and with a tall thin woman.

5. Genitive plural of nouns (supplement)

A. Nouns with nominative plural stems ending in conson. + [j]. In earlier lessons (Unit 13, p. 201 and Unit 19, p. 300) a list has been given of some masculine and neuter nouns with nominative plural endings spelled **-ья** [soft conson. + j]. (A few feminine nouns also have a [j] in their nominative plural endings.) The genitive plural endings of most of the masculine and neuter nouns in this group are spelled **-ьев** [-j.əf]. Other masculine and feminine nouns take genitive endings spelled **-ей**, e.g., **друзья́—друзе́й**.

Some of the more commonly used nouns of the group are listed below:

GENITIVE OF NOUNS WITH -ья AND -ьи NOMINATIVE PLURAL

	Nominative Singular	*Nominative Plural*		*Genitive Plural*		
Masc.	бра́т	бра́тья	[brátj.ə]	бра́тьев	[brátj.əf]	
	ли́ст	ли́стья	[l̹ístj.ə]	ли́стьев	[l̹ístj.əf]	
	сту́л	сту́лья	[stúl̹j.ə]	сту́льев	[stúl̹j.əf]	-ев
Neut.	де́рево	дере́вья	[dir̹éɣj.ə]	дере́вьев	[dir̹éɣj.əf]	
	перо́	пе́рья	[p̹ér̹j.ə]	пе́рьев	[p̹ér̹j.əf]	
	пла́тье	пла́тья	[plátj.ə]	пла́тьев	[plátj.əf]	
Masc.	дру́г	друзья́	[druz̹j.á]	друзе́й	[druz̹éj.]	
	му́ж	мужья́	[mužj.á]	муже́й	[mužéj.]	
	сы́н	сыновья́	[sínaɣj.á]	сынове́й	[sinaɣéj]	-ей
Fem.	семья́	се́мьи	[s̹ém̹j.i]	семе́й	[sim̹éj.]	
	статья́	статьи́	[statj.í]	стате́й	[stat̹éj.]	

[3] To translate from a language, Russian uses **с** + genitive; to translate into a language, **на** + accusative.

B. Neuters in -мя, Type I (zero ending).

Nominative Singular	Nominative Plural	Genitive Plural
и́мя	имена́	имён
вре́мя	времена́	времён

C. Miscellaneous genitive plurals, with Type II endings (-ей).

Nominative Singular	Nominative Plural	Genitive Plural
(ребёнок)	де́ти	дете́й
(челове́к)	лю́ди	люде́й (ог челове́к)[4]
сосе́д	сосе́ди	сосе́дей
мать	ма́тери	матере́й
дочь	до́чери	дочере́й

PATTERN SENTENCES

1. В столо́вой вокру́г стола́ стоя́т ше́сть сту́льев.
2. Что́ э́то за дере́вья? Я никогда́ не ви́дел таки́х дере́вьев!
3. У на́с в саду́ е́сть два́ таки́х де́рева. На э́тих дере́вьях уже́ мно́го кра́сных ли́стьев.
4. —Ско́лько у ва́с бра́тьев? —У меня́ три́ бра́та. Все́ мои́ бра́тья живу́т о́коло Москвы́.
5. —Кто́ э́ти лю́ди? —Э́то на́ши друзья́. —Я́ не зна́л, что у ва́с сто́лько друзе́й.
6. —Для кого́ вы́ купи́ли ша́хматы? —Я́ купи́л и́х для мои́х сынове́й. —Все́ ва́ши сыновья́ игра́ют в ша́хматы? —Не́т, то́лько два́ сы́на.
7. —У ва́с е́сть де́ти? —Да́, е́сть. —Ско́лько у ва́с дете́й? —У на́с то́лько оди́н ребёнок.
8. Когда́ дете́й не́т до́ма, для матере́й о́тдых. Ма́тери то́же должны́ иногда́ отдыха́ть.

1. In the dining room there are six chairs around the table.
2. What sort of trees are these? I've never seen such trees!
3. We have two trees of that kind in our garden. Those trees already have many red leaves.
4. —How many brothers do you have? —I have three brothers. All my brothers live near Moscow.
5. —Who are those people? —They're our friends. —I didn't know that you had so many friends.
6. —For whom did you buy the chess (set)? —I bought it for my sons. —Do all your sons play chess? —No, only two sons.
7. —Do you have children? —Yes, I do. —How many children do you have? —We have only one child.
8. When the children are not at home it's a rest (relief) for mothers. Mothers have to rest sometimes too.

---

[4] See page 240.

9. —Для кого́ вы купи́ли э́ти блу́зки? —Я купи́ла их для мои́х дочере́й. У меня́ две до́чери.

10. Вчера́ в их до́ме везде́ бы́ли лю́ди: в гости́ной бы́ло де́сять **челове́к**, в столо́вой бы́ло три челове́ка, **не́сколько челове́к** бы́ло в кабине́те и на вера́нде. То́лько в спа́льне не́ было ни одного́ челове́ка.

11. На́ши де́ти пою́т мно́го весёлых пе́сен.[5]

9. —For whom did you buy those blouses? —I bought them for my daughters. I have two daughters.

10. Yesterday in their house there were people everywhere: in the living room were ten people, in the dining room three people, several people were in the study and on the porch. Only in the bedroom there wasn't a single person.

11. Our children sing many lively songs.

DRILL

Translate the words in parentheses.

1. Нам ну́жно купи́ть (new chairs).
2. У нас о́чень ма́ло (chairs).
3. В мое́й ко́мнате то́лько два (chairs).
4. Ско́лько (chairs) у вас?
5. У Ни́ны не́сколько (brothers).
6. Я не зна́ю её (brothers).
7. У меня́ три (brothers).
8. Почему́ все (leaves) жёлтые?
9. На э́том де́реве мно́го жёлтых (leaves).
10. В их саду́ ма́ло (trees).

11. О́коло на́шего до́ма четы́ре (trees).
12. Я люблю́ (trees).
13. У нас здесь нет (friends).
14. Где все ва́ши (friends)?
15. У нас здесь то́лько два (friends).
16. Я не зна́ю её (sons).
17. Я не знал, что у неё есть (sons).
18. У неё два (sons) и две (daughters).
19. Вы зна́ете мно́го ру́сских (songs)?
20. Ско́лько у вас (children)?

6. Nouns and adjectives of nationality

Nouns and adjectives of nationality have been introduced in Unit 6 (see p. 73). Following is a table of some nationalities, together with the names of the corresponding countries and the adjectives and adverbs which refer to them.

Country	Nationals Masculine	Nationals Feminine	Plural	Adjective	Adverb
Росси́я	ру́сский	ру́сская	ру́сские	ру́сский	по-ру́сски
Аме́рика	америка́н.ец	америка́н.ка	америка́н.цы	америка́нский	по-америка́нски
Фра́нция	францу́з	францу́женка	францу́зы	францу́зский	по-францу́зски
Испа́ния (Spain)	испа́н.ец	испа́н.ка	испа́н.цы	испа́нский	по-испа́нски
Ита́лия	италья́н.ец	италья́н.ка	италья́н.цы	италья́нский	по-италья́нски
Герма́ния	не́м.ец	не́м.ка	не́м.цы	неме́цкий	по-неме́цки
Япо́ния (Japan)	япо́н.ец	япо́н.ка	япо́н.цы	япо́нский	по-япо́нски
Кита́й (China)	кита́ец	китая́нка	кита́йцы	кита́йский	по-кита́йски
А́нглия	**англича́н.ин**	**англича́н.ка**	**англича́н.е**	англи́йский	по-англи́йски
Арме́ния (Armenia)	**армя́н.ин**	**армя́н.ка**	**армя́н.е**	армя́нский	по-армя́нски

[5] A few feminines in **-ня** have genitive plurals in **-ен** (hard), **e.g.,** пе́сен, спа́лен (*bedrooms*).

Note that most nouns of nationality are formed either like америка́нец or like англича́нин, that is, with one of two types of suffixes.

(1) Masculine singular **-ец**, plural **-цы**; feminine singular **-ка**, plural **-ки**.

Note that the **е** of the suffix **-ец** is dropped in case forms other than the nominative singular, thus the genitive singular америка́н.**ца**, the genitive plural **-цев**; and the feminine genitive singular америка́н.**ки**, the genitive plural **-ок**.

(2) Masculine singular **-анин/-янин** (for declension of this type see Section 7 below), feminine **-анка/-янка**.

(3) Adverbs formed with **по-** are used with reference to language; however, the preposition **на** plus the locative case is used when the word **язы́к** (*language*) appears:

—**На** како́м **языке́** вы́ говори́те до́ма? —Мы́ говори́м **по-ру́сски**.
—Which language do you speak at home? —We speak Russian.

Э́тот профе́ссор говори́т **на** все́х славя́нских языка́х.
That professor speaks all the Slavic languages.

Observe that neither nouns nor adjectives of nationality are capitalized in Russian.

7. Declension of masculine nouns in -анин/-янин; -ин

A. Masculine nouns ending in **-анин/-янин** are declined regularly in the singular. In the plural, however, they have a special declension based on a shortened stem ending in **-ан./-ян**. The nominative plural ends in **-ане/-яне**; genitive plural in **-ан/-ян** (*zero ending*); dative plural in **-анам/-янам**, etc. Most of them are nouns of nationality; they have feminine equivalents ending in **-анка/-янка**.

To this group belong:

англича́нин	Englishman	nom. pl. англича́не
славяни́н	Slav	nom. pl. славя́не
граждани́н	citizen	nom. pl. гра́ждане
христиани́н	Christian	nom. pl. христиа́не
крестья́нин	peasant	nom. pl. крестья́не

B. The noun **господи́н** *Mr., sir*, has the nominative plural **господа́**, and the genitive plural **госпо́д** *sirs, gentlemen, ladies and gentlemen*.

The noun **хозя́ин** *host, master*, has the nominative plural **хозя́ева** *host and hostess, master and mistress, hosts, masters*, and the genitive plural **хозя́ев**.

PATTERN SENTENCES

1. Не́которые **америка́нцы** и не́которые **англича́не** хорошо́ говоря́т **на** иностра́нных языка́х.

1. Some Americans and some Englishmen speak foreign languages well.

2. На приёме у Орло́вых бы́ли ра́зные иностра́нцы. Та́м бы́ло не́сколько **англича́н**, не́сколько **францу́зов**, и не́сколько **америка́нцев**.

2. At the reception at the Orlovs' there were different kinds of foreigners. There were several Englishmen, several Frenchmen, and several Americans.

3. —С ке́м вы́ хоти́те меня́ познако́мить? —Я́ хочу́ познако́мить ва́с с одни́м о́чень интере́сным **англича́нином**. Мне́ ка́жется, что вы́ с ни́м ещё не знако́мы. Его́ жена́ **испа́нка**.

3. —Whom do you want me to meet (Whom do you want to introduce me to)? —I want you to meet a very interesting Englishman. I don't think that you know him yet. His wife is Spanish.

4. Ива́н Петро́в **ру́сский**. О́н сове́тский **граждани́н**. О́н **славяни́н**.

4. Ivan Petrov is Russian. He is a Soviet citizen. He is a Slav.

| | | 5. | Елéна Петрóва **рýсская**. Онá совéтская **граждáнка**. Онá **славя́нка**. | 5. | Elena Petrova is Russian. She is a Soviet citizen. She is a Slav. |

5. Елéна Петрóва **рýсская**. Онá совéтская **граждáнка**. Онá **славя́нка**.

5. Elena Petrova is Russian. She is a Soviet citizen. She is a Slav.

6. Петрóвы **рýсские**. Они́ совéтские **грáждане**. Они́ **славя́не**.

6. The Petrovs are Russians. They are Soviet citizens. They are Slavs.

7. **Нéмцы** лю́бят пи́ть пи́во. Пи́во в **Гермáнии** óчень хорóшее.

7. Germans like to drink beer. The beer in Germany is very good.

8. Мóй сосéд **рýсский**, а егó женá **нéмка**. Они́ говоря́т дрýг с дрýгом иногдá **по-рýсски**, а иногдá **по-немéцки**.

8. My neighbor is Russian, and his wife is German. Sometimes they speak to each other in Russian, and sometimes in German.

9. Оди́н мóй знакóмый **францýз** хорошó знáет рýсский язы́к и óчень лю́бит говори́ть **по-рýсски**.

9. A French acquaintance of mine knows Russian well and is very fond of speaking Russian.

10. —**На** какóм **языкé** говоря́т в Квебéке? —**По-францýзски**.

10. —What language do they speak in Quebec? —French.

DRILL

Переведи́те с англи́йского на рýсский.

1. Anna is English, and her husband is French.
2. —Is Vadim's wife French or American? —His wife is American and he himself is Russian.
3. The English like to play tennis.
4. Americans like steak.
5. Did you speak with these Englishmen?
6. No, I spoke only with these Frenchmen and Frenchwomen.
7. There are many Slavs here.
8. —Who are these peasants? —They are Italians.
9. I like Italians.
10. —What language do they speak in class? —Only Russian!

8. Review of declension in the plural

A. Nouns. The table below presents the *basic* types of noun declension in the plural. A summary of the other types follows the table.

PLURAL ENDINGS OF NOUNS

		Masc.		Neuter		Fem. I		Fem. II
		Hard	Soft	Hard	Soft	Hard	Soft	
Nom.	{ **-Ы/-И** **-Á/-Я**	столы́	гóсти	делá	поля́	жёны	кýхни	двéри
Gen.	{ *zero* **-ОВ/-ЕВ** **-ЕЙ**	столóв	гостéй	дел	полéй	жён	кýхонь	дверéй
Acc.		Inanimate like Nominative; animate like Genitive.						
Dat.	**-АМ/-ЯМ**	столáм	гостя́м	делáм	поля́м	жёнам	кýхням	дверя́м
Instr.	**-АМИ/-ЯМИ**	столáми	гостя́ми	делáми	поля́ми	жёнами	кýхнями	дверя́ми
Loc.	**-АХ/-ЯХ**	столáх	гостя́х	делáх	поля́х	жёнах	кýхнях	дверя́х

1. *Nominative.* (a) Some masculine nouns take the **-á/-я** ending, common in the neuter gender, rather than the regular **-ы/-и**, e.g. домá, городá, лесá, докторá (see Unit 13, p. 200); see also, in Section 4 above, the plurals господá (sing. господи́н) and хозя́ева (sing. хозя́ин). (b) Spelling Rule 2 applies to the formation of the nominative plural: **ы** is never written after **г, к, х, ж, ч, ш, щ**; thus, ногá—но́ги, рукá—ру́ки, нож—ножи́, врач—врачи́.

2. *Genitive.* For distribution of the endings, *zero*, **-ов/-ев**, and **-ей**, consult Table in Unit 16, p. 235. (a) Note that a number of *masculine* nouns of the hard type have *zero* endings in the *genitive plural*, which coincides with the *nominative singular*: **раз, солдáт, глаз** (see p. 240). (b) All masculine nouns ending in **ж, ш, ч,** and **щ** take the ending **-ей** in the *genitive plural*. (c) Those masculines ending in **-ц** take **-ов** if the stress is on the ending, and **-ев** if the stress is on the stem: отцы́—отцо́в, but мéсяцы—мéсяцев.

3. *Instrumental.* A few nouns of the three genders take, in *the instrumental plural*, the ending **-ьми́** instead of the normal **-ами/-ями**: лю́ди—людьми́, дéти—детьми́, ло́шади—лошадьми́.

Special Groups of Plural Nouns

	Masculine	*Masculine and Neuter*	*Neuter*	*Feminine*
Nom.	друзья́	брáтья (пéрья)	именá (like делá)	мáтери (like двéри)
Gen.	друзéй	брáтьев	имён	матерéй
Dat.	друзья́м	брáтьям	именáм	матеря́м
Acc.	Inanimate like Nominative; animate like Genitive.			
Instr.	друзья́ми	брáтьями	именáми	матеря́ми
Loc.	друзья́х	брáтьях	именáх	матеря́х

Notes to Special Groups

Like друзья́ are declined мужья́ and сыновья́. Like брáтья and пéрья are declined сту́лья, ли́стья, and дерéвья. Like именá is declined временá. Мáтери is declined like до́чери (except the instrumental plural, which is дочерьми́).

B. Pronouns, adjectives, and pronoun-adjectives.

Pronominal and Adjectival Plural Endings

	3rd Person Pronouns	*Hard Adjectives*	*Soft Adjectives*	*Possessives*	*Demonstratives*	
Nom.	они́	но́вые	си́ние	мои́	э́ти	те
Gen.	их	но́вых	си́них	мои́х	э́тих	тех
Dat.	им	но́вым	си́ним	мои́м	э́тим	тем

	3rd Person Pronouns	Hard Adjectives	Soft Adjectives	Possessives	Demonstratives	
Acc.	их	Inanimate like Nominative; animate like Genitive.				
Instr.	и́ми	но́выми	си́ними	мои́ми	э́тими	те́ми
Loc.	(н)их	но́вых	си́них	мои́х	э́тих	тех

"Mixed" adjectives with stems ending in **г, к, х, ж, ч, ш,** and **щ** are declined in the plural with the written endings of soft adjectives (си́ний): ру́сские, etc., хоро́шие, etc. (see Spelling Rule 2, page 68).

> Like мой are declined твой, свой, на́ши, and ва́ши.
> Like э́ти are declined одни́ and чьи.
> Like те is declined все.

9. Adjectival words expressing quantity

The adverbs **мно́го, немно́го, ско́лько, сто́лько,** and **не́сколько** have corresponding adjectival forms; the last three are used only in case forms other than the nominative:

> мно́гие, мно́гих, мно́гим, etc.
> (no nom.), ско́льких, ско́льким, etc.
> (no nom.), не́скольких, не́скольким, etc.

The use of these forms may be seen from the following examples:

> **Ско́лько** музе́ев вы ви́дели в Евро́пе?
> *But:* В **ско́льких** музе́ях вы бы́ли? (In how many . . .?)
>
> **Я** ви́дел **мно́го** стра́н (**не́сколько** стра́н).
> *But:* Та́м бы́ли лю́ди из **мно́гих** стра́н (**не́скольких** стра́н). (. . . from many countries.)

Мно́го the adverb differs from мно́гие the adjective (e.g., мно́го студе́нтов— мно́гие студе́нты) in that мно́го means simply *many* (of), *a large number* (of), whereas мно́гие implies part of a total (*many, but not all*). In this sense мно́гие is less than все, but more than не́которые (*some, a few*), thus:

> **Все́** америка́нские студе́нты зна́ют англи́йский язы́к, **мно́гие** зна́ют оди́н иностра́нный язы́к, а **не́которые** зна́ют два́ или да́же три́ иностра́нных языка́.

The words **все, мно́гие, не́которые,** and **немно́гие** are often used without a noun, the word *people* (**лю́ди**) being then understood:

> **Мно́гие** бы́ли недово́льны э́той пье́сой.
> **Не́которые** её совсе́м не по́няли.

The adverb **ма́ло** has no corresponding declined form. **Немно́гие** (cf. немно́го, *a few*) is used instead: в немно́гих слу́чаях—in (a) few cases.

The singular form **мно́гое,** declined, is used in the sense of *many things*:

> В э́той стране́ мно́гое мне нра́вится.

PATTERN SENTENCES

1. У меня **мно́го** студе́нтов. **Мно́гие** мои́ студе́нты хоро́шие. **Не́которые** замеча́тельные.
2. Ру́сские о́чень лю́бят игра́ть в ша́хматы, и **мно́гие** игра́ют хорошо́.
3. В Ита́лии **мно́го** хоро́ших певцо́в. У **мно́гих** италья́нцев хоро́шие голоса́, но́ не у все́х.
4. Васи́лий Ша́пкин крестья́нин. У него́, как у **мно́гих** крестья́н, тяжёлая жи́знь.
5. Оди́н из мои́х друзе́й хорошо́ говори́т на **не́скольких** языка́х.
6. Во вре́мя на́шего путеше́ствия по Фра́нции мы́ познако́мились с **не́сколькими** англича́нами и с **не́сколькими** америка́нцами.
7. **Не́которые** из ни́х бы́ли о́чень симпати́чные лю́ди, и я́ иногда́ пишу́ **не́которым** из ни́х.
8. В Пари́же **мно́го** хоро́ших рестора́нов; мы́ бы́ли в **не́скольких**. В одно́м из ни́х я́ познако́милась с **не́сколькими** о́чень симпати́чными францу́зами.
9. В **не́которых** слу́чаях о́н быва́ет пра́в, но́ не во все́х.

1. I have many students. Many of my students are good ones. Some are excellent.
2. Russians like to play chess very much, and many of them play well.
3. In Italy there are many (a large number of) fine singers. Many Italians have good voices, but not all.
4. Vasili Shapkin is a peasant. Like many peasants, he has a hard life. (*lit.*, He has, as many peasants have, a hard life.)
5. One of my friends speaks (in) several languages well.
6. During our trip through France we met (with) several English people and several Americans.
7. Some of them were very likable people, and I sometimes write to some of them.
8. In Paris there are many (a large number of) fine restaurants; we went to several. In one of them I met (with) several very likable Frenchmen.
9. In some cases he is right, but not in all.

Conversation

1. Познако́мьтесь пожа́луйста

Я. —Ма́рья Васи́льевна, вы́ зна́ете Серге́я Ива́новича Ка́рпова?

М.В. —Не́т, я́ с ни́м не знако́ма, но́ я́ мно́го слы́шала о нём.

Я. —Вы́ хоти́те с ни́м познако́миться?

М.В. —С больши́м удово́льствием!

Я. —Серге́й Ива́нович! Ма́рья Васи́льевна Ша́пкина хо́чет с ва́ми познако́миться.

С.И. —Бу́ду о́чень ра́д. Я́ слы́шал о ней мно́го хоро́шего.

Я. —Познако́мьтесь пожа́луйста: Серге́й Ива́нович, Ма́рья Васи́льевна.

С.И. —О́чень прия́тно! Я́ так мно́го о ва́с слы́шал.

М.В. —О́чень ра́да с ва́ми познако́миться.

—Maria Vasilyevna, do you know Sergey Ivanovich Karpov?

—No, I'm not acquainted with him, but I've heard a great deal about him.

—Would you like to make his acquaintance?

—With great pleasure!

—Sergey Ivanovich! Maria Vasilyevna Shapkina wants to make your acquaintance.

—I would be very happy. I've heard many fine things about her.

—Let me introduce you then (please be acquainted). Sergey Ivanovich, Maria Vasilyevna.

—How do you do? (I'm pleased to meet you.) I've heard so much about you.

—How do you do? (I'm very glad to meet you.)

2. На приёме у Орло́вых

Влади́мир. —Зо́ечка, в чём де́ло? Ты́ обеща́ла позвони́ть мне́ в суббо́ту днём. Мы́ ведь хоте́ли пойти́ в рестора́н, а пото́м в кино́. Я́ сиде́л до́ма и жда́л и жда́л твоего́ звонка́, и ничего́! Звони́л тебе́—никого́!

Зо́я. —Ра́зве я́ должна́ была́ позвони́ть тебе́ в э́ту суббо́ту? Мне́ каза́лось, что мы́ говори́ли о бу́дущей суббо́те. Прости́ меня́, Воло́дя. Я́ забы́ла!

В. —Не зна́ю, мо́жет быть прощу́. Но сна́ча́ла расскажи́, что́ случи́лось, в чём де́ло?

З. —Де́ло в то́м, что, как ты́ вероя́тно зна́ешь, зде́сь сейча́с дипломати́ческий съе́зд. Э́то пе́рвый тако́й съе́зд зде́сь.

В. —Коне́чно зна́ю. Я́ чита́л об э́том в газе́тах, и, кро́ме того́, всё об э́том говоря́т.

З. —Да́, э́то большо́е собы́тие (event). Прие́хало не́сколько мини́стров иностра́н-ных де́л, представи́телей[6] ООН,[7] и коне́чно иностра́нные корреспонде́нты. Прие́хало о́чень мно́го иностра́нцев. Прие́хали англича́не, францу́зы, не́мцы, испа́нцы, италья́нцы, япо́нцы. Уф! Кто́ ещё? Ну́, ещё мно́го ра́зных други́х.

В. —Съе́зд большо́й, а како́й бу́дет результа́т от всего́ э́того?

З. —Наде́юсь, что хоро́ший. Но когда́ рабо́таешь[8] в Объединённых На́циях, как я́, то коне́чно, как ты́ са́м понима́ешь, рабо́ты сейча́с о́чень мно́го. Ка́ждый де́нь быва́ют заседа́ния (sessions), ну́жно слу́шать дли́нные ре́чи[9] на ра́зных иностра́нных языка́х и дли́нные перево́ды э́тих рече́й. И ка́ждый де́нь обе́ды и приёмы.

В. —А когда́ я́ жда́л твоего́ звонка́, что ты́ де́лала? Произноси́ла ре́чь?

З. —Воло́дя, е́сли ты́ бу́дешь смея́ться надо мно́й, я́ тебе́ ничего́ не бу́ду расска́зывать.

В. —Не бу́ду, Зо́ечка, не бу́ду! Обеща́ю. Расска́зывай!

З. —Ну́, во́т. В суббо́ту бы́ло откры́тие (opening) съе́зда, и бы́л большо́й приём у Орло́вых. Орло́в, как ты́ зна́ешь, занима́ет о́чень ва́жное положе́ние в ООН. И та́к как о́н зна́ет, что я́ говорю́ на мно́гих языка́х, о́н проси́л меня́ придти́. Я́ была́ и ра́да и не ра́да: ра́да, потому́ что интере́сно знако́миться с интере́сными людьми́, но не ра́да, потому́ что, во-пе́рвых, я́ вообще́ не люблю́ больши́х приёмов, а, во-вторы́х, тру́дно не́сколько часо́в говори́ть на иностра́н-ных языка́х.

В. —Да́, но когда́ интере́сно, забыва́ешь о тру́дностях. Ты́ познако́милась со мно́гими интере́сными людьми́? Приём был хоро́ший?

З. —О да́! Приём был замеча́тельный! Орло́вы о́чень гостеприи́мные лю́ди, они́ лю́бят и уме́ют принима́ть. Все́ мно́го пи́ли и е́ли и разгова́ривали. С не́которыми, кто́ бы́л та́м, я́ уже́ была́ знако́ма, а со мно́гими меня́ позна-ко́мили хозя́ева.

В. —С ке́м ты́ познако́милась? Кто́ бы́л са́мый интере́сный?

З. —Тру́дно сказа́ть. О́чень мне́ понра́вился францу́зский мини́стр иностра́нных де́л. Мы́ с ни́м, коне́чно, говори́ли по-францу́зски, и зна́ешь, о́н сказа́л, что я́ говорю́ совсе́м как францу́женка!

---

[6] **Представи́тель** (*masc.*) *representative.*

[7] **ООН** (U.N.), abbreviation of Организа́ция Объединённых На́ций.

[8] The second person singular is often used in the indefinite sense of *one, you.* The pronoun **ты** is then usually omitted.

[9] **речь** (*fem.*) *speech.* **Произноси́ть/произнести́ речь** *to make a speech.*

В. —Францу́зы уме́ют де́лать комплиме́нты же́нщинам.

З. —Глу́пости! (Nonsense!) Он серьёзный, у́мный, и культу́рный челове́к. И, зна́ешь, его́ всё интересу́ет, а не то́лько поли́тика и междунаро́дное (international) положе́ние. Его́ интересу́ет совреме́нная литерату́ра и молодёжь, и студе́нческие пробле́мы. Он говори́л о конфли́кте ме́жду но́вым поколе́нием (generation) и ста́рым. Он говори́т, что Турге́нев уже́ в про́шлом ве́ке хорошо́ об э́том написа́л в своём рома́не «Отцы́ и де́ти».

В. —Молоде́ц францу́з! Чита́л Турге́нева! Да́, коне́чно, конфли́кт поколе́ний де́ло не но́вое.

З. —Да́, но ра́зные лю́ди об э́том говоря́т по-ра́зному. Во́т, наприме́р, Орло́в познако́мил меня́ с испа́нским диплома́том (мы с ни́м говори́ли по-испа́нски, коне́чно), и э́тот испа́нец говори́т, что молодёжь про́сто не зна́ет, чего́ хо́чет.

В. —Э́то, вероя́тно, то́же ча́сто быва́ет.

З. —А пото́м меня́ познако́мили с краси́вой италья́нкой. (Мы, коне́чно, говори́ли по-италья́нски.) Она́ корреспонде́нтка большо́й италья́нской газе́ты, ка́жется социалисти́ческой. И она́ говори́т, что не то́лько молодёжь недово́льна, а что вообще́ недово́льны мно́гие, и что везде́ забасто́вки (strikes) и беспоря́дки (disorders, riots). Высо́кий англича́нин, кото́рый слы́шал, что́ говори́ла италья́нка, сказа́л, что в А́нглии то́ же са́мое (the same thing).

В. —А что́ говори́л Орло́в?

З. —Ничего́. Он, как хозя́ин, слу́шал, улыба́лся (smiled), расска́зывал анекдо́ты, знако́мил люде́й. Жена́ его́, как хозя́йка, де́лала то́ же са́мое. Япо́нский диплома́т, с кото́рым я говори́ла по-англи́йски (о́чень у́мный япо́нец) диплома́тично расска́зывал мне́ о ра́зных япо́нских пробле́мах. Он сказа́л, ме́жду про́чим, что в Япо́нии о́чень лю́бят пье́сы Че́хова! О́чень всё бы́ло интере́сно!

В. —Познако́мь меня́ с Орло́выми. Они́ мне́ нра́вятся, и я слы́шал, что у ни́х всегда́ интере́сное о́бщество.

З. —С удово́льствием познако́млю тебя́ с ни́ми.

В. —Но́ тепе́рь, Зо́ечка, о мое́й пробле́ме: когда́ мы́ с тобо́й пойдём в рестора́н и в кино́ или в теа́тр? Везде́ идёт мно́го интере́сных пье́с и карти́н.

З. —В бу́дущую суббо́ту. Хорошо́? Съе́зд конча́ется за́втра, и официа́льные приёмы и обе́ды конча́ются вме́сте с ни́м. Так до суббо́ты?

В. —До суббо́ты. Не забу́дь!

Answer these questions in Russian.

1. Почему́ Воло́дя звони́л в суббо́ту Зо́е? 2. Почему́ прие́хало так мно́го иностра́нцев? 3. Кто́ они́ все́ бы́ли? 4. Что́ бы́ло в суббо́ту? 5. Где́ рабо́тает Зо́я? 6. Почему́ Орло́в проси́л Зо́ю придти́ на приём? 7. Почему́ она́ была́ и ра́да и не ра́да? 8. Почему́ приём бы́л у Орло́вых? 9. Каки́е они́ лю́ди? 10. Зо́я уже́ была́ знако́ма со все́ми? 11. Почему́ Зо́е так понра́вился францу́зский мини́стр иностра́нных де́л? 12. В како́м рома́не мини́стр чита́л о конфли́кте ме́жду молоды́м поколе́нием и ста́рым? 13. Что́ ду́мает о молодёжи испа́нский диплома́т? 14. Что́ говори́л высо́кий англича́нин? 15. Почему́ Орло́в не говори́л ни о полити́ческом положе́нии, ни о молодёжи, ни о беспоря́дках, ни о забасто́вках? 16. Что́ де́лала Орло́ва? 17. Почему́ в бу́дущую суббо́ту Зо́я и Воло́дя смо́гут пойти́ в рестора́н и в кино́?

DRILLS

A. *Combine each phrase of column* A *with each phrase of column* B, *putting the words of column* B *into the correct case form.*

A.	**B.**
Я́ зна́ю	ста́рый англича́нин.
Она́ познако́милась с	э́ти англича́не.
Мы́ говори́ли о (об)	оди́н америка́нец.
Она́ пи́шет	молодо́й францу́з.
Мы́ бы́ли у	молода́я францу́женка.
	сове́тский граждани́н.
	сове́тские гра́ждане.
	тво́й дя́дя.
	ва́ш де́душка.
	ста́рый крестья́нин.
	его́ бра́тья.
	ру́сские солда́ты.

B. *Переведи́те на ру́сский язы́к.*

There was a big reception at Dr. Smirnov's, our acquaintance's. At that reception we met (got acquainted with) many interesting people. There were many men and women whom I had never yet seen. I spoke for a long while with a very funny, fat Italian, who was sitting on the sofa. I sat down in an armchair next to him. I speak a little Italian. He told funny stories about Italy. We laughed a great deal and had a very good time. I also spoke with my host's uncle, who had just arrived from Germany. He is German and his wife is Italian, but they lived all their life in England, and at home they speak many languages. There were also Englishmen and Russians there. It was a very pleasant reception, and it seemed to me that everybody was very pleased. I've been there many times and it has always been pleasant. I hope that there will be many such receptions.

Vocabulary

вообще́ in general
Герма́ния Germany
гостеприи́мный hospitable
граждани́н (*pl.* гра́ждане; *fem.* гражда́нка) citizen
де́душка (*masc.*) grandfather
дя́дя (*masc.*) uncle
еда́ food
знако́мый familiar; (*as a noun*) acquaintance
иностра́нный foreign
иностра́н.ец (*fem.* -ка) foreigner
испа́н.ец (*fem.* -ка) Spaniard

испа́нский Spanish (*adj.*)
италья́н.ец (*fem.* -ка) Italian
италья́нский Italian (*adj.*)
крестья́н.ин (*pl.* -е; *fem.* -ка) peasant
культу́ра culture
культу́рный cultural, cultured
ла́дно all right, O.K. (*colloq.*)
мужчи́на (*masc.*) man, male[10]
не́которые some (*pl.*), certain ones
не́м.ец (*fem.* -ка) German
неме́цкий German (*adj.*)
немно́го, немно́жко a little (+ *gen.*)[11]

---

[10] The word **мужчи́на** is used mostly in contrast to **же́нщина**. When there is no contrast **челове́к** is much used, not only in the sense of *person, human being*, but also *man, male person*, e.g., «Кто́ э́тот челове́к?» "Who is that man?" Note also **молодо́й челове́к** *a young man*.

[11] Contrast to **ма́ло** (*little, few*). **Ма́ло** has a limiting meaning; **немно́го** is more positive.

о́бщий general, common, mutual
о́бщество society; company
па́па (*masc.*) papa, daddy
приём reception
свет world
симпати́чный likable, appealing
славяни́н (*pl.* славя́не; *fem.* славя́нка) Slav

слу́чай (pronounce [slúčij]) case, incident, event; chance
совреме́нный contemporary, modern
съезд convention, assembly
тётя aunt
тяжёлый (тяжело́) heavy, hard (said of life)
францу́.з (*fem.* -же́нка) Frenchman (-woman)
шу́т.ка (*gen. pl.* -ок) joke

VERBS

знако́мить (imperf., II: знако́м.лю, -ишь), познако́мить (perf., II) to introduce, acquaint (+ *acc. of person introduced*: c + *instr. of person to whom introduced*); знако́миться, познако́миться, to meet, be introduced to (c + *instr.*)
принима́ть (imperf., I), приня́ть (perf., I: приму́, при́мешь; past: при́нял, при́няло, приняла́, при́няли) to accept, receive, take (advice, medicine, etc.)
путеше́ствовать (imperf., I: путеше́ству.ю, -ешь) to travel
случа́ться (imperf., I), случи́ться, (perf., II: случи́тся) to happen, occur

EXPRESSIONS

Ка́к сказа́ть по-ру́сски . . .? How do you say . . . in Russian?
знако́м, -а, -ы c (+ *instr.*) acquainted with
Отку́да вы зна́ете? How do you know?
оди́н из мои́х друзе́й one of my friends[12]
не́которые из мои́х друзе́й some of my friends[12]
Что́ э́то за (+ *nom.*)? What (kind of) . . . is that?
за за́втраком at breakfast
к за́втраку for breakfast
станови́ться/ста́ть в о́чередь to get in line
Я та́к и ду́мал. That's just what I thought.
Мне́ бы́ло ве́село. I had a good time.
во-пе́рвых first, in the first place
во-вторы́х second, in the second place
ни оди́н (одно́, одна́) not a single (one)

VOCABULARY REVIEW AND SUPPLEMENT

FOR REFERENCE

Приве́тствия—Greetings

Здра́вствуй, -те! Hello!
До́брое у́тро! Good morning!
До́брый де́нь (ве́чер)! Good afternoon (evening)!
Ка́к {ты́ пожива́ешь? вы́ пожива́ете?} How are you? How have you been?
Хорошо́. Ничего́. Та́к себе. Нехорошо́. Пло́хо. Well. Fair. So-so. Not so well. Poor.
Что́ у тебя́ (ва́с) но́вого? What's new?
Ка́к дела́? How are things?
О́чень ра́д(а) тебя́ (ва́с) ви́деть! I'm very glad to see you!

Проща́ние—Farewell

До свида́ния! Good-bye (till I see you again)!
До ско́рого (свида́ния)! See you soon!
Проща́й, -те! Good-bye!

---

[12] Note also: оди́н мо́й дру́г *a friend of mine*; не́которые мои́ друзья́ *some friends of mine*.

Всего́ хоро́шего! All the best!
Споко́йной но́чи! Good night!
Пожа́луйста, переда́йте приве́т ва́шей жене́! Please give my regards to your wife!

Пожела́ния—Good wishes

Жела́ю успе́ха! Good luck!
Счастли́вого пути́! Bon voyage!

Фо́рмы ве́жливости; про́сьбы—Forms of politeness; requests

Пожа́луйста (+ *imper.*) Please . . .
Бу́дьте добры́ (любе́зны) (+ *imper. or inf.*) Be so kind as to . . .
Мо́жно ва́с попроси́ть (+ *inf.*)? May I ask you to . . .
Мо́жно ва́с попроси́ть переда́ть мне́ са́хар? May I ask you to pass me the sugar?
Сади́тесь пожа́луйста. Please sit down.
Бу́дьте как до́ма. Make yourself at home.
Приходи́те к на́м в сре́ду. Come and see us on Wednesday.
(Большо́е) спаси́бо (за + *acc.*). (Many) thanks for . . .
Благодарю́ ва́с (за + *acc.*). Thank you for . . .
(Я́ ва́м) о́чень благода́рен (за + *acc.*). I am very grateful for . . .
Не́т, спаси́бо. No, thank you.
Вы́ о́чень любе́зны. You are very kind.
Пожа́луйста. You're welcome.
Не́ за что. ⎫
Не сто́ит благода́рности. ⎬ Don't mention it.

Изве́стие—Information

Ка́к ва́ша фами́лия? What is your (last) name?
Ка́к ва́ше и́мя-о́тчество? What is your first name and patronymic?
Ка́к ва́ш а́дрес? What is your address?
Ка́к ва́ш но́мер телефо́на? What is your telephone number?
Когда́ ва́с мо́жно ви́деть? When may I see you?
Когда́ к ва́м мо́жно прийти́? When may I come and see you?

Ка́к лю́ди знако́мятся—Introductions

Позво́льте/разреши́те ва́с познако́мить с мои́м дру́гом Ива́ном Ива́новичем Ива́новым. Let me introduce my friend Ivan Ivanovich Ivanov.
Позво́льте/разреши́те ва́м предста́вить моего́ дру́га Ива́на Ива́новича Ива́нова. May I present my friend Ivan Ivanovich Ivanov (to an older or more important person).
О́чень ра́д(а) с ва́ми познако́миться. ⎫ How do you do?
О́чень прия́тно. ⎬ (I'm very pleased to meet you.)

Извине́ния—Apologies

Извини́те, пожа́луйста. Excuse me, please.
Прости́те. Excuse me.
Прости́те за беспоко́йство. Excuse me for bothering you.
Извини́те (прости́те) меня́. Forgive me.
Пожа́луйста. ⎫
Что́ вы! ⎬ Certainly. Of course!
Ра́ди Бо́га! ⎭

ILLUSTRATION 20.   Ленингра́д но́чью. (*Tass from Sovfoto.*)

Survey of conjugation patterns • Мо́жно and нельзя́ • Perfective
verbs захоте́ть, уви́деть, услы́шать, and смочь • Cardinal and
ordinal numerals, 20–199 • Reading: Моя́ сосе́дка

Unit 21

Grammar

1. Survey of conjugation patterns

It has been seen earlier that the conjugation pattern of a Russian verb is not determined by its infinitive. The ending of the infinitive does not generally indicate what
type of endings (first or second conjugation) the verb takes in the present (or the
perfective future) tense. The stem found in the conjugation may differ to a greater or
lesser extent from the stem of the infinitive.

In practical terms, it is advisable to memorize for each verb, in addition to its
infinitive, also the first and second singular forms from which, except for a very small
number of irregular verbs, the other forms can be derived. It will, however, be helpful
for the student to have an over-all view of the more important patterns of conjugation
and of their variations in both the stem and personal endings.

In the different forms of a verb its stem appears in two variants; one of them is
found in the infinitive and the past tense, the other in the present (or perfective future)
and in the imperative (they will be hereafter referred to as the *infinitive-past stem* and
the *present stem*).

In verbs of the first conjugation, the present stem may end either in a vowel followed
by the sound [j] or in a consonant; the vowel + [j] type of stem is more common. In
the second conjugation, the consonantal stem-ending is typical and only a few verbs
have present stems ending in a vowel + [j].

A. First conjugation, present stems in vowel + [j]. The verb **чита́ть** may
serve as an example of a first conjugation verb with the present stem ending in a
vowel + [j]. One will also see from the presentation below that the infinitive and the
past tense have one stem—in this case [čitá-]—and that the present stem, which is
[čitáj-], is also found in the imperative:

Inf.	чита́ть	[čitá.t̮]	⎫ *Inf.-past stem:* [čitá-]
Past	чита́л	[čitá.l]	⎭

Pres.	читáю	[čitáj.u]	
	читáешь	[čitáj.iš]	
	читáет	[čitáj.it]	
	читáем	[čitáj.im]	*Present stem:* [čitáj-]
	читáете	[čitáj.iṭi]	
	читáют	[čitáj.ut]	
Imperative	читáй	[čitáj]	

Most (but not all) first conjugation verbs with infinitives in **-ать/-ять** are conjugated like **читáть** and have present stems in [aj]. This pattern is, in particular, that of the numerous prefixed imperfective verbs with **-ыв-** or **-ив-** inserted before the infinitive ending; these verbs fall into the **читáть** type of conjugation regardless of the conjugation pattern of the corresponding perfective verb, e.g.:

Imperfective	*Perfective*
покáзывать: покáзываю, покáзываешь . . .	показáть: покажý, покáжешь . . .
запúсывать: запúсываю, запúсываешь . . .	записáть: запишý, запúшешь . . .
открывáть: открывáю, открывáешь . . .	открыть: открóю, открóешь . . .
спрáшивать: спрáшиваю, спрáшиваешь . . .	спросúть: спрошý, спрóсишь . . .

With only a few exceptions, first conjugation verbs with infinitives in **-еть** (e.g., **умéть** *to know how to*) and **-ять** (e.g., **гулять** *to take a walk, stroll*), have present stems in [j], differing from the **читáть** type only in the vowel preceding the [j], e.g.:

Inf.	умéть	[uṃé.ṭ]	*Stem:* [uṃé-]	гулять	[guḷá.ṭ]	*Stem:* [guḷá-]
Past	умéл	[uṃé.l]		гулял	[guḷá.l]	
Pres.	умéю	[uṃéj.u]	*Stem:* [uṃéj-]	гуляю	[guḷáj.u]	*Stem:* [guḷáj-]
	умéешь	[uṃéj.iš]		гуляешь	[guḷáj.iš]	
	. . .			. . .		
Imperative	умéй	[uṃéj]		гуляй	[guḷáj]	

Among first conjugation verbs with present stems in vowel + [j] there are several groups presenting special patterns of variation between the two stems: the present and the infinitive-past.

(1) *Verbs in* **-овать**. These verbs, like **совéтовать** (*to advise*) replace the [-ova-] element of the infinitive-past stem by the element [-uj-] in the present:

Inf.	совéтовать	[saɣétəvə.ṭ]	*Stem:* [saɣétəvə-]
Past	совéтовал	[saɣétəvə.l]	
Pres.	совéтую	[saɣétuj.u]	
	совéтуешь	[saɣétuj.iš]	
	совéтует	[saɣétuj.it]	
	совéтуем	[saɣétuj.im]	*Stem:* [saɣétuj-]
	совéтуете	[saɣétuj.iṭi]	
	совéтуют	[saɣétuj.ut]	
Imperative	совéтуй	[saɣétuj]	

The same pattern is found in numerous verbs of foreign origin ending in **-и́ровать**, like **телефони́ровать** *to telephone*:

Inf.	телефони́ровать	[ṭiḷifaṇírəvə.ṭ]	} *Stem:* [ṭiḷifaṇírəvə.-]
Past	телефони́ровал	[ṭiḷifaṇírəvə.l]	

Pres.	телефони́рую	[ṭiḷifaṇíruj.u]	
	телефони́руешь	[ṭiḷifaṇíruj.iš]	} *Stem:* [ṭiḷifaṇíruj.-]
	. . .		
Imperative	телефони́руй	[ṭiḷifaṇíruj]	

It must be remembered that only verbs in **-овать** (and some in **-евать**) present the feature described above, *not* those in **-ывать/-ивать** or **-ава́ть**.

(2) *Verbs in* **-ава́ть**. Verbs in **-ава́ть,** with the stress on the last syllable (all imperfective), drop the element [va] in the present stem:

Inf.	дава́ть	[davá.ṭ]	} *Stem:* [davá-]
Past	дава́л	[davá.l]	

Pres.	даю́	[daj.ú]	
	даёшь	[daj.óš]	
	даёт	[daj.ót]	
	даём	[daj.óm]	} *Stem:* [daj-]
	даёте	[daj.óṭi]	
	даю́т	[daj.út]	
But: *Imperative*	дава́й	[daváj]	

(One will recall that the corresponding perfective is the irregularly conjugated verb да́ть: дам, дашь, даст, дади́м, дади́те, даду́т; *imperative* да́й.)

(3) *Verbs in* **-ыть** These verbs, e.g., **мы́ть** *to wash*, which are all monosyllabic (prefixed perfectives, like **вы́мыть**, however, may have two or three syllables), change the [ɨ] vowel of the infinitive and the past to [oj] in the present:

Inf.	мы́ть	[mɨ́.ṭ]	} *Stem:* [mɨ́-]
Past	мы́л	[mɨ́.l]	

Pres.	мо́ю	[mój.u]	
	мо́ешь	[mój.iš]	
	мо́ет	[mój.it]	
	мо́ем	[mój.im]	} *Stem:* [mój-]
	мо́ете	[mój.iṭi]	
	мо́ют	[mój.ut]	
Imperative	мо́й	[mój]	

A verb rarely used in its non-prefixed form, **кры́ть** *to cover*, is conjugated like мы́ть; so are its prefixed perfectives, **откры́ть** *to open*, **закры́ть** *to close*, and some others; откры́ть has the perfective future forms откро́ю, откро́ешь.

(4) *Verbs in* -ить (*monosyllabic: one consonant* + -ить). A group of verbs with infinitives consisting of a consonant + ить, like пить *to drink*, have present stems formed with this consonant + [j]:

Inf.	пить	[pí.t̢]	} *Stem:* [p̢i-]
Past	пил	[p̢í.l]	

Pres.	пью	[p̢j.ú]	
	пьёшь	[p̢j.óš]	
	пьёт	[p̢j.ót]	
	пьём	[p̢j.óm]	} *Stem:* [p̢j-]
	пьёте	[p̢j.ót̢i]	
	пьют	[p̢j.út]	
But: *Imperative*	пей	[p̢éj]	

This pattern is preserved in prefixed perfective forms which may have two or three syllables, e.g., вы́пить (вы́пью).

Note that the verb жить (*to live*) does *not* belong to this group.

B. First conjugation verbs with consonantal present stems. A number of verbs of the first conjugation have present stems which end, not in a vowel + [j], but in a consonant; some of these verbs have infinitives in -ать, like the verb ждать *to wait*:

Inf.	ждать	[ždá.t̢]	} *Stem:* [ždá-]
Past	ждал	[ždá.l]	

Pres.	жду	[žd.ú]	
	ждёшь	[žd̢.óš]	
	ждёт	[žd̢.ót]	
	ждём	[žd̢.óm]	} *Stem:* [žd-]
	ждёте	[žd̢.ót̢i]	
	ждут	[žd.út]	
Imperative	жди	[žd̢.í]	

Consonantal present stems in the first conjugation often present irregularities in their formation; the following are examples of such irregularities in verbs with infinitives in -ать/-ять:

брать, to take, *imperfective*
Inf. брать; *Past* брал   *Stem:* [brá-]
Pres. беру́, берёшь etc.; *Imperative* бери́   *Stem:* [b̢er-]

взять, to take, *perfective*
Inf. взять; *Past* взял   *Stem:* [ɣz̢á-]
Fut. возьму́, возьмёшь etc.; *Imperative* возьми́ *Stem:* [vaz̢m-]

нача́ть, to begin, *perfective*
Inf. нача́ть; *Past* на́чал   *Stem:* [nača-]
Fut. начну́, начнёшь etc.; *Imperative* начни́ *Stem:* [načn-]

поня́ть, to understand, *perfective*

Inf. поня́ть; *Past* по́нял   *Stem:* [poņa-]
Fut. пойму́, поймёшь etc.; *Imperative* пойми́   *Stem:* [pojm-]

уста́ть, to become tired, *perfective*

Inf. уста́ть; *Past* уста́л   *Stem:* [ustá-]
Fut. уста́ну, уста́нешь etc.; *Imperative* уста́нь   *Stem:* [ustán-]

Consonantal present stems are found in all verbs with infinitives in **-уть**; these verbs are of the first conjugation and are mostly perfective; they present no irregularities in their conjugation. The verb **верну́ть** (*to return*, transitive, perfective) may serve as an example:

Inf.	верну́ть	
Past	верну́л	*Stem:* [ɣirnú-]
Fut.	верну́	
	вернёшь	
	. . .	*Stem:* [ɣirn-]
Imperative	верни́	

One may also note that verbs with the following infinitive endings (all first conjugation) have consonantal present stems: **-ереть**, **-ти́**, **-сть**, and **-чь**

C. Second conjugation.   The most frequent infinitive endings in the second conjugation are **-еть** and **-ить**. Both these endings occur in the first conjugation as well; however, first conjugation verbs in **-ить** are mostly those of the monosyllabic пить group. Some verbs in **-ать** belong to the second conjugation; nearly all have stems ending in **ж, ч, ш,** or **щ.**

With only a few exceptions, second conjugation verbs have present stems ending in a consonant.

D. Consonant alternations.   Many verbs of both conjugations appear, in their different forms, with different end consonants of the stem; thus [s] is found in писа́ть, писа́л, but [š] in пишу́; [d] in сиде́ть, сиде́л, but [ž] in сижу́. These consonants are said to "alternate." Alternations of consonants occur not only in verbs, but in other series of words as well. A parallel may be found in English, with the difference that English spelling does not usually reflect the alternations of sounds observed in pronunciation; thus:

in pre*ss* and pre*ss*ure, [s] alternates with [š]
in plea*s*e and plea*s*ure, [z] alternates with [ž]
in na*t*ive and na*t*ural, [t] alternates with [č] etc.

In Russian the following consonantal sounds may alternate:

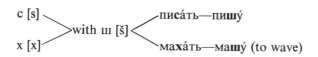

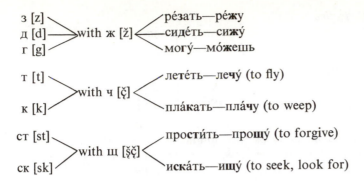

з [z] ⟍
д [d] —— ⟩with ж [ž]⟨ —— ре́зать—ре́жу
г [g] ⟋ сиде́ть—сижу́
могу́—мо́жешь

т [t] ⟍
⟩with ч [č]⟨ —— лете́ть—лечу́ (to fly)
к [k] ⟋ пла́кать—пла́чу (to weep)

ст [st] ⟍
⟩with щ [šč]⟨ —— прости́ть—прощу́ (to forgive)
ск [sk] ⟋ иска́ть—ищу́ (to seek, look for)

In addition, the group of consonantal sounds known as the "labials," [p], [b], [v], [f], and [m], may appear followed by an [ļ], that is, as [pļ], [bļ], [vļ], etc. One finds alternations of this type in:

купи́ть—куплю́   п [p]—пл [pļ]
люби́ть—люблю́   б [ḅ]—бл [bļ]
ста́вить—ста́влю   в [y]—вл [vļ] etc.

(1) *Consonant alternations in the first and in the second conjugations.* It is important to remember that when there is consonant alternation in verbs of the first conjugation, e.g., [s]—[š] in писа́ть—пишу́, the consonant found in the first person singular form ([š] in пишу́) also appears in all the other personal forms: пи́шешь, пи́шет, etc.

In the second conjugation, on the other hand, the alternate consonant is found *in the first person singular only*, the other personal forms having the same consonant as the infinitive. This may be seen in the following examples:

	1st conjugation				2nd conjugation			
Inf.	писа́ть	[s]	дрема́ть (to doze)	[m]	проси́ть	[ş]	люби́ть	[ḅ]
Past	писа́л		дрема́л		проси́л		люби́л	
Pres.	пишу́	[š]	дремлю́	[mļ]	прошу́	[š]	люблю́	[bļ]
	пи́шешь		дре́млешь		про́сишь		лю́бишь	
	пи́шет		дре́млет		про́сит		лю́бит	
	пи́шем		дре́млем		про́сим	[ş]	лю́бим	[ḅ]
	пи́шете		дре́млете		про́сите		лю́бите	
	пи́шут		дре́млют		про́сят		лю́бят	

(2) *Consonant alternations in verbs with infinitives in* -чь. Verbs belonging to this group, all of the first conjugation, have a distinct pattern of consonant alternation. The roots of these verbs all end in either [g] or [k] (historically, the ending [č] derives from [g + ţ] or [k + ţ]). In the conjugation, [g] alternates with [ž] and [k] with [č] according to the following pattern:

Inf.	мочь [č̦]		печь [č̦] (to bake)			
Past	мог, могла́ [g]		пёк, пекла́ [k]			
Pres.	могу́ [g]		пеку́ [k]			

мо́жешь		пече́шь	
мо́жет		пече́т	
мо́жем	[ž]	пече́м	[č̦]
мо́жете		пече́те	
мо́гут	[g]	пеку́т	[k]

Note the past tense masculine forms **мог** and **пёк**; this feature, the absence of **-л** in masculine (but, neuter **-ло**, feminine **-ла**, and plural **-ли**) is common to all verbs with infinitives in **-чь**.

E. The three "key forms" of a verb. It has been stated earlier that three forms of every verb, the infinitive and the first and second persons singular, should be memorized as the "key forms" from which one can predict all the others. The following examples will serve to show this:

1	2	3	4	5	6	7
зна́ть	идти́	писа́ть	мочь	говори́ть	лежа́ть	ходи́ть
зна́ю	иду́	пишу́	могу́	говорю́	лежу́	хожу́
зна́ешь	идёшь	пи́шешь	мо́жешь	говори́шь	лежи́шь	хо́дишь

(1) *Determining the ending.* Whether a verb is of the first or the second conjugation may be seen from the vowel in the ending of the second person singular; the vowel **e** (examples 1, 2, 3, and 4) means first conjugation, while **и** (examples 5, 6, and 7) means second. In two instances, the infinitive ending indicates that the verb is of the first conjugation: **-ти** (example 2) and **-чь** (example 4).

In the first conjugation, the ending of the third person plural is **-ют** if the first person singular ends in **-ю**: зна́ю—зна́ют (example 1); it is **-ут** if the first person singular ends in **-у**: иду́—иду́т (examples 2, 3, and 4). In the second conjugation, **-ю** in the first person singular corresponds to **-ят** in the third person plural: говорю́—говоря́т (example 5); and **-у** to **-ат**: (Spelling Rule 3—page 22): лежу́—лежа́т (example 6). However, verbs with consonant alternations (example 7) have **-у** in the first person singular but **-ят** in the third person plural: хожу́—хо́дят.

(2) *Finding the stem.* In the first conjugation the stem is the same in the six personal forms except for verbs ending in **-чь** (example 4). The special pattern of alternation in these verbs was described before; it will be remembered that the final consonant of the stem of the first person singular appears again in the third person plural: могу́—мо́гут. In the second conjugation, on the other hand, consonant alternations appear in the first person singular only; the final consonant of the second person singular is maintained in the remaining forms (example 7, **д** in the second person singular, хо́дишь, and in the rest of the conjugation: хо́дит, хо́дим, хо́дите, хо́дят).

(3) *Determining the position of the stress.* The stress in the conjugation of a verb may be fixed on the stem (example 1), or fixed on the ending (examples 2, 5, and 6) or it may shift from the ending in first singular to the stem in the other forms (examples 3, 4, and 7). It is, consequently, the position of the stress in the second person singular that determines its position in the remaining forms.

(4) *Irregular verbs.* There are only four verbs in Russian whose endings deviate from

the two types known as the first and second conjugation (they also present certain irregularities in consonant alternations). The conjugation patterns of these verbs cannot be derived from the three "key forms"; the complete conjugation of each of these verbs must be committed to memory. These four verbs are:

дать	есть	хоте́ть[1]	бежа́ть (to run)[1]
дам	ем	хочу́ (1st)	бегу́ (1st)
дашь	ешь	хо́чешь (1st)	бежи́шь (2nd)
даст	ест	хо́чет (1st)	бежи́т (2nd)
дади́м	еди́м	хоти́м (2nd)	бежи́м (2nd)
дади́те	еди́те	хоти́те (2nd)	бежи́те (2nd)
даду́т	едя́т	хотя́т (2nd)	бегу́т (1st)

	дать	есть	хоте́ть	бежа́ть
Past	дал (дала́)	ел	хоте́л	бежа́л
Imper.	дай!	ешь!	хоти́!	беги́! (1st)

F. New verbs, according to conjugation patterns.

(1) *First conjugation verb with infinitive in* **-еть**.

  име́ть (име́.ю, -ешь, *imperf.*; *no perf.*)   to have

This verb is commonly used with abstract nouns and in impersonal constructions. With the negative the object must be in the genitive. It is also used when an infinitive for *to have* is needed.

  Вы́ **име́ете** право (the right) зна́ть всю пра́вду.
  Хорошо́ **име́ть** де́ньги.
  Я́ не **име́л** удово́льствия ва́с ви́деть.

PATTERN SENTENCES

1. Когда́ мы́ бу́дем **име́ть** удово́льствие ва́с ви́деть?
2. Зимо́й ну́жно **име́ть** тёплое пальто́.
3. Они́ **име́ют** возмо́жность пое́хать в Евро́пу на три́ ме́сяца.
4. Я́ **име́ю** пра́во де́лать, что́ хочу́.
5. Я́ ещё **не име́л** слу́чая говори́ть с дире́ктором ва́шего институ́та.
6. Перево́дчик до́лжен **име́ть** хоро́шие словари́.
7. Я́ ничего́ **не име́ю** про́тив э́того.

1. When will we have the pleasure of seeing you?
2. In winter one must have a warm coat.
3. They have the possibility (chance) of going to Europe for three months.
4. I have the right to do whatever I want.
5. I haven't had a chance yet to talk to the director of your institute.
6. A translator must have good dictionaries.
7. I have nothing against that.

DRILL

Переведи́те на ру́сский.

1. You have no right to talk like that!
2. I had the pleasure of meeting your daughter.
3. We never had the opportunity to talk about this matter.
4. You ought to have an evening dress.
5. One must have friends.
6. I have nothing against him.

---

[1] These two verbs mix forms of the first and second conjugations as indicated.

(2) *First conjugation verbs with infinitives in* **-овать/-евать.**

путеше́ствовать (imperf., I: **путеше́ству.ю, -ешь**) to travel

сове́товать (imperf., I: **сове́ту.ю, -ешь**), **посове́товать** (perf., I) (+ *dative of person*) to advise, to give advice to

сове́товаться (imperf., I: **сове́ту.юсь, -ешься**), **посове́товаться** (perf., I) (**с** + *instrumental*) to consult (with)

танцева́ть[2] (imperf., I: **танцу́.ю, -ешь**) to dance

интересова́ть (imperf., I: **интересу́.ю, -ешь**) (+ *accusative of person*) to interest

интересова́ться (imperf., I: **интересу́.юсь, -ешься**), **поинтересова́ться** (perf., I) (+ *instrumental*) to be interested in

телефони́ровать (imperf., I: **телефони́ру.ю, -ешь**), **потелефони́ровать** (perf., I) (+ *dative*) to telephone

PATTERN SENTENCES

1. Ива́н Ива́нович мно́го **путеше́ствует**. Óн бы́л во мно́гих стра́нах.

2. В про́шлом году́ мы́ **путеше́ствовали** по все́й Евро́пе.

3. На́ши друзья́ **интересу́ются** наро́дными та́нцами и хорошо́ и́х **танцу́ют**.

4. —Вы́ хорошо́ **танцу́ете**? —Я́ не уме́ю **танцева́ть** и **танцу́ю** как сло́н.

5. Я́ **сове́тую** мое́й до́чери Катю́ше ме́ньше **танцева́ть** и бо́льше занима́ться.

6. Мно́гие врачи́ **сове́туют** свои́м пацие́нтам ме́ньше е́сть и пи́ть и бо́льше занима́ться спо́ртом. Э́то хорошо́ для здоро́вья.

7. Я́ хочу́ **посове́товаться** с ва́ми об одно́м о́чень ва́жном де́ле.

8. Вчера́ мо́й оте́ц бы́л у своего́ врача́. Вра́ч **посове́товал** ему́ принима́ть горя́чую ва́нну ка́ждый ве́чер и два́ ра́за в де́нь принима́ть аспири́н.

9. Я́ не **сове́тую** ва́м покупа́ть в то́м магази́не— та́м всё о́чень до́рого.

10. —Что́ ва́с **интересу́ет**? —Меня́ **интересу́ют** но́вые пье́сы, а мою́ сестру́ **интересу́ет** но́вая му́зыка.

11. —Че́м **интересу́ются** э́ти ма́льчики? —Не́которые **интересу́ются** то́лько спо́ртом и ма́ло занима́ются, а други́е **интересу́ются** всём.

1. Ivan Ivanovich travels a great deal. He has been in many countries.

2. Last year we traveled all over Europe.

3. Our friends are interested in folk dances, and dance them well.

4. —Do you dance well? —I don't know how to dance, and I dance like an elephant.

5. I advise my daughter Katyusha to dance less and study more.

6. Many doctors advise their patients to eat and drink less and to go in more for sports. It is good for the health.

7. I want to consult you about a very important matter.

8. Yesterday my father went to his doctor's. The doctor advised him to take a hot bath every evening and to take aspirin twice a day.

9. I advise you against shopping in that store; everything there is very expensive.

10. —What are you interested in? —I am interested in new plays, and my sister is interested in new music.

11. —What are those boys interested in? —Some are interested only in sports and study little; others are interested in everything.

DRILLS

A. *Translate the English sentences below in two ways, according to the model.*

Model: —What are you interested in? —In opera.

　　　—Что́ ва́с интересу́ет? —О́пера.

　and: —Че́м вы́ интересу́етесь? —О́перой.

---

[2] The infinitive ending of this verb is spelled **-евать** since unstressed **o** may not be written after **ц** (Spelling Rule 1).

1. —What are you interested in? —In ballet.
2. —What is he interested in? —In sports. In soccer.
3. —What is she interested in? —In folk dances.
4. He is not interested in his students.
5. Our students are interested in Russian literature of the nineteenth century.

B. *Translate the English words in parentheses.*

1. Мо́й учи́тель (advises me) бо́льше занима́ться.
2. Вра́ч (advises Ivan) пое́хать в Кры́м.
3. Что́ они́ (advised you)?
4. О́н лю́бит (to consult with me) обо всём.
5. Я́ зна́ю, что́ они́ (will advise you) в э́том слу́чае.
6. О́н лю́бит (to dance with her), но́ они́ ре́дко (dance).
7. Я́ (dance) то́лько наро́дные та́нцы.
8. Я́ люблю́ (to travel). Я́ мно́го (travel).

(3) *First conjugation verbs with infinitives in* -ава́ть. These are all imperfective; the group also includes the verbs дава́ть (*to give*) and встава́ть (*to get up*), given in previous units.

узнава́ть (imperf., I: узна.ю́, -ёшь), узна́ть (perf., I: узна́.ю, -ешь)[3] to recognize; to find out, learn (about)
устава́ть (imperf., I: уста.ю́, -ёшь), уста́ть (perf., I: уста́н.у, -ешь) to grow tired, weary
перестава́ть (imperf., I: переста.ю́, -ёшь), переста́ть (perf., I: перестан.у, -ешь) to stop, cease (+ imperf. infin.)
достава́ть (imperf., I: доста.ю́, -ёшь), доста́ть (perf., I: достан.у, -ешь) to get, obtain (often with some difficulty)

PATTERN SENTENCES

1. Я́ встре́тил Ива́на на у́лице и не узна́л его́, та́к он измени́лся с тех по́р, как я́ его́ ви́дел.
2. Стра́нно, что она́ меня́ никогда́ не узнаёт!
3. Я́ напишу́ Та́не, как то́лько узна́ю её а́дрес.
4. Я́ то́лько что узна́л, что Ви́ктор уе́хал за грани́цу.
5. Узна́йте, пожа́луйста, когда́ прихо́дит по́чта.
6. Я́ о́чень уста́л.[4] Я́ ля́гу на полчаса́, немно́жко отдохну́, а пото́м мы́ поу́жинаем.
7. Катю́ша, ты́ о́чень уста́ла:[4] ты́ сли́шком мно́го танцева́ла! Ты́ должна́ немно́го от-дохну́ть!
8. —Скажи́те мне́, когда́ вы́ уста́нете—мы́ мо́жем продолжа́ть на́шу рабо́ту по́сле обе́да. —Я́ скажу́ ва́м, е́сли уста́ну.
9. Почему́ о́н вдру́г переста́л на́м писа́ть?
10. Когда́ переста́нет до́ждь, мы́ пойдём погу-ля́ть.

1. I met Ivan on the street and didn't recognize him, he had changed so since I saw him.
2. It's strange that she never recognizes me!
3. I will write Tanya as soon as I find out her address.
4. I have just learned that Victor has gone abroad.
5. Please find out when the mail arrives.
6. I am very tired. I shall lie down for half an hour and rest a bit, and then we shall have supper.
7. Katyusha, you are very tired: you've been dancing too much! You must rest a little!
8. —Tell me when you get tired—we can continue our work after dinner. —I'll tell you if I get tired.
9. Why did he suddenly stop writing to us?
10. When the rain stops, we will go for a walk.

---

[3] Note that the distinction between the imperfective present and the perfective future of this verb is one of place of stress: узна́ю, *but* узна́ю.

[4] Note that the perfective past of this verb may be translated into English with present meaning: Я́ уста́л *I am tired.* In other words, I got tired, and therefore I am tired, but literally, *I have tired* or *I have grown tired.*

11. Де́ти, **переста́ньте** крича́ть!	11. Children, stop shouting!
12. Я узна́л от Ива́на, что о́н наконе́ц **доста́л** для на́с биле́ты на «Лебеди́нное о́зеро».	12. I learned from Ivan that he had finally got tickets for us to *Swan Lake*.

DRILL

Translate the English words in parentheses into Russian.

1. Зо́я та́к (changed), что я её не (recognized).
2. Я не ду́мал, что вы́ (would = will recognize) на́с; мы́ о́чень (changed).
3. Я зна́ю, что она́ пое́хала за грани́цу, но́ я до́лжен (find out) куда́.
4. (Please find out), где́ о́н живёт.

5. Она́ о́чень бы́стро (gets tired).
6. Я (am tired). Я (will go to bed) ра́но.
7. Почему́ вы́ (stopped) на́м писа́ть?
8. Я (will stop) с ва́ми разгова́ривать, е́сли вы́ не (will stop) крича́ть.

(4) *First conjugation verbs with infinitives in* **-нуть.**

отдыха́ть (imperf., I), **отдохну́ть** (perf., I: **отдохн.у́, -ёшь**; past: **отдохну́л**, etc.) to rest, rest up, get rested

привыка́ть (imperf., I), **привы́кнуть** (perf., I: **привы́кн.у, -ешь**; past: **привы́к, -ло, -ла, -ли** [к + *dat.*, *or imperf. infinitive*]) to get used to, grow accustomed to

отвыка́ть (imperf., I), **отвы́кнуть** (perf., I: **отвы́кн.у, -ешь**; past: **отвы́к, -ло, -ла, -ли** [от + *gen.*, *or imperf. infinitive*]) to grow unaccustomed to, lose the habit of

возвраща́ть (imperf., I), **верну́ть** (perf., I: **верн.у́, -ёшь**; past: **верну́л**, etc.)[5] to return (*trans.*), give back

возвраща́ться, верну́ться[5] to return (*intrans.*), go back, come back

Note the absence of the л ending in the masculine past tense in привы́к and отвы́к.

PATTERN SENTENCES

1. Я всегда́ **возвраща́ю** кни́ги, кото́рые беру́ у знако́мых. Я обеща́ю ва́м, что **верну́** ва́шу кни́гу через неде́лю.	1. I always return books which I borrow from friends. I promise you that I'll return your book in a week.
2. —**Верну́ла** ва́м А́нна пятна́дцать рубле́й, кото́рые взяла́ у ва́с тре́тьего дня́? —Не́т ещё. Она́ сказа́ла, что **вернёт** и́х в суббо́ту.	2. —Has Anna returned the fifteen rubles which she borrowed from you the day before yesterday? —Not yet. She said that she would return them on Saturday.
3. Я ча́сто **возвраща́юсь** домо́й вме́сте с мои́м сосе́дом.	3. I often return home with my neighbor.
4. —А́нна уже́ **верну́лась** из Босто́на? —Не́т, она́ **вернётся** послеза́втра.	4. —Has Anna come back from Boston? —No, she will come back the day after tomorrow.
5. Луня́ву бы́ло тру́дно **привы́кнуть** к сиби́рскому кли́мату, но в конце́ концо́в о́н к нему́ **привы́к**. О́н **привы́к** и к жаре́ и к хо́лоду.	5. It was hard for Lunyov to get used to the Siberian climate, but in the end he got used to it. He got used both to the heat and the cold.
6. Я не могу́ **привы́кнуть** к мы́сли, что о́н к на́м не **вернётся**.	6. I can't get used to the idea that he won't return to us.
7. Мы́ уже́ **привы́кли**[6] к на́шей но́вой учи́тельнице, и она́, ка́жется, **привы́кла**[6] к на́м.	7. We're already used to our new teacher, and she, it seems, is used to us.

---

[5] The perfectives have the alternate forms **возврати́ть** (II: **возвра.щу́, -ти́шь**) and **возврати́ться**.
[6] Notice that the perfective past of this verb may correspond to English present: *to be used to*.

8. Мне́ тру́дно **привыка́ть к но́вым места́м и к но́вым лю́дям.**

9. Тёте Ве́ре бы́ло тру́дно **привы́кнуть к жи́зни в го́роде.**

10. Тётя так до́лго жила́ в дере́вне, что она́ совсе́м **отвы́кла от** городско́й жи́зни и **от о́бщества.**

8. I have difficulty getting used to new places and new people.

9. It was hard for Aunt Vera to get used to her life in the city.

10. Auntie lived so long in the country that she became quite unaccustomed to city life and society.

DRILLS

A. *Переведи́те на англи́йский.*

1. Я́ до сих по́р не могу́ привы́кнуть к э́тому го́роду.
2. О́н не ви́дел свои́х роди́телей с тех по́р, как уе́хал из Росси́и, и о́н совсе́м отвы́к от ни́х.
3. А́нна, верни́ де́ньги, кото́рые ты́ взяла́ у меня́ «на два́ дня́».
4. Я́ верну́ и́х тебе́, когда́ ты́ переста́нешь об э́том говори́ть.
5. Верни́сь ра́ньше; не забу́дь, что мы́ сего́дня идём в теа́тр.

B. *Переведи́те на ру́сский.*

1. Andrey has got used to heat and cold.
2. I will return your book when I finish it; I always return books.
3. They will return at 10:00 sharp. When will you return?
4. She returned from Europe two weeks ago.
5. We always come back home together.
6. I must give back your newspaper; I've finished it.

(5) *First conjugation verb* **умере́ть.**

умира́ть (imperf., I), умере́ть (perf., I: умр.у́, -ёшь; past: у́мер, у́мерло, умерла́, у́мерли) to die

Note the absence of the л ending in the masculine past tense.

PATTERN SENTENCES

1. Мо́й де́душка **у́мер** в про́шлом году́, а ба́бушка **умерла́** два́ го́да тому́ наза́д.
2. Роди́тели Ни́ны **у́мерли** во вре́мя войны́.
3. Ты́ бу́дешь пла́кать, когда́ я́ **умру́.**
4. Мы́ все́ **умрём.** Но́ заче́м ду́мать о сме́рти?
5. Э́ти ста́рые дере́вья ме́дленно **умира́ют.**

1. My grandfather died last year, and grandmother died two years ago.
2. Nina's parents died during the war.
3. You will weep when I die.
4. We shall all die. But why think about death?
5. These old trees are slowly dying.

DRILL

Fill in the blanks with proper forms of the verb **умира́ть/умере́ть.**

1. Когда́ о́н . . . ., его́ сыновья́ получи́ли все́ его́ де́ньги.
2. Когда́ о́н . . . ., его́ сыновья́ полу́чат все́ его́ де́ньги.
3. Его́ ма́ть . . . ., когда́ ему́ бы́л го́д.
4. Е́сли ты́ не бу́дешь е́сть, ты́ . . . .!
5. И́х роди́тели давно́ . . . . .
6. Что́ она́ бу́дет де́лать, когда́ её роди́тели . . . .?
7. Э́то ста́рое де́рево ме́дленно . . . . .
8. Его́ де́душка неда́вно . . . . .
9. Мо́й дя́дя не бои́тся сме́рти, но́ о́н не хо́чет . . . . .

(6) *The verbs* **есть** *and* **пить**.

Есть (*to eat*) is conjugated like the verb **дать**, with the exception of the third person plural. But note that **есть** is *imperfective present;* **дать** is *perfective future:*

Perfective Future of **дать** (*to give*)	*Imperfective Present of* **есть** (*to eat*)
дам	ем
дашь	ешь
даст	ест
дади́м	еди́м
дади́те	еди́те
даду́т	едя́т

Past	дал, да́ло, дала́, да́ли	ел, е́ло, е́ла, е́ли
Imperative	дай, да́йте	ешь, е́шьте

Есть[7] has two perfectives: one, **пое́сть** (*to have a meal, have something to eat*); the other always transitive—used with an object—**съесть** (*to eat up, consume* a specific quantity). **Съесть** has its own secondary imperfective, **съеда́ть** (*to eat* a certain quantity of food—often, as a rule).

—Вы́ уже́ е́ли? —Да́, е́л.

Мы́ пое́ли и пошли́ в кино́.

Я́ съе́л два́ куска́ хле́ба. Обыкнове́нно я́ съеда́ю то́лько оди́н.

The same usage applies to **пить** (imperfective)—**вы́пить** (perfective, to drink up a certain quantity)—**выпива́ть** (imperfective, to drink a certain quantity, often, as a rule).[8]

Я́ то́лько что пи́л ко́фе.

Я́ вы́пил две́ ча́шки ко́фе. Обыкнове́нно я́ выпива́ю то́лько одну́.

PATTERN SENTENCES

1. Во́т что мы́ обы́чно еди́м на за́втрак:
2. Му́ж е́ст яи́чницу, иногда́ с ветчино́й, иногда́ с колбасо́й, и пьёт ко́фе.

3. На́ш сы́н И́горь е́ст иногда́ одно́ яйцо́, а иногда́ два́ яйца́, е́ст мно́го хле́ба с ма́слом, и пьёт молоко́.
4. Я́ не е́м яи́ц. Я́ е́м хле́б с сы́ром и пью́ ча́й.

1. Here is what we usually eat for breakfast:
2. My husband eats fried eggs, sometimes with ham and sometimes with sausage, and he drinks coffee.
3. Our son Igor sometimes eats one egg, and sometimes two eggs, eats a great deal of bread and butter, and drinks milk.
4. I don't eat eggs. I eat bread and cheese and drink tea.

---

[7] There is another verb, **ку́шать/поку́шать** (I), which also means *to eat*. It is used chiefly in invitations to eat, e.g., Иди́те ку́шать; Ку́шайте, пожа́луйста. This verb should *never* be used in the first person singular.

[8] Note that *all* perfective verbs with the prefix **вы-** have the stress on **вы-**, but the corresponding imperfective verbs *never* have the stress on **вы-**.

5. Вади́м и Зо́я лю́бят **есть** и мно́го **едя́т**. К у́жину они́ **едя́т** заку́ску, пото́м котле́ты[9] с гре́чневой ка́шей и с кра́сной капу́стой и **пью́т** пи́во за едо́й! А мы́ **еди́м** к у́жину творо́г со смета́ной. Пото́м мы́ **пьём** ча́й. И э́то всё!

6. Ива́н Ива́нович лю́бит **есть** но́чью. Óн ча́сто встаёт с крова́ти среди́ но́чи, идёт на ку́хню, и съеда́ет всё, что е́сть в холоди́льнике.

7. —Ни́на, **хо́чешь е́сть**? —Не́т, спаси́бо, я́ уже́ **е́ла**. —Что́ ты́ **е́ла**? —Я́ **съе́ла** два́ бутербро́да и **вы́пила** ча́шку ко́фе.

8. Как то́лько я́ **пое́м**, я́ приду́ к ва́м. Подожди́те меня́, и мы́ вме́сте пойдём в кино́.

9. Снача́ла **пое́шь**, а пото́м пойди́ игра́ть. **Съе́шь** всё, что у тебя́ на таре́лке.

10. Когда́ моя́ жена́ уе́дет, я́ бу́ду **е́сть** в рестора́не.

5. Vadim and Zoya like to eat and eat a great deal. For supper they eat hors-d'œuvres, then chopped steak with buckwheat porridge and red cabbage, and they drink beer with their meal. And we eat cottage cheese and sour cream for dinner! Then we drink tea. And that's all!

6. Ivan Ivanovich likes to eat at night. He often gets out of bed in the middle of the night, goes to the kitchen, and eats up everything there is in the refrigerator.

7. —Nina, do you want to eat? —No thanks, I've eaten already. —What did you eat? —I ate two sandwiches and drank a cup of coffee.

8. As soon as I've eaten, I'll come to your place. Wait for me and we'll go to the movies together.

9. First eat, and then go and play. Eat up everything that's on your plate.

10. When my wife goes away, I'm going to eat in a restaurant.

DRILL

Переведи́те на ру́сский язы́к.

1. He never eats bread and he never drinks milk.
2. —Vadim, what are you (*familiar*) eating? I am eating meat and (= with) salad.
3. —Ivan Ivanovich, where do you usually eat? —We always eat at home.
4. I ate and went to work.
5. He often eats two steaks at dinner.
6. The French drink a lot of wine.
7. Kolya, drink up your milk!
8. I ate all the meat you gave me.

2. Мо́жно and нельзя́

Мо́жно (мо́жно бы́ло/бу́дет) means *one can*, *one may*, *it is possible to*, etc. It takes an infinitive:

Где́ **мо́жно** купи́ть папиро́сы?
Where can one buy cigarettes?

Вы́ ду́маете, что **мо́жно** бу́дет его́ ви́деть за́втра?
Do you think that one can see him tomorrow?

Óн сказа́л всё, что **мо́жно** бы́ло об э́том сказа́ть.
He said everything that could be said about that.

Мо́жно is used also to request permission:

Мо́жно зде́сь кури́ть?
May one (I) smoke here? (Is smoking permitted here?)

---

[9] A variant of the American hamburger; bread is usually mixed in with the meat.

The person for whom permission is requested is often omitted as obvious. When specified, the person is named in the *dative:*

> Мо́жно **мне́** взя́ть э́ту кни́гу?
> May *I* take that book?

> Мо́жно **на́м с Ива́ном** прийти́ к ва́м сего́дня ве́чером?
> May Ivan and I come to see you this evening?

Нельзя́ (нельзя́ бы́ло/бу́дет) is the negative of **мо́жно:**

> В э́том ваго́не **мо́жно** кури́ть, а в то́м **нельзя́.**
> In this (railroad) car one may smoke, and in that one one may not.

Нельзя́ often corresponds to English *must not, not supposed to.*

> Вра́ч сказа́л, что мне́ **нельзя́ пи́ть вино́.**
> The doctor said that I must not drink wine.

The words **возмо́жно** and **невозмо́жно** also denote possibility or impossibility. But only **мо́жно** and **нельзя́** may be used in requesting or granting permission, and only **возмо́жно** may be used in sentences of the type **Возмо́жно, что....** *It is possible that...,* e.g., Возмо́жно, что о́н сего́дня не придёт на уро́к.

PATTERN SENTENCES

One can—one cannot (possible—impossible)

1. Где́ **мо́жно** купи́ть хоро́шие боти́нки?
2. Зде́сь **нельзя́** купи́ть хоро́шего шокола́да.
3. Что́ **мо́жно** купи́ть за де́сять це́нтов?
4. За э́ти де́ньги тепе́рь ничего́ **нельзя́** купи́ть.
5. **Нельзя́** сказа́ть, что э́то о́чень хоро́шая статья́.
6. Говоря́т, что ско́ро **мо́жно** бу́дет достава́ть кварти́ры в э́том го́роде.
7. У ни́х **мо́жно** встре́тить са́мых интере́сных люде́й.

1. Where can one buy good shoes?
2. One cannot buy good chocolate here.
3. What can one buy for ten cents?
4. You cannot buy anything now for that sum.
5. One can't say that this is a very good article.
6. They say that one will soon be able to get apartments in this city.
7. At their house one can meet the most interesting people.

May—may not (permitted—not permitted)

1. **Мо́жно** попроси́ть ва́с переда́ть мне́ со́ль и пе́рец?
2. —**Мо́жно** зада́ть ва́м оди́н вопро́с? —Пожа́луйста.
3. Во вре́мя ле́кции **нельзя́** задава́ть вопро́сов, а по́сле ле́кции **мо́жно.**
4. —**Мо́жно** мне́ взя́ть бана́н? —Коне́чно!
5. —**Мо́жно** Ива́ну взя́ть э́ту кни́гу? —**Мо́жно.**
6. —**Мо́жно** се́сть ря́дом с ва́ми? —Коне́чно, **мо́жно!**

1. May I ask you to pass me the salt and pepper?
2. —May I ask you a question? —Please do.
3. You may not ask questions during the lecture, but after the lecture you may.
4. —May I take a banana? —Certainly!
5. —May Ivan take this book? —He may.
6. —May I sit down beside you? —Of course you may!

DRILLS

A. *Переведи́те с ру́сского на англи́йский.*

1. —Что́ мо́жно купи́ть в э́том магази́не? —Всё что хоти́те.
2. Вы́ ду́маете, что мо́жно бу́дет ско́ро уйти́?
3. Вра́ч сказа́л, что де́душке нельзя́ мно́го е́сть.
4. Ему́ тепе́рь мо́жно е́сть мя́со то́лько ра́з в неде́лю.
5. Ра́ньше ему́ мо́жно бы́ло е́сть ско́лько о́н хоте́л.
6. Нельзя́ сказа́ть, что Петро́в о́чень у́мный челове́к!
7. Нельзя́ привы́кнуть к э́тому шу́му!
8. Ко всему́ мо́жно привы́кнуть.
9. Мо́й дру́г без труда́ доста́л вчера́ два́ биле́та на места́ во второ́м ряду́, и ему́ сказа́ли, что мо́жно име́ть биле́ты да́же на суббо́ту!
10. Нельзя́ поня́ть, чего́ о́н хо́чет.
11. —Па́па, мо́жно на́м взя́ть тво́й автомоби́ль? —Тебе́ мо́жно, а Ни́не нельзя́.

B. *Переведи́те с англи́йского на ру́сский.*

1. —May I say one word? —Certainly.
2. One can say that he's a very good poet, but one can't say that he is a good teacher.
3. It's not possible to buy even a newspaper here!
4. It will soon be possible to go to the country.
5. You (one) can't believe him!
6. Can one live here?
7. It can't be said yet what kind of student he is.
8. One can't say that he's very clever, but one can say that he's kind.

3. Perfective verbs захоте́ть, уви́деть, услы́шать, and смочь

The perfective verbs захоте́ть (imperf. хоте́ть), уви́деть (imperf. ви́деть), услы́-шать (imperf. слы́шать), and смочь (imperf. мочь), are used as follows:

In most cases calling for the use of the future, in particular after когда́ and е́сли, the perfective is used. The imperfective future of мочь is never used, that of the other three verbs very rarely:

Мы́ уви́дим, кака́я бу́дет пого́да за́втра.
We shall see what the weather is like tomorrow.

Скажи́ мне, когда́ ты́ захо́чешь е́сть.
Tell me when you feel like eating.

Е́сли я́ смогу́, я да́м ва́м де́ньги в понеде́льник.
If I can I shall give you the money on Monday.

The perfectives захоте́ть, уви́деть, and услы́шать refer to the moment when a desire is conceived or a sight or sound caught:

Она́ посмотре́ла в окно́ и уви́дела, что идёт до́ждь.
She looked out the window and saw that it was raining.
Я́ уви́дел его́ то́лько, когда́ о́н бы́л уже́ пе́редо мно́й.
I saw him only when he was already in front of me.
Я́ вдру́г захоте́л пла́кать и пошёл в свою́ ко́мнату.
I suddenly felt like crying and went to my room.

PATTERN SENTENCES

Смочь, захотéть

1. Я боюсь, что не **смогу** хорошó объяснить ему э́то прáвило.
2. Я ничегó ему не обещáл, нó я сказáл, что я дáм ему дéнег, éсли **смогу**.
3. Андрéй обещáл прийти, éсли **смóжет**.
4. Óн надéется, что **смóжет** дáть мнé отвéт во втóрник.
5. Я приду, когдá **захочу**!
6. Éсли вы **захоти́те** меня ви́деть зáвтра, позвони́те мнé, и я приду.
7. —Кóля, éсли ты **захóчешь** éсть, возьми́ хлéб, мáсло и кусóк сы́ра.
8. Я увéрен, что Зóя не **смóжет** прийти зáвтра.
9. Я ду́маю, что **смогу** достáть билéты на зáвтра.

1. I am afraid that I shall not be able to explain that rule well to him.
2. I didn't promise him anything, but I told him that I would give him some money if I could.
3. Andrey promised to come if he can make it.
4. He hopes that he will be able to give me an answer on Tuesday.
5. I shall come when I feel like it!
6. If you feel like seeing me tomorrow, phone me, and I shall come.
7. Kolya, if you feel like eating, take some bread, butter, and a piece of cheese.
8. I am sure that Zoya will not be able to come tomorrow.
9. I think I'll be able (can manage) to get tickets for tomorrow.

Уви́деть, услы́шать

1. Онá **услы́шала** голосá и пошлá к двéри.
2. Я вдру́г **услы́шал** грóмкий кри́к.
3. Я нáчал переводи́ть статью́, но **уви́дел**, что без словаря́ не смогу э́того сдéлать.
4. Я **уви́дел** Бори́са, когдá óн бы́л ещё далекó.
5. Я **услы́шал** об э́том вчерá в пéрвый рáз.
6. Я ви́дел Ни́ну вчерá в три́ часá, и **уви́жу** её зáвтра в четы́ре.
7. Я **уви́жу** егó зáвтра в двá часá, **услы́шу**, чтó óн мнé скáжет, и тогдá **уви́жу**, что я смогу для негó сдéлать.

1. She heard voices and went to the door.
2. I suddenly heard a loud cry.
3. I started to translate the article, but saw that without a dictionary I wouldn't be able to do it.
4. I caught sight of Boris while he was still far away.
5. I heard about that yesterday for the first time.
6. I saw Nina yesterday at three, and shall see her tomorrow at four.
7. I shall see him tomorrow at two o'clock, I shall hear what he has to tell me, and then I shall see what I can do for him.

DRILLS

A. *Translate the words in parentheses, and then the whole sentence into English.*

1. Как тóлько я (shall hear) о тóм, чтó случи́лось на собрáнии, я вáм сейчáс же всё расскажу́.
2. Зи́на (heard) вчерá хорóший анекдóт и рассказáла егó мнé.
3. Éсли вы (should hear) интерéсный анекдóт, расскажи́те егó мнé.
4. Мы́ шли́ вчерá по нáшей у́лице и вдру́г (heard) ужáсный кри́к.
5. Мы́ не в пéрвый рáз (heard) такóй кри́к.
6. Я (saw) вчерá Рóбертса и (shall see) егó опя́ть во втóрник.
7. Éсли через чáс вы (will feel like) погуля́ть—скажи́те мнé.
8. Я ещё не знáю, когдá я (shall be able) прийти к вáм.
9. Я надéюсь, что вы (will be able) прийти в суббóту.

B. *Читáйте и переводúте.*

1. С тех пóр, как Óля поступúла на нóвую слýжбу, онá так устаёт, что ложúтся спáть срáзу пóсле ýжина.

2. —До какúх пóр вы бýдете сегóдня рабóтать? —Я бýду рабóтать до обéда, или до тех пóр, покá не устáну.

3. Я до сих пóр не могý понять, кáк óн мóжет так мнóго рабóтать!

4. Однá моя знакóмая испáнка óчень хорошó танцýет испáнские нарóдные тáнцы и поёт испáнские пéсни. Никтó не знáет стóлько пéсен, как онá.

5. —Ты пóмнишь, что посовéтовал дяде Мúше знаменúтый врáч, у котóрого óн бы́л в Берлúне? —Óн посовéтовал ему́ ходúть двá часá в дéнь.

6. Я сегóдня мнóго рабóтал и óчень устáл. Я пришёл домóй, вы́пил двá стакáна горячего чáю с лимóном и с рóмом, прúнял аспирúн, и лёг в постéль.

7. Éсли я захочý ещё стакáн чáю—я попрошý женý.

8. Зинаúда Михáйловна тóлько что принялá горячую вáнну. Онá óчень устáла и леглá на дивáн отдохнýть.

9. Я не примý у вáс э́тих дéнег! Возьмúте úх обрáтно!

10. Вначáле Ивáну и Áнне бы́ло трýдно привы́кнуть к городскóй жúзни, нó тепéрь онú не тóлько привы́кли к нéй, нó дáже лю́бят её!

11. Садúтесь на э́то крéсло; на э́том крéсле óчень удóбно сидéть.

12. Тепéрь óчень рáно станóвится темнó. Вы́ вúдите, как ужé стáло темнó!

13. По-мóему Вúктор стáл хорóшим ученикóм. Кáк по-вáшему?

14. Éсли вáм стáнет хóлодно, я дáм вáм свóй пиджáк.

15. Трýдно привы́кнуть к мы́сли, что мы́ всé умрём.

4. Cardinal and ordinal numerals, 20–199

	Cardinal	*Ordinal (masc.)*
20	двáдцать	двадцáтый
21	двáдцать одúн (однó, однá)	двáдцать пéрвый
22	двáдцать двá (двé)	двáдцать вторóй
23	двáдцать трú	двáдцать трéтий
24	двáдцать четы́ре	двáдцать четвёртый
25	двáдцать пять	двáдцать пя́тый
	etc.	etc.
30	трúдцать	тридцáтый
31	трúдцать одúн (однó, однá)	трúдцать пéрвый
	etc.	etc.
40	сóрок	сороковóй
50	пятьдеся́т	пятидеся́тый
60	шестьдеся́т	шестидеся́тый
70	сéмьдесят	семидеся́тый
80	вóсемьдесят	восьмидеся́тый
90	девянóсто	девянóстый
100	стó	сóтый
101	стó одúн (однó, однá)	стó пéрвый

110	стó дéсять	стó деся́тый
125	стó двáдцать пя́ть	стó двáдцать пя́тый
	etc.	etc.

It will be remembered that the nominative singular (or other cases as appropriate) is used with **оди́н** and all compound numerals the last digit of which is **оди́н** (21, 31, 101, etc.): двáдцать оди́н студéнт, 21 students; три́дцать однá дéвушка, 31 girls, etc. The *genitive singular* is used with compound numbers the last digit of which is **двá (две)**, **три, четы́ре** (22, 43, 104, etc.): сóрок двá дóма, 42 houses; шестьдеся́т три гóрода, 63 cities. Other cardinal numbers take the *genitive plural*: стó дéсять детéй, 110 children, etc.

Compound ordinals (21st, 135th, etc.) are formed with the *cardinal* of the first part (or parts) and the *ordinal* of the final digit. Only the last digit is declined:

Мы́ живём на двáдцать пéрвом этажé.

Óн живёт на стó три́дцать пя́той у́лице.

Пятьдеся́т (50), шестьдеся́т (60), сéмьдесят (70), and вóсемьдесят (80) are compounds of пять, шесть, etc., but the second element -дéсят lacks -**ь**. Ordinals of these numerals replace the **ь** of the first numeral element with **и**: пятидеся́тый, etc.

DRILL

Translate the English words in parentheses into Russian, spelling out all numerals.

1. Нáшей учи́тельнице (47 years old), а её мáтери (68 years old).
2. Мы́ живём на (76th Street), а нáши роди́тели на (98th Street).
3. В э́том высóтном здáнии (45 floors), и óн рабóтает на (42nd floor).
4. Скóро бýдет (the 21st century). Вы́ бýдете жи́ть в (the 21st century)!
5. Они́ живýт на (132nd Street), а мы́ живём на (165th).

Reading

Моя́ сосéдка

Нельзя́ сказáть, что Вéра Васи́льевна зла́я жéнщина, нó и нельзя́ сказáть, что онá óчень дóбрый и прия́тный человéк.

Во-пéрвых, Вéра Васи́льевна лю́бит сплéтни (gossip). Сплéтничать (to gossip) —э́то её люби́мое заня́тие, и язы́к (tongue) у неё довóльно злóй. Во-вторы́х, онá óчень лю́бит давáть совéты. Цéлый дéнь тóлько и слы́шишь: «Я́ вáм совéтую, сдéлайте э́то; я́ вáм совéтую, не дéлайте э́того.» В-трéтьих, онá лю́бит расскáзывать о рáзных у́жасах, о неприя́тных слýчаях, смертя́х, скандáлах и так дáлее и так дáлее.

Вéра Васи́льевна знакóма не тóлько со всéми жильцáми нáшего дóма, нó почти́ всé жильцы́ сосéдних домóв её хорóшие знакóмые, и онá знáет всё, что у ни́х происхóдит.

В пя́тницу она́ пришла́ ко мне, се́ла на своё люби́мое ме́сто у окна́, та́к чтобы ви́деть всё, что происхо́дит на у́лице (мы́ живём на второ́м этаже́), и сра́зу начала́ расска́зывать:

—Зна́ете, вчера́ я́ возвраща́лась домо́й от Лунёвых. Бы́ло уже́ дово́льно по́здно, и вдру́г ви́жу, идёт Катю́ша Ле́бедева! И идёт она́ не одна́, а с Бори́сом Ка́рповым. Вы́ зна́ете Ка́рповых? Э́то жильцы́, кото́рые живу́т на седьмо́м этаже́. Их кварти́ра пря́мо про́тив ли́фта. Вы́ их зна́ете! У Наста́сьи Ива́новны Ка́рповой о́чень гро́мкий и неприя́тный го́лос, и она́ лю́бит на все́х крича́ть. У ни́х две́ ко́шки.

—Нет, не зна́ю ни Катю́шу Ле́бедеву, ни Ка́рповых, ни и́х ко́шек. И како́е мне́ де́ло, что все́ э́ти лю́ди де́лают?

—Ка́к, како́е де́ло?! Стра́нный вы́ челове́к! Никто́ ва́с не интересу́ет! Прости́те меня́, но та́к нельзя́ жи́ть. Ну́жно принима́ть уча́стие в жи́зни други́х.

Я́ ей ничего́ не отве́тила: она́ всё равно́ не поймёт и начнёт спо́рить. И она́ продолжа́ла.

—Вы́ слы́шали, что инжене́р Ма́слов у́мер?

—Како́й инжене́р Ма́слов? Я́ не зна́ю никако́го инжене́ра Ма́слова.

—Ну что́ вы́ говори́те! Вы́ не зна́ете Ма́слова, кото́рый живёт, то́ есть жи́л, на на́шей у́лице, в тре́тьем до́ме от угла́? Он жи́л на пе́рвом этаже́. Жена́ Ма́слова умерла́ не́сколько ле́т тому́ наза́д (он о́чень люби́л свою́ жену́), и к нему́ из дере́вни прие́хала на неде́лю его́ ску́чная ста́рая тётка. Она́ прие́хала на неде́лю и, поду́майте, до сих по́р живёт у него́! Она́ меня́ почему́-то ненави́дит. За что́? Оди́н Бо́г зна́ет! Я́ ей сове́тую верну́ться в дере́вню, а она́ мне́ говори́т, что э́то не моё де́ло! И оди́н ра́з она́ да́же попроси́ла меня́ к ни́м бо́льше не приходи́ть и не телефони́ровать и́м! Ужа́сная же́нщина! Я́ её про́сто ненави́жу.

—Прости́те меня́, но я́ не понима́ю, ка́к вы́ могли́ посове́товать ей верну́ться в дере́вню? Како́е ва́м де́ло? Како́е пра́во вы́ име́ете та́к говори́ть! Я́ отли́чно понима́ю, что она́ ва́с не лю́бит.

—Вы́ её не зна́ете, вы́ не зна́ете, како́й у неё хара́ктер. Я́ ча́сто говори́ла Ма́слову: —«Андре́й Петро́вич, ну́, почему́ э́та ста́рая ве́дьма (hag, witch) у ва́с живёт? У ва́с така́я ску́чная жи́знь! Я́ ва́м о́чень сове́тую сказа́ть ей, что у ва́с для неё не́т ме́ста. Бу́дьте си́льным челове́ком. Ну́, ра́зве э́то жи́знь?» А о́н, бе́дный, бы́л тако́й до́брый и сла́бый челове́к. Он говори́л: —«Но э́то совсе́м не та́к! Во-пе́рвых, Варва́ра хоро́шая же́нщина, а во-вторы́х, у неё кро́ме меня́ никого́ на све́те не́т. Кро́ме того́, я́ привы́к к ней, и она́ привы́кла ко мне́, и куда́ она́, бе́дная, тепе́рь пое́дет?» А я́ ему́ говори́ла: —«Вы́ никого́ не ви́дите, вы́ не принима́ете уча́стия в жи́зни други́х. Та́к нельзя́ жи́ть. Во́т уви́дите, что э́то пло́хо для ва́с ко́нчится!» И во́т, сего́дня я́ узна́ла, что Ма́слов у́мер!

Пото́м Ве́ра Васи́льевна начала́ говори́ть на одну́ из свои́х люби́мых те́м: о том как бы́ло когда́-то и ка́к тепе́рь. Она́ начала́ издалека́.

—Да́, в моё вре́мя всё бы́ло по-друго́му. Когда́, наприме́р, мне́ бы́ло шестна́дцать ле́т, а мое́й сестре́ О́ле бы́ло семна́дцать, мы́ должны́ бы́ли ложи́ться спа́ть в де́вять часо́в. На́м нельзя́ бы́ло возвраща́ться по́здно домо́й, и на́м нельзя́ бы́ло танцева́ть с ке́м мы́ хоте́ли. А тепе́рь де́вушки де́лают, что хотя́т. Они́ танцу́ют с молоды́ми людьми́, кото́рых и́х роди́тели да́же не зна́ют, и возвраща́ются домо́й в любо́е вре́мя. А бе́дные роди́тели ничего́ свои́м де́тям да́же не говоря́т: они́ тепе́рь и́х боя́тся. Кста́ти, во́т наприме́р, ва́ша Ни́ночка. Ни́ночке четы́рнадцать ле́т, пра́вда? Я́ зна́ю, что она́ хоро́шая де́вочка, но, дорога́я Зинаи́да Миха́йловна! Я́ ведь ва́ш дру́г, пра́вда? Я́ ва́м о́чень сове́тую...

—Дорога́я Ве́ра Васи́льевна, е́сли вы́ хоти́те бы́ть мои́м дру́гом, я́ ва́м о́чень сове́тую не дава́ть мне́ сове́тов и не расска́зывать мне́ о дела́х други́х люде́й. Ла́дно?

Она́ посмотре́ла на меня́ и уви́дела, что я́ не шучу́. Пото́м посмотре́ла на часы́ и сказа́ла: —«Бо́же мо́й! Как по́здно! Споко́йной но́чи, дорога́я! Переда́йте приве́т Ни́ночке.» И она́ ушла́.

Что́ она́ расска́зывает други́м обо мне́? Хотя́, должна́ пра́вду сказа́ть, меня́ э́то не осо́бенно интересу́ет.

Чита́йте э́ти вопро́сы и отвеча́йте на ни́х.

1. Что́ мо́жно сказа́ть о Ве́ре Васи́льевне? Что́ она́ лю́бит? 2. О чём она́ лю́бит расска́зывать? 3. Кого́ она́ зна́ет? 4. Где́ её люби́мое ме́сто в мое́й кварти́ре и почему́? 5. Что́ она́ рассказа́ла про Катю́шу Ле́бедеву и про Ка́рповых? 6. Где́ кварти́ра Ка́рповых? 7. Что́ сказа́ла Ве́ра Васи́льевна, когда́ она́ услы́шала, что я́ не зна́ю все́х э́тих люде́й? 8. Что́ она́ рассказа́ла мне́ про инжене́ра Ма́слова? 9. Почему́ его́ ста́рая тётя Варва́ра живёт у него́? 10. Что́ Ве́ра Васи́льевна о не́й говори́т? 11. Что́ она́ посове́товала тётке? 12. На каку́ю те́му моя́ сосе́дка пото́м начала́ говори́ть? 13. Что́ я́ ей посове́товала? 14. О чём я́ поду́мала, когда́ она́ наконе́ц ушла́?

DRILL

Review Translation.

1. She changed very much since the time I saw her. 2. —When did you see her last? —Last year. 3. When will you give me back my book? 4. I shall return it in two days. 5. I returned to Moscow after a long trip. 6. —When is your husband coming back from France? —In two months. 7. We live opposite the park. 8. My room is opposite Olga's room. 9. —Where is Mama? —She's gone to bed. She is very tired.[10] 10. —May I take part in your conversation? —No, you may not. 11. If I can, I shall find out where he lives. 12. Smirnov is abroad; he will return here next year. 13. He will let us know as soon as he returns (= will return). 14. It was very hard for me to get used to that idea, but I got used to it. 15. She is not used[11] to such noise. 16. By the way, you can take any Russian book. 17. I took a bath, and now good night! 18. This book doesn't interest me. 19. I shall phone you tomorrow. 20. Turgenev and Dostoevsky lived and wrote in the nineteenth century. 21. Tolstoy was eighty-two when he died.

Vocabulary

ва́нна bath
возмо́жность (*fem. II*) possibility, chance
городско́й city, urban, municipal
горя́чий (*adv.* горячо́) hot[12]

до́брый kind, good-hearted
жара́ hot weather, heat
жа́реный fried, roasted
жил.е́ц (*gen.* -ьца́, *fem.* -и́ца) lodger, tenant

---

[10] See note 4 on p. 342.
[11] See note 6 on p. 343.
[12] **Жа́ркий** applies to weather only: жа́ркая пого́да; жа́ркий де́нь, кли́мат, etc. **Горя́чий** applies to objects: горя́чий ко́фе, ча́й, су́п, etc.

заня́тие occupation
заня́тия (*pl.*) occupations, studies, classes
здоро́вье health
злой evil, vicious
издалека́ from afar
ка́ша cooked cereal, porridge
крик cry, shout
кста́ти by the way, à propos
лифт elevator
луна́ moon
любо́й any (at all)
мысль (*fem. II*) thought, idea
наро́дный national; folk
никако́й no, none (at all)
пе́р.ец (*gen.* -ца) pepper
пра́во right (*noun*)

про (+ *acc.*) about, concerning
про́тив (+ *gen.*) opposite, against
связь (*fem. II*) link, tie, connection
си́льный strong
сла́бый weak
слон elephant
сра́зу at once, immediately
та́н.ец (*gen.* -ца) dance
тётка aunt, auntie
у́жас horror, terror
уча́стие participation, part
хо́лод cold
чтобы as to, in order to (+ *inf.*)
яи́чница [jiíšṇicə] omelet
яйцо́ (*nom. pl.* я́йца; *gen. pl.* яи́ц) [jijcó, jájcə, jiíc]
  egg

VERBS

(For other verbs see pages 340–345.)

изменя́ться (imperf., I), измени́ться (perf., II: изменю́сь, изме́нишься) to change (*intrans.*), be altered

крича́ть (imperf., II: крич.у́, -и́шь), кри́кнуть (perf., I: кри́кн.у, -ешь) to cry out, shout

обеща́ть (imperf., I) to promise (+ *dat. of person*)

пла́кать (imperf., I: пла́ч.у, -ешь) to weep, cry

пробы́ть (perf., I: пробу́д.у, -ешь; past: про́был, -о, пробыла́, про́были) to stay, spend (some time)

происходи́ть (imperf., II: происхо́дит), произойти́ (perf., I: произойдёт; past: произошло́) to occur, happen, take place

EXPRESSIONS

сади́ться/се́сть на по́езд to take a (the) train
с тех по́р since then
с тех по́р, как . . . since the time when
до каки́х по́р? how long, how far, till when?
до тех по́р till then
до сих по́р so far, this far, till now, still, till this day
тре́тьего дня́ day before yesterday
по-друго́му otherwise, differently
е́хать за грани́цу (*acc.*) to go abroad
бы́ть за грани́цей (*instr.*) to be abroad
да́ть (+ *dat.*) зна́ть to let someone know
пока́ . . . не (+ *perf. past or future*) until[13]
то́лько и слы́шишь . . . you hear nothing but . . .
в-тре́тьих third, in the third place
и так да́лее (и. т. д.) and so forth (etc.)
принима́ть уча́стие to take part
принима́ть/приня́ть ва́нну to take a bath
принима́ть/приня́ть аспири́н to take aspirin
никогда́ в жи́зни never in (my) life
когда́-то once, at one time

---

[13] E.g. Я бу́ду рабо́тать, пока́ ты́ не придёшь.

The interrogative particle ли • The particles -то and -нибудь •
Prepositions of place or direction (supplement) • Verbs of motion
with prefixes of direction • Verbs of *carrying* • Verbs of *leading*
Translation of *to take* and *to bring* • Prepositions of position and
motion • Reading: На остано́вке авто́буса

Unit 22

Grammar

1. The interrogative particle ли

The particle **ли** is used in indirect questions which may be answered by *yes* or *no*, i.e., in subordinate clauses which, in English, are introduced by *whether* or *if*: *He asked me whether* (or *if*) *I knew.*

In Russian, a direct question is changed into an indirect one as follows:

Direct question: Óн меня́ спроси́л: «Ива́н уже́ прие́хал?»
Indirect question: Óн меня́ спроси́л, прие́хал ли уже́ Ива́н.

One observes that the **ли** particle is placed after the key word of the direct question—which is in this example the predicate **прие́хал**—and that the word order "subject—predicate" (Ива́н прие́хал) is changed to "predicate—subject" (прие́хал ли Ива́н).

The particle **ли** has the significance of *whether or not*:

Óн меня́ спроси́л, прие́хал ли уже́ Ива́н (i.e., прие́хал или не́т).
Я не зна́ю, до́ма ли сейча́с мо́й оте́ц (i.e., до́ма или не́т).
Я его́ спроси́л, чита́л ли о́н «Войну́ и мир» (i.e., чита́л или не́т).

The key word of an indirect question is often but not necessarily always a verb. Compare:

Óн меня́ спроси́л, **е́сть ли** здесь хоро́шая гости́ница.
He asked me if there was a good hotel here.

and: Óн меня́ спроси́л, **хоро́шая ли** э́та гости́ница.
He asked me if this hotel is good.

A very common mistake is made in using **е́сли** instead of **ли**; the confusion arises because both **е́сли** and **ли** may be rendered by *if* in English. **Е́сли** introduces a condition, whereas **ли** means *whether*. Thus if there's the possibility of replacing *if* with *whether* in the English sentence, then **ли**, not **е́сли**, *must* be used in Russian.

Я не зна́ю, есть **ли** э́та кни́га в на́шей библиоте́ке; **е́сли** есть, я её возьму́.[1]

I don't know *if* (or *whether*!) there is this book in our library; *if* (*whether* is impossible!) there is I'll take it.

Ли is sometimes used in direct questions which may be answered by *yes* or *no*, especially in negative questions analogous to polite English requests beginning with *Wouldn't you? Couldn't you?*

Не хоти́те **ли** вы́ ещё ча́ю?
Wouldn't you like some more tea?

Не зна́ете **ли** вы́, где́ живёт до́ктор Петро́в?
Wouldn't you know where Dr. Petrov lives?

Не мо́жете **ли** вы́ мне́ помо́чь?
Couldn't you help me?

In direct questions, generally, **ли** expresses speculation, wonder, or doubt:

По́мнит **ли** о́н, что́ я́ ему́ сказа́л?
Does he remember what I told him?

Зна́ет **ли** о́н об э́том?
Does he know about that?

PATTERN SENTENCES

1. Оте́ц хо́чет зна́ть, **бы́л ли** Ива́н вчера́ в шко́ле.

1. Father wants to know if Ivan was in school yesterday.

2. Я́ ещё не зна́ю, **уезжа́ю ли** я́ во вто́рник или в сре́ду.

2. I don't know yet if I'm going away on Tuesday or on Wednesday.

3. Спроси́те Со́ню, **бу́дет ли** она́ до́ма в четве́рг. **Е́сли** она́ бу́дет до́ма, я́ приду́.

3. Ask Sonya if she will be at home on Thursday. If she will be at home, I'll come.

4. Я́ не по́мню, **лю́бит ли** ба́бушка я́блоки. **Е́сли** она́ лю́бит, я́ ей куплю́ кило́.

4. I don't remember if Grandmother likes apples. If she likes them, I'll buy her a kilo.

5. Я́ спрошу́ милиционе́ра, **есть ли** зде́сь по́чта, и **е́сли** есть, **далеко́ ли** она́.

5. I'll ask the policeman if there's a post office here, and if there is, whether it's far or not.

6. Ива́н не по́мнит, **шёл ли** зде́сь до́ждь в воскресе́нье.

6. Ivan doesn't remember if it rained here on Sunday.

7. Ни́на не зна́ет, **бу́дут ли** у её отца́ де́ньги на бу́дущей неде́ле. Но́ **е́сли** у него́ бу́дут, о́н ей да́ст.

7. Nina doesn't know if her father will have any money next week. But if he does, he will give her some.

8. Мне́ интере́сно зна́ть, **хоро́шее ли** сочине́ние написа́л Ива́н.

8. I'd like to know (= I'm interested in knowing) if Ivan wrote a good composition.

9. Прости́те, не **зна́ете ли** вы́, где́ нахо́дится Библиоте́ка и́мени Ле́нина?

9. Excuse me, do you know where the Lenin Library is located?

---

[1] Note that clauses with **ли**, like other subordinate clauses, are set off by commas.

DRILLS

A. *Change the following direct questions to indirect questions according to the model.*

    Model: Óльга спроси́ла: Здéсь **éсть** пóчта?
    Indirect question: Óльга спроси́ла, **éсть ли** здéсь пóчта.

1. Секретáрша меня́ спроси́ла: Дирéктор **знáет**, что товáрищ Смирнóв придёт?
2. Мóй му́ж меня́ спроси́л: Ивáновы **пришли́**?
3. Онá спроси́ла: Ивáн **бы́л** в библиотéке?

    Model: Мóй брáт не знáл, получи́л я́ егó письмó или нéт.
    Change to: Мóй брáт не знáл, получи́л ли я́ егó письмó.

1. Я́ не знáю, у Ивáна éсть маши́на или нéт.
2. Мóй брáт не знáет, достáл я́ билéты в теáтр или нéт.
3. Хозя́йка спроси́ла, хочу́ я́ чáю или нéт.
4. Ктó знáет, зáвтра бу́дет хорóшая погóда или нéт?

B. *Переведи́те на ру́сский.*

1. Do you know if Petrov has returned from Moscow? If he has returned, I hope he will call me.
2. Ask Olga if she needs a black dress. If she needs one, I can give her mine.
3. I don't remember whether Boris was in class.
4. The professor asked Tanya if she had read *Anna Karenina*.
5. Who knows if she has money?
6. We don't know if they want to go to the country. If they want, they can come with us.
7. I want to know if Ivan is at home.
8. I asked him if he worked much.

2. The particles -то and -нибудь

Interrogative pronouns and adverbs are combined with the particles **-то** and **-нибудь,** producing two series of compounds:

чтó-то	something
чтó-нибудь	something, anything
ктó-то	somebody, someone
ктó-нибудь	someone, anyone
гдé-то	somewhere
гдé-нибудь	somewhere, anywhere
куда́-то	(to) somewhere
куда́-нибудь	(to) somewhere, anywhere
какóй-то	some kind of
какóй-нибудь	some (any) kind of
почему́-то	for some reason
почему́-нибудь	for some (any) reason

The series with **-то** is used in referring to objects, persons, places, directions, etc., that are definite and identifiable, but that the speaker is unable (or unwilling) to identify:

Óн **чтó-то** читáл.
He was reading *something* (he knew what it was, but I couldn't see).

Ктó-то позвонúл.
Someone has rung the bell (I don't know yet who it is).

Я́ егó **гдé-то** ужé встречáл.
I have met him *somewhere* before (I don't recall where it was).

Óн **кудá-то** éдет зáвтра.
He is going *somewhere* tomorrow (he knows, but didn't tell me where).

Мнé нýжно вáм **чтó-то** сказáть.
I must tell you *something* (I know what it is, but I shall tell you a little later).

The compounds with **-нибудь** express indefiniteness; the object, person, place, direction, etc., does not have a definable identity:

Я́ гóлоден; éсть у тебя́ **чтó-нибудь** в кýхне?
I'm hungry; do you have *anything* in the kitchen (any kind of food, whatever it is)?

Ктó-нибудь звонúл?
Did *anyone* call?

Мы́ мóжем пообéдать **гдé-нибудь** в гóроде.
We can have dinner *somewhere* in town (we shall choose the place later; for the time being it is "any place").

Лéтом онú всегдá уезжáют **кудá-нибудь** в Еврóпу.
In summer they always go to *some place* in Europe (each time to a different place, so that no single name can indicate where they go).

The compound forms with **что, кто, какóй,** and **чей** are declined:

Óн **с кéм-то** разговáривает.
He is talking to someone.

Óн **от когó-то** получúл письмó.
He has received a letter from someone.

Онú **о чём-то** говорúли.
They were talking about something.

Ты́ **комý-нибудь** говорúл об э́том?
Did you tell anyone about it?

Я́ не знáю, гдé óн живёт; я́ **когó-нибудь** спрошý.
I don't know where he lives; I will ask someone.

Дáйте мнé **какýю-нибудь** кнúгу.
Give me a book (some book or other).

Я нашёл **чью-то** кни́гу на моём столе́.
I found someone's book on my desk.

The forms **когда́-то** and **когда́-нибудь** show a distinction in meaning similar to that of the pairs listed above, but the proper *English* translation of **когда́-то** with a verb in the past tense will be *once, one day, at one time*, etc.:

Я **когда́-то** хорошо́ игра́л в те́ннис.
At one time I played tennis well.

Когда́-то лю́ди всё де́лали рука́ми.
Once people used to do everything with their hands.

Я наде́юсь, что **когда́-нибудь** бу́дет ми́р на земле́.
I hope that some day there will be peace on earth.

Я **когда́-нибудь** всё ва́м расскажу́.
Sometime I shall tell you everything.

PATTERN SENTENCES

1. —**Кто́-нибудь** е́дет в го́род? —Не́т, никто́.
2. —**Кто́-нибудь** мне́ звони́л? —Да́, **кто́-то** звони́л, но не сказа́л своего́ и́мени.
3. —Вы́ **кого́-нибудь** встре́тили, когда́ шли́ сюда́? —Да́, я встре́тил **како́го-то** старика́.
4. Скажи́те мне́ **что́-нибудь** прия́тное!
5. Я **кому́-то** да́л свой ру́сско-англи́йский[2] слова́рь, и тепе́рь не по́мню кому́.
6. —Я наде́юсь, что у **кого́-нибудь** е́сть сего́дняшняя газе́та. —Да́, я её ви́дел у **кого́-то**.
7. Я хочу́ **куда́-нибудь** пойти́ сего́дня ве́чером.
8. За́втра ве́чером мои́х роди́телей не бу́дет до́ма; они́ **куда́-то** иду́т.
9. Вади́м **что́-то** нашёл, но́ не говори́т что́.
10. Я потеря́л часы́. Éсли **кто́-нибудь** и́х найдёт, скажи́те мне́.
11. Не покупа́й чемода́на, а возьми́ **чей-нибудь**.
12. Я нашёл **чей-то** портфе́ль в свое́й ко́мнате.

1. —Is anyone going to town? —No, no one.
2. —Did anybody call me? —Yes, somebody called, but he didn't give his name.
3. —Did you meet anyone on your way here? —Yes, I met an old man.
4. Tell me something nice!
5. I gave someone my Russian-English dictionary, and now I don't remember whom.
6. —I hope that someone's got today's paper. —Yes, I saw someone with it.
7. I want to go somewhere this evening.
8. Tomorrow evening my parents won't be at home; they're going somewhere.
9. Vadim has found something, but he doesn't say what.
10. I lost my watch. If anyone finds it, tell me.
11. Don't buy a suitcase, but take someone else's.
12. I found someone's briefcase in my room.

DRILLS

A. *Add the particle* **-то** *or* **нибудь** *according to the sense.*

1. Бы́л вчера́ кто- .... на ле́кции Петро́ва?
2. Кто- .... мне́ сказа́л, что вы́ та́м бы́ли.
3. Вы́ мо́жете рассказа́ть мне́ что- .... интере́сное?
4. У кого́- .... е́сть папиро́сы?
5. Я где- .... об э́том уже́ слы́шал.
6. Óн ещё не зна́ет, пое́дет ли о́н куда́- .... ле́том.
7. Вы́ бы́ли где́- .... вчера́ ве́чером?
8. Хо́чет кто- .... пойти́ со мно́й?
9. Сего́дня у́тром кто- .... ва́м звони́л.
10. Я где- .... его́ уже́ ви́дел.
11. Я наде́юсь, что я где́- .... найду́ э́то письмо́.

---

[2] The first part of a compound adjective ends in **-o**, and is not declined.

B. *Переведите с английского на русский.*

1. When you go to the store, buy me something.
2. Somebody wrote to my mother about that matter.
3. Do you know anyone who has recently been in the Soviet Union?
4. I heard that someone had just returned from there.
5. —Where is Grandmother? —She went somewhere.
6. He wrote to someone about that question.
7. Somebody's money is lying on the floor.
8. If you find anything interesting in the newspaper, read it to me.
9. Olga found somebody's hat.
10. Buy me some magazine (or other).
11. I've lost my briefcase somewhere.
12. For some reason he doesn't like me.

3. Prepositions of place or direction (supplement)

The preposition **у** (+genitive) expresses possession as well as location ("at someone's place"—see Unit 10, page 140). In the same way, **к** (+dative) expresses "going to someone," going to someone's place" (see Unit 17, page 248).

When used with words denoting physical objects, these two prepositions have the same basic meaning, although the usage may seem slightly different. **У** (+genitive) denotes close proximity to an object (see Unit 10, page 140); **к** (+dative) denotes motion to the vicinity of an object or toward an object:

У with genitive

Я люблю сидеть **у** окна́.
I like to sit by the window.

Учи́тель стои́т **у** доски́.
The teacher is standing at the blackboard.

К with dative

Позвони́л звоно́к. Хозя́ин пошёл **к** две́ри.
The bell rang, and the host went to the door.

Учени́к пошёл **к** доске́.
The student went to (toward) the blackboard.

The preposition **ми́мо** (+genitive) means *by, past*:

Лю́ди шли **ми́мо** це́ркви.
People were walking past the church.

The preposition **через** (+accusative) means *across, through*:

Мы́ шли **через** па́рк.
We were going through the park.

4. Verbs of motion with prefixes of direction

Verbs of motion prefixed with **при-** (*coming to, arriving at*), and **у-** (*going away, leaving*) were given in Unit 18. These verbs appear in regular imperfective-perfective pairs (e.g., уходи́ть-уйти́), without the imperfective indeterminate-imperfective determinate distinction. They are derived as follows:

From imperfective indeterminate:
 ходи́ть → уходи́ть—*imperfective*
From imperfective determinate:
 идти́ (contracted to -йти́) → уйти́—*perfective*

Besides **при-** and **у-**, a number of other prefixes may be added to the basic forms. It must be noted, however, that in prefixed verbs, not éздить, but the variant form **-езжа́ть** is used (cf. приезжа́ть and уезжа́ть); this form *never* occurs without a prefix.

A. Prefixes в-, вы-, под-, от-.

The more important prefixes other than **при-** and **у-** used with the *going-on-foot* verbs can be found in the table below.

в- (во-, въ-)		вы-[3]	
Going (coming) in, entering *(not by vehicle)*		*Going (coming) out, exiting* *(not by vehicle)*	
Imperf. вход́ить	*Perf.* войти́	*Imperf.* выход́ить	*Perf.* вы́йти[3]
Present вхожу́ вхо́дишь	*Future* войду́ войдёшь	*Present* выхожу́ выхо́дишь	*Future* вы́йду вы́йдешь
Past входи́л, etc.	вошёл, вошла́, etc.	*Past* выходи́л, etc.	вы́шел, вы́шла, etc.
Imperative входи́, -те!	войди́, -те!	*Imperative* выходи́, -те!	вы́йди, -те!
(with **в** + *acc.*)		(with **из** + *gen.*)	
Мы́ **вошли́ в** дом.[4] We entered the house.		Мы́ **вы́шли из** до́ма.[4] We left the house.	
под- (подо-, подъ-)		от- (ото-, отъ-)	
Approaching, coming up to *(not by vehicle)*		*Moving away* *(not by vehicle)*	
Imperf. подход́ить	*Perf.* подойти́	*Imperf.* отход́ить	*Perf.* отойти́
Present подхожу́ подхо́дишь	*Future* подойду́ подойдёшь	*Present* отхожу́ отхо́дишь	*Future* отойду́ отойдёшь
Past подходи́л, etc.	подошёл, подошла́, etc.	*Past* отходи́л, etc.	отошёл, отошла́, etc.
Imperative подходи́, -те!	подойди́, -те!	*Imperative* отходи́, -те!	отойди́, -те!
(with **к** + *dat.*)		(with **от** + *gen.*)	
Он **подошёл к** окну́. He went up to the window.		Он **отошёл от** окна́. He moved away from the window.	

[3] The prefix **вы-** is never stressed in the imperfective, but always stressed in the perfective, in all forms. Note especially: Он **вы́шел**, *He went out.* Also note that the perfective imperative ends in unstressed **-и.**

[4] Observe that these verbs are intransitive and require the use of a preposition, though the corresponding English verbs (*enter, leave,* etc.) may often be transitive.

The corresponding verbs for *going in a vehicle* are:

в- (во-, въ-) *Going (coming) in, entering* *(by vehicle)*	вы- *Going (coming) out, exiting* *(by vehicle)*
Imperf. *Perf.* въезжа́ть въе́хать	*Imperf.* *Perf.* выезжа́ть вы́ехать
Present *Future* въезжа́ю въе́ду въезжа́ешь въе́дешь *Past* въезжа́л, etc. въе́хал, etc. *Imperative* въезжа́й, -те! None (with **в** + *acc.*) Они́ **въезжа́ют во** дво́р. They are driving into the yard.	*Present* *Future* выезжа́ю вы́еду выезжа́ешь вы́едешь *Past* выезжа́л, etc. вы́ехал, etc. *Imperative* выезжа́й, -те! None (with **из** + *gen.*) Мы́ **вы́ехали из** го́рода. We drove out of the city.
под- (подо-, подъ-) *Approaching, coming up to* *(by vehicle)*	от- (ото-, отъ-) *Moving away* *(by vehicle)*
Imperf. *Perf.* подъезжа́ть подъе́хать	*Imperf.* *Perf.* отъезжа́ть отъе́хать
Present *Future* подъезжа́ю подъе́ду подъезжа́ешь подъе́дешь *Past* подъезжа́л, etc. подъе́хал, etc. *Imperative* подъезжа́й, -те! None (with **к** + *dat.*) Маши́на **подъе́хала к** до́му. The car drove up toward the house.	*Present* *Future* отъезжа́ю отъе́ду отъезжа́ешь отъе́дешь *Past* отъезжа́л, etc. отъе́хал, etc. *Imperative* отъезжа́й, -те! None (with **от** + *gen.*) Маши́на **отъе́хала от** до́ма. The car moved away from the house.

B. Prefixes. за-, про-, пере-, до-.

These prefixes, too, are frequently used with verbs of motion.

заходи́ть/зайти́
заезжа́ть/зае́хать
}
to call on, to drop in to see (for a brief informal visit) (к + *dative*);
to call for, come for (за + *instrumental*)

После обе́да мы́ **зайдём** к ва́м.
After dinner we'll drop in to see you.

Они́ **зайду́т** за на́ми, и мы́ вме́сте пойдём поу́жинать.
They'll come for us and together we'll go to supper.

The prefix **про-** forms perfective verbs whose actions are performed for a certain, and often a rather long, period of time (see p. 312). With verbs of motion, this prefix has the meaning of *by, past:*

проходи́ть/пройти́
проезжа́ть/прое́хать
}
to go (come) by, past, through, pass
(+ ми́мо + *genitive*—by, past)
(+ че́рез + *accusative*—through)

Они́ **прошли́** ми́мо на́с.
They passed by us.

Де́нь **прошёл** бы́стро.
The day passed rapidly.

Мы́ **прошли́** че́рез па́рк.
We walked through the park.

The prefix **пере-** has the meaning of *across:*

переходи́ть/перейти́
переезжа́ть/перее́хать
}
to cross (+ *accusative*) or (+ че́рез + *accusative*)

Мы́ **перешли́** у́лицу.
We crossed the street.

The prefix **до-** has the meaning *as far as, reach.*

доходи́ть/дойти́
доезжа́ть/дое́хать
}
to reach, get as far as (+ до + *genitive*)

Мы́ **дошли́** до угла́ и верну́лись.
We went as far as the corner and came back.

Мы́ наконе́ц **дое́хали** до го́рода.
We finally reached the city.

На́ш са́д **дохо́дит** до реки́.
Our garden stretches as far as the river.

PATTERN SENTENCES

1. Ка́ждый де́нь я́ **выхожу́ и́з** дому в во́семь.
2. У Ива́на бы́л гри́пп; о́н вчера́ **вы́шел** в пе́рвый ра́з.
3. Ра́ньше мы́ **выходи́ли** ка́ждый ве́чер, а тепе́рь мы́ о́чень ре́дко **выхо́дим**.
4. —Где́ Ко́ля? —О́н то́лько что **вы́шел из** ко́мнаты.
5. —Мо́жно **войти́**? —Коне́чно, мо́жно!
6. Когда́ о́н **вошёл** в ко́мнату, она́ **вы́шла** (из ко́мнаты).
7. Я́ никогда́ не **вхожу́** в его́ кабине́т.
8. По доро́ге домо́й я́ **зашёл** в апте́ку на гла́вной у́лице.
9. О́н ча́сто **захо́дит** ко мне́ «на мину́ту», а пото́м сиди́т о́чень до́лго. Я́ никогда́ не **захожу́** к нему́.
10. —**Зайди́те** ко мне́ по доро́ге в университе́т. —Хорошо́, я́ **зайду́** к ва́м, но́ не надо́лго.
11. Кто́ бы́л э́тот стари́к, кото́рый **подошёл** к тебе́ в рестора́не?
12. Я́ наде́юсь, что о́н не **подойдёт** к на́м.
13. Мы́ должны́ бу́дем **пройти́** че́рез его́ ко́мнату.
14. Как бы́стро **прошёл** э́тот го́д!
15. Когда́ мы́ **дошли́ до** и́х до́ма, начался́ до́ждь.

1. Every day I leave home at eight.
2. Ivan had the flu; yesterday he went out for the first time.
3. We used to go out every evening, but now we go out very rarely.
4. —Where is Kolya? —He just left (went out of) the room.
5. —May I come in? —Of course you may!
6. When he entered the room, she left it.
7. I never go into his study.
8. On the way home I stopped in at a drugstore on the main street.
9. He often drops in to see me "for a minute," and then stays a long time. I never drop in at his place.
10. —Stop in to see me on your way to the university. —All right, I'll stop in, but not for long.
11. Who was that old man who came up to you in the restaurant?
12. I hope he will not come up to us.
13. We shall have to pass through his room.
14. How quickly this year has gone by!
15. When we got to their house, the rain began.

DRILL

A. *Choose the proper form of the verbs* **выходи́ть/вы́йти**, **выезжа́ть/вы́ехать**, **входи́ть/войти́**, *and translate into English.*

1. Ни́на то́лько что .... из ко́мнаты.
2. До́ктор сказа́л А́нне, что е́й ещё нельзя́ .....
3. Ка́ждое у́тро я́ .... в се́мь часо́в.
4. Мы́ должны́ .... о́чень ра́но, е́сли мы́ хоти́м прие́хать в Босто́н пока́ ещё светло́.
5. Она́ .... в свою́ ко́мнату и че́рез мину́ту .... отту́да.
6. Откро́йте две́рь и .... в мо́й кабине́т.
7. Да́ма и соба́чка .... в магази́н.
8. Они́ ско́ро .... из магази́на.
9. Я́ .... и́з дому че́рез полчаса́.
10. Когда́ вы́ .... из ко́мнаты, закро́йте две́рь.
11. Когда́ мы́ .... из го́рода, мы́ остано́вимся и поза́втракаем.
12. Они́ .... из Москвы́ в понеде́льник.

B. *Choose the proper form of the verb* **заходи́ть/зайти́**, *and translate into English.*

1. Мо́жно .... к ва́м на пя́ть мину́т?
2. Я́ тепе́рь ча́сто .... к нему́ по доро́ге домо́й.
3. Вчера́ о́н .... ко мне́ за кни́гой.
4. У́тром Ни́на .... к подру́ге, но́ её не́ было до́ма.
5. Она́ тепе́рь ре́дко .... к на́м.
6. Я́ тепе́рь живу́ бли́зко и бу́ду ча́сто .... к ва́м.
7. .... ко мне́ сего́дня ве́чером.
8. Я́ .... за ва́ми, и мы́ вме́сте пойдём в кино́.

C. *Choose the proper form of the verbs* **подходи́ть/подойти́**, **отходи́ть/отойти́**, *and translate into English.*

1. . . . . к столу́ и возьми́те кни́гу.
2. По́сле уро́ка о́н . . . . ко мне́, за́дал вопро́с и сейча́с же . . . . от меня́.
3. Я́ никогда́ не . . . . к его́ пи́сьменному столу́.
4. Она́ . . . . к доске́ и начала́ писа́ть, пото́м она́ . . . . от доски́ и се́ла.
5. Мы́ ча́сто и́х встреча́ем, но́ никогда́ не . . . . к ни́м.
6. Я́ . . . . к не́й, е́сли она́ бу́дет одна́.

5. Verbs of *carrying*

As with verbs of *going*, Russian has two series of verbs of *carrying*, one for carrying on foot (corresponding to **ходи́ть/идти́**), the other in a vehicle (hauling, transporting, corresponding to **е́здить/е́хать**).

Also like the *going* verbs, the basic verbs denoting carrying have two kinds of imperfectives: a determinate, denoting carrying on one trip in one direction; and an indeterminate. denoting carrying in general, on more than one trip, or in more than one direction. Compare:

to go (*not by vehicle*):

Indeterminate Imperfective	Determinate Imperfective	Perfective
ходи́ть	**идти́**	**пойти́**
хожу́	иду́	пойду́
хо́дишь, etc.	идёшь, etc.	пойдёшь, etc.

to carry (*not by vehicle*):

	носи́ть		**нести́**		**понести́**
Pres.	ношу́	*Pres.*	несу́	*Fut.*	понесу́
	но́сишь		несёшь		понесёшь
	но́сит		несёт		etc.
	но́сим		несём		
	но́сите		несёте		
	но́сят		несу́т		
Past	носи́л, etc.	*Past*	нёс, несло́, несла́, несли́	*Past*	понёс, понесло́, etc.

Indeterminate imperfective **носи́ть** (*more than one direction*):

Ма́ть **ходи́ла** по ко́мнате и **носи́ла** больно́го ребёнка.
The mother was walking about the room and was carrying the sick child.

Determinate imperfective **нести́** (*one direction*):

Она́ **шла́** по у́лице и **несла́** в руке́ паке́т.
She was walking along the street and was carrying a package in her hand.

Perfective **понести́**

Óн взя́л у неё паке́т и **понёс** его́.

He took the package from her and carried it (= began to carry it).[5]

to go (*by vehicle*):

Indeterminate Imperfective	Determinate Imperfective	Perfective
éздить	**éхать**	**поéхать**
éзжу	éду	поéду
éздишь, etc.	éдешь, etc.	поéдешь, etc.

to carry (*by vehicle*):

	вози́ть		**везти́**		**повезти́**
Pres.	вожу́	*Pres.*	везу́	*Fut.*	повезу́
	вóзишь		везёшь		повезёшь, etc.
	вóзит		везёт		
	вóзим		везём		
	вóзите		везёте		
	вóзят		везу́т		
Past	вози́л, etc.	*Past*	вёз, везло́, везла́, везли́	*Past*	повёз, повезло́, etc.

Indeterminate imperfective **вози́ть**:

Такси́ **éздят** по гóроду и **вóзят** пассажи́ров.

Taxis drive about the city and transport passengers.

Determinate imperfective **везти́**:

Вóт **éдет** пустóе такси́; онó никогó не **везёт**.

There goes an empty taxi; it's not carrying anybody.

Perfective **повезти́**:

Когда́ он **поéдет** на ю́г, óн **повезёт** с собóй стáрого отцá.

When he goes south, he will take his old father along.

A. Prefixed compounds of verbs of *carrying*. Like prefixed compounds of verbs of motion, the compounds of the verbs of *carrying* have *only two* forms: *imperfective* and *perfective*. Imperfectives are formed by adding a prefix to the imperfective *indeterminate*; perfectives by adding a prefix to the imperfective *determinate*:

	to bring	*to take/carry away*	*to take to*
(when walking)			
Imperf.	приноси́ть	уноси́ть	относи́ть
Perf.	принести́	унести́	отнести́
(when riding)			
Imperf.	привози́ть	увози́ть	отвози́ть
Perf.	привезти́	увезти́	отвезти́

[5] The perfectives with **по-** sometimes have an inchoative meaning, emphasizing the beginning of the action, e.g.: Пóезд останови́лся и через мину́ту опя́ть **пошёл**. The train stopped, and after a minute *started* again. But: Ивáн **пошёл** на пóчту; Ivan *went* to the post office.

The conjugation is the same as for the simple (non-prefixed) verbs:

Bringing *(when walking)*	
Imperfective *Inf.* **приноси́ть**	*Perfective* *Inf.* **принести́**
Present	*Future*
приношу́ прино́сим прино́сишь прино́сите прино́сит прино́сят	принесу́ принесём принесёшь принесёте принесёт принесу́т
Past	*Past*
приноси́л, etc.	принёс, принесл.о́, -а́, -и́

Bringing *(when riding)*	
Imperfective *Inf.* **привози́ть**	*Perfective* *Inf.* **привезти́**
Present	*Future*
привожу́ приво́зим приво́зишь приво́зите приво́зит приво́зят	привезу́ привезём привезёшь привезёте привезёт привезу́т
Past	*Past*
привози́л, etc.	привёз, привезл.о́, -а́, -и́

Ка́ждый ра́з, когда́ о́н **прихо́дит** к на́м, о́н на́м что́-нибудь **прино́сит**.
Every time he comes to see us he brings us something.

За́втра о́н **придёт** к на́м и **принесёт** на́м расска́зы Че́хова.
Tomorrow he will come to see us and will bring us Chekhov's stories.

Ка́ждый ра́з, когда́ о́н **приезжа́ет** из Пари́жа, о́н **приво́зит** игру́шки де́тям.
Every time he comes from Paris he brings toys for the children.

О́н **прие́дет** за́втра из Пари́жа и **привезёт** ва́м пода́рок.
Tomorrow he will arrive from Paris, and will bring you a present.

Compounds with **от-** have the meaning of *to take* (carry, drive, etc.) *someone or something to a given place*, invariably specified:

Отнеси́те э́ти таре́лки в ку́хню.
Take these plates to the kitchen.

Вы́ мо́жете **отвезти́** меня́ на вокза́л?
Can you drive (take) me to the station?

Compounds with **у-** simply mean *take away*, with the place often unspecified:

> Унеси́ э́ти гря́зные таре́лки отсю́да.
> Take these dirty dishes away from here.

B. Носи́ть meaning to wear. The indeterminate imperfective **носи́ть** has the secondary meaning *to wear* (habitually), *to wear around* (the determinate **нести́** is *never* used in this sense):

> Зимо́й я́ всегда́ **ношу́** тёплое пальто́.
> I always wear a warm overcoat in winter.

> Почему́ вы́ не **но́сите** шля́пы?
> Why don't you wear a hat?

> *But* (*single occasion*):

> Почему́ вы́ не в но́вом пальто́?
> Why aren't you wearing your new coat (now)?

PATTERN SENTENCES

Носи́ть/нести́.

1. Студе́нты **хо́дят** из кла́сса в кла́сс и **но́сят** свои́ кни́ги.
2. Я́ уже́ два́ дня́ **ношу́** с собо́й э́то письмо́ и забыва́ю его́ посла́ть.
3. Во́т **идёт** стари́к и **несёт** тяжёлый паке́т. Бе́дный стари́к!
4. —Куда́ ты́ **идёшь** и кому́ ты́ **несёшь** э́ти чу́дные цветы́? —Я́ **иду́** к Со́не и **несу́** ей э́тот буке́т.
5. В понеде́льник, когда́ я́ **шёл** на по́чту, я́ встре́тил Лунёвых. Они́ то́же **шли́** туда́ и **несли́** посы́лки. О́н **нёс** две́ тяжёлых посы́лки, а она́ **несла́** одну́ лёгкую.
6. Ле́том де́вушки **но́сят** све́тлые пла́тья.

1. The students go from class to class and carry their books.
2. For two days I've been carrying this letter around and forgetting to mail it.
3. Here comes an old man carrying a heavy package. Poor old man!
4. —Where are you going and to whom are you taking those marvelous flowers? —I'm going to Sonya's and taking her this bouquet.
5. On Monday, when I was on my way to the post office, I met the Lunyovs. They were going there too and were carrying packages. He was carrying two heavy packages, and she was carrying one light one.
6. In summer girls wear light-colored dresses.

DRILL

Replace the blanks by the correct form of the verb.

1. Де́душка шёл по у́лице и .... чемода́н.
2. Ни́на шла́ по у́лице и .... цветы́.
3. Я́ ви́дел ва́с вчера́. Что́ вы́ ....?
4. Мы́ сейча́с .... э́ти кни́ги в библиоте́ку.
5. Я́ тепе́рь никогда́ не .... тёмных костю́мов.

PATTERN SENTENCES

Приноси́ть/принести́ (у-, от-).

1. Ка́ждый ра́з, когда́ они́ **прихо́дят** к на́м, они́ на́м что́-нибудь **прино́сят**.
2. Когда́ я́ **прихожу́** к ни́м, я́ всегда́ что́-нибудь и́м **приношу́**.

1. Every time they come to see us they bring us something.
2. When I go to see them, I always take them something.

3. Я бу́ду **приходи́ть** к ва́м ка́ждое у́тро и бу́ду **приноси́ть** ва́м газе́ту.

4. Я не зна́ю, **придёт** ли о́н во вто́рник и **принесёт** ли о́н пласти́нку, кото́рую о́н обеща́л. Наде́юсь, что о́н не забу́дет её **принести́**.

5. —Что́ вы́ **принесли́**? —Я́ **принёс** две́ буты́лки вина́, а Со́ня **принесла́** всё, что ну́жно к обе́ду.

6. **Уйди́** отсю́да и **унеси́** отсю́да всё твои́ игру́шки!

7. **Отнеси́** и́х в де́тскую и́ли в ку́хню, куда́ хо́чешь, и игра́й та́м!

8. Она́ вы́шла из ко́мнаты и **унесла́** газе́ту.

Вози́ть/везти́, привози́ть/привезти́ (у-, от-).

1. Поезда́ **во́зят** пассажи́ров. Они́ **во́зят** и́х на се́вер, на ю́г, на восто́к, и на за́пад.

2. Андре́й **е́дет** на Сре́дний Восто́к и **везёт** с собо́й свою́ семью́. О́н ещё никогда́ не́ был на восто́ке.

3. Я́ ча́сто **е́зжу** на ю́г и **вожу́** туда́ свою́ до́чь. Моя́ ма́ть живёт на ю́ге. Она́ лю́бит ю́жный кли́мат.

4. Пя́ть дне́й в неде́лю я́ у́тром **отвожу́** дете́й в шко́лу, а ве́чером **привожу́** и́х из шко́лы домо́й.

5. Когда́ я́ **вёз** и́х вчера́, начался́ до́ждь, и я́ бы́стро **привёз** и́х домо́й.

6. Моя́ сестра́ **прие́хала** из За́падной Герма́нии и **привезла́** на́м все́м пода́рки.

7. Ка́ждый ра́з, когда́ она́ **приезжа́ет** отту́да, она́ на́м что́-нибудь **приво́зит**.

8. Когда́ вы́ **прие́дете** из Кры́ма, **привези́те** на́м буты́лку кры́мского вина́.

9. Когда́ вы́ **пое́дете** на вокза́л, пожа́луйста, **отвези́те** туда́ э́тот чемода́н.

10. Они́ уе́хали на Кавка́з и **увезли́** всё свои́ ве́щи.

3. I shall come to see you every morning and shall bring you a paper.

4. I don't know if he'll come on Tuesday and bring the record which he promised. I hope he won't forget to bring it.

5. —What have you brought? —I've brought two bottles of wine, and Sonya has brought everything we need for dinner.

6. Get out of here and take all your toys!

7. Take them to the nursery or the kitchen, wherever you like, and play there!

8. She left the room and took away the paper.

1. Trains carry passengers. They carry them north, south, east, and west.

2. Andrey is going to the Middle East and is taking his family with him. He has never yet been in the East.

3. I often go south and take my daughter there. My mother lives in the south. She likes the southern climate.

4. In the morning, five days a week, I take the children to school, and in the evening I bring them home from school.

5. When I took them yesterday, it started to rain, and I brought them home at once.

6. My sister came from West Germany and brought us all presents.

7. Every time she comes from there she brings us something.

8. When you come from the Crimea, bring us a bottle of Crimean wine.

9. When you drive to the station, please take this suitcase there.

10. They went off to the Caucasus and took all their things.

DRILLS

A. *Choose the correct verb in parentheses and give the correct form.*

1. Куда́ вы́ е́хали сего́дня, и куда́ вы́ (вози́ть/везти́) дете́й в во́семь часо́в утра́?

2. —Вы́ ча́сто (вози́ть/везти́) дете́й к мо́рю в про́шлом году́? —Да́, мо́й му́ж ча́сто и́х (вози́ть/везти́).

3. Бори́с е́хал на автомоби́ле и (вози́ть/везти́) куда́-то свою́ ма́ть.

4. —Почему́ ты́ всегда́ (носи́ть/нести́) с собо́й э́тот тяжёлый портфе́ль? —Я́ ре́дко его́ (носи́ть/нести́).

5. Зо́я, что́ ты́ (носи́ть/нести́), и что́ (носи́ть/нести́) Бори́с, когда́ я вас встре́тил?
6. Я не ви́жу, что́ он (носи́ть/нести́).
7. Через полчаса́ я (относи́ть/отнести́) кни́ги в библиоте́ку.
8. Пожа́луйста, (относи́ть/отнести́) молоко́ на ку́хню.
9. Е́сли вы е́дете на вокза́л, (отвози́ть/отвезти́) меня́ туда́.
10. Я тепе́рь ка́ждый де́нь (отвози́ть/отвезти́) дете́й в шко́лу.
11. Ра́ньше он всегда́ (привози́ть/привезти́) нам что́-нибудь из заграни́цы.
12. Он обеща́л, что когда́ он вернётся, он что́-нибудь нам (привози́ть/привезти́).
13. Вчера́ он прие́хал и ничего́ нам не (привози́ть/привезти́).
14. Когда́ я верну́сь из Пари́жа, я вам что́-нибудь (привози́ть/привезти́).
15. За́втра он придёт к обе́ду и (приноси́ть/принести́) вино́.
16. Когда́ он прихо́дит к обе́ду, он всегда́ что́-нибудь (приноси́ть/принести́).
17. Ива́н уе́хал в Кры́м и (увози́ть/увезти́) с собо́й все́ свои́ кни́ги.

B. *Given the correct form of the verb compound:* (**при-, у-, от-**) **-носи́ть, -нести́; -вози́ть, -везти́.**

1. О́н обеща́л, что придёт за́втра и .... свою́ статью́.
2. О́н пришёл, но ничего́ не .....
3. Приходи́ к на́м за́втра и .... на́м твою́ статью́.
4. Е́сли ты́ е́дешь на автомоби́ле, ты́ мо́жешь .... э́тот паке́т на по́чту.
5. Е́сли я пое́ду на автомоби́ле, я .... паке́т на по́чту.
6. О́н обеща́л .... мне́ из Пари́жа мо́дное пла́тье.
7. Приезжа́й к на́м в дере́вню и .... твою́ сестру́.
8. Я прие́ду к ва́м в понеде́льник и .... сестру́.
9. Я наде́юсь, что она́ ско́ро уе́дет отсю́да и .... своего́ сы́на.
10. Она́ уе́хала и .... сы́на.
11. Мы́ .... ва́м из Евро́пы что́-нибудь интере́сное.
12. Что́ я могу́ ва́м .... из Ме́ксики? .... мне́ пожа́луйста мексика́нскую ва́зу.

6. Verbs of *leading*

Like other unprefixed verbs of motion, the basic verb denoting leading has two imperfectives: *indeterminate* and *determinate*.

to lead, take, bring (*a person or an animal*)

Indeterminate Imperfective		Determinate Imperfective		Perfective	
води́ть		**вести́**		**повести́**	
Pres.	вожу́[6]	*Pres.*	веду́	*Fut.*	поведу́
	во́дишь, etc.		ведёшь, etc.		поведёшь, etc.
Past	води́л, etc.	*Past*	вёл, вел.о́, -а́, -и́	*Past*	повёл, повел.о́, -а́, -и́

Indeterminate imperfective **води́ть:**

Она́ ка́ждый де́нь **во́дит** своего́ ма́ленького сы́на в па́рк.
Every day she takes her little son to the park.

---

[6] This form coincides with the first person singular of **вози́ть**, *to transport.*

Determinate imperfective **вести́**:

> Она́ **шла** по у́лице и **вела́** за́ руку своего́ ма́ленького сы́на.
> She was walking along the street and was leading her young son by the hand.

Compounds with **при-, у-, от-**, etc. have only a single imperfective (formed from the *indeterminate* imperfective) and a perfective (formed from the *determinate* imperfective). The meaning is analogous to the compounds of **носи́ть/нести́** and **вози́ть/везти́**:

Imperfective:

> Она́ лю́бит **приводи́ть** домо́й свои́х подру́г.
> She likes to bring her friends home.

Perfective:

> Он **пришёл** к на́м и **привёл** своего́ мла́дшего бра́та.
> He came to see us and brought his younger brother.

These verbs have many idiomatic meanings, e.g., **вести́ войну́** *to carry on war*, **вести́ разгово́р** *to carry on a conversation*, **проводи́ть/провести́ вре́мя, ле́то** *to spend time, the summer*, etc.

The verb **переводи́ть/перевести́** is most frequently used with the meaning of *to translate*.

PATTERN SENTENCES

1. Вну́чка **во́дит** тепе́рь ка́ждый де́нь свою́ ба́бушку в па́рк погуля́ть.
2. Зимо́й, когда́ вну́чка рабо́тала, она́ **води́ла** ба́бушку в па́рк то́лько два́ ра́за в неде́лю.
3. Я́ ви́дел, как она́ **вела́** её туда́ сего́дня ра́но у́тром.
4. Ни́на, **уведи́** дете́й отсю́да; они́ ужа́сно шумя́т! **Отведи́** и́х в де́тскую.
5. Вчера́ ве́чером Лунёв **пришёл** к ча́ю и **привёл** свою́ сестру́.

1. The granddaughter takes her grandmother to the park every day now for a walk.
2. In winter, when the granddaughter was working, she took her grandmother to the park only twice a week.
3. I saw her taking (= as she took) her there early this morning.
4. Nina, take the children away (from here); they're making a terrible noise! Take them to the children's room.
5. Last evening Lunyov came to tea and brought his sister.

DRILLS

A. *Fill in the blanks with the proper forms of* **води́ть/вести́**.

1. Я́ . . . . ка́ждый де́нь дете́й в па́рк.
2. Ги́д . . . . тури́стов по го́роду.
3. Роди́тели ча́сто . . . . дете́й за́ руку.
4. Он идёт по у́лице и . . . . своего́ ма́ленького сы́на.
5. Мы́ идём в музе́й и . . . . туда́ на́шу до́чь.

B. *Translate the words in parentheses.*

1. Ива́н ча́сто (brings) друзе́й к обе́ду.
2. Ива́н вчера́ (brought) к на́м своего́ бра́та.
3. Е́сли хоти́те, я́ (will bring) к ва́м мою́ до́чь.
4. Коне́чно, (bring) её!

Some additional comments on verbs of motion. Observe that all the above verbs belonging to the *indeterminate imperfective* series of unprefixed verbs of motion, **ходи́ть, е́здить, носи́ть, вози́ть, води́ть** belong to the second conjugation. They all have consonant mutations in the first person singular: хожу́, е́зжу, ношу́, вожу́, вожу́. All except е́здить have shifting stress in the present.

The corresponding members of the *determinate imperfective* series belong to the first conjugation (consonant stems): **идти́, е́хать, нести́, везти́, вести́.** All of their infinitives end in **-ти́** (except е́хать). The past tenses must be learned specially: **шёл (шло), нёс (несло́), вёз (везло́), вёл (вело́);** only **е́хал** is formed regularly.

Simple *perfectives* which do not specify direction are formed with **по-** and the *determinate* imperfective, e.g., they are conjugated like the determinate imperfective except that their "present" tense form has future meaning. All of them may have an inchoative meaning, i.e., the *beginning* of the going, carrying, or leading is emphasized. This inchoative meaning is especially marked with **понести́, повезти́,** and **повести́. Пойти́** and **пое́хать** may or may not emphasize beginning action, e.g.:

По́езд вдру́г **пошёл.**	The train suddenly started.
О́н взя́л чемода́н и **понёс** его́.	He took the suitcase and started to carry it.

7. Translation of *to take* and *to bring*

As has been seen, *to take* is very often rendered in Russian by an appropriate verb of *carrying* or *leading*. This is the case when something or someone is to be moved from one place to another:

Унеси́те э́ти кни́ги.
Take these books away.

Отнеси́те и́х куда́ хоти́те.
Take them wherever you wish.

Отведи́те э́того господи́на в его́ ко́мнату.
Take this gentleman to his room.

With **брать/взять** the emphasis is rather on taking something in order to use it:

Я́ взя́л э́ту кни́гу у Бори́са.
I took that book from Boris.

Я́ взя́л э́ту кни́гу в библиоте́ке.
I took the book at (from) the library.

In these two sentences Boris or the library functions as a source of supply; the emphasis is not on moving the book from place to place, but on having it available to read.

Learn the idiom **бра́ть/взя́ть с собо́й** *to take along*:

Вы́ **взя́ли с собо́й** портфе́ль?
Did you take your briefcase along (with you)?

Принима́ть/приня́ть is used in some expressions equivalent to English phrases with *take:*

п. уча́стие (в + *locative*)	to take part in
п. ва́нну	to take a bath
п. лека́рство	to take medicine

To bring corresponds to a verb of *carrying,* or *leading,* with the prefix **при-:**

Принеси́те вино́; у на́с не́т вина́.	Bring ....
Привези́ мне́ что́-нибудь из Пари́жа.	Bring ....

Приведи́те к на́м ва́шу до́чь; мы́ хоти́м   Bring . . . .
с не́й познако́миться.

DRILL

Translate the words in parentheses.

1. Ива́н (brought) стака́н молока́ из ку́хни.
2. Вади́м (brought) ва́м что́-то из Ита́лии.
3. Я́ (shall bring) тебе́ газе́ту на вера́нду.
4. Я́ (shall bring) тебе́ за́втра цветы́ из дере́вни.
5. О́льга (brought) подру́гу к обе́ду.
6. Она́ всегда́ (brings) кого́-нибудь к обе́ду.

7. (Take) э́ту кни́гу в библиоте́ку.
8. (Take) э́тот чемода́н на вокза́л.
9. Ма́ма (took) посу́ду в столо́вую.
10. Кто́ (took) моё пальто́?
11. Я́ (shall take) за́втра автомоби́ль Ива́на.
12. (Take) мою́ маши́ну; она́ сего́дня мне́ не нужна́.

8. Prepositions of position and motion

A. Position.

(1) *Prepositions with the locative case.*

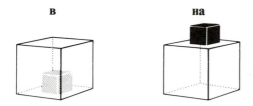

(2) *Prepositions with the instrumental case.*

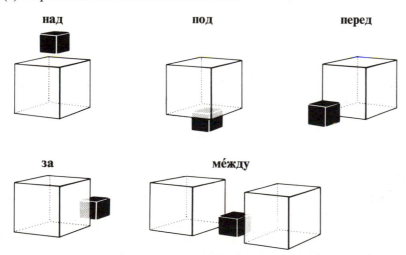

(3) *Prepositions with the genitive case.* Prepositions of location governing the genitive describe proximity or closeness, but do not specify exact position.

Immediate proximity is indicated by **у**. **О́коло** is used to denote any position *nearby, in the neighborhood.* **Вокру́г** is used in reference to a circle around some object.

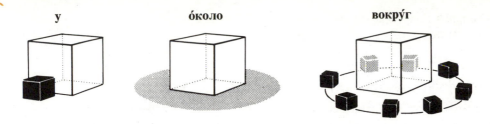

у   óколо   вокру́г

B. Motion.

(1) *Moving into position.* The positions described above will now be considered as goals of motion: moving into position in, on, at, etc.

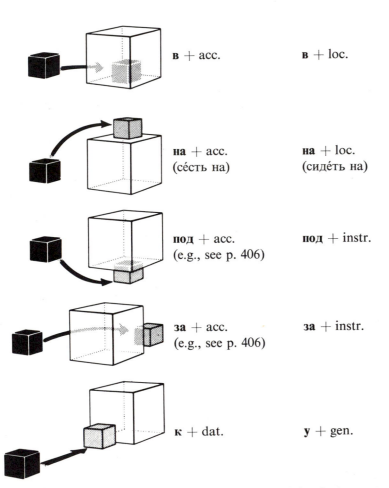

	Motion to Position	Position Reached
	в + acc.	в + loc.
	на + acc. (сéсть на)	на + loc. (сидéть на)
	под + acc. (e.g., see p. 406)	под + instr.
	за + acc. (e.g., see p. 406)	за + instr.
	к + dat.	у + gen.

Other preposition + case combinations are used for *both position and motion* into position: **над, перед,** and **мéжду** + instrumental; and **óколо** and **вокру́г** + genitive, e.g.,

Óн шёл **вокру́г** óзерa.
He was walking around the lake (*motion*).

Вокру́г о́зера лес.
Around the lake there is a wood (*position*).

(2) *Moving away from or out of position.* For motion away from or out of something, the following prepositions are used, all governing the genitive:

Position	*Moving out of Position*	
в + loc.	из	
на + loc.	с	
под + instr.	из-под	} + gen.
за + instr.	из-за	
у + gen.	от	

Most important are the three series:

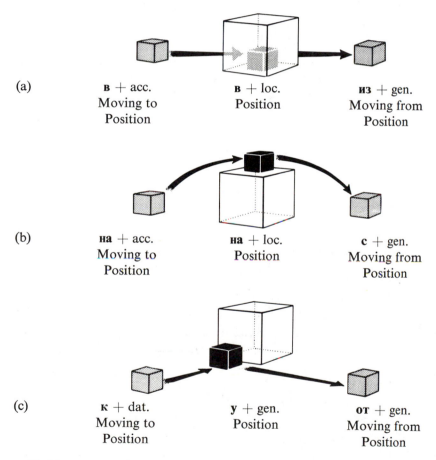

(a) в + acc. | в + loc. | из + gen.
Moving to Position | Position | Moving from Position

(b) на + acc. | на + loc. | с + gen.
Moving to Position | Position | Moving from Position

(c) к + dat. | у + gen. | от + gen.
Moving to Position | Position | Moving from Position

(3) *Movement other than into or out of position.*
(a) **Через** + accusative: *across, through, via.*
(b) **По** + dative: motion within a space not directed to any goal (walking back and forth in a room, strolling in a city, a park, etc.). This is also used to denote motion (which may or may not have a direction) *along* a road, street, by a stream, etc.

(4) *Expression of limits* (*in space or time*).

от . . . . до   from . . . . to (space or time)
с . . . . до   from . . . . to (time; see Unit 26)

All these prepositions take the genitive.

Prepositions of Motion

3. Óн идёт че́рез пло́щадь.

4. Óн прохо́дит ми́мо це́ркви.

5. Óн подхо́дит к рестора́ну и вхо́дит в рестора́н.

2. Óн пьёт ча́й у дру́га и разгова́ривает с дру́гом. Пото́м óн ухо́дит от дру́га. Óн идёт по у́лице, и выхо́дит на пло́щадь.

6. Óн сади́тся на сту́л (за сто́л) и éст. Пото́м óн пла́тит, встаёт со сту́ла, идёт к две́ри и выхо́дит из рестора́на.

1. Ива́нов идёт к дру́гу.

7. Пото́м óн гуля́ет по па́рку.

Other preposition + case combinations are used for *both position and motion* into position: **над, перед,** and **между** + instrumental; and **около** and **вокруг** + genitive.

Prepositions of Position

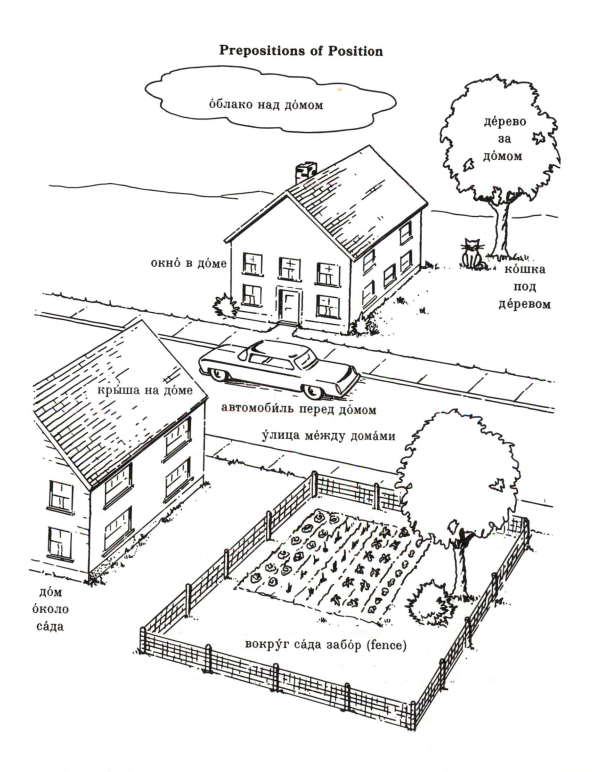

облако над домом

дерево
за
домом

окно в доме

кошка
под
деревом

крыша на доме

автомобиль перед домом

улица между домами

дом
около
сада

вокруг сада забор (fence)

Reading

На остановке автобуса

Я стоя́л на углу́ гла́вной у́лицы и жда́л авто́буса но́мер пя́ть. По гла́вной у́лице всегда́ хо́дят то́лпы люде́й. Одни́ несу́т в рука́х портфе́ли или су́мки, други́е несу́т паке́ты, не́которые веду́т за́ руку дете́й.

Я стоя́л и жда́л, а лю́ди проходи́ли ми́мо. Они́ ходи́ли из магази́на в магази́н, заходи́ли в апте́ки и рестора́ны. К гости́нице подъезжа́ли такси́, и из такси́ выходи́ли лю́ди со свои́ми чемода́нами. Одни́ входи́ли в гости́ницу, а други́е выходи́ли из гости́ницы, сади́лись в такси́, и уезжа́ли. Не́которые покупа́ли газе́ты и спо́рили о после́дних полити́ческих новостя́х, или о футбо́льном ма́тче ме́жду туре́цкой кома́ндой и сове́тской кома́ндой «Локомоти́в», други́е покупа́ли цветы́, кото́рые на углу́ продава́ла то́лстая стару́ха в платке́.

На э́той у́лице всегда́ мо́жно встре́тить знако́мых. Во́т по друго́й стороне́ идёт Лунёв со свое́й жено́й Лизаве́той. Он несёт како́й-то тяжёлый паке́т. Вероя́тно, он несёт на по́чту посы́лку для племя́нницы, кото́рая живёт в ма́леньком селе́ в Восто́чной Сиби́ри.

А во́т идёт Ве́ра Васи́льевна с како́й-то стару́шкой, кото́рая несёт небольшо́й чемода́н. Е́сли не ошиба́юсь, э́то тётка инжене́ра Ма́слова, кото́рый неда́вно у́мер. Ве́ра Васи́льевна что́-то о́чень энерги́чно ей объясня́ет. Куда́ она́ ведёт э́ту стару́шку с печа́льным лицо́м? Вероя́тно на вокза́л. Они́ прохо́дят ми́мо меня́, но сла́ва Бо́гу, меня́ не замеча́ют.

Како́й-то молодо́й челове́к с бородо́й, кото́рый нёс портфе́ль, подошёл ко мне́ и спроси́л, не зна́ю ли я кото́рый ча́с? Я сказа́л ему́, и он пошёл да́льше. Кто́ э́тот молодо́й ге́ний? Поэ́т? Писа́тель? Чита́ет ли кто́-нибудь его́ про́зу или его́ поэ́зию? Е́сть ли у него́ де́ньги на обе́д? Что́ о́н несёт в своём портфе́ле? Мо́жет быть како́й-нибудь замеча́тельный рома́н, кото́рый сде́лает его́ знамени́тым. А мо́жет быть он тала́нтливый учёный и сде́лал како́е-нибудь ва́жное откры́тие, и я ско́ро уви́жу его́ портре́т на пе́рвых страни́цах газе́т?

Ми́мо меня́ прошла́ молода́я де́вушка. Она́ несла́ в руке́ ма́ленький буке́т. Она́ о́чень спеши́ла. Её кто́-то жда́л. А что́ е́сли э́тот «кто́-то» до́лго жда́л и ушёл, и тепе́рь они́ бо́льше никогда́ не уви́дятся?

К остано́вке, где́ я стоя́л, оди́н за други́м подъезжа́ли ра́зные авто́бусы: все́ кро́ме того́, кото́рого я жда́л! Они́ привози́ли и увози́ли пассажи́ров. Авто́бусы остана́вливались. Одни́ пассажи́ры выходи́ли из авто́бусов, други́е входи́ли в ни́х, и авто́бусы е́хали да́льше. Одни́ везли́ пассажи́ров на ю́г, други́е везли́ и́х на се́вер, на за́пад, на восто́к.

Пошёл до́ждь. Я всё стоя́л[7] и жда́л своего́ авто́буса. Я стоя́л под дождём и ду́мал о ра́зных веща́х: отку́да, наприме́р, мо́й авто́бус зна́ет, что я его́ жду́ и поэ́тому не спеши́т за мно́й прие́хать? Кто́ все́ э́ти лю́ди, кото́рые хо́дят по э́той у́лице, подхо́дят к витри́нам, вхо́дят в магази́ны, но́сят поку́пки, су́мки, портфе́ли? Отку́да они́ пришли́, и куда́ пойду́т отсю́да? Ждёт ли и́х кто́-нибудь до́ма?

---

[7] **Я всё стоя́л**, *I continued standing.*

Но где́ же мо́й авто́бус? Что́ с ни́м случи́лось?

Во́н та́м, перед витри́ной како́го-то магази́на, стои́т высо́кая молода́я же́нщина. Она́ мне́ нра́вится. Она́ смо́трит на каки́е-то ве́щи в витри́не. Хо́чет ли она́ что́-нибудь купи́ть, и́ли про́сто смо́трит? Во́т она́ вхо́дит в магази́н и через не́которое вре́мя выхо́дит отту́да с поку́пками. Она́ перехо́дит у́лицу и подхо́дит к друго́й витри́не. Она́ останови́лась на мину́ту перед витри́ной и вошла́ в магази́н. Е́сть ли у неё му́ж? Че́м о́н занима́ется? О́н вероя́тно занима́ет ва́жное положе́ние, и, вероя́тно, о́н о́чень занято́й челове́к, а она́, мо́жет быть, це́лый де́нь быва́ет одна́? Е́сли она́ пое́дет на авто́бусе, подойдёт ли она́ к остано́вке, где́ я́ стою́, и ся́дет ли она́ в то́т же авто́бус что́ я́?

Же́нщина вы́шла из магази́на, останови́ла такси́, и уе́хала. Я́ бо́льше никогда́ её не уви́жу!

О́коло меня́ стоя́л како́й-то стари́к. Я́ его́ ра́ньше не заме́тил. Я́ сказа́л ему́, что я́ уже́ полчаса́ жду́ авто́буса но́мер пя́ть. Стари́к посмотре́л на меня́ с удивле́нием и сказа́л, что прое́хало не́сколько авто́бусов «5», и о́н не понима́ет, ка́к я́ мо́г и́х не ви́деть.

Чита́йте э́ти вопро́сы и отвеча́йте на ни́х.

1. Что́ я́ де́лал на гла́вной у́лице? 2. Расскажи́те, что́ де́лают лю́ди на большо́й центра́льной у́лице? 3. Расскажи́те о то́м, каки́х знако́мых я́ та́м ви́дел, и что́ они́ де́лали? 4. Опиши́те (describe) молодо́го челове́ка, кото́рый ко мне́ подошёл, что́ о́н нёс, что́ я́ о нём ду́мал. 5. Расскажи́те о де́вушке, кото́рая прошла́ ми́мо меня́. 6. Что́ я́ ду́мал о моём авто́бусе? 7. Кто́ мне понра́вился? 8. Что́ я́ хоте́л зна́ть про э́ту же́нщину? 9. Почему́ я́ не заме́тил своего́ авто́буса?

DRILL

Review Translation.

1. I am going to the north and am taking my family there. 2. We shall live in the north for a year. 3. Our doctor told our granddaughter that she may not go out yet. 4. When you go out, please shut the door. 5. The old woman entered the room and came up to me. 6. —Who was that tall young man who approached you on the street? —My grandson. 7. I shall go into the house; it is raining. 8. When I come to see you on Tuesday, I'll bring you the latest magazines. 9. He came from the west and brought a nice toy for our little son. 10. Hello, Vanya! Where are you going and what are you carrying? 11. I am going to my grandmother's and am taking her apples and candies. 12. Our grandson came for us, and we went together to the opera. 13. She used to drop in on us quite often. 14. Yesterday she dropped in for a few minutes and brought her niece and her nephew. 15. My husband was walking along our street and found a watch. 16. I never find anything. 17. When I go to school I usually go through the park. 18. I will cross the street at the corner. 19. I don't know if my nephew will bring me anything from northern Italy. 20. Why does that scientist always carry a briefcase? Have you noticed that? 21. My niece, who lives in the south, always wears a hat. 22. It began to rain; I stopped a taxi, the taxi stopped, I got (= went) in and went home.

Vocabulary

буке́т bouquet
витри́на shop window
внук grandson
вну́ч.ка (*gen. pl.* -ек) granddaughter
вон over there (at a rather great distance)
восто́к east
восто́чный eastern, oriental
де́тская (*adj. used as noun*) children's room, nursery
заня́той busy, occupied
за́пад west
за́падный western
игру́ш.ка (*gen. pl.* -ек) toy, plaything
кома́нда team
матч match, game
остано́в.ка (*gen. pl.* -ок) stop (bus)
паке́т package
пассажи́р (*fem.* -ка) passenger
печа́льный sad
плат.о́к (*gen. sing.* -а́) kerchief, shawl, handkerchief
племя́нник nephew
племя́нница niece

поку́п.ка (*gen. pl.* -ок) purchase
полчаса́ half an hour
портре́т portrait, picture
портфе́ль (*masc.*) briefcase
посы́л.ка (*gen. pl.* -ок) parcel, package
се́вер north
се́верный northern
село́ (*nom. pl.* сёла, *gen. pl.* сёл) village, town
сре́дний middle, center, average
стари́к old man
стару́ха, стару́шка old woman
су́м.ка (*gen. pl.* -ок) bag, purse
толпа́ crowd
туре́цкий Turkish
удивле́ние surprise, amazement
учёный scholarly, scientific; (*adj. used as noun*) scholar, scientist
фотоаппара́т camera
чемода́н suitcase
юг south
ю́жный southern
энерги́чный energetic
я́блок.о (*nom. pl.* -и, *gen. pl.* я́блок) apple

VERBS

замеча́ть (imperf., I), заме́тить (perf., II: заме́.чу, -тишь) to notice, observe
занима́ть (imperf., I), заня́ть (perf., I: займ.у́, -ёшь; past: за́нял, -о, заняла́, за́няли) to occupy
находи́ть (imperf., II: нахожу́, нахо́дишь), найти́ (perf., I: найд.у́, -ёшь; past: нашёл, нашло́, etc.) to find
находи́ться to be located
ода́лживать (imperf., I), одолжи́ть (perf., II: одолжу́, одолжи́шь) to lend
оставля́ть (imperf., I), оста́вить (perf., II: оста́в.лю, -ишь) to leave (*trans.*)
остана́вливать (imperf., I), останови́ть (perf., II: остан.овлю́, -о́вишь) to stop (*trans.*)
остана́вливаться, останови́ться to stop (*intrans.*)
ошиба́ться (imperf., I), ошиби́ться (perf., I: ошиб.у́сь, -ёшься; past: оши́бся, оши́блась, etc.) to make a mistake, be mistaken
серди́ться (imperf., II: сержу́сь, се́рдишься), рассерди́ться (perf., II) to get angry (на + *acc.*) at
теря́ть (imperf., I), потеря́ть (perf., I) to lose

EXPRESSIONS

Не пра́вда ли? Isn't it so? Isn't that true?
с собо́й with oneself, along; брать/взять с собо́й to take along
на се́вер, на юг, на восто́к, на за́пад (to the) north, south, east, west
на се́вере, на юге, на восто́ке, на за́паде in the north, south, east, west
из грани́цы from abroad
за́ руку by the hand

Начался́ до́ждь.⎫
Пошёл до́ждь. ⎭ It began to rain.

VOCABULARY REVIEW

Семья—Family

па́па	сын (*pl.* сыновья́)	двою́родный бра́т ⎱ cousin	внук, вну́чка
ма́ма	дочь (*pl.* до́чери)	двою́родная сестра́ ⎰	дя́дя
оте́ц (*pl.* отцы́)	брат (*pl.* бра́тья)	де́душка	тётя
мать (*pl.* ма́тери)	сестра́ (*pl.* сёстры)	ба́бушка	племя́нник
			племя́нница

Unit **23**

Grammar

1. Short forms of adjectives

Adjectives in Russian, as in English, have two uses, the attributive and the predicative. The adjective is used attributively in:

В на́шем го́роде есть **краси́вые** зда́ния.
In our town there are *beautiful* buildings.

It is used predicatively in:

Э́ти зда́ния о́чень **краси́вые**.
These buildings *are* very *beautiful*.

Most Russian adjectives have special forms known as *short* or *predicative*, which are used when an adjective plays the part of a predicate. The short (predicative) form is mandatory for certain adjectives when they are used predicatively; it is merely optional for many others.

A. Forms of short adjectives. Short adjectives have the following endings:

Masc.	*zero* instead of **-ый/-ий/-ой**	краси́в, хоро́ш, мо́лод
Neut.	**-о** instead of **-ое/-ее**	краси́во, хорошо́, мо́лодо
Fem.	**-а** instead of **-ая**	краси́ва, хороша́, молода́
Pl.	**-ы/-и** instead of **-ые/-ие**	краси́вы, хороши́, мо́лоды

Note that shifts of stress are frequent with short forms. Common are stress shifts to the ending, particularly in the feminine singular.

Only one predicate adjective has a soft stem: **синь, си́не, синя́, си́ни.**

The masculine short form is a base stem form. The stem of a number of adjectives end in a consonantal cluster, and many of these adjectives insert a vowel **e** or **o** in the masculine short form:

интере́сн.ый	интере́сен	у́мн.ый	умён
холо́дн.ый	хо́лоден	лёгк.ий	лёгок
больн.о́й	бо́лен	etc.	

Since short adjectives are used only as predicatives, they agree with the subject of the sentence and therefore occur in the *nominative* case *only*.

B. Optional use of the short forms.   The following illustrates the optional use of the short form:

Э́тот па́рк о́чень **краси́вый** or (short form) **краси́в**.

Э́то зда́ние о́чень **краси́вое** or (short form) **краси́во**.

Э́та це́рковь о́чень **краси́вая** or (short form) **краси́ва**.

Э́ти цветы́ о́чень **краси́вые** or (short form) **краси́вы**.

It is not possible to give any hard and fast rules for the choice between the long and the short (predicative) form for an adjective used predicatively. One may observe, however, that:

(1) The short forms generally suggest a more formal style, while the long ones are more colloquial, and are used more frequently.

(2) The short forms are often preferred when the adjective does not denote a permanent, intrinsic quality, but one that appears only as temporary, or limited to certain circumstances, or present if some special point of view is taken, a special purpose considered, etc.

Их са́д бы́л о́чень **краси́в** весно́й.   (Time)

О́н тогда́ бы́л **мо́лод**.   (Time)

Э́ти цветы́ бу́дут **краси́вы** на столе́ в на́шей гости́ной.   (Circumstance)

О́н **мо́лод** для э́той ро́ли.   (Purpose)

О́н **ста́р** для э́той рабо́ты.   (Purpose)

The adjectives **ма́ленький** (*small*) and **большо́й** (*large*) lack short forms. The short forms of **ма́лый** (*small*) and **вели́кий** (*great*) are often used instead in the sense of "too small" or "too big" for a particular purpose (with dative or для + genitive):

Хотя́ э́та кварти́ра не **ма́ленькая**, но́ она́ **мала́** для на́с.

Э́тот костю́м мне́ **вели́к**.

The neuter short form of the adjective also serves as the adverb:

Adverb:

О́н **свобо́дно** говори́т по-ру́сски.

He speaks Russian *fluently* (*freely*).

Predicate adjective:

Э́то ме́сто **свобо́дно**.

This seat is *free* (*vacant*).

Many adjectives lack short forms entirely. Among these are almost all soft adjectives (после́дний, весе́нний, etc.), all adjectives ending in **-ский** (ру́сский, америка́нский, etc.), ordinal numerals (пе́рвый, второ́й, etc.), and many others. Such adjectives use only long forms in the predicate.

On the other hand, the adjective **рад** (*glad*) has only short forms: рад, ра́до, ра́да, ра́ды.

Note that the forms **как** (*how*) and **так** (*so*) are used with the *short forms* of adjectives; the forms **какой** and **такой** with the *long forms:*

Ва́ша до́чь **така́я** краси́вая!
Она́ была́ **так** краси́ва в но́вом бе́лом пла́тье.

C. Mandatory use of the short forms. A few adjectives must always be used in the short form in the predicate, or are used with a distinct shade of meaning. Some of these are:

(1) **Занято́й** (long form) means *busy* in general:

Он о́чень **занято́й** челове́к.   He is a very busy man.

За́нят (short form) means *busy* or *occupied* at a given moment:

Он тепе́рь **за́нят**.   He is busy now.

The same distinction applies to **свобо́дный** *free* (long form)—**свобо́ден** (short form).

Я сейча́с **за́нят**, но́ ве́чером я́ бу́ду **свобо́ден**.

(2) **Здоро́вый** (long form) means *healthy, enjoying good health.*
Здоро́в (short form) means *being well* at a given time.
Больно́й (long form) means *ailing, having poor health* (used also as a noun it means *a patient*).
Бо́лен (short form) means *being sick* at, or during, a specified time.

—Я слы́шал, что ва́ша жена́ была́ **больна́** (ill).
—Да́, и она́ и де́ти бы́ли **больны́**; у ни́х бы́л гри́пп, но́ тепе́рь они́ уже́ всё **здоро́вы** (well) (short form).
Вообще́ на́ши де́ти о́чень **здоро́вые** (healthy) (long form).

(3) **Любе́зный** (long form) means *gracious, courteous* (in general).

Ива́н Ива́нович о́чень **любе́зный** челове́к.
Ivan Ivanovich is a very gracious person.

Любе́зен (short form) means *kind, courteous* (in a given situation).

Он бы́л о́чень **любе́зен** со мно́й.
He was very nice (considerate, courteous) to me.

Благода́рный (long form) means *grateful, thankful* (in general).

Как ма́ло **благода́рных** люде́й на све́те!
How few grateful people there are in the world!

Благода́рен (short form) means thankful (in a particular situation).

Они́ бы́ли на́м о́чень **благода́рны** за по́мощь.
They were very grateful for our help.

Бу́дьте **любе́зны**, переда́йте мне́ са́хар. Спаси́бо, я́ ва́м о́чень **благода́рен**.
Be so kind as to pass me the sugar. Thank you, I am very grateful to you.

(4) **Пра́вый** (long form) means *right* (as opposed to *left*).
   Прав (short form) means *right* (as opposed to *wrong*).

Вы́ бы́ли **пра́вы**, когда́ сказа́ли, что бу́дет до́ждь.
You were right when you said that it was going to rain.

The following adjectives are normally used in the short form when the adjective is predicative:

знако́м, знако́мо, знако́ма, знако́мы	acquainted
дово́лен, дово́льно, дово́льна, дово́льны	satisfied, content
свобо́ден, свобо́дно, свобо́дна, свобо́дны	free
здоро́в, здоро́во, здоро́ва, здоро́вы	well, healthy
бо́лен, больно́, больна́, больны́	sick, ill
любе́зен, любе́зно, любе́зна, любе́зны	kind, gracious
добр, добро́, добра́, добры́	kind
благода́рен, благода́рно, благода́рна, благода́рны	grateful
за́нят, за́нято, занята́, за́няты	busy, occupied[1]
уве́рен, уве́рено, уве́рена, уве́рены	sure[1]
удивлён, удивлено́, удивлена́, удивлены́	surprised[1]
согла́сен, согла́сно, согла́сна, согла́сны	agreed
гото́в, гото́во, гото́ва, гото́вы	ready
прав, пра́во, права́, пра́вы	right, correct
похо́ж, похо́же, похо́жа, похо́жи	similar, resembling
го́лоден, го́лодно, голодна́, го́лодны	hungry
сча́стлив, сча́стливо, сча́стлива, сча́стливы	happy, lucky

PATTERN SENTENCES

1. **Свобо́да** хоро́шая ве́щь. Всё лю́бят **свобо́ду**.
2. Мо́й прия́тель Пти́цын **свобо́дный** челове́к: у него́ не́т ни жены́ ни дете́й.
3. —Е́сли вы́ бу́дете **свобо́дны** в бу́дущую сре́ду, приходи́те к на́м. —Большо́е спаси́бо, но́ мне́ тру́дно сказа́ть зара́нее, бу́ду ли я́ **свобо́ден**.
4. Ни́ночка обеща́ла мне́, что бу́дет **свобо́дна** во вто́рник ве́чером.
5. Я́ нашёл **свобо́дное** ме́сто и се́л.
6. Э́то ме́сто **свобо́дно**.
7. Сми́т тепе́рь дово́льно **свобо́дно** говори́т по-ру́сски.
8. До́ктор Смирно́в о́чень **занято́й** челове́к.
9. К сожале́нию Ви́ктор бу́дет **за́нят** в воскре́сенье и не смо́жет прийти́.
10. Как жа́ль, что Зо́я была́ **занята́** в сре́ду ве́чером.

1. Freedom is a fine thing. Everyone likes freedom.
2. My friend Ptitsyn is a free man: he has neither wife nor children.
3. —If you are free next Wednesday, come to see us. —Thank you very much, but it's hard for me to tell in advance if I'll be free.
4. Ninochka promised me that she'd be free Tuesday evening.
5. I found a vacant seat and sat down.
6. This seat is vacant.
7. Smith speaks Russian quite fluently now.
8. Dr. Smirnov is a very busy man.
9. Unfortunately Victor will be busy on Sunday and won't be able to come.
10. It's too bad that Zoya was busy Wednesday night.

---

[1] **За́нят, уве́рен, удивлён** are actually past passive participles (explained in Unit 27), but their predicative use does not differ from any other adjectives presented in this lesson.

11. Ве́ра Васи́льевна была́ о́чень **удивлена́**, когда́ услы́шала э́ту но́вость.
12. Мно́гие бы́ли **удивлены́**. На мно́гих ли́цах мо́жно бы́ло ви́деть **удивле́ние**.
13. Профе́ссор Па́влов бы́л **бо́лен** в про́шлом ме́сяце, но́ тепе́рь о́н **здоро́в**.
14. —Вы́ **уве́рены**, что ва́ша жена́ **согла́сна** с ва́ми? —Да́, я соверше́нно **уве́рен** в э́том.
15. Мы́ с О́льгой соверше́нно **согла́сны** с отцо́м, но́ ма́ть с ни́м не **согла́сна**.
16. Вы́ бы́ли **пра́вы**, когда́ сказа́ли, что Зо́я опозда́ет на ле́кцию.
17. Коне́чно, я всегда́ **пра́в**!
18. По-мо́ему вы о́чень **похо́жи на** ва́шего отца́.
19. Ра́зве? А все́ говоря́т, что я **похо́ж на** ма́ть, а сестра́ **похо́жа на** отца́.
20. Я́ о́чень **го́лоден**. Е́сли обе́д не **гото́в**, пойдём в рестора́н. Зо́я, ты́ **гото́ва** идти́?
21. Обе́д бу́дет **гото́в** че́рез де́сять мину́т, и мы́ смо́жем пое́сть, хотя́ я совсе́м не **голодна́**.

11. Vera Vasilievna was very surprised when she heard that piece of news.
12. Many people were surprised. One could see surprise on many faces.
13. Professor Pavlov was sick last month, but now he's well.
14. —Are you sure that your wife agrees with you? —Yes, I am absolutely sure of it.
15. Olga and I are in complete agreement with Father, but Mother does not agree with him.
16. You were right when you said that Zoya would be late to the lecture.
17. Of course, I am always right!
18. To me you look very like your father.
19. Really? But everyone says that I look like my mother, and my sister looks like Father.
20. I am very hungry. If dinner isn't ready, let's go to a restaurant. Zoya, are you ready to go?
21. Dinner will be ready in ten minutes, and we can eat, although I'm not the least bit hungry.

DRILLS

A. *Переведи́те на ру́сский.*

1. We are glad that you could come.
2. I don't agree with you that Ivan is a poor student.
3. Are you satisfied with my work?
4. —Olga, are you sure of that? —Yes, I am absolutely sure.
5. I am busy this evening, and I don't know when I will be free. I never know in advance; I am a very busy person.
6. —I think that this seat is taken. —Yes, you are right.
7. I am very grateful to you for your help. You are very kind.
8. This young man is a little young for that role.
9. This suit is too small for you.
10. All these dresses are either too large or too small for me.
11. I was sure that they would come. But they didn't come.
12. Is supper ready? We are very hungry.

B. *Choose from the following predicate adjectives one which makes correct sense, and supply the proper form:* **го́лоден, удивлён, похо́ж, согла́сен, уве́рен, любе́зен, гото́в, за́нят, свобо́ден**

1. —Я́ не . . . . с ва́ми, что о́н тако́й глу́пый. —А О́льга . . . . со мно́й.
2. Мы́ бы́ли о́чень . . . ., когда́ о́н сказа́л, что о́н не зна́ет, кто́ бы́л Толсто́й.
3. Ни́на была́ . . . ., что пришёл то́лько Вади́м: она́ была́ . . . ., что Бори́с то́же придёт.
4. Я́ совсе́м не . . . ., что о́н по́нял, что́ я сказа́л. А вы́ . . . ., что о́н меня́ по́нял?
5. Ва́ша статья́ уже́ . . . .?
6. Мо́й сы́н о́чень . . . . на меня́.

7. —Америка́нские города́ не .... на европе́йские, пра́вда? —Да́, я ....
с ва́ми.
8. Бу́дьте ...., принеси́те мне́ воды́.
9. —Ни́на ничего́ ещё не е́ла, и она́ о́чень ..... Обе́д ....? —Да́, всё .....
10. Е́сли вы́ бу́дете .... за́втра ве́чером, приходи́те к на́м.
11. Ве́ра не мо́жет прийти́; она́ .....
12. Все́ бы́ли о́чень ...., что ва́с не́ было у Орло́вых.
13. Я́ сказа́л и́м зара́нее, что мы́ бу́дем .... в сре́ду.
14. —Зо́я, ты́ ...., что Серге́й придёт к обе́ду? —Да́, я ...., и я́ бу́ду о́чень
...., е́сли о́н не придёт.

2. Months of the year

The names of the months are all masculine in gender. **В** + *locative* is used to express
"in such and such a month":

	Name of Month	In
January	янва́рь	в январе́
February	февра́ль	в феврале́
March	ма́рт	в ма́рте
April	апре́ль	в апре́ле
May	ма́й	в ма́е
June	ию́нь	в ию́не
July	ию́ль	в ию́ле
August	а́вгуст	в а́вгусте
September	сентя́брь	в сентябре́
October	октя́брь	в октябре́
November	ноя́брь	в ноябре́
December	дека́брь	в декабре́

Note also:

в про́шлом ⎫
в э́том   ⎬ декабре́, ма́е, и т. д.   last ⎫ December, May, etc.
в бу́дущем ⎭   this ⎬
                                                       next ⎭

DRILL

Напиши́те отве́ты на э́ти вопро́сы.

1. Како́й тепе́рь ме́сяц?
2. Како́й пе́рвый ме́сяц го́да? Како́й после́дний?
3. Каки́е ле́тние ме́сяцы вы́ зна́ете?
4. В како́м ме́сяце начина́ется уче́бный (school) го́д?
5. В како́м ме́сяце о́н конча́ется?
6. В како́м ме́сяце вы́ роди́лись?
7. В како́м ме́сяце де́нь рожде́ния Вашингто́на?
8. Како́й ва́ш люби́мый ме́сяц?
9. В како́м ме́сяце начина́ется весна́?
10. В како́м ме́сяце начина́ется ле́то?
11. Како́й пе́рвый зи́мний ме́сяц?
12. В каки́х ме́сяцах три́дцать дне́й, а в каки́х три́дцать оди́н де́нь?

3. Reflexive pronoun себя

The reflexive pronoun **себя** (*oneself*) refers back to the subject of the sentence. It has no nominative case. It corresponds to all three persons and both numbers in English (*myself, himself, ourselves, themselves*, etc.).

Gen.	себя
Dat.	себе
Acc.	себя
Instr.	собой (-ою)
Loc.	себе

E.g.: Я купил всё это для **себя** (for myself).
Она иногда покупает **себе** (for herself) цветы́.

Он очень доволен **собой** (with himself).
Она никогда не думает о **себе** (about herself).

Себя is used as the object of transitive verbs which otherwise are normally not reflexive, that is, which only in exceptional cases direct action back to the subject:

Никто **себя** не знает.
No one knows himself.

Она очень любит **себя**.
She is very fond of herself.

Note: The suffix **-ся**, rather than **себя**, appears with many verbs that are generally or always reflexive, e.g., Он моет**ся**, *he is washing himself*. Note that English frequently omits the reflexive pronoun with such verbs.

Note especially: **чувствовать себя** *to feel* (oneself):

—Как вы **себя чувствуете**?
How are you feeling?

—Я **чувствую себя** очень хорошо.
I am feeling very well.

Note also the idiom **с собой** *along, with oneself*:

Возьми **с собой** тёплое пальто.
Take a warm coat along (with you).

Он возьмёт **с собой** портфель.
He will take a briefcase along.

4. Intensive pronoun сам

This pronoun corresponds to the various English *intensive* pronouns ending in *-self: myself, yourself, himself, ourselves, themselves*, etc., used to identify or emphasize a particular noun or pronoun. **Сам** is declined like **один**:

	SINGULAR			PLURAL
	Masculine	*Neuter*	*Feminine*	*All Genders*
Nom.	сам	самó	самá	сáми
Gen.	самогó	like masc.	самóй	самúх
Dat.	самомý	like masc.	самóй	самúм
Acc.	like Nom. or Gen.	самó	самý (самоё)	like Nom. or Gen.
Instr.	самúм	like masc.	самóй	самúми
Loc.	самóм	like masc.	самóй	самúх

The intensive pronoun must not be confused with the reflexive pronoun **себя**, although both have the same form in English; the intensive pronoun identifies, isolates, or emphasizes:

> Я́ сáм не знáю, что́ я́ бýду дéлать лéтом.
> I don't know myself what I'll be doing in summer.

But: Я́ себя́ не знáю.
> I don't know myself (I have no knowledge of myself).

PATTERN SENTENCES

1. Вóт идёт **сáм** дирéктор!
2. Я́ получúл письмó от **самогó** президéнта.
3. Вы́ должны́ это сказáть **самомý** профéссору.
4. Зúне никтó не помогáет; онá всё дéлает **самá**.
5. Я́ никогдá не читáл **самóй** кнúги, нó я́ слы́шал о нéй.
6. Я́ говорúл об э́том не с **самóй** Зúной, а с её сестрóй.
7. Я́ иногдá ненавúжу **себя́**.
8. Пóсле экзáмена Зúна былá óчень недовóльна **собóй**.
9. Когдá я́ уезжáл из Москвы́, я́ сказáл **себé**, что я́ дóлжен скóро вернýться.

1. Here comes the director himself!
2. I got a letter from the president himself.
3. You must tell that to the professor himself.
4. No one helps Zina; she does everything herself.
5. I have never read the book itself, but I've heard about it.
6. I discussed it not with Zina herself, but with her sister.
7. Sometimes I hate myself.
8. After the exam Zina was very dissatisfied with herself.
9. When I was leaving Moscow, I told myself that I must return soon.

DRILL

Переведúте на рýсский.

1. I did that myself.
2. He bought that picture for himself.
3. Tell that to the director himself!
4. They are always very satisfied with themselves!
5. My teacher told me that herself.
6. I myself don't know what I want.
7. Don't think so much about yourself! It's bad for the health.
8. Did you bring your briefcase with you?
9. Take a coat with you; it will be cold.
10. Who understands himself?
11. I shall take you along.
12. Buy yourself (*dat.*) a new hat!

5. Expressions of health

Learn the following words and expressions:

здоро́вый челове́к	a healthy person
больно́й челове́к	a sick person
бо́лен, больна́, больны́	(be) sick, ill
здоро́в, -а, -ы	(be) well
чу́вствовать себя́ хорошо́/пло́хо/ лу́чше/ху́же, и т. д.	to feel well/ill/better/worse, etc.
Мне хорошо́/пло́хо/лу́чше/ ху́же, и т. д.	I am (feel) well/ill/better/worse, etc.
Мне ста́ло хорошо́/пло́хо, лу́чше/ху́же, и т. д.	I got well/ill/better/worse, etc.
боле́ть (imperf., I: боле́.ю, -ешь)	to be sick, ailing (often or for a period of time)
Ива́н ча́сто боле́ет.	Ivan is often ill.
боле́ть (imperf., II: бол.и́т, -я́т)	to hurt, have a pain
У меня́ боли́т голова́/живо́т/ нога́, и т. д.	I have a headache/a stomach-ache; my foot hurts, etc.
заболева́ть (imperf., I), заболе́ть (perf., I)	to be taken sick, fall ill (with)
Она́ заболе́ла на про́шлой неде́ле.	She was taken sick last week.
Что с ва́ми?	What's the matter with you?
Что у него́?	What (illness) does he have?
У него́ ревмати́зм/грипп/ боле́знь се́рдца, и т. д.	He has rheumatism/grippe/heart disease, etc.
Он простуди́лся.	He caught a cold.
Я просту́жен(а).	I have a cold.
Всё прошло́.	It's (the illness, pain) all gone away.
Э́та боле́знь прошла́.	That illness went away.
Он вы́здоровел.	He recovered.

PATTERN SENTENCES

1. Ири́на **заболе́ла: у неё жа́р**. Температу́ра 38°.

   1. Irina has taken sick: she has a fever. Her temperature is 38° centigrade (= 100.4° Fahrenheit).

2. Ири́на ре́дко **боле́ет**, и ма́ть, коне́чно, беспоко́ится.

   2. Irina is rarely ill, and her mother, of course, is worried.

3. Ири́на **больна́** уже́ два дня́, и та́к как ей не **стано́вится лу́чше**, ма́ть вызыва́ет врача́.

   3. Irina has been sick for two days now, and since she is getting no better, her mother is calling in a physician.

4. Пришёл врач. Это молодая женщина. Она спрашивает Ирину, **что у неё болит**: **болит** ли горло, трудно ли ей дышать, **болят** ли у неё уши.

5. Ирина говорит, что у неё **болит** голова, что есть маленькая **боль** в животе, и **болят** глаза. У неё лёгкий насморк и она немножко **кашляет**.

6. Врач её осматривает и говорит, что ничего серьёзного нет: это вероятно **простуда** или **вирус**. Может быть она **простудилась**, когда ждала автобуса.

7. Она выписывает рецепт и говорит, что Ирина должна **принимать** это **лекарство** три раза в день после еды.

8. Она советует Ирине полежать ещё день, два в постели, и думает, что через три дня она совсём **выздоровеет**.

4. The physician has come. It is a young woman. She asks Irina what hurts her: whether her throat hurts, if it's hard for her to breathe, whether her ears hurt.

5. Irina says that her head aches, that she has a slight pain in her stomach, and her eyes hurt. She has a slight head cold and she coughs a little.

6. The physician examines her and says that there is nothing serious: it is probably a chest cold or a virus. Perhaps she has caught cold when she was waiting for the bus.

7. She writes out a prescription and says that Irina must take the medicine three times a day after meals.

8. She advises Irina to stay in bed another day or two and thinks that in three days she will be completely well.

DRILLS

A. *Choose the word which makes correct sense and give the proper form:* **болеть, больной, болен, здоров.**

1. Вчера у меня .... голова.
2. Во вторник у Нины .... глаза.
3. Теперь у Ивана .... уши.
4. Если у неё опять будет что-нибудь ...., она не придёт.
5. В субботу у меня очень .... правая рука.
6. Если у вас будут .... глаза, пойдите к врачу.
7. Бедная Анна! Она была .... и не могла выходить целую неделю.
8. В это время года все .....
9. Андрей, если ты завтра ещё будешь ...., позвони мне.
10. Мне сказали, что они старые и .... люди.
11. Я была ...., но теперь я совсём .... и могу выходить.
12. Доктор говорит, что папа очень .... человек.
13. У нас весёлые, ... дети.
14. Они, слава Богу, никогда не .....
15. Иван был простужен, но теперь он уже .....

B. *Choose the proper form of the following words:* **себя чувствовать; мне/ему, и т. д. плохо/хорошо/хуже/лучше.**

1. —Как вы ....? —Спасибо, я .... хорошо.
2. —Как .... сегодня ваш брат? —Он .... плохо.
3. Если вы будете плохо ...., позвоните врачу.
4. Вчера Ольга плохо ...., а сегодня ей ...., и она может выйти.
5. Во вторник Борису было очень ...., и мы отвезли его в больницу.
6. К сожалению, ему сегодня ...., и мы не знаем, когда он сможет выйти из больницы.
7. Я надеюсь, что завтра он будет .... немного .....

6. Образова́ние—*Education*: Verbs of *learning, studying,* and *teaching*

A. Учи́ть (II: учу́, у́чишь) *to teach, learn.*

(1) *To teach:* person taught in accusative; subject matter taught in dative (or infinitive):

> Учи́тель **у́чит** на́с ру́сскому языку́.
> The teacher teaches us Russian.

> Ма́ть **у́чит** ребёнка **ходи́ть**.
> The mother teaches the child to walk.

> Учи́тель **у́чит** на́с **говори́ть** и **писа́ть** по-ру́сски.
> The teacher teaches us to speak and write Russian.

(2) *To learn (memorize);* thing learned in accusative:

> Учени́к **у́чит** уро́к.
> The student learns the lesson.

> Актёр **у́чит** ро́ль.
> The actor learns his part.

B. Учи́ться (II: учу́сь, у́чишься), *to learn, study, go to school.*

(1) Subject matter in dative (or infinitive):

> Где́ **у́чится** ва́ш сы́н?
> Where does your son study (go to school)?

> Мо́й сы́н **у́чится** в Моско́вском университе́те.
> My son studies at Moscow University.

> О́н лю́бит **учи́ться**.
> He likes to study.

> —Ка́к о́н **у́чится**? —О́н **у́чится** о́чень хорошо́.
> —How is he doing in school? —Very well.

> —**Чему́** вы́ тепе́рь **у́читесь**? —Я́ **учу́сь** ру́сскому языку́ и матема́тике.
> —What are you studying now? —I am studying Russian and mathematics.

> Мои́ сёстры **у́чатся** танцева́ть.
> My sisters are learning to dance.

(2) The teacher with whom one studies is expressed by the preposition **у** + genitive:

> О́н **учи́лся** му́зыке у хоро́шего учи́теля.
> He studied music with a good teacher.

C. Научи́ть (perf., II: научу́, нау́чишь) (+ accusative of person being taught; dative or infinitive of subject) *to teach, impart* knowledge or skill.

> Ива́н **научи́л** меня́ говори́ть по-ру́сски.
> Ivan taught me to speak Russian.

> Ма́ть **научи́ла** на́с всему́.
> Mother taught us everything.

D. **Научи́ться** (perf., II: научу́сь, нау́чишься) (+ dative or infinitive) *to learn, to acquire* knowledge or skill.

> Я́ **научи́лся** ру́сскому языку́ у Ива́на.
> I learned Russian from Ivan.

> Мы́ **научи́лись** всему́ у ма́тери.
> We learned everything from our mother.

> Я́ пое́ду в Ита́лию, когда́ **научу́сь** говори́ть по-италья́нски.
> I shall go to Italy when I have learned to speak Italian.

E. **Изуча́ть** (imperf., I), **изучи́ть** (perf., II: изучу́, изу́чишь) (+ accusative) *to study* a subject, a question, etc. (perfective past implies that mastery has been acquired).

> —Что́ вы́ **изуча́ете**? —Я́ **изуча́ю** ка́рту (э́ту пробле́му, ру́сский язы́к, и т. д.).
> —What are you studying? —I am studying the map (this problem, Russian, etc.).

> Бори́с **изучи́л** пла́н го́рода.
> Boris mastered the map of the city.

F. **Занима́ться** (imperf., I). *to study* a given subject (subject studied in instrumental case); also used of doing homework, preparing for class, etc.

> —Че́м вы́ **занима́етесь**? —Ру́сским языко́м.
> —What are you studying? —Russian.

> —Где́ вы́ **занима́етесь**? —У себя́ в ко́мнате.
> —Where do you study (do your homework)? —In my room.

More broadly, **занима́ться** (+ instrumental) is used to describe the practice of an occupation:

> —Че́м **занима́ется** ва́ш оте́ц? —О́н архите́ктор.
> —What does your father do? —He's an architect.

G. **Преподава́ть** (imperf., I: conjugated like **дава́ть**), *to teach, give instruction in* (subject matter in the accusative; person(s) taught in the dative).

> Где́ вы́ **преподаёте**?
> Where do you teach?

> Кто́ ва́м **преподаёт** матема́тику?
> Who teaches you mathematics?

> Что́ **преподаёт** э́тот преподава́тель?
> What does that teacher teach?

Observe that with **учи́ть** (= *to teach*; see paragraph A1 above) the person(s) taught *must always be specified* (*in the accusative*), while with **преподава́ть** the person(s) taught may be specified (in the dative) or only implied.

DIALOGUE

—Где́ **преподаёт** Петро́в?

—В на́шей шко́ле. О́н прекра́сный **преподава́тель**.

—Что́ о́н **преподаёт**?

—Му́зыку. Я́ **учу́сь** у него́.

—Я́ не зна́л, что вы́ **у́читесь** в э́той шко́ле, и я́ не зна́л, что вы́ **у́читесь** му́зыке.

—О́ да́, и я́ о́чень мно́го **занима́юсь**, но́ мне́ ещё до́лго ну́жно бу́дет **учи́ться**.

—Вы́ **изуча́ете** компози́цию и гармо́нию?

—Коне́чно. Когда́ я́ око́нчу э́ту шко́лу, я́ поступлю́ в консервато́рию и бу́ду та́м **учи́ться** три́ го́да.

—А пото́м бу́дете дава́ть конце́рты?

—Наде́юсь. А мо́жет быть бу́ду **преподава́ть** му́зыку.

—Where does Petrov teach?

—In our school. He is an excellent teacher.

—What does he teach?

—Music. I study under him.

—I didn't know you were studying at that school, and I didn't know that you were learning music.

—Oh, yes, and I study very hard, but I still have a long way to go (a lot to learn).

—Are you studying composition and harmony?

—Of course. When I finish this school I shall enter the conservatory and shall study there for three years.

—And then you will give concerts?

—I hope so. Or perhaps I'll teach music.

DRILLS

A. *Answer the following question by placing the nouns in the right-hand column in the dative case.*

—Чему́ ты́ у́чишься?

—Исто́рия.
—Матема́тика.
—Му́зыка.
—Францу́зский язы́к.
—Геогра́фия.

B. *Translate into Russian.*

1. My sister teaches in this school.
2. She likes to teach.
3. I am teaching him to play the piano.
4. He studied a great deal.
5. We are studying this new map.
6. I like to study in my room.

7. Dr. Smirnov studied at this university.
8. I am learning to speak Russian.
9. Where did you learn to play tennis so well? Who taught you?
10. I have been studying this problem for a whole month.

Conversation

Об уче́нии

А́нна. —Здра́вствуйте, Зинаи́да Миха́йловна! Ра́да ва́с ви́деть! Ка́к вы́ пожива́ете? Ка́к де́ти?

Зинаи́да. —Спаси́бо, всё хорошо́. Но́ де́ти уже́ не де́ти, а совсе́м взро́слые.

А. —Да́, вре́мя идёт бы́стро. А что́ они́ де́лают? Где́ у́чатся?

З. —Мой ста́рший, Ми́ша, в ию́не око́нчил десятиле́тку[2] и в сентябре́ поступи́л в университе́т.

А. —На како́м факульте́те[3] он у́чится?

З. —На медици́нском.

А. —На медици́нском нелегко́, и ну́жно учи́ться мно́го ле́т.

З. —Да́, но он лю́бит учи́ться и у́чится хорошо́. Он получи́л стипе́ндию, так что его́ уче́ние на́м ничего́ не сто́ит. Я не зна́ю, ка́к бу́дет пото́м, но на пе́рвом ку́рсе[4] он о́чень мно́го рабо́тает. Он тепе́рь изуча́ет анато́мию и иногда́ занима́ется до по́здней но́чи. Но он о́чень дово́лен. Его́ всегда́ интересова́ла медици́на, и, кро́ме того́, он зна́ет, что врачи́ о́чень нужны́.

А. —Коне́чно! Страна́ растёт. Всё ну́жно. А где́ у́чится ва́ш мла́дший сы́н?

З. —Вади́м ещё не ко́нчил семиле́тки. Сейча́с, на кани́кулы, он пое́хал в колхо́з и рабо́тает та́м. Он проведёт та́м ию́ль и а́вгуст. Пока́ он провёл та́м то́лько две́ неде́ли и о́чень всем дово́лен. Он принима́ет акти́вное уча́стие в колхо́зной жи́зни и мно́гому та́м у́чится.

А. —Чему́ же он та́м у́чится?

З. —Он изуча́ет практи́ческую жи́знь, у́чится жи́ть в коллекти́ве, у́чится пользо-ваться маши́нами (тра́ктором и комба́йном). В колхо́зе е́сть инструктора́, кото́рые у́чат шко́льников, всё и́м объясня́ют и пока́зывают.

А. —Он в большо́м колхо́зе?

З. —Да́, колхо́з дово́льно большо́й. У ни́х мно́го земли́ и скота́. Вади́м о́чень лю́бит приро́ду и живо́тных. Он в ка́ждом письме́ пи́шет мне́ про одну́ коро́ву, кото́рую зову́т[5] «Черну́шка» ("Blackie"). Он её про́сто обожа́ет. Он пи́шет, что он изучи́л всё её привы́чки, что она́ о́чень у́мная и понима́ет ка́ждое его́ сло́во. Я не зна́ла, что коро́ва тако́е у́мное живо́тное.

А. —Он вероя́тно бу́дет хоро́шим агроно́мом или ветерина́ром.

З. —Он ещё са́м не зна́ет, ке́м[6] он хо́чет бы́ть. Он та́кже о́чень лю́бит поэ́зию и пи́шет стихи́, и, мо́жет быть, бу́дет поэ́том. Э́то то́же неплохо́е заня́тие. Поэ́ты ведь то́же нужны́. Пра́вда?

А. —Коне́чно, нужны́. А где́ Ни́ночка? Что́ она́ де́лает?

З. —Ни́ночка око́нчила педагоги́ческий институ́т и в октябре́ уе́хала в Казахста́н.[7] Она́ живёт в небольшо́м селе́ и преподаёт в се́льской шко́ле. Она́ у́чит ребя́т ру́сскому языку́, арифме́тике и вообще́ всему́. Она́ та́м то́лько четы́ре ме́сяца, и уже́ научи́ла и́х дово́льно свобо́дно и пра́вильно говори́ть по-ру́сски.

А. —Во́т, молоде́ц! А я по́мню её, когда́ она́ сама́ была́ ещё совсе́м ма́ленькой, и я учи́л её говори́ть! Ско́лько ей тепе́рь ле́т?

---

[2] There are two types of secondary schools in the Soviet Union. **Десятиле́тка** (*ten-year school*) prepares the student for the university (medicine, law, philosophy, etc.), while **семиле́тка** (*seven-year school*) gives the student a minimum required education and prepares him for vocational schools.

[3] **Факульте́т**, a school within a university.

[4] **Пе́рвый ку́рс**, first year in a school of higher education.

[5] **Кото́рую зову́т** (past: **зва́ли**) *Whose name is . . .* Ка́к тебя́ зову́т, де́вочка? *What is your name little girl?* This is a very frequent and very informal expression used only for animates. For more formal address, Ка́к и́мя (ка́к и́мя-о́тчество)? Ка́к фами́лия? are used. For inanimates the question is: Ка́к называ́ется? e.g., Ка́к называ́ется э́та пло́щадь? or Ка́к назва́ние э́того уче́бника?

[6] Russian idiom has **ке́м** он бу́дет; **ке́м** он хо́чет бы́ть; note the use of the instrumental.

[7] **Педагоги́ческий институ́т**, teachers' college. **Kazakhstan**, a Soviet republic in Central Asia.

ILLUSTRATION 21.   Но́вое зда́ние Моско́вского Госуда́рственного
Университе́та. (*Tass from Sovfoto*.)

З. —Ей уже́ два́дцать два́ го́да.

А. —Бо́же мо́й, ка́к вре́мя идёт! Ра́да слы́шать, что у ва́с всё хорошо́.

З. —Да́, сла́ва Бо́гу, жа́ловаться не могу́.

Чита́йте э́ти вопро́сы и отвеча́йте на ни́х.

1. В како́м ме́сяце Ми́ша око́нчил десятиле́тку? 2. Что́ он сде́лал в сентябре́? 3. Бу́дет ли его́ уче́ние до́рого сто́ить его́ роди́телям? 4. Почему́ он поступи́л на медици́нский факульте́т? 5. В како́й шко́ле у́чится Вади́м? 6. Почему́ Вади́м сейча́с в колхо́зе? 7. Каки́е ме́сяцы он проведёт в колхо́зе? 8. Чему́ он та́м у́чится? 9. Что́ он пи́шет в свои́х пи́сьмах? 10. Ке́м он бу́дет? 11. Что́ де́лает до́чь Зина́йды Миха́йловны? 12. Како́й результа́т её преподава́ния? 13. Чему́ вы́ са́ми у́читесь? 14. Ке́м вы́ хоти́те бы́ть?

Reading

Она́ обожа́ет говори́ть о себе́

Вы́ ещё не всё зна́ете про Ве́ру Васи́льевну.

Одна́ из её люби́мых те́м, э́то те́ма о здоро́вье. Она́ о́чень интересу́ется боле́знями все́х, но бо́льше всего́ она́ лю́бит говори́ть о свои́х боле́знях.

По-мо́ему, она́ о́чень здоро́вая же́нщина, но она́ всегда́ жа́луется на своё здоро́вье все́м, кто то́лько хо́чет её слу́шать.

Е́сли, не да́й Бо́г, вы́ задади́те Ве́ре Васи́льевне бана́льный вопро́с: «Ка́к пожива́ете?», вы́ сейча́с же от неё услы́шите, что, хотя́ она́ вообще́ не лю́бит жа́ловаться и никогда́ не жа́луется, она́ должна́ сказа́ть, что она́ сего́дня пло́хо себя́ чу́вствует; она́ заболе́ла в понеде́льник: у неё ве́сь де́нь боле́ла голова́ и боле́ло го́рло. Ве́чером ей ста́ло немно́жко лу́чше, но но́чью ей ста́ло опя́ть ху́же. Она́ всю́ но́чь принима́ла аспири́н, пила́ горя́чий ча́й с лимо́ном, но́ ничего́ не помога́ло. Во вто́рник она́ ве́сь де́нь лежа́ла в посте́ли. Пото́м, сла́ва Бо́гу, всё э́то прошло́ и она́ ду́мала, что она́ вы́здоровела. Но в четве́рг у неё та́к боле́ли но́ги и спина́, что она́ совсе́м не могла́ ходи́ть, и сосе́ди хоте́ли вы́звать (call in) врача́ или отвезти́ её в больни́цу. Но к сча́стью ей ста́ло немно́жко лу́чше, и ве́чером она́ пошла́ в го́сти к сосе́дям.

Я бо́льше никогда́ не спра́шиваю её «ка́к пожива́ете» и ва́м сове́тую э́того не де́лать.

Чита́йте э́ти вопро́сы и отвеча́йте на ни́х.

1. О чём В. В. бо́льше всего́ лю́бит говори́ть? 2. Что́ она́ говори́т о своём хара́ктере? Чего́ она́ никогда́ не де́лает? 3. Что́ у неё боле́ло в понеде́льник? 4. Ка́к ей бы́ло но́чью, и что́ она́ де́лала? 5. Что́ у неё боле́ло в сре́ду? 6. Почему́ в четве́рг её хоте́ли отвезти́ в больни́цу? 7. Почему́ её туда́ не отвезли́? 8. Како́е у ва́с здоро́вье? 9. Ско́лько ра́з в э́том году́ вы́ бы́ли больны́? 10. Что́ ну́жно де́лать, когда́ у челове́ка гри́пп?

DRILL

Review Translation.

1. —How is your father feeling now? —Thank you, fortunately he is better today. 2. Unfortunately, our grandmother is feeling worse today. In the doctor's opinion, she is very sick. 3. My aunt was sick and my uncle took her to the hospital, and now I've learned that my uncle himself is sick. 4. I don't feel well this evening; I have a headache. 5. —Where did you study? —I studied at Moscow University, and besides I studied for a year in England. I studied history. 6. —Does your son like to study? —Yes, very much. 7. —We are studying French this year. —What textbook do you use? —We are using a new textbook; I've forgotten its name. 8. Every year we spend our vacation at the seashore. We adore the sea! 9. My father spent this summer in the mountains. He adores mountains! 10. My aunt often complains of her health; she is a very sick woman. 11. It's impossible to tell in advance who will receive a scholarship for next year. 12. My father's birthday is in August, and my mother's in September. 13. —Tell me something about yourself. —I myself don't know what to tell you. 14. It is a bad habit to speak about oneself. 15. The dog is a very intelligent animal. 16. Your daughter, according to my wife, looks very like you. 17. This city resembles Paris. 18. This kolkhoz has much land and much cattle. 19. Thank God, my grandfather is better today. 20. Fortunately, we took him to the hospital.

Vocabulary

(See also p. 390.)

боле́знь (*fem. II*) illness, disease
боль (*fem. II*) pain
больни́ца hospital
взро́слый (*adj. used as noun*) adult
го́рло throat
живо́т stomach, belly
живо́тное (*adj. used as noun*) animal
зара́нее in advance
земля́ (*gen. pl.* земе́ль) earth, land
инстру́ктор (*nom. pl.* -а́), *fem.* -ша (practical) instructor
кани́кулы (*fem. pl. only*) school holidays, vacation
ка́шель (*m.*) cough
коро́ва cow
лека́рство medicine
лу́чше better
мно́гое (*declined as a neut. adj.*) much, many things
на́сморк chest cold
образова́ние education
поэ́зия poetry

практи́ческий practical
преподава́ние teaching
привы́ч.ка (*gen. pl.* -ек) habit
просту́да cold, chill
ребя́та (*nom. pl.; gen. pl.* ребя́т) kids, fellows (*colloq.*)
рожде́ние birth, birthday
свобо́да freedom, liberty
свобо́дный free
свобо́дно freely, fluently
се́льский village (*adj.*)
се́рдце heart
скот livestock, cattle
соверше́нно completely, absolutely
спина́ back (of an animate being)
стипе́ндия scholarship
температу́ра temperature
уче́ние study, learning, schooling, education
у́ши (*nom. pl. of* у́хо) ears
ху́же worse
шко́льн.ик (*fem.* -ица) schoolboy (girl)

VERBS

беспоко́иться (imperf., II: беспоко́.юсь, -ишься) to worry
жа́ловаться (imperf., I: жа́лу.юсь, -ешься), пожа́ловаться (perf., I) to complain (+ *dat.*) to; (на + *acc.*) of, about

обожа́ть (imperf., I) to adore, worship

ока́нчивать (imperf., I), око́нчить (perf., II: око́нч.у, -ишь) (+ acc.) to graduate, be graduated from

по́льзоваться (imperf., I: по́льзу.юсь, -ешься), воспо́льзоваться (perf., I) to use, take advantage of (+ instr.)

поступа́ть (imperf., I), поступи́ть (perf., II: поступлю́, посту́пишь) to enter, enroll in (+ в/на + acc.)

проводи́ть (imperf., II: провожу́, прово́дишь), провести́ (perf., I: провед.у́, -ёшь; past: провёл, провели́, etc.) to pass, spend (time)

простужа́ться (imperf., I), простуди́ться (perf., II) to catch a cold

рожда́ться (imperf., I), роди́ться (perf., II: рожу́сь, роди́шься; past: роди́лся, родил.о́сь, -а́сь, -и́сь) to be born

чу́вствовать (imperf., I: чу́вству.ю, -ешь), почу́вствовать (perf., I) to feel (trans.)

чу́вствовать себя́ to feel (intrans.: well, ill, etc.)

EXPRESSIONS

к сча́стью fortunately

к сожале́нию unfortunately

уве́рен в (+ loc.) sure of

похо́ж на (+ acc.) look like, resemble

Пойдём! Let's go!

де́нь рожде́ния birthday

бо́льше всего́ most of all

всем, кто то́лько хо́чет to everyone who is the least bit willing

Не да́й Бо́г! God forbid!

по мнению (+ gen.) in the opinion of . . . , according to . . .

кро́ме того́ besides (adv.), in addition

The hypothetical mood • The English conditional and its equivalent in Russian • Verbs of *placing* • Prepositions за and под with accusative • *Going* verbs (continued) • Reading: Áх, éсли бы у негó был порядок!

Unit 24

Grammar

1. The hypothetical mood

The particle **бы** is used with verb forms of the past tense (or the infinitive) to express the *hypothetical mood* (also called the conditional or subjunctive).

The sentence «Я пошёл бы в теáтр» is in the hypothetical mood; the form «**пошёл бы**» means that the speaker considers going to the theater as a possibility, as something he might do (or might have done), would like (or would have liked) to do, would do (or would have done), circumstances permitting.

These meanings may be contrasted with those expressed by the *indicative mood*, which is used to state that an action was, is, or will actually be performed: Я пошёл (went) в теáтр, Я идý (am going) в теáтр, Я пойдý (will go) в теáтр; or in questions, e.g., Вы пойдёте в теáтр? etc.

It must be clearly understood that in hypothetical constructions (past tense forms plus **бы**), the verb is *not* past in meaning; it is actually neither past, nor present, nor future, since this construction does not have the means to differentiate tenses.

A. The hypothetical mood in conditions. It has been seen earlier that the word **éсли** in Russian (like *if* in English) means that one event is contingent on another one:

Éсли отéц мнé пришлёт дéньги, я куплю автомобúль.
If Father sends me the money, I shall buy a car.

In this example, both verbs (**куплю** and **пришлёт**) are in the future tense and the indicative mood. Substituting the hypothetical mood for the indicative, we have:

Éсли бы отéц прислáл мнé дéньги, я **бы** купúл автомобúль.

This construction emphasizes the hypothetical nature of the condition; the speaker here has no particular reason to believe that the money will be forthcoming and is merely expressing a wish or speculating on what he would do if he did receive it. The indicative (Éсли отéц пришлёт . . . я куплю) would suggest, on the other hand, that there is some reason for expecting or hoping that the money will arrive.

The Russian hypothetical construction does not differentiate between conditions that, however improbable, might come true, and those that are known to have failed (or are regarded as impossible); only the context can indicate whether the condition is possible or contrary to fact. The sentence above, given a context, may correspond in English either to "If Father *sent* (or *would send*) me the money, I *would buy* a car" (possible, though perhaps unlikely), or to "If Father *had sent* me the money, I *would have bought* a car" (impossible).

A clearly "unreal" condition is stated in the phrase "If I were you . . .":

> Éсли бы я бы́л на ва́шем ме́сте, я **бы** ему́ э́того не расска́зывал.
> If I were in your place, I shouldn't have told him that.

B. Wishing, hoping, and considering with бы. (1) The words **éсли бы** or the particle **бы** alone are often used colloquially as expressions of a wish, hope, uncertainty, tentative consideration, etc.

> Éсли бы я то́лько бы́л бога́т!
> If only I were rich!

> Хорошо́ (было) **бы** пое́хать куда́-нибудь к мо́рю.
> It would be nice to go somewhere to the seaside.

> На́до (было) **бы** написа́ть отцу́; мы́ давно́ ему́ не писа́ли.
> I think (or: Don't you think) we ought to write to Father; it has been a long
>   time since we wrote to him.

(2) In questions:

> Где́ **бы** на́м пообе́дать сего́дня?
> Where could we (or: I wonder where we could) have dinner tonight?

> Куда́ **бы** на́м пойти́ ве́чером?
> Where could we (or: I wonder where we could) go tonight?

(3) Very often the phrase **я хоте́л бы** is used rather than the more assertive **я хочу́**; the difference between the two is very much the same as that between *I would like to* and *I want to*.

C. Wishes, commands, requests, applied to another person. The hypothetical mood is also used in Russian in sentences of the type *John wants Peter to come*:

> Ива́н хо́чет, **чтобы** Пётр **пришёл**.

In this construction the subordinate clause is introduced by **чтобы** (**что** combined with the **бы** particle), and the verb in this clause is in the past tense form (not past in *meaning*).

Observe that **хоте́ть** is used with the infinitive in sentences of the type Я́ хочу́ прочита́ть э́ту кни́гу, or Бори́с хо́чет прочита́ть э́ту кни́гу; in such sentences the person who wants and the person who will read are the same. Contrast: Я́ хочу́, чтобы **Бори́с** прочита́л э́ту кни́гу; here the persons are different and the hypothetical mood *must* be used.

The same pattern is followed with other verbs, such as telling, writing, requesting, commanding, etc.:

Я́ скажу́ ему́, **что́бы** о́н **принёс** кни́гу.
I shall tell him to bring the book.

О́н мне́ написа́л, **что́бы** я́ **привёз** кни́ги.
He wrote me to bring the books.

Thus, when someone wants *someone else* to do something, **что́бы** + the past tense form (= hypothetical mood) *must* be used.

D. Purpose clauses. The word **что́бы** or the prepositional construction **для того́, что́бы** is generally used to express the purpose of an action (*in order that, in order to*); the verb in the subordinate clause then has the past tense form when there are different subjects in the two clauses:

Я́ да́л ему́ де́нег (для того́), **что́бы** о́н **мо́г** пое́хать на Кавка́з.
I gave him money so that he could go to the Caucasus.

Я́ не зна́ю, что́ я́ до́лжен сде́лать, **что́бы** она́ наконе́ц **отве́тила** на письмо́ ма́тери.
I don't know what I must do so that she will finally answer her mother's letter.

If the subject in the two clauses is the same, the *infinitive* is used:

О́н мно́го занима́ется (для того́), **что́бы** хорошо́ **сда́ть** (pass) экза́мены.
He studies a great deal (in order) to get good grades on his exams.

Она́ идёт в магази́н (для того́), **что́бы** всё **купи́ть** на за́втра.
She is going to the store (in order) to buy everything for tomorrow.

2.   The English conditional and its equivalent in Russian

As has already been pointed out (Unit 15, page 229), in Russian the tense used in reported discourse is the same as in the original statement, e.g.:

Ivan speaking: «Я́ приду́ за́втра.»
Reported: Ива́н сказа́л, что **придёт** за́втра.
(Contrast English: He said that he *would* come.)

The English auxiliary verb *would* corresponds here to the Russian future in past reported speeches, and not, as in the examples in Section 1, to the hypothetical mood.[1]
A third use of English *would* is to denote habitual action in the past; this corresponds to the Russian *imperfective past*:

О́н ка́ждый де́нь **приходи́л** к на́м.
Every day he *would* come to see us.

Care must be taken when translating *would* into Russian to determine whether the future, imperfective past, or the hypothetical mood is appropriate.

---

[1] The same rule applies to constructions which are not, strictly speaking, reported speeches, and for which there is no actual "original statement"; the principles involved, however, are the same as if an actual statement had been made, e.g., Я́ ду́мал, что о́н **придёт**. I thought that he *would* come.

PATTERN SENTENCES

Hypothetical conditions: **éсли бы**.

1. **Éсли бы** у меня́ **бы́ло** мно́го де́нег, мне́ не ну́жно **бы́ло бы** рабо́тать.
2. **Éсли бы** вы́ вчера́ **сказа́ли**, что ва́м нужны́ де́ньги, я́ **бы** ва́м сего́дня и́х **принёс**.
3. **Они́ купи́ли бы** э́того Рембра́ндта, **éсли бы** у ни́х **бы́ло** бо́льше де́нег.
4. Как **бы́ло бы** хорошо́, **éсли бы** вы́ **прие́хали** к на́м, когда́ мы́ жи́ли на да́че! Почему́ вы́ не прие́хали?
5. —Как жа́ль, что вы́ вчера́ **не́ были** у Смирно́вых! —**Éсли бы** я́ **зна́л**, что вы́ та́м бу́дете, я́ **бы** то́же **пришёл**.
6. Что́ **бы** вы́ **сде́лали**, **éсли бы** о́н ва́м сказа́л, что вы́ ему́ бо́льше не нужны́?
7. Что́ **бы** мы́ **де́лали** без ва́с?[2]

Wishes, commands, etc.: **что́бы**.

1. Я́ хочу́, **что́бы** Па́вел **написа́л** обо всём свои́м роди́телям.
2. **Я́ хочу́, что́бы** ты́ **отве́тил** на мо́й вопро́с.
3. Учи́тель **хо́чет, что́бы** мы́ **сде́лали** э́тот перево́д на за́втра.
4. Они́ **хотя́т, что́бы** я́ и́м **принёс** два́дцать пя́ть до́лларов во вто́рник.
5. Мы́ о́чень **хоти́м, что́бы** вы́ **пришли́** к на́м в э́то воскресе́нье к обе́ду.
6. Мы́ все́ **хоти́м, что́бы** вы́ на́м **сыгра́ли** балла́ду Шопе́на.
7. Ири́на **про́сит, что́бы** я́ **привёз** ей часы́ из Швейца́рии.
8. Ива́н **написа́л** мне́, **что́бы** я́ **привёз** ему́ но́вые пласти́нки.
9. **Я́ сказа́л** Со́не, **что́бы** она́ **купи́ла** цвето́в.

Purpose clauses: **что́бы**.

1. **Принеси́те** мне́ письмо́, **что́бы** я́ **мо́г** его́ подписа́ть.
2. **Для того́ что́бы купи́ть** биле́ты в теа́тр, ва́м ну́жно бу́дет пое́хать в го́род.
3. **Что́бы** о́н со мно́й не **спо́рил**, я́ сра́зу скажу́ ему́, что я́ с ни́м согла́сен.
4. **Для того́, что́бы** свобо́дно **говори́ть** по-ру́сски, ва́м нужна́ пра́ктика.
5. **Что́бы** Пе́тя лу́чше **éл**, ма́ть расска́зывает ему́ ска́зки за обе́дом.

1. If I had a lot of money, I wouldn't have to work.
2. If you had said yesterday that you needed money, I would have brought it to you today.
3. They would have bought that Rembrandt if they had had more money.
4. How nice it would have been if you had come to see us when we were living in the country! Why didn't you?
5. —Too bad you weren't at the Smirnovs' yesterday! —If I had known that you would be there, I would have come too.
6. What would you do if he should tell you that he doesn't need you anymore?
7. What would we do without you?

1. I want Paul to write to his parents about everything.
2. I want you to answer my question.
3. The teacher wants us to do that translation for tomorrow.
4. They want me to bring them $25 on Tuesday.
5. We would very much like you to come to our house this Sunday for dinner.
6. We all want you to play a ballade by Chopin for us.
7. Irene is asking me to bring her a watch from Switzerland.
8. Ivan wrote me to bring him some new records.
9. I told Sonya to buy some flowers.

1. Bring me the letter so that I can sign it.
2. In order to buy tickets for the theater, you'll have to go downtown.
3. To keep him from arguing with me, I'll tell him right away that I agree with him.
4. In order to speak Russian fluently, you need practice.
5. So that Petya should eat better (more), his mother tells him fairy tales at dinner.

---

[2] In this sentence the condition with **éсли бы** is implied. Compare: Что́ бы мы́ де́лали, éсли бы ва́с не́ было?

Wishes, advice, etc. with **бы**.

1. **Я́ бы́л бы** ра́д его́ ви́деть.	1. I would be glad to see him.
2. Как **бы́ло бы** хорошо́ пое́хать к мо́рю в таку́ю пого́ду!	2. How nice it would be to go to the seashore in such weather!
3. На́до **бы** написа́ть дя́де Ва́не! Мы́ так давно́ ему́ не писа́ли.	3. We ought to write to Uncle Vanya! We haven't written to him for such a long time.
4. О́н не до́лжен **бы́л бы** э́того говори́ть.	4. He shouldn't have said that.
5. Вы́ **бы пошли́** погуля́ть.	5. You should go for a walk.
6. Я́ **бы хоте́л** забы́ть своё про́шлое.	6. I would like to forget my past.
7. Как **бы́ло бы** хорошо́, **е́сли бы** вы́ **могли́** к на́м прийти́ в воскресе́нье! Вы́ придёте?	7. How nice it would be if you could come to see us on Sunday! Will you come?
8. **Бы́ло бы** хорошо́, **е́сли бы** вы́ ему́ **помогли́**.	8. It would be good if you would help him.

DRILLS

A. *Translate the words in parentheses into Russian.*

1. Мы́ о́чень хоти́м, (you to come) в суббо́ту.
2. Моя́ ма́ть хо́чет, (me to write) отцу́.
3. Я́ не зна́ю, что́ сде́лать, (so that he should speak) бо́льше по-ру́сски!
4. Они́ (would have been) о́чень ра́ды ва́с ви́деть.
5. Бы́ло бы хорошо́, (if he would come).
6. Вы́ должны́ попроси́ть его́, (that he should bring) пятьдеся́т рубле́й.
7. (In order to do) перево́д, мне́ ну́жен слова́рь.
8. О́н хоте́л, (me to read) ему́ э́то письмо́. Но́, (in order to read) э́то письмо́, мне́ ну́жно взя́ть его́ у сестры́.
9. Они́ та́к (would like) пое́хать на Кавка́з!

B. *Translate into Russian.*

1. She said that she would buy me a present.
2. If he had the money, he would have bought me a present. But unfortunately he has no money!
3. If he has (will have) the money tomorrow, he'll buy me something.
4. How nice it would have been if you had written to Olga! Why didn't you write to her?
5. I would like to see him.
6. In order to see him, you must go to Moscow.
7. Mother doesn't want me to go to Moscow.
8. She wants to go there herself.
9. You should have written to her husband.

3. Verbs of *placing*

Russian makes a sharp distinction between placing something in a standing position and placing it in a lying position. The student translating English verbs such as *to put* or *to place* must make this distinction.

Transitive verbs of *placing* are related to corresponding intransitive verbs of *standing* or *lying* (see pages 313–314).

	Intransitive Verbs (Being in a Position)	Transitive Verbs (Putting into Position)	
		Imperfective	*Perfective*
Standing	**стоя́ть** (II: сто.ю́, -и́шь)	**ста́вить** (II: ста́в.лю, -ишь)	**поста́вить** (II: поста́в.лю, -ишь)
Lying	**лежа́ть** (II: леж.у́, -и́шь)	**класть**[3] (I: клад.у́, -ёшь; *Past:* кла́л, -о, -а, -и)	**положи́ть**[3] (II: положу́, поло́жишь)

Transitive verbs of *placing* take the prepositions **в** or **на** with the accusative, or **к** with the dative, or adverbs of direction:

Я положи́л э́то письмо́ **на** пи́сьменный сто́л, и оно́ ещё та́м **лежи́т**.
I put (laid) that letter on the desk, and it's still lying there.

Поста́вьте э́тот сту́л **сюда́**. Пу́сть о́н здесь **стои́т**.
Put (stand) this chair here. Let it stand here.

REVIEW: VERBS OF POSITION

	I Being in a Standing, Sitting, or Lying Position		II Taking a Standing, Sitting, or Lying Position		III Putting Something or Someone in a Standing, Sitting, or Lying Position	
	Imperf.	*Perf.*	*Imperf.*	*Perf.*	*Imperf.*	*Perf.*
A *Standing*	**стоя́ть** стою́ стои́шь стоя́л	**по-** **про-**	**встава́ть** встаю́ встаёшь встава́л	**встать** вста́ну вста́нешь вста́л	**ста́вить** ста́влю ста́вишь ста́вил	**по-**
			станови́ться становлю́сь стано́вишься станови́лся	**стать** ста́нешь ста́нет ста́л		
B *Sitting*	**сиде́ть** сижу́ сиди́шь сиде́л	**по-** **про-**	**сади́ться** сажу́сь сади́шься сади́лся	**сесть** ся́ду ся́дешь сел	**сажа́ть**[4] сажа́ю сажа́ешь сажа́л	**посади́ть**[4] посажу́ поса́дишь посади́л
C *Lying*	**лежа́ть** лежу́ лежи́шь лежа́л	**по-** **про-**	**ложи́ться** ложу́сь ложи́шься ложи́лся	**лечь** ля́гу ля́жешь лёг	**класть** кладу́ кладёшь клал	**положи́ть** положу́ поло́жишь положи́л

[3] The imperfective-perfective pair **класть/положи́ть** is a third suppletive pair (like **говори́ть/сказа́ть** and **брать/взять**). Note the relationship between the perfective **положи́ть**, *to put in a lying position, put down*, and **лежа́ть**, *to lie*.

[4] These verbs mean *to seat*, also *to plant*.

4. Prepositions за and под with accusative

The prepositions **за** and **под** take the *instrumental* case to indicate location (see Unit 19, page 303). When they indicate direction of motion, however, they take the *accusative*:

Я поста́вил велосипе́д **за** де́ре**во**.   Во́т о́н стои́т **за** де́рев**ом**.
Я положи́л газе́ту **под** кни́**гу**.   Она́ лежи́т **под** кни́**гой**.

Note the following expressions:

е́хать за́ го́род[5]	to go out of town, go to the country
жи́ть за́ го́родом	to live in the country
е́хать за грани́цу	to go abroad (literally, beyond the border)
жи́ть за грани́цей	(*instr.*) to live abroad

PATTERN SENTENCES

1. Ты́ забы́ла **положи́ть** на сто́л ло́жки и забы́ла **поста́вить** стака́ны для воды́.

2. —Кто́ **поста́вил** на сто́л э́ту пусту́ю буты́лку? —Э́то я́ **поста́вила** её. Мне́ показа́лось, что она́ по́лная.

3. Я́ **поста́влю** э́то кре́сло в кабине́т; оно́ мо́жет **стоя́ть** в кабине́те.

4. Не **клади́** все́ э́ти ве́щи на дива́н, а **положи́** и́х в шка́ф. Они́ должны́ **лежа́ть** в шкафу́.

5. Я́ **положи́л** письмо́ на тво́й пи́сьменный сто́л, туда́, куда́ я́ всегда́ **кладу́** пи́сьма. Во́т оно́ лежи́т.

6. Я́ **поста́вил** твою́ кни́гу на по́лку. Во́н она́ **стои́т**.

7. —Куда́ О́льга **кладёт** де́ньги? —Она́ всегда́ **кладёт** де́ньги **за** э́ту ва́зу. Ви́дишь, они́ лежа́т **за** ва́зой.

8. Ма́ма **поло́жит** твои́ платки́ в шка́ф **за** руба́шки. По́мни, что они́ **бу́дут лежа́ть за** руба́шками на второ́й по́лке.

9. Я́ **поста́влю** твои́ боти́нки **под** крова́ть. Ты́ и́х найдёшь **под** крова́тью.

10. Мо́крый зо́нтик **стои́т за** кре́слом. Кто́ **поста́вил** зо́нтик **за** кре́сло? Не **ста́вьте** его́ туда́!

11. Не **ста́вь** пусты́е буты́лки **под** сто́л!

1. You forgot to put spoons on the table and to put out water glasses.

2. —Who put this empty bottle on the table? —I did. I thought it was full.

3. I'll put that easy chair in the study; it can stand in the study.

4. Don't put all those things on the sofa, but put them in the dresser. They must stay in the dresser.

5. I put the letter on your desk, in the place where I always put letters. There it is.

6. I put your book on the shelf. There it is.

7. —Where does Olga put money? —She always puts it behind this vase. You see it's lying behind the vase.

8. Mama will put your handkerchiefs in the dresser behind the shirts. Remember that they'll be lying behind the shirts on the second shelf.

9. I shall put your shoes under the bed. You'll find them under the bed.

10. A wet umbrella is standing in back of the armchair. Who put an umbrella in back of the armchair? Don't put it there!

11. Don't put empty bottles under the table!

---

[5] Prepositions sometimes take the stress from the noun, especially in certain common adverbial expressions; note also: Кни́га упа́ла **на́ пол**. The book fell on the floor; and Ма́ть вела́ ребёнка **за́ руку**. The mother led the child by the hand.

DRILLS

A. *Replace the blank with a suitable verb* (класть/положи́ть, ста́вить/поста́вить, лежа́ть, стоя́ть).

1. —Кто́ .... э́ти пи́сьма на мо́й сто́л? —Ве́ра .... и́х сюда́.
2. —Почему́ ты́ всегда́ .... всё пи́сьма на мо́й сто́л? —Я́ обыкнове́нно ....
   и́х сюда́, потому́ что я́ не зна́ю куда́ и́х .....
3. Чьи́ пи́сьма .... на моём столе́?
4. —Вади́м, куда́ ты́ .... ви́ски? —Я́ .... его́ туда́, куда́ я́ всегда́ его́ .....
5. Е́сли хоти́те, я́ сейча́с .... ви́ски в буфе́т, туда́, где́ .... во́дка.
6. Возьми́те э́ти докуме́нты и .... и́х в шка́ф, а слова́рь .... на по́лку туда́,
   где́ .... францу́зские кни́ги.
7. Не клади́ газе́ты на́ пол! .... её сейча́с же на то́т сто́лик!
8. —Ива́н, ты́ .... маши́ну в гара́ж? —Да́, маши́на .... в гараже́.

B. *Translate into Russian.*

1. He always puts the newspaper under the bed.
2. Vanya went behind the garage.
3. Kolya, why did you put your bicycle behind the door?
4. Who put my notebook under the dictionary?

5. *Going* verbs (continued)

Three more commonly used verbs of motion have paired imperfective forms: *determinate* and *indeterminate* (see Unit 17, page 251):

	Indeterminate Imperfective	Determinate Imperfective		Perfective
to run				
Inf.	**бе́гать** (I)	**бежа́ть**[6]		**побежа́ть** (I)
Pres.	бе́гаю	бегу́	*Fut.*	побегу́
	бе́гаешь	бежи́шь		побежи́шь
	etc.	. . .		. . .
		бегу́т		побегу́т
to fly				
Inf.	**лета́ть** (I)	**лете́ть** (II)		**полете́ть** (II)
Pres.	лета́ю	лечу́	*Fut.*	полечу́
	лета́ешь	лети́шь		полети́шь
	etc.	. . .		. . .
		летя́т		полетя́т
to swim, float				
Inf.	**пла́вать** (I)	**плыть** (I)		**поплы́ть** (I)
Pres.	пла́ваю	плыву́	*Fut.*	поплыву́
	пла́ваешь	плывёшь		поплывёшь
	etc.	etc.		etc.

[6] The verb **бежа́ть** is irregular: its forms are second conjugation, except for the third person plural which is first conjugation.

Prefixed compounds of these verbs are formed analogously to those of other verbs, e.g., **прилета́ть/прилете́ть** *to come* (*arrive*) *by flying*; **улета́ть/улете́ть** *to fly away*, etc. Note the stress shift in compounds of **бе́гать**: **прибега́ть/прибежа́ть** *to come running*. Compounds of **пла́вать** are found with **-плыва́ть**: **подплыва́ть/подплы́ть** *to sail* (*swim*) *toward*.

PATTERN SENTENCES

Лета́ть/лете́ть (у-, при-, вы-).

1. Над на́шим го́родом це́лый де́нь **лета́ют** самолёты.
2. Посмотри́те, как ни́зко **летя́т** э́ти два́ самолёта!
3. Я **лета́ю** в Оде́ссу по де́лу два́ ра́за в ме́сяц.
4. За́втра я **лечу́** туда́. Моя́ секрета́рша **лети́т** со мной.
5. Е́сли я **вы́лечу** в се́мь утра́, я **прилечу́** в Оде́ссу в де́сять.
6. Я обы́чно **вылета́ю** и **прилета́ю** в э́то вре́мя.
7. Со́ня не лю́бит **лета́ть**; она́ предпочита́ет е́здить по́ездом или парохо́дом.
8. Мой племя́нник **прилете́л** вчера́ у́тром из Се́верной А́фрики и ве́чером **улете́л** в Ю́жную Аме́рику.
9. Вре́мя **лети́т** бы́стро.

1. All day airplanes fly over our town.
2. Look how low those two planes are flying!
3. I fly to Odessa twice a month on business.
4. Tomorrow I'm flying there. My secretary is coming with me.
5. If I set out at seven, I shall land in Odessa at ten.
6. I usually leave and arrive by plane at that time.
7. Sonya doesn't like to fly; she prefers to travel by train or by boat.
8. My nephew flew in yesterday morning from North Africa and left by plane in the evening for South America.
9. Time flies quickly.

Бе́гать/бежа́ть (при-, у-, в-, вы-).

1. Как мно́го эне́ргии у дете́й! Они́ **бе́гают** це́лый де́нь и никогда́ не устаю́т.
2. Куда́ **бегу́т** э́ти ма́льчики?
3. Я ви́дел, как Ива́н Ива́нович **бежа́л** по у́лице. Я останови́л его́ и спроси́л: «Куда́ вы́ **бежи́те?**» Он останови́лся и отве́тил: «Я **бегу́** на вокза́л; я бою́сь опозда́ть на по́езд.»
4. Вероя́тно, когда́ он **прибежа́л** на вокза́л, по́езд уже́ ушёл.
5. Мы с Ни́ной стоя́ли и споко́йно разгова́ривали. Вдру́г **вбежа́л** в ко́мнату Ко́ля с телегра́ммой в руке́.
6. Ни́на прочла́[7] телегра́мму и **вы́бежала** из ко́мнаты.
7. Еле́на Ива́новна так мно́го вчера́ говори́ла, что я **убежа́л**.

1. How much energy children have! They run about all day long and never get tired.
2. Where are those boys running?
3. I saw Ivan Ivanovich running down the street. I stopped him and asked, "Where are you running?" He stopped and answered, "I am running to the station; I'm afraid I'll be late for the train."
4. When he arrived at the station, the train had probably left already.
5. Nina and I were standing talking peacefully. Suddenly Kolya ran into the room with a telegram in his hand.
6. Nina read the telegram and ran out of the room.
7. Yelena Ivanovna talked so much yesterday that I rushed (ran) away.

---

[7] The perfective verb **прочесть** is interchangeable with the perfective verb **прочита́ть**: past: прочёл, прочло́, прочла́, прочли́; future: проч.ту́, -тёшь.

Пла́вать/плы́ть (до-,[8] у-, под-).

1. —Вы́ лю́бите **пла́вать**? —О́чень, но́ я пло́хо **пла́ваю**.	1. —Do you like to swim? —Very much, but I swim badly.
2. Бори́с вчера́ сли́шком мно́го **пла́вал** и о́чень уста́л.	2. Boris swam too much yesterday and got very tired.
3. Я **плы́л** полчаса́ до того́ ма́ленького о́строва. Я ду́мал, что я никогда́ не **доплыву́ до** него́.	3. I swam for half an hour to that small island. I thought I'd never reach it.
4. Огро́мная ры́ба **подплыла́** к бе́регу, и бы́стро **уплыла́**.	4. A huge fish swam up to the shore and quickly swam away.

DRILLS

Choose the correct form.

Лета́ть/лете́ть

1. Я люблю́ (лета́ть/лете́ть), но я ре́дко (лета́ю/лечу́).
2. Я слы́шал, что вы́ куда́-то (лета́ете/лети́те) сего́дня ве́чером.
3. Да́, я (лета́ю/лечу́) в Я́лту.
4. Посмотри́те! Куда́ (лета́ют/летя́т) э́ти самолёты?
5. В кото́ром часу́ вы́ вчера́ (прилета́ли/прилете́ли)?
6. Дя́дя Ми́ша ча́сто (прилета́л/прилете́л) к на́м на Кавка́з.

Бе́гать/бежа́ть

1. Соба́чка лю́бит (бе́гать/бежа́ть).
2. Э́та соба́ка (бе́гает/бежи́т) домо́й.
3. Я ви́дел у́тром Серёжу. О́н куда́-то (бе́гал/бежа́л).
4. О́н (прибега́л/прибежа́л) ко мне́ сего́дня у́тром.
5. И́х соба́ка ча́сто (убега́ет/убежи́т) от ни́х.
6. Я ду́маю, что она́ ско́ро опя́ть (убега́ет/убежи́т).
7. Она́ всегда́ (прибега́ет/прибежи́т) обра́тно.

Пла́вать/плы́ть

1. Я люблю́ (пла́вать/плы́ть).
2. Ле́том я ка́ждый де́нь (пла́вал/плы́л) в о́зере.
3. Оди́н ра́з, когда́ я (пла́вал/плы́л) к бе́регу, я уви́дел ры́бу, кото́рая (пла́вала/плыла́) ко мне́. Она́ посмотре́ла на меня́, и бы́стро (уплыва́ла/уплыла́) от меня́.

Reading

А́х, е́сли бы у него́ бы́л поря́док!

Ива́н Ива́нович Пти́цын живёт за́ городом, и ка́ждый де́нь е́здит на слу́жбу, снача́ла по́ездом, а пото́м на метро́.

Что́бы не опа́здывать на слу́жбу, он до́лжен встава́ть о́чень ра́но, и ка́ждый де́нь, кро́ме выходно́го дня́, он ста́вит буди́льник на ше́сть часо́в. А о́сенью и зимо́й в э́то вре́мя на дворе́ быва́ет хо́лодно и темно́ как но́чью.

---

[8] Доплыва́ть/доплы́ть + до + genitive, *cf.* доходи́ть/дойти́ + до + genitive.

У Птицына была бы довольно спокойная и даже лёгкая жизнь, если бы он вставал сразу, когда звонит будильник, и если бы у него был порядок в вещах. Тогда он всегда приходил бы вовремя на работу, ему не нужно было бы каждый раз спешить, и у него не было бы неприятных разговоров, ни со своим начальником на службе, ни дома со своей квартирной хозяйкой (landlady). Утром он мог бы спокойно принять душ, мог бы спокойно побриться и спокойно позавтракать. Но этого почти никогда не бывает.

Возьмём для примера одно утро, и вот что мы увидим и услышим.

Будильник звонит ровно в шесть и будит Птицына. Птицын просыпается, открывает один глаз, берёт будильник, кладёт его под подушку и немедленно опять засыпает. Бедный будильник беспокоится и громко тикает (ticks) под подушкой, но разбудить Птицына не может.

Через некоторое время Птицын просыпается от стука в дверь. Это стучит Вера Васильевна, его хозяйка, вдова, у которой он снимает комнату. Птицын слышит за дверью её неприятный, громкий голос.

Хозяйка. (кричит) —Иван Иванович! Пора вставать! Вы опять опоздаете на службу. Вам не стыдно?

Птицын. (громко, чтобы она слышала) —Я встаю! Я уже почти готов.

Хозяйка. —Почти готов! Ха, ха! Как вам не стыдно! А я, как только услышала ваш будильник, сразу поставила кофейник на плиту. Кофейник уже полчаса стоит на плите. А вы знаете, сколько я должна платить за газ?

Птицын. (громко) —Знаю, знаю, всё теперь дорого стоит. (Не очень громко, так, чтобы она не слышала) —Например моя комната. (Громко) —Вера Васильевна, снимите пожалуйста кофейник с плиты и поставьте его на стол. Я буду готов через пять минут. Я уверен, что кофе будет ещё горячий.

Хозяйка. —Знаю я ваши пять минут. (Уходит).

Птицын встаёт с кровати и начинает спешить. Он бежит в ванную, быстро моется (у него нет времени чтобы принять душ), чистит зубы, бреется и бежит обратно в свою комнату, чтобы одеться. Он надевает рубашку, хочет надеть брюки, но не может их найти. Он помнит, что вечером положил их на кресло. Где же они? Оказывается, они упали за кресло. Он находит их за креслом в довольно печальном виде, надевает их, и начинает искать галстук. Он ищет галстук минут пять.[9] Оказывается, галстук упал за диван. Он находит его за диваном. Куда же он поставил вечером свои ботинки? Он помнит, что он сидел на том стуле, когда их снимал. Он ищет их и, наконец, находит один ботинок в одном углу, а другой в другом. Пиджак его в ужасном виде, так как на нём всю ночь спала кошка хозяйки. Наконец он готов и бежит на[10] кухню.

Там его ждёт хозяйка. Она давно сняла кофейник с плиты, и, пока Птицын пьёт холодный кофе, она произносит целую речь.

Хозяйка. —Я не могу убирать комнату, в которой всегда такой беспорядок. Вы ничего не кладёте в шкаф, и всё бросаете на пол: бельё, чистое и грязное, носки, чистые и грязные, книги, газеты. Всё лежит на полу! Спички вы бросаете под стол, под диван, за диван. А вчера, когда я убирала комнату, я нашла за диваном сигареты и две рубашки. И вчера вы поставили мокрый

---

[9] About five minutes. Inverting the noun and the numeral is one method (a colloquial one) of indicating approximation.

[10] The preposition **на** is often used with **кухня**.

зо́нтик в у́гол ко́мнаты, на парке́т (parquet floor)! Вы́ не в пе́рвый ра́з его́ туда́ ста́вите! Я всегда́ ста́влю свой зо́нтик в у́гол в пере́дней. Я не хочу́, чтобы мо́крые зонты́ стоя́ли в ко́мнатах. Вы́ меня́ слы́шите? А мо́крую шля́пу вы́ положи́ли на но́вое кре́сло! Пожа́луйста, клади́те ва́ши ве́щи на ме́сто.

—О́ Го́споди! — говори́т Пти́цын. О́н выпива́ет ча́шку холо́дного ко́фе, съеда́ет кусо́к сухо́го хле́ба, надева́ет пальто́, и выбега́ет и́з дому. Когда́ о́н прибега́ет на вокза́л, после́дний ваго́н его́ по́езда бы́стро прохо́дит ми́мо него́.

Чита́йте э́ти вопро́сы и отвеча́йте на ни́х.

1. Почему́ Пти́цын до́лжен так ра́но встава́ть? 2. Всегда́ ли о́н ста́вит буди́льник на ше́сть часо́в? 3. Что́ бы́ло бы, е́сли бы о́н сра́зу встава́л, когда́ буди́льник его́ бу́дит? 4. Что́ о́н де́лает, когда́ звони́т буди́льник? 5. Что́ о́н слы́шит за две́рью? 6. Что́ она́ ему́ говори́т? 7. Что́ о́н хо́чет, чтобы она́ сде́лала с кофе́йником? 8. Что́ о́н де́лает, когда́ встаёт? 9. Что́ о́н де́лает в ва́нной? 10. Почему́ о́н не мо́жет бы́стро оде́ться? 11. Что́ случи́лось с брю́ками и с га́лстуком? Где́ о́н и́х нашёл? 12. Почему́ хозя́йка не хо́чет убира́ть его́ ко́мнату? 13. Что́ о́н сде́лал с мо́крым зонто́м? 14. Что́ о́н сде́лал с мо́крой шля́пой? 15. Кто́ ва́с бу́дит у́тром? 16. Продолжа́ете ли вы́ лежа́ть в крова́ти, и́ли сра́зу встаёте? 17. Броса́ете ли вы́ ва́ши ве́щи на́ пол, и́ли кладёте и́х на ме́сто? 18. Что́ вы́ де́лаете с ва́шим зонто́м? 19. Кто́ убира́ет ва́шу ко́мнату?

DRILL

Review Translation.

1. If you want me to come on Tuesday, I shall come and read you the second part of the letter. 2. I asked Boris to write to the director of your school, but he still hasn't done it. 3. I want Olga to buy an evening dress. 4. It would be good if there were a park opposite our house. 5. Her brothers see each other very seldom. 6. He doesn't want me to go with him to the Middle East. 7. Take off your coat, put your wet hat on the table, and put your wet umbrella in the corner. 8. I shall take off my coat, put my hat on the table, and put my umbrella in the corner. 9. Don't put all those bottles on the floor! Put them in the cupboard (there) where I usually put them. 10. I am sure that if he wanted to get a good grade, he would have studied all day Sunday. 11. If they had helped their children, their children would have loved them. 12. I would very much have liked to live in some eastern country. 13. The saleslady asked me whether I wanted the black shoes. 14. We shall go to the country on Wednesday if the weather is nice. 15. We would have gone to the country if the weather had been nice. 16. I shall take off my hat. 17. I put the newspaper on the table underneath the book. 18. Your pen fell behind the piano.

Vocabulary

бельё underwear, linen, laundry
беспоря́д.ок (*gen.* -ка) disorder
буди́льник alarm clock
ваго́н railroad car
вдова́ widow

велосипе́д bicycle
вид appearance, condition, air, view, aspect
во́время on time
газ gas
га́лстук necktie

душ shower
зонт, зо́нтик umbrella
зуб tooth
кофе́йник coffeepot
мо́крый wet
нос.о́к (*gen.* -ка́) sock
оде́жда clothing
о́стров (*nom. pl.* -а́) island
пере́дняя (*adj. used as noun*) vestibule, anteroom
плита́ stove
поду́ш.ка (*gen. pl.* -ек) pillow
по́лный full (+ *gen.*)

поря́д.ок (*gen.* -ка) order
про́шлое (*adj. used as noun*) the past
пусто́й empty
речь (*f.*) speech
самолёт airplane
сигаре́та[11] cigarette
ска́з.ка (*gen. pl.* -ок) fairy tale
спи́ч.ка (*gen. pl.* -ек) match
споко́йный peaceful, calm
стук knock, rap
сухо́й dry
шкаф (*loc.* в шкафу́) cupboard, closet

VERBS

бри́ться (imperf., I: бре́.юсь, -ешься), побри́ться (perf., I) to shave (oneself)
броса́ть (imperf., I), бро́сить (perf., II: бро́шу, бро́сишь) to throw, fling; to throw away, give up, abandon
буди́ть (imperf., II: бужу́, бу́дишь), разбуди́ть (perf., II) to wake up (*trans.*), arouse
засыпа́ть (imperf., I), засну́ть (perf., I: засн.у́, -ёшь) to fall asleep
иска́ть (imperf., I: ищу́, и́щешь) to look for, seek
надева́ть (imperf., I), наде́ть (perf., I: наде́н.у, -ешь) to put on
ока́зываться (imperf., I), оказа́ться (ока́жется) to turn out (to be)
па́дать (imperf., I), упа́сть (perf., I: упад.у́, -ёшь) to fall
снима́ть (imperf., I), снять (perf., I: сниму́, сни́мешь) to take off; rent
стуча́ть (imperf., II: стуч.у́, -и́шь), постуча́ть (perf., II) to knock, rap
убира́ть (imperf., I), убра́ть (perf., I: убер.у́, -ёшь) to clean up, off; tidy
чи́стить (imperf., II: чи́щу, чи́стишь), почи́стить (perf., II) to clean

EXPRESSIONS

по де́лу on business
(по)е́хать за́ город to drive out of town
бы́ть за́ городом to be out of town
выходно́й де́нь day off, holiday
(по)ста́вить буди́льник на (+ *acc.*) to set an alarm clock for
на дворе́ out of doors
возьмём let's take
за две́рью on the other side of the door
Ва́м не сты́дно? Aren't you ashamed?
на ме́сто to its proper place
на ме́сте in its place; on the spot

VOCABULARY REVIEW

Оде́жда—Clothing

пальто́	шля́па	ша́пка (cap)	плато́к

Мужска́я оде́жда
мужско́й костю́м
пиджа́к
брю́ки (*gen. pl.* брюк)
руба́шка
носо́к (*nom. pl.* носки́)
боти́нок (*nom. pl.* боти́нки; *gen. pl.* боти́нок)

Же́нская оде́жда
да́мский костю́м (жаке́т с ю́бкой)
пла́тье
блу́зка
чуло́к (*nom. pl.* чу́лки; *gen. pl.* чуло́к) stocking
ту́фля (*nom. pl.* ту́фли; *gen. pl.* ту́фель) shoe, slipper

---

[11] The word **сигаре́та** is used for a cigarette without a built-in mouthpiece. **Папиро́са** rather refers to the well-known typical "Russian" cigarette with such a mouthpiece.

Comparative adjectives and adverbs • Superlative adjectives •
Reading: Несколько слов о географии СССР • The verbal prefixes
за-, с-, раз- • Translation of the imperative *let* • Conversation: Чем
бо́льше я тебя́ зна́ю, тем ме́ньше я тебя́ понима́ю

Unit 25

Grammar

1. Comparative adjectives and adverbs

The adjectives and adverbs given in earlier lessons were in the *positive* degree. Besides the positive degree, Russian, like English, also has a *comparative* degree (formed in English with the ending *-er: bigger, taller, sooner;* or with the word *more: more interesting*). Russian and English also have a *superlative* degree (formed in English with the ending *-est: biggest, tallest, soonest;* or with the word *most: most interesting*). The following are some examples of Russian comparatives (they are given beside the corresponding positive forms):

Positive Degree		*Comparative Degree*	
но́вый	new	нове́е	newer
дли́нный	long	длинне́е	longer
большо́й	large, big	бо́льше	larger, bigger
бы́стрый	fast	быстре́е	faster

Comparatives are indeclinable: their endings do not change to express gender, number, or case. The same form serves as comparative both of the adjective and of its corresponding adverb; e.g., **быстре́е** means both *more rapid* and *more rapidly.* Most comparatives are formed with the ending **-ее** (sometimes shortened to **-ей**), like **нове́е** from **но́вый,** and **длинне́е** from **дли́нный.** The stress shifts to the ending **-ее** if the adjective has a monosyllabic stem, e.g., нове́е; it does not shift when the stem has more than one syllable, e.g., краси́вее. There are a few exceptions: холодне́е, веселе́е, etc.

Other comparatives are formed with **-е** (never stressed) e.g., **бо́льше** from **большо́й,** or **бога́че** from **бога́тый.** In the latter type (one **-е**) consonant mutations occur, as from бога́тый—бога́че or молодо́й—моло́же, etc.; these consonant changes and irregular formations will be given below.

In a statement of comparison such as *He is younger than I*, or *The Volga is longer than the Don*, English *than I* or *than the Don* may be rendered in Russian in two different ways:

(1) With the second term of a comparison in the same case as the first term to which it is compared; the second term is placed in a subordinate clause introduced by **чем**:

Во́лга длинне́е, чем **До́н**. (two nominatives).
The Volga is longer than the Don.

О́н помога́ет **мне́** бо́льше, чем **ва́м**. (two datives).
He helps me more than (he does) you.

(2) With the second term of comparison, which is part of the main clause, in the *genitive*:

Во́лга длинне́й **До́на**.
The Volga is longer than the Don.

Ва́ш костю́м нове́е мо**его́**.
Your suit is newer than mine.

The latter construction (with the genitive) obviously serves only for declinable words; it may be used in comparing someone or something to the subject of the sentence (or sometimes to the direct object, particularly when the direct object is inanimate):

О́н умне́е **меня́**. (comparison with subject).
He is more intelligent than I.

Я́ люблю́ **мя́со** бо́льше **ры́бы**. (comparison with object).
I like meat better than fish.

Otherwise the construction with **чем** is mandatory; thus:
(1) Comparison between adverbs:

О́н говори́т **по-ру́сски** лу́чше, чем **по-англи́йски**.
He speaks Russian better than English.

(2) Comparison between infinitives:

Говори́ть по-ру́сски трудне́е, чем **чита́ть**.
It's harder to speak Russian than to read it.

(3) Comparison between adverbial clauses:

В Крыму́ тепле́е, чем **в Москве́**.
It's warmer in the Crimea than in Moscow.

A. Use of comparatives. Comparatives have two uses: predicative and adverbial.

Predicative use.

Э́та шля́па **деше́вле** то́й (or чем та́).
This hat is *cheaper* than that one.

То зда́ние **вы́ше** э́того (or чем э́то).
That building is *taller* than this one.

На́ша ста́рая кварти́ра была́ **деше́вле**, но́ **ме́ньше** э́той.
Our old apartment was *cheaper* but *smaller* than this one.

Adverbial use. The comparative forms are also used adverbially; thus **интере́снее** is the comparative of the adjective **интере́сный** and also of the adverb **интере́сно**.

Adjectival use:

Его́ докла́д бы́л **интере́сный**, но́ докла́д Петро́ва бы́л ещё **интере́снее**.
His report was *interesting*, but Petrov's was still *more interesting*.

Adverbial use:

О́н говори́т **интере́сно**, но́ пи́шет ещё **интере́снее**.
He speaks *interestingly*, but he writes still *more interestingly*.

B. Comparatives with бо́лее and ме́нее. An alternative means for expressing comparison in Russian is provided by the words **бо́лее** (*more*) and **ме́нее** (*less*), placed before an adjective in the positive degree which is declined; they require the use of the construction with **чем**:

Э́та гости́ница **бо́лее дорога́я**, чем та́, в кото́рой мы́ живём.
This hotel is more expensive than the one in which we live.

Мы́ жи́ли в **ме́нее дорого́й** гости́нице, чем та́, в кото́рой жи́ли Кали́нины.
We lived in a less expensive hotel than the one in which the Kalinins lived.

Generally comparisons with **бо́лее** are less idiomatic than those using the comparative forms; in some instances, however, the use of **бо́лее** may be preferable, or even necessary, as in the case when a comparative appears in the *attributive* function (i.e., not predicatively or adverbially):

Мне́ ну́жен **бо́лее о́стрый** но́ж.
I need a sharper knife.

Я́ никогда́ не чита́л **бо́лее интере́сной** кни́ги.
I have never read a more interesting book.

C. Comparatives with the prefix по-. Comparatives prefixed with **по-** are often used in requests, commands, suggestions, etc., indicating, *without any specific comparison*, the wish for better, more, quicker, cheaper, etc.:

Купи́ **побо́льше** моро́женого: они́ приду́т со свои́ми детьми́.
Buy more (be sure to buy enough) ice cream; they are bringing their children.

Приходи́те к на́м **поча́ще**.
Come to see us more often.

Не́т ли у ва́с чего́-нибудь **подеше́вле**?
Don't you have anything (a bit) cheaper?

Да́й мне́ но́ж **поостре́е**.
Give me a sharper knife.

D. Consonant mutations and irregularities in the comparatives in -e.

Comparatives ending in **-e** (not **-ee**) often undergo changes of the final consonant of the stem. These follow the usual pattern of consonant mutations and are the same mutations as those which occur in the present conjugation of verbs (see Unit 21, page 337).

г > ж	дорого́й—доро́же	dearer, more expensive
х > ш	ти́хий—ти́ше	quieter
х > ш	сухо́й—су́ше	drier
т > ч	бога́тый—бога́че	richer, wealthier
д > ж	молодо́й—моло́же	younger
ст > щ	просто́й—про́ще	simpler
	ча́стый—ча́ще	oftener
	чи́стый—чи́ще	cleaner
	то́лстый—то́лще	thicker, fatter
в > вл	дешёвый—деше́вле	cheaper

A number of adjectives have a **-к-**, or **-ок-**, element between the stem and the ending; in the comparative form some adjectives preserve the **-к-** element (which undergoes a mutation and appears as **ч**), while in others it disappears; the **-ок-** element always disappears: **-к-** changes to **ч**:

гро́мкий—гро́мче	louder
жа́ркий—жа́рче	hotter
лёгкий—ле́гче	lighter, easier
мя́гкий—мя́гче	softer

-к- disappears; final stem consonant changed:

т > ч	коро́ткий—коро́че	shorter
з > ж	бли́зкий—бли́же	nearer
	ни́зкий—ни́же	lower
	у́зкий—у́же (note stress)	narrower
д > ж	ре́дкий—ре́же	more rarely, less often

-ок- disappears:

высо́кий—вы́ше	higher, taller
широ́кий—ши́ре	wider, broader

Observe also the following comparatives formed with **-ше** or **-же**:

глубо́кий—глу́бже	deeper
далёкий—да́льше	farther, further
по́здний (по́здно)—по́зже	later
ра́нний (ра́но)—ра́ньше	earlier
то́нкий—то́ньше	thinner
до́лгий (до́лго)—до́льше	longer (in time)
ста́рый—ста́рше	older

A small number of adjectives have special attributive forms made without **бо́лее**. In most of these the comparative stem is distinct from that of the positive:

Positive	Comparative Attributive	Predicative and Adverbial	
хоро́ший	лу́чший	лу́чше	better
плохо́й	ху́дший	ху́же	worse
ста́рый	ста́рший	ста́рше	older, elder, senior
молодо́й	мла́дший	мла́дше, моло́же	younger, junior
большо́й	бо́льший[1]	бо́льше[2]	greater, bigger, larger; more
ма́ленький	ме́ньший	ме́ньше[2]	smaller; less, fewer

Attributive:

Сего́дня мы́ нашли́ **лу́чший** рестора́н.

Today we found a better restaurant (better than our usual one).

Predicative:

Э́тот слова́рь **лу́чше** ва́шего.

Adverbial:

О́н пи́шет **лу́чше** меня́, но́ ме́дленнее.

PATTERN SENTENCES

Predicate and Adverbial Comparatives.

1. Ленингра́д **краси́вее** Москвы́.
2. Ва́ш до́м **нове́е** на́шего.
3. Ле́на **умне́е** О́льги.
4. О́льга **глупе́е** Ле́ны.
5. Вади́м, хотя́ **моло́же**, **сильне́е** Бори́са.
6. Бори́с **ста́рше** и **вы́ше**, но́ **слабе́е его́**.
7. Ю́жное не́бо **сине́е** се́верного.
8. Сего́дня немно́жко **тепле́е**, чем бы́ло вчера́. Но́ говоря́т, что за́втра бу́дет опя́ть **холодне́е**.
9. **Ти́ше!** Не шуми́те!
10. Говори́те немно́жко **гро́мче**—я́ ва́с пло́хо слы́шу.

1. Leningrad is more beautiful than Moscow.
2. Your house is newer than ours.
3. Lena is more intelligent than Olga.
4. Olga is stupider than Lena.
5. Vadim, though younger, is stronger than Boris.
6. Boris is older and taller, but weaker than he is.
7. The southern sky is bluer than the northern one.
8. Today it's a bit warmer than yesterday. But they say that tomorrow will be colder again.
9. Quiet(er)! Don't make noise!
10. Speak a little louder. I can't hear you well.

Attributive with **бо́лее** *or* **ме́нее**.

1. Что́ э́то за те́ма! Поговори́м на **бо́лее интере́сную** те́му!
2. Пообе́даем в **бо́лее дешёвом** рестора́не. Рестора́н про́тив моего́ до́ма **деше́вле** э́того.
3. Я́ счита́ю, что э́то **ме́нее ва́жный** вопро́с, чем то́т, о кото́ром мы́ говори́ли вчера́.
4. В э́тот ра́з мы́ останови́лись в **бо́лее дорого́й** гости́нице.

1. What kind of subject is that! Let's talk about a more interesting subject!
2. Let's dine in a cheaper restaurant. The restaurant across from my house is cheaper than this one.
3. I consider this question less important than the one we talked about yesterday.
4. This time we stopped (stayed) at a more expensive hotel.

---

[1] Note the distinction in place of stress between the positive **большо́й** and the comparative **бо́льший**.

[2] **Бо́льше** serves as the comparative form of both **большо́й** (*big*) and **мно́го** (*much, many*). Similarly, **ме́ньше** is the comparative of both **ма́ленький** and **ма́ло**.

DRILLS

A. *Complete the sentences.*

$$
\text{Семёновы богаче} \begin{cases} \text{я.} \\ \text{ты.} \\ \text{он.} \\ \text{она́.} \\ \text{мы.} \\ \text{вы.} \\ \text{они́.} \\ \text{до́ктор Смирно́в.} \\ \text{на́ша но́вая учи́тельница.} \\ \text{Ива́н Петро́вич Андре́ев.} \\ \text{ва́ши друзья́.} \\ \text{ва́ши подру́ги.} \end{cases}
$$

$$
\text{Москва́ бо́льше} \begin{cases} \text{Оде́сса.} \\ \text{Ки́ев.} \\ \text{ва́ша столи́ца.} \\ \text{э́тот го́род.} \end{cases}
$$

B. *Supply the comparatives of the adjectives in boldface and then give their opposites in the comparative, according to the model.*

		Opposite comparatives	
Model:	Ива́н **си́льный**, но Па́вел **сильне́е** Ива́на.	**Ива́н**	**слабе́е.**
1.	Днепр **дли́нный**, но Во́лга	. . . .	. . . .
2.	Мы́ **бога́тые**, но Рокфе́ллер	. . . .	. . . .
3.	Воло́дя **высо́кий**, но Серёжа	. . . .	. . . .
4.	Моя́ кварти́ра **хоро́шая**, но ва́ша	. . . .	. . . .
5.	Ка́тя **у́мная**, но Зи́на	. . . .	. . . .
6.	Мне́ **удо́бно** прийти́ в два́, но в три́ мне́	. . . .	. . . .
7.	Мо́й костю́м **дорого́й**, но тво́й	. . . .	. . . .
8.	Я́ пишу́ **пло́хо**, но ты́ пи́шешь	. . . .	. . . .
9.	Мы́ живём **далеко́**, но вы́ живёте	. . . .	. . . .
10.	Ла́вка **бли́зко**, но апте́ка	. . . .	. . . .
11.	Моё пла́тье **коро́ткое**, но твоё	. . . .	. . . .
12.	Моя́ ко́мната **тёмная**, но твоя́	. . . .	. . . .
13.	Сего́дня **тепло́**, но вчера́ бы́ло	. . . .	. . . .
14.	Си́няя ю́бка **широ́кая**, но чёрная	. . . .	. . . .
15.	Зи́на поёт **хорошо́**, но ты́ поёшь	. . . .	. . . .

C. *Supply correct forms of the comparative.*

1. До́ктор Смирно́в (хоро́ший), чем до́ктор Кры́мов.
2. Я́ (пло́хо) гото́влю, чем Ли́за.
3. Толсто́й писа́л «Войну́ и ми́р» (до́лго), чем «А́нну Каре́нину».
4. Си́няя ю́бка (коро́ткая) чёрной.
5. Я́ живу́ (далеко́) от университе́та, чем вы́.
6. Мне́ (легко́) чита́ть по-францу́зски, чем говори́ть.
7. Э́то вече́рнее пла́тье (но́вое) того́.
8. Алёша (у́мный) Ви́ктора.
9. Во́лга (широ́кая) Днепра́.
10. На́ша у́лица (у́зкая) ва́шей.
11. Река́ Амазо́нка (дли́нная) Во́лги.
12. Ва́ш до́м (высо́кий) на́шего.
13. Э́та гора́ (ни́зкая) то́й.
14. На́ша гости́ная (больша́я) столо́вой.
15. Э́ти боти́нки (дешёвые) чёрных.
16. Твоя́ кварти́ра (дорога́я) мое́й.
17. Кто́ (си́льный), Бори́с или Вади́м?
18. Вади́м (сла́бый) Бори́са.
19. На́ши сосе́ди (бога́тые) на́с.
20. Мы́ (бе́дные) на́ших сосе́дей.

E. Adverbs and conjunctions with the comparative. Гора́здо is used with comparatives for emphasis much as the word о́чень is used with adjectives or adverbs in the positive degree; о́чень тру́дный—гора́здо трудне́е (*much harder*); о́чень высо́кий—гора́здо вы́ше (*much higher*); о́чень мно́го—гора́здо бо́льше (*much*—or *many—more*).

Ещё means *still* (*more*):

> Он о́чень у́мный, но его́ брат **ещё умне́е.**
> He is very intelligent, but his brother is still more so.

Всё before a comparative adjective means *more and more*, *all* the time:

> Дни стано́вятся **всё коро́че.**
> The days keep getting shorter.

На ско́лько? means *by how much?* The answer is also made with на:

> —**На ско́лько** вы **ста́рше** меня́? —**На два́ го́да.**
> —How much older are you than I? —Two years.

> —**На ско́лько** страни́ц вы прочита́ли **бо́льше,** чем я? —Я прочита́л на оди́ннадцать страни́ц **бо́льше.**
> —How many pages more than I did you read? —I read eleven pages more.

Чем . . . тем is equivalent to English *the . . . the . . .* with comparatives:

> **Чем** бо́льше, **тем** лу́чше.
> The more the better.

> **Чем** скоре́й, **тем** лу́чше.
> The sooner the better.

PATTERN SENTENCES

Гора́здо *with comparatives.*

1. Ле́том в Сре́дней А́зии **гора́здо жа́рче,** чем в Крыму́.
2. Сове́тский Сою́з **гора́здо бо́льше** и **бога́че** По́льши.
3. Кавка́зские го́ры **гора́здо вы́ше** Ура́льских и Кры́мских гор.
4. Ура́льские го́ры **гора́здо ни́же** Кавка́зских.
5. Э́ти рабо́чие рабо́тают тепе́рь **гора́здо бы́стрей,** но всё же недоста́точно бы́стро.

1. In summer it's much hotter in Central Asia than in the Crimea.
2. The Soviet Union is much larger and wealthier than Poland.
3. The Caucasus Mountains are much higher than the Urals or those of the Crimea.
4. The Ural Mountains are much lower than those of the Caucasus.
5. These workers work much faster now, but still not fast enough.

Ещё *with comparatives.*

1. Хотя́ Днепр и о́чень дли́нная река́, но Во́лга **ещё длинне́е** (Днепра́).
2. О́зеро Ми́чиган глубо́кое, но Байка́л **ещё глу́бже.**
3. Вчера́ бы́ло жа́рко, но сего́дня, ка́жется, бу́дет **ещё жа́рче.**
4. Мы живём о́чень бли́зко от университе́та, но вы живёте **ещё бли́же.**

1. Though the Dnieper is a very long river, the Volga is still longer (than the Dnieper).
2. Lake Michigan is deep, but Baikal is still deeper.
3. It was hot yesterday, but I think today will be still hotter.
4. We live very close to the university, but you live still closer.

Всё *with comparatives.*

1. Óн **всё ре́же** и **ре́же** быва́ет в на́шем го́роде.
2. Тепе́рь **всё ча́ще** и **ча́ще** идёт снéг.
3. Алёша занима́ется **всё ме́ньше** и **ме́ньше**.

1. He visits our city more and more rarely.
2. It snows more and more often now.
3. Alyosha is studying less and less.

На ско́лько *with comparatives.*

1. —**На ско́лько** э́та кварти́ра **доро́же** ста́рой? —Она́ **доро́же на** пятна́дцать до́лларов в ме́сяц.
2. Мы́ живём тепе́рь в **бо́лее дешёвой** кварти́ре. Она́ **на** три́дцать рубле́й **деше́вле** ва́шей.
3. **На ско́лько** ле́т Ни́на **моло́же** О́льги? —Она́ **моло́же на** четы́ре го́да.

1. —How much more expensive is this apartment than the old one? —It's fifteen dollars a month more.
2. We're now living in a cheaper apartment. It's thirty rubles cheaper than yours.
3. —How much younger is Nina than Olga? —She is four years younger.

Чем . . . тем *with comparatives.*

1. **Чем бо́льше** вы́ бу́дете говори́ть по-ру́сски, **тем лу́чше** вы́ бу́дете говори́ть.
2. **Чем скоре́е** о́н вернётся, **тем лу́чше**.

1. The more you (will) speak Russian, the better you will speak it.
2. The sooner he comes back, the better.

DRILL

Переведи́те на ру́сский.

1. How much younger is your brother than you (are)?
2. He is two years younger than I (am).
3. —How much older is your son than mine? —He is much older.
4. —How much shorter is the second story than the first one? —Three pages.
5. —How much closer do you live to (к + dative) the border than we do? —Forty-two kilometers.
6. —How many kilometers farther from (от + genitive) the border is your town than theirs? —Only a few (several) kilometers.
7. —How many more books do you have now than you had before? —Fifty or sixty.
8. The sooner you (will) finish this book, the sooner you'll start another one.
9. The oftener I see him the less I like him.
10. He makes mistakes more and more often.
11. I like meat much more than fish.
12. He writes many more letters than I do.
13. The grandmother talks much more than the granddaughter.
14. She talks more and more.

2. Superlative adjectives

One type of superlative was presented in Unit 12, page 187. Another type is formed by adding **-ейший** or **-айший** to the stem of the adjective. This superlative usually does *not imply* any comparison, but merely asserts a very high degree of the quality in question. The ending is regularly **-ейший**, but **-айший** is used after **ж, ч, ш**, occurring as the result of mutation of the final stem consonant, e.g., ближа́йший, велича́йший, глубоча́йший, тиша́йший, etc.

в **ближа́йшем** вре́мени
in the very near future

Very often this form of the superlative has an emotional coloring:

Э́то **интере́снейшая** рабо́та!
That's extremely interesting work!

Я́ то́лько что ви́дел **замеча́тельнейший** фи́льм!
I've just seen the most wonderful film!

By contrast, the superlative formed with **са́мый** is used chiefly to denote superiority to others (contrast English *the most* = **са́мый**, as opposed to *a most* = **-ейший/-айший**):

Э́то **са́мая интере́сная** кни́га на э́ту те́му.
This is *the most interesting* book on the subject.

Э́то **интере́снейшая** кни́га!
This is *a most interesting* book.

The forms **лу́чший, ху́дший, ста́рший**, and **мла́дший** are frequently used with superlative meaning:

мо́й лу́чший дру́г   my best friend
мо́й ста́рший бра́т   my elder (or eldest) brother

Са́мый is also used with these comparatives and makes the statement somewhat stronger:

О́н **са́мый лу́чший** учени́к в кла́ссе.
He is the (very) best student in the class.

PATTERN SENTENCES

Superlatives in **-ейший/-айший**.

1. О́н за́дал мне́ **глупе́йший** вопро́с.
2. Луне́в рассказа́л на́м **интере́снейшую** исто́рию.
3. Его́ де́душка **умне́йший** стари́к.
4. Дире́ктор произне́с на банке́те **длинне́йшую** ре́чь.
5. Пу́шкин **велича́йший** ру́сский поэ́т.
6. В Сре́дней А́зии нахо́дятся **высоча́йшие** го́ры. Они́ вы́ше все́х го́р в ми́ре.
7. —Что́ о́н за челове́к? —О́н **миле́йший** челове́к.

1. He asked me an extremely foolish question.
2. Lunyov told us a most interesting story.
3. His grandfather is an extremely clever old man.
4. The director gave a terribly long speech at the banquet.
5. Pushkin is the greatest Russian poet.
6. In Central Asia there are very high mountains. They are the highest (higher than any other) mountains in the world.
7. —What kind of person is he? —He's a most pleasant person.

Superlatives with **са́мый**.

1. Во́лга **са́мая дли́нная** река́ в Евро́пе.
2. **Са́мые высо́кие** го́ры в СССР нахо́дятся о́коло грани́цы Афганиста́на. Э́ти го́ры **гора́здо вы́ше** Кавка́зских го́р.

1. The Volga is the longest river in Europe.
2. The highest mountains in the U.S.S.R. are located near the frontier of Afghanistan. These mountains are much higher than those of the Caucasus.

Grammar   421

3. Байка́л **са́мое большо́е** о́зеро Сове́тского Сою́за, и в пе́снях его́ да́же называ́ют мо́рем. Э́то **са́мое глубо́кое** о́зеро в ми́ре. Нет о́зера **глу́бже** Байка́ла.

4. —**Са́мое лу́чшее** что вы́ мо́жете сде́лать, э́то верну́ть ему́ э́то письмо́.

5. Я́ разгова́ривал вчера́ с **са́мым у́мным** челове́ком, кото́рого я́ когда́-либо зна́л.

Лу́чший, ху́дший

1. Андре́й **лу́чший** учени́к в кла́ссе, а Ива́н **ху́дший**.

2. Э́то **лу́чшая** кни́га, кото́рую я́ когда́-либо чита́л.

3. Baikal is the largest lake in the Soviet Union, and in songs it is even called a sea. It is the deepest lake in the world. There is no deeper lake than Baikal.

4. —The best thing that you can do is to return that letter to him.

5. Yesterday I talked to the most intelligent man I have ever known.

1. Andrey is the best pupil in the class, and Ivan is the poorest.

2. That's the best book that I have ever read.

Reading

Не́сколько сло́в о геогра́фии СССР

Сове́тский Сою́з гора́здо бо́льше всех стра́н ми́ра. О́н бо́льше Соединённых Шта́тов и Кита́я.

Одна́ часть Сове́тского Сою́за лежи́т в Евро́пе, а друга́я часть, бо́льшая (the greater), в А́зии. Европе́йская часть занима́ет, с за́пада на восто́к, террито́рию от Балти́йского мо́ря до Ура́ла, а азиа́тская часть от Ура́ла до Ти́хого океа́на (Pacific Ocean). На кра́йнем (extreme) се́веро-восто́ке Бе́рингов проли́в (strait) отделя́ет СССР от Аля́ски, т. е.[3] от США.

Се́верная грани́ца Сою́за—Ледови́тый океа́н (Arctic Ocean), и его́ моря́. В азиа́тской ча́сти, в Сиби́ри, вдоль (along) э́той грани́цы идёт ту́ндра. Та́м кли́мат аркти́ческий, на земле́ лёд (ice) и снег. Та́м почти́ ничего́ не растёт. Южне́е идёт тайга́; э́то огро́мные се́верные леса́.

В центра́льной европе́йской ча́сти кли́мат уме́ренный (temperate); есть четы́ре вре́мени го́да, и расти́тельность (vegetation) та́м сре́дне-европе́йская. В Крыму́ и на Кавка́зе гора́здо тепле́е—та́м кли́мат субтропи́ческий, и субтропи́ческая расти́тельность.

На ю́ге СССР грани́чит с (borders on) Ту́рцией, Ира́ном, Афганиста́ном, Монго́льской Наро́дной Респу́бликой, Кита́ем и Се́верной Коре́ей. В Сове́тской центра́льной А́зии гора́здо жа́рче, чем в Крыму́ или на Кавка́зе.

Са́мые высо́кие го́ры европе́йской ча́сти Сою́за нахо́дятся на Кавка́зе. Кавка́з нахо́дится ме́жду Чёрным и Каспи́йским моря́ми. Са́мая высо́кая гора́ Кавка́за Эльбру́с.[4] Монбла́н,[5] са́мая высо́кая гора́ в за́падной Евро́пе, ни́же Эльбру́са. Ура́льские го́ры, кото́рые отделя́ют на се́вере европе́йскую часть СССР от азиа́тской, и та́кже Кры́мские го́ры гора́здо ни́же кавка́зских.

---

[3] **т. е.**, abbreviated form of **то́ есть** *that is.*
[4] **Эльбру́с,** *Mt. Elbrus,* 18,481 feet (5,667 meters).
[5] Mont Blanc, 15,781 feet (4,832 meters).

Са́мая больша́я река́ не то́лько в европе́йской Росси́и, но́ и во все́й Евро́пе— это Во́лга. Во́лга длинне́е и ши́ре Днепра́ и До́на и длинне́е и ши́ре Дуна́я (Danube) и Ре́йна (Rhine). В Сиби́ри е́сть ре́ки, кото́рые гора́здо бо́льше Во́лги; это О́бь, Енисе́й, Ле́на и Аму́р.

Са́мые больши́е города́ нахо́дятся в европе́йской ча́сти Сою́за, и городо́в в э́той ча́сти бо́льше чем в азиа́тской ча́сти.

Но́ и в Сиби́ри, и в Сре́дней А́зии е́сть та́кже больши́е города́ и больши́е индустриа́льные це́нтры, и везде́ открыва́ется всё бо́льше и бо́льше шко́л, институ́тов, и изыска́тельных (research) це́нтров.

Москва́, столи́ца СССР, гора́здо бо́льше Вашингто́на, и в Москве́ гора́здо бо́льше жи́телей, чем в Вашингто́не. Но́ Москва́ ме́ньше Нью-Йо́рка, Ло́ндона, и То́кио.

Населе́ние СССР бо́льше населе́ния Соединённых Шта́тов, но ме́ньше населе́ния Кита́йской Наро́дной Респу́блики.

Answer these questions in Russian.

1. Каки́е европе́йские ре́ки бо́льше Во́лги? 2. Са́мая ли больша́я река́ Сове́тского Сою́за Во́лга? 3. Пра́вильно ли сказа́ть, что Москва́ са́мый большо́й го́род в ми́ре? 4. Пра́вильно ли сказа́ть, что СССР страна́ с са́мым больши́м населе́нием? 5. Пра́вильно ли сказа́ть, что в СССР кли́мат холо́дный? 6. Како́е са́мое за́падное мо́ре СССР? 7. Что́ отделя́ет европе́йскую ча́сть Сою́за от азиа́тской? 8. Что́ отделя́ет СССР от США, и где́ э́то ме́сто?

DRILL

Translate the words in parentheses.

1. Кака́я (longest) у́лица в э́том го́роде?
2. Како́й из э́тих домо́в (oldest)?
3. Вади́м танцева́л вчера́ с (most pretty) де́вушкой.
4. Андре́й лю́бит (the silliest) де́вушку из все́х.
5. Я пишу́ э́то письмо́ моему́ (most intelligent) студе́нту.
6. Я расска́зывал о моём (oldest) дру́ге.
7. Зелёное пла́тье (most expensive) из все́х.
8. Вади́м (much taller) Ива́на.
9. Алёша (much more intelligent) Ле́ны.

Set expressions with the superlative.

са́мое лу́чшее
the best (thing)

са́мое ху́дшее
the worst (thing)

са́мое гла́вное
the most important (thing), the main thing

в лу́чшем/ху́дшем слу́чае
at best (worst)

с велича́йшим удово́льствием
with the greatest pleasure

в ближа́йшем бу́дущем
in the very near future

в ближа́йшие дни́
in the next few days

в ближа́йшем магази́не
in the nearest store

бо́льше всего́
most of all, more than anything else

бо́льше все́х
most of all, more than anyone else

These last two forms, though comparative, are frequently used in the function of an adverbial and predicative superlative. Similarly used are **лу́чше всего́**, *better than anything else*, and **лу́чше все́х**, *better than anyone else*.

PATTERN SENTENCES

1. **Са́мое лу́чшее**, что вы́ мо́жете сде́лать, э́то написа́ть письмо́ самому́ дире́ктору.

2. Да́, я то́же ду́маю, что э́то бу́дет **са́мое лу́чшее**. Я́ напишу́ ему́ в **ближа́йшие дни́**.

3. **В ху́дшем слу́чае** о́н ва́м не отве́тит.

4. **В ху́дшем слу́чае** я́ опозда́ю к нача́лу его́ ре́чи.

5. Мы́ зашли́ в **ближа́йший** рестора́н и пое́ли та́м.

6. **Бо́льше всего́** мо́й сы́н лю́бит му́зыку. О́н игра́ет на роя́ле **лу́чше все́х** свои́х друзе́й.

7. Молодо́й италья́нский певе́ц пе́л **лу́чше все́х**. **Лу́чше всего́** о́н пе́л неаполита́нские серена́ды.

1. The best thing you can do is to write to the director himself.

2. Yes, I think too that would be the best. I'll write to him in the next few days.

3. At worst he won't answer you.

4. At worst I'll miss (be late for) the beginning of his speech.

5. We stopped at the nearest restaurant and ate there.

6. Most of all my son likes music. He plays the piano better than any of his friends.

7. The young Italian singer sang the best of anyone. Best of all he sang Neapolitan serenades.

DRILLS

A. *Переведи́те с ру́сского на англи́йский.*

1. Профе́ссор счита́ет Вади́ма свои́м лу́чшим студе́нтом.

2. Ленингра́д бли́же к грани́це, чем Москва́.

3. Мно́гие счита́ют Петра́ Вели́кого велича́йшим ру́сским царём.

4. Как то́лько верну́сь, я́ сейча́с же расскажу́ обо всём э́том мои́м лу́чшим друзья́м.

5. Мы́ зашли́ в ближа́йшую ла́вку, купи́ли лу́чшее вино́, како́е у ни́х бы́ло, и верну́лись домо́й.

6. О́н отве́тил мне́ глупе́йшим письмо́м, кото́рое я́ ему́ верну́, как то́лько его́ уви́жу.

7. Я люблю всех их детей, но больше всех я люблю Вёрочку.
8. Я больше всего люблю говорить по-французски.
9. Самое лучшее будет никому об этом не говорить.
10. Надеюсь, что он поговорил с ним о самом главном.
11. Мы ляжем сегодня гораздо раньше, чем обычно, так как завтра нужно будет очень рано встать.
12. —На сколько эта дорога короче той? —Эта дорога, кажется, на пять километров короче.
13. Новый словарь дороже старого на шесть рублей; правда, он толще, то есть полнее. Старый дешевле, но тоньше: он менее полный.
14. Граница между Советским Союзом и Китаем длиннее, чем граница между Соединёнными Штатами и Канадой.
15. Я зайду к вам в ближайшие дни.
16. Зинаида Михайловна милейший человек.
17. Я получил интереснейшее письмо от одного немецкого учёного.
18. К чёрту всё! Нужно жить веселей.
19. Он теперь работает гораздо больше, чем раньше, но всё же недостаточно.

B. *Переведите на русский.*

1. Most of all Petrov likes to play chess. He plays the best (better than anyone) in our town.
2. I shall finish the article in the next few days.
3. The best that you can do is to write to him at once.
4. I shall help you with the greatest pleasure.
5. At the worst I shall be a few minutes late.
6. A young French journalist told me that the war in Africa would end in the near future.
7. I told him the main thing.
8. He is my best friend.
9. —How much more do you pay for your room than I do? —Ten rubles more.
10. He's a most wonderful person!

3. The verbal prefixes за-, с-, раз-

За-. A special class of perfectives denotes only the start of an action; such perfectives are known as inchoatives. They are formed with several prefixes, among which is the prefix **за-**:

> играть——**за**играть   to start playing
> говорить——**за**говорить   to speak up, begin to speak
> Оркестр **за**играл весёлый марш.
> Ниночка вдруг **за**плакала.

This prefix is not always inchoative, e.g., **заходить—зайти**, *to drop in to see.*

С- *and* **раз-**. The prefix **с-** (**съ-**, **со-**) adds to verbs of motion the idea of *together*, whereas the prefix **раз-** (**рас-**, **разо-**), its opposite, means *apart*. Intransitive verbs of motion use the suffix **-ся** with these prefixes: **сходиться/сойтись, съезжаться/съехаться**.

PATTERN SENTENCES

1. Все ста́рые друзья́ **сошли́сь** вчера́ у Смирно́ва; был день его́ рожде́ния.

2. Ле́том вся на́ша семья́ **съе́дется** в Крыму́.

3. Толпа́ ме́дленно **расходи́лась**.

4. На́ши вку́сы **схо́дятся**.

5. Его́ роди́тели **разошли́сь**, когда́ ему́ бы́ло пять лет.

6. Почтальо́н **разно́сит** пи́сьма по дома́м.

7. Ну́жно **снести́** все твои́ ве́щи в э́ту ко́мнату.

1. All the old friends came together yesterday at Smirnov's; it was his birthday.

2. In summer our whole family will get together in the Crimea.

3. The crowd slowly dispersed.

4. Our tastes agree.

5. His parents separated when he was five.

6. The postman delivers letters to the houses.

7. You must bring together all your things in this room.

4. Inclusive imperative (*let us*) and 3rd person imperative (*let him*, etc.)

Let us, that is, an invitation or command to perform an action in which the speaker will participate, may be rendered by a verb in the future tense of the first person plural without a pronoun subject; when one person is addressed by the formal **вы**, or when several persons are addressed, **-те** is added.

Perfective future:

> **Пойдём!** (пойдёмте!)
> Let's go!

> **Возьмём** (возьмёмте) маши́ну и **пое́дем**.
> Let's take the car, and let's go.

Imperfective future:

> *Positive:*

> **Бу́дем наде́яться.**
> Let's hope.

The imperfective is more frequent when the meaning is negative, *Let's not*.

> *Negative:*

> **Не бу́дем** об э́том **спо́рить**.
> Let's not argue about that.

With imperfective verbs it is, however, more common to use the *infinitive* preceded by **дава́й** or **дава́йте** (the imperative of **дава́ть**); **дава́й/дава́йте** may also be used together with *future tense* forms of both aspects:

> Дава́й/те писа́ть.
> Let's write.

> Дава́й/те бу́дем ходи́ть гуля́ть вме́сте ка́ждое у́тро.
> Let's go for a walk together every morning.

> Дава́й/те поговори́м об э́том де́ле.
> Let's have a talk about this matter.

Unprefixed verbs of motion are used in the first person plural of the *present* tense as the inclusive imperative:

Идём/те!⎫
Éдем/те! ⎭ Let's go!

Бежи́м/те   Let's run!

In the third person, singular and plural (*let him*, *let her*, *let them*), **пусть** (or, more colloquially, **пуска́й**) is used:

Пу́сть она́ придёт.
Let her come (Tell her to come; or I don't mind if she comes).

Éсли о́н мне́ не ве́рит, **пуска́й** спро́сит у моего́ отца́.
If he doesn't believe me, let him ask my father.

PATTERN SENTENCES

First person plural, perfective future.

1. Ко́нчим перево́д. На́м оста́лось то́лько три́ стро́чки.
2. Начнём рабо́тать. Пора́!
3. Пойдём ве́чером в кино́. Ла́дно?
4. Уйдёмте отсю́да! Мне́ ску́чно.
5. Зайдём к Ива́ну.
6. Пое́дем за́ город.
7. Напи́шем А́нне.

1. Let's finish the translation. We have only three lines left.
2. Let's start work. It's time!
3. Let's go to the movies tonight. O.K.?
4. Let's get out of here! I'm bored.
5. Let's go to see Ivan.
6. Let's go out of town.
7. Let's write Anna.

Дава́й(те).

1. Дава́йте говори́ть то́лько по-ру́сски!
2. Дава́й(те) напи́шем пье́су!
3. Дава́йте чита́ть.
4. Дава́йте занима́ться.
5. Дава́й(те) сде́лаем э́тот перево́д вме́сте.

1. Let's speak only Russian!
2. Let's write a play!
3. Let's read.
4. Let's study.
5. Let's do that translation together.

Пусть (пуска́й) + *third person.*

1. Пу́сть А́нна да́ст ва́м сво́й слова́рь.
2. Пу́сть Андре́й са́м э́то сде́лает.
3. Éсли они́ хотя́т, пуска́й приведу́т своего́ дру́га.
4. Пу́сть (она́) говори́т, что́ хо́чет.
5. Пу́сть всё э́то зна́ют.

1. Let Anna give you her dictionary (tell her to).
2. Let Andrey do that himself.
3. If they want to, let them bring their friend.
4. Let her say what she wants.
5. Let everyone know that.

DRILL

Переведи́те с англи́йского на ру́сский.

1. Let him do what he wants!
2. Let her tell you what she saw.
3. Let them think what they want.
4. Let's play.
5. Let's go abroad!
6. Let's start studying. It's time!
7. Let's go to the restaurant.
8. Let's finish the article.
9. Let's tell them about our plans.
10. Let them come if they want.
11. Let's not think about war.
12. Let's write to him today.
13. Let Anna buy the newspaper this evening.
14. Let's not talk about it.

Conversation

Чем бо́льше я тебя́ зна́ю, тем ме́ньше я тебя́ понима́ю

Ви́ктор. —А, Алёша! Ра́д тебя́ ви́деть! Сади́сь в то́ кре́сло! Мы́ тепе́рь всё ре́же и ре́же ви́димся, а когда́ ви́димся, то то́лько и́здали, на ле́кциях. Зимо́й ты́ заходи́л ко мне́ гора́здо ча́ще. Ты́, по-мо́ему, да́же в клу́бе не́ был бо́льше ме́сяца. В чём де́ло?

Алёша. —Учи́ться в ву́зе[6]—не шу́тка. У меня́ ма́сса рабо́ты. Я́ занима́юсь с ра́ннего утра́ и до по́зднего ве́чера. Я́ тепе́рь ложу́сь по́зже и встаю́ ра́ньше и всё-таки у меня́ не́т доста́точно вре́мени не то́лько, чтобы ходи́ть в го́сти, но да́же чтобы газе́ту почита́ть! Возьмём для приме́ра сего́дняшний де́нь. Сего́дня воскресе́нье, пра́вда? Я́ вста́л в ше́сть, как то́лько позвони́л буди́льник. Я́ при́нял холо́дный ду́ш, побри́лся, оде́лся, вы́пил стака́н ча́ю, съе́л кусо́к хле́ба с колбасо́й, се́л за сто́л и просиде́л за столо́м ве́сь де́нь. И то́лько тепе́рь вы́шел на полчаса́.

В. —Ты́ сумасше́дший! Ты́ всегда́ рабо́таешь бо́льше все́х и хо́чешь бы́ть лу́чше все́х. Чем бо́льше я тебя́ зна́ю, тем ме́ньше я тебя́ понима́ю. Мне́ ка́жется, что е́сли я проживу́ с тобо́й сто́ ле́т, я́ всё равно́ не пойму́, что ты́ за челове́к! Кста́ти, мо́жно узна́ть, над че́м ты́ рабо́таешь?

А. —Я́ рабо́таю сейча́с над докла́дом, и хочу́ поскоре́й ко́нчить его́, чтобы прочита́ть его́ на после́днем семина́ре. Я́ нашёл гора́здо бо́льше интере́сных материа́лов, чем я ду́мал и, поэ́тому, я́ рабо́таю над докла́дом до́льше, чем предви́дел. Докла́д оказа́лся длинне́й, но зато́ гора́здо интере́сней. В ближа́йшие не́сколько дне́й я́ бу́ду о́чень за́нят. Во́т и всё.

В. —Ты́ молоде́ц! Настоя́щий учёный! Но́ что э́то за жи́знь? Коне́чно, э́то де́ло вку́са, но́, по-мо́ему, та́к нельзя́ жи́ть. Жи́знь сли́шком коротка́. Ну́жно же иногда́ поговори́ть с прия́телем, поигра́ть в ша́хматы, послу́шать му́зыку, вы́йти с де́вушкой потанцева́ть. Но ты́, ви́дно, бо́льше всего́ лю́бишь тру́д. Чу́вство до́лга в тебе́ сильне́е всего́. До́лг пре́жде всего́!

А. —Ты́ о́чень похо́ж на мою́ сестру́ Ле́ну. Она́ говори́т то́ же са́мое. Я́ слы́шу от неё те́ же слова́. Она́ счита́ет меня́ сухи́м и ску́чным челове́ком. А я́ счита́ю, что она́ гора́здо скучне́й меня́. Но́, как ты́ говори́шь, э́то де́ло вку́са, а о вку́сах не спо́рят. Пу́сть она́ говори́т, что хо́чет. И ты́ мо́жешь ду́мать, что хо́чешь. Мне́ всё равно́.

В. —Ты́ говори́шь, что я́ похо́ж на Ле́ну, а Ле́ну ты́ счита́ешь ску́чной? Зна́чит, и я́ ску́чный? Спаси́бо за комплиме́нт! Дава́й лу́чше поговори́м о чём-нибудь бо́лее интере́сном. Что́ ты́ бу́дешь де́лать на пра́здниках? У на́с ведь бу́дут три́ свобо́дных дня́. Ты́ куда́-нибудь пое́дешь на э́ти дни́?

А. —Не ду́маю, хотя́ я́ и получи́л приглаше́ние от Смирно́вых. Они́ приглаша́ют меня́ прие́хать к ни́м на да́чу и пожи́ть у ни́х не́сколько дне́й. Они́ тепе́рь живу́т на берегу́ Балти́йского мо́ря. Они́ пи́шут, что у ни́х бу́дет о́чень интере́сное о́бщество.

---

[6] **Ву́з**, acronym for **вы́сшее уче́бное заведе́ние** (*higher educational institution*); the term is applied to all schools on the college or university level. Note that the word **вуз** is declined as a masculine noun.

В. —И ты́ не при́нял э́того приглаше́ния? Стра́нный ты́ челове́к! Я́ бы пое́хал, е́сли бы меня́ пригласи́ли! Смирно́вы—миле́йшие лю́ди, и говоря́т, что у и́х до́чери замеча́тельнейший го́лос. Не лу́чше ли бы́ло бы тебе́ пое́хать туда́, чем сиде́ть в ду́шном го́роде?

А. —Не́т, не пое́ду. Я́ поблагодари́л за приглаше́ние и написа́л, что прие́хал бы с велича́йшим удово́льствием, е́сли бы кани́кулы бы́ли подлинне́е. Э́то бы́ло бы друго́е де́ло. Но́ та́к—не сто́ит. Смирно́вы живу́т недалеко́ от фи́нской грани́цы. Э́то о́чень дли́нное путеше́ствие; я́ не смо́г бы верну́ться ра́ньше среды́ и потеря́л бы мно́го вре́мени. А что́ ты́ бу́дешь де́лать?

В. —Я́ ещё не реши́л. Я́ бы о́чень хоте́л пое́хать в прия́тном о́бществе куда́-нибудь за́ город. Хорошо́ бы погуля́ть на све́жем во́здухе, попла́вать в ре́чке, полежа́ть на зелёной траве́ под зелёными дере́вьями, послу́шать, ка́к пти́цы пою́т. Про́сто забыва́ешь, что е́сть цветы́, дере́вья, трава́, сло́вом—приро́да. Я́ уже́ счита́ю часы́, когда́ всё э́то уви́жу. Ну́жно бы поча́ще е́здить за́ город.

А. —Да́, бы́ло бы хорошо́ провести́ де́нь в дере́вне. Э́то не плоха́я мы́сль.

В. —Так почему́ же на́м не пое́хать? Пое́дем! Пое́дем хо́ть на рыба́лку (fishing) куда́-нибудь под Москво́й. Э́то гора́здо бли́же и про́ще, чем е́хать на фи́нскую грани́цу. Вы́едем ра́но у́тром и, е́сли хо́чешь, вернёмся ве́чером пора́ньше. Ла́дно?

А. —А докла́д? И я́ ведь, кро́ме того́, уже́ на́чал рабо́тать над диссерта́цией... Я́ потеря́ю це́лый де́нь, и мне́ пото́м бу́дет трудне́е...

В. —К чёрту всё! Оди́н де́нь на во́здухе да́ст тебе́ бо́льше эне́ргии, си́л и мы́слей, чем витами́ны, кото́рые врачи́ сове́туют на́м принима́ть. Е́дем?

А. —Ре́чка, дере́вья, си́нее не́бо. Е́дем! То́лько не говори́ ничего́ Ле́не. Пу́сть она́ ду́мает, что я́ сижу́ в библиоте́ке.

Чита́йте вопро́сы и отвеча́йте на ни́х.

1. Всегда́ ли Ви́ктор и Алёша так ре́дко ви́делись? 2. Ско́лько вре́мени Алёша не́ был в клу́бе? 3. Когда́ Алёша тепе́рь занима́ется? 4. О́н тепе́рь ложи́тся и встаёт в то́ же вре́мя, как пре́жде? 5. Почему́ Алёша тепе́рь не чита́ет газе́т? 6. Ка́к о́н провёл воскресе́нье? 7. Что́ сказа́л Ви́ктор, когда́ услы́шал э́тот расска́з? 8. Ка́к А. объясня́ет своё поведе́ние (behavior)? 9. Почему́ его́ рефера́т бу́дет длинне́е, чем о́н ду́мал? 10. Кака́я филосо́фия жи́зни у В., и что́ о́н говори́т о вку́сах А.? 11. Что́ говори́т Ле́на? 12. От кого́ А. получи́л приглаше́ние, и что́ бы́ло в письме́? 13. Почему́ о́н не при́нял приглаше́ния? 14. Что́ В. хоте́л бы сде́лать на пра́здниках? 15. Что́ об э́том пла́не ду́мает А.? 16. Ка́к реаги́рует (reacts) В., когда́ о́н слы́шит, что А. никуда́ не хо́чет е́хать? 17. Че́м конча́ется э́тот разгово́р?

DRILL

Review Translation.

1. —How old is this little boy? —He is only five years old. He is two years younger than my son. 2. The climate of that country is much worse and colder than the climate of our country. 3. We live a little closer to the border than you. 4. His elder sister is seven years older than he. 5. I have never heard him play, but they say that he plays much better than his father. 6. Our kolkhoz is wealthier than

yours; and theirs is still wealthier.   7. He promised to return in an hour, but he returned much later.   8. Nature is much richer in southern Russia than in northern Russia.   9. She always used to go to bed late, but yesterday she went to bed still later.   10. Sit down near me and let's have a talk.   11. We shall sit and smoke for a while until he returns.   12. He sat down at his table, worked for a while, and went to the restaurant.   13. The longer you (will) work at your novel, the better your novel will be.   14. I've read a most interesting story.   15. This is the most interesting story in this book.   16. Let's go to the movies this evening.   17. Let them pay for the tickets.   18. He is seventy-five years old already; if he were younger, he would travel more.   19. I paid 145 rubles for this suit; formerly I used to pay much less for suits.   20. I saw Nina from afar.   21. —Everyone will think you are crazy if you don't accept their invitation! —Let them think what they wish!   22. Victor has not yet accepted the invitation which we sent him two and a half weeks ago.   23. But I hope he will accept it and will come for the holidays.   24. Let's go to the country tomorrow.   25. You're crazy! I have to work on my article.

Vocabulary

арти́ст (*fem.* **-ка**) performing artist (singer, dancer, etc.)

ви́дно apparent(ly), evident(ly)

долг debt; moral duty (*no pl. in this sense*)

жи́тель (*masc.*) (*fem.* **-ница**) inhabitant

зато́ on the other hand, however

и́здали from afar

киломе́тр kilometer (0.621 mile)

когда́-либо ever, at any time

ла́в.ка (*gen. pl.* **-ок**) shop, small store

населе́ние population

недоста́точно insufficient(ly), not enough

пре́жде formerly, before (*adv.*)

приглаше́ние invitation

ре́ч.ка (*gen. pl.* **-ек**) small river, stream

си́ла power, force (*often used in plural*)

спортсме́н athlete

строка́, **стро́чка** line (of writing or print)

сумасше́дший crazy, insane, mad (person), madman

хоть if only

чу́вство (*gen. pl.* **чувств**) feeling

VERBS

остава́ться (imperf., I: **оста.ю́сь**, **-ёшься**), **оста́ться** (perf., I: **оста́н.усь**, **-ешься**) to remain, stay, be left

приглаша́ть (imperf., I), **пригласи́ть** (perf., II: **пригла.шу́**, **-си́шь**) to invite

шуме́ть (imperf., II: **шум.лю́**, **-и́шь**) to make noise

EXPRESSIONS

Что́ за[7] What sort of . . .? **Что́ это за кни́га?** What sort of book is that?

далеко́ от (+ *gen.*) far from

недалеко́ от (+ *gen.*) not far from

бли́зко от (+ *gen.*) near (to)

бли́же к (+ *dat.*) nearer (to)

произноси́ть/произнести́ ре́чь to give a speech

с утра́ до ве́чера from morning till evening

три́ (**пя́ть, и т. д.**) **с полови́ной** three (five, etc.) and a half

Ти́ше! Quiet! Silence!

когда́ . . . то́ when . . . then

---

[7] Here **за** is a particle and not a preposition.

сего́дняшний де́нь today (*used as noun*)

Во́т и всё. That's all (there is to it).

ра́ньше всего́⎫
пре́жде всего́⎭ first of all

то́ же са́мое the same (thing)

на пра́здники for the holidays

на пра́здниках during the holidays

принима́ть/приня́ть приглаше́ние to accept an invitation

сло́вом in a word

К чёрту! The devil with it!

К чёрту всё! To the devil with everything!

на во́здухе in the (open) air

ILLUSTRATION 22.   Фёдор Михáйлович Достоéвский (1821–1881). По
фотогрáфии 1879-го гóда. (*Sovfoto*).

Declension of numerals • Cardinal and ordinal numerals (review and completion) • Óба/óбе *both* • Dates • Fractions • Time of day • Time in schedules • Expressions of time (review and supplement) • Conversation: Приéзд Елéны Ивáновны • Reading: Письмó: Чáсть пéрвая

Unit 26

Grammar

1. Declension of numerals

Like nouns, pronouns, and adjectives, Russian numerals are declined.

A. Declension of 1.

	Masculine	Neuter	Feminine
Nom.	одúн	однó	однá
Gen.	одногó	like Masc.	однóй
Dat.	одномý	like Masc.	однóй
Acc.	like Nom. or Gen.	однó	однý
Instr.	однúм	like Masc.	однóй
Loc.	однóм	like Masc.	однóй

B. Declension of 2, 3, and 4.

	2		3	4
	Masc.–Neut.	*Fem.*		
Nom.	два	две	три	четы́ре
Gen.	двух		трёх	четырёх
Dat.	двум		трём	четырём
Acc.	Like Nom. or Gen.			
Instr.	двумя́		тремя́	четырьмя́
Loc.	двух		трёх	четырёх

Note the stem in oblique cases of **два—две**: **дву-**; of **три**: **трё—тре-**.

C. Declension of numerals above 4 ending in -ь.
These are declined like Fem. II nouns in the *singular*:

	5	8
Nom.	пять	во́семь
Gen.	пяти́	восьми́
Dat.	пяти́	восьми́
Acc.	пять	во́семь
Instr.	пятью́	восемью́
Loc.	пяти́	восьми́

D. Phrases "Numeral + Noun."
As we know, after 2, 3, and 4 nouns are in the genitive *singular*; after 5 and above in the genitive *plural*, e.g., два́ стола́, три́ кни́ги, четы́ре окна́; *but:* пя́ть столо́в, ше́сть кни́г, се́мь о́кон, etc.

These rules apply only when the numeral is in the *nominative* case, that is, most commonly when the word group "numeral + noun" is the subject of a sentence:

> Мой **два́** бра́та живу́т здесь.
>
> На по́лке стоя́т **два́дцать пя́ть** кни́г.

Used in case forms other than the nominative (and the accusative, which is treated below), the numeral and the noun appear in the case form required, the noun in the *plural* of the case.

Gen.	Во́т до́м мои́х дву́х профессоро́в.
Dat.	Я́ написа́л дву́м профессора́м.
Instr.	Я́ говори́л с двумя́ профессора́ми.
Loc.	Мы́ говори́ли о дву́х профессора́х.

In the accusative case of the group "numeral + noun," the animate-inanimate distinction applies to all genders for the numbers 2, 3, and 4: inanimate is like nominative; animate is like genitive.

Inanimate:	Я́ ви́дел **два́** до́м**а** (**две́** кни́ги).
Animate:	Я́ ви́дел **дву́х** студе́нтов.

The numbers 5 and above, however, have but one form of the accusative for *both* animate and inanimate:

Inanimate:	Я́ ви́дел **пя́ть** домо́в.
Animate:	Я́ ви́дел **пя́ть** студе́нт**ов**.

SUMMARY TABLE OF NUMERAL DECLENSIONS

1. **Два (две), три, четы́ре** *with inanimate nouns.*

Nom.	Во́т (**два́, три́, четы́ре**) до́ллара, (**две́**) шля́пы.
Gen.	У меня́ не́т (**дву́х, трёх, четырёх**) до́лларов, шля́п.

Dat.	Я ра́д[1] э́тим (дву́м, трём, четырём) до́лларам, шля́пам.
Acc.	Я получи́л (два́, три́, четы́ре) до́ллара, (две́) шля́пы.
Instr.	Что́ я́ сде́лаю с (двумя́, тремя́, четырьмя́) до́лларами, шля́пами?
Loc.	Я ду́маю о (дву́х, трёх, четырёх) до́лларах, шля́пах.

2. **Два (две), три, четы́ре** *with animate nouns.*

Nom.	Во́т на́ши (два́, три́, четы́ре) ма́льчика, (две́) де́вочки.
Gen.	Э́то кни́ги для (дву́х, трёх, четырёх) ма́льчиков, де́вочек.
Dat.	Ко́ля пи́шет (дву́м, трём, четырём) ма́льчикам, де́вочкам.
Acc.	Я зна́ю (дву́х, трёх, четырёх) ма́льчиков, де́вочек.
Instr.	Мы́ бы́ли та́м с (двумя́, тремя́, четырьмя́) ма́льчиками, де́вочками.
Loc.	Мы́ говори́м о (дву́х, трёх, четырёх) ма́льчиках, де́вочках.

3. *Numerals above* **5** (*ending in soft sign*): *nominative and accusative are alike* (*no distinction for animate and inanimate*); *genitive, dative, and locative all end in* **-и**.

Nom.	Во́т пя́ть **столо́в, по́лок, студе́нтов**.
Gen.	Зде́сь не́т пяти́ столо́в, по́лок, студе́нтов.
Dat.	Я подошёл к пяти́ стола́м, по́лкам, студе́нтам.
Acc.	Я ви́жу пя́ть **столо́в, по́лок, студе́нтов**.
Instr.	Что́ мне́ де́лать с пятью́ стола́ми, по́лками, студе́нтами?
Loc.	Мы́ говори́м о пяти́ стола́х, по́лках, студе́нтах.

E. Approximation is expressed by о́коло + genitive.

Я та́м жи́л о́коло дву́х ле́т.
I lived there about two years.

У меня́ бы́ло о́коло пяти́ рубле́й.
I had about five rubles.

F. Declension of compound cardinal numerals. All parts of a compound cardinal numeral are declined, e.g.:

ме́ньше двадцати́ трёх фу́нтов
less than 23 pounds

о́коло тридцати́ пяти́ киломе́тров
about 35 kilometers

It will be recalled that in the nominative and accusative inanimate, the final part of a compound numeral determines the case and number of the following noun:

В э́том кла́ссе два́дцать **оди́н** студе́нт (nom. sing.).
Я ви́жу на ка́рте три́дцать **два́** го́род**а** (gen. sing.).
На собра́нии бы́ло со́рок **пя́ть** учителе́й (gen. pl.).

---

[1] **Ра́д** + dative means *to be glad of* (*glad to get/to see*).

When pronoun-adjectives (**все, мой, наши, эти, те,** etc.) and some adjectives such as **первые, последние, другие,** etc., *precede* numerals, they agree with the *numeral* in case:

Вы читали **всé мой три** ромáна?
Я прочитáл **вáши пять** книг.
Вы знáете **мойх трёх** дочерéй?
Я познакóмился со **всéми твойми пятью** детьми́.
Я читáл его **пéрвые двá** ромáна.

2. Cardinal and ordinal numerals (review and completion)

		Cardinal	*Ordinal*
0		ноль (masc.), нуль (masc.)	нолевóй, нулевóй
1		оди́н, однó, однá	пéрвый
2		два, две	вторóй
3		три	трéтий
4		четы́ре	четвёртый
5		пять	пя́тый
6		шесть	шестóй
7		семь	седьмóй
8		вóсемь	восьмóй
9		дéвять	девя́тый
10		дéсять	деся́тый
11		оди́ннадцать	оди́ннадцатый
12		двенáдцать	двенáдцатый
13		тринáдцать	тринáдцатый
14		четы́рнадцать	четы́рнадцатый
15		пятнáдцать	пятнáдцатый
16		шестнáдцать	шестнáдцатый
17		семнáдцать	семнáдцатый
18		восемнáдцать	восемнáдцатый
19		девятнáдцать	девятнáдцатый
20		двáдцать	двадцáтый
21		двáдцать оди́н (однó, однá)	двáдцать пéрвый
22		двáдцать двá (двé)	двáдцать вторóй
		etc.	etc.
25		двáдцать пять	двáдцать пя́тый
		etc.	etc.
30		три́дцать	тридцáтый
40		сóрок	сороковóй
50		пятьдеся́т	пятидеся́тый
60		шестьдеся́т	шестидеся́тый
70		сéмьдесят	семидеся́тый
80		вóсемьдесят	восьмидеся́тый
90		девянóсто	девянóстый
100		сто	сóтый

	Cardinal	Ordinal
200	двести	двухсо́тый
300	три́ста	трёхсо́тый
400	четы́реста	(gen. sing. ста)	четырёхсо́тый
500	пятьсо́т	пятисо́тый
600	шестьсо́т	шестисо́тый
700	семьсо́т	(gen. pl. сот)	семисо́тый
800	восемьсо́т	восьмисо́тый
900	девятьсо́т	девятисо́тый
1,000	(одна́) ты́сяча (fem. noun)	ты́сячный
2,000	две́ ты́сячи (gen. sing. ты́сячи) etc.	двухты́сячный etc.
5,000	пя́ть ты́сяч (gen. pl. ты́сяч) etc.	пятиты́сячный etc.
1,000,000	миллио́н (masc. noun)	миллио́нный

Observe that the teens drop the soft sign (ь) after the first numeral element. The numerals 50, 60, 70, and 80 retain the soft sign in the middle (after the first numeral element), but have *no* soft sign at the end. There are never two soft signs in a Russian numeral in the nominative case.

Сто (100) has the form **ста** in all cases except the nominative and accusative. Like **сто** are declined **со́рок** (40) and **девяно́сто** (90).

Пятьдеся́т (50), **шестьдеся́т** (60), **се́мьдесят** (70), and **во́семьдесят** (80) are declined like **пять**, though they lack final **-ь** in the nominative and accusative. In the genitive, dative, and locative all of them replace the **-ь** of the first numeral element with **-и**, e.g., пятьдеся́т: genitive–dative–locative, пяти́десяти; in the instrumental they have **-ью**: пятью́десятью.

Numerals for 200, 300, 400, 500, etc., have both parts declined, e.g., две́сти, двухсо́т, двумста́м, две́сти, двумяста́ми, двухста́х; or пятьсо́т, пятисо́т, пятиста́м, пятьюста́ми, пятиста́х.

Ты́сяча (1,000) is declined as a hard feminine noun; **миллио́н** (1,000,000) as a hard masculine. These two numerals always govern the genitive plural, regardless of the case of the numeral itself, e.g.: С ты́сячей солда́т. В миллио́не слу́чаев (in a million cases).

The higher ordinals generally are formed by combining the *genitive* of the cardinal of the first numeral element with the ordinal of the second, e.g., пятидеся́тый, шестидеся́тый, двухсо́тый, пятиты́сячный, etc. Note the forms with double accents: трёхсо́тый, четырёхты́сячный, etc.

It will be recalled that ordinals are adjectives, and are declined as adjectives. All of them are hard adjectives, except **тре́тий** (for the declension of which see Unit 18, page 275). Cardinals ending in **-ь** drop **-ь** before adding the adjective ending **-ый (-о́й)**.

With compound ordinals, only the final part is declined as an ordinal adjective. All other parts are *cardinals* (as in English), and remain in the *nominative* case:

На́ша конто́ра нахо́дится на **два́дцать пя́том** этаже́.

Я́ ва́м э́то уже́ говори́л сто́ ра́з; я́ повторя́ю э́то в **сто́ пе́рвый** и в после́дний!

DRILLS

A. *Translate the following cardinal or ordinal numerals.*

1. Двáдцать дéвять.
2. Сóрок вóсемь.
3. Сéмьдесят сéмь.
4. Девянóсто седьмóй.
5. Стó двенáдцать.
6. Стó двáдцать дéвять.
7. Стó сóрок девя́тый.
8. Сóтый.
9. Стó сéмьдесят вторóй.
10. Стó семидеся́тый.
11. Двéсти сороковóй.
12. Двухсóтый.
13. Четы́реста шестьдеся́т четы́ре.
14. Четырёхсóтый.
15. Четы́реста шестьдеся́т четвёртый.

16. Пятьсóт двá.
17. Пятисóтый.
18. Семьсóт сóрок вторóй.
19. Восьмисóтый.
20. Ты́сяча девятисóтый.
21. Ты́сяча девятьсóт шестьдеся́т четвёртый.
22. Ты́сячный.
23. Двé ты́сячи восемьсóт пятьдеся́т оди́н.
24. Шéсть ты́сяч двéсти сóрок седьмóй.
25. Двéсти три́дцать три́ ты́сячи семьсóт девянóсто вóсемь.
26. Три́ миллиóна восемьсóт сéмьдесят шéсть ты́сяч три́ста сóрок двá.
27. Пя́ть биллиóнов шестьсóт двенáдцать миллиóнов.

B. *Read and write the following numerals as both cardinals (nominative) and ordinals (masculine singular nominative).*

Model: Cardinals: 1,781, ты́сяча семьсóт вóсемьдесят оди́н.
Ordinals: 1,781st, ты́сяча семьсóт вóсемьдесят пéрвый.

10	37	69	141	666	2,000
11	40	70	200	777	100,000
14	44	77	225	800	1,000,000
20	50	80	300	999	
21	56	90	330	1,000	
22	60	99	400	1,851	
30		100	500	1,962	

C. *Переведи́те с англи́йского на ру́сский.*

1. She cannot live without her three dogs.
2. She buys the best meat for her three dogs.
3. These are the wives of their four sons.
4. Zina is the wife of their fourth son.
5. Anna is their fourth daughter.
6. I didn't know the name of your fourth daughter.
7. I don't have $7.
8. I don't have $25.
9. Why do you speak about $25?
10. In a year there are 12 months, 52 weeks, 365 days.
11. Vladimir has 1,000 rubles, I have 1,500, and Zina has 2,250.
12. We have about $1,000.
13. Here is 102nd Street.
14. Who lives on 102nd Street?
15. Her husband is twenty-two years older than she is.
16. The new road is 130 kilometers longer than the old one.
17. I read 1,000 pages less than Andrey.
18. In this town there are 11,335 inhabitants.
19. In this small village there are only 92 homes, and in ours there are 112 homes.
20. This church is 400 years old.

3. Óба/óбе *both*

This numeral, like **два/две**, has a masculine/neuter and a feminine form.

	Masculine—Neuter	Feminine
Nom.	óба	óбе
Gen.	обóих	обéих
Dat.	обóим	обéим
Acc.	Like Nom. or Gen.	
Instr.	обóими	обéими
Loc.	обóих	обéих

E.g.: Я́ прочёл **óба** журнáла, котóрые вы́ мнé дáли.

У **обéих** нáших дочерéй éсть дéти.

У нáс двá дóма; мы́ живём в **обóих** домáх.

DRILLS

A. *Переведи́те на англи́йский.*

1. Я́ прочёл óбе газéты.
2. У Елéны Ивáновны двá сы́на и двé дóчери. Óба её сы́на живýт на ю́ге, а óбе дóчери живýт с мáтерью.
3. Я́ хорошó знáю обóих сыновéй и обéих дочерéй.
4. Я́ учи́лся в шкóле с её обóими сыновья́ми, а моя́ сестрá учи́лась с обéими дочерьми́.
5. Онá чáсто пи́шет свои́м обóим сыновья́м.
6. Онá чáсто получáет пи́сьма от свои́х обóих сыновéй.
7. Я́ написáла и емý и éй.
8. Бори́с и истóрик и математик.

B. *Переведи́те на рýсский.*

1. I liked both pictures.
2. I want to buy both tables.
3. I wrote to both sisters.
4. He loves both his mother and his father.
5. I spoke with both professors.
6. I was there with both my sisters.
7. I bought these briefcases for both our boys.

4. Dates

Days of the month are expressed by the neuter ordinal (the noun **числó**, *number, date,* is understood). The month is in the genitive (such and such a day *of* the month):

—Какóе сегóдня числó?
—What is the date today?

—Сегóдня двáдцать шестóе ию́ня.
—Today is the twenty-sixth of June.

—Пéрвое октября́.
—October the first.

"Time when" (on such and such date) is expressed by the genitive:

Двáдцать шестóго ию́ня мы́ поéдем на дáчу.
On June 26th we go to the country.

Заня́тия начинáются пéрвого сентября́.
Classes begin on September 1.

Note that in Russian dates the numeral of the date always *precedes* the name of the month.

From . . . to . . . is expressed by **от** + genitive . . . **до** + genitive.

От пятнáдцат**ого** мáя **до** три́дцать пéрв**ого** áвгуст**а**.
From May 15 to August 31.

From . . . (that date on) is expressed by **с** + genitive:

С пéрв**ого** сентября́ мы́ бýдем в гóроде.

Years are expressed by ordinal numerals with the noun **год**:

Ты́сяча девятьсóт сóрок пя́**тый** гó**д**.
The year 1945.

Time when in years is expressed by the preposition **в** and the locative case of the ordinal with **годý**.

В ты́сяча девятьсóт сóрок пя́**том** годý.
In 1945. (In the 1,945th year.)

But when an exact date or more specific time of the year is given, the *genitive must* be used:

Толстóй роди́лся двáдцать восьмóг**о** áвгуст**а** ты́сяча восемьсóт двáдцать восьмóг**о** гóд**а** (1828 г.) и ýмер седьмóг**о** ноября́ ты́сяча девятьсóт деся́т**ого** гóд**а** (1910 г.).
Tolstoy was born on August 28, 1828, and died on November 7, 1910.

DRILL

D. *Переведи́те на рýсский.*

1. Today is December 25th.
2. We are going abroad on December 25th.
3. We shall be in Italy from May 15th to June 6th.
4. Who said that yesterday was the 15th?
5. What date will it be tomorrow, the 21st or the 22nd?
6. Our exam is on the 22nd.
7. Where were you in 1945?
8. In August, 1945, I was in the South.
9. —What date is it today? —It is September 28th.
10. This semester (семéстр) began in September.
11. They say that it will rain from the 28th to the 30th.
12. It rained from the 15th to the 23rd.
13. In what month were you born?
14. I was born in February.
15. —In what year and on what date?
    —February 13, 1927.

5. Fractions

Following are several important Russian fractions; all of them take the genitive case.

пол; полови́на	one half, e.g., по́л стака́на
(одна́) че́тверть (fem.)	one quarter, e.g., че́тверть фу́нта
три че́тверти	three quarters, e.g., три че́тверти го́да
(одна́) тре́ть (fem.)	one third, e.g., тре́ть семе́стра
две́ тре́ти	two thirds, e.g., две́ тре́ти доро́ги

Other fractions are formed with a *cardinal* numeral (feminine)[2] as the numerator, and an *ordinal* numeral (feminine)[2] as the denominator, e.g., **одна́ пя́тая** *one fifth*, **две́ седьмы́х** *two sevenths*, **три деся́тых** *three tenths*.

Пол is used with measures. With precise measures, **пол** is spelled as one word together wih the genitive of the noun-measure:

полчаса́, полдня́, полго́да, и т. д.
half an hour/a day/a year, etc.

When the measure is not precise, it is spelled separately:

по́л стака́на, по́л ча́шки, и т. д.   half a glass/a cup, etc.

Полови́на (feminine noun) is generally used to denote half of something which is not itself a unit of measure:

полови́на де́нег	half of the money
полови́на веще́й	half of the things

Russian has a special term to denote $1\frac{1}{2}$. This is **полтора́** with masculine and neuter nouns; **полторы́** with feminine nouns. The noun following it is in the genitive singular:

Masc./Neut.   полтора́ го́да/рубля́/я́блока
Fem.   полторы́ неде́ли/мину́ты/ты́сячи

With other numerals:

for $2\frac{1}{2}$, $3\frac{1}{2}$, $4\frac{1}{2}$, два/три/четы́ре **с полови́ной**, followed by a noun in the genitive singular: два́ **с полови́ной** часа́; with five and above followed by a noun in the genitive plural: се́мь **с полови́ной** часо́в.

Полтора́ *with numerals:*

150	полтора́ста рубле́й
1,500	полторы́ ты́сячи жи́телей
1,500,000	полтора́ миллио́на челове́к

---

[2] The word **часть** (*part*), which is feminine in gender, is understood with fractions.

6. Time of day

A. Fractions of the hour.

чéтверть часá	a quarter of an hour
полчасá	half an hour
трѝ чéтверти часá	three quarters of an hour
полторá часá	an hour and a half
двá с половѝной часá	two and a half hours

The expression of hours in Russian has been presented in Unit 16 (page 242).The phrases двá часá, пя́ть часóв, etc., denote an exact hour: *2:00, 5:00*; also в двá часá, в пя́ть часóв, *at 2:00, at 5:00*, etc. Periods of one hour, i.e., the sixty minutes beginning at 12:00, 1:00, 2:00, etc., are denoted by *ordinal* numerals as follows:

пéрвый чáс	the hour beginning at 12 o'clock
вторóй чáс	the hour beginning at 1 o'clock
трéтий чáс	the hour beginning at 2 o'clock
etc.	

Expressing time by means of ordinals is comparable to English *after three, after four*, etc.:

вторóй чáс—во вторóм часý	after one
трéтий чáс—в трéтьем часý	after two

More important, ordinal numerals for hours are used for *quarter past, half past*, as well as, e.g., five minutes past an hour:

—Котóрый чáс?   —What time is it?

"*Past*" or "*after*": Nominative + genitive of *ordinal* of hour:

2:15	чéтверть трéтьего (lit., a quarter of the third hour)
2:30	половѝна[3] трéть**его** (a half of the third hour)
3:05	пя́ть минýт четвёрт**ого** (five minutes of the fourth)
4:20	двáдцать минýт пя́т**ого** (twenty minutes of the fifth)

"*Of*" or "*to*": бе́з + genitive of *cardinals* for minutes; hour (*cardinal*) in *nominative*:

2:45	бе́з чéтверти трѝ (quarter to three)
2:57	бе́з трёх трѝ (three minutes to three)
3:35	бе́з двадцатѝ пятѝ четы́ре (twenty-five minutes to four)

The next illustration represents a series of times between the hours of twelve and one (the hour hand is to the right of twelve). The various times given in Russian correspond to the different positions of the minute hand shown:

---

[3] **Половѝна** is correctly used instead of **пол** for time of day.

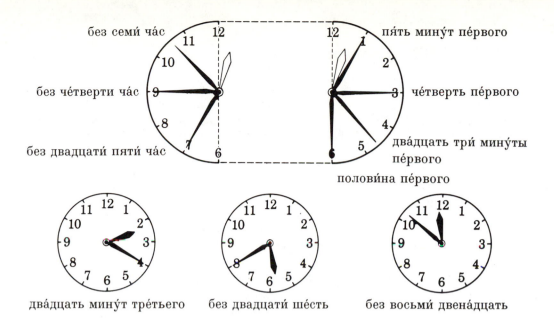

без семи́ час

пя́ть мину́т пе́рвого

без че́тверти час

че́тверть пе́рвого

без двадцати́ пяти́ час

два́дцать три́ мину́ты пе́рвого

полови́на пе́рвого

два́дцать мину́т тре́тьего

без двадцати́ шесть

без восьми́ двена́дцать

два́дцать три́ мину́ты второ́го

без че́тверти три́

B. At what time?

—В кото́ром часу́?   —At what time?

The answer employs the preposition **в. Полови́на** is preferably used in the locative case: **в полови́не**:

at 2:15   в че́тверть тре́тьего
at 2:30   в полови́не тре́тьего
at 3:05   в пя́ть мину́т четвёртого
at 4:20   в два́дцать мину́т пя́того

With **без** the preposition **в** is usually omitted; the *genitive* case is used:

at 2:45   без че́тверти три́
at 2:57   без трёх три́
at 3:35   без двадцати́ пяти́ четы́ре

DRILLS

A. *Переведите на английский.*

1. Половина первого.
2. В половине первого.
3. Четверть первого.
4. Без четверти час.
5. Без двадцати час.
6. Десять минут второго.
7. Двадцать пять минут второго.
8. Без двадцати пяти два.
9. Пять минут третьего.
10. В половине третьего.
11. Без трёх (минут) три.

12. Половина пятого.
13. Половина седьмого.
14. В половине девятого.
15. В половине одиннадцатого.
16. В четверть одиннадцатого.
17. Без четверти одиннадцать.
18. Без десяти (минут) одиннадцать.
19. Двадцать три минуты десятого.
20. В половине двенадцатого.
21. Без двадцати трёх двенадцать.
22. Двадцать три минуты первого.

B. *Читайте по-русски.*

at 12:00	1:45	3:45	7:45	10:57
12:30	2:00	5:30	at 8:30	10:59
1:00	3:15	6:30	at 9:30	at 11:00
at 1:35	3:40	7:15	at 9:10	

7. Time in schedules

For *schedules* and *timetables* the time is often expressed by the hour followed by the number of minutes.

> Лекция начинается в девять тридцать.
> The lecture starts at 9:30.

For transportation a twenty-four hour schedule is used:

> Поезд уходит в двадцать три десять.
> The train leaves at 23:10 (= 11:10 p.m.).

8. Expressions of time (review and supplement)

Different types of time expressions use different grammatical cases, some with prepositions, some without.

A. Accusative.   The length of time an action endures is expressed by the *accusative* (*no* preposition).

> Он жил в Москве неделю/всю зиму/ целый месяц.
> He lived in Moscow (for) a week/the whole winter/a whole month.

The preposition **на** + *accusative* expresses the duration of an implied state or condition which is to *follow* the action of the verb.

> Он приехал в Москву **на** неделю/**на** всю зиму/**на** месяц.
> He came to Moscow for a week/for the whole winter/for a month (planning to stay a week, etc.).

A period of time at the end of which an action is performed is expressed by **через** + *accusative*.

> **Через** неде́лю мы́ пое́дем за грани́цу.
> In (after) a week we shall go abroad.

The time *when* a given action occurs is expressed differently, depending on several factors. One is the relative length of the unit of time.

With short units of time (minutes, hours, days) **в** + *accusative* is used:

в то́т моме́нт	at that moment
в ту́ мину́ту	at that minute
в то́т ча́с	at that hour
в три́ часа́	at 3:00
в то́т де́нь	that day
в пя́тницу	on Friday

Words meaning *time*, *period*, *epoch*, *occasion*, etc., also take **в** + *accusative*:

в то́ вре́мя	at that time
в ту́ эпо́ху	in that epoch
в то́т пери́од	at that period
в то́т ра́з	on that occasion

B. Instrumental. With parts of the day and seasons of the year, the *instrumental* is used:

> вчера́ у́тром, за́втра ве́чером
> про́шлым ле́том, э́той весно́й, бу́дущей о́сенью

C. Locative. With longer units of time (months, years, centuries) **в** + *locative* is used:

в про́шлом ме́сяце	last month
в э́том ме́сяце	this month
в бу́дущем ме́сяце	next month
в апре́ле	in April
в про́шлом году́	last year
в э́том году́	this year
в бу́дущем году́	next year
в ты́сяча девятьсо́т шестьдеся́т второ́м году́	in 1962
в двадца́том ве́ке	in the 20th century
в про́шлом ве́ке	in the last century

на + *locative with weeks*:

> **на** э́той/на про́шлой/на бу́дущей неде́ле   this/last/next week

D. Genitive. With dates, the *genitive* is used:

пятна́дцатого апре́ля	on April 15
два́дцать тре́тьего января́ ты́сяча девятьсо́т шестьдеся́т четвёртого го́да	on January 23, 1964

When one unit of time falls within another, the second and larger unit is in the *genitive* (compare English *of*):

Сего́дня пе́рвое февраля́.
Today is February 1 (the first of February).

в после́дний де́нь про́шл**ого** ме́сяц**а**
on the last day of last month

DRILLS

A. *Complete the sentence by translating the English phrases on the right.*

Я бы́л/бу́ду в Я́лте

- last year.
- last month.
- last January.
- last week.
- next week.
- this week.
- a month and a half.
- a week and a half.
- last summer.
- last winter.
- for the last time.
- for a whole week.
- the whole winter.
- the whole month of May.
- in May.
- next year.
- next spring
- this Wednesday.
- this Sunday.
- on Tuesday.

Я е́ду за грани́цу

- for the week.
- for two weeks.
- for two months.
- for half a year.
- for five months.
- for a year and a half.
- for three and a half years.

B. *Write out the numerals in the correct case; translate dates.*

Его́ конто́ра на 15; 19; 20; 21; 27; 30; 40; 50; 102 этаже́.

—На како́й э́то страни́це? —На 15; 19; 20; 21; 30; 33; 40; 50; 90; 102.

О́н роди́лся on May 1, 1923; in 1923; on Sept. 12, 1847; in 1947; on July 28, 1942; in 1962; in 1951.

Мы́ уезжа́ем на кани́кулы ме́жду (June 25 and 30); (July 1 and 5); (May 13 and 19); (August 20 and 22).

Мы́ пробу́дем заграни́цей от (August 15 to September 27); (October 1 to November 21); (January 3 to February 12).

C. *Translate the words in parentheses.*

1. О́н прие́хал (that day).
2. (At that hour) на у́лице никого́ не́ было.
3. Она́ пришла́ (at four).
4. (At that time) я ещё ходи́л в шко́лу.
5. (Next month) я пое́ду в Вашингто́н.
6. (Last month) я провёл два́ дня́ в Ки́еве.
7. Андре́й око́нчил семиле́тку (last year).
8. Мы́ ещё не зна́ем, куда́ мы́ пое́дем (next spring).
9. (Next week) моя́ тётя приезжа́ет сюда́.

10. —Мы́ идём в теа́тр (this week).
    —(On what day)? —(On Saturday.)
11. (Next week) у на́с бу́дут экза́мены.
    —(On what day)? —(On Tuesday.)
12. Толсто́й у́мер (in the twentieth century).

D. *Переведи́те на ру́сский.*

1. This year I am working much more than I worked last year.
2. I don't know yet what I will be doing next year.
3. Last month my sister arrived from China.
4. There will be many holidays this month.
5. I would like to go to the seashore next month.
6. It will be much warmer in a month.
7. We were at the seashore last week.
8. This week I must go to Kharkov for two weeks.
9. I will return next week.

13. Она́ прие́хала (last week) и уезжа́ет (next week).
14. Каки́е знамени́тые писа́тели жи́ли (in the last century)?
15. Бы́ло о́чень хо́лодно (last January).

10. They told us that they are going to the Crimea for a week, and that in a week they will come back here.
11. I will return from there in three days.
12. Last time I explained that rule to you.
13. Last summer we spent a month in the Caucasus, on the shore of the Black Sea.
14. Next summer we'll go to the mountains.
15. Next spring we want to go to the Ukraine.
16. I am going there for three days.

Conversation

Прие́зд Еле́ны Ива́новны

(Ве́чер. Вокза́л. Больши́е часы́. На часа́х два́дцать пя́ть мину́т девя́того. Напра́во на стене́ расписа́ние поездо́в. Два́ молоды́х челове́ка, Смирно́в и Зло́бин.)

Смирно́в (Зло́бину). —А́, здра́вствуйте! Что́ вы́ ту́т де́лаете? Пришли́ встреча́ть кого́-нибудь или куда́-нибудь е́дете?

Зло́бин. —Я́ пришёл встреча́ть одну́ знако́мую, кото́рая приезжа́ет из Ха́рькова. А что́ вы́ ту́т де́лаете?

С. —Я́ то́же встреча́ю одну́ знако́мую из Ха́рькова. Мо́жно спроси́ть, кто́ ва́ша знако́мая?

З. —Еле́на Ива́новна Во́лкова.

С. —Я́ то́же пришёл её встреча́ть!

З. —Я́ получи́л от неё письмо́, в кото́ром она́ пи́шет, что приезжа́ет во вто́рник, семна́дцатого декабря́, и про́сит меня́, её лу́чшего дру́га, встре́тить её. Но́ она́ забы́ла написа́ть в письме́, каки́м по́ездом она́ е́дет, и в кото́ром часу́ её по́езд прихо́дит! А мо́жет быть она́ вообще́ реши́ла оста́ться в Ха́рькове и забы́ла да́ть мне́ зна́ть.

С. —Я́ получи́л от неё то́чно тако́е же письмо́! Она́ пи́шет мне́ то́ же са́мое, что ва́м: она́ про́сит меня́, своего́ лу́чшего дру́га, встре́тить её, и мне́ то́же не пи́шет, в кото́ром часу́ она́ приезжа́ет!

З. —Кака́я исто́рия! Вчера́ ве́чером я́ позвони́л на вокза́л, и мне́ сказа́ли, что из Ха́рькова прихо́дит не́сколько поездо́в в де́нь! Е́сть у́тренний по́езд, о́н прихо́дит без десяти́ во́семь, е́сть оди́н дневно́й в че́тверть пя́того, пото́м е́сть вече́рний по́езд, кото́рый прихо́дит без че́тверти де́вять (в два́дцать со́рок пять), и последний, ночной, приходит в одиннадцать (в двадцать три). (На стене расписание поездов. Они останавливаются перед расписанием.) Вот видите, всё, как я вам говорил.

С. —Да, вижу. В котором же часу вы сюда пришли?

З. —Я боялся опоздать и пришёл в половине восьмого утра. Я здесь с половины восьмого!

С. —Несчастный человек!

З. —Да, глупо. Но почему вы пришли только сейчас? Откуда вы знали, что она приезжает вечером?

С. —Я знаю Елену Ивановну. Она не любит ни рано вставать, ни поздно ложиться, и я решил поэтому, что она приедет вечерним поездом.

З. —Поезд приходит без четверти девять, а сейчас уже без двадцати пяти. Мы должны спешить. У нас осталось десять минут, а мы даже ещё не знаем номера платформы.

С. —Я никогда не спешу и всегда прихожу вовремя. У нас есть ещё много времени. Я думаю, полчаса, или даже три четверти.

З. —Я вас не понимаю! Посмотрите на часы! Сейчас уже без двадцати девять, а поезд должен прийти без четверти. У нас есть только пять минут.

С. —Я хорошо знаю Елену Ивановну. Она всегда опаздывает.

З. —Вы хотите сказать, что поезд опоздает, потому что на нём едет Елена Ивановна?

(Голос громкоговорителя = loudspeaker.) Внимание! Внимание! Поезд из Харькова опоздает на полчаса и придёт в двадцать один пятнадцать.

С. —Ну, вот видите, в четверть десятого! Значит, я был прав! У нас ещё много времени. Пойдёмте в буфет, и выпьем за здоровье Елены Ивановны.

Читайте эти вопросы и отвечайте на них.

1. Где встретились два молодых человека? 2. Зачем они оба пришли на вокзал? 3. Пришли ли они оба в то же время? 4. Который час на больших часах? 5. Что мы видим на стене направо? 6. Что Елена Ивановна написала обоим молодым людям? 7. В какой день она должна была приехать и какого числа? 8. Что Смирнов говорит о Е. И.? 9. Что сказал громкоговоритель?

Reading

Письмо: Часть первая[4]

Ялта, 2-ое июля 1971 г.[5]

Дорогой Павел!

Ты вероятно будешь очень удивлён, когда получишь это письмо от меня, Матвея Желябина. Столько лет прошло с тех пор, как мы с тобой виделись в последний раз.

---

[4] Чтобы легче было читать это длинное письмо, мы разделили (divided) его на главы.

[5] This date may also be abbreviated as 2/VII/71. In Russian dates the day comes first, then the month, then the year.

Я то́лько что случа́йно узна́л твой а́дрес и реши́л сейча́с же тебе́ написа́ть. Мне́ так хо́чется мно́гое тебе́ рассказа́ть, мно́гое узна́ть о тебе́, и так хо́чется вме́сте с тобо́й вспо́мнить про́шлое!

Я пишу́ тебе́, как ви́дишь, из Я́лты, где́ я провожу́ кани́кулы с мое́й семьёй. Мы́ провели́ здесь ле́то в про́шлом году́ и нам так понра́вилась Я́лта, что мы́ реши́ли в э́том году́ опя́ть сюда́ прие́хать.

Мы́ прилете́ли сюда́ 21-ого ию́ня из Свердло́вска,[6] где́ мы́ живём. 23-го ию́ля конча́ется мо́й о́тпуск, и я до́лжен бу́ду верну́ться в Свердло́вск и нача́ть опя́ть рабо́тать в больни́це; я та́м гла́вный вра́ч. Но семья́ моя́ пробу́дет здесь до 15-го а́вгуста.

Я слы́шал, что ты́ жена́т, и что у тебя́ сы́н и до́чь. Как хорошо́ бы́ло бы, е́сли бы ты́ прие́хал сюда́ со свое́й семьёй! Я не зна́ю, был ли ты́ уже́ когда́-нибудь в Я́лте. Я уве́рен, что Я́лта тебе́ бы о́чень понра́вилась. Приро́да здесь чуде́сная: мо́ре, го́ры, везде́ ма́сса цвето́в.

Я пишу́ э́то письмо́ на балко́не, кото́рый выхо́дит[7] в са́д. Ви́д с балко́на замеча́тельный: за са́дом мо́ре, спра́ва и сле́ва го́ры. На одно́й горе́ ста́рая тата́рская[8] дере́вня. Над голово́й глубо́кое, си́нее, ю́жное не́бо. Над мо́рем лета́ют и крича́т ча́йки. Люблю́ ю́г!

Тепе́рь немно́го о себе́. Я то́же жена́т. Мою́ жену́ зову́т Любо́вь. Лю́ба[9] чу́дный челове́к. Она́ краси́вая, у́мная, и у неё золото́е се́рдце. У нас две́ де́вочки и ма́льчик. О́бе де́вочки о́чень сла́вные и хорошо́ у́чатся. Ста́ршей, Ве́ре,[9] 11 ле́т; мла́дшей, Наде́жде[9] 9, а сы́ну 4 го́да. Мы́ пра́здновали его́ де́нь рожде́ния на про́шлой неде́ле. Сы́на зову́т Па́влом, в че́сть тебя́. Па́влик[10] то́лстый, о́чень смешно́й и задаёт ма́ссу заба́вных вопро́сов. Во́т тебе́ не́сколько приме́ров:

1. Ма́ма, кто́ роди́лся ра́ньше: ты́ или я́?
2. Па́па, заче́м мне́ учи́ться чита́ть? Я всегда́ могу́ попроси́ть ма́му, и она́ прочита́ет мне́ всё, что мне́ захо́чется.
3. Ма́ма, когда́ я роди́лся, я не уме́л говори́ть, ве́рно? Так ка́к же ты́ и па́па узна́ли, что меня́ зову́т Па́влик?
4. Па́па, а кто́ сильне́е: леопа́рд или тра́ктор?

И та́к без конца́! Он о́чень заба́вный па́рень, но пове́рь мне́, не всегда́ легко́ отвеча́ть на все́ его́ вопро́сы. Приезжа́й, Павлу́ша! Мы́ с тобо́й должны́ сно́ва познако́миться и познако́мить на́ши се́мьи. Бы́ло бы так хорошо́ нам все́м ту́т собра́ться! Мо́жешь ли ты́ получи́ть о́тпуск?

Продолже́ние сле́дует (to be continued).

Чита́йте э́ти вопро́сы и отвеча́йте на ни́х.

1. Почему́ Матве́й ду́мает, что Па́вел бу́дет удивлён, когда́ полу́чит от него́ письмо́? 2. Почему́ Матве́й то́лько тепе́рь пи́шет своему́ дру́гу? 3. Почему́ он пи́шет э́то письмо́? 4. Почему́ Желя́бины второ́й ра́з прово́дят кани́кулы

---

[6] Sverdlovsk, a city in the Urals.
[7] Here this verb has the meaning of *look out on*, *face*.
[8] Tartar, or, more correctly, Tatar (*adj. form*).
[9] **Любо́вь** (diminutive, **Лю́ба**) *Love*; **Ве́ра** *Faith*; **Наде́жда** *Hope*.
[10] Diminutive of **Па́вел**.

в Я́лте? 5. Верну́тся ли все́ Желя́бины вме́сте в Свердло́вск? А е́сли не́т, то почему́? 6. Почему́ сы́на Матве́я зову́т Па́влом? 7. Куда́ выхо́дит балко́н, и како́й с него́ ви́д? 8. Запо́мнили ли вы́ како́й-нибудь вопро́с Па́влика, и како́й из ни́х вам бо́льше всего́ понра́вился? 9. Почему́ Матве́й так хо́чет, чтобы его́ дру́г прие́хал в Я́лту?

Vocabulary

ве́рно right, true; probably
дневно́й afternoon, daytime (*adj.*)
дура́к (*fem.* ду́ра) fool
жена́т, -ы (на + *loc.*) married (to)[11]
за́мужем (за + *instr.*) married (to)[11]
заба́вный amusing, entertaining
закры́тый closed, shut[12]
золото́й gold (*adj.*), golden
копе́йка (*gen. pl.* копе́ек) copeck (1/100 of a ruble)
красота́ beauty
о́тпуск leave (from work), vacation

прие́зд arrival (by vehicle)
расписа́ние schedule
сон (*gen.* сна) sleep; dream
сла́вный (*colloq.*) fine, nice
сле́ва on (from) the left
сно́ва again, anew
спра́ва on (from) the right
страни́ца page
том volume
у́тренний morning (*adj.*)
ча́йка (*gen. pl.* ча́ек) gull
число́ number, date

VERBS

вспомина́ть (imperf., I), вспо́мнить (perf., II: вспо́мн.ю, -ишь) to recollect, recall
опи́сывать (imperf., I), описа́ть (perf., I: опишу́, опи́шешь) to describe
пра́здновать (imperf., I: пра́здну.ю, -ешь) to celebrate
свети́ть (imperf., II: свечу́, све́тишь) to shine
хоте́ться (imperf.: хо́чется), захоте́ться (perf.: захо́чется) to want to, feel like (+ *dat. and inf.*).
    Мне́ хо́чется е́сть. I feel like eating, I am hungry.

EXPRESSIONS

расписа́ние поездо́в railway timetable
тако́й же of the same sort
вы́пить за здоро́вье (+ *gen.*) to drink someone's health

зна́чит (*as adverb*) so then, then, hence
в честь (+ *gen.*) in someone's honor
ви́деть со́н to have a dream

---

[11] A man says Я жена́т, but a woman says Я за́мужем; a married couple say Мы́ жена́ты.
[12] The short form is obligatory in the predicate, e.g., Две́рь закры́та.

Participles • Russian equivalents for English words ending in -*ever* •
Conjunctions of time in subordinate clauses • Negative pronouns and
adverbs with the element не- • Reading: Письмо́: Ча́сть втора́я

Unit 27

Grammar

1. Participles

Russian participles are words derived from verbs and having the verbal characteristics of tense, past or present (but not future), and aspect, perfective or imperfective.

There are two kinds of participles:

Adjectival participles, which are similar to adjectives in form and function.

Adverbial participles, which are indeclinable and similar in function to adverbs.

A. Adjectival participles. Adjectival participles may be active or passive, past or present; they have the aspect of the verb from which they are derived.

(1) *Active adjectival participles*, *past*. The words in boldface in the sentences below are *past* active adjectival participles; they may replace a clause introduced by **кото́рый** and containing a verb in the *past* tense, imperfective or perfective, from which the participle is derived (in the following examples this clause is given in parentheses after each participle). It will be observed that participles agree, like adjectives, with the nouns they modify, in number, gender, and case.

Все́ мои́ хоро́шие студе́нты, **чита́вшие** (кото́рые чита́ли) э́ту кни́гу, говоря́т, что она́ о́чень интере́сная.

Я́ зна́ю писа́теля, **написа́вшего** (кото́рый написа́л) э́ту кни́гу.

Я́ познако́мился с одни́м америка́нским журнали́стом, до́лго **жи́вшим** (кото́рый до́лго жи́л) в Москве́.

Я́ написа́л письмо́ в Вашингто́н моему́ хоро́шему дру́гу, **бы́вшему** (кото́рый бы́л) неда́вно в Москве́ и **ви́девшему** (кото́рый ви́дел) та́м моего́ бра́та.

О́н спроси́л молодо́го челове́ка, **сиде́вшего** (кото́рый сиде́л) ря́дом с ни́м в авто́бусе, идёт ли э́тот авто́бус на Кра́сную пло́щадь.

Мы́ ви́дели де́вушку, **бежа́вшую** (кото́рая бежа́ла) по у́лице и гро́мко **пе́вшую** (кото́рая гро́мко пе́ла) каку́ю-то пе́сню.

451

Past active participles are formed from the past stem by dropping the **-л** ending and adding the element **-вш-** (in the case of some verbs **-ш-** only), then the adjectival ending:

чита́(л)	чита́.**вш**.ий
написа́(л)	написа́.**вш**.ий
бы(л)	бы́.**вш**.ий
ви́де(л)	ви́де.**вш**.ий
сиде́(л)	сиде́.**вш**.ий
принёс	принёс.**ш**.ий
шёл	шёд.**ш**.ий (irregular)

(2) *Active adjectival participles, present.* The words in boldface in the sentences below are *present* active participles; they may replace a clause introduced by **кото́рый** and containing a verb in the *present* tense from which the participle is derived; this clause is given in parentheses after the participle.

Я́ зна́ю инженéра, **рабо́тающего** (кото́рый рабо́тает) на э́том заво́де.

Она́ получи́ла письмо́ от свое́й сестры́, **живу́щей** (кото́рая живёт) в Москве́.

Мне́ нужна́ секрета́рша, **зна́ющая** (кото́рая зна́ет) ру́сский язы́к.

Молодо́й челове́к, **иду́щий** (кото́рый идёт) по то́й стороне́ у́лицы, похо́ж на ва́шего бра́та.

У на́с е́сть не́сколько студе́нтов, хорошо́ **говоря́щих** (кото́рые хорошо́ говоря́т) по-ру́сски.

Соба́ка подошла́ к челове́ку, **сидя́щему** (кото́рый сиди́т) у окна́.

Уче́бник для **начина́ющих** (для те́х, кто начина́ет) (for beginners).

Ваго́н для **куря́щих** (для те́х, кто ку́рит) (for smokers).

Present active participles are formed from the present tense conjugation stem as it appears in the third person plural; final **-т** is dropped, and to this stem is added the element **-щ-**, then an adjectival ending:

рабо́таю(т)	рабо́таю.**щ**.ий
живу́(т)	живу́.**щ**.ий
зна́ю(т)	зна́ю.**щ**.ий
иду́(т)	иду́.**щ**.ий
говоря́(т)	говоря́.**щ**.ий
сидя́(т)	сидя́.**щ**.ий

DRILL

Replace adjectival participles by clauses with **кото́рый**, *and translate.*

Model: Актри́са, **игра́вшая** ро́ль Офе́лии, о́чень тала́нтлива.
Актри́са, **кото́рая игра́ла** ро́ль Офе́лии, о́чень тала́нтлива.

1. Я́ зна́ю да́му, **сидя́щую** про́тив на́с.
2. Вы́ по́мните де́вушку, **сиде́вшую** ря́дом с Серге́ем?
3. Ва́м ну́жно найти́ ги́да, **зна́ющего** португа́льский язы́к.
4. Я́ спроси́л одну́ же́нщину, **слы́шавшую** Ле́нина, хорошо́ ли о́н говори́л.
5. Мы́ познако́мились с писа́тельницей, мно́го **пи́шущей** о де́тях.

6. Учи́тельница, **даю́щая** мне́ уро́ки му́зыки—францу́женка.
7. Вы́ зна́ете люде́й, **сня́вших** кварти́ру на пя́том этаже́?
8. Да́ма, **снима́вшая** пальто́ когда́ вы́ вошли́, до́чь хозя́йки.
9. Господи́н, **покупа́вший** руба́шки и **кури́вший** большу́ю сига́ру, изве́стный певе́ц.
10. Я́ зна́ю ма́ленького ма́льчика, хорошо́ **игра́ющего** на роя́ле.
11. **Сидя́щий** в углу́ челове́к—бра́т мое́й сосе́дки.
12. Семья́, **жи́вшая** над на́ми, перее́хала в другу́ю кварти́ру.
13. Ты́ ви́дишь старика́, **иду́щего** с чемода́ном в руке́?
14. Мы́ ча́сто пи́шем сы́ну, **живу́щему** на Кавка́зе.
15. Андре́й зна́ет журнали́стку, **написа́вшую** э́ту статью́.
16. Ребёнок, **ше́дший** оди́н, упа́л.
17. **Входя́щий** в ко́мнату челове́к—знамени́тый учёный.
18. **Воше́дшая** с ни́м же́нщина—его́ жена́.

(3) *Passive adjectival participles*, *past*.   *Passive* adjectival participles, which can be derived from transitive verbs only, modify the *object* of an action; the agent by whom the action was performed may be described by a noun (or pronoun) in the instrumental case; thus:

Construction with *active* participle:

Журнали́ст, **написа́вший** статью́ . . .
The newspaperman who wrote the article . . .

Construction with *passive* participle:

Статья́, **напи́санная** журнали́стом . . .
The article written (which was written) by the newspaperman . . .

It will be observed that all the participles occurring in the examples below are derived from *perfective* verbs; past passive participles from *imperfective* verbs are rarely used.

In these sentences, the words in boldface are *past passive* adjectival participles:

Я́ прочита́л статью́, **напи́санную** мои́м знако́мым (кото́рую написа́л мо́й знако́мый).

Мы́ е́здили в Босто́н на автомоби́ле, неда́вно **ку́пленном** мои́м бра́том (кото́рый мо́й бра́т неда́вно купи́л).

Я́ ещё не получи́л **по́сланных** ва́ми кни́г (кни́г, кото́рые вы́ посла́ли).

Я́ возврати́л в библиоте́ку всё **прочи́танные** мно́й кни́ги (всё кни́ги, кото́рые я́ прочита́л).

Я́ чита́ю кни́гу, **взя́тую** мно́ю (кото́рую я́ взя́л) в библиоте́ке.

Портфе́ль, **привезённый** отцо́м (кото́рый привёз оте́ц) из А́нглии, мне́ о́чень нра́вится.

Я́ ви́дел письмо́, **подпи́санное** гла́вным реда́ктором (кото́рое подписа́л гла́вный реда́ктор).

Past passive participles are formed by inserting the element **-нн-**, or **-енн-**, or **-т-** between the infinitive stem and the adjectival ending. Formation of these participles is complicated, and the student is advised to learn the forms below as vocabulary. Note that all the forms below are *perfective*.

The following are among the more frequently used forms:

Element **-нн-** (*mostly first conjugation*):

написа́ть	напи́санный	written (which was, has been written)
прода́ть	про́данный	sold
прочита́ть	прочи́танный	read (which has been read)
сказа́ть	ска́занный	said, spoken
показа́ть	пока́занный	showed
рассказа́ть	расска́занный	told, narrated
подписа́ть	подпи́санный	signed
сде́лать	сде́ланный	done, made
услы́шать	услы́шанный	heard
сыгра́ть	сы́гранный	played
потеря́ть	поте́рянный	lost

Element **-енн-** (*mostly second conjugation, often with consonant mutations similar to those in the first person singular*):

получи́ть	полу́ченный	received, obtained
купи́ть	ку́пленный	bought, purchased
поста́вить	поста́вленный	placed, stood
положи́ть	поло́женный	placed, set down
постро́ить	постро́енный	built
пригото́вить	пригото́вленный	prepared
око́нчить	око́нченный	finished
возврати́ть	возвращённый	returned, given back
окружи́ть	окружённый	surrounded
принести́	принесённый	brought (on foot)
привезти́	привезённый	brought (in a vehicle)
найти́	на́йденный	found

Element **-т-** (*occurs with a limited number of first conjugation verbs*):

заня́ть	за́нятый	occupied; busy
сня́ть	сня́тый	taken off; rented
забы́ть	забы́тый	forgotten
взя́ть	взя́тый	taken
за-/откры́ть	за-/откры́тый	closed/open, opened
оде́ть	оде́тый	dressed
уби́ть	уби́тый	killed
нача́ть	на́чатый	begun, started
вы́пить	вы́питый	consumed, drunk

(4) *Predicative forms of passive adjectival participles.* Passive adjectival participles, past and present, have predicative (short) forms which are mandatory when these participles are used predicatively. As with adjectives, the predicative forms are obtained by dropping the adjectival endings and adding zero for masculine, **-o** for neuter, **-a** for feminine, and **-ы** for plural. Past passive participles formed with the element **-нн-** preserve only the first **-н-** of this element:

	Attributive		Predicative
	написанный	*Masc.*	написан
		Neut.	написано
		Fem.	написана
		Plural	написаны

PATTERN SENTENCES

1. Э́то письмо́ бы́ло **напи́сано** мно́й в ма́е.
2. Я́ ду́маю, что о́н бу́дет о́чень **удивлён** те́м, что услы́шит.
3. Аме́рика была́ **откры́та** Колу́мбом.
4. Э́тот писа́тель тепе́рь все́ми **забы́т**.
5. Э́та телегра́мма была́ **полу́чена** в два́ часа́.
6. На́ш до́м **окружён** поля́ми и леса́ми.

1. This letter was written by me in May.
2. I think that he will be very amazed by what he is going to hear.
3. America was discovered by Columbus.
4. That writer is now forgotten by everyone.
5. This telegram was received at two o'clock.
6. Our house is surrounded by fields and woods.

DRILL

Переведи́те на англи́йский.

1. Письмо́, **возвращённое** мне́ А́нной, лежи́т на полу́.
2. Почему́ э́то письмо́ бы́ло **возвращено́**?
3. Я́ не могу́ найти́ на ка́рте го́рода, **взя́того** враго́м.
4. Мо́жет быть вы́ по́мните, когда́ э́тот го́род бы́л **взя́т**?
5. Куда́ ты́ положи́ла проду́кты, **ку́пленные** на за́втра?
6. **Полу́ченные** вчера́ журна́лы лежа́т на сто́лике в кабине́те.
7. Ке́м была́ **ку́плена** карти́на, о кото́рой вы́ говори́ли?
8. Э́та карти́на была́ **ку́плена** одни́м музе́ем.
9. Э́тот до́м бы́л **постро́ен** в конце́ про́шлого ве́ка.
10. В нача́ле э́того ве́ка о́н бы́л **про́дан** бога́тому иностра́нцу.
11. На фотогра́фии де́душка и ба́бушка, **окру-жённые** детьми́ и вну́ками.
12. Сто́л, **поста́вленный** посреди́ ко́мнаты, занима́ет сли́шком мно́го ме́ста.
13. Куда́ вы́ положи́ли **прочи́танные** газе́ты?
14. Я́ уви́дел на дива́не кни́гу, **забы́тую** Ива́ном.
15. Всё э́то бы́ло **сде́лано** мои́м отцо́м.
16. Я́ никогда́ не забу́ду сло́в, **ска́занных** ва́ми.
17. Она́ бои́тся, что её сы́н бу́дет **уби́т** на фро́нте.
18. Кто́ ко́нчит **на́чатую** ва́ми рабо́ту?
19. Э́та кни́га была́ **напи́сана** и́м до войны́.
20. Ста́рое зда́ние Моско́вского университе́та бы́ло **постро́ено** в 1755 г.

(5) *Passive adjectival participles*, *present*. Present tense passive participles are less common than the past tense forms discussed in the preceding paragraph; only a limited number of verbs, all transitive, produce this type of participle. While most *past* passive participles are formed from perfective verbs, all *present* passive participles are formed from *imperfective* verbs. Their use emphasizes that an action continues to be performed over a period of time. They are derived from present tense stems and have a vowel plus the element **-м-** (**-ем-** with most verbs of the first conjugation, **-им-** for those of the second conjugation).

Note: Examples of passive, present tense, participial constructions:

Я́ не чита́л кни́ги, **критику́емой** а́втором э́той статьи́ (кото́рую критику́ет а́втор . . .).

I have not read the book criticized (under criticism) by the author of this article.

Пра́вила, **изуча́емые** на́ми, ча́сто ка́жутся мне́ тру́дными (кото́рые мы́ изуча́ем . . .).
The rules studied by us (which we are studying) often seem difficult to me.

More common than the pattern illustrated above is the adjectival use of present passive participles with no agent in the instrumental case. Compare the passive construction with a passive participle and the agent in the instrumental:

Во́т после́дний рома́н **люби́мого мно́й** писа́теля.
   (*literally*, of the loved [or preferred] by me writer.)

with the more idiomatic construction in which the passive participle is used simply as a modifier:

Во́т после́дний рома́н **моего́ люби́мого** писа́теля.
   (*literally*, of my favorite [or preferred] writer.)

The following are among the more common present passive participles, used mostly as adjectives:

ви́деть	ви́димый	seen, visible, apparent
ви́деть	неви́димый	invisible
забыва́ть	незабыва́емый	unforgettable
называ́ть	называ́емый	called; так называ́емый, so-called; *abbrev.*, т. н.
уважа́ть	уважа́емый	respected, esteemed; уважа́емый, многоуважа́емый (much respected) or глубокоуважа́емый (deeply respected), followed by a name or title, is the standard official form of address in Russian—used in letters, in addressing a meeting, etc.
обходи́ть	необходи́мый	indispensable (from обходи́ть, to by-pass, get around)
обвиня́ть	обвиня́емый	(the) accused (the defendant in a criminal trial; used as a noun)

The present passive participle is also used in the predicative short form:

Его́ оте́ц бы́л все́ми **люби́м** и **уважа́ем**.
His father was loved and respected by everyone.

B. Adverbial participles. In a sentence with one subject and two predicate verbs, one of these verbs may usually be replaced by an adverbial participle derived from it. Thus, in О́н **сиде́л** у окна́ и **чита́л** (He *sat* by the window and *read*), either verb may be replaced by an adverbial participle (**сиде́л** by **си́дя**, or **чита́л** by **чита́я**), producing the two variants:

О́н сиде́л у окна́ **чита́я** газе́ту.
He sat by the window (*while*) *reading* the newspaper.

О́н чита́л газе́ту **си́дя** у окна́.
He read the newspaper (*while*) *sitting* by the window.

In the first variant above, the action expressed by the verb **сиде́л** is given more prominence than the other action of the original sentence; the latter is now referred to by an adverbial participle, **чита́я**, which is a modifier describing the circumstances in which the action «сиде́л» is performed. The reverse is true of the second variant, where **си́дя** is an adverbial modifier of the predicate **чита́л**.

Adverbial participles are said to be *past* when they refer to actions performed prior to the action of the predicate verb, and *present* when their action is in progress at the time of the action of the predicate verb.

(1) *Past adverbial participles.* The words in boldface in the sentences below are *past* adverbial participles; each example is followed by the infinitive of the verb which appears here as an adverbial participle:

Прочита́в кни́гу, я́ верну́л её в библиоте́ку. (прочита́ть)
Having read the book, I returned it to the library.

Верну́в кни́гу, я́ пошёл в рестора́н. (верну́ть)
Having returned the book, I went to a restaurant.

Написа́в письмо́, я́ отнёс его́ на по́чту. (написа́ть)
Having written the letter, I took it to the post office.

Купи́в всё, что е́й бы́ло ну́жно, она́ пошла́ домо́й. (купи́ть)
Having bought all she needed, she went home.

Узна́в в како́й гости́нице о́н останови́лся, я́ посла́л ему́ телегра́мму. (узна́ть)
Having found out in what hotel he was staying, I sent him a wire.

Посла́в телегра́мму, я́ лёг спа́ть. (посла́ть)
Having sent the wire, I went to bed.

Прие́хав в Москву́, я́ пошёл осма́тривать Кре́мль. (прие́хать)
Arriving (having arrived) in Moscow, I went to visit the Kremlin.

О́н ушёл, никому́ не **сказа́в** куда́ о́н идёт. (сказа́ть)
He left without telling (having told) anyone where he was going.

Не **получи́в** отве́та на моё письмо́, я́ написа́л ему́ опя́ть. (получи́ть)
Receiving no reply to my letter, I wrote to him again.

Formation. Past adverbial participles are derived from the past tense stem and take the suffix **-в**: написа́(л)—написа́в; прочита́(л)—прочита́в; купи́(л)—купи́в; узна́(л)—узна́в; получи́(л)—получи́в. (A less commonly used variant is formed with **-вши**: написа́в—написа́вши; прочита́в—прочита́вши; прие́хав—прие́хавши.)

Past adverbial participles (referring to an action terminated before that of the predicate verb) are, as a general rule, derived from perfective verbs.

The use of a past adverbial participle instead of a verb for an action performed prior to the action of the predicate is a means of indicating that some connection is felt to exist between the two actions, the one referred to by the past adverbial participle being regarded as the circumstance that has caused, or made possible, necessary, desirable, etc., the action expressed by the predicate verb.

DRILL

Replace the verbs in boldface by past adverbial participles and rework the sentence according to the example.

Model: Óн **написа́л** сво́й пе́рвый рома́н и сра́зу ста́л знамени́тым.
Написа́в сво́й пе́рвый рома́н, о́н сра́зу ста́л знамени́тым.

1. Óн **про́жил** не́сколько ле́т в Москве́ и тепе́рь хорошо́ говори́т по-ру́сски.
2. Óн **получи́л** телегра́мму из Чика́го и сейча́с же туда́ вы́ехал.
3. Óн **вы́пил** дово́льно мно́го во́дки и на́чал гро́мко и ве́село пе́ть.
4. Я́ **поза́втракал** и пошёл погуля́ть.
5. Мы́ **пообе́дали** в рестора́не и пошли́ в кино́.
6. Мы́ **ко́нчили** рабо́тать и на́чали чита́ть газе́ту.
7. Я́ **написа́ла** письмо́ и позвони́ла Óльге.
8. Я́ **прочита́л** газе́ту и да́л её Áнне.
9. Óн **спроси́л** меня́, гото́в ли обе́д, и пошёл в столо́вую.
10. Она́ **начала́** говори́ть и не могла́ останови́ться.
11. Я́ **отве́тил** на её вопро́с и вы́шел из ко́мнаты.
12. Зи́на **откры́ла** окно́ и легла́ на дива́н.

(2) *Present adverbial participles.* The words in boldface in the sentences below are present adverbial participles:

Ду́мая о де́тстве, я́ всегда́ вспомина́ю ба́бушку.
Thinking about my childhood, I always remember my grandmother.

Вспомина́я ба́бушку, я́ иногда́ пла́чу.
(When) remembering my grandmother, I sometimes cry.

Óн лю́бит чита́ть газе́ту, **лёжа** на дива́не.
He likes to read the paper lying on the sofa.

Чита́я газе́ту, о́н лю́бит кури́ть.
(When) reading the paper, he likes to smoke.

Говоря́ со мно́й, о́н всё вре́мя смотре́л на часы́.
(While) talking with me, he constantly looked at his watch.

Не **получа́я** отве́та на на́ши пи́сьма, мы́ посла́ли телегра́мму.
Not receiving any answer to our letters, we sent a telegram.

Посыла́я телегра́мму, мы́ не спроси́ли когда́ она́ придёт.
When sending the telegram, we didn't ask when it would arrive.

Не **зна́я** его́ а́дреса, я́ не мо́г посла́ть ему́ кни́гу.
I couldn't send him the book without knowing his address.

Отвеча́я на вопро́с учи́теля, учени́к сде́лал две́ оши́бки.
In answering the teacher's question, the pupil made two mistakes.

Де́лая оши́бки, о́н всегда́ красне́ет.
When making mistakes, he always blushes.

У на́с бы́ло мно́го вре́мени, и мы́ шли́ не **спеша́**.
We had a great deal of time and we walked along without hurrying.

Живя́ так далеко́, я́ ре́дко ви́жу мои́х роди́телей.
Living so far away, I seldom see my parents.

Negative adverbial participles in Russian often correspond to the English use of *without* and the verbal noun in *-ing*, e.g.:

Óн отвéтил **не дýмая**.
He answered without thinking.

Не говоря́ ни слóва, óн вы́шел из кóмнаты.
Without saying a word he left the room.

Не зна́я чтó сказа́ть, она́ спроси́ла, хóчет ли óн ещё ча́ю.
Not knowing what to say, she asked if he wanted some more tea.

Adverbial participles past and present may be used in constructions in which the main action is expressed by a verb in the infinitive; constructions of this type are impersonal:

Нельзя́ **переходи́ть** у́лицу, **чита́я** газéту. (Compare: Óн переходи́л у́лицу, **чита́я** газéту.)
One must not (ought not to) cross a street reading a newspaper.

Лéтом прия́тно **чита́ть, лёжа** на травé.
In the summer it is pleasant to read lying on the grass.

Кóнчив чита́ть кни́гу, на́до сейча́с же **верну́ть** её в библиотéку.
Having finished reading a book, one should at once return it to the library.

Formation. Present adverbial participles are formed from the present stem of the verb (third person plural, less **-ут/-ют** or **-ат/-ят**), to which is added the ending **-я** (**-а** after **ж, ч, ш, щ**):

начина́(ют)	начина́я	нес(у́т)	неся́
чита́(ют)	чита́я	ид(у́т)	идя́
говор(я́т)	говоря́	леж(а́т)	лёжа
кýр(ят)	куря́	спеш(а́т)	спеша́

A number of perfective verbs (in particular the prefixed perfective forms of идти́, нести́, везти́) usually form their *past* adverbial participle on the pattern of the present adverbial participle, that is, not the past tense stem with the element **-в-**, but the present-future stem with **-я** (or **-а**):

Past adv. participle (*from perf.*)

уйти́: уйд(у́т)—**уйдя́** (having left)
принести́: принес(у́т)—**принеся́** (having brought)
отвезти́: отвез(у́т)—**отвезя́** (having driven to)

Pres. adv. participle (*from imperf.*)

уходи́ть: ухóд(ят)—**уходя́** (leaving)
приноси́ть: проинóс(ят)—**принося́** (bringing)
отвози́ть: отвóз(ят)—**отвозя́** (driving to)

DRILLS

A. *Replace the clauses with* **когда́** *by present or past adverbial participles and rework the sentence according to the examples.*

Model: **Когда́** де́душка **говори́л** с врачо́м, о́н забы́л рассказа́ть ему́ о са́мом гла́вном.

Говоря́ с врачо́м, де́душка забы́л рассказа́ть ему́ о са́мом гла́вном.

1. **Когда́** о́н **жи́л** в Я́лте, о́н ча́сто е́здил в Севасто́поль.
2. **Когда́** она́ **говори́т** по телефо́ну, она́ всегда́ ку́рит.
3. **Когда́** я́ **приезжа́ю** в Нью-Йо́рк, я́ сейча́с же звоню́ ма́тери.
4. **Когда́** А́нна **расска́зывает** о свои́х де́тях, она́ всегда́ смеётся.
5. **Когда́** Алёша **слу́шает** му́зыку, о́н отдыха́ет.
6. **Когда́** о́н **отдыха́ет**, о́н слушает му́зыку.
7. **Когда́** она́ **ду́мает** о сы́не, она́ ча́сто пла́чет.
8. **Когда́** о́н **рабо́тает**, о́н никогда́ не шу́тит.
9. **Когда́** она́ **сняла́** пальто́, она́ вошла́ в гости́ную.
10. **Когда́** о́н **уходи́л**, о́н сказа́л, что ско́ро вернётся.

B. *Replace the first verb with a present or past adverbial participle, according to the model.*

Model: Ива́н **шёл** по у́лице и пе́л.

Идя́ по у́лице, Ива́н пе́л.

1. Она́ **сиде́ла** в кре́сле и говори́ла по телефо́ну.
2. О́льга **чита́ла** кни́гу и кури́ла.
3. О́н **прочита́л** кни́гу и да́л её мне́.
4. О́н **расска́зывал** о свое́й жи́зни в Сиби́ри и кури́л папиро́су за папиро́сой.
5. О́н **рассказа́л** всё и ушёл.
6. Она́ **снима́ла** пальто́ и разгова́ривала с Зо́ей.
7. Она́ **говори́ла** с Бори́сом и ве́село смея́лась.
8. О́н **сказа́л**, что ему́ ску́чно, и ушёл.
9. Она́ **поспала́** и начала́ рабо́тать.
10. Она́ **игра́ла** на роя́ле и пе́ла.

C. *Переведи́те на ру́сский.*

1. Speaking with me, she was looking at my husband.
2. Having said a few words, she left the room.
3. Having read the letter, he put it on the desk.
4. (While) reading the letter, he laughed.
5. Lying on the divan, he was looking at the wall.
6. While living with his family, he never worked.
7. He said it without thinking.
8. He was walking along the street, not seeing anyone.
9. Not knowing what to do, she stood near the door.
10. Having finished our work, we went home.

C. Participles from verbs in -ся. Active adjectival and adverbial participles, past and present, may be formed from verbs in **-ся**.

Adjectival participles from verbs in **-ся** preserve **-ся** in all forms (it is *not* contracted to **-сь** even after vowels). In the case of adverbial participles the ending always appears as **-сь**.

Past adverbial participles of **-ся** verbs are formed with **-вши-** (see page 457), to which **-сь** is added.

To take an example, the verb **смея́ться** (perfective, засмея́ться *to burst out laughing*) gives the following participial forms:

Act. adj., past imperf. masc. смея́вш.ийся
Act. adj., past perf. masc. засмея́вш.ийся ⎰ (*neut.* -ееся; *fem.* -аяся; *pl.* -иеся)

Act. adj., pres.	смеющ.ийся—(*neut.* -ееся; *fem.* -аяся; *pl.* -иеся)
Adverbial, past perf.	засмеявшись
Adverbial, pres.	смеясь

(1) *Active adjectival participles, present*

На фотогра́фии бы́ло молодо́е, краси́вое, **смею́щееся** лицо́.
In the photograph was a young, handsome, laughing face.

Её ма́ленький сы́н подошёл на у́лице к незнако́мому **смею́щемуся** челове́ку и спроси́л его́, почему́ о́н смеётся.
Her little son went up on the street to a stranger who was (= is) laughing and asked him why he was laughing.

(2) *Adverbial participles, past*

Засмея́вшись, ма́ть попроси́ла меня́ продолжа́ть расска́з.
Laughing (having broken out laughing), Mother asked me to continue the story.

Бы́стро **оде́вшись**, она́ пошла́ открыва́ть две́рь.
Having dressed quickly, she went to open the door.

(3) *Adverbial participles, present*

Смея́сь, Ни́на рассказа́ла мне́ о то́м, что случи́лось вчера́.
Laughing, Nina told me about what happened yesterday.

Умыва́ясь и **одева́ясь,** Ко́ля ве́село пе́л.
Kolya was cheerfully singing while washing and dressing.

Verbs in **-ся** may correspond to English passives when the verb without **-ся** is transitive, e.g.:

Зде́сь **стро́ится** мно́го домо́в.
Many homes are being built here.

Э́то зда́ние **стро́илось** два́ го́да.
This building was under construction for two years.

Что́ **продаётся** в э́том магази́не?
What is sold in this store?

Ско́лько кни́г в го́д **пи́шется** в э́той стране́?
How many books a year are written in this country?

Such verbs may form active participles corresponding in meaning to English passives:

О́н подошёл к **стро́ящемуся** до́му.
He approached the building which was being constructed.

Мы́ ви́дели дово́льно большо́й до́м, **продаю́щийся** о́чень дёшево.
We saw a fairly large house which was being sold at a very cheap price.

DRILLS

A. *Translate.*

Надéжда Вѝкторовна зáмужем за архитéктором Ковалéвским. Гóрод, в котóром онѝ живýт, бы́л совершéнно разрýшен во врéмя войны́. Тепéрь тáм стрóится мнóго домóв, шкóл, открывáется мнóго рáзных магазѝнов, и т. д. Мнóго здáний ужé пострóены, и стрóится ещё мнóго нóвых.

Сыновья́ Ковалéвских, Андрéй и Борѝс, бы́ли с родѝтелями, когдá врáг окружѝл гóрод. Гóрод бы́л окружён со всéх сторóн. Трýдно себé предстáвить, кáк жѝли лю́ди, окружённые врагáми!

Во врéмя защѝты гóрода, стáрший сы́н Ковалéвских, Андрéй, бы́л убѝт, а млáдший, Борѝс, бы́л тяжелó рáнен. Портрéт убѝтого сы́на висѝт над дивáном в кабинéте отцá.

B. *Translate. Identify the participles in boldface as adjectival or adverbial, active or passive, present or past.*

1. Старýха, **снимáющая** пальтó в передней—бáбушка хозя́йки.
2. **Снимáя** пальтó, онá вéсело разговáривала с внýчкой.
3. **Сня́в** пальтó, онá пошлá в гостѝную.
4. **Входя́** в гостѝную, онá замéтила своегó внýка, **стоя́щего** óколо красѝвой молодóй блондѝнки, **сидя́щей** на дивáне.
5. **Войдя́**, бáбушка срáзу подошлá к нѝм, и, не **говоря́** ни слóва, сéла в крéсло **стоя́вшее** ря́дом с дивáном.
6. Мы́ осмотрéли нóвый музéй, **пострóенный** знаменѝтым архитéктором.
7. Э́тот музéй бы́л **пострóен** в прóшлом годý.
8. **Убѝтая** собáка лежáла на дорóге. Никтó не знáет, кéм онá былá **убѝта**.
9. Вóт телегрáмма, тóлько что **полýченная** мнóй из Бакý.
10. Телегрáмма былá **полýчена** в двá часá.
11. Лю́ди, **получáющие** мнóго пѝсем, не всегдá на нѝх отвечáют.
12. **Отвечáя**, я́ всегдá благодарю́ за **полýченное** мнóй письмó.

C. *Translate and form participles with the words in italics.*

1. I know your cousin Anna *who lives* in Odessa.
2. *Living* there, I used to meet her and your cousin Paul quite often.
3. *Not speaking* Italian, I couldn't explain to him the mistakes *made* by him in his speech.
4. *Knowing* that he would come at half-past five, I placed the *signed* papers on the desk.
5. The director *who signed* them left the room *without saying* a word.
6. I saw a woman *who was smoking* a pipe.
7. *Smoking, crying, and talking*, she walked about the room.
8. Do you know that the man *who lives* downstairs is my cousin?
9. *Having taken* all our money, he went abroad.
10. *Having heard* the terrible news, her grandson and her granddaughter returned all the presents *received* from her.
11. I must finish the article *begun* last week.
12. He is a *forgotten* man.
13. Why does the woman *who is speaking* with your grandson shout so?

14. The house *which is being built* (use **-ся** form of verb) on the corner will obstruct (закроет) the view of (to) the river.
15. Tomorrow I will return the money *taken* by my cousin from (at) the bank.
16. The umbrella *found* by me is standing in the corner.

2. Russian equivalents for English words ending in -ever

The particle **ни** is used in Russian where English adds *-ever* to pronouns and adverbs:

> **Кого́** о́н **ни** проси́л о по́мощи, никто́ не хо́тел ему́ помо́чь.
> Whomever he asked (no matter whom he asked) for help, no one wanted to help him.

> **Что́ я́ ни** говорю́, о́н говори́т обра́тное.
> Whatever I say (no matter what I say), he says the contrary.

The hypothetical mood (past tense form + **бы**) is common in this construction:

> **Где́ бы** о́н **ни** жи́л, о́н всегда́ бы́л сча́стлив.
> Wherever he lived (no matter where he lived), he was always happy.

> **Где́ бы я́ ни** был, я всегда́ по́мню мои́х друзе́й.
> No matter where *I am*, I always remember my friends.

> **С ке́м бы** о́н **ни** говори́л, о́н всем расска́зывал о своём сы́не.
> Whomever he talked to, he talked about his son.

Что́ бы—*whatever*, is written as two words to distinguish it from **чтобы**—*in order*:

> **Что́ бы** я́ ни говори́л, о́н говори́т, что я́ не пра́в.
> Whatever I say, he says that I am wrong.

DRILL

Переведи́те на англи́йский.

1. Где́ я́ ни спра́шивал, нигде́ не́ было э́той кни́ги.
2. Что́ она́ ни де́лает, её му́жу э́то не нра́вится.
3. Что́ бы она́ ни де́лала, она́ всё де́лает хорошо́.
4. Кому́ бы я́ об э́том ни расска́зывал, мне́ никто́ не ве́рит.
5. О ко́м бы о́н ни говори́л, о́н всех называ́ет дурака́ми.
6. Куда́ бы они́ ни приезжа́ли, они́ везде́ встреча́ли э́того челове́ка.
7. Кого́ бы я́ ни спра́шивал об Ива́не, никто́ ничего́ о нём не зна́ет.
8. Когда́ бы я́ её ни ви́дел, она́ всегда́ куда́-то спеши́т.
9. Что́ бы я́ ни купи́ла сестре́, ей никогда́ ничего́ не нра́вится.

3. Conjunctions of time in subordinate clauses

The Russian words **до**, **перед**, and **по́сле** are prepositions. They may be used as conjunctions only by inserting the connective phrase **то́, как**, with **то** in the case governed by the preposition employed. These combinations are usually followed by an infinitive when one subject only is given. When there are two distinct subjects, they introduce a subordinate clause with a conjugated verb in the required tense.

До того́, как приня́ть реше́ние, я́ до́лжен посове́товаться с отцо́м.
Before making a decision, *I* must consult with Father (one subject).

Перед те́м, как уйти́, мне́ ну́жно бу́дет позвони́ть в конто́ру.
Before leaving *I* must call the office (one subject).

Я́ до́лжен с ва́ми поговори́ть **до того́, как** о́н придёт.
I must speak to you before *he* comes (will come) (two subjects).

По́сле того́, как о́н верну́лся из-за грани́цы, мы́ ни ра́зу у него́ не́ были.
Since *he* has come back from abroad, *we* haven't been to see him once (two
subjects).

Verbal nouns are sometimes used in place of such clauses:

Перед свои́м **отъе́здом** о́н зашёл к ма́тери прости́ться.
Before his departure (before he left) he went to see his mother to say good-bye.

По́сле ва́шего **прихо́да** Андре́й не сказа́л ни сло́ва.
Since your arrival (since you came) Andrey hasn't said a word.

4. Negative pronouns and adverbs with the element не-

Negative constructions with the dative and infinitive are formed from the pronouns
кто and **что** (gen. **кого́** and **чего́**) and the adverbs **когда́**, **где́**, and **куда́**, by prefixing
the negative particle **не-**, e.g.: **не́чего** *there is nothing*, **не́кого** *there is no one*, **не́когда**
there is no time, etc.

Мне́ **не́чего** де́лать.	I have nothing to do.
Мне́ **негде́** рабо́тать.	I have nowhere to work.
Мне́ **не́когда** ему́ помога́ть.	I have no time to help him.

In impersonal uses the dative may be omitted:

Не́чего де́лать!
There is nothing to be done!

В э́том го́роде **не́куда** ходи́ть.
There's nowhere to go in this town.

Не́чего and **не́кого** lack nominatives but have all other cases. Prepositions are
written between **не-** and the pronoun element:

Мне́ **не́кому** расска́зывать про своё го́ре.
I have no one to tell about my sorrow.

Ей **не́ с кем** говори́ть.
She has no one to talk to.

Care must be taken to distinguish the series of negatives with **не-** from the general
negatives with **ни-**: **ничего́**, **никого́**, **нигде́**, etc. In particular, the series formed with
не- *never* requires a second negative, required for the series with **ни-** when used with
verbs, e.g.,

Э́тому ребёнку **не́чего** е́сть.
This child has nothing to eat.

But: Э́тот ребёнок **ничего́ не** е́ст.
This child doesn't eat anything.

Мне́ **не́кому** пока́зывать, что́ я́ пишу́.
I have no one to show what I write.

But: Я́ **никому́ не** пока́зываю, что́ я́ пишу́.
I show what I write to no one.

Переведи́те на англи́йский.

Перед те́м, как нача́ть говори́ть, докла́дчик посмотре́л на челове́ка, **стоя́вшего** спра́ва от него́, пото́м спроси́л о чём-то **стоя́вшую** сле́ва от него́ и **кури́вшую** де́вушку, и на́чал говори́ть. Я́ смотре́л на **говори́вшего** челове́ка, слу́шал его́, и мне́ вдру́г ста́ло так ску́чно, что я́ реши́л уйти́. **Перед те́м, как** уйти́, я́ сказа́л **сиде́вшему** у вы́хода господи́ну, что я́ верну́сь то́лько **по́сле того́, как говоря́щий** сейча́с дура́к переста́нет говори́ть. **Говоря́** э́то, я́ вы́шел, **не заме́тив**, что о́коло **сиде́вшего** у вы́хода челове́ка сиде́ла жена́ **говори́вшего** и слы́шала, что я́ назва́л её му́жа дурако́м. Пото́м мне́ расска́зывали, что **услы́шав** мои́ слова́, она́ **смея́сь** сказа́ла **стоя́вшей** о́коло неё молодо́й же́нщине, что ей всё равно́, ка́к я́ называ́ю её му́жа: та́к как, **бу́дучи** его́ ста́рым полити́ческим враго́м и **ви́дя**, како́й успе́х име́ла его́ ре́чь, я́ ничего́ друго́го не мо́г сде́лать, как уйти́, и что **называ́я** её му́жа дурако́м, я́ то́лько дока́зываю, что я́ са́м не осо́бенно умён. Я́ узна́л обо всём э́том из письма́, **полу́ченного** мно́й вчера́, и **напи́санного** одни́м мои́м дру́гом, то́же **бы́вшим** на собра́нии. Э́то письмо́ **бы́ло напи́сано** сра́зу **по́сле того́, как** собра́ние ко́нчилось. **До того́, как** я́ получи́л э́то письмо́, я́ не зна́л, что́ произошло́ по́сле моего́ ухо́да. «Дру́г», **написа́вший** э́то письмо́, ду́мал, что **чита́я** письмо́, мне́ бу́дет неприя́тно узна́ть обо всём э́том, но **прочита́в** о слу-**чи́вшемся**, я́ сейча́с же обо всём забы́л.

Reading

Письмо́: Ча́сть втора́я

Получи́в твой а́дрес, я́ неме́дленно се́л за письмо́ да́же не спроси́в себя́, о чём я́ бу́ду писа́ть, и реши́л писа́ть всё, что придёт в го́лову.

Стра́шно поду́мать, ско́лько ле́т мы́ с тобо́й не ви́делись! Мы́ ви́делись в после́дний ра́з в 1939 году́: ты́, я́, и ещё не́сколько бы́вших шко́льных това́рищей собрали́сь у Васи́лия Кузнецо́ва. По́мнишь? Э́то бы́ло в Москве́, 3-го ию́ня 1939 го́да. Ви́дишь, я́ да́же то́чно по́мню число́ и ме́сто так я́сно, как бу́дто э́то бы́ло вчера́!

А ка́к лети́т вре́мя! С тех по́р прошло́ уже́ сто́лько ле́т! Как бы́стро пролете́ли э́ти го́ды! Мы́ с тобо́й ско́ро бу́дем старика́ми... Но́ не́чего жа́ловаться.

А ка́к мы́ ещё бы́ли мо́лоды в 1939 году́! Мы́ о́ба ещё учи́лись в ву́зе: я́ учи́лся на медици́нском факульте́те, а ты́ поступи́л в педагоги́ческий институ́т. Ты́ с ра́нних лет мечта́л стать преподава́телем. Я по́мню, что тебя́ гла́вным о́бразом интересова́ло преподава́ние иностра́нных языко́в. Ты всегда́ говори́л о том, как зна́ние языко́в ва́жно и поле́зно в на́ше вре́мя. Мне по́мнится,[1] что в институ́те ты гла́вным о́бразом занима́лся англи́йским языко́м. Научи́лся ли ты свобо́дно говори́ть на э́том языке́? Тепе́рь э́то бы́ло бы так поле́зно! Я слы́шал, что есть большо́й спрос на люде́й, зна́ющих англи́йский. Зна́я англи́йский, мо́жно быть не то́лько поле́зным, но мо́жно та́кже и хорошо́ зараба́тывать.

Челове́к, да́вший мне твой а́дрес и живу́щий в той же гости́нице, что мы, тебя́ ли́чно не зна́ет. Он говори́т, что слы́шал от како́го-то твоего́ ро́дственника, что ты служи́л одно́ вре́мя перево́дчиком в Интури́сте.[2] Пра́вда ли э́то? Ещё кто́-то говори́л, что ты перевёл с англи́йского како́й-то совреме́нный рома́н, кото́рый бу́дто бы име́л здесь огро́мный успе́х.

Но э́то всё слу́хи, и я о́чень хочу́ поскоре́й услы́шать обо всём от тебя́ самого́.

Но вернёмся к на́шему после́днему свида́нию.

Собра́вшись в ма́ленькой ко́мнатке[3] у Кузнецо́ва, жи́вшего у каки́х-то свои́х ро́дственников на ве́рхнем этаже́ ста́рого четырёхэта́жного (four-story) до́ма, си́дя на крова́ти и́ли на полу́, окружённые облака́ми таба́чного ды́ма, мы е́ли хлеб с колбасо́й, пи́ли пи́во, и говори́ли и говори́ли... Смея́сь, спо́ря и куря́, мы мечта́ли о бу́дущем и стро́или грандио́зные пла́ны.

Мы с тобо́й мечта́ли о том, что, око́нчив уче́ние и до того́, как нача́ть серьёзно рабо́тать по специа́льности, мы вме́сте пое́дем путеше́ствовать по на́шей ро́дине. Что́бы лу́чше познако́миться с ней и с жи́знью наро́да, мы собира́лись порабо́тать не́которое вре́мя в колхо́зах и на произво́дстве. Мы счита́ли, что, сде́лав э́то, мы смо́жем в бу́дущем принести́ стране́ бо́льше по́льзы.

Мы та́кже хоте́ли вме́сте посети́ть наш родно́й го́род, где мы о́ба роди́лись, где провели́ де́тство. По́мнишь, как детьми́[4] мы бе́гали по поля́м и леса́м с сосе́дними ма́льчиками, как мы лови́ли птиц и игра́ли в войну́? По́мнишь, как мы возвраща́лись домо́й голо́дные, гря́зные, но счастли́вые? На́ши ма́тери не всегда́ встреча́ли нас с улы́бкой; вме́сто улы́бки и поцелу́я нас ча́сто жда́ло наказа́ние. Но на сле́дующий день, несмотря́ на наказа́ние—всё опя́ть начина́лось снача́ла.

В день на́шей после́дней встре́чи никто́ из нас не мог ни предви́деть, ни предсказа́ть, что ро́вно через три ме́сяца произойдёт мирова́я катастро́фа—начнётся война́ со все́ми её у́жасами, кото́рых никто́ тогда́ не мог да́же себе́ предста́вить. Война́ положи́ла коне́ц на́шим мечта́м.

Но зна́ешь, где бы я ни был, что бы со мной ни случа́лось, я всегда́ вспомина́л тебя́, на́ше де́тство, и гла́вным о́бразом шко́лу, учителе́й и шко́льных това́рищей.

Я вспомина́л об э́том да́же на фро́нте, где я провёл бо́льше трёх лет, с 1941-го до 1944-го го́да; да́же в са́мые стра́шные дни, когда́ на́ша ро́дина была́ в серьёзной опа́сности, когда́ враг иногда́ окружа́л нас со всех сторо́н.

Во вре́мя защи́ты Сталингра́да, я был серьёзно ра́нен и пролежа́л в го́спитале до середи́ны 1945-го го́да. Когда́ я ещё лежа́л в го́спитале, я получи́л изве́стие,

---

[1] I seem to remember.

[2] **Служи́ть**, **рабо́тать**, etc., take the instrumental in the sense of *to serve as*, *to work as*. **Интури́ст**, Intourist, the Soviet travel agency (from иностра́нный тури́ст).

[3] Diminutive of **ко́мната**.

[4] **Детьми́** *as children*.

что мо́й оте́ц бы́л уби́т на за́падном фро́нте, что ма́ма умерла́ в Ленингра́де во вре́мя блока́ды.

Во все́ го́ды войны́ и по́сле её оконча́ния, я не мо́г найти́ тебя́. Но тепе́рь, когда́ я наконе́ц тебя́ нашёл, мне́ захоте́лось поговори́ть с тобо́й о про́шлом, да́же до того́, как я тебя́ уви́жу. Ты́ ведь еди́нственный челове́к, с кото́рым я могу́ об э́том поговори́ть. Но́ мне́ давно́ пора́ останови́ться. Отве́ть поскоре́е и приезжа́й!

Тво́й дру́г,
Матве́й Желя́бин.

Чита́йте э́ти вопро́сы и отвеча́йте на ни́х.

1. Бы́л ли у Матве́я гото́вый пла́н в голове́, когда́ о́н се́л за письмо́? 2. Почему́ о́н пи́шет, что они́ о́ба ско́ро бу́дут старика́ми? 3. Почему́ сове́тскому гражда́нину поле́зно зна́ть англи́йский язы́к? 4. Почему́ Матве́й почти́ ничего́ не зна́ет о своём дру́ге? 5. Почему́ они́ собира́лись рабо́тать в колхо́зах и на произво́дстве? 6. Како́й го́род они́ хоте́ли посети́ть? 7. Почему́, око́нчив заня́тия, они́ не смогли́ пое́хать путеше́ствовать, как они́ об э́том мечта́ли? 8. Собра́вшись у Кузнецо́ва, чего́ они́ не могли́ предви́деть? 9. Когда́ Матве́й бы́л ра́нен? 10. До́лго ли о́н пролежа́л в го́спитале? 11. О чём о́н про́сит своего́ дру́га в конце́ письма́?

Vocabulary

бу́дучи (*pres. adv. participle of* быть) being
бы́вший (*past adj. participle of* быть) former
ве́рхний top, upper
враг enemy
встре́ча meeting, encounter
вы́ход exit, way out
го́спиталь (*masc.*) (army) hospital
двою́родный бра́т cousin (male)
двою́родная сестра́ cousin (female)
де́тство childhood
докла́дч.ик (*fem.* -ица) lecturer, speaker
дым smoke
еди́нственный the only (one)
защи́та defense
зна́ние knowledge
ина́че otherwise, different(ly)
изве́стие (piece of) news, information
ли́чный personal
мечта́ (day)dream, reverie
мо́лодость (*fem.*) youth
наде́жда hope; наде́жда на (+ *acc.*) hope for
наказа́ние punishment
наро́д nation, people

необходи́мый essential, indispensable, necessary
о́блако (*gen. pl.* облако́в) cloud
оконча́ние termination, ending
опа́сность (*fem.*) danger
по́льза use, profit
поле́зный useful, profitable
посреди́ (+ *gen.*) in the middle of
произво́дство production
ра́нний early
ро́дина homeland, fatherland
родно́й native, own
ро́дственн.ик (*fem.* -ица) relative
свида́ние meeting, rendezvous
сле́дующий next, following
слух rumor; hearing
спасе́ние salvation
спрос demand; спро́с на (+ *acc.*) demand for
стра́шный terrible, frightening
улы́б.ка (*gen. pl.* -ок) smile
усло́вие condition
успе́х success
ухо́д departure (on foot)
шко́льный school (*adj.*)

VERBS

висе́ть (imperf., II: вишу́, виси́шь) to hang (*intrans.*)
дока́зывать (imperf., I), доказа́ть (perf., I: докажу́, дока́жешь) to prove[5]
зараба́тывать (imperf., I), зарабо́тать (perf., I) to earn
лови́ть (imperf., II: ловлю́, ло́вишь) to catch
мечта́ть (imperf., I) to (day)dream, muse
окружа́ть (imperf., I), окружи́ть (perf., II: окруж.у́, -и́шь) to surround
переноси́ть (imperf., II: переношу́, перено́сишь), перенести́ (perf., I: like нести́) to bear, endure
попутеше́ствовать (perf., I: попутеше́ству.ю, -ешь) to travel (a little, a while)
посеща́ть (imperf., I), посети́ть (perf., II: посещу́, посети́шь) to visit
почу́вствовать (perf. of чу́вствовать, I: почу́вству.ю, -ешь) to feel
предви́деть (imperf., II: предви́жу, предви́дишь) to foresee
предска́зывать (imperf., I), предсказа́ть (perf., I: предскажу́, предска́жешь) to foretell, predict
представля́ть (imperf., I), предста́вить (perf., II: предста́в.лю, -ишь) to present, represent; п. себе́
    to imagine, suppose
пролета́ть (imperf., I), пролете́ть (perf., II: проле.чу́, -ти́шь) to fly (past)
разруша́ть (imperf., I), разру́шить (perf., II: разру́ш.у, -ишь) to destroy
ра́нить (imperf. and perf., II: ра́н.ю, -ишь) to wound
стро́ить (imperf., II: стро́.ю, -ишь), постро́ить (perf., II) to build
убива́ть (imperf., I), уби́ть (perf., I: убью́, убьёшь) to kill
уважа́ть (imperf., I) to respect
целова́ть (imperf., I: целу́.ю, -ешь), поцелова́ть (perf., I) to kiss

EXPRESSIONS

со всех сторо́н from all sides
се́сть за письмо́ to sit down to write a letter
та́к же . . . как (just) as . . . as
как бу́дто (бы) as if
бу́дто бы seemingly
по специа́льности in one's field
несмотря́ на (+ *acc.*) in spite of
по-сво́ему in its (my, your, his) own way, in one's own way
Не́чего жа́ловаться. It's no use complaining.

---

[5] The imperfective often means only *try to prove*. This weakening of force is common with many imperfectives.

Appendix A—Declensions

The tables below present the basic declension patterns for nouns, pronouns, pronoun-adjectives, and adjectives. Numerals have in general not been included, since they are summarized in Unit 26; some supplementary numeral forms are given in Appendix E.

1. Nouns

A. Masculines.

	Sing.		*Pl.*	
	Hard	Soft	Hard	Soft
Nom.	стол	дождь	столы́[4]	дожди́[4]
Gen.	стола́[1]	дождя́[1]	столо́в[5]	дожде́й[5]
Dat.	столу́	дождю́	стола́м	дождя́м
Acc.	стол (anim. до́ктора)	дождь (anim. го́стя)	столы́ (anim. докторо́в)	дожди́ (anim. госте́й)
Instr.	столо́м[2]	дождём	стола́ми	дождя́ми
Loc.	столе́[3]	дожде́[3]	стола́х	дождя́х

---

[1] Genitive singular са́хару, шокола́ду, ча́ю, and some others in partitive sense.

[2] Instrumental singular has unstressed **-ем** instead of **-ом** after ж, ч, ц, ш, щ, e.g., ме́сяцем, това́рищем, etc.

[3] Locative singular в саду́, на берегу́, на мосту́, на полу́, в лесу́, в/на углу́, в году́, на краю́, and some others. Locative singular о ге́нии (see below).

[4] Masculine plural has **-и** instead of **-ы** after г, к, х, ж, ч, ш, щ, e.g., куски́, ножи́, etc. Many nouns end in **-а́/-я́** (stressed); леса́, дома́, города́, вечера́, берега́, голоса́, цвета́, адреса́, глаза́, поезда́, доктора́, профессора́, учителя́, etc. See Unit 13:4 page 200. Сосе́д (*neighbor*) is soft throughout the plural: сосе́ди, сосе́дей, etc. Note also the plural of чёрт (*devil*): че́рти, черте́й, etc.

[5] Genitive plural—see Units 16, page 234, and 20, page 319.

It will be recalled that many masculines ending in the nominative singular in **o** + consonant or **e** + consonant drop the **o** or **e** in other cases of the singular and plural (except accusative singular inanimate); this is particularly true of nouns ending in **-ок** and **-ец**, e.g., кусо́к, genitive куска́; оте́ц, genitive отца́, etc.

B. Masculine and neuter plurals in -ья. These are formed from a few masculine and neuter hard nouns: друг, муж, сын, стул, лист, перо́, брат, де́рево, etc.

	Pl.	*Pl.*
Nom.	друзья́	сту́лья
Gen.	друзе́й	сту́льев
Dat.	друзья́м	сту́льям
Acc.	друзе́й	сту́лья (anim. бра́тьев)
Instr.	друзья́ми	сту́льями
Loc.	друзья́х	сту́льях

Like друзья́ are declined мужья́ and сыновья́ (stress on ending and genitive in **-е́й**).

Like сту́лья are declined ли́стья, бра́тья, and дере́вья (stress on stem and genitive in **-ьев**).

C. Masculines in -анин/-янин. This type of declension is used for a few masculine animates, most of which denote nationality or place of origin (see page 322).

	Sing.	*Pl.*
Nom.	граждани́н	гра́ждане
Gen.	граждани́на	гра́ждан
Dat.	граждани́ну	гра́жданам
Acc.	граждани́на	гра́ждан
Instr.	граждани́ном	гра́жданами
Loc.	граждани́не	гра́жданах

D. Masculines in -ёнок, plural -я́та. Nouns in this class designate the young of animals.

	Sing.	*Pl.*
Nom.	котёнок (kitten)	котя́та
Gen.	котёнка	котя́т
Dat.	котёнку	котя́там
Acc.	котёнка	котя́т
Instr.	котёнком	котя́тами
Loc.	котёнке	котя́тах

To this group belongs **ребёнок** *child*. The plural **ребя́та** serves in colloquial speech in the meaning of *fellows, kids, guys,* while **де́ти** meaning *children* is the proper plural of **ребёнок**.

Plurals of **господи́н** *and* **хозя́ин**. The plurals of **господи́н** (*master, sir, Mr.*) and **хозя́ин** (*host, landlord, owner, proprietor*) are declined like the above group: nominative plural, господа́, хозя́ева; genitive plural, госпо́д, хозя́ев; dative plural, господа́м, хозя́евам, etc.

E. Neuters.

	Sing.		Pl.	
	Hard	Soft	Hard	Soft
Nom.	ме́сто	по́ле	места́[7]	поля́
Gen.	ме́ста	по́ля	мест[8]	поле́й[9]
Dat.	ме́сту	по́лю	места́м	поля́м
Acc.	ме́сто	по́ле	места́	поля́
Instr.	ме́стом	по́лем	места́ми	поля́ми
Loc.	ме́сте	по́ле[6]	места́х	поля́х

F. Neuters in -мя.

	Sing.	Pl.	Sing.	Pl.
Nom.	и́мя	имена́	вре́мя	времена́
Gen.	и́мени	имён	вре́мени	времён
Dat.	и́мени	имена́м	вре́мени	времена́м
Acc.	и́мя	имена́	вре́мя	времена́
Instr.	и́менем	имена́ми	вре́менем	времена́ми
Loc.	и́мени	имена́х	вре́мени	времена́х

G. Feminine I.

	Sing.		Pl.	
	Hard	Soft	Hard	Soft
Nom.	ко́мната	неде́ля	ко́мнаты[13]	неде́ли
Gen.	ко́мнаты[10]	неде́ли	ко́мнат[14]	неде́ль[14]
Dat.	ко́мнате	неде́ле[11]	ко́мнатам	неде́лям
Acc.	ко́мнату	неде́лю	ко́мнаты[13]	неде́ли
			(animate like gen.)	
Instr.	ко́мнатой (-ою)[12]	неде́лей (-ею)	ко́мнатами	неде́лями
Loc.	ко́мнате	неде́ле[11]	ко́мнатах	неде́лях

---

[6] Neuters ending in **-ие** have **-ии** in the locative singular, e.g., зда́нии, собра́нии, etc. (see below).

[7] Я́блоко (*apple*), плечо́ (*shoulder*), and коле́но (*knee*) end in **-и** in the plural. У́хо (*ear*) has the plural у́ши, уше́й, etc. Не́бо (*sky, heaven*) has the plural небеса́, небе́с, etc.

[8] Genitive plural may add fleeting **o** or **e**, e.g., о́кон, пи́сем. О́блако has облако́в.

[9] Neuters ending in **-ие** have **-ий** in the genitive plural: зда́ний, собра́ний, etc. The genitive plural of пла́тье is пла́тьев.

[10] Genitive singular has **-и** instead of **-ы** after г, к, х, ж, ч, ш, and щ, e.g., кни́ги, да́чи, etc.

[11] Feminines ending in **-ия** have **-ии** in dative and locative singular: Росси́и, фотогра́фии, etc. (see below).

[12] Instrumental singular has **-ей (-ею)** instead of unstressed **-ой (-ою)** after ж, ч, ц, ш, щ, e.g., да́чей, у́лицей, etc.

[13] Nominative plural has **-и** instead of **-ы** after г, к, х, ж, ч, ш, and щ, e.g., кни́ги, да́чи, etc.

[14] Genitive plural—see Units 16, page 235, and 20, page 319.

H. Feminine II. These include all feminines ending in **-ь** in the nominative singular.

	Sing.	*Pl.*
Nom.	дверь	две́ри
Gen.	две́ри	двере́й
Dat.	две́ри	дверя́м
Acc.	дверь	две́ри
Instr.	две́рью	дверя́ми[15]
Loc.	две́ри	дверя́х

Two Fem. II nouns ending in **-овь** drop **o** in all cases other than the nominative-accusative and instrumental singular, e.g., любо́вь (*love*), genitive любви́, but instrumental любо́вью; це́рковь (*church*), genitive це́ркви, but instrumental це́рковью.

I. Feminine nouns мать and дочь.

	Sing.	*Pl.*	*Sing.*	*Pl.*
Nom.	мать	ма́тери	дочь	до́чери
Gen.	ма́тери	матере́й	до́чери	дочере́й
Dat.	ма́тери	матеря́м	до́чери	дочеря́м
Acc.	мать	матере́й	дочь	дочере́й
Instr.	ма́терью	матеря́ми	до́черью	дочерьми́
Loc.	ма́тери	матеря́х	до́чери	дочеря́х

J. Masculines, neuters and feminines with stems ending in -ij.

Singular

	Masc.	*Neut.*	*Fem.*
Nom.	ге́ний	зда́ние	исто́рия
Gen.	ге́ния	зда́ния	исто́рии
Dat.	ге́нию	зда́нию	исто́рии
Acc.	ге́ния	зда́ние	исто́рию
Instr.	ге́нием	зда́нием	исто́рией
Loc.	ге́нии	зда́нии	исто́рии

Plural

	Masc.	*Neut.*	*Fem.*
Nom.	ге́нии	зда́ния	исто́рии
Gen.	ге́ниев	зда́ний	исто́рий
Dat.	ге́ниям	зда́ниям	исто́риям
Acc.	ге́ниев	зда́ния	исто́рии
Instr.	ге́ниями	зда́ниями	исто́риями
Loc.	ге́ниях	зда́ниях	исто́риях

---

[15] Instrumental plural of this noun has the alternate form дверьми́. Ло́шадь has only лошадьми́. Note also instrumental plural людьми́ from лю́ди (*people*) and детьми́ from де́ти (*children*); also дочерьми́ from дочь (*daughter*)—see the next table.

2. Pronouns

A. Personal pronouns.

		1st pers.	2nd pers.	Masc.	3rd pers. Neut.	Fem.
Sing.	Nom.	я	ты	он	онó	онá
	Gen.	меня	тебя	егó	егó	её
	Dat.	мне	тебé	емý	емý	ей
	Acc.	меня	тебя	егó	егó	её
	Instr.	мной (-óю)	тобóй (-óю)	им	им	ей (éю)
	Loc.	мне	тебé	нём	нём	ней
Pl.	Nom.	мы	вы		онú	
	Gen.	нас	вас		их	
	Dat.	нам	вам		им	
	Acc.	нас	вас		их	
	Instr.	нáми	вáми		úми	
	Loc.	нас	вас		них	

B. Reflexive pronoun себя *oneself*.

Gen.	себя
Dat.	себé
Acc.	себя
Instr.	собóй (-óю)
Loc.	себé

C. Reciprocal pronoun дрýг дрýга *each other*.

Gen.	дрýг дрýга
Dat.	дрýг дрýгу
Acc.	дрýг дрýга
Instr.	дрýг дрýгом
Loc.	дрýг (о) дрýге[16]

D. Interrogative pronouns.

Nom.	кто	что
Gen.	когó	чегó
Dat.	комý	чемý
Acc.	когó	что
Instr.	кем	чем
Loc.	ком	чём

---

[16] Other prepositions also come between the two words, é.g., дрýг **у** дрýга, дрýг **с** дрýгом, etc.

3. Pronoun-adjectives

A. Possessive мой.

	Masc.	Sing. Neut.	Fem.	Pl. All genders
Nom.	мой	моё	моя	мои
Gen.	моего́	Like masc.	моей	моих
Dat.	моему́	Like masc.	моей	моим
Acc.	мой (anim. моего́)	моё	мою	мои (anim. моих)
Instr.	моим	Like masc.	моей (-éю)	моими
Loc.	моём	Like masc.	моей	моих

Like **мой** are declined **твой** and **свой**.

B. Possessive наш.

	Masc.	Sing. Neut.	Fem.	Pl. All genders
Nom.	наш	на́ше	на́ша	на́ши
Gen.	на́шего	Like masc.	на́шей	на́ших
Dat.	на́шему	Like masc.	на́шей	на́шим
Acc.	наш (anim. на́шего)	на́ше	на́шу	на́ши (anim. на́ших)
Instr.	на́шим	Like masc.	на́шей (-ею)	на́шими
Loc.	на́шем	Like masc.	на́шей	на́ших

Like **наш** is declined **ваш**.

C. Demonstrative э́тот.

	Masc.	Sing. Neut.	Fem.	Pl. All genders
Nom.	э́тот	э́то	э́та	э́ти
Gen.	э́того	Like masc.	э́той	э́тих
Dat.	э́тому	Like masc.	э́той	э́тим
Acc.	э́тот (anim. э́того)	э́то	э́ту	э́ти (anim. э́тих)
Instr.	э́тим	Like masc.	э́той (-ою)	э́тими
Loc.	э́том	Like masc.	э́той	э́тих

Like **э́тот** are declined the numeral **оди́н, одно́, одна́** (stem **одн-**), and the intensive pronoun **сам, само́, сама́**. Besides the feminine singular accusative **саму́** the latter has a partly archaic form **самоё**.

D. Demonstrative тот.

	Masc.	Sing. Neut.	Fem.	Pl. All genders
Nom.	тот	то	та	те
Gen.	того́	Like masc.	той	тех
Dat.	тому́	Like masc.	той	тем
Acc.	тот (*anim.* того́)	то	ту	те (*anim.* тех)
Instr.	тем	Like masc.	той (то́ю)	те́ми
Loc.	том	Like masc.	той	тех

E. Definite весь.

	Masc.	Sing. Neut.	Fem.	Pl. All genders
Nom.	весь	всё	вся	все
Gen.	всего́	Like masc.	всей	всех
Dat.	всему́	Like masc.	всей	всем
Acc.	весь (*anim.* всего́)	всё	всю	все (*anim.* всех)
Instr.	всем	Like masc.	всей (-éю)	всéми
Loc.	всём	Like masc.	всей	всех

F. Interrogative possessive pronoun чей? *whose?*

	Masc.	Sing. Neut.	Fem.	Pl. All genders
Nom.	чей	чьё	чья	чьи
Gen.	чьего́	Like masc.	чьей	чьих
Dat.	чьему́	Like masc.	чьей	чьим
Acc.	чей (*anim.* чьего́)	чьё	чью	чьи (*anim.* чьих)
Instr.	чьим	Like masc.	чьей (-éю)	чьи́ми
Loc.	чьём	Like masc.	чьей	чьих

4. Adjectives

A. Hard adjectives.

	Sing. Masc.	Neut.	Fem.	Pl. All genders
Nom.	нóвый[17]	нóвое	нóвая	нóвые
Gen.	нóвого	Like masc.	нóвой	нóвых
Dat.	нóвому	Like masc.	нóвой	нóвым
Acc.	нóвый (anim. нóвого)	нóвое	нóвую	нóвые (anim. нóвых)
Instr.	нóвым	Like masc.	нóвой (-ою)	нóвыми
Loc.	нóвом	Like masc.	нóвой	нóвых

B. "Mixed" adjectives with stems ending in г, к, х.

Since only и, never ы, can be written after г, к, and х, the masculine singular nominative (and inanimate accusative), the masculine and neuter singular instrumental, and the entire plural deviate in spelling from the hard adjective declension:

	Sing. Masc.	Neut.	Fem.	Pl. All genders
Nom.	рýсский	рýсское	рýсская	рýсские
Gen.	рýсского	Like masc.	рýсской	рýсских
Dat.	рýсскому	Like masc.	рýсской	рýсским
Acc.	рýсский (anim. рýсского)	рýсское	рýсскую	рýсские (anim. рýсских)
Instr.	рýсским	Like masc.	рýсской (-ою)	рýсскими
Loc.	рýсском	Like masc.	рýсской	рýсских

C. "Mixed" adjectives with stems ending in ж, ц, ч, ш, щ.

Since only и, never ы, can be written after ж, ч, ш, щ, the same changes apply as for adjectives with stems in г, к, х. In addition, unstressed е, not о, must be written after ж, ч, ш, щ, *and also* ц:

	Sing. Masc.	Neut.	Fem.	Pl. All genders
Nom.	свéжий	свéжее	свéжая	свéжие
Gen.	свéжего	Like masc.	свéжей	свéжих
Dat.	свéжему	Like masc.	свéжей	свéжим
Acc.	свéжий (anim. свéжего)	свéжее	свéжую	свéжие (anim. свéжих)
Instr.	свéжим	Like masc.	свéжей (-ею)	свéжими
Loc.	свéжем	Like masc.	свéжей	свéжих

---

[17] The ending for masculine singular nominative and accusative inanimate is **-óй** when the stress is on the ending, e.g., больш**óй**.

D. Soft adjectives in -ний.

	Sing. Masc.	Sing. Neut.	Fem.	Pl. All genders
Nom.	си́ний	си́нее	си́няя	си́ние
Gen.	си́него	Like masc.	си́ней	си́них
Dat.	си́нему	Like masc.	си́ней	си́ним
Acc.	си́ний (anim. си́него)	си́нее	си́нюю	си́ние (anim. си́них)
Instr.	си́ним	Like masc.	си́ней (-ею)	си́ними
Loc.	си́нем	Like masc.	си́ней	си́них

E. Soft adjectives in -ий, -ье, -ья, -ьи. The ordinal numeral **тре́тий** (*third*) follows a special declension, limited to a few adjectives. The pronoun **чей?** (*whose?*— see Table 3F), also follows this declension.

	Sing. Masc.	Sing. Neut.	Fem.	Pl. All genders
Nom.	тре́тий	тре́тье	тре́тья	тре́тьи
Gen.	тре́тьего	Like masc.	тре́тьей	тре́тьих
Dat.	тре́тьему	Like masc.	тре́тьей	тре́тьим
Acc.	тре́тий (anim. тре́тьего)	тре́тье	тре́тью	тре́тьи (anim. тре́тьих)
Instr.	тре́тьим	Like masc.	тре́тьей (-ею)	тре́тьими
Loc.	тре́тьем	Like masc.	тре́тьей	тре́тьих

F. Possessive adjectives in -ин. Some nouns denoting specific persons and ending in **-а/-я** form possessive adjectives in **-ин**, **-ино**, **-ина**. These include nouns designating members of the family such as ма́ма (*mama*), ба́бушка (*grandmother*), де́душка (*grandfather*), тётя (*aunt*), дя́дя (*uncle*), etc.; feminine names: Ле́на, О́льга Зо́я, etc.; and masculine nicknames: Ко́ля, Алёша, etc.

	Sing. Masc.	Sing. Neut.	Fem.	Pl. All genders
Nom.	ма́мин	ма́мино	ма́мина	ма́мины
Gen.	ма́мина (-ого)	Like masc.	ма́миной	ма́миных
Dat.	ма́мину (-ому)	Like masc.	ма́миной	ма́миным
Acc.	ма́мин (anim. ма́мина)	ма́мино	ма́мину	ма́мины (anim. ма́миных)
Instr.	ма́миным	Like masc.	ма́миной (-ою)	ма́миными
Loc.	ма́мином	Like masc.	ма́миной	ма́миных

5. Declension of Surnames

A. Surnames in -ин and -ов/-ев. These were originally possessive adjectives similar to those described above. They too have a mixed declension: some case forms have noun endings; others adjectival endings.

| | *Sing.* | | *Pl.* |
	Masc.	*Fem.*	*Both genders*
Nom.	Петро́в	Петро́ва	Петро́вы
Gen.	Петро́ва	Петро́вой	Петро́вых
Dat.	Петро́ву	Петро́вой	Петро́вым
Acc.	Петро́ва	Петро́ву	Петро́вых
Instr.	Петро́вым	Петро́вой	Петро́выми
Loc.	Петро́ве	Петро́вой	Петро́вых

B. Surnames of males. Surnames (as well as first names) which denote males are declined in Russian *unless* they end in -е, -и, -о,[18] -у or stressed -а́. Other Russian masculine names *are* declined.

Я́ зна́ю Па́бло Пика́ссо́. (undeclined)

Óн зна́л { президе́нта Ке́ннеди. (Ке́ннеди undeclined, but note his title.)
Алекса́ндра Дюма́.

C. Surnames of females. Surnames which denote females are declined in Russian *only* when they end in -ова/-ева, -ина (see above) or in -а́я or -ская (which are declined as adjectives). No other names denoting women are declined.

Males		*Females*
Óн зна́л { Джо́на Сми́та,	*but*	А́нну Сми́т.
Жа́на Море́ля,	*but*	Жа́нну Море́ль.
Ма́кса Блю́менфельда,	*but*	Ли́зу Блю́менфельд.
Никола́я Станке́вича,	*but*	Мари́ю Станке́вич.

Note the declinable first names.

Appendix B—Diminutives

1. Diminutives of nouns

Russians have a strong tendency to use so-called diminutives either to express the smallness of an object, or to convey a certain emotional attitude (affection, intimacy, sometimes condescension) toward an object or a person. Diminutives are much used in speaking to children and animals, for example. Diminutives are also frequently used for food, thus: вода́—води́чка, во́дка—во́дочка, яйцо́—яи́чко, ры́ба—ры́бка, кусо́к—кусо́чек, etc.

Diminutives end in -ок, -ёк, -ик for masculine, -ко for neuter, -ка for feminine. Final г, к, х of the stem become ж, ч, ш respectively:

---

[18] But first names and family names ending in -o are sometimes declined as feminines, e.g., Я́ зна́ю Миха́йла Зо́щенку or Я́ зна́ю Миха́йла Зо́щенко.

друг—дружо́к
круг—кружо́к (circle; club or society)
го́род—городо́к
дом—до́мик
ко́мната—ко́мнатка
кварти́ра—кварти́рка
у́лица—у́личка
стол—сто́лик (especially in restaurants)
кни́га—кни́жка (this diminutive is as much used as the regular form)
рука́—ру́чка (also denotes a handle)
нога́—но́жка (also denotes the leg of a piece of furniture)
спина́—спи́нка (also denotes the back of a chair or sofa)
стару́ха—стару́шка
стари́к—старичёк
соба́ка—соба́чка

So-called diminutives of second degree take a variety of endings of two syllables, including **-очек** or **-ушек** for masculine; **-очка** or **-ушка** for feminine. They convey greater tenderness than diminutives of first degree, and are much used among members of a family group:

ма́ма—ма́мочка
дед—де́душка (this diminutive has become more common than the root word)
дя́дя—дя́дюшка
etc.

The words ба́бушка, де́вушка, and де́вочка are actually secondary diminutives which have replaced the words from which they are derived.

Some secondary diminutives have a pejorative shade of meaning:

ма́льчик—мальчи́шка   urchin
де́вочка—девчёнка   girlie

Russian also has *augmentatives* in **-йще, -йща**, denoting large size (or contempt); these are much less used:

дом—доми́ще   a huge house
рука́—ручи́ща   a big strong hand

2.   Diminutives of adjectives

Not only nouns, but also adjectives have diminutive forms. These diminutives have the same functions as have the diminutives of nouns, i.e., to show small size, affection, etc.:

ти́хонький   nice and quiet
ху́денький   little and thin
etc.

The suffixes are: **-енький (-онький)** masculine, **-енькое (-онькое)** neuter, **-енькая (-онькая)** feminine.

нóвый—нóвенький   мѝлый—мѝленький
сѝний—сѝненький   крáсный—крáсненький
бéлый—бéленький   дешёвый—дешёвенький
глýпый—глýпенький   ýмный—ýмненький
стáрый—стáренький   молодóй—молодéнький

But: хорóший—хорóшенький (pretty)

Russian adjectives in **-овáтый/-евáтый** often correspond to English adjectives ending in *-ish*.

желтовáтый	yellowish
синевáтый	bluish
красновáтый	reddish
слабовáтый	rather weak (weakish)
глуповáтый	rather silly
тепловáтый	lukewarm, tepid

Appendix C—Index of Prepositions

1. Prepositions with genitive

без, безо	without	Мы̀ бы́ли в теáтре **без Áнны**. Я̀ пью̀ чáй **без сáхара**. Óн сдéлал э́то **без нáшей пóмощи**.
близ	near	**Близ** нáшей шкóлы большóй пáрк.
вдоль	along	Мы̀ дóлго шлѝ **вдоль** бéрега рекѝ.
вмéсто	instead, in place of	**Вмéсто** письмá óн прислáл телегрáмму. **Вмéсто** Áнны пришлá её сестрá.
вне	outside of	Óн дóлго жѝл **вне Россѝи**.
внутрѝ	inside of	Мы̀ не знáли, чтó происхóдит **внутрѝ** страны́.
вóзле	near, alongside	Аптéка **вóзле** нáшего дóма.
вокрýг	around	Ктó-то всю̀ нóчь ходѝл **вокрýг** дóма. **Вокрýг** столá стоя́ли стýлья.
впередѝ	ahead of	Óн éхал **впередѝ** всéх.
для	for, for the sake of	Я̀ э́то сдéлал **для** отцá. Э́то плóхо **для** страны́. Вóт нóж **для** хлéба.

до	before, until, up to, as far as	До войны́ они́ жи́ли на Кавка́зе. Я бу́ду рабо́тать до пяти́. Мы́ дошли́ до це́ркви.
из (изо)	from (place), out of	Во́т письмо́ из Москвы́. О́н пьёт из буты́лки. Э́тот сто́л сде́лан из дорого́го де́рева (wood).
из-за	because of, from behind	Я опозда́л из-за Ива́на. Соба́ка вы́бежала из-за угла́.
кро́ме	besides, except	Кро́ме расска́зов, Че́хов писа́л пье́сы. Кро́ме О́льги, все́ бы́ли до́ма.
ми́мо	past, by	Ми́мо на́с прошёл высо́кий челове́к. Мы́ прое́хали ми́мо це́ркви.
накану́не	on the eve of	Накану́не пра́здника мы́ пошли́ в це́рковь.
о́коло	near, about	Я живу́ тепе́рь о́коло университе́та. У меня́ бы́ло о́коло пяти́ до́лларов.
от (ото)	from (a person), from the house of, away from; from . . . (to); from (due to)	Во́т письмо́ от А́нны. Я иду́ от до́ктора. Отойди́ от окна́! От девяти́ до десяти́. Ско́лько киломе́тров от Москвы́ до Ки́ева? О́н дрожа́л от стра́ха. (He was trembling from fear.)
по́сле	after	По́сле у́жина мы́ бу́дем игра́ть в бри́дж. О́н пришёл по́сле слу́жбы.
посреди́	in the middle of	Посреди́ разгово́ра она́ вдру́г замолча́ла (fell silent). До́м стоя́л посреди́ па́рка.
про́тив	opposite; against, opposed to	Рестора́н про́тив теа́тра. Я про́тив э́того кандида́та.
ра́ди	for the sake of	Я э́то сказа́л ра́ди ва́с. О́н всё де́лает ра́ди де́нег.
с, со	from, off, down from; since; beginning with	Мы́ идём с конце́рта. Сними́ всё со стола́. Они́ сошли́ (got down) с авто́буса. Мы́ здесь с пя́того ма́я. С понеде́льника я́ бу́ду приходи́ть регуля́рно.
среди́	among, in the midst of	Среди́ мои́х друзе́й мно́го враче́й. Я не заме́тил его́ среди́ толпы́.

| y | "to have"; at the house of; by, near, at | У до́ктора но́вый автомоби́ль.
Мы обе́даем сего́дня у ба́бушки.
Учи́тель стои́т у доски́. |

2. Prepositions with dative

благодаря́	thanks to, due to	Жизнь ста́ла ле́гче **благодаря́** прогре́ссу. Я смог э́то сде́лать **благодаря́** ва́шей по́мощи. Он нашёл рабо́ту **благодаря́** зна́нию языко́в.
к, ко	to, toward (motion); to (going to a person), to the house of; by (time)	Я иду́ **к** дире́ктору. Автомоби́ль подъе́хал **к** до́му. Я ко́нчу рабо́ту **к** концу́ ме́сяца.
навстре́чу	toward, to meet	**Навстре́чу** мне́ шла́ стару́ха. Он вы́шел **навстре́чу** ма́тери.
по	about, along; according to; in the/on (time); distribution ("to each"); by (phone, mail, radio)	Мы це́лый день е́здили **по** го́роду. Ко́шки лю́бят ходи́ть **по** кры́ше. **По** гла́вной у́лице ходи́ли то́лпы люде́й. **По**-мо́ему вы́ не пра́вы. Мы **по** вечера́м всегда́ до́ма. Я посла́л посы́лку **по** по́чте. Он да́л ка́ждому **по** рублю́.
согла́сно	according to, in accordance with	**Согла́сно** э́тому до́говору . . . Всё бы́ло сде́лано **согла́сно** его́ жела́нию.

3. Prepositions with accusative

в, во	into, to (direction); per, a; at, on (time)	Она́ **вошла́ в** ко́мнату. Маши́на въе́хала **во** дво́р. Он рабо́тает во́семь часо́в **в** де́нь. Мы бу́дем та́м **в** сре́ду.
за	behind (direction); for (exchange); for (opposite of against); for (in place of)	Соба́ка побежа́ла **за** до́м. Кни́га упа́ла **за** кре́сло. Я плачу́ сто́ рубле́й **за** кварти́ру. В спо́ре я бы́л **за** О́льгу, а Ива́н бы́л про́тив неё. Он мо́жет э́то сде́лать **за меня́** (in my place).
на	on; to (direction); for (time); with comparison of quantities	Мы идём **на** собра́ние. Кто́ положи́л письмо́ **на** мо́й сто́л? Я е́ду в Ло́ндон **на** неде́лю. Э́то перево́д **на** за́втра. Бра́т **на** два́ го́да ста́рше меня́.

о (об)	against	Парохо́д уда́рился **о** ска́лу. (The ship struck against a rock.)
по	until (date), up to	Я́ бу́ду та́м с пе́рвого **по** пятна́дцат**ое**. Зде́сь вода́ **по** коле́но (knee).
под	under (direction)	Положи́ де́ньги **под** кни́гу. Каранда́ш упа́л **под** сто́л.
про	about, concerning	О́н мне́ всё рассказа́л **про** сестру́.
с	about (with quantities)	Мы́ жи́ли та́м **с** неде́лю.
сквозь	through	Све́т прохо́дит **сквозь** занаве́ску (curtain). Вода́ протекла́ (flowed) **сквозь** потоло́к.
через	across, through; after, in (time); via, by way of; every other	Мы́ живём **через** у́лицу. Они́ прое́хали **через** на́ш го́род. Ива́н вернётся **через** неде́лю. Я́ переда́л ему́ приглаше́ние **через** Ива́на. Ле́том я́ игра́л в те́ннис **через** де́нь (every other day).

4. Prepositions with instrumental

за	behind (static); go for/after; at (during) (with meals)	На́ше село́ **за** реко́й. Гара́ж **за** до́мом. Я́ иду́ **за** молоко́м и **за** папиро́сами. Соба́ка бежа́ла **за** на́ми. **За** обе́дом мы́ говори́ли о поли́тике.
ме́жду	between, among	Я́ бу́ду до́ма **ме́жду** тремя́ и пятью́. Я́ сиде́л **ме́жду** Ива́ном и О́льгой. Э́то, коне́чно, **ме́жду на́ми**.
над, надо	above, over; (work) on; (laugh) at	На́ша кварти́ра **над** магази́ном. О́н рабо́тает **над** диссерта́цией. Почему́ ты́ смеёшься **над на́ми**?
перед, передо	before; in front of	О́н пришёл **перед** обе́дом. **Перед** на́шей да́чей—доро́га. **Передо мно́й** тру́дная пробле́ма.
под, подо	under (static)	Кни́га лежи́т **под** столо́м. Она́ **под** влия́нием ма́тери. Они́ живу́т **подо мно́й**.

| с, со | with | Я́ бы́л в теа́тре **с сестро́й**.
На столе́ стои́т ва́за **с цвета́ми**.
О́н е́л **с больши́м аппети́том**.
Я́ э́то сде́лаю **с удово́льствием**.
Она́ была́ **со мно́й** в теа́тре.
Мы́ **с жено́й** . . . (my wife and I) |

5. Prepositions with locative

в, во	in, at	Она́ тепе́рь **в Москве́**. Вы́ **во всём** пра́вы. Мы́ бы́ли вчера́ **в теа́тре**.
на	on; at (event); by (vehicles)	Кни́га **на по́лке**. Я́ ви́дел его́ **на конце́рте**. Я́ прие́хал **на по́езде**.
о, об, обо	about, concerning	Мы́ говори́ли **о но́вой** пье́се. Она́ забы́ла **обо всём**. Не бу́дем **об э́том** говори́ть.
по	after, upon, on	**По** прие́зде о́н сейча́с же на́м позвони́л. **По** оконча́нии университе́та о́н поступи́л на слу́жбу.
при	at the time of; under (a ruler or government); in the presence of; attached to	**При** царе́ Никола́е Второ́м. О́н э́то сказа́л **при мне́**. **При** на́шем университе́те е́сть библиоте́ка.

Appendix D—Suffixes

1. Certain types of nouns denoting persons

A. Agent.

(1) **-тель**, feminine **-тельница**. This suffix is added to verbal stems to denote persons performing an action or engaged in an occupation:

писа́тель, -ница	writer
учи́тель, -ница	teacher
преподава́тель, -ница	teacher
чита́тель, -ница	reader
строи́тель, -ница	builder

(2) The suffix **-ик**, feminine **-ица** (or **-ник/-ница**, **-чик/-чица**) also serves for nouns of agent or occupation:

лётчик, -ица	flier, pilot
носи́льщик, -ица	porter
колхо́зник, -ица	collective farmer
перево́дчик, -ица	translator

(3) The suffix **-ик** is also used to designate the practitioners of sciences with words of non-Russian origin. There is no special form for feminine:

исто́рик	historian
хи́мик	chemist
матема́тик	mathematician
фи́зик	physicist

(4) Many foreign words in *-ist* preserve this *-ist* in Russian; feminine in **-ка**:

социали́ст, -ка	socialist
коммуни́ст, -ка	communist
импрессиони́ст	impressionist

(5) Words formed in English with *-logist* lack the element *-ist* in Russian. There is no distinct feminine:

археоло́г	archaeologist
физио́лог	physiologist
зоо́лог	zoologist
био́лог	biologist

The corresponding science denoted by *-ology* in English has **-оло́гия** in Russian:

зооло́гия	zoology
физиоло́гия	physiology
филоло́гия	philology
биоло́гия	biology

(6) Words formed in English with *-ographer* correspond to Russian words with **-о́граф**. There is no distinct feminine:

гео́граф	geographer
фото́граф	photographer
био́граф	biographer

The corresponding subject denoted in English by *-ography* has **-огра́фия** in Russian:

геогра́фия	geography
фотогра́фия	photography; also photograph
биогра́фия	biography

B. Origin.

(1) Patronymics. These end in **-ич** (feminine **-ична**) for fathers' Christian names ending in **-а/-я**; in **-ович/-евич** (feminine **-овна/-евна**) for all other fathers' names:

Ники́тич	son of Nikita	Ники́тична	daughter of Nikita
Ива́нович	son of Ivan	Ива́новна	daughter of Ivan
Алексе́евич	son of Alexey	Алексе́евна	daughter of Alexey

The actual pronunciation of those in **-ович/-евич** is usually slurred to [-ič̟]/[-ič̟] when the vowel **-o-** or **-e-** is not stressed, e.g., [iván̟ič̟], [aḽikṣéič̟] etc. Feminines in **-овна/-евна** are also more or less slurred.

(2) The suffix **-анин/-янин** (feminine **-анка/-янка**) is used principally to denote certain nationalities or inhabitants of certain countries or cities:

англича́нин, англича́нка	Englishman (-woman)
армяни́н, армя́нка	Armenian
датча́нин, датча́нка	Dane
парижа́нин, парижа́нка	Parisian

The masculine plural of these end in **-ане/-яне** (see Unit 20, page 322).

(3) The suffixes, **-ец**, feminine **-ка**, and **-ич**, feminine **-ичка**, are also used to denote inhabitants or natives of countries, regions, cities:

америка́нец, америка́нка	American
голла́ндец, голла́ндка	Dutchman
испа́нец, испа́нка	Spaniard
кавка́зец, кавка́зка	Caucasian
ленингра́дец, ленингра́дка	inhabitant of Leningrad
москви́ч, москви́чка	Muscovite

(4) The suffix **-ёнок** (plural **-я́та/-а́та**) is used for the names of young animals (see Appendix A, Table 1D):

котёнок, pl. котя́та	kitten
гусёнок, pl. гуся́та	gosling

2. Abstract nouns

A. Verbal nouns. These end in **-ние** (or **-нье**) for those classes of verbs which have past passive participles in **-нный**; the connecting vowel **-e-** or **-a-/-я-** remains the same, except that the **-ё-** of the participle becomes **-é-**. Intransitive verbs, which lack past passive participles, may nevertheless possess verbal nouns, formed analogously.[19]

понима́ние	(process of) understanding
объясне́ние	explanation
чте́ние	reading
гуля́нье	walking, strolling

Verbal nouns end in **-тие (-тье)** for those groups of verbs which have a past passive participle in **-тый**:

откры́тие	discovery	заня́тие	occupation

---

[19] The student is warned that not all verbs form verbal nouns, nor can the exact meaning be predicted for those which do form them.

Very often these nouns have come to denote not only the generalized process of verbal action, but also a specific case of it, e.g., чтéние, a given piece of reading; объяснéние, a given explanation; открытие, a given discovery; поня́тие, an idea. Sometimes their meaning becomes entirely concrete, e.g., имéние, an estate; расписáние, a timetable.

B. Other abstract nouns.

(1) The suffix **-ость** (feminine) (occasionally **-есть**) is added to adjectives (sometimes participles) to denote qualities:

рáдость	joy	нóвость	newness; news
стáрость	old age	глýпость	stupidity, foolishness
мóлодость	youth	свéжесть	freshness
бéдность	poverty		

(2) The suffix **-ство** is used to form abstract nouns which link individual situations or instances to create a single concept, sometimes one which is relatively concrete:

дéтство	childhood
родствó	kinship
знакóмство	acquaintance
óбщество	society; a company
госудáрство	state (from госудáрь, sovereign)

(3) The foreign suffix **-изм** is used in words of foreign origin corresponding to English *-ism*; it is sometimes also used for words of native origin:

социали́зм	socialism	большеви́зм	Bolshevism
коммуни́зм	communism		

(4) The suffix **-ция** corresponds in words of foreign origin to English *-tion*:

нáция	nation	цивилизáция	civilization
револю́ция	revolution	конститу́ция	constitution

(5) Suffixes **-олóгия**, **-огрáфия**: see paragraphs 5 and 6 on page 485.

3. Diminutives and Augmentatives—see Appendix B

4. Adjectives

A. Derivations from nouns, adverbs, and verbal stems.

(1) The suffix **-ный (-нóй)** is used to derive adjectives from nouns (mostly inanimate). The final stem consonant may change (see page 337).

ум—у́мный	intelligent
вкус—вку́сный	delicious, tasty
шум—шу́мный	noisy
страх—стрáшный	frightful
труд—трýдный	difficult

ло́гика—логи́чный	logical
у́жас—ужа́сный	terrible
свобо́да—свобо́дный	free
хо́лод—холо́дный	cold
ме́сто—ме́стный	local
век—ве́чный	eternal
сон—со́нный	sleepy

This suffix is also used for some adjectives of foreign origin:

серьёзный	serious
консервати́вный	conservative
норма́льный	normal

This suffix sometimes has the form **-енный**, or **-онный**:

жизнь—жи́зненный	vital
о́бщество—обще́ственный	social
револю́ция—революцио́нный	revolutionary

(2) The suffix **-ний** (soft) is used for adjectives of time and a few adjectives of place; the form **-шний** is frequent in derivations from adverbs:

зима́—зи́мний	вчера́—вчера́шний
весна́—весе́нний	сего́дня—сего́дняшний
ле́то—ле́тний	за́втра—за́втрашний
о́сень—осе́нний	здесь—зде́шний (local, of here)
у́тро—у́тренний	тепе́рь—тепе́решний (present, of this time)
ве́чер—вече́рний	сосе́д—сосе́дний (neighboring)
по́здний	ра́нний

(3) The suffix **-ский (-ско́й)** is used to derive adjectives from some animate nouns, as well as from inanimates. It is most common with adjectives of place:

жена́—же́нский	women's, feminine
муж—мужско́й	men's, masculine
Аме́рика—америка́нский	American
Нью-Йо́рк—нью-йо́ркский	New York (adj.)
Москва́—моско́вский	of Moscow
Ленингра́д—ленингра́дский	of Leningrad

(4) The suffix **-и́ческий** is used in many adjectives of foreign origin corresponding to English -ic or -ical.

юмористи́ческий	электри́ческий
драмати́ческий	коммунисти́ческий
траги́ческий	социалисти́ческий
истори́ческий	капиталисти́ческий

(5) The suffix **-имый** or **-емый** is added to verbal stems (of the infinitive) to form adjectives (identical with the present passive participle: see Unit 27, page 455) com-

parable to English adjectives ending in *-able*, *-ible*. They are most common in the *negative*:

незабыва́емый   unforgettable
необъясни́мый   inexplicable

(6) Possessive suffix **-ин**—see Appendix A, Table 4F.

(7) Diminutives—see Appendix B.

Appendix E—Numerals: Supplement

1. Collective numerals

Russian has a special set of numerals from 2 to 10, the so-called collective numerals: **дво́е, тро́е, че́тверо, пя́теро, ше́стеро, се́меро, во́сьмеро, де́вятеро, де́сятеро.** The numerals above 5 are relatively little used. They all (including дво́е, тро́е, and че́тверо) take the genitive plural.

(1) Collectives are used with masculine animates when a group is thought of as a unit.

Тро́е солда́т вы́шли и́з лесу.
Дво́е на́ших сосе́дей бы́ли у на́с.
Её че́тверо сынове́й живу́т заграни́цей.

(2) Collectives are used with certain masculine animate nouns, including де́ти and мужчи́ны.

У ни́х пя́теро дете́й.
В конто́ре слу́жат тро́е мужчи́н.

(3) With nouns which are used only in the plural, such as *scissors*, *trousers*, the collective numeral is mandatory.

тро́е часо́в   (часы́—clock, watch)
че́тверо су́ток   (су́тки—24 hours)
дво́е воро́т   (воро́та—gate)

(4) The collective numeral is used with personal pronouns and sometimes without a noun.

На́с бы́ло дво́е.   There were two of us.
И́х бу́дет че́тверо.   There will be four of them.
Мы́ все́ тро́е бы́ли та́м.   All three of us were there.
Тро́е стоя́ли у доски́.   Three were standing by the blackboard.

(5) With adjectives used as nouns, for 2, 3, 4, the collective is similarly used.

Тро́е рабо́чих рабо́тали во дворе́.
Three workmen were working in the yard.

Двóе больны́х жда́ли врачá.

Two patients were waiting for the doctor.

In oblique cases (except for accusative inanimate) collective numerals are usually replaced by the oblique cases of the cardinal numerals (see Unit 26), e.g., двóе детéй, *two children*, but двýх детéй—more common for *of the two children*. If the collectives are declined, they take endings of the soft adjectives (двóе, трóе) or hard adjectives (чéтверо . . . дéсятеро). The accent shifts to the ending in declension: двóе, двои́х, двои́м, etc. In oblique cases the noun agrees with the numeral in case, e.g., Мы́ подошли́ к двои́м дéтям.

2. Collective units

A second type of collective numeral is used for collective units (compare English *dozen, score, gross*). These are declined as hard or soft nouns; they always govern the genitive plural:

деся́ток   ten (eggs, fruit, etc.)
дю́жина   dozen (handkerchiefs, sheets, etc.)
сóтня   hundred (military unit, money, etc.)

E.g.: деся́ток папирóс, двá деся́тка, пя́ть деся́тков яи́ц (eggs), etc.; дю́жина платкóв, двé дю́жины платкóв, пя́ть дю́жин, etc.; сóтня папирóс, двé сóтни, пя́ть сóтен, etc.

3. Adverbial numerals

(1) One type describes action performed by a number of people *as a group*:

Они́ пришли́ к нáм втроём.   They came to see us, the three of them together.
В бри́дж игрáют вчетверóм.   Bridge is played by four people.
Мы́ бýдем вдвоём весь вéчер.   We will be alone (just the two of us) all evening.
Мы́ остáлись вдвоём.   We were left alone.

(2) With comparatives either the forms вдвóе, втрóе, вчéтверо, впя́теро, or the phrases в двá рáза, в пя́ть рáз are used.

вдвóе (в двá рáза) бóльше   twice as much
в шéсть рáз мéньше   six times as small

4. Substantivized numerals

These designate numerals used as nouns; cf. English *a one, a three*, etc., as in cards, or in numeral grades:

едини́ца	a one	шестёрка	a six	семёрка	a seven
двóйка	a two	четвёрка	a four	восьмёрка	an eight
трóйка[20]	a three	пятёрка	a five	девя́тка	a nine
				деся́тка	a ten

---

[20] Also used for a team of three horses abreast.

The grading system in Russian schools goes from едини́ца to пятёрка: едини́ца corresponds to an F; пятёрка to an A.

5. Numerals used distributively

The preposition **по** is used with cardinal numerals in a distributive sense (compare English *one each*, *three apiece*, etc.). With the number **оди́н** (expressed or implied), **по** takes the dative; with other numerals it takes the accusative:

> Оте́ц да́л сыновья́м **по** рублю́ (masc. dat.).
> The father gave his sons a ruble each.

> Ка́ждый из на́с купи́л **по две́** кни́ги.
> Each of us bought two books (apiece).

Russian-English Vocabulary

The following vocabulary is complete, except for a few words used in the readings which are similar in form and meaning in both Russian and English, and for certain numerals which are listed in Unit 26. Thus, ordinals above *tenth* are not included, nor are compound numerals denoting hundreds. Also, a few special words used in Pattern Sentences and Readings and translated there are not included.

The number of the unit in which a given word or expression is first used appears in parentheses. This number is italicized when the unit gives important information concerning a word's inflection, usage, or meaning.

Perfective verbs are given following the corresponding imperfective verb with the same meaning. Imperfectives and perfectives are both marked as such.

First conjugation verbs like читáть are indicated simply by the number I, e.g., объясня́ть, I. For other verbs of the first or second conjugations, the first and second persons singular are given after the infinitive, e.g., сказа́ть (perf., I: скажу́, ска́жешь), or говори́ть (imperf., II: говор.ю́, -и́шь). Where prefixed perfectives are conjugated like the corresponding imperfectives, the conjugation pattern is given only for the imperfective, e.g., писа́ть (imperf., I: пишу́, пи́шешь), на- (perf., I). Imperative and past tense forms are given only when they cannot be derived according to the usual rules. A dot is sometimes used to separate stems from endings.

Forms of adverbs in **-o** are given in parentheses after the corresponding adjectives when their stress is distinct from that of the adjective, e.g., лёгкий (легко́).

a and; but (*4*); **a то́** otherwise, or else
абза́ц paragraph
а́вгуст August (*23*)
авто́бус autobus, bus (17); **на авто́бусе** by (on the) bus
автомоби́ль (*m.*) automobile, car (6); **на автомоби́ле** by car (17)
а́втор author (7)
авторучка fountain pen (7)

а́дрес (*nom. pl.* **-á**) address (7). **Ка́к а́дрес** (+ *gen.*)? What is the address of . . . ? (7)
алло́! Hello! (on the telephone) (11)
Аме́рика America (5)
америка́н.ец (*gen.* **-ца**) (*f.* **-ка**, *gen. pl.* **-ок**) American (*noun*) (6)
америка́нский American (*adj.*) (6)
а́нгел angel (18)
А́нглия England (12)

английский English (*adj.*) (9)

англича́н.ин (6, *decl.* 20) (*fem.* -ка, *gen. pl.* -ок) Englishman (-woman) (6, 20)

анекдо́т anecdote

аппети́т appetite (11)

апре́ль (*m.*) April (23)

апте́ка drugstore (12)

арти́ст (*f.* -ка) (performing) artist, actor (25)

аудито́рия auditorium, lecture room (13)

А́фрика Africa (11)

ах! ah! oh! (3)

ба́буш.ка (*gen. pl.* -ек) grandmother (17)

бале́т ballet

банк bank (11)

бе́гать (indeterm. imperf., I), бежа́ть (determ. imperf.: бегу́, бежи́шь, . . . бегу́т), побежа́ть (perf.), to run (24)

бе́дный poor, unfortunate (13)

без (+ *gen.*) without (10)

бе́лый white (6)

бельё linen, laundry, underwear (24)

бер-, *see* брать

бе́рег (*loc.* на берегу́; *nom. pl.* -а́) shore, bank (12)

беспоко́иться (imperf., II: беспоко́.юсь, -ишься) to worry, be concerned (23)

беспоря́д.ок (*gen.* -ка) disorder (24)

библиоте́ка library (5)

биле́т ticket (17)

бифште́кс beefsteak (18)

благодари́ть (imperf., II: благодар.ю́, -и́шь), по- (perf., II) (+ *acc.*) to thank (18) б. за (+ *acc.*) to thank for

благода́рный grateful (23); б. за (+ *acc.*) grateful for (23)

благода́рность (*f.*) gratitude. Не сто́ит благода́рности. Don't mention it. (18)

бли́же nearer (25); б. к (+ *dat.*) nearer to (25)

бли́зко near(by) (5); б. от (+ *gen.*) near (to) (*prep.*) (25)

блонди́н (*f.* -ка, *gen. pl.* -ок) blond(e) (8)

блу́з.ка (*gen. pl.* -ок) blouse (8)

Бог God (18) Бо́же мо́й! My God! Good heavens! (18) Сла́ва Бо́гу! Thank God! (18)

бога́тый rich, wealthy (10)

боле́знь (*f.*) sickness, illness (23)

боле́ть (imperf., II: боли́т, боля́т) to ache, pain. У меня́ боли́т голова́. I have a headache (23)

боле́ть (imperf., I: боле́.ю, -ешь) to be ailing, get sick (often) (23), за- (perf., I), to be taken ill (25)

боль (*f.*) pain (23)

больни́ца hospital

больно́й sick, ill; a patient (*adj. used as noun*) (23)

бо́льше (+ *gen.*) more, bigger (8); б. не no more, no longer (10); б. всего́ (всех) most of all (23, 25) б. ничего́ nothing more (8, 27)

бо́льший bigger, larger, greater (25)

большо́й big, large (6); большо́е спаси́бо many thanks (10)

борода́ beard (20)

борщ borsch (soup) (11)

боти́н.ок (*gen.* -ка; *gen. pl.* боти́нок) shoe (13)

боя́ться (imperf., II: бо.ю́сь, -и́шься) (+ *gen.*) to fear, be afraid of (19)

брат (*nom. pl.* бра́тья; *gen. pl.* бра́тьев) brother (4, 20)

брать (imperf., I: бер.у́, -ёшь), взять (perf., I: возьм.у́, -ёшь) to take (14), бра́ть/взя́ть у (+ *gen.*), take from (15)

бри́ться (imperf., I: бре́.юсь, -ешься), по- (perf., I) to shave (24)

броса́ть (imperf., I), бро́сить (perf., II: бро́.шу, -сишь) to throw, throw away; to give up, abandon (24)

брю́ки (*pl. only, gen. pl.* брюк) trousers (13)

брюне́т (*f.* -ка, *gen. pl.* -ок) brunet(te) (8)

буди́льник alarm clock (24)

буди́ть (imperf., II: бужу́, бу́дишь) (24), разбуди́ть (perf., II) (24) to awake (*trans.*)

бу́дто: как бу́дто (бы) as if (27); бу́дто бы seemingly (27)

бу́ду I shall be (*see* быть)

бу́дучи being (27)

бу́дущий future, next (14); бу́дущее (*adj. used as noun*) the future (25)

в бу́дущем году́ next year (12)

буке́т bouquet (22)

бума́га paper (2)

бутербро́д sandwich (17)

буты́л.ка (*gen. pl.* -ок) bottle (11)

буфе́т buffet (13)

бы particle indicating the hypothetical mood (24)

быва́ть (imperf., I) to be, happen, visit (sometimes, often), frequent (5, 8). Это быва́ет. That (sort of thing) happens. (5)

бы́вший former (27)

бы́стро fast, quickly (8)

быть (imperf.) to be (5, 14); б. в (+ *loc.*) to wear (6)

в, во (+ *loc.*) in, inside, at (5); (+ *acc.*) to, into (17); per, a (17); (+ *acc. or loc.*) at, in (time) (26)

ваго́н railway car (24)

ва́жный important (12)

ва́нна bath (21); принима́ть/приня́ть ва́нну to take a bath (21)

ва́нная (*declined as an adj.*) bathroom (10)

варе́нье jam (11)

ваш your, yours (4, 12, 20)

вбега́ть (imperf., I), вбежа́ть (perf., I: вбегу́, вбежи́шь . . . вбегу́т) to run in (24)

вдова́ widow (24)

вдоль (+ gen.) along

вдруг suddenly (13)

вед-, see вести́

ведь but, why, you know, since, you realize (implies that a fact is well known or obvious) (18)

везде́ everywhere (11)

везти́ (determ. imperf., I: вез.у́, -ёшь; past вёз, везло́, etc.), по- (perf., I) to carry, take, drive (22)

век (nom. pl. -á) century (18)

вели́кий great (18)

велосипе́д bicycle (24)

вера́нда porch, veranda (16)

ве́рить (imperf., II: ве́р.ю, -ишь), по- (perf., II) (+ dat.) to believe (14)

ве́рно right, true; probably (26)

верну́ть (perf., I: верн.у́, -ёшь) to return (trans.), give back (21); верну́ться to return (intrans.), go back, come back (21)

вероя́тно probably (5)

ве́рхний upper, top (27)

весёлый (ве́село) merry, lively, cheerful (16). Мне́ ве́село. I'm having a good time (20).

весе́нний spring (adj.)

весна́ spring (11); весно́й in spring (11)

вести́ (determ. imperf., I: вед.у́, -ёшь; past вёл, вело́, etc.), по- (perf., I) to lead, take, conduct, carry on (22)

весь all, the whole; (pl.) every (12, 20); весь де́нь all day (7)

вет.ер (gen. -ра) wind; it's windy (11)

ветчина́ ham (17)

ве́чер (nom. pl. -á) evening; evening party (7); в де́вять часо́в ве́чера at 9:00 P.M.; ве́чером in the evening (11)

вечери́н.ка (gen. pl. -ок) (informal) evening party (8)

вече́рний evening (adj.) (8)

вещь (f.) thing (13); work (of art, etc.) (14)

взро́слый adult (23)

взять (perf.), see брать

вид appearance, condition, air, view, aspect; в. на (+ acc.) view of (24)

ви́деть (imperf., II: ви́жу, ви́дишь) (11), у- (perf., II) (21) to see

ви́дно apparent(ly), evident(ly) (25)

ви́л.ка (gen. pl. -ок) fork (16)

вино́ wine (7)

висе́ть (imperf., II: вишу́, виси́шь) to hang (intrans.) (27)

витри́на shop window (22)

вкус taste (19)

вку́сный delicious, tasty (11)

вме́сте together (5)

вме́сто (+ gen.) instead of, in place of (23)

внима́ние attention (13)

внима́тельный attentive (19)

внук grandson (22)

вну́ч.ка (gen. pl. -ек) granddaughter (22)

во, see в

во́время on time (24)

во-вторы́х second, in the second place (20)

вода́ water (7)

води́ть (indeterm. imperf., II: вожу́, во́дишь), вести́ (determ. imperf., I: вед.у́, -ёшь; past вёл, вело́, etc.), повести́ (perf., I) to lead, take, conduct (22)

во́дка vodka (11)

вождь (m.) leader (12)

возвраща́ть (imperf., I), возврати́ть (perf., II: возвра.щу́, -ти́шь) or верну́ть (perf., I: верн.у́, -ёшь) to return (trans.), give back (21); возвраща́ться, возврати́ться or верну́ться, to return (trans.), go back, come back (21)

во́здух air (12); на во́здухе in the (open) air (25)

вози́ть (indeterm. imperf., II: вожу́, во́зишь), везти́ (determ. imperf., I: вез.у́, -ёшь; past вёз, везло́, etc.), повезти́ (perf., I) to carry, take, drive, transport (22)

возмо́жно possible (18, 21)

возмо́жность (f.) possibility (21)

возьм-, see взять

война́ war (10)

войти́ (perf.), see входи́ть

вокза́л terminal, large station (17); на вокза́ле at the station

вокру́г (adv. or prep. + gen.) around, all around (16)

волейбо́л volleyball (8)

вон over there (22)

вообще́ in general (20)

во-пе́рвых first, in the first place (20)

вопро́с question (6); задава́ть/зада́ть в. to ask a question (13)

восемна́дцать eighteen (16, 26)

во́семь eight (16, 26)

во́семьдесят eighty (22, 26)

воскресе́нье Sunday (18)

воспо́льзоваться (perf.), see по́льзоваться

восто́к east (22); на в. to the east; на восто́ке in the east

восто́чный eastern, oriental (22)

восьмо́й eighth (18)

вот here is (are); there is (are) (2). Во́т и всё. That's all (25).

враг enemy (27)

врач physician (16)

вре́мя (n.) time (7, decl. 12); во вре́мя (+ gen.) during (12); ско́лько вре́мени? how long? what time is it? (12); вре́мя го́да season (13) всё (*n. sing.*) everything, all (3); всё, что everything that (7); ра́ньше всего́ first of all (25); о́н всё ду́мает he keeps thinking; Мне́ всё равно́. It's all the same to me (9); Во́т и всё. That's all (25); Всего́ хоро́шего! Good-bye! (7)

все (*pl.*) everyone, everybody, all (8)

всегда́ always (5)

всё-же still, all the same (25)

всё-таки still, nevertheless, all the same (19)

вспомина́ть (imperf., I), вспо́мнить (perf., II: вспомн.ю, -ишь) to recollect, recall (26)

встава́ть (imperf., I: встаю́, -ёшь; imperative встава́йте), встать (perf., I: вста́н.у, -ешь) to get up, stand up, arise (16)

встреча́ть (imperf., I) (19), встре́тить (perf., II: встре́.чу, -тишь) (24) to meet (*trans*), encounter; встреча́ться, встре́титься с (+ *instr.*) to meet (with) (19)

вто́рник Tuesday (18)

второ́й second (15); во-вторы́х second, in the second place (20)

в-тре́тьих third, in the third place (21)

входи́ть (imperf., II: вхожу́, вхо́дишь), войти́ (perf., I: войд.у́, -ёшь; past вошёл, вошло́, etc.) to go in, come in, enter (on foot) (22)

вчера́ yesterday (5)

вчера́шний yesterday's (6)

въезжа́ть (imperf., I), въе́хать (perf., I: въе́д.у, -ешь; imperative въезжа́й/-те) to go in, drive in (22)

вы you (2)

выбега́ть (imperf., I), вы́бежать (perf., вы́бегу, вы́бежишь...вы́бегут) to run out (24)

вы́бор choice, selection (13)

выезжа́ть (imperf., I), вы́ехать (perf.: I: вы́ед.у, -ешь; imperative выезжа́й/те) to drive out, set out (22)

выздора́вливать (imperf., I), вы́здороветь (perf., II: вы́здоров.лю, -ишь) to get well, recover (23)

вы́йти (perf.), *see* выходи́ть

вылета́ть (imperf., I), вы́лететь (perf., II: вы́ле.чу, -тишь) to fly out, set out by plane (24)

вы́мыть (perf.), *see* мыть

выраже́ние expression (13)

высо́кий high, tall (10)

вы́ход exit, way out (27)

выходи́ть (imperf., II: выхожу́, выхо́дишь), вы́йти (perf., I: вы́йд.у, -ешь; past вы́шел, вы́шло, etc.) to go out, set out, exit, come out (on foot) (22)

выходно́й де́нь day off, holiday (24)

вы́ше higher, taller (25)

газ gas (24)

газе́та newspaper (4)

га́лстук necktie (24)

гара́ж garage (6)

где where (2)

где́-нибудь, где́-то anywhere, somewhere (22)

ге́ний genius (9)

Герма́ния Germany (20)

герои́ня heroine (5)

геро́й hero (5)

гид guide (12)

глава́ chapter; head, chief (14)

гла́вный main, chief (12); гла́вным о́бразом for the most part, chiefly (19)

глаго́л verb (13)

глаз (*nom. pl.* -а́; *gen. pl.* глаз) eye (3)

глу́бже deeper (25)

глубо́кий deep (13)

глу́пый foolish, stupid, silly (9)

говори́ть (imperf., II: говор.ю́, -и́шь) (8, 14), to speak, talk; tell, say (perfs., *see* сказа́ть and поговори́ть)

год (*loc.* в году́; *gen. pl.*, *see* 16) year; в э́том году́ this year (12); в бу́дущем году́ next year (12)

голова́ head (3)

го́лод hunger, famine

голо́дный hungry (23)

го́лос (*nom. pl.* -а́) voice (11)

гора́здо much (used with comparatives) (25)

гора́ mountain (13)

го́рло throat (23)

го́род (*nom. pl.* -а́) city, town (3); за́ город to the country (17); за́ городом out of town (24)

городско́й city (*adj.*), urban

горя́чий (горячо́) hot (21)

го́спиталь (*m.*) (army) hospital (27)

господи́н (*nom. pl.* господа́; *gen. pl.* госпо́д) Mr., gentleman, master (11); (*in plural*) ladies and gentlemen (20)

госпожа́ Mrs. (11)

гостеприи́мный hospitable (20)

гости́ная (*declined as an adj.*) living room (10)

гости́ница hotel (7)

гость (*m.*) guest (4); ходи́ть/идти́/пойти́ в го́сти to go visiting (17)

гото́вить (imperf., II: гото́в.лю, -ишь) (13), при- (perf., II) (14) to prepare, cook

гото́в/ый ready (13, 23)

граждани́н (*decl.* 20) (*f.* гражда́н.ка, *gen. pl.* -ок) citizen (12)

грамма́тика grammar (2)

грани́ца boundary, frontier (13); (по)е́хать за грани́цу to go abroad (21); бы́ть за грани́цей to be abroad (21)

гро́мкий loud (19)

гру́стный mournful, sad (17)

гря́зный dirty (15)

гуля́ть (imperf., I) (16), по- (perf., I) to stroll, take a walk

ГУМ: госуда́рственный универса́льный магази́п state department store

да yes (2); and; but (emphatic)

дава́ть (imperf., I: да.ю́, -ёшь; imperative: дава́й/те) (9), дать (perf., see 15; imperative: дай/те), to give; д. зна́ть (+ dat.) to let know (21); дава́й(те) let's (25)

давно́ long ago, long since (7, 9, 11). Вы́ давно́ здéсь? Have you been here long? (7) Давно́ пора́ (+ inf.). It's high time to . . .

да́же even (5)

да́лее further; и так да́лее and so forth (21); и т. д. etc. (21)

далеко́ far (away) (5); д. от (+ gen.) far from

да́льше farther, further (25). Что́ идёт д.? What comes next? (19) идти́/éхать д. to go on, continue (one's journey, etc.)

да́ма lady (15)

дать (perf.), see дава́ть

да́ча summer house, cottage (12); (по)éхать на да́чу to go to the country (for the summer, on weekends, etc.)

два (m. and n.), две (f.) two (10, 26)

два́дцать twenty (16, 26)

двена́дцать twelve (16, 26)

дверь (f.) door (5)

двор court, yard (16); на дворé out of doors (24)

двою́родный бра́т (f. двою́родная сестра́) cousin (27)

дéвоч.ка (gen. pl. -ек) (little) girl (13)

дéвуш.ка (gen. pl. -ек) girl, young girl (8)

девяно́сто ninety (21, 26)

девятна́дцать nineteen (16, 26)

девя́тый ninth (18)

дéвять nine (16, 26)

дед, дéдуш.ка (gen. pl. -ек) grandfather (20)

действи́тельно indeed, in fact, actually (14)

дека́брь (m.) December (23)

дéлать (imperf., I) (5, 8), с- (perf., I) (14), to do, make. Что́ на́м д.? What are we to do? (9)

дéло matter, affair, business (14); дела́ (pl.) business (14). В чём д.? What is it? Д. в то́м, что . . . The thing is . . . (14) Как дела́? How are you? How are things? по дéлу on business (24)

день (m., gen. дня) day (6) До́брый д.! Good day! (greeting) (3); днём in the daytime, in the afternoon (11); весь д. all day (7); в два часа́ дня́ at 2:00 p.m. (16)

дéньги (pl. only, gen. дéнег) money (15)

дерéвня village; country (6)

дéрево (nom. pl. дерéвья; gen. pl. дерéвьев) tree, wood (13, 20)

дерева́нный wooden (16)

держа́ть (imperf., II: держу́, дéржишь) to hold (11); д. экза́мен to take an exam (13)

деся́тый tenth (18)

дéсять ten (16, 26)

дéти (gen. pl. детéй) children (13)

дéтская (adj. used as noun) nursery, children's room (22)

дéтство childhood (27)

дешёвый (дёшево) cheap, inexpensive (7)

джаз jazz (9)

дива́н sofa, couch (11)

дирéктор (nom. pl. -á) director (9)

дли́нный long (11)

для (+ gen.) for, for the sake of (16, 17)

дн-, see день

дневно́й afternoon, daytime (adj.); daily (26)

днём in the daytime; in the afternoon (11)

до (+ gen.) before; until, up to; as far as (10); до свида́ния good-bye (3)

до́бр/ый kind, good-hearted (21). Д. дéнь! Good day! (greeting) (3) Бу́дьте добры́ (+ imperative). Be so good as to . . . (17)

дово́льный (+ instr.) pleased, satisfied (with) (10, 23); дово́льно rather, fairly, enough (10)

дождь (m.) rain (17). Идёт д. It's raining. (17); под дождём in the rain

дока́зывать (imperf., I), доказа́ть (perf., I: докажу́, дока́жешь) to prove (27)

докла́д report, speech (12); чита́ть д. to give a talk (12)

докла́д.чик (f. -чица) speaker, lecturer (27)

до́ктор (nom. pl. -á) doctor (4)

долг debt; (moral) duty (no pl. in this meaning) (25)

до́лгий long

до́лго long, for a long time (11)

до́лжен must, have to, ought to (8, 9); д. был had to, was supposed to (8); д. был бы should have (24)

до́ллар dollar (15)

дом (nom. pl. -á) house, building, home (2); до́ма at home (2); домо́й (to) home, homewards (17); и́з дому from home (17)

доплыва́ть (imperf., I), доплы́ть (perf., I: доплыв.у́, -ёшь) (до + gen.) to sail, swim (to, as far as), reach by swimming (24)

доро́га way, road, route (17); по доро́ге on the way

дорого́й (до́рого) dear; expensive (7)

дос.ка́ (gen. pl. -ок) blackboard, board (2)

достава́ть (imperf., I: доста.ю́, -ёшь; imperative: достава́й/-те), доста́ть (perf., I: доста́н.у, -ешь) to get, obtain (at times with difficulty) (21)

доста́точно enough, sufficiently (16)

дочь (f.) daughter (4, decl. 12, 20)

друг (*nom. pl.* друзья́; *gen. pl.* друзе́й) friend (6, *20*)

дру́г дру́га each other, one another (*13*)

друго́й another, a different, other (10); по-друго́му otherwise, differently (21)

ду́мать (imperf., I) (5, 8), по- (perf., I) (20), to think

дура́к (*f.* ду́ра) fool (26)

душ shower (24)

ду́шно stuffy; it's stuffy (17)

дым smoke (27)

дя́дя (*m.*) uncle (20)

Евро́па Europe (5)

европе́йский European (7)

ед-, *see* е́хать; есть

еда́ food (20)

еди́нственный the only (one) (27)

е́здить (indeterm. imperf., II: е́зжу, е́здишь), е́хать (determ. imperf., I: е́д.у, -ешь; imperative езжа́й/те), пое́хать (perf., I) to go, ride, drive (*17*)

ел ate (past tense of есть) (7)

е́сли if (10, *14*); е́сли бы if (*24*)

есть there is (are) (7); то́ есть that is (17); У меня́ есть . . . (+ *nom.*) I have . . . (*10*)

есть (imperf., 7, 8, *conj. 21*), по- (perf., *21*), съ- (perf. trans., *21*) to eat

е́хать (indeterm. imperf., I: е́д.у, -ешь), по- (perf., I) to go, ride, drive (*17*)

ещё still, yet (7); in addition, more, another (10); кто́ ещё who else? что́ ещё what else? ещё оди́н one more (10) Ещё бы! I should say so! (8); ещё не (не́т) not yet

жа́ловаться (imperf., I: жа́лу.юсь, -ешься), по- (perf., I) (+ *dat.*) to complain to; (на + *acc.*) to complain (of) (23)

жаль: Жа́ль, что . . . It's too bad that . . . (6) Как жа́ль! What a pity! Мне́ его́ (*acc.*) жа́ль. I feel sorry for him. (18)

жара́ heat (21)

жа́реный fried (21)

жа́ркий hot (of weather) (7) Жа́рко. It's hot. (9)

ждать (imperf., I: жду, ждёшь), подожда́ть (perf., I) (+ *gen. or acc., see 18*) to wait for (*18*)

же particle expressing identity, contrast, emphasis, emotional intensity, etc. что́ же? what then, but what? где́ же? just where? то́т же the same (18); та́к же . . . как just as . . . as (27)

жёлтый yellow (11)

жена́ (*nom. pl.* жёны) wife (4)

жена́т married (said of men; in plural of a married couple) (26); ж. на (+ *loc.*) married to

же́нщина woman (4)

жест gesture (11)

живо́т stomach, belly (23)

живо́тное (*adj. used as noun*) animal (23)

жизнь (*f.*) life (11)

жил.е́ц (*gen.* -ьца́) (*f.* -и́ца) lodger, tenant (21)

жи́тель (*m.*) (*f.* -ница) inhabitant (25)

жить (imperf., I: жив.у́, -ёшь) to live (9)

журна́л magazine (3)

журнали́ст (*f.* -ка, *gen. pl.* -ок) reporter, newspaperman (woman) (4)

за (+ *instr.*) behind, beyond, on the other side of (*19*), for (after) (17); (+ *acc.*) beyond, to the other side of (27); (in exchange) for (*16, 17*). Не́ за что. Don't mention it. (10) Что́ э́то за (+ *nom.*)? What (kind of) . . . ? (22)

заба́вный amusing, entertaining (26)

заболева́ть (imperf., I), заболе́ть (perf., I) to fall ill (23)

забыва́ть (imperf., I), забы́ть (perf., I: забу́д.у, -ешь) to forget (16)

заво́д plant, factory (12)

заводско́й factory (*adj.*) (14)

за́втра tomorrow (10); До з. Good-bye until tomorrow. (19)

за́втрак breakfast; lunch (11)

за́втракать (imperf., I) (11), по- (perf., I) (17) to have breakfast, lunch

заграни́ца abroad (22); из заграни́цы from abroad (22)

задава́ть (imperf., I: зада.ю́, -ёшь; imperative задава́й/те) (13), зада́ть (perf.; *conj.* like дать) (24): to assign; з. вопро́с to ask a question (13); з. уро́к/и to assign homework (13)

зада́ние assignment, task (13)

заинтересова́ть(ся) (perf.), *see* нитересова́ть(ся)

зайти́ (perf.), *see* заходи́ть

закрыва́ть (imperf., I) (8), закры́ть (perf., I: закро́.ю, -ешь) (15) to close, shut

закры́т/ый closed, shut (26)

заку́с.ка (*gen. pl.* -ок) appetizer, hors d'œuvres (11)

замеча́тельный wonderful, remarkable (12)

замеча́ть (imperf., I), заме́тить (perf., II: заме́.чу, -тишь) to notice, observe (22)

за́мужем married (of women only) (26); з. за (+ *instr.*) married to (26)

занима́ть (imperf., I), заня́ть (perf., I: займ.у́, -ёшь; past за́нял, etc.) to occupy (22); занима́ться, заня́ться to be occupied with, study (imperf. only) (+ *instr.*) (19, 23)

заня́тие occupation (21); заня́тия studies, classes, occupations (21)

занято́й busy, occupied (22, *23*)

за́пад west (22); на з. to the west; на за́паде in the west

за́падный western (22)

запи́с.ка (*gen. pl.* -ок) note, jotting

запи́сывать (imperf., I) (13), **записа́ть** (perf., I: **запишу́, запи́шешь**) (15) to write down, note down

заплати́ть (perf.), *see* **плати́ть**

запомина́ть (imperf., I), **запо́мнить** (perf., II: **запо́мн.ю, -ишь**) to memorize, learn (by heart) (18)

зараба́тывать (imperf., I), **зарабо́тать** (perf., I) to earn (27)

зара́нее in advance, ahead (23)

засыпа́ть (imperf., I), **засну́ть** (perf., I: **засн.у́, -ёшь**) to fall asleep (24)

зато́ on the other hand, however (25)

заходи́ть (imperf., II: **захожу́, захо́дишь**), **зайти́** (perf., I: **зайд.у́, -ёшь**; past **зашёл, зашло́**, etc.) to call on, stop in, drop in (to see) (**к** + *dat.*) (22); to stop for (**за** + *instr.*) (22)

захоте́ть (perf.), *see* **хоте́ть**

заче́м why, what for (10)

защи́та defense (27)

звать (imperf., I: **зов.у́, -ёшь**) **на-** (perf., I), to name, call (+ *nom. or instr.*); **Ка́к его́ зову́т?** What is his name? (26) **Его́ зову́т Па́вел (Па́влом).** His name is Pavel. (26)

звони́ть (imperf., II: **звон.ю́, -и́шь**), **по-** (perf., II) (14) to ring, telephone (+ *dat.*) (9)

звон.о́к (*gen.* -ка́) bell, ring (3)

зда́ние building (12)

здесь here (4)

здо́рово! (*colloq.*) wonderful! terrific! (7)

здоро́в/ый healthy, well (*23*)

здоро́вье health (21); **Ка́к ва́ше здоро́вье?** How is your health? (21) (**вы́)пить за з.** (+ *gen.*) to drink someone's health (26)

здра́вствуй(те)! hello! (4)

зелёный green (12)

земля́ (*gen. pl.* **земе́ль**) land, earth (23)

зима́ (6); **зимо́й** in winter (11)

зи́мний winter (*adj.*) (6)

злой evil, wicked, vicious, ill-tempered (21)

знак sign (19)

знако́мить (imperf., II: **знако́м.лю, -ишь**), **по-** (perf., II) to acquaint, introduce (*acc. and* **с** + *instr.*) (20); **знако́миться, по-** to be introduced, meet, make the acquaintance of (**с** + *instr.*) (20)

знако́м/ый familiar; an acquaintance (*adj. used as noun*) (20, 23); **знако́м, -а, -ы с** (+ *instr.*) acquainted with (20, 23). **Мы́ знако́мы.** We are acquainted. (20)

знамени́тость (*f.*) celebrity (25)

знамени́тый famous (12)

зна́ние knowledge (27)

знать (imperf., I) to know (5)

зна́чит (*as adv.*) so, then, hence (26). **Что́ зна́чит . . . ?** What does . . . mean? (18)

зов-, *see* **звать**

золото́й gold, golden (26)

зонт, зо́нтик umbrella (24)

зуб tooth (24)

и and (2); also, too, as well (7); even (7); **и . . . и** both . . . and (4); **и так да́лее** and so forth; **и т. д.** etc.

игра́ть (imperf., I) (6, 8), **сыгра́ть** (perf., trans., I) (14) to play; **и. на роя́ле** to play the piano (6); **и. в те́ннис** to play tennis (6); **и. в ша́хматы** to play chess (14); **и. в ка́рты** to play cards (14)

игру́ш.ка (*gen. pl.* -ек) toy (22)

иде́я idea (16)

идти́ (determ. imperf., I: **ид.у́, -ёшь**; past **шёл, шло**, etc.), **пойти́** (perf., I: **пойд.у́, -ёшь**; past **пошёл, пошло́**, etc.) to go, walk (17); **Идём (пойдём)!** Let's go (23). **Идёт до́ждь.** It's raining (17). **Фи́льм/пье́са идёт.** The picture/the play is running (playing) (17)

из (+ *gen.*) out of, from (*15, 17*)

изве́стие (piece of) news, information (27)

изве́стный well-known (16)

извиня́ть (imperf., I), **извини́ть** (perf., II: **извин.ю́, -и́шь**) to excuse (18)

издалека́, и́здали from afar (21, 25)

изда́тель (*m.*) publisher (11)

изменя́ться (imperf., I), **измени́ться** (perf., II: **изменю́сь, изме́нишься**) to change (*intrans.*), be altered (21)

изуча́ть (imperf., I), **изучи́ть** (perf., II: **изучу́, изу́чишь**) (+ *acc.*) to study, learn (12, 23)

и́ли or (2); **и́ли . . . и́ли** either . . . or (5)

име́ть (imperf., I: **име́.ю, -ешь**) to have (21)

и́мя (*n.*) (first, Christian) name (7, *decl.* 12); **Ка́к ва́ше и́мя?** What is your (first) name? (7)

ина́че otherwise, differently (27)

инжене́р engineer (9)

иногда́ sometimes (8)

иностра́н.ец (*gen.* -ца) (*f.* -ка, *gen. pl.* -ок) foreigner (20)

иностра́нный foreign (20)

инстру́ктор (*nom. pl.* -а́) (*f.* -ша) (practical) instructor (23)

интере́с interest (11); **и. к** (+ *dat.*) interest in

интере́сный interesting (5)

интересова́ть (imperf., I: **интересу́.ю, -ешь**), **за-** (perf., I) to interest (+ *acc. of person, instr. of object of interest*) (21); **интересова́ться, за-** to be interested in (+ *instr.*)

иска́ть (imperf., I: **ищу́, и́щешь**) to look for, seek (24)

иску́сство art

испа́н.ец (*gen.* -ца) (*f.* -ка, *gen. pl.* -ок) Spaniard (20)

испа́нский Spanish (*adj.*) (20)

историк historian (11)

история history; story, event (9)

Италия Italy (12)

итальян.ец (*gen.* -ца) (*f.* -ка, *gen. pl.* -ок) Italian (20)

итальянский Italian (*adj.*) (20)

июль (*m.*) July (*23*)

июнь (*m.*) June (*23*)

к, ко (+ *dat.*) to, toward; to the house of (*17, 22*)

кабинет study (5)

Кавказ Caucasus (3); на Кавказе in the Caucasus (12, 25)

каждый each, every (8)

казаться (imperf., I: кажусь, кажешься), по- (perf., I) to seem (+ *instr.*) (19)

как how, like, as (3); what do you mean? (surprise); как только as soon as (14); так как since, because, as (14); как и as well as, along with

как-нибудь, как-то somehow (*22*)

какой what (a); which; what kind of; how (6); к. большой how large, what a large (6); к.-нибудь, к.-то any, some, sort of (*22*)

каникулы (*pl. only, gen.* каникул) (school) vacation (23)

карандаш pencil (3)

карта map; card (3); играть в карты to play cards (14)

картина picture; motion picture (5)

картофель (*m., no pl.*) potato(es) (11)

каша porridge, cooked cereal, kasha (21)

квартира apartment (5)

килограмм (*masc.,* or кило, *neut.*) kilogram, kilo (7)

километр kilometer (25)

кино (*neut. indecl.*) movie house, cinema (*12*)

киоск newsstand, kiosk (8)

Китай China (11, 25)

китайский Chinese (*adj.*) (20)

класс class, classroom (2)

класть (imperf., I: клад.у́, -ёшь; past клал, etc.), положить (perf., II: положу, положишь) to put, place, lay down (24)

климат climate (12)

клуб club (12)

книга book (2)

книжный book (*adj.*) (10); к. магазин bookstore (10); книжная полка bookshelf, bookcase (10)

ко, *see* к

ков.ёр (*gen.* -ра́) rug, carpet (10)

когда when (4, *14*); к.-либо ever, at all (25); к.-нибудь, к.-то at one time, at some time, one day (*22*)

колбаса sausage (17)

колхоз collective farm (17)

колхозн.ик (*f.* -ица) collective farmer

колхозный collective farm (*adj.*)

команда team (22)

комната room (4)

кон.ец (*gen.* -ца́) end, finish (7); в конце at the end (7); в конце концов in the end, in the last analysis

конечно of course, certainly (5)

контора office

конфета a piece of candy (20); конфеты (*pl.*) candy (20)

концерт concert (5); на концерте at a concert (5)

кончать (imperf., I) (8), кончить (perf., II: конч.у, -ишь) (15) to finish, end

копейка (*gen. pl.* копеек) copeck (1/100 of a ruble) (26)

коридор corridor, hall (16)

корова cow (23)

королева queen (18)

король (*m.*) king (18)

короткий (коротко) short, brief (11)

костюм suit (6)

который (*rel. pron.*) who, which, that (6); (*interrog. pron.*) which (one)? (6) К. час? What time is it? (16) В котором часу? At what time? (16)

кофе (*m. indecl.*) coffee (11)

кофейник coffeepot (24)

кош.ка (*gen. pl.* -ек) cat (16)

красивый beautiful, handsome, pretty (6)

красный red (8)

красота beauty (26)

кресло armchair (6)

крестьян.ин (*decl.* 20) (*f.* -ка, *gen. pl.* -ок) peasant (*20*)

крик cry, shout (21)

кричать (imperf., II: крич.у́, -ишь), крикнуть (perf., I: крикн.у, -ешь) to cry out, shout (21)

кровать (*f.*) bed (5)

кроме (+ *gen.*) except, besides (*prep.*) (10); к. того besides (*adv.*) (23)

Крым (*loc.* в Крыму́) Crimea (12)

крыша roof (7)

кстати by the way; apropos (21)

кто who (3)

кто-нибудь, кто-то anybody, somebody (22)

куда where, whither (17)

куда-нибудь, куда-то somewhere (22)

культура culture (20)

культурный cultured, cultural (20)

купить (perf.), *see* покупать

курить (imperf., II: курю, куришь) to smoke (11)

кус.ок (*gen.* -ка́) piece, bit (7)

кухня kitchen (4)

ла́в.ка (*gen. pl.* **-ок**) shop, small store (25)

ла́дно all right, O.K. (*colloq.*) (20)

ла́мпа lamp, electric light (2)

ле́вый left (11)

лёгкий (легко́) easy, light (6)

лежа́ть (imperf., II: леж.у́, -и́шь) to lie, be lying (11)

ле́кция lecture (12); чита́ть ле́кцию to give a lecture (12)

лени́вый lazy (10)

лень: Мне́ бы́ло л. (+ *inf.*) I didn't feel like . . .; I felt too lazy to . . . (18)

лес (*loc.* в лесу́; *nom. pl.* леса́) woods, forest (12)

лета́ть (indeterm. imperf., I), лете́ть (determ. imperf., II: лечу́, лети́шь), полете́ть (perf., II) to fly (24)

ле́тний summer (*adj.*) (6)

ле́то summer (6); ле́том in summer (11); пя́ть ле́т five years (16)

лечь (perf.), *see* ложи́ться

ли, interrogative particle used in "yes-or-no" questions (22)

лимо́н lemon (11)

лист (*nom. pl.* листы́; *gen. pl.* листо́в) sheet (13); (*nom. pl.* ли́стья; *gen. pl.* ли́стьев, etc.) leaf (13, 20)

литерату́ра literature (20)

литерату́рный literary (20)

лифт elevator (21)

лицо́ face; person (3)

ли́чный personal (27)

лови́ть (imperf., II: ловлю́, ло́вишь), пойма́ть (perf., I) to catch (27)

ложи́ться (imperf., II: лож.у́сь, -и́шься; imperative ложи́.сь/тесь), лечь (perf., I: ля́гу, ля́жешь . . . ля́гут; imperative ля́г/те; past лёг, легло́, etc.) to lie down, go to bed (21); л. спа́ть to go to bed (21)

ло́ж.ка (*gen. pl.* **-ек**) spoon (11)

ло́шадь (*f., instr. pl.* лошадьми́) horse (16)

луна́ moon (21)

лу́чше better (23, *25*). Мне́ л. I am (feel) better (23); л. всего́ (все́х) best of all (25)

лу́чший better, best (*25*); Всего́ лу́чшего! All the best! Good-bye!

любе́зный kind, gracious (17, *23*). Бу́дьте любе́зны (+ *imperative*). Be so kind as to . . . (17)

люби́мый favorite, beloved (12, *27*)

люби́ть (imperf., II: люблю́, лю́бишь) to love, like (11, *19*)

любо́вь (*f., gen.,* любви́; *instr.* любо́вью) love (12)

любо́й any (whatsoever), any you like (21)

лю́ди (*pl., gen. pl.* люде́й) people (13)

мавзоле́й mausoleum (18)

магази́н store, shop (9)

май May (23)

ма́ленький little, small (6)

ма́ло (+ *gen.*) little, few (*5*)

ма́льчик boy (13)

ма́ма mama (5)

ма́р.ка (*gen. pl.,* **-ок**) stamp (17)

март March (23)

ма́сло butter; oil (6)

ма́сса mass; great quantity of (*colloq.*) (17)

матч match, game (22)

мать mother (4, *decl. 12, 20*)

маши́на machine; car, auto (10)

машини́ст (*f.* **-ка**, *gen. pl.* **-ок**) machinist; typist (14)

ме́бель (*f. collect.*) furniture (10)

ме́дленно slowly (8)

ме́жду (+ *instr.*) between, among (19); м. про́чим incidentally, by the way (19)

мел chalk (11)

ме́ньше (+ *gen.*) less, fewer (*8*)

ме́ньший smaller (25)

ме́сто place, seat (11); на м. to its proper place (24); на ме́сте in its place; on the spot (24)

ме́сяц month; moon (7); в э́том ме́сяце this month (23)

метро́ (*n. indecl.*) subway (12); на метро́ by subway

мечта́ (day)dream, reverie, fancy (27)

мечта́ть (imperf., I) to daydream, dream, muse

миллио́н million (26)

ми́лый nice, likable, dear (9)

ми́мо (+ *gen.*) past, by (22)

мину́та minute (18)

мир world; peace (6)

мирово́й world (*adj.*) (18)

мла́дший younger, youngest (9, *25*)

мне́ние opinion; по мне́нию (+ *gen.*) in the opinion of . . . (23)

мно́го (+ *gen.*) much, many (5, *7, 20*); так мно́го (+ *gen. pl.*) so many (*16, 20*); мно́го хоро́шего many good things (9)

мно́гое (*declined as a neut. adj.*) much, many things (23)

мог-, мож-, *see* мочь

мо́да fashion, style (13)

мо́жет быть maybe, perhaps (10)

мо́жно it is possible to; one can (may) (21). Мо́жно (мне́)? May I? (*21*)

мой my, mine (4, *12, 20*)

мо́крый wet (24)

молодёжь (*f., collect.*) young people (16)

молоде́ц! (*used both for men and women*) Good for you (him, her)! (8)

молодо́й young (6)

мо́лодость (*f.*) youth (27)

молоко́ milk (7)

молочный milk (*adj.*)

море sea (12)

мороженое (*adj. used as noun*) ice cream (11)

Москва Moscow (3)

московский (of) Moscow (12)

мост (*loc.* на мосту) bridge (12)

мочь (imperf., I: могу, можешь . . . могут; past мог, могло, etc.) (10) с- (perf., I) (21) to be able (+ *inf.*); я могу I can (10); я смогу I shall be able, shall manage (21); может быть maybe, perhaps (10). Я не могу не (+ *inf.*) I can't help . . . (11)

мою(сь), *see* мыть(ся)

муж (*nom. pl.* мужья, *gen. pl.* мужей) husband (4, 20)

мужчина (*m.*) man (male) (20)

музей museum (2)

музыка music (9)

музыкант musician (6)

мы we (3)

мысль (*f.*) thought, idea (21)

мыть (imperf., I: мою, -ешь), по- or вы- (perf., I) to wash (*trans.*) (19), мыться, по- or вы- to wash (oneself) (19)

мягкий soft (19)

мясник butcher (19)

мясо meat (6)

на (+ *loc.*) on, at (5); (+ *acc.*) onto, to (16); (+ *acc.*) for (time) (18); by (with vehicles) (17)

наверно(е) likely, probably, for sure (18)

над, надо (+ *instr.*) above, over (19)

надевать (imperf., I), надеть (perf., I: наден.у, -ешь) to put on (24)

надежда hope; н. на (+ *acc.*) hope for, reliance on (27)

надеяться (imperf., I: наде.юсь, -ешься) to hope (19); н. на (+ *acc.*) to rely on

надо (+ *inf.*) it is necessary to . . . , one must (has to) . . . (10); Мне надо (+ *inf.*). I must (have to, need to) . . . (10)

надо, *see* над

надолго for a long time (22)

назад back; (тому) н. ago (16)

название name, title (7); Как название (+ *gen.*)? What is the name of (an object)? (7)

называть (imperf., I), назвать (perf., I: назов.у, -ешь) to name, call (18)

найти (perf.), *see* находить

наказание punishment (27)

наконец finally, at last (14)

налево on (to) the left (12)

население population (25)

написать (perf.), *see* писать

направо on (to) the right (12)

например for example (8)

народ nation, people (27)

народный national, folk (21)

настоящий real (9), present

находить (imperf., II: нахожу, находишь), найти (perf., I: найд.у, -ёшь; past нашёл, нашло, etc.) to find; находиться to be located (22)

начало beginning (7); в начале (+ *gen.*) at the beginning of . . . (7)

начальник superior, chief, boss (9)

начинать (imperf., I) (8), начать (perf., I: начн.у, -ёшь) (15) to begin, start (+ *inf.*)

наш our, ours (4, 12, 20)

не not (2); Не за что. Don't mention it. (10)

небо (*pl.* небеса) sky, heaven (7)

невозможно impossible (18, 20)

недавно recently, not long ago (7)

недалеко not far (away) (6); н. от (+ *gen.*) not far from (25)

неделя week (8)

недоволен dissatisfied (10); н. (+ *instr.*) dissatisfied with . . .

недостаточно insufficiently (16)

некоторые (*pl. adj.*) some, certain (ones) (20)

нелегко not easy, hard (9)

нельзя (+ *inf.*) it is impossible (forbidden); one can (may) (must) not (21); н. не (+ *inf.*) one can't help but . . .

немедленно immediately

нем.ец (*gen.* -ца) (*f.* -ка, *gen. pl.* -ок) German

немецкий German (*adj.*) (20)

немного, немножко (+ *gen.*) a little (7, 20)

ненавидеть (imperf., II: ненави.жу, -дишь) to hate (14)

необходимый essential, indispensable, necessary (27)

неплохо not bad(ly) (11)

неправ wrong (in predicate only) (14)

неправда untruth; (it is) not true (5)

неправильно incorrect(ly) (19)

неприятный unpleasant (8)

несколько (+ *gen. pl.*) several, a few, some, a number of (16, 20)

несмотря на (+ *acc.*) in spite of (27)

несчастный unhappy, unfortunate (13)

нет no (2); (+ *gen.*) there is (are) no; (at end of sentence) not (7); нету (+ *gen.*) (*colloq.*) there is (are) no (7)

нетерпение impatience (18); с нетерпением impatiently

ни not even; ни . . . ни neither . . . nor (8)

-нибудь, *see* 22

нигде nowhere (8)

низкий low (10)

никакой no, none (at all) (21)

никогда never (8)

никто no one (8, 10)

ничего́ nothing (8, 10); never mind; it doesn't matter; it's not so bad; so-so (16); бо́льше н. nothing else (8)

но but (5)

но́вый new (6); Что́ (у ва́с) но́вого? What's new (with you)?

но́вость (f.) news, a piece of news (14); но́вости (pl.) the news (14)

нога́ foot, leg (10)

нож knife (16)

но́мер (nom. pl. -а́) number, hotel room (6, 7, 12)

норма́льный normal (6)

нос (loc. на носу́) nose (3)

нос.о́к (gen. -ка́) sock (24)

ночно́й night (adj.)

ночь (f.) night (6); но́чью at night (11); в два́ часа́ но́чи at 2:00 A.M. (16); Споко́йной но́чи! Good night! (20)

ноя́брь (m.) November (23)

нра́виться (imperf., II: нра́в.люсь, -ишься), по- (perf., II) to please, like (see 19); Мне́ нра́вится (+ nom.) I like . . . (19)

ну well (interjection expressing mild surprise, impatience or encouragement) (5)

ну́жен necessary, needed (10); Мне́ нужна́ кни́га. I need a book (10). Ну́жно (+ inf.). It is necessary to; one must (has to, needs to) . . . (9). Мне́ ну́жно (+ inf.). I must (have to . . .) (9)

о, об, обо (+ loc.) about, concerning (5, 12)

о́ба, о́бе both (26)

обе́д dinner (10); к обе́ду to (for) dinner (18)

обе́дать (imperf., I); по- (perf., I) to dine, have dinner (11)

обеща́ть (imperf., I) (21) to promise (+ dat. of person)

о́блако (gen. pl. облако́в) cloud (27)

обо, see о

обожа́ть (imperf., I) (23) to adore, worship

о́браз image, picture; way, form; гла́вным о́бразом for the most part, chiefly (19)

образова́ние education (23)

обра́тно back, in return (17)

о́бщество (gen. pl. о́бществ) society; company (20)

о́бщий common, mutual, general (20)

объясне́ние explanation (13)

объясня́ть (imperf., I) (8), объясни́ть (perf., II: объясн.ю́, -и́шь) (15) to explain

обыкнове́нный ordinary, usual (12)

обы́чно usually (9)

о́вощи (pl., gen. pl. овоще́й) vegetables (19)

огро́мный huge, enormous, immense (12)

ода́лживать (imperf., I), одолжи́ть (perf., II: одолж.у́, -и́шь) to lend (22)

одева́ть (imperf., I), оде́ть (perf., I: оде́н.у, -ешь) to dress (trans.) (19); одева́ться, оде́ться to dress (intrans.) (19)

оде́жда clothing (24)

оди́н one (8, 12); only, alone (8, 12); a certain (8); одни́ only, alone; some, certain (8, 12); ни оди́н not a single (20); одни́ . . . други́е some . . . others (13); оди́н его́ дру́г a friend of his (15); оди́н из его́ друзе́й one of his friends (20)

одина́ково equally (19)

оди́ннадцать eleven (16, 26)

одино́кий lonely (18)

одна́жды once, at one time

одни́, see оди́н

одолжи́ть, perf., see ода́лживать

о́зеро (nom. pl., озёра) lake (13)

ока́зываться (imperf., I), оказа́ться (perf., I: окажу́сь, ока́жешься) to turn out (to be) (24); Он оказа́лся (+ instr.). He turned out to be . . . . Оказа́лось, что . . . . It turned out that . . . .

ока́нчивать (imperf., I), око́нчить (perf., II: око́нч.у, -ишь) to complete, graduate from (+ acc.) (23)

окно́ (gen. pl. о́кон) window (2)

о́коло (+ gen.) near, about, approximately (16, 26)

окружа́ть (imperf., I), окружи́ть (perf., II: окруж.у́, -и́шь) to surround (27)

октя́брь (m.) October (23)

он he; it (3, 4)

она́ she; it (3, 4)

они́ they (3, 4)

оно́ it (3, 4)

опа́здывать (imperf., I), опозда́ть (perf., I) to be late (17); о. в кла́сс to be late for class; о. на по́езд to be late for the train; о. на ча́с to be an hour late

опа́сность (f.) danger (27)

опа́сный dangerous (17)

описа́ние description

опи́сывать (imperf., I), описа́ть (perf., I: опишу́, опи́шешь) to describe (26)

опя́ть again (14)

оригина́льный original (9)

осе́нний autumn, fall (adj.)

о́сень (f.) autumn, fall; о́сенью in fall (11)

осно́вывать (imperf., I), основа́ть (perf., I: осну.ю́, -ёшь) to found, establish (18)

осо́бенно especially (12)

остава́ться (imperf., I: оста.ю́сь, -ёшься), оста́ться (perf., I: оста́н.усь, -ешься) to remain, stay, be left (25)

оставля́ть (imperf., I), оста́вить (perf., II: оста́в.лю, -ишь) to leave (trans.) (22)

остана́вливать (imperf., I), останови́ть (perf., II: остановлю́, остано́вишь) to stop (trans.); остана́вливаться, останови́ться to stop (intrans.) (22)

остано́в.ка (*gen. pl.* -ок) stop (bus) (22)

о́стров (*nom. pl.* -á) island (24)

о́стрый sharp (16)

от (+ *gen.*) from, away from, from the house of (15, *17*)

отве́т answer, reply (9)

отвеча́ть (imperf., I) (9), отве́тить (perf., II: отве́.чу, -тишь) (15) to answer, reply (+ *dat. of persons or* на + *acc., see 15*)

отвози́ть (imperf., II: отвожу́, отво́зишь), отвезти́ (perf., I: отвез.у́, -ёшь; past отвёз, отвезло́, etc.) to take, drive, transport (to) (*22*)

отвыка́ть (imperf., I), отвы́кнуть (perf., I: отвы́кн.у, -ешь; past отвы́к, отвы́кло, etc.) to grow unaccustomed to (от + *gen. or inf.*) (21)

отде́л department, section (13)

о́тдых rest, relaxation (8)

отдыха́ть (imperf., I) (8), отдохну́ть (perf., I: отдохн.у́, -ёшь) (21) to rest, relax

от.е́ц (*gen.* -ца́) father (4)

открыва́ть (imperf., I) (8), откры́ть (perf., I: откро́.ю, -ешь) (24) to open

откры́тие discovery (17)

откры́тый open, opened (26)

отку́да from where (*17*)

отли́чный excellent (18)

отме́т.ка (*gen. pl.* -ок) mark, grade (13)

относи́ть (imperf., II: отношу́, отно́сишь), отнести́ (perf., I: отнес.у́, -ёшь; past отнёс, отнесло́, etc.) to take, carry (to, on foot) (22)

о́тпуск leave (from work), vacation (26)

отсю́да from here (*17*)

отту́да from there (*17*)

отходи́ть (imperf., II: отхожу́, отхо́дишь), отойти́ (perf., I: отойд.у́, -ёшь; past отошёл, отошло́, etc.) to move away, withdraw (on foot), stand back (от + *gen.*) (22)

о́тчество patronymic (*11*)

офице́р officer (11)

о́чень very (3, *10*)

о́чередь (*f.*) line, queue, turn (18, 20); ста́ть в о. to get in line (20)

ошиба́ться (imperf., I), ошиби́ться (perf., I: ошиб.у́сь, -ёшься; past оши́бся, оши́блось, etc.) (22) to be mistaken

оши́б.ка (*gen. pl.* -ок) mistake, error; (с)де́лать оши́бку to make a mistake (14)

па́дать (imperf., I), упа́сть (perf., I: упад.у́, -ёшь; past упа́л, -о, -а, -и) to fall (24)

паке́т package (22)

па́л.ец (*gen.* -ьца) finger; toe (11)

пальто́ (*n. indecl.*) coat, overcoat (12)

па́мятник monument, memorial (7)

па́мять (*f.*) memory (11)

па́па papa (*20*)

папиро́са cigarette (15)

па́ра pair, couple (13)

па́р.ень (*gen.* -ня) (*colloq.*) fellow

парк park (6)

парохо́д ship, steamboat (18)

па́ртия game; political party (14)

пассажи́р (*f.* -ка, *gen. pl.* -ок) passenger (22)

пев.е́ц (*gen.* -ца́) (*f.* -и́ца) singer (16)

пе́рвый first (6); в п. ра́з (for) the first time (16) во-пе́рых first, in the first place (20)

перево́д translation (10)

переводи́ть (imperf., II: перевожу́, перево́д-ишь) (5, *19*), перевести́ (perf., I: перевед.у́, -ёшь; past перевёл, перевело́, etc.) (19) to translate

перево́д.чик (*f.* -чица) translator, interpreter (12)

перед, передо (+ *instr.*) before, in front of (*19*)

передава́ть (imperf., I: переда.ю́, -ёшь), переда́ть (perf., *conj. like* дать) to convey, transmit, give (18); п. приве́т to give, send (someone) one's regards (18)

пере́дняя (*adj. used as noun*) vestibule, anteroom (24)

переноси́ть (imperf., II: переношу́, перено́сишь), перенести́ (perf., I: перенес.у́, -ёшь; past перенёс, перенесло́, etc.) to bear, endure, carry (over) (27)

перепи́сывать (imperf., I), переписа́ть (perf., I: перепишу́, перепи́шешь) to rewrite (15)

перестава́ть (imperf., I: переста.ю́, -ёшь), переста́ть (perf., I: перестáн.у, -ешь) to stop, cease (+ *imperf. inf.*) (21, 22)

переходи́ть (imperf., II: перехожу́, перехо́дишь), перейти́ (perf., I: перейд.у́, -ёшь; past перешёл, перешло́, etc.) to cross (22)

пе́р.ец (*gen.* -ца) pepper (21)

перо́ (*nom. pl.* пе́рья, *gen. pl.* пе́рьев) pen; nib; feather (2)

пе́сня (*gen. pl.* пе́сен) song (13)

петь (imperf., I: по.ю́, -ёшь), с- (perf., trans., I) to sing (16)

печа́льный sad (22)

пешко́м on foot (17)

пи́во beer (17)

пиджа́к coat, jacket (13)

писа́ние writing (14)

писа́тель (*f.* -ница) writer (5)

писа́ть (imperf., I: пишу́, пи́шешь) (9), на-(perf., I) (14) to write

пи́сьменный сто́л desk (7)

письмо́ (*gen. pl.* пи́сем) letter (4)

пить (imperf., I: пью, пьёшь; imperative пей/те) (11), вы́- (perf., trans., I) (past, 7; present, 21) to drink; (вы́)пить за здоро́вье (+ *gen.*) to drink to the health of . . . (26)

пла́вать (indeterm. imperf., I), плыть (determ. imperf., I: плыв.у́, -ёшь), поплы́ть (perf., I) to float, sail, swim (*24*)

пла́кать (imperf., I: пла́ч.у, -ешь) to weep, cry (21)

план plan (14)

пласти́н.ка (*gen. pl.* -ок) phonograph record

плати́ть (imperf., II: плачу́, пла́тишь), за- (perf., II) to pay (+ *dat. of person*) (16); (за)п. за (+ *acc.*) to pay for (16)

плат.о́к (*gen.* -ка́) kerchief, handkerchief (22)

пла́тье (*gen. pl.* пла́тьев) dress (6)

племя́нник nephew (22)

племя́нница niece (22)

плита́ stove (24)

плохо́й (пло́хо) bad, poor (6); Мне́ пло́хо. I feel sick (23)

пло́щадь (*f.*) square (12)

по (+ *dat.*) about, around, along (motion) (*17*); по го́роду around (back and forth through) the city; по у́лице along the street

по-англи́йски (in) English (*5*); говори́ть по-англи́йски to speak English, in English (*5*)

побежа́ть (perf.), *see* бежа́ть

поблагодари́ть (perf.), *see* благодари́ть

по-ва́шему in your opinion

повезти́ (perf.), *see* везти́

пове́рить (perf.), *see* ве́рить

повести́ (perf.), *see* вести́

повторе́ние repetition (18)

повторя́ть (imperf., I) (18), повтори́ть (perf., II: повтор.ю́, -и́шь) (24) to repeat

поговори́ть (perf., II: поговор.ю́, -и́шь) (*20*), perf. of говори́ть = to speak, talk

погово́р.ка (*gen. pl.* -ок) saying, proverb (18)

пого́да weather; Кака́я сего́дня п.? What is the weather today? (6)

по́д, подо (+ *instr.*) under, below (19)

пода́р.ок (*gen.* -ка) gift (9)

подожда́ть (perf.), *see* ждать

подплыва́ть (imperf., I), подплы́ть (perf., I: подплыв.у́, -ёшь) to approach by sailing, swimming; to swim/sail up to (24)

подру́га (girl) friend (8)

по-друго́му otherwise, differently (21)

поду́мать (perf.), *see* ду́мать

поду́ш.ка (*gen. pl.* -ек) pillow (24)

подходи́ть (imperf., II: подхожу́, подхо́-дишь), подойти́ (perf., I: подойд.у́, -ёшь; past подошёл, подошло́, etc.) to approach, go (come) up, come near (on foot) (к + *dat.*) (22)

подъезжа́ть (imperf., I), подъе́хать (perf., I: подъе́д.у, -ешь; imperative подъезжа́й/те) to approach, drive up to (к + *dat.*) (22)

по́езд (*nom. pl.* -а́) train (13)

пое́хать (perf.), *see* е́хать

пожа́луйста please, if you please; you're welcome (3)

пожива́ть (imperf., I) to live, get along; Ка́к вы пожива́ете? How are you? (3)

поза́втракать (perf.), *see* за́втракать

позавчера́ day before yesterday (18)

позвони́ть (perf.), *see* звони́ть

по́здно late (9)

по́зже later (15, 25)

пойти́ (perf.), *see* идти́

пока́ so far, till now; for the time being (14); п. . . . не (+ *perf.*) until (*21*)

пока́зывать (imperf., I) (9), показа́ть (perf., I: покажу́, пока́жешь) (15) to show

показа́ться (perf.), *see* каза́ться

покупа́тель (*f.* -ница) customer, shopper (13)

покупа́ть (imperf., I) (8), купи́ть (perf., II: куплю́, ку́пишь) (16) to buy

поку́п.ка (*gen. pl.* -ок) purchase (22)

пол (*loc.* на полу́) floor (2)

по́лдень (*m.*) noon (19)

по́ле field (4)

поле́зный useful (27)

полете́ть (perf.), *see* лете́ть

поли́тика politics, policy (7)

по́л.ка (*gen. pl.* -ок) shelf, bookshelf (2)

по́лночь (*f.*) midnight (19)

по́лный full (+ *gen.*) (*24*)

полови́на half (14, *26*); три́ с полови́ной three and a half

положе́ние position, situation (18)

положи́ть (perf.), *see* класть

полтор.а́ (*m.*), -ы́ (*f.*) one and a half (*26*)

получа́ть (imperf., I) (13), получи́ть (perf., II: получу́, полу́чишь) (15) to receive, get, obtain

полчаса́ half an hour (22)

по́льза use, profit (27)

по́льзоваться (imperf., I: по́льзу.юсь, -ешься), вос- (perf., I) to use, take advantage of (+ *instr.*) (23)

по́мнить (imperf., II: по́мн.ю, -ишь; imperative по́мни/те) to remember (11)

помога́ть (imperf., I) (9), помо́чь (perf., I: помогу́, помо́жешь . . . помо́гут (18); imperative помоги́/те; past помо́г, помогло́, etc.) to help (+ *dat.*)

по-мо́ему in my opinion (14)

по́мощь (*f.*) help (10)

помы́ть(ся) (perf.) *see* мы́ть(ся)

понеде́льник Monday (18)

понести́ (perf.), *see* нести́

понима́ть (imperf., I) (8), поня́ть (perf., I: пойм.у́, -ёшь) (19) to understand, grasp, comprehend

понра́виться (perf.), *see* нра́виться

пообе́дать (perf.), *see* обе́дать

поплы́ть (perf.), *see* плыть

попроси́ть (perf.), *see* проси́ть

популя́рный popular (7)

попутеше́ствовать (perf., I: попутеше́ству.ю, -ешь) to travel (for a while) (27) порá (+ *dat. and inf.*) it is time to . . . (17); с тех пóр since then; с тех пóр, как . . . since the time when . . . ; до каки́х пóр? how long, how far, till when? до тех пóр till then; до сих пóр so far, thus far, till now, still (21)

портрéт portrait (22)

портфéль (*m.*) briefcase (22)

по-рýсски (in) Russian; чита́ть по-рýсски to read (in) Russian (5)

поря́д.ок (*gen.* -ка) order (24)

по-свóему in one's (its) own way (9)

посеща́ть (imperf., I), посети́ть (perf., II: посе.щý, -ти́шь) to visit (27)

посла́ть (perf.), *see* посыла́ть

пóсле (+ *gen.*) after (10); (*adv.*) later, afterwards

послéдний last, latest (6)

послеза́втра day after tomorrow (17)

послýшать (perf.), *see* слýшать

посмотрéть (perf.), *see* смотрéть

посовéтовать(ся) (perf.), *see* совéтовать(ся)

поспеши́ть (perf.), *see* спеши́ть

посреди́ (+ *gen.*) in the middle of (27)

поста́вить (perf.), *see* ста́вить

постéль (*f.*) bed, bedding (18)

пострóить (perf.), *see* стрóить

поступа́ть (imperf., I), поступи́ть (perf., II: поступлю́, посту́пишь) to enroll, enter (23)

постуча́ть (perf.), *see* стуча́ть

посýда (*collect.*) dishes, china (13)

посыла́ть (imperf., I) (9), посла́ть (perf., I: пошл.ю́, -ёшь) (19) to send

посы́л.ка (*gen. pl.* -ок) package, parcel (22)

потеря́ть (perf.), *see* теря́ть

потол.óк (*gen.* -ка́) ceiling

потóм then, next, later (11)

потомý что because (4)

поýжинать (perf.), *see* ýжинать

похóж/ий similar, like; п. на (+ *acc.*) similar to, like; Он похóж на своегó отца́. He looks like his father (23)

поцелова́ть, perf. of целова́ть

поцелýй kiss (27)

почемý why (4); почемý-то for some reason (12)

почи́стить (perf.), *see* чи́стить

пóчта post office; post, mail (12); на пóчте at the post office

почти́ almost, nearly (8)

почýвствовать (perf.), *see* чýвствовать

пошути́ть (perf.), *see* шути́ть

поэ́зия poetry (23)

поэ́т poet (16)

поэ́тому therefore (9)

прав right, correct (said of persons in predicate only) (14, 23); Он пра́в. He's right (13, 23)

пра́вда truth; justice (5, 13); П., что . . . It's true that . . . Это пра́вда. That's right (5).

пра́вило rule (9)

пра́вильный correct (3, 18)

пра́во right (*noun*) (21)

пра́вый right (*adj.*) (11)

пра́здник holiday (9); на пра́здники for the holidays (25)

пра́здновать (imperf., пра́здну.ю, -ешь) to celebrate (26)

пра́ктика practice (14)

практи́ческий practical (23)

предви́деть (imperf., II: предви́.жу, -дишь) to foresee (27)

предложéние sentence, proposition (19)

предпочита́ть (imperf., I) to prefer (+ *acc. or inf.*) (18)

предска́зывать (imperf., I), предсказа́ть (perf., I: предскажý, предска́жешь) to foretell, predict (27)

представля́ть (imperf., I), предста́вить (perf., II: предста́в.лю, -ишь) to present, represent; п. себé to imagine (27)

прéжде formerly, before (*adv.*) (25)

президéнт president (11)

прекра́сный fine, wonderful, excellent (7)

преподава́ние teaching (23)

преподава́ть (imperf., I: препода.ю́, -ёшь; imperative преподава́й/те) to teach (23)

прéсса press (7)

прибега́ть (imperf., I), прибежа́ть (perf.: прибегý, прибежи́шь . . . прибегýт) to come running, rush up (24)

привéт greeting(s) (9)

привози́ть (imperf., II: привожý, приво́зишь), привезти́ (perf., I: привез.ý, -ёшь; past привёз, привезло́, etc.) to bring (by vehicle) (22)

привыка́ть (imperf., I), привы́кнуть (perf., I: привы́кн.у, -ешь; past привы́к, привы́кло, etc.) to get used to (к + *dat. or inf.*) (21)

привы́ч.ка (*gen. pl.* -ек) habit (23)

приглаша́ть (imperf., I), пригласи́ть (perf., II: пригла.шý, -си́шь) to invite (25)

приглашéние invitation (25)

пригото́вить (perf.), *see* гото́вить

приéзд arrival (by vehicle) (26)

приезжа́ть (imperf., I), приéхать (perf., I: приéд.у, -ешь, imperative приезжа́й/те) to come, arrive (by vehicle) (*18*)

приём reception (20)

прийти́ (perf.), *see* приходи́ть

прилéжный diligent, studious (10)

прилета́ть (imperf., I), прилетéть (perf., II: приле.чý, -ти́шь) to fly in, arrive (by flying) (*24*)

принима́ть (imperf., I), приня́ть (perf., I: примý, при́мешь) to accept, receive, take (20) приноси́ть (imperf., II: приношу́, прино́сишь), принести́ (perf., I: принес.у́, -ёшь; past принёс, принесло́, etc.) to bring (on foot) (22)

принц prince

принце́сса princess

приро́да nature (16)

приходи́ть (imperf., II: прихожу́, прихо́дишь), прийти́ (perf., I: прид.у́, -ёшь; past пришёл, пришло́, etc.) to come, arrive (on foot) (18)

прия́тель (f. -ница) friend (7)

прия́тный pleasant (6)

про (+ acc.) about, concerning (21)

пробы́ть (perf., I: пробу́д.у, -ешь) to stay, spend (some time) (21, 25)

прова́ливаться (imperf., I), провали́ться (perf., II: провалю́сь, прова́лишься) to fail; п. на зкза́мене to fail an exam (19)

проводи́ть (imperf., II: провожу́, прово́дишь), провести́ (perf., I: провед.у́, -ёшь; past провёл, провело́, etc.) to spend/pass time, lead (through) (23)

продава́ть (imperf., I: прода.ю́, -ёшь; imperative продава́й(те) (9), прода́ть (perf., conj. like дать) (15) to sell. Что́ продаю́т? What is sold? (9)

продав.е́ц (gen. -ца́) salesman, sales clerk (13)

продавщи́ца saleslady (13)

продолжа́ть (imperf., I) to continue, go on (+ inf.) (16)

проду́кты (m. pl.) produce, products (19)

произво́дство production (27)

произноси́ть (imperf., II: поризношу́, произно́сишь), произнести́ (perf., I: произнес.у́, -ёшь; past произнёс, произнесло́, etc.) to pronounce; п. ре́чь to give a speech (19)

произноше́ние pronunciation (19)

происходи́ть (imperf., II: происхожу́, происхо́дишь), to come from (originate); произойти́ (perf., I: произойдёт; past произошёл, произошло́) to occur, take place (21)

пройти́ (perf.), see проходи́ть

пролета́ть (imperf., I), пролете́ть (perf., II: проле.чу́, -ти́шь) to fly past (27)

проси́ть (imperf., II: прошу́, про́сишь), по- (perf., II) to ask for, beg (18)

прости́(те) (imp.) Pardon! (Forgive me!) (4)

просто́й simple (12); про́сто simply; only (10)

просыпа́ться (imperf., I), просну́ться (perf., I: просн.у́сь, -ёшься) to wake up (intrans.) (19)

про́тив (+ gen.) opposite, opposed to (21)

прохла́дно cool; it's cool (12)

проходи́ть (imperf., II: прохожу́, прохо́дишь), пройти́ (perf., I: пройд.у́, -ёшь; past прошёл, прошло́, etc.) to cross, go through, finish; п. ми́мо (+ gen.) to pass (22); Это пройдёт. That will pass (23)

прочита́ть, проче́сть (perf.), see чита́ть

про́шлый past, last (12); в про́шлом году́ last year (12); про́шлое (adj. used as noun) the past (24)

про́ще simpler (25)

пря́мо straight, direct(ly) (17)

пти́ца bird (16)

пусто́й (пу́сто) empty (24)

пусть, пуска́й(те) (imp.) let (25)

путеше́ствие travel, journey, trip (20)

путеше́ствовать (imperf., I: путеше́ству.ю, -ешь) to travel (20)

пье́са play, drama (7)

пятна́дцать fifteen (16, 26)

пя́тница Friday (18)

пя́тый fifth (18)

пять five (16, 26)

пятьдеся́т fifty (21, 26)

рабо́та work (5); на рабо́те at work (5)

рабо́тать (imperf., I) to work (5); р. над (+ instr.) to work at (on) (19)

рабо́чий work, working (adj.); workman (adj. used as noun) (19)

равно́: Мне́ всё равно́. I don't care. (9)

рад glad (5); Я э́тому ра́д. I'm glad of that.

ра́дио (n. indecl.) radio (9)

раз (gen. pl. раз) time, occasion (16); в пе́рвый р. for the first time; (оди́н) р. once; два́ ра́за twice

разбуди́ть (perf.), see буди́ть

ра́зве can it be that . . . ? (expresses surprise or disbelief); р . . . . не surely (18)

разгова́ривать (imperf., I) to converse (11)

разгово́р conversation (7)

раздева́ть (imperf., I), разде́ть (perf., I: разде́н.у, -ешь) to undress (trans.); раздева́ться, разде́ться to undress (intrans.)

разме́р size, measure (13)

ра́зный various (13)

разруша́ть (imperf., I), разру́шить (perf., II: разру́ш.у, -ишь) to destroy (27)

ра́нить (imperf. and perf., II: ра́н.ю, -ишь) to wound (27)

ра́нний early (adj.) (27)

ра́но early (adv.) (9)

ра́ньше earlier, before (adv.) (12)

расписа́ние schedule; р. поездо́в train timetable (26)

рассерди́ться (perf.), see серди́ться

расска́з story, tale (10)

расска́зывать (imperf., I) (11), рассказа́ть (perf., I: расскажу́, расска́жешь) (15) to tell, narrate

расти́ (imperf., I: раст.у́, -ёшь; past рос, росло́, etc.) to grow (16)

ребён.ок (gen. -ка; pl., see де́ти) child (13)

ребя́та (m. pl.: gen. pl. ребя́т) (colloq.) fellows, kids (23) револю́ция revolution (12)

реда́ктор editor (7)

ре́дкий rare, uncommon (16); ре́дко seldom, rarely (9)

ре́же less often, rarer (25)

ре́зать (imperf., I: ре́ж.у, -ешь) to cut (19)

река́ river (3)

рестора́н restaurant (7)

ре́ч.ка (gen. pl. -ек) stream, small river (25)

речь (f.) speech (24)

реша́ть (imperf., I), реши́ть (perf., II: реш.у́, -и́шь) to decide (17)

рис rice (12)

ро́вно exactly (with numerals) (16); р. в се́мь (часо́в) at 7:00 sharp (16)

ро́дина fatherland (27)

роди́тел.и (pl., gen. -ей) parents (16)

родно́й native, own (27)

ро́дствен.ник (f. -ница) relative (27)

рожда́ться (imperf., I), роди́ться (perf., II: рожу́сь, роди́шься) to be born (23)

рожде́ние birth, birthday (23); де́нь рожде́ния birthday; на р. for (on) one's birthday

ро́зовый pink, rosy (16)

роль (f.) role (12); игра́ть р. to play a part

рома́н novel (6)

Росси́я Russia (11)

рот (gen. рта, loc. во рту́) mouth (3)

роя́ль (m.) piano (6)

руба́ш.ка (gen. pl. -ек) shirt (13)

рубль (m.) ruble (14, 15)

рука́ hand; arm (3); за́ руку by the hand (22)

ру́сский Russian; a Russian (6, 20)

ры́ба fish (7)

ря́дом next door, beside, side by side; р. с (+ instr.) beside, next to, next door to (11)

с, со (+ instr.) with, together with (11); (+ gen.) off, down from, from, beginning with (17); (+ acc.) about, approximately

сади́ться (imperf., II: сажу́сь, сади́шься), сесть (perf., I: ся́д.у, -ешь; past сел, -о, -а, -и) to sit down (20); с. за сто́л to sit down at the table; с. на по́езд to take a train

сала́т salad (11)

сам oneself, myself, himself, etc. (14, 23)

самолёт airplane (24)

са́мый the very, the most (superlative) (13, 25); то́ же са́мое the same thing (25)

са́хар sugar (11, 12)

све́жий (свежо́) fresh; cool, chilly; it is cool (6, 9)

свет world, light (20)

свети́ть (imperf., II: свечу́, све́тишь) to shine (26)

све́тлый (светло́) light, bright (9)

свида́ние meeting, rendezvous (27); до свида́ния good-bye (lit. till we meet again) (3)

свобо́да freedom (23)

свобо́дный free; fluent (23)

свой my, his, our, etc. (refers back to subject of sentence; see 9) (12, 20)

связь (f.) link, tie, connection (21)

сде́лать (perf.), see де́лать

себя́ oneself (23)

се́вер north (22); на с. to the north; на се́вере in the north

се́верный northern (22)

сего́дня today (5)

сего́дняшний today's (6); с. де́нь today (used as noun) (25)

седьмо́й seventh (18)

сейча́с now, just now (5); right away, just a minute (14); с. же at once, immediately (14)

секре́т secret (14)

секрета́рша secretary (4)

село́ (nom. pl. сёла, gen. pl. сёл) village, town (22)

се́льский village (adj.) (23)

семе́йный family (adj.) (20)

семна́дцать seventeen (16, 26)

семь seven (16, 26)

се́мьдесят seventy (21, 26)

семья́ (gen. pl. семе́й) family (9, 20)

сентя́брь (m.) September (23)

серди́ться (imperf., II: сержу́сь, се́рдишься), рас- (perf., II) to get angry at (на + acc.) (22)

се́рдце (gen. pl. серде́ц) heart (23)

середи́на middle (18)

се́рый gray (7)

серьёзный serious (6)

сестра́ (nom. pl. сёстры, gen. pl. сестёр) sister (4)

сесть (perf.), see сади́ться

Сиби́рь (f.) Siberia (3)

сигаре́та cigarette (24)

сиде́ть (imperf., II: сижу́, сиди́шь) (11) to sit, be seated; с. до́ма to stay at home (11)

си́ла power, force (25)

си́льный strong (21)

симпати́чный likable, pleasant (20)

си́ний blue (6)

сказа́ть (perf., I: скажу́, ска́жешь), perf. of говори́ть = to say, tell (14); Я хочу́ сказа́ть . . . I mean (to say) . . . (14)

ска́з.ка (gen. pl. -ок) fairy tale (24)

ско́лько (+ gen. pl.) how much, how many (7, 16, 20); с. вре́мени how long (12)

ско́ро soon (5). Скоре́й! Hurry!

скот cattle, livestock (23)

ску́чный dull, boring (6). Мне́ ску́чно. I'm bored. (9)

сла́вный nice, likable (26)

славяни́н (decl. 20) (f. славя́н.ка, gen. pl. -ок) Slav (20)

сле́ва on (from) the left (26)

сле́дующий next, following (27)

сли́шком too, excessively (8)

слова́рь (*m.*) dictionary, vocabulary (4)

сло́во word (6); сло́вом in a word (25)

слон elephant (21)

слу́жба job, work; service (9)

служи́ть (imperf., II: служу́, слу́жишь), to serve (+ *dat.*); be employed, work (12)

слух rumor; hearing (27)

слу́чай case, incident, event; chance (20)

случа́йно by chance (19)

случа́ться (imperf., I), случи́ться (perf., II: случи́тся) to happen, occur (20)

слу́шать (imperf., I) (5, 8), по- (perf., I) (18) to listen to, obey (+ *acc.*)

слы́шать (imperf., II: слы́ш.у, -ишь) (11), у- (perf., II) (21) to hear

смерть (*f.*) death (11)

смех laughter (16)

смешно́й funny (19)

смея́ться (imperf., I: сме.ю́сь, -ёшься) to laugh; (над + *instr.*) to laugh at, make fun of (19)

смотре́ть (imperf., II: смотрю́, смо́тришь), по- (perf., II) to look; (по)с. на (+ *acc.*) to look at (17)

смочь (perf.), *see* мочь (*21*)

сна, *see* сон

снача́ла at first (11)

снег (*loc.* в снегу́; *nom. pl.* -а́) snow (11, *12*); Идёт снег. It's snowing (17).

снима́ть (imperf., I), снять (perf., I: сниму́, сни́мешь) to take off; rent (24)

сно́ва again, anew (26)

со, *see* с

соба́ка dog (10)

собира́ть (imperf., I), собра́ть (perf., собер.у́, -ёшь) to collect, gather (*trans.*) (19); собира́ться, собра́ться to collect, assemble, come together, prepare to (*intrans.*) (19)

собра́ние meeting, gathering (12)

соверше́нно completely, perfectly (23)

сове́т advice, counsel; council (9)

сове́товать (imperf., I: сове́ту.ю, -ешь), по- (perf., I) to advise (someone + *dat. and inf.*) (21); сове́товаться, по- to consult with (с + *instr.*) (21)

сове́тский Soviet (7); С. Сою́з Soviet Union (3)

совреме́нный contemporary, modern (20)

совсе́м quite, entirely, completely (11); с. не (нет) not at all (11); не с. not quite (11)

согла́сный agreed, in agreement (*23*)

Соединённые Шта́ты Аме́рики United States of America (13)

сожале́ние regret; к сожале́нию unfortunately (23)

солда́т (*gen. pl.* солда́т) soldier (16)

со́лнце sun (16)

соль (*f.*) salt (7)

сон (*gen.* сна) sleep; dream; ви́деть с. to have a dream (26)

со́рок forty (*21, 26*)

сосе́д (*pl.* сосе́ди) neighbor; сосе́д.ка (*gen. pl.* -ок) neighbor woman (10)

соси́с.ка (*gen. pl.* -ок) frankfurter (17)

сочине́ние composition (5)

сою́з alliance, union

спа́льня (*gen. pl.* спа́лен) bedroom (10)

спасе́ние salvation (27)

спаси́бо thank you (3); с. за (+ *acc.*) thanks for (16)

спать (imperf., II: сплю, спишь) to sleep (7, 11)

специа́льность (*f.*) speciality; по специа́льности in one's field (27)

спеши́ть (imperf., II: спеш.у́, -и́шь), по- (perf., II) to hurry, hasten; Часы́ спеша́т. The watch (clock) is fast (17)

спина́ back (of a person) (23)

спи́ч.ка (*gen. pl.* -ек) match

споко́йный peaceful, calm (24). Споко́йной но́чи! Good night! (20)

спор argument (13)

спо́рить (imperf., II: спо́р.ю, -ишь), по- (perf., II) to argue (13)

спортсме́н athlete (25)

спра́ва on (from) the right (26)

спра́шивать (imperf., I) (8), спроси́ть (perf., II: спрошу́, спро́сишь) (15) to ask, question (*acc. or* у + *gen.*)

спрос demand; с. на (+ *acc.*) demand for (27)

сра́зу at once, immediately (21)

среда́ Wednesday (18)

среди́ among, amidst (17)

сре́дний average, medium, middle (22)

СССР (*indecl.*); Сою́з Сове́гских Социалисти́ческих Респу́блик Union of Soviet Socialist Republics; U.S.S.R. (13)

ста́вить (imperf., II: ста́в.лю, -ишь), по- (perf., II) to put, stand (*trans.*) (24); (по)с. буди́льник на (+ *acc.*) to set an alarm clock for . . . (24)

стака́н glass, tumbler (7)

станови́ться (imperf., II: становлю́сь, стано́вишься), стать (perf., I: ста́н.у, -ешь) to stand (take a standing position); to become (+ *instr.*) (*20*); Мне ста́ло лу́чше. I got better (23)

ста́нция station (12)

стари́к old man (22)

старомо́дный old-fashioned (16)

ста́рость (*f.*) old age (18)

стару́ха old woman (22)

ста́рше older (25)

ста́рший older, elder; oldest, eldest (8, *25*)

ста́рый old (6)

стать, perf., *see* **станови́ться**; стать (+ *imperf. inf. only*) to start . . . (*20*)

статья́ (*gen. pl.* статéй) article (*5*)

стена́ wall (*2*)

степь (*f.*) steppe, prairie (*13*)

стипе́ндия scholarship (*23*)

стих (line of) verse; стихи́ verse(s) (*16*)

сто hundred (*21, 26*)

сто́ить (imperf., II: сто́.ю, -ишь) to cost, be worth (*16*)

стол table (*2*); за столо́м at the table (*19*)

столи́ца capital (city) (*7*)

столо́вая (*adj. used as noun*) dining room (*10*)

сто́лько (+ *gen. pl.*) so much, so many (*16, 20*)

сторона́ side; direction (*17*); с ва́шей стороны́ on your part (*18*); со все́х сторо́н from all sides (*27*)

стоя́ть (imperf., II: сто́.ю, -и́шь) to stand (*5, 11*)

страда́ние suffering (*27*)

страна́ country (*7*)

страни́ца page (*11*)

стра́нный strange (*6*)

стра́шный terrible, frightful (*27*)

стро́ить (imperf., II: стро́.ю, -ишь), по- (perf., II) to build (*27*)

строка́, стро́ч.ка (*gen. pl.* -ек) line (of writing) (*25*)

студе́нт (*f.* -ка) student (*2*)

студе́нческий student (*adj.*) (*13*)

стук knock, rap (*24*)

стул (*nom. pl.*, сту́лья, *gen. pl.* сту́льев) chair (*2*)

стуча́ть (imperf., II: стуч.у́, -и́шь), по- (perf., II) to knock, rap (*24*)

сты́дно: Мне́ сты́дно. I am ashamed (*24*)

суббо́та Saturday (*18*)

сумасше́дший insane, mad (person), madman (*25*)

су́м.ка (*gen. pl.* -ок) bag, purse (*22*)

суп soup (*7*)

сухо́й dry (*24*)

су́ше drier (*25*)

счастли́вый happy, fortunate (*13, 23*)

сча́стье happiness, luck; к сча́стью fortunately (*23*)

счита́ть (imperf., I) to count, consider as (+ *instr.*) (*17*)

США (*indecl.*) U.S.A. (*13*)

съезд convention (*20*)

сыгра́ть (perf.), *see* **игра́ть**

сын (*nom. pl.* сыновья́, *gen. pl.* сынове́й) son (*4*)

сыр cheese (*7, 12*)

сюда́ (to) here, hither (*17*)

сюрпри́з surprise (*7*)

так so, thus (*4*); that's right; т. себе́ so-so (*19*); т. как since, because, as (*12*); т. же . . . как (just) as . . . as (*27*); т. что so that; и т. да́лее and so forth

та́кже also, in addition (*17*)

тако́й such (*2*), so (*6*); т. большо́й so large (*6*); т. же similar, of the same sort (*26*)

такси́ (*n. indecl.*) taxi; на т. by taxi, in a taxi (*12*)

тала́нтливый talented (*9*)

там there, over there (*2*)

та́н.ец (*gen.* -ца) dance (*21*)

танцева́ть (imperf., I: танцу́.ю, -ешь), по- (perf., I) to dance (*21*)

таре́л.ка (*gen. pl.* -ок) plate (*12*)

тата́рский Tartar (*26*)

твёрдый firm, hard (*19*)

твой your, yours (*4, 12, 20*)

теа́тр theater (*5*)

телеви́зор television set (*9*)

телегра́мма telegram (*9*)

телефо́н telephone; по телефо́ну by (on the) telephone (*9*)

те́ма theme, subject; на э́ту те́му on that subject (*11*)

тёмный (темно́) dark; it is dark (*9*)

температу́ра temperature (*23*)

те́ннис tennis (*8*)

тепе́рь now (*2, 5*)

тепе́решний present, of the present time (*6*)

тёплый (тепло́) warm; it's warm (*6*)

терпе́ние patience (*18*)

теря́ть (imperf., I), по- (perf., I) to lose (*22*)

тетра́дь (*f.*) notebook, copybook (*13*)

тётя, тёт.ка (*gen. pl.* -ок) aunt (*21*)

ти́кать (imperf., I) to tick (*24*)

ти́хий quiet, low (in voice) (*8*)

ти́ше quieter (*25*); Ти́ше! Silence! (*25*)

то that (*4*); то́, что that which, what (*13*); е́сли . . . , то́ if . . . , then; когда́ . . . , то́ when . . . , then (*25*); то́ есть that is (*17*)

-то, *see* 22

това́рищ comrade (*8*)

тогда́ then, at that time (*8, 11*)

то́же also, too (*3, 17*)

толпа́ crowd (*22*)

то́лстый fat, stout, thick (*8*)

то́лько only (*4*); как т. as soon as (*14*); т. что (have) just (*14*)

том volume (*26*)

тому́ наза́д ago (*16*)

то́нкий thin, fine, delicate (*13*)

тот that (one) (*4, 12, 20*); т. же the same (*18*); то́, что that which, what (*13*)

то́чно exactly (*19*); just like, just as if

трава́ grass (*17*)

тре́тий third (*18*); тре́тьего дня́ the day before yesterday (*21*); в-тре́тьих third, in the third place (*21*)

три three (*10, 26*)

три́дцать thirty (*21, 26*)

трина́дцать thirteen (*16, 26*)

тру́б.ка (*gen. pl.* -ок) pipe (11)

труд work, labor (11); **с трудо́м** with difficulty (11)

тру́дный difficult, hard (6)

туда́ (to) there, thither (*17*)

туре́цкий Turkish (11)

тури́ст (*f.* -ка) tourist (7)

тут here (2)

ту́ча (storm) cloud (19)

ты you, "thou" (intimate) (*4*)

ты́сяча thousand (*26*)

тяжёлый (тяжело́) heavy; hard (said of life, fate, etc.) (20)

у at the house (apartment, etc.) of (*10*); at, near, by (*22*); **У меня́ (есть)** (+ *nom.*). I have . . . . (*10*)

убега́ть (imperf., I), убежа́ть (perf.: убегу́, убежи́шь . . . убегу́т) to run away (27)

убива́ть (imperf., I), уби́ть (perf., I: убью́, убьёшь) (24) to kill (27)

убира́ть (imperf., I), убра́ть (perf., I: убер.у́, -ёшь) (24) to clean up (off), tidy

уважа́ть (imperf. only, I) to respect (27)

уве́рен/ный sure, certain (18, *23*); **уве́рен в** (+ *loc.*) sure of

уви́деть (perf. of ви́деть), *see 21*

увози́ть (imperf., II: увожу́, уво́зишь), увезти́ (perf., I: увез.у́, -ёшь; past увёз, увезло́, etc.) to carry, transport away (*22*)

у́гол (*gen.* угла́, *loc.* в/на углу́) corner, angle (12)

ударе́ние accent, stress (19)

удивле́ние surprise (22)

удивлён/ный surprised (*23*)

удо́бный comfortable, convenient (7); **Мне́ удо́бно.** I am comfortable (9).

удово́льствие pleasure (11)

уезжа́ть (imperf., I), уе́хать (perf., I: уе́д.у, -ешь; imperative уезжа́й/те), to ride away, leave (in a vehicle) (*18*)

у́жас horror, terror (21)

ужа́сный horrible, terrible (13)

уже́ already (3); **у. не** no longer

у́же narrower (25)

у́жин supper (16)

у́жинать (imperf., I), по- (perf., I) to have supper (11)

у́зкий narrow, tight (8)

узнава́ть (imperf., I: узна.ю́, -ёшь), узна́ть (perf., I) to find out, learn (*21*)

уйти́ (perf.), *see* уходи́ть

Украи́на Ukraine (12); **на Украи́не** in the Ukraine

улета́ть (imperf., I), улете́ть (perf., II: уле.чу́, -ти́шь) to fly away (24)

у́лица street (5); **на у́лице** on the street, outdoors

улыба́ться (imperf., I) to smile (19)

улы́б.ка (*gen. pl.* -ок) smile (27)

уме́ть (imperf., I) to know how to (+ *inf.*) (11)

умира́ть (imperf., I), умере́ть (perf., I: умр.у́, -ёшь; past у́мер, -ло, etc.) to die (21)

у́мный (умно́) clever, intelligent (9)

универса́льный магази́н (универма́г) department store (13)

университе́т university (12)

уноси́ть (imperf., II: уношу́, уно́сишь), унести́ (perf., I: унес.у́, -ёшь; past унёс, унесло́, etc.) to take away, carry away (on foot) (22)

упа́сть (perf.), *see* па́дать

упражне́ние exercise (9)

Ура́л Urals (12); **на Ура́ле** in the Urals

уро́к lesson (5); **на уро́ке** at the lesson, in class

усло́вие condition (27)

услы́шать, perf. of слы́шать

успе́х success (27)

устава́ть (imperf., I: уста.ю́, -ёшь), уста́ть (perf., I: уста́н.у, -ешь) to get tired; (in perf. past) to be tired (21)

у́тренний morning (*adj.*) (8)

у́тро morning (7); **у́тром** in the morning (11); **в де́вять часо́в утра́** at 9:00 A.M. (16); **с утра́ до ве́чера** from morning to evening (25)

у́хо (*nom. pl.* у́ши; *gen. pl.* уше́й) ear (10, *19*)

ухо́д departure (on foot) (27)

уходи́ть (imperf., II: ухожу́, ухо́дишь), уйти́ (perf., I: уйд.у́, -ёшь; past ушёл, ушло́, etc.) to leave, go away (on foot) (*18*)

уча́стие participation (21)

уче́бник textbook (9)

уче́ние studies, studying, learning, schooling (18, *23*)

учен.и́к (*f.* -и́ца) pupil, schoolboy (-girl) (*10*)

учёный scholarly, scientific; (*adj. used as noun*) scholar, scientist (22)

учи́тель (*f.* -ница, *nom. pl.* учителя́) teacher (3)

учи́ть (imperf., II: учу́, у́чишь), на- (perf., II) to teach (*acc. of person*; *dat. of subject matter*); **учи́ться, на-** to learn, study (+ *dat.*) (23)

у́ши, *see* у́хо

ую́тный cozy (9)

фами́лия family name (4); **Ка́к ва́ша фами́лия?** What is your (last) name?

февра́ль (*m.*) February (23)

фильм film, motion picture (12)

фоне́тика phonetics (3)

фотоаппара́т camera (9)

фотогра́фия photograph (16)

Фра́нция France (12)

францу́.з (*f.* -же́нка, *gen. pl.* -же́нок) Frenchman (-woman) (20)

францу́зский French (*adj.*); **по-францу́зски** in French (7)

фрукт a fruit; **фру́кты** (*pl.*) fruits, fruit (*collect.*) (17)

футбо́л football; soccer; **на футбо́ле** at a football game (5)

хара́ктер disposition, character (10)

хи́мик chemist (14)

хлеб bread (7)

ходи́ть (indeterm. imperf., II: **хожу́, хо́дишь**), **идти́** (determ. imperf., I: **ид.у́, -ёшь**; past **шёл, шло**, etc.), **пойти́** (perf., I: **пойд.у́, -ёшь**; past **пошёл, пошло́**, etc.) to go (on foot, perf.) (17)

хозя́ин (*f.* **хозя́йка**, *gen. pl.* **хозя́ек**) master, host, landlord, owner (11); **хозя́ева** (*m. pl.*) masters, etc.; *also* master and mistress, host and hostess, landlord and landlady, etc. (20)

хозя́йство household; management; business; economy (9); **помога́ть по хозя́йству** to help with the housework (9)

хо́лод cold (21)

холоди́льник refrigerator (7)

холо́дный (**хо́лодно**) cold (*adj.*) (6); **Хо́лодно.** It is cold. (9). **Мне́ хо́лодно.** I am cold. (9)

хоро́ший (**хорошо́**) good, fine, nice, well (6)

хорошо́ good, well, fine, all right (3); **Э́то х.** That's good. **Х., что . . .** It's good that . . . (3). **Мне́ х.** I feel well, good, all right. (23)

хоте́ть (imperf., *conj. 10*), **за-** (perf., *21*) to want, wish; intend (+ *inf.*); **х. сказа́ть** to mean (14); **хоте́ться, за-** (*see 26*)

хоть if only (25)

хотя́ (**и**) although (10)

худо́жник artist, painter

худо́й thin, lean (20)

ху́дший worse, worst (25)

ху́же worse (23, 25); **Мне́ х.** I am (feel) worse. (23)

царь (*m.*) tsar (14)

цвет (*nom. pl.* **-а́**) color (7); **Како́го цве́та** (+ *nom.*)? What is the color of . . .? (7)

цвет.о́к (*gen.* **-ка́**; *nom. pl.* **цветы́**) flower (19)

целова́ть (imperf., I: **целу́.ю, -ешь**), **по-** (perf., I) to kiss (27)

це́лый (a) whole (6)

цена́ price (7); **Кака́я цена́** (+ *gen.*)? What is the price of . . .? (7)

центр center (7)

це́рк.овь (*f.*, *gen.* **-ви**, *instr.* **-овью**) church (12)

чай tea (11, 12)

ча́йка (*gen. pl.* **ча́ек**) gull (26)

час hour (14); **в ч.** at one o'clock (16); **Кото́рый ч.?** What time is it? **В кото́ром часу́?** At what time? (16); **часы́** (*pl.*) hours; clock, watch (17)

ча́сто often (9)

часть (*f.*) part (12)

ча́ш.ка (*gen. pl.* **-ек**) cup (10)

ча́ще more often, more frequently (25)

чей whose (4, 18)

челове́к (*pl.*, *see* **лю́ди**) man, person, human being (8)

чем . . . тем the . . . the (25)

чемода́н suitcase (22)

через (+ *acc.*) from now, after, at the end of; **ч. ча́с** in an hour (18); across, through (22); **ч. у́лицу** across the street

чёрный black (6)

чёрт (*nom. pl.* **че́рти**) devil; **К чёрту!** The devil with it! (25)

честь (*f.*) honor; **в ч.** (+ *gen.*) in honor of (26)

четве́рг Thursday (18)

четвёртый fourth (18)

че́тверть (*f.*) quarter, one-fourth (26)

четы́ре four (10, 26)

четырёхэта́жный four-story (27)

четы́рнадцать fourteen (16, 26)

число́ number; date (26)

чи́стить (imperf., II: **чи́щу, чи́стишь**), **по-** (perf., II) to clean (24)

чи́стый clean, pure (15)

чита́тель (*f.* **-ница**) reader (18)

чита́ть (imperf., I) (5, 8), **про-** (perf., I) (14) *or* **прочесть** (perf., I: **прочт.у́, -ёшь**; past **прочёл, прочло́**, etc.) (24) to read; **чита́йте!** read! (3); **(про)ч. ле́кцию** to lecture, give a lecture (12); **(про)ч. докла́д** to give a talk, report (12)

чи́ще cleaner (25)

чте́ние reading (*noun*) (6)

что what; that (3, 5, 15); **Что́ э́то (тако́е)?** What is this (that)? (3) **Что́ э́то за** (+ *nom.*)? What, what kind of . . . is that? (22) **Что́ де́лать?** What can one do? What should we do? (10) **Что́ нам де́лать?** What can (should) we do? (9) **Что́ тако́е . . . ?** What is . . . ? **Что́ с ва́ми?** What is the matter with you? (23); **Что́ вы!** You don't say!

чтобы (in order) to (that) (24)

что́-нибудь, что́-то anything, something (22)

чу́вство (*gen. pl.* **чувств**) feeling (25)

чу́вствовать (imperf., I: **чу́вству.ю, -ешь**), (23) **по-** (perf., I) (27) to feel; **Как вы́ себя́ чу́вствуете?** How do you feel? **Я́ себя́ чу́вствую хорошо́.** I feel well. (23)

чу́дный, чуде́сный wonderful, marvelous (17, 19)

чуло́к (*gen. pl.* **чуло́к**) stocking (24)

ша́хматы (*pl. only*, *gen.* **ша́хмат**) chess; **игра́ть в ш.** to play chess (14)

шестна́дцать sixteen (16, 26)

шесто́й sixth (18)

шесть six (16, 26)

шестьдеся́т sixty (*21, 26*)

ши́ре wider, broader (*25*)

широ́кий wide, broad (8)

шкаф (*loc.* в шкафу́) cupboard; closet (24)

шко́ла school (5)

шко́льный school (*adj.*) (27)

шко́ль.ник (*f.* -ница) schoolboy (-girl) (11)

шля́па hat (6)

шокола́д chocolate (*12*)

шум noise (16)

шуме́ть (imperf., II: шум.лю́, -и́шь) to make noise, be noisy (25)

шу́мный noisy (16)

шути́ть (imperf., II: шучу́, шу́тишь), по- (perf., II) to joke

шу́т.ка (*gen. pl.* -ок) joke (20)

эгои́ст (*f.* -ка, *gen. pl.* -ок) egoist, selfish person (14)

экза́мен examination (5); держа́ть э. to take an exam. (13); вы́держать э. to pass an exam.; провали́ться на экза́мене to fail an exam. (19)

энерги́чный energetic (22)

эпо́ха epoch (8)

эта́ж floor, story (12)

э́тот this, that (*4, 12, 20*); Э́то . . . . This (that) is . . . (*2*).

ю́б.ка (*gen. pl.* -ок) skirt (8)

юг south (22); на юг to the south; на ю́ге in the south

ю́жный southern (22)

я́блоко (*nom. pl.* я́блоки, *gen. pl.* я́блок) apple (22)

яи́чница omelet; fried or scrambled eggs (21)

яйцо́ egg (*21*)

язы́к language, tongue (12, 20)

янва́рь (*m.*) January (23)

япо́нский Japanese (19)

я́сный clear (18)

English-Russian Vocabulary

As in the Russian-English Vocabulary, the numbers in parentheses refer to the units in which words or expressions are first used or are explained. Where the number is italicized, additional information on inflection or on usage may be found by referring to the unit indicated.

Verbs are designated as imperfective (imperf.), or perfective (perf.), except when two verbs related in form are given together: in the latter case the first verb of the pair is always imperfective, the second always perfective. Verb conjugation patterns are not given in this vocabulary; they can be found by referring to the Russian-English Vocabulary, or to the units listed after the verbs.

All cardinal numerals are given except the compound forms denoting the hundreds. Ordinals are given up to *tenth* only. Other numerals can be found by referring to Unit 26.

a (*not translated—see 2*); **(a certain)** один; какóй-то (*22*); **(any)** какóй-нибудь (*22*); **(not a single)** ни одúн (*20*); **(per)** в (+ *acc.*) (*17*)

able, to be мочь (*10*), с- (*21*)

about (concerning) о, об, обо (+ *loc.*) (*5, 12*), про (+ *acc.*) (*21*); **(approximately)** óколо (+ *gen.*) (*26*); **a. five students** студéнтов пять (*colloq.*), *or* óколо пятú студéнтов; **a. the town** по гóроду; **a. the room** по кóмнате (*17*)

above над (+ *instr.*) (*19*)

abroad, to go (по)éхать за гранúцу; **to be a.** быть за гранúцей (*21*)

accent ударéние, акцéнт (*19*)

to accept принимáть, принять (*20*)

accident, by случáйно (*19*)

acquaintance (friend) знакóм/ый (*20*)

acquainted with знакóм с (+ *instr.*) (*20*)

across чéрез (+ *acc.*) (*22*)

addition, in ещё (*10*); крóме тогó (*23*)

address áдрес (*nom. pl.* -á) (*7*); **What is the a. of . . .?** Кáк áдрес (+ *gen.*)? (*7*)

to adore обожáть (*imperf. only*) (*23*)

adult взрóслый (*23*)

advance, in зарáнее (*23*)

advertisement объявлéние (*8*)

advice совéт (*9*)

to advise совéтовать, по- (*21*)

affair дéло (*14*)

afraid of, to be боя́ться (*imperf. only*) (+ *gen.*) (*19*)

Africa Áфрика (*11*)

after пóсле (+ *gen.*) (*10*); **(at the end of a period of time)** чéрез (+ *acc.*) (*18*); **(afterwards)** потóм, пóсле (*11*)

afternoon, in the днём (*11*); (*adj.*) дневнóй (*26*); **Good a.!** Дóбрый дéнь!

again опя́ть (*14*); ещё рáз; **(anew)** снóва (*26*)

against (opposed to) прóтив (+ *gen.*) (*21*)

age, old ста́рость (*f.*) (18); **What is your a.?** Ско́лько вам ле́т?

ago (тому́) наза́д (16)

to agree: I a. with you. Я с ва́ми согла́сен (23).

air во́здух (12)

airplane самолёт (24)

alarm clock буди́льник (24); **to set an a. c. for . . .** (по)ста́вить буди́льник на (+ *acc.*) (24)

alike (in the same way) одина́ково (19)

all весь (*12*); **(everyone)** все (*8, 20*); **(everything)** всё (*7, 14*); **a. (everything) that . . .** всё, что . . . (*7*); **a. the** весь, це́лый (*6*); **not at a.** совсе́м не (не́т) (11); **a. the same** всё-таки (19); **in a.** всего́; **a. day (long)** весь де́нь (*7*); **a. night (long)** всю но́чь (*7*); **a. right** хорошо́ (3), ла́дно (*colloq.*) (20); **first of a.** ра́ньше/пре́жде всего́ (25); **best of a.** лу́чше всего́ (все́х) (25). **That's a.** Во́т и всё! (25)

almost почти́ (8)

alone оди́н (*8, 20*)

along (the street, river, etc.) по (+ *dat.*) (17); вдоль (+ *gen.*); **to take a.** взя́ть с собо́й (22)

already уже́ (3, 7)

also и (*7*); то́же (3, 17); та́кже (*17*)

although хотя́ (и) (*10*)

always всегда́ (5)

am, *see* **be**

A.M. утра́ **(in the morning)** (*16*); но́чи **(at night)** (*16*)

America Аме́рика (5)

American (*adj.*) америка́нский (6)

American, an америка́н.ец, *f.* -ка (6)

among ме́жду (+ *instr.*) (*19*); среди́ (+ *gen.*) (17)

amusing заба́вный (26)

and и (2, 3); а (*3*)

anecdote анекдо́т

angel а́нгел (18)

angry, to get серди́ться, рас- (*22*)

animal живо́тное (23)

announcement объявле́ние (8)

another друго́й (13); **(in addition)** ещё (*10*); **one a.** дру́г дру́га (*13*)

answer отве́т (9); **to a.** отвеча́ть (9), отве́тить (15)

any: (at all) како́й-нибудь (22), любо́й (21); *with a negative verb* никако́й (21), *or omit*

anyone, anybody кто́-нибудь (22); **not . . . a.** никто́ не (*8, 10*)

anything что́-нибудь (22); **not . . . a.** ничего́ не (*8, 10*)

anywhere где́-нибудь (22); **(go)** куда́-нибудь (22); **not . . . a.** нигде́ не (*8*); **not (go) a.** никуда́ не

apartment кварти́ра (5)

apparent(ly) ви́дно (25)

to appear (seem) каза́ться (*19*)

appetite аппети́т (11)

appetizer заку́ска (11)

apple я́блоко (*22*)

to approach (on foot) подходи́ть, подойти́ к (+ *dat.*) (*22*); **(not on foot)** подъезжа́ть, подъе́хать к (+ *dat.*) (*22*)

approximately о́коло (+ *gen.*) (26)

April апре́ль (*m.*) (23)

apropos кста́ти (21)

are, *see* **be**

to argue спо́рить, по- (13)

argument спор (13)

arm рука́ (2)

armchair кре́сло (6)

around вокру́г (+ *gen.*) (*16*); **(with numerals)** о́коло (+ *gen.*) (26); **to walk a. town** ходи́ть по го́роду (*17*)

arrival (on foot) прихо́д; **(not on foot)** прие́зд (26)

to arrive (on foot) приходи́ть, прийти́ (18); **(not on foot)** приезжа́ть, прие́хать (*18*); **(flying)** прилета́ть, прилете́ть (*24*)

art иску́сство

article статья́ (5)

artist (performer) арти́ст, *f.* -ка (25); **(painter)** худо́жник

as как (*4*); **(because)** та́к как (12); **as soon as** как то́лько (14), **as . . . as** та́к же . . . как (27); **as if** как бу́дто (бы) (27)

ashamed: I am a. Мне́ сты́дно (24).

Asia А́зия (11)

to ask спра́шивать (8), спроси́ть (15); **to a. for** проси́ть, по- (*18*); **to a. a question** задава́ть/ зада́ть вопро́с (13)

asleep, to fall засыпа́ть, засну́ть (24)

assemble (*trans.*) собира́ть, собра́ть (*19*); (*intrans.*) собира́ться, собра́ться (*19*)

to assign задава́ть (13), зада́ть (24)

assignment зада́ние (13)

at в (+ *loc.*) (*5*); на (+ *loc.*) (5, 12); у (+ *gen.*) (*10*); **(near)** у (+ *gen.*) (22); **a. the house of (a.—'s)** у (+ *gen.*) (*10*); **a. home** до́ма (2); **a. once** сейча́с же (14), сра́зу (21); **a. last** наконе́ц (14); **a. that time** в то́ вре́мя (17), тогда́ (10); **a. one o'clock** в ча́с (*17*); **(a. a given time of day—see 26)**

athlete спортсме́н (25)

attention внима́ние (13)

attentive внима́тельный (19)

auditorium аудито́рия (13)

August а́вгуст (23)

aunt тётя (21)

author а́втор (7)

automobile автомоби́ль (*m.*) (6), маши́на (10); **by a.** на автомоби́ле, на маши́не (17)

autumn о́сень (11); (*adj.*) осе́нний; **in a.** о́сенью (11)

to **awake** (*trans.*) буди́ть, раз- (24); (*intrans.*) просыпа́ться, просну́ться (*19*)

awful(ly) ужа́сно (13)

back (in return) обра́тно (17); **(of a person)** спина́ (23); **to give b., come b.,** *see* **to return**

bad плохо́й (пло́хо) (5, 6); **not b.** непло́хо; **It's too b. that . . . .** Жаль, что . . . (6).

badly пло́хо (5); **not b.** непло́хо

bag су́мка (22)

ballet бале́т

bank банк (12); **(of a river, etc.)** бе́рег (12)

bath ва́нна (21); **to take a b.** принима́ть/приня́ть ва́нну (21)

bathroom ва́нная (10)

to be *usually not translated in present tense, see 2*; *past, see 7*; *future, see 17*; **there is, there are (pointing)** вот (*2*), **(not pointing)** есть (*10*); **there is (are) not** нет (+ *gen.*) (*10*); **to b. (often, sometimes)** быва́ть (imperf.) (5, 8)

to bear переноси́ть, перенести́ (27)

beard борода́ (20)

beautiful краси́вый (6)

beauty красота́ (26)

because потому́ что (4)

to become станови́ться, стать (+ *instr.*) (*20*)

bed крова́ть (*f.*) (5), посте́ль (*f.*) (18); **to go to b.** ложи́ться/лечь спать (*21*)

bedroom спа́льня (10)

beefsteak бифште́кс (18)

beer пи́во (17)

before до (+ *gen.*) (*10, 19*); перед (+ *instr.*) (*19*); **(earlier)** ра́ньше (12), пре́жде (25)

to beg for проси́ть, по- (*18*)

to begin (*trans.*) начина́ть (8), нача́ть (*15*); (*intrans.*) начина́ться, нача́ться (*19*); **It began to rain.** Начался́ дождь (23).

beginning нача́ло (7); **in/at the b. (first)** снача́ла (11); **in/at the b. of** в. нача́ле (+ *gen.*) (7)

behind за (+ *instr.*) (*19*); (+ *acc.*) (*27*)

being бу́дучи (27)

to believe ве́рить, по- (+ *dat.*) (*14*)

bell звоно́к (3, 19)

beneath под (+ *instr.*) (*19*); (+ *acc.*) (*24*)

besides (*prep.*) кро́ме (+ *gen.*) (10); (*adv.*) кро́ме того́ (23)

best (са́мый) лу́чший (*25*); **the b. thing** са́мое лу́чшее (25); **b. of all** лу́чше всего́ (всех) (*25*)

better лу́чший (*25*); лу́чше (23, *25*); **I feel b.** Мне лу́чше (23).

between ме́жду (+ *instr.*) (*19*)

beyond за (+ *instr.*) (*19*); (+ *acc.*) (*24*)

bicycle велосипе́д (24)

big большо́й (6)

bigger бо́льший (*25*); бо́льше (*25*)

bird пти́ца (16)

birth рожде́ние (23)

birthday день рожде́ния (23); **for (on) one's b.** на рожде́ние

black чёрный (6)

blackboard доска́ (2)

blond(e) блонди́н, *f.* -ка (8)

blouse блу́зка (8)

blue си́ний (6)

book кни́га (2)

bookcase по́лка (2), кни́жная по́лка (10)

bookstore кни́жный магази́н (10)

bored: I am b. Мне ску́чно (9)

boring ску́чный (8)

born, to be рожда́ться, роди́ться (*23*)

borsch борщ (11)

boss нача́льник (9), шеф

Boston Босто́н (5)

both о́ба, о́бе (*26*); **b. . . . and** и . . . и (4)

bottle буты́лка (11)

boundary грани́ца (13)

bouquet буке́т (22)

boy ма́льчик (13)

bread хлеб (7)

breakfast за́втрак (11); **to have b.** за́втракать (11), по- (17)

bridge мост; **on the b.** на мосту́ (12)

brief коро́ткий (коро́тко) (11)

briefcase портфе́ль (*m.*) (22)

bright све́тлый (светло́) (9)

to bring, *see 22*

broad широ́кий (широко́) (8)

broader ши́ре (*25*)

brother брат (4, *20*)

brunet(te) брюне́т, *f.* -ка (8)

buffet буфе́т (13)

to build стро́ить, по- (*27*)

building зда́ние (12)

bus авто́бус (17); **by b.** на авто́бусе

business де́ло, дела́ (*pl.*) (14); **on b.** по де́лу (24), по дела́м

busy заня́то́й, за́нят (22, 23)

but но (*5*); а (*4*); **(except)** кро́ме (+ *gen.*) (10)

butcher мясни́к (19)

butter ма́сло (6)

to buy покупа́ть (8), купи́ть (*16*)

by *instr. case* (*11*); **(near)** у (+ *gen.*) (22); **(past)** ми́мо (+ *gen.*) (22); **(by vehicle)** на (+ *loc.*) (*17*); **by (phone, radio, etc.)** по (+ *dat.*)

to call (by phone) звони́ть (9), по- (+ *dat.*) (*15*); **to c. on (for)** заходи́ть, зайти́ (22); **(to name)** звать, на- (*26*)

calm споко́йный (24)

camera фотоаппара́т (9)

can мочь (10), с- (21); **one c.** мо́жно (21); **one cannot** нельзя́ (21); **One can't help but . . . .** Нельзя́ не (+ *inf.*). **I can't help but . . . .** Я не могу́ не (+ *inf.*).

candy конфе́ты (*f. pl.*); (**a piece**) конфе́та (20)

capital столи́ца (7)

car автомоби́ль (*m.*) (6), маши́на (10); (**railway**) c. ваго́н (24); **by c.** на автомоби́ле, на маши́не (17)

card ка́рта (5); **to play cards** игра́ть в ка́рты (14)

care: I don't c. Мне́ всё равно́ (9)

carpet ковёр (10)

to carry, *see* 22

case слу́чай (20)

cat ко́шка (16)

to catch лови́ть (imperf.) (27), пойма́ть (perf.)

cattle скот (*collect.*) (23)

Caucasus Кавка́з (11); **in the C.** на Кавка́зе (12)

ceiling потоло́к (2)

to celebrate пра́здновать (imperf.) (26)

celebrated знамени́тый (13)

celebrity знамени́тость (*f.*) (25)

center центр (7)

century век (*nom. pl.* -а́) (18)

cereal ка́ша (21)

certain (sure) уве́рен/ный (18, 23); **c. of** уве́рен в (+ *loc.*) (23); **a c.** оди́н (8), како́й-то (22); **c. (ones)** не́которые (20)

chair стул (2); (**armchair**) кре́сло (6)

chalk мел (11)

chance, by случа́йно (19)

to change (*intrans.*) изменя́ться, измени́ться (21)

chapter глава́ (14)

character хара́ктер (10)

charming ми́лый (9)

cheap дешёвый (дёшево) (7)

cheaper деше́вле (25)

cheerful весёлый (ве́село) (16)

cheese сыр (7, 12)

chemist хи́мик (14)

chess ша́хматы (*pl. only*); **to play c.** игра́ть в ша́хматы (14)

chief (*adj.*) гла́вный (12, 19); (*noun*) нача́льник (9)

child ребёнок (*pl., see* **children**) (13)

childhood де́тство (27)

children де́ти (*13*)

chilly све́жий (6, 9)

China Кита́й (11, 25)

Chinese кита́йский (20)

chocolate шокола́д (*12*)

choice вы́бор (13)

Christian name и́мя (*n.*) (7, 12, 20)

church це́рковь (*f.*) (12)

cigarette папиро́са (*15*), сигаре́та (*24*)

cinema кино́ (12)

citizen граждани́н, *f.* гражда́нка (*11, 12, 20*)

city го́род (*nom. pl.* -а́) (3); (*adj.*) городско́й (21)

class класс (2); уро́к (3)

classroom класс (2)

clean чи́стый (15); **cleaner** чи́ще (*25*)

to clean чи́стить, по- (*24*); **to c. up (off)** убира́ть, убра́ть (*24*)

clear я́сный (18)

climate кли́мат (12)

clock часы́ (*pl.*) (17)

close бли́зко (5); **c. to** бли́зко от (+ *gen.*) (25); **closer** бли́же; **c. to** бли́же к (+ *dat.*) (25)

to close (*trans.*) закрыва́ть (8), закры́ть (*15*); (*intrans.*) закрыва́ться, закры́ться (*19*)

closed закры́т/ый (*26*)

closet шкаф (24); **in the c.** в шкафу́

clothing оде́жда (24)

cloud о́блако (27); **storm c.** ту́ча (19)

club клуб (12)

coast бе́рег (*nom. pl.* -а́) (12); **on the c.** на берегу́ (12)

coat (overcoat) пальто́ (*n. indecl.*) (*12*); (jacket) пиджа́к (13)

coffee ко́фе (*m. indecl.*) (*11*)

coffeepot кофе́йник (24)

cold холо́дный (хо́лодно); (*noun*) хо́лод (21); **It is c.** Хо́лодно (9). **I am c.** Мне́ хо́лодно (9).

to collect (*trans.*) собира́ть, собра́ть, (*19*); (*intrans.*) собира́ться, собра́ться (*19*)

collective farm колхо́з (17); (*adj.*) колхо́зный

collective farmer колхо́зн.ик, *f.* -ица

color цвет (*nom. pl.* -а) (7). **What c. is . . .?** Како́го цве́та (+ *nom.*) (7)

to come (on foot) приходи́ть, прийти́ (*18*); (not on foot) приезжа́ть, прие́хать (*18*); **to c. in, out, up to, etc.** (*see* 22); **to c. back,** *see* **return** (*intrans.*)

comfortable удо́бный (7); **I am c.** Мне́ удо́бно (9).

common (mutual) о́бщий (20)

company о́бщество (20)

to complain жа́ловаться, по- (*23*)

completely совсе́м (11); соверше́нно (23)

compliment комплиме́нт; **Thanks for the compliment!** Спаси́бо за комплиме́нт! (8)

composition сочине́ние (5)

comrade това́рищ (8)

concerning о, об, обо (+ *loc.*) (5, 12); про (+ *acc.*) (21)

concert конце́рт (5); **at the c.** на конце́рте (5)

condition усло́вие (27)

connection связь (*f.*) (21)

to consider счита́ть (imperf.) (17)

to consult сове́товаться с (+ *instr.*) (21), по- (21)

contemporary совреме́нный (20)

to continue продолжа́ть (imperf.) (16)

convenient удо́бный (7)

convention съезд (20)

conversation разгово́р (7)

to converse разгова́ривать (imperf.) (11)

to cook гото́вить (*13*), с-

cool: It's cool. Прохла́дно (12). Свежо́ (6, 9).

copeck копе́йка (*26*)

corner у́гол (12); **in the c.** в углу́; **on the c.** на углу́

correct (of things) пра́вильный (18)

correspondent корреспонде́нт, *f.* -ка (8)

corridor коридо́р (16)

to cost сто́ить (imperf.) (*16*)

cottage (summer) да́ча (12); **at the c.** на да́че

couch дива́н (11)

could, *see* **can**

council, counsel сове́т (9)

to count счита́ть (imperf.) (17)

country (nation) страна́ (7); **country(side)** дере́вня (6); **to go to the country** е́здить/е́хать/пое́хать в дере́вню/на да́чу/за́ город (17)

couple па́ра (13)

course, of коне́чно (5)

court двор (16)

cousin (male) двою́родный бра́т; **(female)** двою́родная сестра́ (27)

cow коро́ва (23)

cozy ую́тный (9)

Crimea Крым; **in the C.** в Крыму́ (12)

to cross переходи́ть, перейти́ (*22*)

crowd толпа́ (22)

cry крик (21)

to cry (out) крича́ть, кри́кнуть (*21*); **(to weep)** пла́кать (imperf.) (*21*)

culture культу́ра (20)

cultured, cultural культу́рный (20)

cup ча́шка (10)

cupboard шкаф, (24); буфе́т; **in the c.** в шкафу́

customer покупа́тель, *f.* -ница (13)

to cut ре́зать (imperf.) (*19*)

daddy па́па

daily дневно́й (26)

dance та́нец (21)

to dance танцева́ть, по- (*21*)

danger опа́сность (*f.*) (27)

dangerous опа́сный (17)

dark тёмный (темно́) (9); **It is d.** Темно́ (9)

date число́; **What is the d. today?** Како́е сего́дня число́? (*26*)

daughter дочь (4, *12, 20*)

day день (6); **all d. (long)** весь де́нь (7); **in the daytime** днём (11); **d. off** выходно́й де́нь (24); **d. after tomorrow** послеза́втра (17); **d. before yesterday** позавчера́ (18), тре́тьего дня́ (21). **Good d.! (greeting)** До́брый де́нь! **What d. is it today?** Како́й сего́дня де́нь?

daydream мечта́ (27)

daytime (*adj.*) дневно́й (26)

daytime, in the днём (11)

deal, a great мно́го (+ *gen.*) (5)

dear дорого́й (до́рого) (7); **dearer** доро́же (*25*)

death смерть (*f.*) (12)

debt долг (25)

December дека́брь (*m.*) (23)

to decide реша́ть, реши́ть (*17*)

deep глубо́кий (13); **deeper** глу́бже (*25*)

defense защи́та (27)

delicious вку́сный (11)

demand спрос, **d. for** спро́с на (+ *acc.*) (27)

department отде́л (13); **d. store** универса́льный магази́н (универма́г) (13)

departure (on foot) ухо́д (27)

to describe опи́сывать, описа́ть (*26*)

description описа́ние

desk стол (2), пи́сьменный сто́л (7)

to destroy разруша́ть, разру́шить (*27*)

devil чёрт (25)

dictionary слова́рь (4)

to die умира́ть, умере́ть (*21*)

different друго́й (10); **(various)** ра́зный (13)

differently ина́че; по-друго́му (21)

difficult тру́дный (6)

difficulty, with с трудо́м (11)

diligent приле́жный (10)

to dine обе́дать (11), по- (17)

dining room столо́вая (10)

dinner обе́д (10); **at d.** за обе́дом; **to (for) d.** к обе́ду (18); **to have d.,** *see* **to dine**

diplomat диплома́т (11)

direct(ly) пря́мо (17)

director дире́ктор (*nom. pl.* -а́) (9), нача́льник (9)

dirty гря́зный (15)

discovery откры́тие (14)

to discuss говори́ть о (+ *loc.*) (5, 8), по- (20)

dish таре́лка (13); **dishes** посу́да (*collect.*) (13)

disorder беспоря́док (24)

displeased, dissatisfied недово́лен (*10*)

disposition хара́ктер (10)

division отде́л (13)

to do де́лать (5, 8, 9), с- (14); **What can one d.?** Что де́лать? (10); **What can we d.?** Что нам де́лать? (9)

doctor до́ктор (*nom. pl.* -а́) (4); врач (16)

dog соба́ка (10)

dollar до́ллар (15)

Don Дон (*12*); **on the D.** на Дону́

door дверь (*f.*) (5, *13*); **out of doors (static)** на у́лице (7), на дворе́ (24)

down from (off) с (+ *gen.*) (17)

dream сон (26); **(daydream)** мечта́ (27); **to have a d.** ви́деть со́н (26); **to daydream** мечта́ть (imperf.) (27)

dress пла́тье (6, *20*)

to dress (*trans.*) одева́ть, оде́ть (*19*); (*intrans.*) одева́ться, оде́ться (*19*)

drier су́ше (25)

to drink пить (7, 21), вы́- (7, 21)

to drive (= to ride), *see 17, 18*; **to d. (someone)**, *see 22*

to drop in to see заходи́ть, зайти́ к (+ *dat.*) (22)

drugstore апте́ка (12)

dry сухо́й (су́хо) (24)

dull ску́чный (6)

during во вре́мя (+ *gen.*) (12)

duty долг (*no pl.*) (25)

each ка́ждый (8); **e. other** друг дру́га (13)

ear у́хо (10, 19)

early (*adv.*) ра́но (9); (*adj.*) ра́нний (27); **It's e.** Ра́но (9); **earlier** ра́ньше (12, 25)

to earn зараба́тывать, зарабо́тать (27)

easier ле́гче (25)

east восто́к; **to the e.** на восто́к; **in the e.** на восто́ке (22)

eastern восто́чный (22)

easy лёгкий (легко́) (6); **It's e. to . . . .** Легко́ (+ *inf.*) (9); **not e.** нелегко́ (9)

to eat есть (imperf.) (7, 8, 21), по- (perf.) (21), съ- (perf.) (21) **to e. breakfast, lunch, supper,** *see* **breakfast, lunch, supper; to e. dinner,** *see* **dine**

editor реда́ктор (7)

education образова́ние (23); **(studies)** уче́ние (23)

egg яйцо́ (21)

eight во́семь (17, 26)

eighteen восемна́дцать (17, 26)

eighth восьмо́й (18)

eighty во́семьдесят (21, 26)

either . . . or и́ли . . . и́ли (5)

elder ста́рший (25)

eldest (са́мый) ста́рший (8, 25)

elephant слон (21)

elevator лифт (21)

eleven оди́ннадцать (17, 26)

else: who e.? кто́ ещё? **what e.?** что́ ещё? **or e.** а то́

empty пусто́й (пу́сто) (24)

end коне́ц (7); **at the e. of** в конце́ (+ *gen.*) (7); **in the e., in the final analysis,** в конце́ концо́в

to end (*trans.*) конча́ть (8), ко́нчить (15); (*intrans.*) конча́ться, ко́нчиться (19)

to endure переноси́ть, перенести́ (27)

enemy враг (27)

engineer инжене́р (9)

England А́нглия (12)

English (*adj.*) англи́йский (9); **(language)** англи́йский язы́к; **(in) E.** по-англи́йски (5); **the E.** англича́не (20)

Englishman англича́нин (6, 20)

Englishwoman англича́нка (20)

enough дово́льно (19), доста́точно (25)

to enter (on foot) входи́ть, войти́ в (+ *acc.*) (22); **(not on foot)** въезжа́ть, въе́хать в (+ *acc.*) (22); **(enroll in)** поступа́ть, поступи́ть в/на (+ *acc.*) (23)

entertaining заба́вный (26)

entirely совсе́м (11), соверше́нно (23)

epoch эпо́ха (8)

equally одина́ково (19)

error оши́бка (14)

especially осо́бенно (12)

essential необходи́мый (27)

etc. и т. д. (и так да́лее) (21)

Europe Евро́па (5)

European европе́йский

even да́же (5), и (7)

evening ве́чер (*nom. pl.* -а́) (7); **in the e.** ве́чером (11); **e. party** вечери́нка (8); (*adj.*) вече́рний (8); **Good e.!** До́брый ве́чер!

ever (in questions) когда́-нибудь (22), когда́-либо (25); **not e.** никогда́ не (8)

every ка́ждый (8); все (8, 20)

everybody, everyone все (8, 20); **e. who** всё, кто . . .

everything всё; **e. that** всё, что . . . (7)

everywhere везде́ (11)

evident(ly) ви́дно (25)

evil (*adj.*) злой (21)

exactly то́чно (21); **(with numerals)** ро́вно (16, 21)

examination экза́мен (5); **to take an e.** держа́ть экза́мен (13); **to pass an e.** вы́держать экза́мен; **to fail an e.** провали́ться на экза́мене (19)

example, for наприме́р (8)

excellent отли́чный (18); **(fine)** прекра́сный (7)

except кро́ме (+ *gen.*) (10)

to excuse извиня́ть, извини́ть (18); **E. me!** Извини́те! (18). Прости́те! (4)

exercise упражне́ние (9)

exit вы́ход (27)

expensive дорого́й (до́рого) (7); **more e.** доро́же (25)

to explain объясня́ть (8), объясни́ть (15)

explanation объясне́ние (13)

expression выраже́ние (13)

eye глаз (*nom. pl.* -а́; *gen. pl.* глаз) (3)

face лицо́ (20)

fact факт; **in f.** действи́тельно

factory заво́д; **at the f.** на заво́де (12); (*adj.*) заводско́й (14)

to fail прова́ливаться, провали́ться; **to f. an exam** провали́ться на экза́мене (19)

fairly (rather) дово́льно (10)

fairy tale ска́зка (24)

fall (autumn) о́сень; **in f.** о́сенью (11); (*adj.*) осе́нний

to fall па́дать, упа́сть (24); **to f. asleep** засыпа́ть, засну́ть (24); **to f. ill** заболева́ть, заболе́ть (23)

falsehood непра́вда (5)

familiar знако́м/ый (20)

family семья́ (9, 20); (adj.) семе́йный; **f. name** фами́лия; **What is your f. name?** Ка́к ва́ша фами́лия? (4)

famous знамени́тый (12)

far (away) далеко́; **f. from** далеко́ от (+ gen.); **not f. (away)** недалеко́ (6); **not f. from** недалеко́ о́т (+ gen.) (25); **so f. (to now, up to here)** до сих по́р (21); **from f.** издалека́ (21), и́здали (25)

farther да́льше (25)

fashion мо́да (13)

fast бы́стрый (8); **The clock is f.** Часы́ спеша́т (17)

fat то́лстый (8)

father оте́ц (4, 7)

fatherland ро́дина (27)

fatter то́лще (25)

favorite люби́мый (12)

to fear боя́ться (imperf.) (19)

February февра́ль (m.) (23)

to feel—often expressed by an impersonal construction + dat., (see 9, 23); (trans.) чу́вствовать, по- (23); (intrans.) чу́вствовать себя́ (imperf.); **How do you f.?** Ка́к вы́ себя́ чу́вствуете? **I f. well.** Я́ хорошо́ себя́ чу́вствую (23); **to f. like (want)** хоте́ть (10), за- (21); хоте́ться, за- (26)

feeling чу́вство (25)

fellow па́рень (14)

few ма́ло (+ gen. pl.) (16); **a f.** не́сколько (+ gen. pl.) (16, 20); немно́гие (nom. pl.) (20)

fewer ме́ньше (+ gen. pl.) (25)

field по́ле (4)

fifteen пятна́дцать (17, 26)

fifth пя́тый (18)

fifty пятьдеся́т (21, 26)

film фильм (12)

finally наконе́ц (14)

to find находи́ть, найти́ (22); **to f. out, learn** узнава́ть, узна́ть (21)

fine хоро́ший (хорошо́) (6); прекра́сный (7); сла́вный (26); (delicate, thin) то́нкий (13)

finger па́лец (11)

to finish (trans.) конча́ть (8), ко́нчить (15); (intrans.) конча́ться, ко́нчиться (19)

firm твёрдый (19)

first пе́рвый (6); **at f.** снача́ла (11); **f. name** и́мя (n.) (7, 12, 20); **What is your f. name?** Ка́к ва́ше и́мя? (7); **the f. time** пе́рвый ра́з (16); **for the f. time** в пе́рвый ра́з (16); **in the f. place** во-пе́рвых (20)

fish ры́ба (7)

five пять (16, 26)

to float, see 24

floor пол (2, 12); (story) эта́ж (12)

flower цвет.о́к (nom. pl., -ы́) (19)

fluently свобо́дно (23)

to fly, f. in, out, away, past, etc., see 24, 27

folk (adj.) наро́дный (21)

following сле́дующий (27)

fond of, to be люби́ть (imperf., 11, 19)

food еда́ (20)

fool дура́к, f. ду́ра (26)

foolish глу́пый (9)

foot нога́ (10); **on f.** пешко́м (17)

football футбо́л; **at a f. game** на футбо́ле (5); **to play f.** игра́ть в футбо́л

for (f. the sake of) для (+ gen.) (16, 17); **(in exchange f.)** за (+ acc.) (16, 17); **(a period of time)** simple acc. (18), на (+ acc.) (18); **(= to get)** за (+ instr.) (17)

forbidden, it is нельзя́ (+ inf.) (20)

force си́ла (25)

foreign иностра́нный (20)

foreigner иностра́н.ец, f. -ка (20)

to foresee предви́деть (imperf.) (27)

forest лес (nom. pl. -а́) (12, 13); **in the f.** в лесу́

to foretell предска́зывать, предсказа́ть (27)

to forget забыва́ть, забы́ть (16)

fork ви́лка (16)

former бы́вший (27)

formerly ра́ньше (12), пре́жде (25)

fortunate счастли́вый (13)

fortunately к сча́стью (23)

forty со́рок (21, 26)

to found осно́вывать, основа́ть (18)

fountain pen авторучка (7)

four четы́ре (10, 26)

four-story четырёхэта́жный (27)

fourteen четы́рнадцать (17, 26)

fourth четвёртый (18)

France Фра́нция (12)

free свобо́дный (23)

freedom свобо́да (23)

French (adj.) францу́зский (7); **(language)** францу́зский язы́к; **(in) F.** по-францу́зски; **the F.** францу́зы (20)

Frenchman францу́з (20)

Frenchwoman францу́женка (20)

frequently ча́сто (9); **more f.** ча́ще (25)

fresh све́жий (свежо́) (6, 9)

Friday пя́тница (18)

fried жа́реный (21)

friend прия́тель, f. -ница (7); друг (6, 20), f. подру́га (8)

frightening стра́шный (27)

from (a person) от (+ gen.) (15, 17); **(out of)** из (+ gen.) (15, 17); **down f.** с (+ gen.) (17); **f. where** отку́да (15, 17); **f. the house of** от (+ gen.) (17)

front of, in перед (+ *instr.*) (19)

frontier грани́ца (13)

fruit, a фрукт; **fruit** (*collect.*) фру́кты (*pl.*) (*17*); (*adj.*) фрукто́вый

full по́лный (24)

fun весе́лье; **to make f. of** смея́ться (imperf.) над (+ *instr.*) (*19*)

funny смешно́й (19)

furniture ме́бель (*f. collect.*) (10)

further да́льше (25)

future (*adj.*) бу́дущий (*14*); **the f.** бу́дущее (*25*); **in the near f.** в ближа́йшем бу́дущем (25)

game (contest) матч (22); па́ртия (14)

garage гара́ж (6)

garden сад (*12*); **in the g.** в саду́

gas газ (24)

general (*adj.*) о́бщий (20); **in g.** вообще́ (20)

genius, a ге́ний (9)

gentleman господи́н (*11, 20*)

German (*adj.*) неме́цкий (20); **G. language** неме́цкий язы́к; **in G.** по-неме́цки (*20*); **a G.** не́мец, *f.* не́мка (*20*)

Germany Герма́ния (20)

gesture жест (11)

to get (receive) получа́ть, получи́ть (*13*); **(obtain)** достава́ть, доста́ть (*21*); **(arrive on foot)** приходи́ть, прийти́ (*21*); **(not on foot)** приезжа́ть, прие́хать (*21*); **to g. up** встава́ть, встать (*16*); **(to become)** станови́ться, стать (+ *instr.*) (*21*); **to g. dressed** одева́ться, оде́ться (*19*); **to g. undressed** раздева́ться (*19*); **to g. used** привыка́ть, привы́кнуть (*21*); **to g. well** выздора́вливать, вы́здороветь (23)

gift пода́рок (22)

girl де́вушка (8); **(little) g.** де́вочка (13)

to give дава́ть (9), дать (*15*); **to g. back,** *see* **return** (*trans.*); **to g. up (doing something)** перестава́ть, переста́ть (+ *inf.*) (27)

glad рад (*51*); **I'm g. of that.** Я э́тому ра́д.

glass (tumbler) стака́н (7)

to go, *see 17, 18, 22*; **let's g.** идём(те), пойдём(те) (*23*); **to g. away,** *see 18*; **to g. in, out, up to, away, through, past, across,** *see 22*; **to g. back,** *see* **return** (*intrans.*); **to g. on, continue** продолжа́ть (+ *inf.*) (imperf.) (16); **to g. to bed** ложи́ться/ лечь спа́ть (*21*); **going to** (+ *inf.*) = *future tense* (*see* 14)

God Бог (18). **Thank God!** Сла́ва Бо́гу! (18)

gold(en) золото́й (26)

good хоро́ший (хорошо́) (4, 6); **It's g. that . . . .** Хорошо́, что . . . . (4). **That's g.** Э́то хорошо́ (4). **G. morning!** До́брое у́тро! (7). **G. night!** Споко́йной но́чи! (20). **G. for you (him, her, etc.)!** Молоде́ц! (8); **g.-hearted** до́брый (21)

good-bye до свида́ния (3), проща́й(те)! всего́ хоро́шего! (7); **g. till tomorrow** до за́втра (19)

grade (mark) отме́тка (13)

grammar грамма́тика (2)

granddaughter вну́чка (22)

grandfather дед, де́душка (*20*)

grandmother ба́бушка (17)

grandson внук (22)

grass трава́ (17)

grateful благода́рный (23)

gray се́рый (7)

great большо́й (6); вели́кий (18); **a g. deal** мно́го (+ *gen.*) (5); **greater** бо́льший, бо́льше (25)

green зелёный (12)

greeting(s) приве́т (9); **to give (someone) g. from . . .** переда́ть п. от . . . (+ *gen.*)

ground земля́ (23)

to grow (*intrans.*) расти́ (imperf.) (*21*); **(to become)** станови́ться, стать (*21*)

guest гость (*m.*) (4)

guide гид (12)

guitar гита́ра (8)

habit привы́чка (23)

half полови́на (14, 26); пол (26); **h. an hour** полчаса́ (22); **one and a h.** полтора́ (26); **five and a h.** пять с полови́ной (25)

hall коридо́р (16); **(vestibule)** пере́дняя (24)

ham ветчина́ (17)

hand рука́ (2); **by h.** за́ руку (22)

handkerchief плато́к (22)

handsome краси́вый (6)

to hang (*intrans.*) висе́ть (imperf.) (27)

to happen случа́ться, случи́ться (20); **to h. sometimes/often** быва́ть (imperf.) (8)

happy счастли́вый (13, 23)

hard тру́дный (6); **(firm)** твёрдый (19); **(not easy)** нелегко́ (9); **h. life** тяжёлая жизнь (20); **It is h. to . . . .** Тру́дно (+ *inf.*) (9)

hardly: h. anyone почти́ никто́ (6); **h. anything** почти́ ничего́ (6)

hard-working приле́жный (10)

hat шля́па (6)

to hate ненави́деть (imperf.) (*14*)

to have у (+ *gen.*) (10); **I h . . . .** У меня́ (есть) (+ *nom.*) (10). **I h. no . . .** У меня́ нет (+ *gen.*) (10). **I h. to . . .** Я до́лжен (+ *inf.*) (8); Мне на́до (ну́жно) (+ *inf.*) (10); **to h. breakfast, lunch, supper,** *see* **breakfast, lunch, supper; to h. dinner,** *see* **dine; to h. a talk** поговори́ть (perf.) (25); **to h. a nap** поспа́ть (perf.) (25)

he он (2, 12)

head голова́ (3, 10); **(chief)** глава́

headache: I have a h. У меня́ боли́т голова́ (23)

health здоро́вье (21); **How is your h.?** Как ва́ше здоро́вье? (21)

healthy здоро́в/ый (*23*)

to hear слы́шать (*11*), y- (*21*)

heart сéрдце (*23*)

heat жарá (21)

heaven нéбо (7)

heavy тяжёлый (тяжелó) (20)

hello здрáвствуй(те) (*4*); **(on the telephone)** аллó (11)

help пóмощь (*f.*) (10)

to help помогáть (*9*), помóчь (*18*) (+ *dat.*); **to h. with the housework** помогáть на хозя́йству (9); **One can't h. but . . .** Нельзя́ не (+ *inf.*). **I can't h. but . . .** Я́ не могу́ не (+ *inf.*) (11)

her, hers её (7)

here тут (*2*), здесь (*4*); **h. is (are)** вот (*2*); **(to) h., hither** сюда́ (*17*); **from h.** отсю́да (*17*)

hero герóй (*5*)

heroine героúня (5)

herself, *see* **self**

high высóкий (10); **higher** вы́ше (25)

himself, *see* **self**

his егó (7)

historian истóрик (11)

history истóрия (9)

to hold держáть (imperf.) (*11*)

holiday прáздник (9); **(day off)** выходнóй дéнь (24); **for the holidays** на прáздники (25); **school holidays** каникулы (*pl.*) (23)

home дом (*nom. pl.* -á) (2); **at h.** дóма (2); **(to) h., homewards** домóй (*17*); **from h.** и́з дому (*17*)

honor честь (*f.*); **in h. of** в честь (+ *gen.*) (26)

hope надéжда (27)

to hope надéяться (imperf.) (*19*); **to h. for** надéяться на (+ *acc.*) (19)

horrible ужáсный (13)

horror у́жас (21)

horse лóшадь (*f.*) (16, *20*)

hospitable гостеприи́мный (20)

hospital больни́ца (23); гóспиталь (*m.*) (27)

host хозя́ин (11, *20*)

hostess хозя́йка (9)

hot (of weather) жáркий (7); **It's h.** Жáрко (9); **(of objects)** горя́чий (горячó) (21); **hotter (of weather)** жáрче (25)

hotel гости́ница (7); **h. room** нóмер (7)

hour час (14); **half an h.** полчасá (22)

house дом (*nom. pl.* -á) (2); **at the h. of** у (+ *gen.*) (10); **to the h. of** к (+ *dat.*) (17); **from the h. of** от (+ *gen.*) (15); **to help around the h.** помогáть по хозя́йству (21)

housewife хозя́йка (9)

housework хозя́йство (9)

how как (3); какóй (*with adjectives in long form*) (6); **h. much, h. many** скóлько (+ *gen.*) (7, 15); **h. large!** какóй большóй! (6); **h. long (time)?** скóлько врéмени? (12); **H. much is**

(are) . . . ? Скóлько стóит (стóят)? (16). **H. are you?** Кáк вы поживáете? (3)

however затó (25)

huge огрóмный (12)

hundred сто (21, 26)

hunger гóлод

hungry голóдный (23)

to hurry спеши́ть, по- (*17*); **H. up!** Скорéй!

to hurt (*intrans.*) болéть (imperf.) (*23*)

husband муж (3, *20*)

I я (2)

ice cream морóженое (11)

idea мысль (*f.*) (21), идéя (16)

identically одинáково (19)

if éсли (10, *14*, *24*); **in indirect questions** ли (22); **in hypothetical conditions** éсли бы (*24*)

ill бóлен (23); **to be taken i.** заболевáть, заболéть (23)

illness болéзнь (*f.*) (23)

to imagine (suppose) представля́ть/предстáвить себé (27)

immediately срáзу (21), немéдленно (20)

immense огрóмный (12)

impatience нетерпéние (18)

important вáжный (12)

impossible невозмóжно (18, *20*); **it is i.** нельзя́ (20); невозмóжно (20)

in в (+ *loc.*) (5); **with expressions of time,** *see* 26; **in front of** перед (+ *instr.*) (19)

incident случáй (20)

incidentally мéжду прóчим (19)

incorrectly непрáвильно (19)

inexpensive дешёвый (дёшево) (7)

information извéстие (27)

infrequently рéдко (9)

inhabitant жи́тель, *f.* -ница (22)

insane (person) сумасшéдший (25)

instead of вмéсто (+ *gen.*) (23)

instructor инстру́ктор (*nom. pl.* -á), *f.* -ша (23)

insufficiently недостáточно (16)

intelligent у́мный (умнó) (9)

interest интерéс (11); **i. in** интерéс к (+ *dat.*)

to interest интересовáть, за- (*21*); **to be interested in** интересовáться, за- (+ *instr.*) (*21*)

interesting интерéсный (5)

interpreter перевóдч.ик, *f.* -ица (12)

into в (+ *acc.*) (*17*)

to introduce знакóмить, по- (*20*); **to be introduced** знакóмиться, по- (*20*)

invitation приглашéние (25)

to invite приглашáть, пригласи́ть (*25*)

is, *see* **be**

island óстров (24)

it э́то (2); он, онó, онá (4); **with impersonals not translated** *see* 7, 9

Italian (*adj.*) италья́нский (12); **I. language** италья́нский язы́к; **in I.** по-италья́нски (12); **(an) I.** италья́н.ец, *f.* -ка (20)

Italy Ита́лия (12)

its его́ (7); её (7)

itself, *see* **self**

jacket пиджа́к (13)

jam варе́нье (11)

January янва́рь (*m.*) (23)

Japanese (*adj.*) япо́нский (19)

jazz джаз (9)

job рабо́та (5); **(service)** слу́жба (9)

joke шу́тка (20)

to joke шути́ть, по-

journalist журнали́ст, *f.* -ка (4)

July ию́ль (*m.*) (23)

June ию́нь (*m.*) (23)

just (only) то́лько (4); **(exactly)** ро́вно (16); **have j.** то́лько что (+ *past tense*) (14); **j. now** сейча́с (5)

to keep (hold) держа́ть (imperf.) (*11*)

kerchief плато́к (22)

Kiev Ки́ев

to kill убива́ть, уби́ть (27)

kilogram килогра́мм, кило́ (7)

kilometer киломе́тр (25)

kind до́брый (21); любе́зный (18, 23); **Be so k. as to . . . .** Бу́дьте добры́ (18, 23). Бу́дьте любе́зны (18, 23) (+ *imperative*). **What k. of . . .?** Како́й . . .? (6); Что э́то за (+ *nom.*)? (20)

king коро́ль (18)

kiss поцелу́й (27)

to kiss целова́ть, по- (27)

kitchen ку́хня (4, 20)

knife нож (16)

knock стук (24)

to knock стуча́ть, по- (24)

to know знать (imperf.) (5, 8); **to k. how to** уме́ть (imperf., + *inf.*) (11)

knowledge зна́ние (27)

kolkhoz колхо́з (17)

labor (work) труд (11)

lady да́ма (15); **ladies and gentlemen** господа́ (20)

lake о́зеро (*13*)

lamp ла́мпа (2)

land земля́ (23); **(country)** страна́ (7)

landlady хозя́йка (9)

landlord хозя́ин (11, 20)

language язы́к (12, 20)

large большо́й (6)

larger бо́льший, бо́льше (25)

last после́дний (6); **at l.** наконе́ц (14); **(past)** про́шлый (12); **(in) l. year** в про́шлом голу́ (12); **l. name** фами́лия (4); **What is your l. name?** Ка́к ва́ша фами́лия? (4)

late (*adv.*) по́здно (9); (*adj.*) по́здний; **It's l.** По́здно (9). **to be l.** опа́здывать, опозда́ть (17, 19); **later** по́зже (15, 25), поздне́е; **(afterwards)** пото́м (11), по́сле; **latest** после́дний (6)

to laugh смея́ться (imperf.) (*19*); **to l. at** смея́ться над (+ *instr.*) (19)

laughter смех (16)

laundry бельё (24)

to lay down класть (imperf.), положи́ть (perf.) (24)

lazy лени́вый (10). **I felt too l. to . . . .** Мне́ бы́ло ле́нь (+ *inf.*) (18).

leader вождь (*m.*) (12)

leaf лист (13, 20)

to learn учи́ться, на- (+ *dat.*) (23); **(to find out)** узнава́ть, узна́ть (21); **(to memorize)** запомина́ть, запо́мнить (18)

leave (vacation) о́тпуск (26)

to leave (go away), *see* 18, 22; **to l. behind, l. for someone** оставля́ть, оста́вить (22)

lecture ле́кция (12), докла́д (12); **to give a l.** (про)чита́ть ле́кцию (докла́д) (12)

lecturer докла́дч.ик, *f.* -ица (27)

left ле́вый (11); **on the l.** нале́во (12), сле́ва (26); **to the l.** нале́во (12); **to be l.** остава́ться, оста́ться (25)

leg нога́ (10)

lemon лимо́н (11)

to lend ода́лживать, одолжи́ть (22)

Leningrad Ленингра́д (5)

less ме́ньше (+ *gen.*) (8); ме́нее (25)

lesson уро́к (3); **at the l.** на уро́ке (5)

let пусть, пуска́й(те); **l. us** дава́й(те) (25); **let's go** идём(те), пойдём(те) (23); **l. me know** да́й(те) мне́ зна́ть (21)

letter письмо́ (4)

library библиоте́ка (5)

to lie, be lying лежа́ть (imperf.) (11); **to l. down** ложи́ться (imperf.) (20), лечь (perf.) (20)

life жизнь (*f.*) (11)

light (*noun*) свет; (*adj.*) **(bright)** све́тлый (светло́) (9); **(not heavy)** лёгкий (легко́) (6); **lighter (not so heavy)** ле́гче (25)

likable ми́лый (9), симпати́чный (20)

like как (4); **(similar to)** похо́ж на (+ *acc.*) (23); **l. this (that)** так; **He looks l. . . . .** Он похо́ж на (+ *acc.*) (23).

to like люби́ть (imperf.) (11, 19); нра́виться, по-; **I l. that.** Э́то мне́ нра́вится (19). **I would l. to . . . .** Я́ бы хоте́л (+ *inf.*) (24).

likely вероя́тно (5)

line (of writing) строка́, стро́чка (25); **l. (queue)** о́чередь (*f.*) (18, 20), **to get in l.** (20)

linen бельё (24)

to listen (to) слу́шать (5, 8), по- (18)

literary литерату́рный

literature литерату́ра

little ма́ленький (6); l. (of) ма́ло (+ gen.) (5); a l. немно́го, немно́жко (+ gen.) (7, 20)

to live жить (imperf.) (5, 9)

lively весёлый (ве́село) (16)

livestock скот (collect.) (23)

living room гости́ная (10)

located, to be находи́ться (imperf.) (22)

London Ло́ндон (5)

lonely одино́кий (18)

long (adj.) дли́нный (11); a l. while/time до́лго (11); for a l. time до́лго (11), надо́лго (22); l. ago, l. since давно́ (7, 9, 11); not l. ago неда́вно (7); how long? (time) ско́лько вре́мени? (12); Have you been here l.? Вы давно́ здесь? (7). I haven't written for so l. Я так давно́ не писа́л (9).

to look смотре́ть, по- (17); to l. at (по) смотре́ть на (+ acc.) (17); He looks like . . . . Он похо́ж на (+ acc.) (23). to l. for иска́ть (imperf.) (24)

to lose теря́ть, по- (22)

lot: a lot (of) мно́го (+ gen.) (5)

loud гро́мкий (гро́мко) (19); louder гро́мче (25)

love любо́вь (f.) (12)

to love люби́ть (imperf.) (11, 19)

low ни́зкий (10); (quiet) ти́хий (8); lower ни́же (25); (quieter) ти́ше (25)

lunch за́втрак (11); to have l. за́втракать, по- (17)

machine маши́на (10)

machinist машини́ст, f. -ка (14)

mad (person) сумасше́дший (25)

magazine журна́л (3)

mail по́чта (12)

main гла́вный (12)

to make де́лать (5, 8), с- (14)

mama ма́ма (5)

man (person, human being) челове́к (8, 13, 16); (male) мужчи́на (20)

many мно́го (+ gen. pl.) (16); мно́гие (nom. pl.) (20); how m. ско́лько (+ gen. pl.) (16, 20); so m. так мно́го (+ gen. pl.); сто́лько (+ gen. pl.) (16, 20); m. thanks большо́е спаси́бо (10); m. good things мно́го хоро́шего (9)

map ка́рта (3)

March март (23)

mark (grade) отме́тка (13)

married (of men) жена́т (26); (of women) за́мужем (26)

marvelous чу́дный (17), чуде́сный (19)

mass, a ма́сса (17)

match спи́чка (24); (sports) матч (22)

matter де́ло; What is the m. with you? Что с ва́ми? (23)

mausoleum мавзоле́й (18)

may мочь (imperf.) (10); one m. мо́жно (21); one m. not нельзя́ (21); M. I? Мо́жно (мне) (+ inf.)? (21)

May май (23)

maybe мо́жет быть (10)

mean: What does that m.? Что э́то зна́чит? (18). I m. . . . . Я хочу́ сказа́ть (14).

meat мя́со (6)

to meet (encounter) встреча́ть, встре́тить (16); to m. (each other) встреча́ться, встре́титься (19); (to be introduced to each other) знако́миться, по- (20)

meeting собра́ние (12); съезд (20)

memorial па́мятинк (7)

to memorize запомина́ть, запо́мнить (18)

memory па́мять (f.) (11)

mention: Don't m. it. Не́ за что (10). Не сто́ит благода́рности (18).

merry весёлый (ве́село) (16)

Mexico Ме́ксика (18)

middle (noun) середи́на (18); (adj.) сре́дний (22); in the m. of посреди́ (+ gen.) (27)

midnight по́лночь (f.) (19)

milk молоко́ (7)

million миллио́н (26)

mind: I don't mind. Мне всё равно́ (10).

mine мой (4, 12, 20)

minute мину́та (18)

mistake оши́бка (14); to make a m. (с)де́лать оши́бку (14)

mistaken, to be ошиба́ться, ошиби́ться (22)

modern совреме́нный (20)

Monday понеде́льник (18)

money де́ньги (pl.) (15)

month ме́сяц (7); (in) this m. в э́том ме́сяце (23)

monument па́мятник (7)

moon ме́сяц (7), луна́ (21)

more бо́льше (+ gen.) (8); бо́лее (25); (in addition) ещё (10); one m. ещё оди́н (10); no m. бо́льше не (10); comparative, see 25

morning у́тро (7); in the m. у́тром (11); from m. to evening с утра́ до ве́чера (25); Good m.! До́брое у́тро! (7). (adj.) у́тренний (8)

Moscow Москва́ (5); (adj.) моско́вский (12)

most са́мый (+ adj.) (13, 25); m. of all бо́льше всего́ (всех) (25)

mostly: (for the most part) гла́вным о́бразом (19)

mother мать (4, 12, 20)

motion picture фильм (12), карти́на; m. p. house кино́ (12)

mountain гора́ (13)

mournful гру́стный (17)

mouth рот (2)

movie фильм (12), карти́на; **to go to a m.** идти́/пойти́ в кино́

movie house кино́ (12)

Mr. господи́н (11)

Mrs. госпожа́ (11)

much мно́го (+ gen.) (5, 20); **how m.** ско́лько (+ gen.) (7, 20); **so m.** так мно́го (+ gen.), сто́лько (+ gen.) (16); **(with comparatives)** гора́здо (25); **to like very m.** о́чень люби́ть; **to want very m.** о́чень хоте́ть (10); **How m. is (are) . . .?** Ско́лько сто́ит (сто́ят)? (16)

municipal городско́й (21)

museum музе́й (2)

music му́зыка (8)

musician музыка́нт (6)

must до́лжен (8); на́до, ну́жно (9)

mutual о́бщий (20)

my мой (4, 12, 20)

myself, see **self**

name (first n.) и́мя (n.) (7, 12, 20); **(last n.)** фами́лия (4); **(of an object)** назва́ние (7); **What is your n.? (first n.)** Ка́к ва́ше и́мя? (7); **(last n.)** Ка́к ва́ша фами́лия? (4); **What is the n. of (an object, book, etc.)?** Ка́к назва́ние (+ gen.) (7), Ка́к называ́ется (+ nom.)?

to name называ́ть, назва́ть (18); **to be named, called (of an object)** называ́ться, назва́ться

to narrate расска́зывать, рассказа́ть (15)

narrow у́зкий (8)

narrower у́же (25)

nation наро́д (20)

national наро́дный (21), национа́льный

native родно́й; **one's n. town** родно́й го́род (27)

nature приро́да (16)

near (adv.) бли́зко (5), ря́дом (11); **n. (to)** бли́зко от (+ gen.) (25), ря́дом с (+ instr.) (11); (prep.) о́коло (+ gen.) (16); (adj.) бли́зкий; **in the n. future** в ближа́йшем бу́дущем (25); **nearer** бли́же; **n. to** бли́же к (+ dat.) (25)

nearby ря́дом (11)

necessary ну́жен (10); необходи́мый (27); **It is n. to . . .** Ну́жно (на́до) (+ inf.) (9)

necktie га́лстук (24)

need: I need . . . Мне́ ну́жен (+ nom.) (10)

neighbor сосе́д (nom. pl. -и) (10, 20)

neither . . . nor ни . . . ни (8)

nephew племя́нник (22)

never никогда́ (не) (8)

nevertheless всё-таки (19)

new но́вый (6); **What's new (with you)?** Что́ (у ва́с) но́вого?

New York Нью-Йо́рк (5)

news но́вость (f.), но́вости (pl.) (14); изве́стие (27); **That's n.** Это́ но́вость. (14)

newspaper газе́та (4)

newsstand кио́ск (8)

next (adv.) пото́м (11); (adj.) сле́дующий (27); **(future)** бу́дущий (14); **(in the) n. year** в бу́дущем году́ (12); **What's n.?** Что́ да́льше? (14); **n. to, n. door to** ря́дом с (+ instr.) (11)

nice хоро́ший (хорошо́) (6); **(of persons)** ми́лый (9)

niece племя́нница (22)

night ночь (f.) (6); **at n.** но́чью (11); **all n. (long)** всю́ но́чь (6); (adj.) ночно́й; **Good n.!** Споко́йной но́чи! (20)

nine де́вять (17, 26)

nineteen девятна́дцать (17, 26)

ninety девяно́сто (21, 26)

ninth девя́тый (18)

no нет (2), (adj.) никако́й (не) (21), **There is (are) n.** нет (+ gen.) (10), **n. more** бо́льше не (нет) (10); **n. longer** уже́ не (нет); **n. one** никто́ (не) (8, 10)

nobody никто́ (не) (8, 10)

noise шум (16); **to make n.** шуме́ть (imperf.) (25)

noisy шу́мный (16)

noon по́лдень (m.) (19)

nor ни (8)

normal норма́льный (6)

north се́вер; **to the n.** на се́вер; **in the n.** на се́вере (22)

northern се́верный (22)

nose нос (2, 12)

not не (2); нет (at end of sentence): **Of course n.** Коне́чно не́т. **Why n.?** Почему́ не́т? **n . . . but** не . . . , а (4); **n. at all** совсе́м не (нет) (11)

to note down запи́сывать (13), записа́ть (15)

notebook тетра́дь (f.) (13)

notes запи́ски (f. pl.) (13)

nothing ничего́ (не) (8, 10); **n. more** бо́льше ничего́ (8, 27)

to notice замеча́ть, заме́тить (22)

novel рома́н (6)

November ноя́брь (m.) (23)

now тепе́рь (2, 5), сейча́с (5, 14); **to n.** до сих по́р (21); пока́ (14)

nowhere нигде́ (не) (8); **(going) n.** никуда́ (не) (17)

number число́ (26); но́мер (nom. pl. -а́) (6, 7, 12); **a n. of** не́сколько (+ gen. pl.) (16, 20)

nursery де́тская (22)

to obey (trans.) слу́шать (5), по- (18)

to obtain получа́ть (13), получи́ть (15), достава́ть, доста́ть (21)

occupation заня́тие (21)

occupied заня́той (22), за́нят (23); **to be o. with** занима́ться, заня́ться (+ instr.) (19)

to occupy занима́ть, заня́ть (22)

to occur случа́ться, случи́ться (20); происходи́ть, произойти́ (21)

o'clock, see 16, 26

October октя́брь (m.) (23)

of—genitive case (7); (about) о, об, обо (+ loc.) (5, 12); o. course коне́чно (5); a friend o. his оди́н его́ друг (15); one o. his friends оди́н из его́ друзе́й (20)

off (prep.) с (+ gen.) (17)

office конто́ра

officer офице́р (11)

often ча́сто (9); more o. ча́ще (25); less o. ре́же (25)

oil ма́сло (6)

O.K. ла́дно (20)

old ста́рый (6); o. age ста́рость (f.) (18); o.-fashioned старомо́дный (16); o. man стари́к (22); o. woman стару́ха (22); older ста́рший (8, 25), ста́рше (25); oldest ста́рший (8, 25), са́мый ста́рый (ста́рший) (25)

omelet яи́чница (21)

on на (+ loc.) (5); with expressions of time, see 17; (further) да́льше; Read o. Чита́йте да́льше!; to go o. (continue) продолжа́ть (+ inf.) (16)

once (one time) (оди́н) раз (16); (in the past) одна́жды, когда́-то (22)

one оди́н (8, 12); not translated after adjectives— see 6; o. . . . another оди́н . . . друго́й (13); the o. who (which, that) тот, кото́рый (7); o. = you (indefinite)—2nd pers. sing. verb (20); o. can (may) мо́жно (+ inf.) (21); o. cannot (may not) нельзя́ (+ inf.) (21); o. must на́до (ну́жно) (+ inf.) (9); o. must (should) not нельзя́ (+ inf.) (21); o.'s own свой (9, 12, 20); at o. time одно́ вре́мя; o. another друг дру́га (13); o. of my friends оди́н из мои́х друзе́й (20); no o. никто́ (8, 10)

oneself, see self

only то́лько (4); the o. (one) еди́нственный (27)

onto на (+ acc.) (17)

open откры́т/ый

to open (trans.) открыва́ть (8), откры́ть (15); (intrans.) открыва́ться, откры́ться (19)

opinion мне́ние (23); in the o. of по мне́нию (+ gen.) (23); in my o. по-мо́ему (14); in your o. по-ва́шему

opposite про́тив (+ gen.) (21)

or и́ли (2)

order поря́док (24); in o. to/that что́бы (24)

ordinary обы́чный (9), обыкнове́нный (12)

original (adj.) оригина́льный (9)

other друго́й (10); each o. друг дру́га (13); some . . . others одни́ . . . други́е (13)

otherwise (or else) а то; (differently) ина́че (22); по-друго́му (21)

ought to до́лжен (+ inf.) (8); до́лжен был бы (+ inf.) (24)

our, ours наш (4, 12, 20)

ourselves, see self

out of из (+ gen.) (15)

outside, out of doors (static) на у́лице (7), на дворе́ (24)

over над (+ instr.) (19); o. there там (2); вон (там)

overcoat пальто́ (n. indecl.) (12)

own: one's o. свой (9, 12, 20); (related, native) родно́й (27); со́бственный

package паке́т (22), посы́лка (22)

page страни́ца (11)

pain боль (f.) (23)

to pain боле́ть (imperf.) (23)

painter худо́жник

pair па́ра (13)

papa па́па (20)

paper бума́га (2); (newspaper) газе́та (4)

paragraph абза́ц (18)

parcel посы́лка (22)

to pardon извиня́ть, извини́ть (18); p. me прости́те (4), извини́те (18)

parents роди́тели (pl.) (16)

Paris Пари́ж (5)

park парк (6)

part часть (f.) (12); on your p. с ва́шей стороны́ (18); (role) роль (f.) (12); to take p. in принима́ть уча́стие в (+ loc.) (21); for the most p. гла́вным о́бразом (19)

party (evening) ве́чер (7); вечери́нка (8); political p. па́ртия (14)

to pass (go by) проходи́ть, пройти́ ми́мо (+ gen.) (22); (time) проводи́ть, провести́ (23)

passenger пассажи́р, f. -ка (22)

past (by) ми́мо (+ gen.) (22); (former) про́шлый (12); the p. про́шлое (24)

patience терпе́ние (18)

patient (sick person) больно́й (23)

patronymic о́тчество (11); What is your p.? Как ва́ше о́тчество? (20)

to pay плати́ть, за- (16); to p. for (за)п. за (+ acc.) (16)

peace мир (6)

peasant крестья́н.ин, f. -ка (20)

pen перо́ (2, 20); fountain p. авторучка (7)

pencil каранда́ш (3)

people лю́ди (13, 16); (nation) наро́д (27); young p. молодёжь (f., collect.) (16); (in general) 3rd. pers. pl. of verb, p. say говоря́т (9)

pepper пе́рец (21)

per в (+ acc.) (17)

perhaps мо́жет быть (10)

person челове́к (pl., see лю́ди) (8, 13, 16)

personal ли́чный (27)

pessimist пессими́ст, f. -ка

photograph фотогра́фия (16)

physician врач (16)

piano роя́ль (*m.*) (6)

picture карти́на (5); **(photo)** фотогра́фия (16)

piece кусо́к (7)

pillow поду́шка (24)

pink ро́зовый (16)

pipe тру́бка (11)

pity: it's a p. жаль (6). **I p. him.** Мне́ его́ (*acc.*) жа́ль. **What a p.!** Как жа́ль! (6)

place ме́сто (11); **at someone's p. (house, etc.)** у (+ *gen.*) (10); **to someone's p.** к (+ *dat.*) (17); **from someone's p.** от (+ *gen.*) (17); **in the first p.** во-пе́рвых (20); **to its (proper) p.** на ме́сто (24); **in its p.** на ме́сте (24); **in p. of** вме́сто (+ *gen.*) (23)

to place, *see 24*

plan план (14)

plant (factory) заво́д (12); **at the p.** на заво́де (12)

plate таре́лка (12)

play (drama) пье́са (7)

to play игра́ть (6), сыгра́ть (perf. *trans.*) (14); **to p. the piano** игра́ть на роя́ле (6); **to p. chess** игра́ть в ша́хматы (14); **to p. cards** игра́ть в ка́рты (14); **to p. tennis** игра́ть в те́ннис (6, 8)

pleasant прия́тный (6)

please пожа́луйста (3)

to please нра́виться, по- (19) (+ *dat.*)

pleased дово́лен (*11, 23*)

pleasure удово́льствие (11)

P.M. дня **(in the afternoon)** (16); ве́чера **(in the evening)** (16)

poet поэ́т (16)

poetry поэ́зия (16)

policy: (political) поли́тика (7)

politics поли́тика (7)

poor бе́дный (13); **(bad)** плохо́й (ило́хо) (5, 6)

popular популя́рный (7)

population населе́ние (25)

porch вера́нда (16)

portrait портре́т (22)

position положе́ние (18)

possibility возмо́жность (*f.*) (21)

possible возмо́жно (18, *21*); **it is p. (one can)** мо́жно (*21*); возмо́жно (18, *21*)

post office по́чта (12); **at the p. o.** на по́чте (12)

potato(es) карто́фель (*m., no pl.*) (*11*)

power си́ла (25)

practical практи́ческий (23)

practice пра́ктика (14)

to predict предска́зывать, предсказа́ть (*27*)

to prefer предпочита́ть, предпоче́сть (*18*)

to prepare гото́вить (*13*), при- (*14*)

present (gift) пода́рок

present (time) настоя́щее; (*adj.*) настоя́щий (9), тепе́решний (6)

to present представля́ть, предста́вить (*27*)

president президе́нт (11)

press (newspapers) пре́сса (7)

pretty краси́вый (6)

price цена́ (7); **What is the p. of . . .?** Кака́я цена́ (+ *gen.*)? (7)

prince принц

probably вероя́тно (5), наве́рно(е) (18)

produce проду́кты (*pl.*) (19)

production произво́дство (27)

professor профе́ссор (*nom. pl.* -а́) (4)

to promise обеща́ть (imperf.) (*21*)

to pronounce произноси́ть, произнести́ (*19*)

pronunciation произноше́ние (19)

proposition предложе́ние (19)

to prove дока́зывать, доказа́ть (*27*)

publisher изда́тель (*m.*) (11)

punishment наказа́ние (27)

pupil учен.и́к, *f.* -и́ца (10)

purchase поку́пка (22)

purse су́мка (22)

to put (down), *see 24*; **to p. on** надева́ть, наде́ть (24)

quarter че́тверть (*f.*) (26)

queen короле́ва (18)

question вопро́с (6); **to ask a q.** задава́ть/зада́ть вопро́с (*13*)

to question спра́шивать (6), спроси́ть (*15*)

quick бы́стрый (8)

quiet ти́хий (8); **quieter** ти́ше (*25*)

quite совсе́м (11), дово́льно (10)

radio ра́дио (*9*); **on the r.** по ра́дио

rain дождь (*m.*) (17); **It is raining.** Идёт дождь (17). **It began to r.** Начался́ до́ждь (22)

rare ре́дкий (16); **rarely** ре́дко (9); **more r.** ре́же (*25*)

rather (fairly) дово́льно (10)

to read чита́ть (imperf.) (5), про- (perf., *14*) *or* проче́сть (perf.) (*24*); **Read!** Чита́й(те)! (3)

reader чита́тель, *f.* -ница (18)

reading чте́ние (8)

ready гото́в/ый (*13, 23*)

real настоя́щий (9)

reason: for some r. почему́-то (12)

to recall, recollect вспомина́ть, вспо́мнить (*26*)

to receive получа́ть, получи́ть (*15*); **(receive guests)** принима́ть, приня́ть (*20*)

recently неда́вно (7)

reception приём (20)

to recognize узнава́ть, узна́ть (*21*)

record (phonograph) пласти́нка (8)

to recover: (get well) выздора́вливать, вы́здо- роветь (23)

red кра́сный (8)

refrigerator холоди́льник (7)

regards привет (9); **Give my r. to . . . .** Передайте от меня привет (+ *dat.*)

relative ро́дствен.ник, *f.* -ница (27)

to relax отдыха́ть (8), отдохну́ть (*21*)

relaxation о́тдых (8)

to rely on наде́яться (imperf.) на (+ *acc.*) (*19*)

to remain остава́ться (25)

remarkable замеча́тельный (12)

to remember по́мнить (imperf.) (*16*)

to rent снима́ть, снять (*24*)

to repeat повторя́ть, повтори́ть (*18*); **Repeat!** Повтори́(те)! (3)

repetition повторе́ние (18)

reply отве́т (9)

to reply отвеча́ть (9), отве́тить (*15*); **to r. to** (+ *dat.* or на + *acc.*—15)

report (oral) докла́д (12)

reporter журнали́ст, *f.* -ка (4)

to represent представля́ть, предста́вить (27)

to resemble: He resembles . . . . Он похо́ж на (+ *acc.*) (23).

to respect уважа́ть (imperf. only) (27)

rest о́тдых (8)

to rest отдыха́ть (8), отдохну́ть (*21*)

restaurant рестора́н (7)

to return (*trans.* **to give back**) возвраща́ть (imperf.), возврати́ть (perf.) *or* верну́ть (perf.); (*intrans.,* **to go/come back**) возвраща́ться, возврати́ться ог верну́ться (*21*)

revolution револю́ция (12)

to rewrite перепи́сывать, переписа́ть (*15*)

rice рис (*12*)

rich бога́тый (10); **richer** бога́че (*25*)

to ride, *see 17, 18, 22*

right пра́вый (11, *23*); **on (to) the r.** напра́во (12), спра́ва (26); **(correct)** пра́вильный (*18*); прав **(of people,** *in pred. only*) (14, 23); **r. away** сейча́с же (14); **That's r.** Э́то пра́вда (5). **the r.** пра́во (21)

to ring звони́ть (9), по- (*14*)

river река́ (3)

road доро́га (17)

role роль (*f.*) (12)

roof кры́ша (7)

room ко́мната (4); **hotel r.** но́мер (12)

ruble рубль (*m.*) (14, 15)

rug ковёр (10)

rule пра́вило (9)

rumor слух (27)

to run бе́гать (indeterm. imperf.), бежа́ть (determ. imperf.), побежа́ть (perf.) (*24*); **to r. out** выбега́ть, вы́бежать (*24*)

Russia Росси́я (11)

Russian ру́сский (6, *20*); **R. language** ру́сский язы́к (12); **in R.** по-ру́сски (5)

sad гру́стный (17), печа́льный (22)

to sail, *see 24*

salad сала́т (11)

saleslady продавщи́ца (13)

salesman продаве́ц (13)

salt соль (*f.*) (7)

salvation спасе́ние (27)

same тот же (са́мый) (18); **the s. thing** то́ же са́мое (25); **all the s. (nevertheless)** всё-таки (19); **It's all the s. to me.** Мне всё равно́. (9)

sandwich бутербро́д (17)

satisfied дово́лен (10, *11, 23*); **s. with** (+ *instr.*) (*11*)

Saturday суббо́та (18)

sausage (bologna) колбаса́ (17); **(frankfurter)** соси́ска (17)

to say говори́ть (imperf.) (5, *8*), сказа́ть (perf.) (*14*); **I should s. so!** Ещё бы! (8); **You don't say!** Что вы!

saying погово́рка (18)

schedule расписа́ние (26)

scholar, scholarly учёный (*22*)

scholarship стипе́ндия (*23*)

school шко́ла (3); (*adj.*) шко́льный (27)

schoolboy учени́к (*10*), шко́льник (11)

schoolgirl учени́ца (*10*), шко́льница (11)

scientist учёный (*22*)

sea мо́ре (12)

seagull ча́йка (26)

seashore бе́рег мо́ря (12)

season вре́мя го́да (13)

seat ме́сто (11)

second (*adj.*) второ́й (15); **in the s. place** во-вторы́х (20)

secret секре́т (14)

secretary секрета́рша (4)

section отде́л (13)

to see ви́деть (*11*), у- (*21*); **to s. one another** ви́деться, у- (*19*); **go (come) to s. someone** быть у (+ *gen.*) (*10*); ходи́ть/идти́/пойти́ к (+ *dat.*) (*17*), приходи́ть/прийти́ к (+ *dat.*) (*18*)

to seem каза́ться, по- (+ *instr.*) (*19*)

seldom ре́дко (9); **more s.** ре́же (*25*)

selection вы́бор (13)

-self—*see suffix* -ся (*17*); *reflexive pronoun* себя́ (*23*); *intensive pronoun* сам (14, *23*)

selfish person эгои́ст, *f.* -ка (14)

to sell продава́ть (9), прода́ть (*15*)

to send посыла́ть (9), посла́ть (*19*)

sentence предложе́ние (*19*)

September сентя́брь (*m.*) (23)

serious серьёзный (6)

to serve служи́ть (*12*)

service слу́жба (9)

to set an alarm clock for . . . (по)ста́вить буди́льник на (+ *acc.*) (24)

seven семь (*17, 26*)

seventeen семнáдцать (*17, 26*)

seventh седьмóй (*18*)

seventy сéмьдесят (*21, 26*)

several нéсколько (+ *gen. pl.*) (*16, 20*)

Shakespeare Шекспúр (*14*)

sharp óстрый (*16*); **at two o'clock s.** póвно в двá часá (*16*)

to shave (*trans.*) брить, по-; (*intrans.*) брúться, по- (*24*)

she онá (*2*)

sheet (of paper) лист (*13*)

shelf пóлка (*2*)

to shine (*intrans.*) светúть (imperf.) (*26*)

ship парохóд (*18*)

shirt рубáшка (*13*)

shoe ботúнок (*13, 16*)

shop магазúн (*8*); **(small)** лáвка (*25*)

shore бéрег (*nom. pl.* -á) (*12*); **on the s.** на берегý

short корóткий (кóротко) (*11*); **(for) a s. time** недóлго

shorter корóче (*25*)

should: he s. . . . . Óн дóлжен (бы́л бы) (+ *inf.*). He s. have . . . . Óн дóлжен бы́л (бы) (+ *inf.*) (*8, 9, 24*). **I s. say so!** Ещё бы! (*8*)

to shout кричáть, крúкнуть (*21*)

to show покáзывать (*9*), показáть (*15*)

shower душ (*24*)

shut закры́т/ый (*26*)

to shut (*trans.*) закрывáть (*8*), закры́ть (*15*); (*intrans.*) закрывáться, закры́ться (*19*)

Siberia Сибúрь (*f.*) (*12*)

sick бóлен (*23*); **a s. person** больнóй (*23*); **to be s. (sometimes, often)** болéть (imperf.) (*23*); **to fall s.** заболéть (perf.) (*23*)

sickness болéзнь (*f.*) (*23*)

side сторонá (*17*); **on all sides** со всéх сторóн (*27*)

sight: to catch s. of увúдеть (perf.) (*21*)

sign (mark, symptom) знак (*19*)

to sign подпúсывать, подписáть (*15*)

silly глýпый (*9*)

simple простóй (*12*); **simpler** прóще (*25*)

simply прóсто (*10*); **more s.** прóще (*25*)

since (after) пóсле (+ *gen.*) (*10*); **(because)** так как (*12*); **s. the time that** с тех пóр, как (*21*)

to sing петь, с- (*16*)

singer пев.éц, *f.* -úца (*16*)

single: not a s. ни одúн (ни однóго) (*20*)

sister сестрá (*4, 13*)

to sit, be seated сидéть (imperf.) (*11*); **to sit at table** сидéть за столóм

to sit down садúться, сесть (*20*); **to s. d. to table** садúться/сéсть за стол (*21*)

situation положéние (*18*)

six шесть (*17, 26*)

sixteen шестнáдцать (*17, 26*)

sixth шестóй (*18*)

sixty шестьдеся́т (*21, 26*)

size (measure) размéр (*13*)

skirt ю́бка (*8*)

sky нéбо (*7*)

Slav славянúн, *f.* славя́нка (*20*)

sleep сон (*26*)

to sleep спать (imperf.) (*7, 11*); **to s. a little** поспáть (perf.) (*25*)

slender тóнкий (*13*)

slowly мéдленно (*8*)

small мáленький (*6*); **smaller** мéньше (*25*)

smile улы́бка (*27*)

to smile улыбáться (*19*)

smoke дым (*27*)

to smoke курúть (imperf.) (*11*)

snow снег (*11, 12*)

snowing: It's s. Идёт снéг (*17*)

so так (*4*); (*with attributive adjs.*) такóй (*6*); **s. far (till now)** до сих пóр (*21*); **s. much (many)** стóлько (+ *gen.*) (*16, 20*); **s. that** (тáк), чтóбы (*with hypothetical mood*) (*24*); **s. -s.** тáк себе (*19*); **and s. forth** и. так дáлее (*20*)

soccer футбóл (*5*)

society óбщество (*20*)

sock носóк (*24*)

sofa дивáн (*11*)

soft мя́гкий (*19*); **softer** мя́гче (*25*)

sold: What is sold? Чтó продаю́т ? (*9*)

soldier солдáт (*gen. pl.* солдáт) (*16*)

some (several) нéсколько (+ *gen. pl.*) (*16, 20*); **(certain ones)** нéкоторые (*20*); **s. of my friends** нéкоторые из моúх друзéй (*20*); **(a quantity of)**—*partitive gen.* (*10*); **Do you want s. bread?** Вы́ хотúте хлéба ? (*10*); **s . . . others** однú . . . другúе (*13*)

somehow кáк-то, почемý-то (*12*)

someone, something, somewhere, etc., *see* 22

sometimes иногдá (*8*)

son сын (*4, 20*)

song пéсня (*13, 20*)

soon скóро (*5*); **as s. as** как тóлько (*14*)

sorry: I feel s. for him. Мнé егó (*acc.*) жáль (*18*)

soup суп (*7*)

south юг; **to the s.** на юг; **in the s.** на юге (*22*)

southern ю́жный (*22*)

Soviet совéтский (*7*); **S. Union** Совéтский Сою́з (*7*)

Spaniard испáн.ец, *f.* -ка (*20*)

Spanish (*adj.*) испáнский (*20*); **in S.** по-испáнски (*20*)

to speak говорúть (*5, 8*), по- (*20*)

speaker (public) доклáд.чик, *f.* -чица (*27*)

speech речь (*f.*) (*24*); доклáд (*12*); **to give a s.** произносúть/произнестú рéчь (*24*); (про)читáть лéкцию/доклáд (*12*)

to spell: This word is spelled so. Это слóво пúшется тáк (*19*)

to spend (time) проводи́ть, провести́ (23); пробы́ть (perf.) (21)

spite: in spite of несмотря́ на (+ acc.) (27)

spoon ло́жка (11)

spring весна́; (in s.) весно́й (11); (adj.) весе́нний (19)

square (public) пло́щадь (f.) (12)

stamp ма́рка (17)

to stand стоя́ть (imperf.) (5, 11); **to s. up** встава́ть, встать (16); **(to take up a standing position)** станови́ться, стать (20); (trans.— **to place standing)** ста́вить, по- (24)

to start (trans.) начина́ть (8), нача́ть (15) **to** (+ inf.); (intrans.) начина́ться, нача́ться (19); стать (+ perf. inf. only) (20)

station ста́нция (12); **(terminal)** вокза́л (17); **at the s.** на ста́нции, на вокза́ле

to stay (remain) остава́ться, оста́ться (25); **(live, dwell)** жить (9), по- (25) or про- (perf.) (25); **(spend time)** проводи́ть, провести́ (час, ле́то, etc.) (23); **to s. at home** сиде́ть до́ма (11); **to s. in a hotel, etc.** остана́вливаться, остано-ви́ться (22)

steak бифште́кс (18)

steppe степь (f.) (13)

still ещё (7); **(nevertheless)** всё-таки (19), всё-же (25)

stomach живо́т (23); желу́док

stop (bus) остано́вка (22)

to stop (trans.) остана́вливать, останови́ть (22); (intrans.) остана́вливаться, останови́ться (22); **(to cease)** переставaть, переста́ть (+ imperf. inf.) (22); **to s. in to see** заходи́ть, зайти́ к (+ dat.) (22)

store магази́н (8)

story расска́з (10); **(floor)** эта́ж (12)

stout то́лстый (8)

stove плита́ (24)

straight (adv.) пря́мо (17)

strange стра́нный (5, 6)

street у́лица (5)

to stroll гуля́ть, по- (16)

strong си́льный (21)

student студе́нт, f. -ка (2); (adj.) студе́нческий (13)

studious приле́жный (10)

study уче́ние (18); **(room)** кабине́т (5)

to study занима́ться (imperf.) (+ instr.) (19, 23); учи́ться (imperf.) (+ dat.) (23); изуча́ть, изучи́ть (+ acc.) (12, 23)

stuffy ду́шный (17)

stupid глу́пый (9)

style (fashion) мо́да (13)

subject те́ма; **on that s.** на э́ту те́му (12)

subway метро́ (n. indecl.); **by s.** на метро́ (12)

success успе́х (27)

such (a) тако́й (6)

suddenly вдруг (13)

suffering (noun) страда́ние (27)

sufficiently доста́точно (16)

sugar са́хар (11, 12)

suit костю́м (6)

suitcase чемода́н (22)

summer ле́то (6); **in s.** ле́том (11); (adj.) ле́тний (6); **s. house** да́ча (12)

sun со́лнце (16)

Sunday воскресе́нье (18)

superior (noun) нача́льник (9); (adj.) ве́рхний (27)

supper у́жин (11); **to (for) s.** к у́жину; **to have s.** у́жинать, по- (16)

sure уве́рен (18, 23); **s. of** уве́рен в (+ loc.) (23)

surely наве́рно (18)

surprise удивле́ние (22); **(a) s.** сюрпри́з (7)

surprised удивлён (23)

to surround окружа́ть, окружи́ть (27)

to swim, see 24

table стол (2); **to sit down at t.** сади́ться/сесть за стол (19); **to be at the t.** сиде́ть за столо́м

to take брать (imperf.), взять (perf.) (14); **to t. from** бра́ть/взя́ть у (+ gen.) (14); **(carry, transport, etc.)**—see 22; **to t. off** снима́ть, снять (24); **to t. an exam** держа́ть экза́мен (13); **to t. place (occur)** происходи́ть, произойти́ (21); **to t. part in** принима́ть уча́стие в (+ loc.) (21); **to t. a train** сесть на по́езд (21); **to t. a walk** гуля́ть, по- (16)

talented тала́нтливый (9)

talk: (a conversation) разгово́р (4)

to talk говори́ть (5, 8), по- (20); **t. to** (по-)говори́ть с (+ instr.) (11)

tall высо́кий (10); **taller** вы́ше (25)

taste вкус (19)

taxi такси́ (n. indecl.) (12); **by t.** на такси́

tea чай (11, 12)

to teach учи́ть, на- (23); преподава́ть (imperf.) (23)

teacher учи́тель (nom. pl. учителя́), f. -ница (3)

teaching преподава́ние (23)

team (sports) кома́нда (22)

telegram телегра́мма (9)

telephone телефо́н (9); **on the t.** по телефо́ну (9)

to telephone звони́ть (9), по- (по телефо́ну) (14) (+ dat.)

television set телеви́зор (9)

to tell (say) говори́ть (imperf.) (5, 8), сказа́ть (perf.) (14); **(narrate, recount)** расска́зывать, рассказа́ть (15); **T. me about . . . .** Расскажи́те мне о (+ loc.)

temperature температу́ра (23)

ten де́сять (17, 26)

tenant жиле́ц, f. -и́ца (21)

tennis те́ннис (8)

tenth деся́тый (18)

terminal вокза́л; **at the t.** на вокза́ле (17)

terrible ужа́сный (13); **(frightening)** стра́шный (27)

terrific: That's t.! Э́то здо́рово! (7)

terror у́жас (21)

textbook уче́бник (9)

than чем (or *gen.*) (25)

to thank благодари́ть, по- (+ *acc.*) (18); **t. you** спаси́бо (3); благодарю́ ва́с (18); **thanks for** спаси́бо за (+ *acc.*) (16); **many thanks** большо́е спаси́бо (10)

thankful благода́рный (18, 23)

that (*demonstr.*) э́тот; тот (4, 12, 20); **T. is . . .** Э́то . . . (2); (*conj.*) что (5, 15); (*rel. pronoun*) кото́рый (6); **t. which** то́, что (13); **in t. way** так (4)

the—*definite article not translated* (2); **t. . . . t.** чём . . . тём (25); **t. more t. better** чём бо́льше, тём лу́чше

theater теа́тр (5); **motion picture t.** кино́ (*n. indecl.*) (12)

their, theirs их (7)

theme те́ма (12)

themselves, *see* **self**

then (at that time) тогда́ (8, *11*); **(next)** пото́м (*11*); **if . . . t.** е́сли . . . то́ (19)

there там (2); **(to) t., thither** туда́ (*17*); **from t.** отту́да (*17*); **t. is/are (pointing)** вот (2); **(not pointing)** есть (+ *nom.*) (10); **t. is/are not** нет (+ *gen.*) (10); **over t.** там, во́н (та́м)

therefore поэ́тому (9)

they они́ (2); **t. say** говоря́т (9)

thick то́лстый (8); **thicker** то́лще (25)

thin (slender) то́нкий (13); **(lean)** худо́й (20); **thinner** то́ньше (25)

thing вещь (*f.*) (13); **(matter)** де́ло (14); **not a t.** ничего́ (не) (8); **The t. is that . . . .** Де́ло в то́м, что . . . (14). **How are things?** Ка́к дела́?

to think ду́мать (5, 8), по- (20)

third тре́тий (*18*)

thirteen трина́дцать (*17, 26*)

thirty три́дцать (*21, 26*)

this (*demonstr.*) э́тот (4, 12, 20); **t. is . . .** э́то . . . (2); **in t. way** так (4); **(in) t. year** в э́том году́ (12)

though хотя́ (и) (10)

thought мысль (*f.*) (21)

thousand ты́сяча (26)

three три (*10, 26*)

throat го́рло (23)

to throw броса́ть, бро́сить (*24*)

Thursday четве́рг (18)

thus так (4)

to tick ти́кать (imperf.) (24)

ticket биле́т (17)

till (*prep.*) до (+ *gen.*) (10); (*conj.*) пока́ . . . не (*21*); **t. now** до сих по́р (21)

time вре́мя (*12, 20*); **(occasion)** раз (*gen. pl.* раз) (16); **for the first t.** в пе́рвый ра́з (16); **many times** мно́го ра́з (16); **at that t.** в то́ вре́мя (17); **at one t.** одно́ вре́мя; **on t.** во́время (24); **at times** иногда́ (8); **for a long t.** до́лго (11), надо́лго (22); **for some t.** не́которое вре́мя (14); **for the t. being** пока́ (14); **a long t. ago** давно́ (7); **at what t.?** в кото́ром часу́? (16); **at any t.** когда́-либо (25); **all the t.** всё вре́мя (17); **I'm having a good t.** Мне́ ве́село (20). **It's t. to . . . .** Пора́ (+ *dat. and inf.*) (17); **It's high t. to . . . .** Давно́ пора́ (+ *inf.*). **What t. is it?** Кото́рый ча́с? (16)

timetable (train) расписа́ние поездо́в (26)

tired: to grow t. устава́ть, уста́ть; **to be t.**—*past tense of* уста́ть (21)

title назва́ние (7); **What is the t. of . . . ?** Ка́к назва́ние (+ *gen.*) (7)

to—*dative case* (9); в (+ *acc.*); на (+ *acc.*); к (+ *dat.*) (*17, 22*); **t. the house of** к (+ *dat.*) (17)

today сего́дня (5); **t.'s** сего́дняшний (6)

together вме́сте (5)

tomorrow за́втра (10); **day after t.** послеза́втра (17)

tongue язы́к (12)

tonight (this evening) сего́дня ве́чером (11)

too (also) и (7); то́же (3); та́кже (*17*); **(excessively)** сли́шком (8)

tooth зуб (24)

tourist тури́ст, *f.* -ка (7)

toward к (+ *dat.*) (22)

town го́род (*nom. pl.* -а́) (5); село́ (22); **to go out of t.** (по)е́хать за́ город (17)

toy игру́шка (22)

train по́езд (*nom. pl.* -а́) (13); **by t.** по́ездом, на по́езде (17)

to translate переводи́ть, перевести́ (*19*)

translation перево́д (10)

translator перево́д.чик, *f.* -чица (12)

to transport, *see* 22

travel путеше́ствие (20)

to travel е́здить (indeterm. imperf.) (*17*); путеше́ствовать (imperf.) (20); **to t. around (a country, region)** е́здить по (+ *dat.*)

tree де́рево (13, *20*)

trousers брю́ки (*pl.*) (*13*)

true пра́вда (5); **That's t.** Э́то пра́вда (5). **It's t. that . . . .** Пра́вда, что . . . . **That's not t.** Э́то непра́вда (5).

truth пра́вда (5)

tsar царь (11)

Tuesday вто́рник (18)

to turn out ока́зываться, оказа́ться (*24*); **He turned out . . . .** О́н оказа́лся (+ *instr.*). **It turned out that . . . .** Оказа́лось, что . . . .

twelve двена́дцать (*17, 26*)

twentieth двадца́тый (18)

twenty два́дцать (*17, 26*)

twice два́ ра́за (16)

two два (*m. and n.*), две (*f.*) (*10, 26*)

typist машини́стка (14)

Ukraine Украи́на; **in the U.** на Украи́не (12)

Ukrainian (*adj.*) украи́нский

umbrella зонт, зо́нтик (24)

unaccustomed: to become u. to отвыка́ть, отвы́кнуть (от + *gen. or inf.*) (*21*); **to be u. to—** *past tense of* отвы́кнуть (*21*)

uncle дя́дя (20)

under под (+ *instr. or acc.*) (*19, 24*)

to understand понима́ть (8), поня́ть (*19*)

to undress (*trans.*) раздева́ть, разде́ть (*19*); (*intrans.*) раздева́ться, разде́ться (*19*)

unfortunate несча́стный (13)

unfortunately к сожале́нию (23)

unhappy несча́стный (13)

union сою́з; **Soviet U.** Сове́тский Сою́з; **U. of Soviet Socialist Republics** Сою́з Сове́тских Социалисти́ческих Респу́блик (СССР) (7)

United States of America Соединённые Шта́ты Аме́рики (13); **U.S.A.** США (*indecl.*) (13)

university университе́т (12)

unnecessary нену́жно (11)

unpleasant неприя́тный (8)

until (*prep.*) до (+ *gen.*) (10); (*conj.*) пока́ . . . не (*21*)

untruth непра́вда (5)

up to до (+ *gen.*) (10); **u. t. now** до сих пор (25)

Urals Ура́л (12); **in the U.** на Ура́ле

urban городско́й (21)

use по́льза (27)

to use по́льзоваться (+ *instr.*) (*imperf.*) (23)

used to—past tense of imperf. aspect* (5); **to get u. to** привыка́ть, привы́кнуть (+ *dat. or inf.*) (*21*); **to be u. to—**past tense of* привы́кнуть (*21*)

useful поле́зный (27)

U.S.S.R. СССР (*indecl.*) (13)

usual: as u. как всегда́ (5), как обы́чно (9); **(ordinary)** обыкнове́нный (12); **more than u.** бо́льше обыкнове́нного

usually обы́чно (9), обыкнове́нно (12)

vacation (school) кани́кулы (*pl.*) (*23*); **(leave from work)** о́тпуск (26)

various ра́зный (13)

vegetables о́вощи (*pl.*) (*19*)

verb глаго́л (14)

verse стих (*16*)

very о́чень (*3, 10*)

vestibule пере́дняя (24)

view вид; **v. of** вид на (+ *acc.*) (24)

village дере́вня (6); село́ (*22*); (*adj.*) се́льский (23)

to visit быть у (+ *gen.*) (*10*); **(sometimes, often)** быва́ть у (+ *gen.*) (5, 8); **to go to v.** ходи́ть/ идти́/пойти́ к (+ *dat.*) (*17*); **to go visiting** ходи́ть/идти́/пойти́ в го́сти (*17*)

vocabulary слова́рь (*m.*) (4)

vodka во́дка (11)

voice го́лос (*nom. pl.* -á) (11)

volleyball волейбо́л (8)

volume том (26)

to wake (*trans.*) буди́ть, раз- (*19*); (*intrans.*) просыпа́ться, просну́ться (*19*)

to walk, *see 17, 18, 22*; **(stroll)** гуля́ть, по- (16)

wall стена́ (2)

to want хоте́ть (*10*), за- (*21*)

war война́ (10)

warm тёплый (тепло́) (6)

was, *see* be

to wash (*trans.*) мыть, по- *or* вы́-; (*intrans.*) мы́ться, по- *or* вы́- (*19*)

watch часы́ (*pl.*) (*17*); **by my w.** на мои́х часа́х

water вода́ (7)

way доро́га (*17*); **on the w.** по доро́ге (*17*); **in this (that) w.** так (4); **by the w.** ме́жду про́чим (*19*); кста́ти (*21*); **in the same w.** одина́ково (*19*)

we мы (2)

weak сла́бый (*21*)

wealthy бога́тый (10); **wealthier** бога́че (*25*)

to wear быть в (+ *loc.*) (6); **(often, habitually)** носи́ть (imperf.) (*22*)

weather пого́да (6); **What is the w. today?** Кака́я сего́дня пого́да? (6)

Wednesday среда́ (18)

week неде́ля (8); **(in) this w.** на э́той неде́ле (26)

to weep пла́кать (imperf.) (*21*)

welcome, you're пожа́луйста (3); не́ за что (10)

well (good) хорошо́ (3); (*particle at beginning of sentences*) ну (3); **(in good health)** здоро́в/ый (*23*)

well-known изве́стный (16)

were, *see* be

west за́пад (*22*); **to the w.** на за́пад (*22*); **in the w.** на за́паде (*22*)

western за́падный (*22*)

wet мо́крый (24)

what (*pronoun*) что (*3, 5*); **W. is . . .?** Что тако́е . . . ? **W. is that?** Что э́то (тако́е)? (3); **W. a** како́й (*6*); **w kind of** како́й (*6*), что э́то за (+ *nom.*) (12); **(which one)** како́й (*6*), кото́рый (*6*); (= *that which*) то́, что (13); **W. are we to do?** Что нам де́лать? (9); **W. can one do?** Что де́лать? (10)

when когда́ (4, *14*)

where где (2); **(to) w., whither** куда́ (*17*); **from w.** отку́да (*17*)

whether ли (*22*)

which (*rel. pronoun*) кото́рый (*6*); (*interrog.*) како́й (*6*); кото́рый (*6*)

while (when) когда́ (*4*); for a long w. до́лго (*11*); read, work, etc. for a w. почита́ть, порабо́тать, etc. (*25*)

white бе́лый (*6*)

who (*interrog.*) кто (*3*); (*relative*) кото́рый (*6*)

whole це́лый (*6*)

wholly совсе́м (*11*)

whose (*interrog.*) чей? (*4, 12, 18*); (*relative*) кото́рого, кото́рой, кото́рых (*6*)

why почему́ (*4*); (opening sentences, an expression of mild surprise) ведь

wide широ́кий (широко́) (*8*); wider ши́ре (*25*)

widow вдова́ (*24*)

wife жена́ (*4, 13*)

wind ве́тер (*11*)

window окно́ (*2*); shop w. витри́на (*22*)

wine вино́ (*7*)

winter зима́ (*6*); in w. зимо́й (*11*); (*adj.*) зи́мний (*6*)

to wish хоте́ть (*10*), за- (*21*) (+ *inf.*)

with—*instrumental case* (*11*); с (+ *instr.*) (*11*)

within (time) че́рез (+ *acc.*) (*18*)

without без (+ *gen.*) (*10*); (with verbs) не + *pres. adv. part.* (*27*)

woman же́нщина (*4*)

wonderful прекра́сный (*7*), замеча́тельный (*12*), чу́дный (*17*), чуде́сный (*19*), здо́рово! (*colloq.*) (*7*)

wooden деревя́нный (*16*)

woods лес (*nom. pl.* -а́) (*12*); in the w. в лесу́ (*12*)

word сло́во (*6*); in a w. (одни́м) сло́вом (*25*); in other words други́ми слова́ми

work рабо́та (*5*), слу́жба (*9*); at (one's place of) w. на рабо́те (*5*), на слу́жбе; (*adj.*) рабо́чий (*19*)

to work рабо́тать (imperf.) (*5, 8*); to w. on рабо́тать над (+ *instr.*) (*19*)

workman рабо́чий (*19*)

world мир (*6*), свет (*20*); (*adj.*) мирово́й (*18*)

to worry беспоко́иться (imperf.) (*23*)

worse ху́же (*23, 25*), ху́дший (*25*); I feel w. Мне́ ху́же (*23*); worst (са́мый) ху́дший (*25*); at the w. в ху́дшем слу́чае (*25*)

to worship обожа́ть (imperf.) (*23*)

worth, to be сто́ить (imperf.) (*16*)

would—*future tense or hypothetical mood* (*15, 24*); He w. not . . . . Он не хоте́л (+ *inf.*) (*10*)

to wound ра́нить (imperf. and perf.) (*27*)

to write писа́ть (*5, 9*), на- (*14*); to w. down запи́сывать, записа́ть (*15*)

writer писа́тель, *f.* -ница (*5*)

writing писа́ние (*14*)

wrong непра́в (of persons, *in pred. only*) (*14*); (of things) непра́вильно

yard двор (*16*)

year год (*12*); (in) this y. в э́том году́; (in) last y. в про́шлом году́ (*12*); (in) next y. в бу́дущем году́ (*12*)

yellow жёлтый (*11*)

yes да (*2*)

yesterday вчера́ (*5*); y.'s вчера́шний (*6*); day before y. позавчера́ (*18*), тре́тьего дня (*21*)

yet ещё (*7*); not y. ещё не (*with pred.*); ещё нет (*final in sentence*) (*16*)

you ты, вы (*2*); indefinite (= one), *2nd pers. sing. verb* (*20*)

young молодо́й (*6*); y. people молодёжь (*f., collect.*) (*16*); younger мла́дший (*8, 25*), мла́дше, моло́же (*25*); youngest (са́мый) мла́дший (*25*)

your, yours твой; ваш (*4, 12, 20*)

yourself, *see* self

youth мо́лодость (*f.*) (*27*); молодёжь (*f.*) (*16*)

zero ноль (*m.*), нуль (*m.*) (*26*)

Index

Russian and English vocabulary listings have not been included in this index; for them the student should consult the vocabularies, which give the pertinent unit numbers.

The abbreviation *n.* used below indicates a reference to a footnote.

Masculine, nouns in [-a/-ja], 318
   See also under separate cases
Months, 387
Motion, adverbs and prepositional
      phrases of. *See* Destination,
      Going verbs

Names, 168–169, 395n., 477–478
   See also Titles
Nationality, nouns and adjectives of,
      73, 321–322
Negation, 16–17, 48, 107–108
   object of negated verb in genitive, 246
Negative expressions, 107–108, 464–465
Neuters. *See* under separate cases
Nominative, plural, 197–198, 200–202
   singular, of adjectives, 199–200
      of nouns, 51
      of pronoun-adjectives, 199
Nouns, cases of. *See* under separate cases
   declension in plural, review, 323–324,
      469–472
   declension in singular, review, 175–181
   gender classes of, 39–42
   indeclinable, 180–181
Numerals, approximation with, 410n.,
      435
   cardinal, *1*, 108–109
      2–4, 147
      5–39, 239–240
      20–199, 350–351
   ordinal, *1–20*, 274–275
      20–199, 350–351
      above *199*, 435–437
   review and declension of, 433–439,
      489–491

Ordinal numerals. *See* Numerals

Palatalization, 9–10, 14, 24
Participles, adjectival, 451–456, 460–461
   adverbial, 456–461
Partitive genitive, 175–176
Passive voice, 453–456
   expressed by third person plural, 129

expressed by verbs in [-sja], 292
Past tense. *See* Verbs
Patronymics. *See* Names
Perfective aspect. *See* Verbs
Personal pronouns. *See* Pronouns
Phonetics, 1–15, 19–25
Place where, prepositions and adverbs
      of, 53, 138–139, 252–253,
      258–259, 303–305, 360, 373–377
   with events or activities, 54
Plural, review of declension, 323–325,
      469–479
Position, verbs of, 313–315, 405
Possession, expressed by genitive, 81–83
   expressed by pronoun-adjectives,
      43–45, 130–131
   expressed by [u] + genitive, 139–141
Possessive, reflexive, 130–131
Possessive adjectives, 477
Predicate forms of adjectives, 382–386
Predicate instrumental, 166–167
Prefixes, verbal, [po-] and [pro-], 311–312
   [za-], [pro-], [pere-], [do-], 363
   [za-], [s-], [raz-], 425–426
   See also Going verbs, Verbs, aspects of
Prepositional case. *See* Locative
Prepositions, pronunciation of, 53–54
   review of, 480–484
   with various cases, *see* under separate
      cases
Present tense, in place of future, 261
   See also Verbs
Pronoun-adjectives, demonstratives,
      45–46
   possessives, 43–45
   review of declension in plural,
      324–325, 474–475
   review of declension in singular,
      184–186
Pronouns, intensive, 388–389
   interrogative, 102, 141
   personal, 43
   reciprocal, 203–204
   reflexive, 388
   relative, 76
   review of declension, 183, 473
   third person, 39–40
Purpose clauses, 402